THE UNIVERSITY OF TORONTO

A HISTORY

FACULTY OF MEDICINE
University of Toronto

Presented to

Michael Bronskill

with gratitude for contributions
to the achievement of
our academic mission
by the Faculty of Medicine, University of Toronto

DEPARTMENT CHAIR .

DEAN

June 2003
DATE

GREAT MINDS FOR
A GREAT FUTURE

MARTIN L. FRIEDLAND

THE
UNIVERSITY
OF TORONTO

A HISTORY

UNIVERSITY OF TORONTO PRESS
Toronto Buffalo London

© University of Toronto Press Incorporated 2002
Toronto Buffalo London
Printed in Canada

ISBN 0-8020-4429-8

∞

Printed on acid-free paper

The endpapers reproduce a portion of a map of the University, painted in 1937 by
A. Scott Carter. The map was commissioned by the Massey Foundation and hangs on the
east wall of the Map Room of Hart House. This image was created with the assistance of the
Map Room and Preservation Services of Robarts Library.

National Library of Canada Cataloguing in Publication Data

Friedland, M.L. (Martin Lawrence), 1932–
The University of Toronto : a history

Includes bibliographical references and index.
ISBN 0-8020-4429-8

1. University of Toronto – History.   I. Title.

LE3.T52F75 2002   378.713′541   C2001-903301-X

University of Toronto Press acknowledges the financial assistance to its publishing
program of the Canada Council for the Arts and the Ontario Arts Council.

This book has been published with the help of a grant from the Humanities and
Social Sciences Federation of Canada, using funds provided by the Social Sciences
and Humanities Research Council of Canada.

University of Toronto Press acknowledges the financial support for its publishing
activities of the Government of Canada, through the Book Publishing Industry
Development Program (BPIDP).

CONTENTS

PART THREE: ASPIRATIONS

PART FOUR: TURBULENCE

PART FIVE: GROWTH

PART SIX: EXPANDING HORIZONS

PART SEVEN: ADJUSTMENT

Contents

PART EIGHT: RAISING THE SIGHTS

PROLOGUE

In early June 1997, I received a telephone call from Ron Schoeffel, the editor-in-chief at the University of Toronto Press, asking if I would be interested in submitting a proposal to a university committee charged with deciding who would be invited to write a history of the University of Toronto. The committee, chaired by Father James McConica of the Pontifical Institute of Mediaeval Studies, wanted a scholarly yet accessible one-volume history. The last history of the University had been published in 1927. In the 1970s, material had been collected for a history, but the project was abandoned. The new history would be published in the year 2002 – the 175th anniversary of the granting of a charter to King's College, the predecessor of the University of Toronto.

I wasn't sure at first that I wanted to undertake the task. Was there enough archival material from which to draw? Could the story be told adequately in one volume? How would the information be organized? Would I find the endeavour intellectually rewarding? Over the course of the following six weeks, I prepared a detailed proposal, helped by my two summer research assistants, Graham Rawlinson and Katrina Wyman, who had just completed first year law school and who were working with me on various legal projects. It became clear that an almost overwhelming amount of primary material was available in the University of Toronto archives and at other locations. Moreover, there was an abundance of secondary material, such as autobiographical writing by former administrators – President Claude Bissell, Dean Ernest Sirluck of the graduate school, Chief Librarian Robert Blackburn, and many others. An extensive collection of doctoral theses, biographies, taped interviews, and departmental and other histories relative to the University of Toronto could also be used.

A one-volume history would pose problems of selection, but that would make the task more interesting. The presentation of the material would also be a challenge. I hoped to make the history one that people would want to read from beginning to end, rather than just concentrate on their own areas of interest. A chronological approach seemed the best way to accomplish this. The faculty of medicine, for example, would be dealt with in a number of places rather than within a single chapter. Similarly, instead of treating broad themes, such as academic freedom or curriculum development, as individual chapters, I would discuss these themes in appropriate places throughout the book.

I planned relatively short chapters that would look at specific issues and events – often turning points – in the University's history. A chapter would start on a particular date and look backwards at what led up to an issue or event, and then take the story forward in time. I would approach the writing in much the same way I had approached the three true-crime murder books I had written: I would try to tell a story in an interesting manner and also make a scholarly contribution to the literature.

The proposal was presented to the committee in late July 1997, and I was eventually informed that I had been selected. The contract with the University of Toronto Press allowed me about 200,000 words of text and the equivalent of 100 pages of pictures. Notes – there are about 500 pages of notes – would be published separately by the Press and would also appear on the University of Toronto Press' website (www.utppublishing.com).

In 1997, I was about to turn 65, and at the University of Toronto one officially retires at the end of June of the year in which one reaches that age. This history has turned out to have been a perfect post-retirement project. Over the next four years, I spent perhaps 90 per cent of my research time on the endeavour. I can't think of a more intellectually stimulating project to have undertaken.

The history of the University of Toronto is the history of Toronto, the history of Ontario, and the history of Canada. It is intimately connected with events outside the University. One can trace over the years, for example, both Canada's and the University's transition from dependence on Great Britain and fear of the United States to a lessening of British influence and acceptance of

American culture and ideas. Life at the University clearly was affected by the two world wars, the cold war, and the Vietnam war. The opening up of the University to various groups as students and as faculty members also reflects developments in society generally. What was happening in society can be seen, for example, in the admission of women to University College in the 1880s, or in the expansion of the University in the 1960s to accommodate the 'baby boomers' born after the Second World War. And it can be seen in the growing ethnic, cultural, and religious diversity of the University in the 1990s, a reflection of Canadian immigration patterns in the 1960s and 1970s. And so on.

The project has also been an exploration of the history of ideas. The early periods show the fierce conflicts in the country and in the University over the role of the Christian religion in public institutions, and the tensions among the different Christian denominations. Charles Darwin's ideas permeate much of the intellectual debate in the second half of the nineteenth century. The ideas of many of the major intellectual figures on the world's stage make their way onto Toronto's. Thomas Huxley, a Darwinian, was turned down for a position at the University in the 1850s. James Mavor, a follower of Karl Marx, was hired as the professor of political economy in the 1880s. Ernest Jones, Sigmund Freud's biographer, taught psychoanalysis in the medical school before the First World War, and Leopold Infeld, one of Albert Einstein's collaborators, taught in the mathematics department in the 1940s.

On what date should the history end? I decided to bring the history up to the year 2000. I wanted the story to have a happy ending. I could have ended at an earlier point, one at which I had neither known the key players nor participated in the events. But that would hardly have been the history the University wanted, or one I was interested in undertaking. I came to the University in 1951 and knew Sidney Smith in the 1950s. I worked closely with Claude Bissell on university governance in the 1960s. I was dean of law in the 1970s when John Evans was president. I hired Robert Prichard as a law teacher, and so on. I grew up in Toronto and went to the University for both my undergraduate and law degrees. After my post-graduate work at Cambridge University and teaching at Osgoode Hall Law School, I returned to the faculty of law in 1965. For better or worse, I am not a detached observer. But then, who would be?

Over the course of the project, I have had excellent research assistance. The quantity of material collected was enormous. I ended up with over a hundred file boxes of material, some of which has been deposited in the University of Toronto

Archives along with forty binders containing photocopies of the precise pages of the source material on which I relied. The main sources used are set out in an appendix. Historian Charles Levi was my principal research assistant for almost three years. He had helped Michiel Horn with his book on academic freedom in Canada and was described in Horn's preface as 'incomparable.' I would echo that view. If there was a document that had to be found, Charles found it. Other first-class research assistants who worked on the project at various times are David Bronskill, Sara Burke, Colin Grey, Kelly de Luca, Michael McCulloch, Tim Meadowcroft, Patrick Okens, and Sam Robinson. The University of Toronto Archives, headed by Garron Wells, was always helpful. I am particularly indebted to archivist Harold Averill, the great font of historical knowledge about the University, who helped me and my research assistants find material and photographs. Harold also read drafts of the manuscript, as did my research assistants.

The manuscript was read by numerous people at various stages of the project. The advice I received was invariably helpful to me in my many revisions. I have listed in the endmatter the names of those people connected with the University of Toronto who received the entire manuscript and sent me comments. The contributions of those who commented on individual chapters or parts of chapters are mentioned in the relevant footnotes. Here, I will mention only those from outside the University of Toronto who read the manuscript: Alan Cairns and Anne Innis Dagg of the University of Waterloo, Jacalyn Duffin of Queen's University, Robert Gidney and Wynn Millar of the University of Western Ontario, James Greenlee of Memorial University, Michiel Horn of York University, and Brian McKillop of Carleton University. I also benefited greatly from the detailed comments of the reviewers for the University of Toronto Press and the Social Sciences and Humanities Research Council. I am grateful to all those who generously contributed ideas for improving the manuscript.

I am also indebted to those at the University of Toronto Press who have given me encouragement and advice over the past few years: Ron Schoeffel, in charge of the project for the Press; Bill Harnum, the vice-president of scholarly publishing; and Melissa Pitts, the head of marketing. Many others contributed their care and expertise to the production of the book, including Valerie Cooke, who designed the book, Theresa Griffin, who copy-edited the manuscript, and Ruth Pincoe, who did the index. One person whom I asked to read a draft of the manuscript is a former managing editor of the Press, Francess Halpenny. Her comments were so helpful that she was asked to become the principal manu-script editor of the book, a task to which she brought the same skill and care she brought to another book of mine about thirty-five years ago. Finally, I am indebted to my wife, Judy, for her substantive and editorial advice as well as her encouragement throughout the project. I dedicated the book that grew out of my doctoral thesis to Judy. This present work I dedicate to our three children – like Judy and me, proud graduates of the University of Toronto.

Martin L. Friedland
University Professor and Professor of Law Emeritus
University of Toronto

July 1, 2001

PART ONE

BEGINNINGS

chapter one

1826

A CHARTER FOR KING'S COLLEGE

On the sixteenth of March, in the seventh year of the reign of George the Fourth – that is, in 1826 – John Strachan left the town of York, later called Toronto, for England. His principal mission was to obtain a charter for a proposed university for Upper Canada. The result of his trip was a royal charter, and twenty-five years of intense conflict on the question of the place of an established church in higher education in the colony.

Strachan was part of the so-called Family Compact that ran the colony of Upper Canada for much of the first half of the nineteenth century. He was a member of the non-elected legislative council from 1820 until 1841. The lieutenant governor, with whom he was very close, had appointed him in 1823 as the president of the general board of education for the province. It is not surprising, then, that he was the person selected to go to England to seek a charter for a university.

He had come to Upper Canada from Scotland as a teacher, and later became a minister of the Church of England and, eventually, the bishop of Toronto. Strachan's switch from the Presbyterian Church of Scotland to the Church of England continued to raise the eyebrows of his opponents over the years. His dual interest in religion and in education – to Strachan they were inseparable – continued until his death in 1867 at the age of 90.

Many thought he should stay out of politics. The radical reformer William Lyon Mackenzie – remembered for his role in the 1837 rebellion and as Prime

Town of York, drawn by James Gray in 1828, viewed from Gibraltar Point,
now part of Centre Island.

Minister Mackenzie King's grandfather – made this point in his newspaper, the
Colonial Advocate. 'Our countryman, Doctor Strachan,' he wrote in 1826, 'is
about to proceed to England on a political embassy ... Can the society who
uphold this clergyman really approve of the active part he takes in politics? What
will become of his flock?' Then, directing his remarks to Strachan, Mackenzie
warned, 'Like Cardinal Wolsey, you may, when too late, wish you had served
your Heavenly King with that ardour with which you now obey the nod of a
Colonial Governor.'

The 'colonial governor' was Sir Peregrine Maitland, who had become lieutenant governor of Upper Canada in 1818. He had led one of the brigades in the
Battle of Waterloo three years earlier and was knighted later that year. Maitland
agreed with Strachan's views that the Church of England should be the established church in Upper Canada. Both believed that the use of the clergy reserves
that had been set aside for the 'Protestant Clergy' (one-seventh of the public

lands in the province) should be restricted to the Church of England and that the education endowment for the new university should be used to build an Anglican institution.

The education endowment had been established in the late 1790s in the recently created province of Upper Canada, then with a population of perhaps 25,000 Europeans. Five hundred thousand acres of 'waste lands' scattered throughout the new province had been set aside as an endowment for the support of schools and 'a college or university, for the instruction of youth in the different branches of liberal knowledge.'

John Graves Simcoe, the first lieutenant governor, had been in favour of a college in the colony. Even before he had left England for Canada in 1792, the Oxford-educated Simcoe had written about establishing 'a college of a higher class,' a vision that even earlier had been expressed by the United Empire Loyalists who had come after the American Revolution to what would later be called Upper Canada. Such an institution, wrote Simcoe, 'would give a tone of principle and manners that would be of infinite support to government.' Of perhaps more importance, it would also help prevent students from picking up subversive ideas in the United States, where, 'owing to the cheapness of education ... the gentlemen of Upper Canada will send their children.' Simcoe had fought against the Americans in the revolutionary war and obviously had no wish to lose the rest of British North America as well.

'I have no idea that a University will be established,' Simcoe wrote to the Anglican bishop of Quebec in 1796, 'though I am daily confirmed in its necessity.' Such an institution, he felt, would 'strengthen the union with Great Britain and preserve a lasting obedience to His Majesty's authority.' He also stated that a university would 'have a great influence in civilising the Indians,' and then added, 'and what is of more importance, those who corrupt them.'

A report by the Upper Canada Executive Committee in 1798 recommended that a university be established in the town of York and that half the education endowment be used for that purpose. Little was done, however, until after Maitland arrived. In 1819, he referred the issue to his executive council, and in 1822 he sent a request to England for the use of the endowment lands for a university. The British government, however, appeared to favour the development of a university in Montreal to serve both Upper and Lower Canada. McGill College had received its royal charter in 1821, with Strachan himself having played a major role in its establishment. In 1807, Strachan had married the widow of the brother of James McGill, who brought with her a welcome annuity of £300 a year (Strachan had lavish tastes). Strachan had helped persuade James McGill to leave his fortune to found an educational institution. McGill had thought that Strachan would be its first principal, but Strachan probably felt that he had greater prospects in Upper Canada.

At the end of 1825, Maitland sent a further dispatch to the colonial secretary, Lord Bathurst, asking for the establishment of a university, and coupled with it a request that the endowment lands be exchanged for better lands that could be sold or rented for a higher price. Much of the existing endowment lands, he wrote, 'lie in tracts at present remote from settlements, and a considerable portion of them is not of the first quality.' Moreover, the government was giving away free blocks of land to settlers, and that made it difficult to sell the 'waste lands.' The solution requested was for the colonial office to allow the exchange of some of these waste lands for the more valuable crown reserves. As no reply was forthcoming from the colonial office, it was decided that someone must go to England to lobby for the charter, and, of equal if not greater importance, for the proposed change in the endowment.

Strachan was asked by Maitland to prepare a document to take to England, outlining why a university was necessary. As Simcoe had done a quarter of a century earlier, Strachan warned of the danger faced by sending students to the United States for their education. In the United States, he wrote, 'politics pervade the whole system of instruction. The school books ... are stuffed with praises of their own institutions, and breathe hatred to everything English ... Some may become fascinated with that liberty which has degenerated into licentiousness, and imbibe, perhaps unconsciously, sentiments unfriendly to things of which Englishmen are proud.' Three-quarters of the doctors in the province, he went on to say, had studied in the United States. Moreover, he wanted to be able to train Church of England clergy to act as teachers: 'It is of the greatest importance that the education of the Colony should be conducted by the Clergy,' that is, the Church of England clergy. 'Nothing can be more manifest,' he wrote, 'than that this Colony has not yet felt the advantage of a religious establishment.'

His 1826 mission was apparently not widely known outside the inner circle. With characteristic irreverence, Mackenzie's *Colonial Advocate* stated several days after Strachan left to set sail for England: 'Dr. Strachan set out for England last Thursday. The episcopal clergy of these colonies enjoy themselves right

Portrait of John Strachan, painted about 1827, now hanging in Trinity College.

pleasantly trotting and sailing backwards and forwards between the land of promotion and British America ... His real errand is best known to himself and those who act with him upon the petite theatre here.'

Strachan arrived in England about a month after he had left Toronto. He began discussions with colonial office officials, whom he had known from a previous visit to England relating to the clergy reserves. It is not known in detail what took place on this later trip. There were discussions with the colonial secretary, Bathurst, whom Strachan found 'a man of talent ... but shy and of feeble health.' It is also known that he met on a number of occasions with the archbishop of Canterbury, who strongly insisted that the Church of England be firmly in control of the university. The technical details of the charter were worked out with James Stephen, the counsel to the colonial office, who likely took a more liberal position on religious questions than Bathurst – 'a tory of the old school' – or the archbishop. Stephen 'was indefatigable,' Strachan later said, 'in removing difficulties and meeting objections raised.'

While overseas, Strachan visited the University of Aberdeen, from which he had graduated and had received an honorary doctorate – hence the title 'Dr Strachan.' He also spent time on immigration matters and had dinner with the great population expert Thomas Malthus, whom he described in a letter as 'rather an ugly man, and speaks very thick and through his nose.'

On March 15, 1827, the charter was issued under the Great Seal for the 'establishment of a College ... for the education of youth in the principles of the Christian Religion, and for their instruction in the various branches of Science and Literature ... at or near our town of York ... to continue for ever, to be called "King's College."'

The university was to be run by members of the Church of England. The president, the charter stated, would for 'all times' be the archdeacon of York, who at that time was Strachan. The governing council would be made up of seven professors, along with a chancellor and a president. All members of the council would have to 'sign and subscribe' to the Thirty-Nine Articles of Religion of the Church of England. Students, however, could be of any faith. This last provision was more liberal than at Oxford or Cambridge and the King's Colleges in Nova Scotia and New Brunswick. Strachan later said that it was 'the most open charter for a University that had ever been granted.' The charter, however, was in fact less liberal than the one granted to McGill College earlier in the decade, which, being in a largely Catholic province, did not restrict either students or professors to the Church of England. It is true that Strachan did not want the presidency to be necessarily restricted to the archdeacon of York, but he certainly wanted the holder to be a Church of England clergyman. Indeed, he probably wanted the president to be a Church of England cleric from England so that the institution would have a strong English flavour.

Whatever Strachan's views, it is likely that nothing more liberal could have been obtained for Upper Canada at the time. The religious nature of universities was then a major issue in England. The non-sectarian University of London had been established by Henry Brougham, James Mill, and others in 1826, the year Strachan arrived in England. But it had to be established as a limited liability company and not by royal charter and did not have the right to grant degrees.

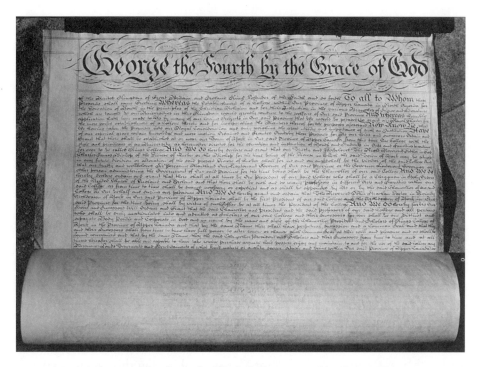

An original copy of the charter for King's College, granted by George IV in 1827.

The Commons supported Brougham's position that degrees be permitted, but the Lords rejected it. In 1836, however, the University of London was turned into an examining body, and the original University of London – 'the godless institution of Gower Street' – was granted a charter as University College. As will be seen later, this was the solution eventually adopted, in 1853, for the University of Toronto.

The charter said nothing about the endowment, but in the dying days of Lord Liverpool's ministry, Bathurst, who was about to leave office, agreed to the proposal to exchange crown reserves for the far less valuable 'waste lands.' Subsequently, 225,944 acres of crown reserves in well-settled districts were transferred to King's College. Moreover, the relatively substantial sum of £1,000 a year for sixteen years was to be given to King's for building purposes. It was primarily the decision about the endowment lands that created public controversy over the next half century, as representatives of other religious faiths fought for access to the income from these lands.

Strachan was back in Toronto in July 1827 – sixteen months after he had left – having returned to his large family and his grand house, a lavish brick building known as 'The Palace' overlooking Toronto harbour at the north-west corner of the present Front Street and University Avenue. But his reception by his critics was decidedly cool. The *Colonial Advocate* referred to Strachan's 'Judas like work' and asked, 'Can such charters be given by the king in Upper Canada without the consent of parliament?' There was particular concern about a pamphlet that Strachan had circulated in England to raise funds, which described the proposed university as a Church of England 'missionary college,' and greatly exaggerated the number of members of the Church of England in Upper Canada – they were in a clear minority in comparison with the total number of members of other Christian faiths.

When the Upper Canada legislature opened in January 1828, the elected legislative assembly sought an inquiry to determine whether 'the principles upon which [the university] has been founded shall, upon enquiry, prove to be conducive to the advancement of true learning and piety, and friendly to the civil and religious liberty of the people.' In mid-March, the assembly passed by a vote of 21 to 9 an address to be dispatched to the King and the colonial secretary stating that 'as the great body of Your Majesty's subjects in this Province are not members of the Church of England, they have seen, with grief, that the Charter contains provisions which are calculated to render the institution subservient to the particular interest of that Church, and to exclude, from its offices and honours, all who do not belong to it.' The address went on to ask that the charter be cancelled, and a new one granted to meet the assembly's concerns.

The assembly's address was referred to a select committee of the House of Commons in London, which issued a report that summer, agreeing with the Upper Canada assembly and stating that 'in a country where only a small proportion of the inhabitants adhere to [the Church of England], a suspicion and jealousy of religious interference would necessarily be created.' The committee wanted the charter to be changed so that 'with respect to the President, professors, and all others connected with the College, no religious test whatever should be required.' 'If Dr. Adam Smith were alive,' one member pointed out in the debate, 'he could not fill the professor's chair of political economy.'

In spite of these concerns, the planning for King's College proceeded at a rapid pace. Before the legislative assembly had met to request the cancellation of the charter and pending the appointment of professors, a council of 'seven discreet and proper persons' was selected by Maitland to join him (as chancellor)

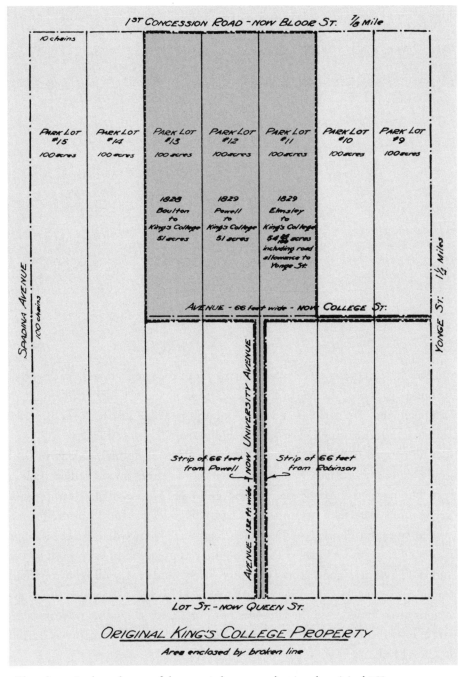

Plan, drawn in the early part of the twentieth century, showing the original 150-acre property obtained by King's College in 1828, plus the University-owned roads that became University Avenue and College Street.

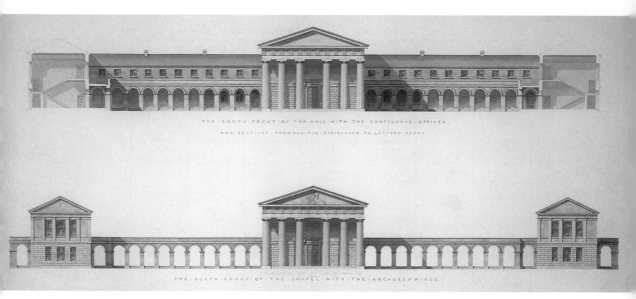

THE·SOVTH·FRONT·OF·THE·HALL·WITH·THE·CONTIGVOVS·OFFICES
AND·SECTIONS·THROVGH·THE·STAIRCASES·TO·LECTVRE·ROOMS.

THE·SOVTH·FRONT·OF·THE·CHAPEL·WITH·THE·ARCADES & WINGS.

Charles Fowler's 1829 design for King's College.

and Strachan (as president) in planning the acquisition of land and the design of the buildings. These 'discreet and proper persons' included Chief Justice William Campbell and the attorney general and future chief justice John Beverley Robinson, a former pupil of Strachan's and perhaps his closest friend.

The council had many choices for a site. They examined a block of land beside the Humber River, west of the town, not far from an old Indian trading post, but rejected it partly on medical grounds because of its swampy soil. Negotiations were then begun to purchase 150 acres of land from the former chief justice John Elmsley – offered at £25 an acre – somewhere between Yonge Street and the present Queen's Park. The site was unanimously approved by the council. There was good access to Yonge Street, and it was on relatively high ground and considered healthy. Elmsley changed his mind, however; the negotiations broke down, and the land was not purchased. A number of years later, part of it was acquired by St Michael's College, and St Basil's Church was erected on Clover Hill, the highest part of the property.

Another large tract of 150 acres – between St George Street and Spadina Avenue – was offered by the wealthy Baldwin family for £3,750. This offer was rejected, and instead the council chose the present site, consisting of 150 acres of vacant forest land: 50 acres from Chief Justice Dummer Powell, 50 acres from D'Arcy Boulton (the owner of the 'Grange' residence, now part of the Art Gallery of Ontario), and 50 acres from the Elmsley family. All three properties were obtained for £25 an acre for a total of £3,750, a sum about equal to the cost of John Strachan's home. Had the university also purchased and kept the Baldwin property and the remaining Elmsley property, all of which, including the site actually purchased, could have been obtained for a little over £10,000, the University of Toronto's financial future would have been considerably more secure – perhaps even today.

In 1829, plans were completed in England by the eminent architect Thomas Fowler, who was then designing Covent Garden Market. A model showing a Greek revival design resembling Thomas Jefferson's University of Virginia was sent to Upper Canada. The plans met with the approval of the colonial secretary in London. Some of the land was cleared, and stone for the building selected. Title to a grand avenue 132 feet wide (now University Avenue) leading from Queen Street to the site where the Parliament Buildings of Ontario now stand was purchased, and, in addition, a route along the present College Street was obtained and cleared from Yonge Street to the new site. Strachan wrote to a friend in Scotland in October 1829, 'We have procured plans – purchased a good site ... for the building, garden, and pleasure grounds three quarter of a mile from my house; and we are fencing, clearing, and planting and shall next summer, I think, commence to put up a portion of the general design.'

On Maitland's departure from Upper Canada as lieutenant governor in the fall of 1828, Strachan reported that King's College was about to open its doors.

chapter two

1842

LAYING THE CORNERSTONE

The building of King's College – for reasons that will be discussed shortly – in fact was not begun until fifteen years after the charter had been obtained in 1827. The cornerstone for the college was laid by the governor general, Sir Charles Bagot, in an impressive ceremony on April 23, 1842, a brilliantly sunny, cloudless spring day. A civic holiday was observed in the City of Toronto, whose increasingly affluent population had now grown to about 6,000 from the 2,000 or so in the town of York when Maitland left in 1828.

This was Bagot's first visit to Toronto since coming to the new province of Canada at the beginning of the year. A union of Upper and Lower Canada had taken place the previous year, following Lord Durham's famous report on conditions in the two provinces. Bagot had come with a considerable reputation for diplomacy. He had been the British ambassador to the United States after the War of 1812 and had negotiated the Rush-Bagot treaty, which controlled the number of naval vessels on the Great Lakes. If anyone could bring a measure of peace to the warring factions that had led to the 1837 rebellions against the ruling elites in both Upper and Lower Canada and continued to plague Canadian politics, it would be Bagot.

A few days before the ceremony, Bagot had arrived at the Queen's Wharf at the foot of Bathurst Street on HMS *Traveller* from Kingston, the new seat of government for the United Province. He was taken to the home of the attorney general, William Henry Draper, an open-minded conservative, who was leader

Approach to King's College, now the site of the provincial legislative buildings, viewed from the present Queen Street, about 1868.

of the legislative assembly. Draper had warned Bagot of the 'almost certainly injurious political conclusion which would be deduced' if Bagot were to accept Strachan's invitation to stay at 'The Palace.' Such was the delicate nature of Canadian politics of the period. Bagot and Draper wanted to give the ceremony 'as little of an exclusive character as possible.'

The ceremony for the laying of the cornerstone began with a procession that started at the preparatory school, Upper Canada College, at the corner of King and Simcoe streets, and proceeded to the King's College gates at the corner of the present Queen Street and University Avenue. At precisely 1 o'clock, Bagot arrived at the gates 'in an open carriage and four, escorted by a party of the First Incorporated Dragoons' and 'was placed on a slightly raised platform, over which was suspended a canopy, tastefully decorated with ever-green boughs.' An innocuous address in Latin by Dr John McCaul, the principal of Upper Canada College, and a similar reply by Bagot – a cultured Oxford graduate – were given. The procession then continued up University Avenue, accompanied by the tolling of the Upper Canada College bells, to the site of the present legislative building. Soldiers of the 43rd Regiment, bearing arms, lined the route. Dr Henry Scadding, who earlier in the day had preached a sermon from the pulpit of the Anglican St James' Cathedral, described the procession as 'such as had never before been seen in these parts.' He went on:

> The Governor's rich Lord-Lieutenant's dress, the Bishop's sacerdotal robes, the Judicial Ermine of the Chief Justice, the splendid Convocation robes of Dr. McCaul ... the accoutrements of the numerous Firemen ... the grave habiliments of the Clergy and Lawyers, and lances and waving plumes of the First Incorporated Dragoons, all formed one moving picture of civic pomp, one glorious spectacle which can never be remembered but with satisfaction by those who had the good fortune to witness it.

At the site of the laying of the corner stone was a wooden amphitheatre accommodating 1,500 persons, 'densely filled with ladies, who thus commanded a view of the whole ceremony.' The only other structure on the grounds of King's College was a log-built magnetic observatory, which had been erected by the province in 1840 on 2 acres of land given by King's just south-east of the present Convocation Hall. The observatory would have been barely visible through the trees, some of which, including the giant elms just east of Whitney Hall, are still standing today.

Again, various speeches were delivered, this time in English, extolling the 'glorious models, furnished by the Parent State' of what a university should be. The 'godless' University of London was not mentioned. Bagot cemented into the cornerstone a bottle filled with coins, various Bibles, the charter, and other papers, and the ceremony concluded with a nineteen-gun salute, the singing of God Save the Queen, and three cheers for Her Majesty.

From the moment Bagot had come to Canada earlier in the year, he had given high priority to bringing to life King's College, which he described as 'this hitherto imaginary college.' He had written to the colonial secretary immediately after his arrival that 'the delay has caused a great deal of dissatisfaction, while, by driving the youth of this Province to seek in the neighbouring States

Governor General Charles Bagot.

for the higher branches of education, it has had a tendency to produce results of a very objectionable nature,' no doubt referring to the 1837 rebellion. The students would be going there, he stated in a later letter, 'at the very time when their minds were most ductile, and their feelings most enthusiastic to the influence of democratic associations and principles.' After the laying of the cornerstone, he wrote to his brother in England, 'If I have ever done any good which is to outlive me, I verily believe that it has been this act.'

Bagot wrote to the colonial secretary a few days after the event: 'Nothing could exceed my reception there. From the moment that I landed, on the 21st, till I reembarked on the evening of the 25th, I never saw a thing, nor heard a word which could have led any one to imagine that there were two parties in the town.' Many of the dissidents, of course, including William Lyon Mackenzie, had fled to the United States after the 1837 rebellion, a large number had been convicted and transported, and two in Upper Canada had been hanged.

❧

The fifteen-year delay in starting the construction of King's College had been caused by great concern over the dominance of the Church of England in the control of the college as well as by a series of important political events in Upper Canada. After Maitland had left Upper Canada, Sir John Colborne, also a hero of the Battle of Waterloo, arrived in York in late 1828. He served eight years as lieutenant governor, under seven colonial secretaries, and for an additional three years he was head of the military in Canada. Described today as 'Upper Canada's ablest governor,' he kept his distance from the Family Compact leaders, particularly from Strachan.

Following the British House of Commons' strongly worded endorsement in 1828 of the Upper Canada Assembly's condemnation of the charter, a new colonial secretary told Colborne that the British government would welcome a request from the province for a change in the charter, and that such a request '[would] not fail to receive the most prompt and serious attention.' Colborne cautiously and skilfully diverted attention from King's College by stopping progress on the college and moving to establish a strong preparatory school, Upper Canada College.

The King's College charter had continued to disturb many in Upper Canada. Robert Baldwin, a member of a prominent reform-minded family who was elected to the legislative assembly in 1829, chaired, for example, a large public meeting in the town of York in 1830 on the university question. The meeting, sponsored by the Friends of Religious Liberty, petitioned Her Majesty 'to modify the Charter of King's College ... so as to exclude all sectarian tests and preferences.' More than 10,000 persons signed the petition. Baldwin, a member of the Church of England who had been a student of Strachan's, would continue his efforts to change the charter. Members of other denominations, such as Egerton Ryerson, a Methodist minister, were also strong opponents of the King's charter.

In 1831, the colonial secretary, Lord Goderich, asked for the surrender of the charter, indicating that any new Upper Canada legislation would be approved by the British government. The Upper Canada assembly, however, did not want to give up the dignity of a 'Royal' charter. Meanwhile, the King's College council was willing to modify some of the offending clauses. The president, the council said, need not be the archdeacon, and later it conceded that the president need not hold any ecclesiastical office. It was also willing to modify the requirement that members of the King's council subscribe to the Thirty-Nine Articles.

A liberalizing bill was passed by the elected legislative assembly in 1835, but was rejected by the appointed legislative council. In 1837, however, under a new lieutenant governor, Sir Francis Bond Head, and with a more conservative assembly, an act to amend the King's College charter was passed by both houses. Among the amendments was one eliminating subscription to the Thirty-Nine

Articles, but requiring a solemn declaration that members of the council 'believe in the authenticity and divine inspiration of the Old and New Testament and in the Doctrine of the Holy Trinity.' The college council was increased to twelve members and would include the solicitor general and the attorney general as well as the two speakers in the legislature, thus bringing the government directly into the running of the university.

With the amended charter, it once again looked as though King's was close to opening. The curriculum of the university was approved, and plans were made for the construction of the college. Thomas Young, who was in the process of designing St James' Cathedral after one of its fires, was engaged to plan the building. Fowler's original plan had been abandoned. The classical design, using half columns, envisioned three buildings: a centre block containing the library, a convocation hall, and a museum, with classrooms in the west block and a residence in the east block. All three would be connected by a covered walkway.

Construction was delayed, however, by a series of events. A number of months after the passing of the amendment, the 1837 rebellion took place. Then, in 1839, an investigation into the King's College finances found serious irregularities. The bursar, who acknowledged that he had engaged in 'censurable conduct,' had made large loans, without adequate security, to various individuals, including Strachan. One of the loans to Strachan was for £5,250, of which £1,875 was outstanding. To add to the complications, the union of the provinces of Upper and Lower Canada in 1841 was posing new political problems.

The members of other denominations were establishing universities in Upper Canada and so increasing the pressure to bring King's College into operation. The Methodists, led by Egerton Ryerson, got legislation passed in 1841 to convert the preparatory academy in Cobourg, which he had had founded by royal charter in 1836, into Victoria College. The college was officially opened in Cobourg in 1842, with Ryerson as principal. The Presbyterians received a royal charter for Queen's College in Kingston in 1841, which opened in the spring of 1842 with two professors and eleven students. Regiopolis College was founded in 1837 in Kingston by the Roman Catholic bishop of Kingston.

❦

This was the situation Bagot faced when he came to Upper Canada in early 1842, determined to make the construction of King's College a priority in his administration. Statutes were passed for the erection of the two wings of King's.

Victoria College in Cobourg, opened in 1842. The building is still standing
and is used as a retirement home.

In the meantime, Bagot authorized the use of the unoccupied parliament
buildings on Front Street, overlooking the bay, as the temporary quarters for
King's until the new buildings were completed. Moreover, following the laying
of the cornerstone, he actively took steps, as chancellor of the university, to hire
professors for the college. During this period, as his engrossing correspondence
makes clear, the 62-year-old Bagot knew that he was dying.

Against the wishes of President Strachan, Bagot hired the Reverend John
McCaul, the principal of Upper Canada College and a graduate of Trinity
College, Dublin, as vice-president of King's and professor of classics. Strachan
wanted only English staff. 'If we are to commence King's College in an imposing, popular, and effective manner,' Strachan wrote Bagot, 'the President and
leading professors must without exception be from England.' The Irish McCaul
was hired, however, and later became the first president of the University of
Toronto.

A number of staff were hired from England, though often with considerable

Engraving of John McCaul, done while he was president of King's College.

Photograph of Henry Croft, who taught chemistry from 1843 until 1880, and after whom University College's Croft Chapter House is named. Date uncertain, but towards the end of his career.

difficulty. To make recruiting easier, the college council had fixed the summer vacation period so as 'in these days of steam navigation [to] allow a visit to England.' Bagot had asked specific persons in England in whom he had confidence to find suitable professors. The great scientist Michael Faraday, for example, filled that role in the finding of a chemistry professor. After four chemists turned down Faraday's invitation to come to King's College, an offer was accepted by the 22-year-old Henry Croft, who had worked with Faraday and then had spent more than three years studying at the University of Berlin under a number of distinguished professors. Croft taught effectively and imaginatively in the University of Toronto until his retirement in 1880. (The round Croft Chapter House attached to University College and initially used as a chemistry laboratory is named after him.)

A Cambridge graduate – the son of a good friend of Bagot's – helped find a professor of mathematics and physics. Graduates standing high in the math-

Drawing of the legislative buildings, built in 1829 on what became Front Street, between Simcoe and John streets. The buildings were demolished in 1903.

ematics program at Cambridge are called 'wranglers.' 'Can you,' Bagot wrote, 'amongst the wrangling triangling Cantabs of your acquaintance, fix upon some man, eminent for his knowledge of Mathematics pure and mixed whose prospects in England are not either brilliant or certain ... who you think can be persuaded to come out to this Country as the Mathematical Professor.' High-ranking wrangler after wrangler turned down the invitation. They finally secured a person who had stood sixth in his year. He came out to Canada but left after a year. A wrangler who had stood second in his class, James Sylvester, had actually applied for the job, but was not acceptable because he was Jewish and therefore could not subscribe to the doctrine of the Trinity, a requirement for King's College professors. Sylvester, it should be noted, went on to be the brilliant Savilian Professor of Mathematics at Oxford University and the winner of the highest academic honour accorded to British mathematicians, the Copley Medal of the Royal Society.

Other teachers selected for King's included a tutor in Hebrew, Jacob Hirshfelder, a Jew who, unlike Sylvester, had converted to Christianity. The professor of divinity was to be selected by Bagot's brother, the bishop of Oxford. Bagot thought it would be easy to find a suitable person in 'the crowded state of the ecclesiastical profession,' but the person selected, the Reverend James Beaven, who came with his wife and seven children, was at least their third choice.

After Attorney General Draper had turned it down, the chair in law was given on a part-time basis to William Hume Blake, a future chancellor of the University of Toronto and the father of Edward Blake, another future chancellor. Chairs in medicine were given to various local doctors, including Dr William Gwynne, one of Bagot's doctors during his fatal illness, who became the professor of anatomy and physiology, and John King, a doctor 'of the Catholic persuasion,' who, Bagot wrote Strachan, would 'perhaps afford us the best and safest answer to the charges of exclusion and intolerance which, as you probably know, have already been loudly, but very unwarrantably directed against us.'

King's College officially opened in its temporary quarters in the unused legislative building on Front Street on June 8, 1843. Strachan had written to Bagot that 'the University should begin with some degree of solemnity.' Bagot was not there, however, having died in Kingston before the ceremony. Eight professors and 26 students took part. In a long speech, Strachan attacked those who had taken pains 'by calumnies and misrepresentation, to poison the minds of the people against the charter.' He went on to draw attention to the University of London, stating that 'the infidel attempt called the London University has signally failed, as all such godless imitations of Babel ever must.'

chapter three

1849

❦

THE CREATION OF THE UNIVERSITY OF TORONTO AND TRINITY COLLEGE

On April 3rd, 1849, Robert Baldwin introduced a bill into the parliament of the province of Canada to convert King's College into the University of Toronto. It would completely secularize the university, eliminating any publicly funded chairs of divinity and all religious tests for any member of the university, whether student or professor. Queen's and Victoria and other denominational colleges could affiliate with the university 'with some vague status, perhaps as divinity halls,' without assured government funding or the power to grant degrees, except in divinity. If passed, the bill would represent, in the words of historian J.M.S. Careless, 'an entire victory for the forces of secularisation and centralism in Upper Canadian higher education.'

In the meantime, King's College had been limping along in the unused red-brick legislative building on Front Street. The south-east wing of its own building had been completed in 1845 and turned into a residence, with the Reverend James Beaven in charge. Residence rules were established, such as one requiring students to be back in the residence before the gates were closed at 9:30 in the evening during the winter, and others requiring students to attend a certain number of chapel services. Not surprisingly, the students complained about the food, one later reminiscing that 'day after day the same pies and puddings made their appearance.'

The curriculum borrowed heavily from that of Trinity College, Dublin, the school from which the Reverend John McCaul and several others had graduated.

Photograph taken in 1886 of the start of the demolition of what was originally the residence for King's College, which had been completed in 1845 on the site of the present legislative buildings.

A number of scholarships were established, including one from the Duke of Wellington, who donated £500 worth of shares in the Welland Canal Company for that purpose. The students were overwhelmingly Anglicans – 22 of the first 26 students – and entrance examinations to the college were so demanding that only graduates of Upper Canada College had much chance of admission. In order to gain admission, it was said, students would have had to know 'nearly all the chief classics of ancient times.'

Baldwin had introduced a similar bill back in 1843. He and his Lower Canadian partner in the United Provinces, Louis-Hyppolite LaFontaine, had been asked by Governor General Bagot to head the government in the fall of

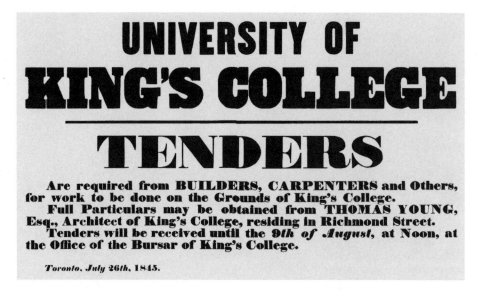

Public poster calling for tenders for King's College in 1845.

1842. Even before King's officially opened in June 1843, Baldwin had felt it his duty to tell the dying Bagot that he was opposed to the college as at present constituted. 'I do not, particularly considering the present state of His Excellency's health,' Baldwin wrote Bagot, 'feel called upon to do more ... than, for my own future justification, to express my entire though respectful dissent from the scheme adopted.' The Government, he went on to state, 'will find themselves called upon' to give the University 'less of a sectarian and more of a provincial character.' The proposed 1843 legislation would 'destroy King's College as a visible symbol of Anglican privilege and class favouritism.' The proportion of Church of England supporters in the population was continuing to decline. The bill of 1843 did not go quite as far as the 1849 bill, in that it contemplated having several theological chairs. The bill died, however, when the government resigned on other grounds in November 1843.

During the next six years, there were many schemes and bills to reform King's College. The new leader of the government, William Draper, introduced a series of bills in 1845 to establish a University of Upper Canada, with King's, Queen's, Victoria, and other institutions surrendering their powers to the new university and becoming affiliated colleges. Each would receive an annual income according to the number of students it attracted, a 'formula funding' proposal that

Robert Baldwin, the person primarily
responsible for the creation of the
University of Toronto.
Lithograph printed in 1845.

would not emerge again until the 1960s. Baldwin argued against Draper's proposal, saying that the scheme 'would necessarily encourage a multiplicity of small colleges, instead of large well endowed ones.' Bishop Strachan, of course, was opposed to this solution. Draper's concept was defeated. Two years later, John A. Macdonald – who would become Canada's first prime minister after Confederation – introduced a bill that would have given the income from the endowment (that is, the crown reserves that had been given to King's College in 1827) to the four existing colleges, with King's receiving £3,000 a year and Queen's, Victoria, and Regiopolis each receiving £1,500. Representatives of other religious denominations, however, complained that they were being shut out. The bill was withdrawn before reaching second reading, when it became clear that it would be defeated by a unified reform party and two defecting conservatives.

In the election of 1847–8, the reformers under Baldwin and LaFontaine won an overwhelming majority. The 'University Question' was an important issue in the election. The governor general, Lord Elgin, under instructions from London to maintain political neutrality, called on Baldwin and LaFontaine to form the government. They were sworn in on March 11, 1848. This was 'the culmination of a long and gradual process, through which internal self-government was worked out for Canada.' One of Baldwin's first actions was to persuade the King's College Council to order a commission of inquiry into the financial functioning of the college.

The 1849 bill creating the University of Toronto was introduced into the assembly, then meeting in the long, plain St Anne's Market building in Montreal. Baldwin said the bill would ensure 'the abolishment of every religious observance which could possibly prove offensive to any portion of the students attending the University.' Before the bill could reach second reading, however, the market was deliberately burned down by a Tory mob angered by Lord Elgin's signing of the contentious Rebellion Losses Bill (designed to compensate those whose property was damaged in the revolt in Lower Canada) and the apparent rise of French power over the British minority in Canada East. Elgin reported to the Colonial Secretary about 'this thin crust of order which ... covers the anarchical elements that boil and toss beneath our feet.'

The second reading of the bill in May 1849 was conducted in the quickly refurbished Bonsecours Market. It was immediately attacked by William Boulton, the owner of the stately Grange residence in Toronto. Boulton, a leading Orangeman and Strachan's spokesman in the assembly, said the bill was an attempt to make the university 'entirely infidel.' 'This bill,' he stated in the debates, 'instead of amending the charter of King's College as it professed, was intended to destroy King's College altogether, without leaving one vestige of it remaining.' It should, he added, be entitled 'A Bill for the Spoliation and Robbery of the Church.' 'Let the lands be taken away,' he pleaded, 'but let the institution remain; let the Church of England maintain the proud reflection that it still possessed a Royal Charter to educate its youth, as other denominations also possessed one.' Baldwin replied that 'when the Church of England asked for a charter like those of the other colleges he would be prepared to grant it.'

During Boulton's speech, an unidentified voice interjected, 'The College is in favour of it [that is, the 1849 bill].' Ironically, this was true. At the King's council meetings to discuss the college's reaction to the proposed bill, Professors Croft and Gwynne and another medical professor, William Beaumont, expressed themselves in favour of the bill, along with the council members Robert Baldwin and William Hume Blake. In earlier years, Croft and Gwynne, increasingly fed up with the politics of the college, had sent a petition to the assembly about undue clerical influence. Moreover, they had at times tried to obstruct the functioning of the council by depriving it of a quorum. Professors McCaul and

Beaven, however, both Church of England ministers, were strongly opposed to the bill. Bishop Strachan had resigned the presidency of the college in 1848, and McCaul was now its president.

The bill passed by a vote of 44 to 14 and became law on May 30, 1849. The University of Toronto came into existence on January 1, 1850. The 1906 Royal Commission on the University would call the legislation the 'real charter of the institution.' Along with the 1853 changes, to be described in the next chapter, it formed the foundation for the governing of the University for more than fifty years. King's College ceased to exist.

⧉

Within days, the 71-year-old Bishop Strachan started organizing a campaign for funds for his proposed new Church of England institution, Trinity College. He had given the idea considerable thought over the previous decade, as he saw the prospects for King's College rise and fall. Indeed, in as early as 1842 he had written to the brother of the Duke of Northumberland, proposing to call a new college 'Percy College' if the Percy family would put up the money. They declined. Several years later, the attorney general, Henry Sherwood, had offered to introduce a bill to incorporate the Anglican seminary in Cobourg as a college or university, 'say, Trinity College.' Again, nothing came of the offer. Moreover, Strachan was looking into the possibility that the British government would disallow the 1849 legislation, an unrealistic prospect given the new spirit of responsible government.

In February 1850, Strachan sent a letter to members of the Church of England in Upper Canada, seeking their financial support before he travelled to England for further support and a royal charter. 'On the 1st day of January, 1850,' he wrote, 'the destruction of King's College as a Christian Institution was accomplished ... To see it destroyed by stolid ignorance and presumption, and the voice of prayer and praise banished from its halls, is a calamity not easy to bear.' He himself pledged £1,000 to the cause. Other substantial pledges followed, and on April 10, 1850 a large crowd led by Chief Justice John Beverley Robinson saw him depart for New York to take the steamer *Europa* to England. He returned in the autumn of 1850 with considerable private financial support, but this time without a royal charter. Neither the government of the colony nor the University of Toronto wanted a second university in Toronto. A strictly theological college might have been tolerated, but a university was a different matter. Nor did they want a royal charter considered for another denominational college until it was known whether Queen's and Victoria would join the University of Toronto.

Strachan had wanted more than a divinity school because he saw Trinity College as the pinnacle of a system of Church of England education, comparable to the emerging Roman Catholic system of education in the province. Encouraged by Robinson, who would become Trinity's first chancellor, Strachan proceeded with plans to open the college, even though it could not yet grant degrees. On his return from London, he had been approached by a group of prominent doctors who had recently founded the Upper Canada School of Medicine and wanted to bring their school into Trinity as its faculty of medicine. The offer was accepted in early November 1850, and within days the first medical lectures were given at the Mechanics' Institute, near Church and Adelaide streets.

Twenty acres of land were purchased in early 1851 on the north side of Queen Street – now the Trinity Bellwoods Park – for £2,000. Queen Street was a fashionable street at the time, with many fine estates along it. Moreover, it offered a splendid view of the lake and the harbour. Today, the inelegant Strachan Avenue leads from the property to the lake. A college council was formed at about the same time. The architect Kivas Tully was selected over Frederic Cumberland's firm, which would later build University College. Tully's previous major work was the Bank of Montreal – now the Hockey Hall of Fame – at the corner of Yonge and Front streets. Sod was turned in the spring of 1851, and within two months Bishop Strachan, as president of the new university, took part in the laying of another cornerstone. Trinity College opened its doors in a half-completed building to 30 students on January 15, 1852, about two years after the closing of King's.

In the summer of 1851, the government of the United Province had incorporated Trinity College, but it was not until July 1852 that it received a royal charter from London, permitting it to grant degrees. By that time, it was clear that neither Queen's nor Victoria would give up its charter and join the University of Toronto. In these circumstances, as Strachan forcefully argued, it was hard to deny the Church of England the similar privilege of a charter. The institution would now be known formally as the University of Trinity College.

In order to receive their degrees, Trinity College students had to declare

Trinity College on Queen Street West, completed in 1852, now the site of Trinity-Bellwoods Park.

allegiance to the Church of England. Clergymen from Oxford or Cambridge were hired as professors. The first provost, or academic head, was a Cambridge-educated clergyman, George Whitaker, who, coincidentally, like Strachan, was a convert to the Church of England, his parents being Baptists. He had a wife and at least eight children. It appears to be a myth that Bishop Strachan insisted, at least in the early periods, that the professors be celibate. In his opening lecture, Provost Whitaker, who would be provost for another thirty years, told the students, 'The foundation of this College is a solemn protest against the separation of religion from education; we have joined together what others had put asunder.'

On the third reading of the 1849 bill to establish the University of Toronto, John A. Macdonald had predicted that the Act 'would not finally settle the question; that in a very few years some change would be loudly called for.' His prediction would prove correct.

chapter four

1850

⚛

STARTING OVER

When the University of Toronto officially came into existence on January 1, 1850, the King's College faculty, with the exception of the professor of divinity but including the professors of law and medicine, automatically became professors in the University of Toronto. In spite of his opposition to its founding, the Reverend Dr John McCaul continued as professor of classics and president of the new university, where he would remain as a loyal member of the academic community for the next thirty years. He also continued his 'high scholarship,' publishing a volume on Britanno-Roman inscriptions in 1863 and one on Christian epitaphs of the first six centuries a few years later.

The Reverend James Beaven, the professor of divinity at King's, also remained, in spite of his strong abhorrence of the new institution. Although the Act of 1849 had abolished his chair of divinity, he became the professor of metaphysics and ethics. He was elected by his few colleagues in arts as the dean of arts. In an 1851 letter to the first University of Toronto chancellor, the landowner Peter de Blaquière, he expressed his 'entire disapproval of the very principles upon which the University is founded ... an Institution which I abominate.' The chancellor replied that he could not understand how Beaven, in the light of his view of the university, 'could, under any circumstances, remain as one of its Professors.' Beaven explained, 'I submit to the greatest mortification of my life only because I cannot see my way clear to acting otherwise.' He had a large family and the government had not offered him an adequate pension, so he

Cartoon of a celebrated prank involving James Beaven and a monkey, from the
University of Toronto Monthly of 1930.

remained. His statements to the chancellor were brought before the new university senate, but before any dismissal proceedings could be brought, Beaven apologized.

Although Bishop Strachan unsuccessfully tried to find Beaven a pulpit, he did not offer him a position at Trinity College. Beaven was neither a good scholar nor a good teacher. His real interest was in church work. Sir William Mulock, a student at the university in 1859 and later its chancellor, reminisced that 'Dr. Beaven who had the difficult task of teaching fundamental principles of ethics, was as dry as his lectures.' Unfortunately, he remained at the University of Toronto until he was forced to resign in 1871 at the age of 70, after his students had sent a petition to the premier of the province describing Beaven as 'incompetent for the chair.' On one occasion, the students in his class placed a stuffed monkey from the university museum in his seat in the classroom. Beaven entered the lecture room, saw the monkey, and, according to a professor on staff at the time, 'looked first at the monkey and then at the class. Then he made a low bow to his prospective audience and said: "Ah, gentlemen, I see that at last you have a professor suited to your capacity. I wish you a very good morning."' So perhaps he was not as humourless as his contemporaries state.

Croft, the professor of chemistry, was pleased to be in the new university, as were the professors of medicine, who dominated the senate, in which all professors had a place. Croft was elected vice-chancellor by the senate, and Dr William Nicol, a Cambridge graduate who had been on the faculty of King's College since 1843, was elected dean of medicine by his colleagues. The part-time professor and dean of law – there was only one professor of law – was William Hume Blake's brother-in-law and legal partner, George Skeffington Connor. The two had come from Ireland together with their families in 1832. Jacob Hirshfelder, who had not had a permanent position at King's, applied to be a professor of Oriental languages and was appointed a lecturer with a fixed salary, an improvement over his previous position, in which he had had to rely entirely on student fees.

It had been assumed when the Baldwin Act of 1849 was introduced that the University of Toronto would occupy the King's College property in Queen's Park and, until it was completed, the legislative building on Front Street. But things did not work out that way because, after fire had destroyed the building housing parliament in Montreal, parliament returned to Toronto for its sittings. As a result, the University of Toronto was short of space. The east wing of King's College, which had been used as a residence, was converted into lecture rooms, administrative offices, a library, and a museum, as well as Professor Croft's laboratory. The library consisted of about 4,500 books – somewhat smaller than the King's library had been, because the books Bishop Strachan had acquired from the Society for Promoting Christian Knowledge were transferred to Trinity College (along with the Duke of Wellington Scholarship). The faculty of medicine was housed in a Greek revival brick building similar to King's College, constructed in 1850 (later known as Moss Hall) on the site of the present Medical Sciences Building. In addition, a house was rented on Wellington Street for meetings of the senate and other official university bodies.

Architects were invited to submit designs for the centre block at the old King's College site, and once again Thomas Young was selected. He produced an

The university gates at College and Yonge streets, with tracks of the Yonge Street railway in the foreground; photograph taken about 1880. The sign prohibits, among other activities, 'allowing cattle or swine to run at large,' 'discharging firearms,' and erecting a table 'wheron any game of hazard or chance can be played.'

elegant design, but before anything could be done, the government took over the site for a possible permanent parliament building for the United Province of Canada, thinking that Toronto would become the capital. As it turned out, Ottawa was selected as the capital, but the old King's College site was never returned to the University. The building was needed for a women's mental hospital. The University was then forced to occupy the newly constructed medical building, which, for the reasons discussed below, was no longer required for the medical school. The King's College building, perhaps not inappropriately, was named 'The University Lunatic Asylum.' The University obviously needed a new building. The magnificent University College, the building of which commenced in 1856, would be the answer.

About 50 full-time students attended the new university in the 1850s – roughly the same number as had been at King's. The number dropped to 35 in

1851 but rose to 56 in 1857. A somewhat larger number attended lectures as occasional students, many of whom were preparing for the Law Society and medical exams. One student in those early years, George Kennedy, later recalled that 'there was no residence then; the students found accommodation for themselves wherever they pleased in the city. It was the rule that the students should wear the cap and gown not only at the classes, but always.' 'East of the Don was all farming land,' he noted. 'The only railway in my matriculation year was the Northern to Collingwood.' Two other full-time students during the early years were Adam Crooks and Edward Blake, both excellent students who would later play significant roles, first in helping the University survive and later, as vice-chancellor and chancellor respectively, in helping it prosper. Crooks received his BA from the University in 1852, with first-prize medals in both classics and metaphysics. Blake, the son of the first professor of law at King's, William Hume Blake, obtained his BA in 1854, and received the silver medal in classics. Seventy-five years later, the historian Frank Underhill would describe Edward Blake as 'probably the greatest intellectual in our history.' Both Crooks and Blake became lawyers and politicians: Crooks served as Ontario's attorney general under Premier Edward Blake in the early 1870s and, later, as Ontario's first minister of education.

Baldwin's hope that the denominational colleges would join the new University of Toronto was unfulfilled. Queen's College did not want to leave Kingston, both for the sake of the students from that area and because the college in that location would provide a bulwark against the Roman Catholicism of Lower Canada. Victoria College in Cobourg, however, came close to joining, particularly after Baldwin passed an amending Act in 1850, which allowed the denominational colleges to prescribe 'religious requisites' for their students and to require attendance at public worship and religious instruction, provided there was no cost to the university. According to the official historian of Victoria, C.B. Sissons, if a purchaser had been found for the Victoria College buildings at Cobourg, the college might have joined the University of Toronto at that time.

In the summer of 1851, Baldwin suddenly resigned as co-premier, and Francis Hincks was asked to form a government along with a Lower Canadian colleague, Augustin-Norbert Morin. There were plausible political reasons for Baldwin's resignation, but there were also professional and personal reasons. He had for some years been subject to bouts of depression – his wife had died in childbirth in 1836, and his own health was deteriorating at an increasing rate.

John McCaul as president of the
University of Toronto.

Jean Mathieu Soulerin, the founding superior
of St Michael's College.
Photograph taken about 1865.

In 1853, he wrote to his former colleague LaFontaine that he was 'seldom free
for two consecutive days from the disagreeable rumbling noise in my head.' He
ran again for parliament in an election in late 1851 but was defeated, and at the
age of 47 he more or less retired from public life, moving from his large house on
Front Street to his country home, Spadina, just east of the present Casa Loma.

Hincks was sympathetic to proposals for changing the structure of the
University in an attempt to induce the denominational colleges – which were
given representation on the senate – to join the University. He was familiar with
the Queen's University, Belfast, model – similar to the University of London
system – which would make the University an examining body, with the
teaching done by affiliated denominational colleges and a non-denominational
University College. After consulting with the superintendent of education,
Egerton Ryerson, who supported restructuring the University and removing the
endowment from the exclusive benefit of the University of Toronto, Hincks
introduced a bill in September 1852 adopting the University of London model,
with University College as a separate teaching institution in the University. The
University of Toronto would become an examining body.

University College would have its own council, and no religious test would be permitted. McCaul would become president of University College and would no longer be president of the University. The bill was strongly attacked by those who saw it as negating the principles of the Baldwin legislation. George Brown, for example, wrote in the *Globe* that 'it would be a national calamity to split up and destroy Toronto University for a set of little paltry colleges.' The chancellor of the University, de Blaquière, resigned in protest, and Baldwin was invited to take his place. He declined to do so, stating that acceptance 'would imply less hostility than I entertain to the course adopted by the present Government.' The Bill was given royal assent on April 22, 1853.

The 1853 legislation was meant to encourage the denominational colleges to join the University, but apart from Knox College, a Presbyterian divinity school that had broken away from the official Church of Scotland, no other college joined. The other denominational colleges had hoped that in the bill the endowment would be divided, but it was not. Although the legislation provided for use of the endowment income for the non-affiliated colleges, it was only to be the 'surplus' income. There never would be any surplus, particularly after the use of the endowment to construct University College.

St Michael's College expressed an interest in affiliation, but was turned down by the University. The head of the college, Father Jean Mathieu Soulerin, saw significant financial advantages because the University of Toronto was 'so richly endowed,' but the Roman Catholic bishop of Toronto, Armand de Charbonnel, was less sure. He was against affiliation because 'our students might be required to study works contrary to the teaching of the Church ... I am ... completely resolved, whatever my straits may be, to refuse all affiliation with this Protestant University, to preach about its dangers among our Catholics and to turn them away from it as far as possible.' Nevertheless, Father Soulerin wrote to the Senate in 1855 asking for affiliation. The Senate politely said no. Father Lawrence Shook, a later president of St Michael's, states in his history of the college that one possible reason was that 'the affiliation of perhaps the smallest and least influential institution in Toronto was more likely to weaken than strengthen the position of the university in its Toronto constituency.' It is true that in the early period St Michael's was largely a high school, but it is also true that there was strong anti-Catholic feeling among certain members of the university community, just as there was in the larger society. Professor Beaven, for one, had expressed such views.

St Michael's College and St Basil's Church. Photograph taken about 1870.

The Roman Catholic St Michael's College had been founded by the French Basilians in 1852. The Roman Catholic bishop of Toronto had been trained by the Basilians in France, and he had invited four members of the thirty-member French-speaking community to join the one member already in Toronto. They were impressed by the wealth of the city, one of them writing that the houses 'have two or sometimes three stories, very beautiful on the exterior but even more magnificent inside. Everywhere one sees carpets, armchairs, sofas, stuffed chairs, splendid mirrors. Here no one ever waxes floors; the corridors, even the stairs of the houses are carpeted.' The Jesuits had been invited earlier to establish the college but had declined, even though John Elmsley, a convert to Catholicism, had offered them some of his land. In 1853, this land was offered to the Basilians on the condition that they erect a parish church along with a college. St Basil's Church and the attached college on Clover Hill were the result. The church and the college were officially opened in 1856, the oldest surviving buildings in the university. It would not be until 1881 that St Michael's would affiliate with its neighbour, the University of Toronto.

The 1853 Act, which had repealed the 1849 Act, had many defects. The University was now effectively controlled by the government. Appointments and significant expenditures required government approval, a state of affairs that did not change until the 1906 Act – more than fifty years later. The University was now to be headed by a chancellor and a vice-chancellor. McCaul would no longer be president of the University, but president of University College. The chancellor would be appointed by the government and not elected by the graduates, as had been provided for under the 1849 legislation – and would again become the practice thirty years later. William Hume Blake accepted the chancellorship after Baldwin turned it down.

Furthermore, the denominational colleges had an undue influence on the affairs of the University through their participation in the senate, which in turn would elect the vice-chancellor. Whereas about half the members of the former senate had been professors, the only University of Toronto professor on the new senate was McCaul, who was elected as vice-chancellor and chaired the senate's deliberations. Other senators were appointed directly by the government or were there because of their positions in the denominational colleges, even though those colleges had chosen not to affiliate with the University. John Langton, a member of the senate and a future vice-chancellor, remarked that with the exception of himself and two or three others, the senate 'consists of the heads of these other colleges, who bear us no love and, if they attend at all, do it only to obstruct.'

A highly significant feature of the 1853 Act was the elimination of the faculties of medicine and law. Although the university would continue to examine and grant degrees in those fields, it would not offer instruction. The professors who were let go were given a year's extra salary as compensation for their loss of position. To avoid protests, those professors who resigned before the act came into effect were offered an additional year's pay.

There is little doubt that Dr John Rolph, a member of Hincks' cabinet, played a crucial role in the elimination of the medical faculty. Rolph was both a doctor and a lawyer – Baldwin had worked in his law office in the 1820s – and had been forced to flee to the United States because of his part in the 1837 rebellion. In the mid-1830s, he and Hincks had been involved in a major commercial venture. When Rolph returned in 1843, he concentrated on medicine, and started his own medical school, the Toronto School of Medicine, which was incorporated in 1851, the year he agreed to join Hincks' cabinet. In 1853, Rolph's medical school was facing increasing competition from the University of Toronto medical school and the recently established Trinity medical school. No contemporary document has come to light directly stating that

elimination of the Toronto school was a condition of Rolph's continuing participation in Hincks' shaky government, but later reminiscences assert the connection. The University of Toronto medical professors who were let go called the
1853 legislation 'the Rolph Act,' and John A. Macdonald intimated in the
assembly that Rolph was behind the act. Rolph's presence in the cabinet helped
keep Hincks in office. He remained loyal to Hincks when other reformers were
deserting him over his railway deals. When Rolph resigned from the government
after his school's future seemed secure, the government fell.

There were other factors at play. Ryerson, the superintendent of education,
advised Hincks that both law and medicine should be run by private institutions, perhaps housed on the university campus, with special grants from the
government. Moreover, there was concern about the dominance of the medical
faculty in the University, a not uncommon complaint in universities over the
years. John Langton, a member of the senate, later wrote that the 'professors of
various branches of medicine were so numerous as to outwit the rest and they
first lowered the other salaries and then raised their own. Before three years the
University had got into a very bad odour, and had degenerated into a very
expensive and very bad medical school.' Many years later, however, the professor
of anatomy, James Richardson, painted a far different picture in a letter to
President James Loudon, referring to the high quality of the faculty members,
whose duties 'were discharged faithfully and with enthusiasm.' 'Everything was
progressing most favourably,' he wrote, 'when suddenly a blow was struck which
annihilated the medical faculty, and left the University of Toronto without one
for about 30 years.' A faculty of medicine was not established again at the
University until 1887.

The story of Rolph's school is complex. In 1854, he offered his school to
Victoria College, which was happy to provide medical degrees for Rolph's
Victoria Medical School in Toronto – for a share of the fees to be used for their
library in Cobourg. A couple of years later, however, all Rolph's professors
resigned to form their own medical school, using the name 'Toronto School of
Medicine.' Rolph was unsuccessful in his legal action to prevent the use of the
name of his old school. The Victoria school ceased operation in 1874, Rolph
having resigned as dean in 1870 at the age of 76. The Victoria students were
transferred to the Toronto School of Medicine, which eventually became the
resurrected faculty of medicine of the University of Toronto.

The teaching of law was also removed from the University in 1853, though, as with medicine, examinations were still held and degrees could still be awarded. Many hoped that the Law Society of Upper Canada would take over the teaching of law in a serious manner. It had been urged to do so for a number of years by those seeking admission to the bar, who had complained that 'students of the laws are left to grope their way through the intricate labyrinth of legal science, almost without a clue to guide their steps.' Ryerson had suggested to Hincks that the Law Society would receive £500 a year if it set up its own school, a powerful inducement for the habitually cash-strapped Society. The school was established; the money was never given.

One reason why Ryerson wanted legal education transferred to the Law Society was that such a school, he argued, 'would exert a salutary influence upon the whole Legal Profession in Upper Canada – very different from having one Professor of Law in the University, lecturing betimes to some half a dozen students, but not recognised in any way by the incorporated Law Society of Upper Canada.' The new arrangement had the concurrence of the Law Society. Skeffington Connor simply moved from teaching at the University to teaching at Osgoode Hall. But the Law Society did not treat the matter seriously. Its school had a rocky existence: it closed in 1868 for four years and then closed again in 1877. The University did not re-establish a teaching faculty until 1889, but as will be seen, this was short-lived after the Law Society again set up its own school – Osgoode Hall Law School – in 1889. The teaching of law at the University would not officially be recognized as equivalent to the Law Society's Osgoode Hall Law School until 1957.

Baldwin's concept of a faculty-dominated university consisting of both the arts institution and the professional schools had been replaced in reality by a government-dominated arts institution. Appointments and major decisions were in the hands of the government. Moreover, owing to the composition of the senate, the University was an institution vulnerable to attack from within as well as from without.

chapter five

1853

NEW PROFESSORS

Additional staff for University College arrived in the fall of 1853. Two years earlier, advertisements had been placed in the British literary and scientific journal the *Athenaeum* for five new chairs for the University at £350 a year. Whereas a decade earlier Bagot had had difficulty recruiting faculty members, this time there were many first-rate applications from which to choose. Toronto was now a wealthy city of about 40,000 persons and was growing rapidly. The question is whether the University chose the best of the applicants.

There is no doubt that Daniel Wilson, one of those who arrived in 1853, was an excellent choice as the professor of English history and literature, said to be the first such professor in British North America. His appointment was an indication of the shift of the university away from classics to literature and history. He was and continued to be an excellent scholar with wide interests in history, literature, anthropology, art, and archaeology. Before coming from Scotland to Canada, he had published two major works, *Memorials of Edinburgh in the Olden Time* and *The Archaeology and Prehistoric Annals of Scotland*. He is credited with having first used the word 'prehistory.' He is credited also with giving the first course in anthropology in the world. Wilson never completed his university degree in Scotland, though just before coming to Canada, the University of St Andrews awarded him an honorary doctorate. It did not hurt his cause that the Governor General, Lord Elgin, as a member of the Society of Antiquaries of Scotland, was familiar with Wilson's work and career. Wilson, after whom

View of the city of Toronto in 1854. Lithograph by Edwin Whitefield.

a University College residence is named, was a powerful intellectual force in the University, and later became its second president.

Wilson's journal and his letters to his wife reveal his views of Toronto and the University. (His wife and two children did not join him until 1854.) In a letter dated September 21, 1853, he gave his first impressions of the city: 'It is a busy, bustling, active town ... bearing such evident marks of rapid increase that I should not wonder if ten years hence it be found to number nearer a hundred thousand ... Everything indicates wealth and prosperity. As to the shops, many of them are equal to the best in Edinburgh, and if a person has only money, he need want for nothing here that he desires.' He pointed out that one could get a servant for 'just £12 a year' and that he thought his own salary would soon be raised to £400 a year.

Wilson's opinion of the University College president, McCaul, was initially
very favourable. 'Tomorrow I dine with Dr. McCaul,' he wrote, 'a clever, lively,
humorous Irishman ... He seems a shrewd fellow and a good scholar, very well
fitted for his post.' Wilson at first was amused by the great formality insisted
upon by McCaul. 'It is a high crime and misdemeanour,' Wilson wrote, 'to
appear in College hours otherwise than in cap and gown.' On one occasion, he
was forced by McCaul to go back for his cap and gown to administer an exam to
a single student. Wilson's views on McCaul would soon change, however.
Within months, he was calling McCaul 'a confounded intriguer.' Many years
later he would write in his diary that McCaul has 'always been a ridiculously
over-estimated man, and never out of some mean trick or another.' He seemed

Daniel Wilson, shortly after his arrival in Canada in 1853.

to like the other professors, however, calling them 'clever fellows,' but did not think much of Professor Beaven, a 'dreadfully dry stick.'

Wilson appeared to get along well with the students. Several months after his arrival, he wrote to his wife that he 'could not possibly desire a more respectful or gentlemanly set of students.' In early 1854, he helped the students form the University College Literary and Scientific Society. 'I have been engaged this week in helping the students to constitute a College Literary and Debating Society,' he wrote, 'and mediating between them and Dr. McCaul, who had very nearly knocked the whole on the head by some of his stupid and martinet interference, just for the pleasure of exercising a little brief authority. Now however the young gentlemen are fair set agoing, in high spirits, and likely to work well together. The result I anticipate will be to give them a fresh and more lasting interest in the College, a thing greatly needed here.'

George Kennedy, a future lawyer, later reminisced about the founding of what is still called 'the Lit': 'I remember well the meeting of students at which the Literary Society was organised. It was held in Professor Croft's lecture room, which was a wooden building that stood by itself off the west wing of the old Parliament buildings ... There was a long wrangle over the name that should be given to it, and, finally, after several names were proposed and rejected, the late Ernestus Crombie moved that the name be "The University College Literary and Scientific Society" and this was adopted. The first debate took place a few evenings after, and was held in Professor Wilson's lecture room. The subject was "The Relative Merits of the Arts of War and the Arts of Peace."' The name of the society was changed in 1921 to the University College Literary and Athletic Society.

The new professor of mathematics and physics (called natural philosophy in the nineteenth century) was John Cherriman, 'a Cambridge man whom I expect to like,' wrote Wilson. Cherriman was a good teacher and a fine mathematician, though only a 'sixth wrangler' (wranglers, as mentioned, were those standing high in the maths program at Cambridge), but he was not much of a scholar. An historical survey of professors of maths and physics in Canada done in the 1990s refers to his many presentations as having 'no sense of unity' and demonstrating 'a rather eclectic interest in the sciences,' and as often presenting work he had come across in journals 'or reflections on problems that had arisen in the course of his teaching,' sometimes without reference to prior work in the field.' Cherriman was particularly interested in probability theory, and in 1875 he left the

John Cherriman, appointed professor of mathematics and physics (then called natural philosophy) in 1853.

Reverend William Hincks, professor of natural science and the brother of the premier of the United Province.

University to become the first superintendent of insurance for the Dominion of Canada.

An extremely strong candidate for the maths and physics position was the 31-year-old John Tyndall, still remembered today as an important physicist. The so called 'Tyndall effect,' for example, showed the effect of the scattering of light by very small particles suspended in a medium and thus explained why the sky is blue. In a famous speech to the British Association for the Advancement of Science, he traced the origins of life to inorganic compounds and even single atoms. Tyndall had received his doctorate in Marburg, Germany, and had also studied there under Robert Bunsen, the inventor of the Bunsen burner. His scientific work would make him a fellow of the Royal Society of London in 1852 and the following year a professor at the Royal Institution in London, where he later took over as superintendent from the great Michael Faraday. Tyndall's name, however, was not even one of the three passed on by the senate to the government for consideration. Why was Cherriman chosen? Perhaps because he was much more than competent and was already at the University, having been appointed a lecturer in mathematics in 1850 to fill in for the then ailing professor of natural philosophy, whose death in 1853 opened up the professorship.

Overlooking Tyndall is perhaps understandable, but passing up Thomas Huxley for the chair in biology (then called natural history) was unpardonable. After graduating from the University of London as a medical doctor in 1845, he spent four years on HMS *Rattlesnake* as the ship's surgeon doing scientific work in the South Pacific. The publications that resulted earned him election to the Royal Society of London and the Royal Medal for having published 'the most valuable paper' to appeared in the three preceding years in the philosophical transactions of the Society. Huxley's application for the chair included testimonials from Charles Darwin and many other leaders of the scientific world, who all predicted a great future for the 27-year-old scientist. He was optimistic about being appointed, writing, 'Toronto is not very much out of the way, and the pay is decent and would enable me to devote myself wholly to my favourite pursuits.' 'There are, I learn,' he wrote to his fiancée, 'several other candidates, but no one I fear at all, if they only have fair play ... There is no one of the others who can command anything like the scientific influence which is being exercised for me, whatever private influence they may have.'

The position went, however, to the nearly 60-year-old Reverend William Hincks, who had been a professor of natural history in Cork for the previous ten years, having spent most of his earlier career as a Unitarian minister. He also happened to be the much older brother of Francis Hincks, a premier inclined to do what was expedient. Huxley was prepared for the outcome, however; he wrote to his friend Tyndall before the actual appointment: 'I believe the Chair will be given to a brother of one of the members of the Canadian Ministry, who is, I hear, a candidate. Such a qualification as that is, of course, better than all the testimonials in the world.' Fifty years later, in 1901, Professor A.B. Macallum, one of Toronto's most distinguished scientists and the first Canadian-born member of the Royal Society of London, stated that if Huxley and Tyndall had been appointed, 'Toronto, as a seat of learning, today would more than rival the leading universities of this Continent.'

William Hincks did not have a high reputation as a teacher. 'His method of teaching,' one former student wrote, 'left much to be desired.' Like Beaven, he made his students memorize lists of classifications. He did not do fieldwork, 'preferring local strolls in the amateur naturalist tradition.' As did many other naturalists in the early part of the nineteenth century, Hincks believed in the so-called quinarian theory – that all species could be categorized into discernible groups of five, arranged in a circle. The trouble was that he was teaching these antiquated and anachronistic ideas in the second half of the nineteenth century. The students played jokes on him, just as they did on Beaven. On one occasion, they released a foul-smelling gas into his classroom through a hole in the wall.

Behind the Reverend William Hincks' penchant for classification was his understandable desire to show that the world was ordered by divine design in a logical manner. He tried to rebut the Darwinian view of natural selection with his own detailed scheme. In an 1866 paper, for example, he referred to the 'unity of plan and perfection of design' brought about by 'the God of Nature, infinite in power, Supreme in Wisdom and Benevolence.'

Nothing in the history of this or any other relatively modern university equals the impact of Darwin in the nineteenth century on the thinking and research of its professors. Perhaps the Copernican idea that the earth was not the centre of the universe had a similar impact on sixteenth-century universities. One can almost feel the intense struggle in the University of Toronto to come to grips with Darwin's ideas, not just in the natural sciences, but also later in the social sciences, where 'Social Darwinism' would be debated. The University of Toronto may have been a 'godless university,' but almost everyone believed in God, the question always being the precise form of worship required to communicate with God.

Other members of the faculty shared Hincks' view. The Reverend James Beaven obviously did. Indeed, the monkey in the chair incident described earlier may have been a comment on Beaven's views about Darwin. The recently appointed professor of mineralogy and geology, Edward Chapman, a civil engineer who had come to Toronto in 1853 from University College, London, was, however, a relatively quick convert to Darwin's views. In 1860, in a review of *On the Origin of Species*, which had been published the previous year, Chapman took the Hincks line, stating that the differences in the various species 'are regarded by us as parts of a great plan, conceived and carried out by the ALMIGHTY in his wisdom, for some purpose unfathomable to us at present, and perhaps ever to remain unfathomed by our restricted powers of inquiry.' Three years later, however, Chapman was conceding that Darwin's views had 'some strong claims to consideration.'

Daniel Wilson's reaction to Darwin is particularly interesting. After many years of fieldwork and study in American libraries – the library at the University

Edward Chapman, appointed professor of mineralogy and geology in 1853.

James Forneri, appointed professor of modern languages in 1853.

of Toronto was wholly inadequate for his purposes – Wilson wrote his major work, *Prehistoric Man: Research into the Origin of Civilisation in the Old and the New World*. Published in 1862, it has been described by a recent commentator as 'one of the great anthropological syntheses of the nineteenth century.' In a review of *Prehistoric Man* a hundred years after its initial publication, the then chair of the department of anthropology at the University, Thomas McIlwraith, stated that 'our early president is shown as a scholar, a philosopher, and an original thinker, many of whose predictions have been fulfilled.' That such a book could come out of the 'woody depths of Canada' was a surprise to at least one British reviewer. In his early writings, Wilson was not prepared to abandon the biblical chronology that humans were only several thousand years old, even though Darwin might have been right with respect to animals. In a later edition, however, after visiting several Palaeolithic collections in France and England, he accepted the great antiquity of human origins and the likelihood that humans descended from apes. And in his third edition, published in 1876, he removed all reference to biblical chronology. He insisted, however, that 'the transformation from ape to human had been an instantaneous one, in which a soul had been infused into an animal body.' So he tried to have the best of both the scientific and the theological worlds.

Wilson's views led him to view humankind as one. He was shocked at the racist conclusions of prominent American scientists who took the position that humanity consisted of several separate species with differing capabilities, thus justifying the subjugation of blacks. To Wilson, all races were equal, and the mixing of the races was beneficial and would eventually produce a new North American people.

Not until the 1870s and the new generation of Toronto scientists, such as the biologist Ramsay Wright and the physicist James Loudon, do we see an explicit disentangling of science and religion on the part of those teaching at the University. Ramsay Wright publicly expressed the opinion that the origin of species, including humankind, had been 'definitely settled' by Darwin.

Other professorships were established in the 1850s – those of modern languages, agriculture, and engineering. James Forneri, in languages, who seems to have been well liked by his students, was an Italian veteran of the Napoleonic wars. He came to the University in 1853 at age 63 with a family of ten after a one-year teaching position at an academy in Nova Scotia. No doubt Premier Hincks helped in getting him the job because Forneri and Hincks' father had taught together in Belfast. Daniel Wilson wrote to his wife that Forneri 'was a soldier, doing manful deeds at the retreat from Moscow, three years before I was born.' Wilson also noted that Forneri was 'amusingly simple, and much in need of a course in English.' George Kennedy recalled: 'Perhaps the most general favourite of all the professors of that day was old Professor Forneri ... His Italian pronunciation of French was very funny, and I shall never forget the vivacity with which, when a correct answer to a question was given, he would bring down his hand upon his desk and say, "Dat it ees."' William Mulock, a future chancellor of the University, who was Forneri's student in 1859, remembered him as 'a cultured gentleman and an excellent teacher of French, German, Italian and Spanish.' He held his professorship until reaching the age of 77 in 1866.

The professor of agriculture, George Buckland, seemed never to attract many students. Apparently only a handful ever received a diploma in agricultural science. He was responsible for starting an unsuccessful 25-acre experimental farm, located where Hart House now stands, and a botanical garden farther up Taddle Creek, towards Bloor Street. He was more successful, however, in helping establish the Ontario Agricultural College in Guelph in 1874, affiliated with the University of Toronto until 1964, when it became the University of Guelph.

For the chair of engineering, a number of applications were received, including one from Kivas Tully, the architect of Trinity College. A controversy was created when the rival architect, Frederic Cumberland, applied for the position after the deadline. Over the objections of the other applicants, his name was nevertheless one of the three sent to the government from the senate, but without indication of an order of preference. The government, however, never appointed anyone to the chair, no doubt because of the controversy and probably also because they took the same view with respect to engineering that they had taken with respect to law and medicine – that is, that the teaching of such subjects should be the responsibility of the professions, with the schools possibly located on the campus of the University. In 1878, the School of Practical Science – as engineering was to be called – would be physically located on university grounds. As with law and medicine, the University continued to conduct examinations and grant degrees in the fields concerned, but in the twenty-six years during which the course in engineering was available, only seven persons received a diploma.

University College now had a credible group of professors. What was desperately needed was a proper home.

chapter six

1856

BUILDING
UNIVERSITY COLLEGE

The foundation stone for University College was laid without fanfare or publicity or any of the grand ceremony that had accompanied the laying of the stone for the ill-fated King's College. The governor general was not there, and the stone itself was unmarked. As far as anyone now knows, no documents or other objects were inserted in it. Only three people attended the October 4, 1856 event: John Langton, the vice-chancellor of the University, and Professors Croft and Wilson. Wilson later remarked that 'they laid the stone secretly as if engaged in a deed of shame, full of hope, but also full of fear.' He then added, 'Perhaps it was well and wisely done.' They did not want to create controversy and the possibility of renewed opposition from the denominational colleges. They moved quickly. 'Every stone that goes up in the building, every book that is bought,' wrote Langton at the time, 'is so much more anchorage, and so much less plunder to fight for.' The premier of the United Province, John A. Macdonald, is reported to have said, 'Even Methodists can't steal bricks and mortar.'

The three people who can claim the most credit for bringing the magnificent University College building into being are John Langton, Governor General Sir Edmund Walker Head, and the architect Frederic Cumberland. A lesser but still notable contribution was made by Daniel Wilson, who was very knowledgeable about art and architecture. He knew the ancient buildings in Britain and in his youth had spent two years as an engraver, working on an engraving of one of J.M.W. Turner's works. John Langton, a graduate of Cambridge and a member

Stone carvings in the University College rotunda.

of parliament who had developed a reputation for financial acumen, was appointed by Premier John A. Macdonald in 1855 as chairman of the recently created provincial board of audit and later that year to the senate of the University, where he took a strong interest in the institution and its financial affairs. The following year, he defeated McCaul, the president of University College, in the election held for the position of vice-chancellor. It was obvious to him that University College needed a proper home.

Fortunately, Sir Edmund Walker Head had recently been appointed governor general of Canada. He was an Oxford graduate, with a first in classics, who had been a fellow of Merton College, Oxford, for eight years. The 'scholarly governor' – to borrow the title of a biography of Head – had a deep interest in art and literature and put pressure on the government to allow the endowment to be used for a new building, now that King's had become an asylum. Langton wrote at the time that Head was 'about the best friend we have.' Chancellor William Blake's resignation owing to frustration over the lack of a building no doubt helped increase the pressure. The government permitted £95,000 to be used for a new building, to include a library and a museum. Professors Croft and Wilson were subsequently added to the building committee.

Frederic Cumberland, or Fred, as he was called, was an exceptionally good architect who had been appointed by the senate as the university architect in early 1856. No competition was held for the job. Perhaps it was felt he was owed work, having been appointed in 1853 to design the proposed parliament buildings in Queen's Park, which were never built. And, as stated earlier, no one was appointed to the chair of engineering for which Cumberland had applied. Moreover, as a university senator since 1853, he had an inside track with his fellow senators and had recently built the new magnetic observatory, then just south-east of the present Convocation Hall. (The observatory was disassembled in 1908 and the material reassembled for a differently structured building just east of University College, which now serves as the offices of the Students' Administrative Council. Even though the original stones were used for its reconstruction, this building does not have as good a claim as the later St Basil's Church in St Michael's College to be considered the oldest still-standing building at the University.)

Cumberland had come to Canada in 1847 at age 27 with excellent recommendations, including one from the architect of the British parliament buildings, then nearing completion. Within a relatively brief period of time after his arrival, he had been involved in some important projects, including St James' Cathedral, the Adelaide Street Courthouse, and the Seventh Post Office on Toronto Street. While working on University College, he also worked on the equally fine expansion of Osgoode Hall. Unlike those of many architects, almost all Cumberland's buildings survive today, including his residence, Cumberland House, completed in 1860 on the east side of St George Street, just north of College Street, and now the International Student Centre. University College and the buildings mentioned above are considered some of the most splendid buildings in Canada. When Anthony Trollope visited Toronto in 1862, he wrote that 'the two sights of Toronto' were Osgoode Hall and University College, the latter of which he called 'the glory of Toronto.' 'Until I reached Toronto,' said the governor general, Lord Dufferin, in 1872, referring to University College, 'I confess I was not aware that so magnificent a specimen of architecture existed upon the American continent.'

The selection of the architectural style and the siting of the building were described in some detail by Langton in letters to his family in England. Because the King's College site could no longer be used, a move to the west was required. Langton was not unhappy with the move. Having a building at the end of the mile-long approach, now called University Avenue, would have caused problems. 'St Peter's would look magnificent there,' Langton wrote, 'but anything we could build would be but a mushroom at that distance.' One suspects that University College in fact, would have looked majestic on the site where the legislature now stands.

Cumberland was sent by the senate to Great Britain and the Continent in the spring of 1856 to study other buildings, and when he returned, he and his partner, William Storm, designed a Gothic structure. Governor General Head, however, was unhappy with the choice of the Gothic style. 'The site being chosen,' Langton wrote, 'Cumberland drew a first sketch of a gothic building but the Gov. would not hear of Gothic and recommended Italian, [showing] us an example of the style, a palazzo at Siena which, if he were not Gov. Gen. and had written a book on art, I should have called one of the ugliest buildings I ever saw.' Then the governor general suggested a Byzantine style. In his absence, Cumberland, Langton, and Wilson redesigned the building. 'We polished away almost all traces of Byzantine,' Langton wrote, 'and got a hybrid with some features of Norman, of early English etc. with faint traces of Byzantium and the Italian palazzo, but altogether a not unsightly building and on his return His Excellency approved.'

Which way would the building face? It seemed obvious to Cumberland, as it does to us today, that the building should face south, but apparently the governor general wanted it to face west. The three were saved, however, by a tall elm tree when they began to stake out the ground according to the governor general's wishes. The tree would have to be cut down, they informed the governor. This he would not permit, claiming that 'it was the handsomest tree about Toronto,' and adding, 'You Canadians have a prejudice against trees.' So they staked it out facing south, and, Langton wrote, 'when the Gov. paid us a visit next day he was quite satisfied and complimentary, and in congratulating us upon the safety of the tree he said to Cumberland ..., "I am sure that *you* can never put anything up half so pretty."' The tree was toppled in a storm the following year.

The south front of University College is nearly 400 feet long, an imposing structure that then could be seen from the city and the lake. The architectural historian Eric Arthur is probably still correct in saying that its front door is 'the most photographed bit of architecture in Toronto.' Ideas had been taken from many places. The doorway is clearly borrowed from the medieval gate tower to a Benedictine abbey in eastern England, and the round chemistry building – subsequently named the Croft Chapter House, after Croft retired – was patterned after a recently constructed laboratory at the University Museum in Oxford, which itself had been borrowed from an abbot's kitchen in western England, to give two examples. Each part of the building is of great architectural interest, as the art historian Douglas Richardson has shown in his book on University College, *A Not Unsightly Building* – taking the title from the Langton letter cited above. Cumberland said he chose the Norman Romanesque style because he 'believed that its ruggedness was appropriate to Canada.' Langton called it the 'Canadian style.' Cumberland had been influenced by John Ruskin, the well-known nineteenth-century English art and social critic, whom Cumberland knew and who, using the example of English castles, urged young architects 'to conceive and deal with breadth and solidity' and stressed the importance of craftsmanship. These features are found, of course, in University College.

The first structure to be built was the round chemistry laboratory because

Workers in front of Croft Chapter House, University College, about 1857.

Construction of the east wing of University College, about 1857.

The bell tower of University College,
the scene of the well-known incident in which
a cow's tail was tied to the bell.

there was a danger that it might not be built for reasons of economy. It served as the architects' office for the project. A residence for the president, McCaul, to be attached to the college, was never built. The west wing of the building was given over to student residences, and the present Junior Common Room was the dining hall. The bell tower above the dining hall became the subject of a famous Hallowe'en incident in which a number of undergraduates were able to lure a cow up the narrow tower stairs and tie a rope to the bell and the cow's tail. The awakened authorities found it harder to get the cow down than the students had found it getting the cow up. Wooden boards were required to slide the cow down from the top.

The northern part of the eastern wing was a convocation hall, for official ceremonies and, perhaps surprisingly in a 'godless college,' for prayers. 'Every resident student,' according to the calendar, was obliged to 'be present in the Hall at daily Morning and Evening Prayers, with reading of the Scriptures,' unless there was 'conscientious objection.' The upper hall on the east side of the main tower contained the library, with space for about 35,000 books, fewer than half of which were in the library when it opened. The museum was in the west wing on the second floor. Hincks, as curator, was busy collecting and arranging his various specimens, no doubt in groups of five.

Workers in front of University College, about 1857, among them perhaps
Ivan Reznikoff and Paul Diabolos.

Although the building appears to be made of stone, only about one-third of the exterior is stone, the rest being a very pale yellow brick, produced at a brickyard on Yonge Street, where Ramsden Park now stands. Many of the workmen came from German-speaking cantons in Switzerland. The stained glass was produced locally, but only one window – on the landing of the staircase at the west end of the building – survived the 1890 fire. None of the original wooden gargoyles survived. The crests over the main door of the college were carved by a Bavarian Jew, Newman Steiner, who had fled to North America after taking part in the unsuccessful 1848 Hungarian revolution. He learned to be a stone sculptor in New York and then moved to Canada, where he established a major marble supply company. Close inspection of the carved university crest above the doorway, designed by Daniel Wilson in 1857, shows that the tree is a maple. When the crest was later approved by the College of Heralds in England, the maple was removed and an oak substituted. They left the beaver, however.

Two of the workmen, Ivan Reznikoff, a 'Russian Pole,' and Paul Diabolos, a Greek sculptor, are known to recent generations of students because pubs in University College have been named after them. Apparently they were both in love with the same woman. Reznikoff and the woman were said to be planning to marry when Diabolos persuaded her to go west with him, taking Reznikoff's savings. Before they left, a fight ensued at the deserted work site, Reznikoff brandishing an axe and Diabolos a dagger. Reznikoff was reportedly killed and his body thrown down the well over which the circular staircase to the top of the tower was built. Over the years, it is said, his ghost haunted the halls of University College. His bones – so the story goes – were found after the fire and given a proper burial. Reznikoff's ghost then departed from the college.

A dam was built in 1859 in Taddle Creek to form a pond 12 feet deep, known over the years as McCaul's Pond, north-east of the college. The creek, which begins in Wychwood Park on the high ground north of what was then the city, runs beside the present Philosopher's Walk, and makes its way to Lake Ontario, will appear and reappear in this history. It was covered over in 1884 and made a city sewer, having become 'a holding tank for all the sewage discharged into Taddle Creek by residents of Yorkville upstream.' A current planning document proposes to re-create parts of the stream.

Exactly two years after the foundation stone was laid – on October 4, 1858 – the capstone for the 120-foot tower was set in place by Governor General Head. There was no need for stealth on this occasion. Indeed, there was a twenty-one-gun salute and afterwards a banquet in the library. President McCaul eloquently predicted that long after his bones had turned to dust, there would remain 'an institution which freely offers the advantages of an education of the highest order to all who are qualified to avail themselves of its benefits, and enables the son of the poorest and humblest man in the land to compete on equal terms with the children of the most affluent and the most influential.'

chapter seven

1860

SAVING THE UNIVERSITY

With the opening of a grand new building, the number of students began to increase significantly. Moreover, tuition fees were modest, and the University provided many prizes and scholarships. Whereas in 1855 there had been only 35 full-time students, by 1860 the number had increased to more than 100. The college was in a semi-rural retreat, somewhat removed from the city. Many of the full-time students were in residence. The college gardens provided food for the kitchens, and the fields provided pasture for the cows, which supplied milk. Students and professors spent the afternoons taking walks. 'No professor,' claimed William Mulock, a future chancellor who was a student at the time, 'if he could avoid it, lectured in the afternoon, which was reserved for recreation and walking.' Students would often throw a football or play cricket, but it was not until 1869 that the first organized athletic group at the University – a cricket club – was formed.

Beneath the outward tranquillity of the University, however, serious problems were developing. In 1859, the denominational colleges commenced a sustained attack on the University of Toronto that came very close to removing its privileged position. The contest was at times vitriolic. 'A more annoying and distasteful controversy could not well be conceived,' Daniel Wilson noted in his journal, 'conducted as it was with an amount of vulgar personality inconceivable to educated men at home [that is, in Britain].' The controversy was partly about money, but it was also about the proper purpose of a university education.

University College before the fire of 1890.

The economic depression that began in 1857 seriously affected the denominational colleges. Victoria College was going deeply into debt and started agitating for a share in the endowment. The visual grandeur of University College was a constant reminder of the disparity of treatment by the government. The Wesleyan Methodist Conference, the principal supporter of Victoria College, passed a series of resolutions at its 1859 assembly in Hamilton, pointing out the importance of 'religious and moral instruction of youth in the most exposed, critical and eventful period of their lives' and asking for a fair share of government funding, to which, it argued, Victoria College was 'justly entitled.' A number of public meetings throughout the province organized by the Methodists supported the resolutions.

Egerton Ryerson, the founder of Victoria College and from 1845 to 1876 the superintendent of education for Ontario (then called Canada West), played the key role in the challenge to the University of Toronto. It was Ryerson who drafted a petition sent to the government in late 1859, who prepared the extensive background papers on the issues, and who generally was the strategist behind the endeavour. Samuel Nelles, the president of Victoria, was also an important figure. Nelles had been a member of the first undergraduate class at Victoria College in the early 1840s, and he became the professor of classics at the college in 1850 and president in 1854, a position in which he remained until 1884. Trinity College stayed on the sidelines, with Bishop Strachan personally refusing to have any part in what he called 'the present raid.' Similarly, the Roman Catholic institutions were mainly spectators. Queen's University, however, gave Victoria its active support.

In a series of letters to the *Globe* in 1859, President Nelles argued the importance of religious instruction. At a university, he stated, 'there is no father to counsel, no mother to instil, from lips of love, the lessons of Sacred Truth. A stranger has taken the place of both father and mother ... Christian fathers and mothers will want to know who that stranger is.' He pointed out that although under the 1853 Act the denominational colleges were to share in any surplus from the endowment, 'very good care is taken that there shall be no "surplus".' Ryerson noted that in England there is 'one London University, but there are thirty-six Colleges in that University – all standing upon equal footing – some of them Church of England, others Wesleyan, Congregational, Baptist, Roman Catholic, etc.' C.B. Sissons, the official historian of Victoria University, was later to take the position that 'there was much justice in the claims of the outlying colleges as against those of what they designated the Toronto College monopoly.'

A document drafted by Ryerson in 1859 added a new note by criticizing the standards of the University of Toronto. 'The curriculum of the University studies,' it argued, 'has been revised and changed three times since 1853, and reduced by options, and otherwise, [to] below what it was formerly, and below what it is in the British Universities, and below what it is in the best Colleges of the United States.' 'In the best colleges and universities,' Ryerson stated, 'the first and largest place has been given to the study of classics and mathematics.' Toronto's system of options and exemptions, which permitted a degree of specialization after the first year, meant, he wrote, that 'a degree of B.A. can have no definite signification, especially as applied to a man of Honours. He may not have studied a word of Greek, or Latin, or solved a problem of algebra, or demonstrated a proposition of geometry, after the first year of his course of studies, and yet be a B.A. with honours.' The charge was strongly resisted by the University of Toronto.

Under the guidance of John McCaul, Toronto had indeed introduced options, more than at Oxford and Cambridge, though even those universities were slowly moving towards permitting greater specialization. Ryerson would exclude

McCaul's Pond, with University College in the background.
Watercolour by Lucius O'Brien, 1876.

from the curriculum such subjects as modern history and modern languages and, of course, agriculture, meteorology, and similar practical courses. It will be recalled that he did not think even law or medicine belonged in a university. The introduction of the new subjects at Toronto meant that it was obviously not possible for a student to take all the subjects offered, even when the number of years required for graduation was increased from three to four years. Toronto students who received first-class honours in their first year were permitted even greater specialization than the so-called pass students. The distinction between 'honours' and 'pass' gave rise to complaints, not unlike those in later years, that professors spent too much of their time with the honours students. The recognition of 'honours' was the precursor of the honours program, which would be introduced formally in the 1870s and would last for nearly a hundred years. In this earlier period, however, the term 'honour' referred to the student and not the course.

A further charge brought against the University of Toronto was waste and mismanagement, one that also was strenuously resisted. Ryerson complained, moreover, about the lowering of entrance standards. This was readily admitted. Vice-chancellor Langton stated that 'if a much higher matriculation exam were prescribed and acted upon, the young men from many parts of the country would be altogether excluded from the university, unless their parents were able to afford to send them for preparatory training to Upper Canada College or some other superior grammar school.'

A legislative committee was established in 1860 to examine the resolutions put forward by the Wesleyan Methodists. The committee included in its membership the attorney general, John A. Macdonald, who was sympathetic to the denominational colleges, and George Brown, the radical editor of the *Globe*, who was not. Brown was a friend of Daniel Wilson's, having been a schoolmate of his in Edinburgh. The committee held nineteen sittings in Quebec City during March and April 1860. Witnesses appeared for Victoria, Queen's, and Trinity. John Langton, the widely respected vice-chancellor, and Professor Wilson testified for the University of Toronto. The president of University College, John McCaul, did not appear. Although ready to go, he was told that he 'was not required.' He was too closely identified, it was thought, with his former King's colleagues, now at Trinity. Moreover, McCaul was thoroughly disliked by many of the professors at Toronto, including Wilson, whose own administrative star was rising. Langton, who had defeated McCaul in the election for the post of vice-chancellor in 1856, had noted that the professors 'from hatred of McCaul stick to me like bricks.'

At the legislative hearings, much was made of the fact that Ryerson had not attended university. 'Are you a graduate of any university or were you at any time a student at any university?' George Brown asked. 'I never was a student at any university,' Ryerson replied, adding, however, that he had 'both studied and taught many of the branches commonly taught in university education.' Daniel Wilson gave evidence stating that Ryerson was not to blame for not having attended a university, but was to blame 'for insisting on laying down the law in matters in which he has not had the slightest experience.' 'German and French,' Wilson said, 'are now the keys to so much modern philosophy and science that all wise university reformers are learning to give to modern languages the place they justly claim in a liberal education.' The university that had been mentioned in the 1853 Act, he reminded the committee, was not Oxford or Cambridge, but the University of London, 'established in the nineteenth century, with a view to

Engraving of Egerton Ryerson, probably done
in the 1860s.

meeting all the advanced requirements of this age, rather than Oxford University, which is understood from vague tradition to have owed its origin to a meeting of three monks in a barn, some time in the good old times of the Saxon Alfred.' The sons of wealthy English noblemen or gentlemen, he went on, may learn at Oxford and Cambridge 'to be able to compose the most perfect Latin verse ... but that is not what Canada requires. We want an educational institution which shall train our young men for the practical duties of life.'

'Where were you educated?' President Nelles asked Wilson through a member of the committee, knowing, of course, the answer. 'At Edinburgh,' Wilson replied. 'Did you take out a degree in arts?' 'No,' Wilson answered, 'it is rarely the practice at the Scottish universities.' Ryerson then drove the point home, asking the committee 'what claim that gentleman himself has to support his pretensions? Is he a graduate himself?' If graduation from university is a necessity, Ryerson asked – knowing that only one member of the committee had graduated from a university – 'what business have you laymen, who never graduated at a university, with the affairs of the educational institutions of our country?' One can almost feel in the debates the personal animosity between Wilson and Ryerson, the former of whom stated privately that Ryerson was 'the most unscrupulous and jesuitically untruthful intriguer I ever had to do with.'

Two draft reports were prepared by the committee, one with the assistance of Langton and one by the chair of the committee, Malcolm Cameron, 'an old friend' of Victoria College, no doubt with help from Ryerson. The committee could not agree, however, and never brought in a final report. John A. Macdonald, now the premier, requested draft legislation from Ryerson, but the legislation, which would have limited University College to a fixed sum each year from the endowment, was not acted upon. Instead, Macdonald, with the help of Ryerson, appointed a royal commission designed to be sympathetic to the denominational colleges. The commissioners were asked to 'inquire into the expenditure of the funds of [the University and University College], and the best means of reducing such expenditures, without weakening their efficiency.' The three-member commission had a representative of Victoria and of Queen's as well as James Patton, the new vice-chancellor of the University of Toronto. Patton had been elected vice-chancellor in 1860 over Langton, who was occupied with government business in Quebec City. It seems unlikely that most University of Toronto supporters realized how firmly Patton, an early graduate of King's College, was in the camp of the opposition.

The commission did not take formal evidence, but spoke to numerous individuals and sent out various questionnaires. A questionnaire went to all the denominational colleges as well as to the University of Toronto, arguably going beyond the commission's terms of reference in asking for opinions on the best mode of affiliation. The University of Toronto's senate responded, expressing the view that the present system was unsatisfactory and that one 'University of Upper Canada' was desirable, provided that University College had 'a first claim to a fixed endowment amply sufficient to its support in its present state of efficiency,' including faculties of law and medicine. To a considerable extent, the senate's position would have met the needs of the denominational colleges.

When the commission's two-hundred-page report became known in early 1863, the University of Toronto concluded that it had been duped. The commissioners recommended that University College be limited to $28,000 a year. The affiliated colleges would each be given $60,000 to enlarge their premises and maintain their libraries. Moreover, University College's name in the new University of Upper Canada was to become King's College, a name that did not hold fond memories for most supporters of the University of Toronto. Furthermore, professors, who had wanted a greater role in the governance of the University, were to be excluded from the senate. This was not what defenders of the University had expected.

The Toronto supporters' new strategy was to arrange for five persons friendly to the University to be appointed by the government to the university senate, including Edward Blake. John A. Macdonald was no longer the premier, and the new premier of the United Province, Sandfield Macdonald, was willing to comply because he was personally opposed to public support of denominational colleges. Adam Crooks, the president of the University Association, made up of all the graduates of the University, was already a member of the senate, and at an even earlier point three professors, Wilson, Croft, and Cherriman, had been appointed by the government. This gave the supporters of the University a strong position in any future decisions. Ryerson, Nelles, and Vice-chancellor Patton realized this and attempted – unsuccessfully – to have additional persons favourable to the denominational colleges appointed. At a senate meeting of March 4, 1863, Crooks gave notice that he would move that the earlier position of the senate be overturned and the endowment be maintained intact. The commission, Crooks argued, had exceeded its jurisdiction. 'If these resolutions are carried,' Patton wrote to Ryerson, 'the commissioners' report will receive a fatal blow.'

The next evening, a large public meeting of University College students, alumni, and professors, Chancellor Skeffington Connor, and other supporters filled Toronto's St Lawrence Hall. Adam Crooks, as president of the University Association, had called the meeting and was invited to chair it. 'The Commissioners had dealt with matters in their report with which they were not authorised to deal,' he said to great cheers, according to the report in the *Globe*. 'They had set forth a scheme,' he continued to more cheers, 'which, if carried out, could result in nothing less than an entire dismemberment of the endowment and destruction of the University of which we were so proud.' A series of resolutions – similar to those Crooks would introduce in the senate – were passed without dissent. One resolution was moved by Edward Blake, that the professorships of law and medicine be restored, and the last resolution was moved by a 19-year-old student, William Mulock, whose first name the *Globe* reporter did not know. The meeting ended with 'three cheers for Her Majesty the Queen, three for the Chairman, and three groans for the Commissioners.'

Ryerson, Nelles, and Patton attempted to block a subsequent university senate debate on Crooks' motions on procedural grounds, arguing that the senate had no jurisdiction to debate the commissioners' report and, in any event, could not meet until a new chancellor was appointed to replace Skeffington Connor, who had died suddenly. Vice-chancellor Patton ruled against Crooks'

University College 'foot ball team,' 1870, with James Loudon, the future president, in the second row, far left.

motions, but the senate overruled the chair, and all the resolutions were passed with healthy majorities. Patton would not resign, however. 'Their object is to drive me from the Vice Chancellor's Chair,' Patton wrote to Ryerson, 'but ... I have made up my mind not to fall into the trap, as my duty to you and to the other members of the senate, who have acted with me is not to give up a position which to a great extent gives me a controlling power – at least in many things.'

The threat, however, was now over. Daniel Wilson noted in his journal his 'grim satisfaction' in 'seeing the pack turn tail at last and scuttle off ignominiously with their tails between their legs.' He later commented, 'It is very doubtful if the men of our day realize how narrowly their university escaped extinction.' In 1864, Patton stepped aside, and Crooks became vice-chancellor. The financial position of the denominational colleges, however, did improve for a time. The government increased their grants of money without affecting the University of Toronto's endowment.

But government funding of the denominational colleges was not to last long. After Confederation in 1867, education was transferred to provincial jurisdiction, and Premier Sandfield Macdonald's new Ontario government abolished grants to the denominational colleges. He no longer had to worry about the reaction to that measure by legislators in Quebec. Ryerson and his supporters could do little except warn of the 'necessity for the advocates of Christianity ... to buckle on their armour and by prayer and faith and courage to challenge and meet the enemy in open combat.' There was, however, no further fight. Nelles concluded, 'It is I think useless to struggle any more – at least at present.' The opportunity would emerge twenty years later. Ironically, it would be William Mulock as vice-chancellor and Edward Blake as chancellor who would bring Victoria University into the University of Toronto.

❧

The number of full-time students at University College continued to increase during the 1860s. At the time of Confederation, there were 250 full-time students, primarily from the towns and villages of Ontario. One of those who graduated in 1867 was a prize-winning black student, Alfred Lafferty, whose parents probably came from the United States in the 1830s. Lafferty went on to become the headmaster of the Guelph High School and, later, a lawyer. Another member of a minority group was James Ross, who received his MA in 1865, after receiving two gold medals for his BA. Ross, whose grandfather was an Okanagan Indian chief, became a lawyer and was chief justice in Louis Riel's 1869 provisional government at Red River.

The 1860s were not peaceful years for the University. Nor were they peaceful outside the campus. For the first half of the decade, Canada lived under the shadow of the American civil war, which posed a threat to British North America, particularly after American forces forcefully removed Confederate agents from a British ship on the Atlantic Ocean. In view of the threat, Professor Croft organized the University Rifle Corps. Croft was the captain, Cherriman a lieutenant, and the ubiquitous Adam Crooks an ensign. The corps saw action in 1866 in resisting the Fenian raids on the Niagara frontier. Three University College students, Malcolm Mackenzie, I.H. Mewburn, and William Tempest, were killed. The bell in the great tower of University College tolled every minute until their bodies were brought back to the University. A memorial window in their memory can be found in the East Hall of University College, and a monument to those who took part in the battle can be found

Fenian monument, constructed in 1870; Hart House, completed in 1919, is in the background.

on the mound between the legislative buildings and the Sigmund Samuel Library building.

Blake became the Liberal premier of the province in 1871, and Crooks became one of his ministers. When Blake chose federal politics the following year, Oliver Mowat, a strong supporter of the University, became premier, and in 1873 an act was passed that would prevent the senate from ever again being captured by hostile persons. It did so by ensuring that fifteen of the senators as well as the chancellor would be elected by the graduates of the University. The government would appoint nine persons for three-year periods, and the denominational colleges would have no claim to representation unless they affiliated. The first chancellor elected by the graduates was, not surprisingly, Edward Blake.

chapter eight

1871

⁓

SCIENCE AND TECHNOLOGY

In 1871, the 79-year-old professor of natural science, William Hincks, died suddenly. In the same year, the 70-year-old professor of philosophy, James Beaven, was forced to retire. These anti-Darwinians had had an inhibiting effect on science at the University. In the 1870s, new appointments and ideas would create a framework for the future of science and technology.

George Paxton Young, the new professor of philosophy, was an Edinburgh-trained Presbyterian minister who had most recently been the professor of philosophy at Knox College. Unlike Beaven, he exhibited an open-minded approach to such questions as the logical proof of the existence of God. One can lead a 'satisfying Christian life,' he argued, without 'accepting the supernatural aspects of Christianity.' He was, by all accounts, a 'truly great teacher.' Daniel Wilson, his friend from their Edinburgh days, wrote in the student newspaper the *Varsity*, after Young's death in 1889, 'He was, as we all know, an enthusiastic and soul-inspiring lecturer; and the students were astonished to find what they had been accustomed to regard as a dry and arid, if not repulsive, subject transformed into the most popular of all their College studies.'

Young was also interested in mathematics. He published a number of papers over the years on such subjects as Boolean 'mathematical theory of the laws of thought.' His understanding of mathematics was such that he had earlier been offered the professorship of mathematics at Victoria College. From the 1850s, like many of the professors at the University, he was an active participant in the

University College Natural Science Club, 1867–8, with two future deans of engineering:
John Galbraith, second row far left, and William Ellis, second row second from right.

Canadian Institute, later called the Royal Canadian Institute. The Institute, begun in 1849 by professional engineers and surveyors and subsequently devoted to science in general, provided a forum for the presentation of papers and their publication in its journal, the *Canadian Journal*. Most of the professors published in the *Journal*, and some, such as Hincks, published almost exclusively there.

Hincks' eventual replacement in natural science would turn out to be equally important for the development of the University. The appointment first went to H.A. Nicholson, a 27-year-old highly regarded Edinburgh-trained scientist and doctor, who returned to England three years later to take a chair at Durham University. He observed on his arrival that Hincks had left 'a wilderness of stuffed birds.' In the short time he was at Toronto, he managed to publish some twenty-six articles. The position was then taken by Robert Ramsay Wright,

Robert Ramsay Wright, appointed professor of natural science in 1874, retired in 1912.

James Loudon, appointed professor of mathematics and physics in 1875.

another young Edinburgh-trained scientist – he was only 22 – who would remain in Toronto until his retirement in 1912. He particularly impressed his students by his ability to make two drawings on the blackboard simultaneously, using both hands. Wright, as noted earlier, was a Darwinian who took the position that the origin of species had been 'definitely settled' by Darwin. He and his students, such as A.B. Macallum, had an important impact on the later development of the scientific base for medical research in Canada.

Wright was more interested in zoology than botany, and it is appropriate that the present zoology building at the University is named after him. (A separate department of botany was not established until the First World War.) He is also noteworthy as having been appointed the first dean of arts in the University (after the position had been abolished in 1853) and its first vice-president, in 1901 and 1902 respectively. One of his distinguished colleagues, A.G. Huntsman, who, like Wright, studied fish, wrote on Wright's death that 'the influence which this brilliant teacher and investigator exercised in his own department of biology in the University of Toronto and medicine makes him one of the most memorable figures in the history of Canadian education.'

Cherriman, the professor of mathematics and physics, resigned unexpectedly in 1875 to take up the position of superintendent of insurance in Ottawa. For some time he had been a consulting actuary for Confederation Life. To this point, no Canadian-born or Canadian-educated person had been appointed as a professor in the University. Was it not time, Canadian nationalists asked? Graduates of the University, such as Blake and Crooks, were leaders in politics – why not also in the University?

A credible candidate was available – James Loudon. He was both Canadian born and a graduate of the University. He had graduated in 1862 with the gold medal in mathematics and might well have received the medal in classics if his father had not been ill and died during exams. Loudon was heading for a legal career and articled with Thomas Moss, who was then the University College registrar (and in 1873 would become vice-chancellor of the University). While studying law, Loudon tutored in both classics and mathematics, and taught some of Cherriman's classes when he was away. In 1865, Loudon accepted a full-time position in the University as a mathematical tutor and the dean of residence.

When the professorship opened up in 1875, Loudon did not at first apply, hoping that it would be offered to him without a competition, as in the case of George Paxton Young's appointment. He did apply, however, after Daniel Wilson, who thought the University could do better, informed him that 'the matter had already been decided against' him and that there was therefore no need to bother producing testimonial letters. Cherriman shared Wilson's view and recommended that a Cambridge mathematician be brought in for the professorship and a lectureship be established in experimental physics – presumably for Loudon.

Loudon pursued the appointment, however, and produced fifty-five letters, including one from Wilson, who referred to the 'zealous and efficient manner in which you have fulfilled the duties of mathematical tutor in University College.' This was as weak a testimonial letter as Wilson could reasonably openly provide for Loudon. But other important figures, such as Edward Blake and Vice-chancellor Moss, sent strong letters directly to Premier Oliver Mowat, who would make the decision. Wilson urged Mowat to advertise this and other positions, as a 'check against inferior appointments.' Mowat did advertise, in fact, but kept the closing date very short, and Loudon was selected. When President McCaul introduced Loudon for his inaugural lecture, McCaul stated that 'he would rise to a higher position still,' a remark designed to annoy Wilson rather than predict the future, though it happened to do both. Loudon, as we will see, became president of the University after Wilson.

Was Loudon a successful scientist? Certainly he said the right things about research, arguing before the Canadian Institute in 1877 for a commitment to the German research ideal of pursuing knowledge for its own sake. Moreover, it was Loudon who first introduced students to the experimental method. His physics laboratory was the first in Canada for undergraduate students. In contrast, Croft merely lectured, though he would occasionally bring favoured students into his laboratory in the roundhouse. But though Loudon trained people in experimental methods, he was not himself a researcher. As with Cherriman, according to a recent book, *Physics and the Rise of Scientific Research in Canada*, his publications 'originated in the course of reflection on pedagogy ... The originality of his solutions was only that they differed from those offered in traditional textbooks.' Ramsay Wright, on the other hand, was both a major researcher and a splendid teacher. The emphasis on research was growing in the academic world. The British physicist John Tyndall, who, as we saw, had failed to get an appointment at Toronto twenty years earlier, was at this time engaged in path-breaking research, tracing 'the origins of life to inorganic compounds and even single atoms.'

⟨⟩

Throughout this period, there was great interest in applied science in Toronto, just as there was throughout North America. In 1862, the United States federal government had provided the individual states with free land for agricultural and mechanical colleges, usually referred to as A & M's. In 1871, the Ontario government commissioned a report on how best to provide technical education. The two authors of the report, one of whom was Egerton Ryerson's deputy, toured the United States, visiting such institutions as the recently established Massachusetts Institute of Technology, New York's Rensselaer Polytechnic, and various institutions connected with universities – at Columbia, Cornell, and Harvard – to study their programs and operations. The authors favoured the establishment of a school of technology, but one unconnected with an existing institution. 'To attach it as an appendage to any school or college for teaching purposes,' they wrote, 'would be to ensure its ultimate failure ... We would strongly recommend that it be ... left entirely under the care, management and control of the government itself.'

One can see Ryerson's influence in the report, particularly in the recommendation that the new institution be located beside the teachers' college (the Normal School on the site of the present Ryerson Polytechnical University), which was controlled by Ryerson. Instead of constructing a new building, however, Sandfield Macdonald's government appropriated money for the purchase of the Mechanics' Institute on the north-east corner of Church and Adelaide streets. Some have wondered whether Macdonald realized what Ryerson had in mind, because in the debates Macdonald is said to have confused professional engineers with railway engine drivers. 'Was it not time,' he asked in the legislative debates, 'that the drivers of our locomotives, who were entrusted with so many lives, should be thoroughly taught their business?' But the context makes it reasonably clear that locomotive drivers were only some of the people he thought would benefit from such a school.

In late 1871, however, the government changed, and Edward Blake became premier, with Adam Crooks a leading member of his cabinet. Both strongly opposed the creation of a separate institution for technology. Crooks had been a member of a University of Toronto committee that earlier had proposed a school of mines for the University. Blake, as leader of the opposition, had argued against a separate school of technology, describing it as 'a wild and extravagant scheme' instigated by Ryerson, 'who wanted a rival school in the Normal School grounds under his own auspices.' The Mechanics' Institute building, however, had already been purchased and was being used for evening classes for artisans and other workers, beginning in the spring of 1872. Classes were given every weekday evening by this forerunner of the University's School of Practical Science (SPS), covering drawing, mathematics and physics, and chemistry. Loudon, in addition to his duties at University College, handled the maths and physics lectures, and William H. Ellis lectured in chemistry. In 1914, Ellis would become the second dean of the faculty of engineering. He had graduated from University College in 1867 with the gold medal in natural sciences, and he received an MA the following year and a medical degree from the independent Toronto School of Medicine in 1870. He had been an unsuccessful applicant for the chair of natural science after Hincks died.

Crooks, now in Mowat's cabinet, brought in legislation in 1873 to establish a 'School of Practical Science' in Toronto. In the words of the preamble, it would 'promote the development of the mineral and economic resources of the province, and its industrial progress' by the 'establishment of a school for practical

The engineering building (School of Practical Science), in 1927, looking west,
with the physics building and Knox College in the background.

education in such arts as mining, engineering, mechanics and manufacturing.' It
would provide post-matriculation study for the scientific professions (students
would receive a diploma after three years) and also offer evening classes for
artisans and others. The act establishing the School of Practical Science anticipated a close connection between the school and the University. Although
technically independent, the school was effectively under the control of University College professors. The government wanted to help the University of
Toronto without conspicuously appearing to do so. Loudon, especially, wanted
to increase the laboratory facilities available to University College.

The act permitted engineering students to take lectures at University College
and use its library and museum and also permitted the affiliation of SPS with the

University. The arrangement was unsuccessful, however, in part because the Mechanics' Institute was too far from the University. Crooks sought the advice of Loudon, who recommended that the school be established on university grounds, with one new professor being hired to teach engineering while University College professors taught all the other courses. The school would be outfitted with laboratories that could be used by students and professors of both University College and SPS for work in the physical sciences. The report was well received by the government and by Casimir Gzowski, an influential engineer (and the great-great-grandfather of the broadcaster and author Peter Gzowski) who was a member of the university senate. In 1877, therefore, the government – Crooks was now minister of education – decided to sell the Mechanics' Institute and erect a new building on the grounds of the University. The plan had, of course, the strong support of the University, including Chancellor Blake and Vice-chancellor Moss. A site for the building on the south-west part of the campus was rejected as being somewhat out of the way for the evening workingmen's classes, so another was selected at the south-east part of the campus where the Medical Sciences Building now stands. The three-storey red-brick building, known for close to a century as 'the little red Schoolhouse' – and after the Second World War sometimes spelled 'Skulehouse' – was designed by Kivas Tully, the architect of Trinity College. The school opened in 1878.

In 1878, John Galbraith was selected as the first professor of engineering. Loudon had recommended him from among the nine applicants 'on the ground of his scientific attainments and his experience as an Engineer.' Galbraith had received his BA from the University of Toronto in 1868, with the gold medal in mathematics and the Prince of Wales Medal, for overall proficiency, and later received his MA. The story is told that as a freshman at University College, Galbraith refused to accept the usual hazing by upper year students: 'when he learned of some of the performances in the initiation in which he was to take part, he refused to submit to the indignity and defied the whole residence, standing at the door of his room with a sword in one hand and a dagger in the other.'

After graduation, Galbraith gained considerable experience as a railway engineer – the professional kind. Galbraith taught all the engineering subjects and then some. He complained that he had to teach fourteen courses, twelve of them running through both terms. 'I ought not,' he stated, 'to have to teach astronomy to one class and the theory of the steam engine to the next.' He received some help, however, from Eugene Stern, an engineering graduate of

John Galbraith, appointed in 1878 as
the first professor of engineering.
Picture taken about 1900.

1884 who later moved to New York City. Stern was the first of his assistants and probably the first Jewish employee at the University. (Hirshfelder, it will be recalled, had converted.)

The School of Practical Science was controlled by University College. Croft was the first chair of the board and was followed by Daniel Wilson. Ramsay Wright was the secretary. Most of the space was given over to University College professors. Croft had his chemistry lab in the building, and Chapman his geology lab. Loudon, a principal promoter of the new building, ended up not having any space at all in it. He had gone to England during the summer of 1878 to purchase physics equipment, and when he returned, he discovered that Ramsay Wright, with his various fish tanks, had acquired the third floor of the building. Loudon was forced to use Croft's abandoned roundhouse and any other rooms he could get at University College. The whole scheme, in spite of statements to the contrary, seems to have been designed to provide additional science facilities for University College professors. There were, in fact, relatively few engineering students in the early years – only seven in 1878–9 – and no engineering labs. Even the evening lectures to skilled tradesmen were abandoned for a time, until Wilson, after some prodding by the minister, organized a series of public lectures in 1881–2, giving the first one himself – 'The Practical Uses of Science in the Daily Business of Life' – and introducing every other one. 'A good audience, and a fair promise of success,' he wrote in his diary after the first lecture. These may have been the first public 'continuing studies' lectures organized by the University of Toronto.

The number of engineering students began to grow. (The federal government's so-called National Policy of 1878 had set up tariff barriers to encourage industrial development in Canada.) By 1882, there were more than 30 students, and in 1884 more than 40. Students could now get the designation 'CE' (civil engineer) after their names if they completed three years of school and three years of approved engineering work. The bulk of the other students taking courses at the School of Practical Science were University College arts students and students from the private medical schools. The space available became increasingly inadequate. Engineering courses were cut back. By 1886, only civil and mining engineering were being offered as full courses, not mechanical or electrical engineering, despite their increasing importance for the economic growth of the province. (In 1879, Edison had developed a practical light bulb, and in 1882 the annual Toronto Exhibition was lit at night by arc lamps.) An extension to the SPS building was clearly required.

There were conflicts in the school, one of which involved William Ellis, who taught chemistry at SPS, and W.H. Pike, Croft's replacement as professor of chemistry at University College. (Croft had chosen to retire in 1879 and had moved to Texas, where one of his sons had a farm.) The Oxford- and Göttingen-trained Pike had no desire to teach courses at SPS, and Ellis refused to do work for which Pike was being paid. The conflict was partially resolved by making Ellis the professor of applied chemistry and the head of chemistry at SPS. A dispute also arose between Galbraith and the geology professor, Edward Chapman, though the reason for the conflict is not known. It is not surprising, therefore, that a new relationship between SPS and the University was required. This was formed in 1889, when SPS formally 'affiliated' with the University. But, as will be seen in a later chapter, the new relationship, in effect, was more a 'disaffiliation' than an 'affiliation.' SPS now had its own council, headed by Galbraith, and was made up only of SPS members.

In the 1870s, science and technology were becoming important components of university life at the University of Toronto and at other institutions. The expense of hiring competent staff and maintaining proper science laboratories and equipment would soon force Victoria College to affiliate with the University of Toronto. It would also be the primary reason for the affiliation of the Toronto School of Medicine with the University.

chapter nine

1880

~⚬~

THE ADMISSION OF WOMEN

'The question of the co-education of the sexes in Colleges,' stated an article on the front page of the inaugural issue of the *Varsity* in 1880, 'is still a vexed one and some time must elapse before it can be regarded as finally disposed of.' The *Varsity* – 'A Weekly Review of Education, University Politics and Events' – which was run by both graduates and undergraduates, played an important role in shaping opinion in the debate on the admission of women. The aforementioned article, strongly in favour of co-education, was written by William Houston, an 1872 graduate who had been a reporter for the *Globe* and other papers. 'It is only a question of time,' he wrote, 'when female under-graduates will be knocking at the door of University College for admission.' He ended the article with a somewhat unappealing image: 'Let a few young ladies muster courage to break the ice and they will soon find a numerous troop plunging in after them and the young gentlemen generously applauding their intrepidity.'

Although there was nothing in the University of Toronto Act specifically excluding women, they were not admitted to University College. President McCaul certainly did not favour their admission. Emily Stowe, later to be the first Canadian woman licensed to practise medicine, sought to take classes at University College in chemistry and physiology in 1869, but her request was denied by the senate. McCaul conveyed the decision to her. When she predicted that 'these university doors will open some day to women,' McCaul, according to Stowe, answered 'with some vehemence': 'Never in my day Madam!'

William Houston, MA, 1874, an advocate for the admission of women to University College.

Augusta Stowe Gullen, a graduate of Victoria's medical school in 1883.

In the summer of 1879, the 72-year-old McCaul announced his retirement. 'This will be a memorable year,' Daniel Wilson wrote in his diary, 'with a new president and new professors of classics and chemistry. We have much need of a little new blood. Things have been drifting of late.' McCaul had not attended a senate meeting since June 1876. The president 'is now in that stage of touchy irritable senility,' wrote Wilson, 'which makes him an obstruction in every way.' Crooks, the minister of education, along with the University's vice-chancellor, the 39-year-old chief justice of Ontario, Thomas Moss, went to England that summer to find a professor of classics who could also serve as president of University College. Wilson was turning 64 and was probably considered too old. If the new classics professor became president, Wilson would be made vice-president, Crooks told Wilson, 'with a fitting increase of salary.'

Crooks and Moss, however, were unable to find a senior classicist who could also serve as president, and McCaul continued as president during the 1879–80 academic year. In May 1880, they secured a young Cambridge classicist, and Crooks offered the presidency of University College to Wilson. A few days later, however, the offer was withdrawn. Wilson noted in his diary, 'The Cambridge phoenix has on further consideration declined, and Mr. Crooks seems to consider that he is at liberty to back out with me in like fashion.'

Wilson was discouraged. He and his family were travelling to Britain that summer, and, before leaving, Wilson wrote to Crooks, asking to be informed 'on what terms you will allow me to retire.' 'I left Toronto,' Wilson wrote in his diary, 'in the belief that I had delivered my last lecture; and when in Edinburgh revisited my old "Elm Cottage" with the thought and hope of recovering it and ending my days there.' 'I was more than reconciled to the prospect,' he went on, 'when on July 29 came a cable message from the Minister of Education, "Council will advise your appointment as President" and instructing me to proceed at once with efforts to find a fit successor for the classical chair.' (Wilson hired the Oxford-trained Maurice Hutton, who later would be principal of University College.) 'So here I am,' Wilson went on, 'President of University College, with a new lease of Canadian life.' 'I wish I were 10 years younger,' he noted, 'but there's life in the old dog yet.'

One of the first major issues Wilson had to face was that of the admission of women. Houston's article appeared the week after Wilson took office on October 1, 1880. Women were starting to enter the professions, particularly the teaching profession. For the most part, one needed a university degree in order to teach high school. 'Without a University training,' Houston wrote, 'they cannot take charge of High Schools or become even acceptable assistants in them.' Wilson noted in his diary in February 1882: 'A deputation of ladies – strong minded – bent on having the college thrown open to women. Parliament to be appealed to, etc. etc.' The deputation was most probably from the Toronto Women's Literary Club, founded in 1877 by the physician Emily Stowe.

The club, which later reconstituted itself as the Canadian Women's Suffrage Association, had approached the university senate several years earlier, seeking to have it allow women to write university entrance examinations, 'identifying papers by numbers instead of names.' The senate gave permission for women to write examinations in localities with a sufficient number of female candidates, provided there was a local committee to supervise the exams (to be held in June at the same time that male candidates wrote the exams in Toronto), pay all costs, and provide suitable accommodation, and provided also that 'the questions should be precisely the same as those proposed to male candidates in the same subject.'

Women who passed the entrance exams, however, could not attend lectures at University College. There was the odd exception. Croft, it seems, one year had permitted two women to attend his chemistry lectures given at SPS. And Daniel Wilson had permitted two of the daughters of his recently assassinated friend, George Brown, to sit in his office with the door to the lecture room left open and listen to his anthropology lectures. Other women had to rely on private tutors or their own study to prepare themselves for the university exams at the end of the year. Of the 23 women students admitted in the 1870s, only 1, Henrietta Charles, from St Catharines, ever graduated. The senate made things somewhat easier by allowing women who won prizes and scholarships to keep the money for their private education. But most, including the scholarship winner Henrietta Charles, wanted to attend lectures. Their requests to Wilson were turned down.

The Women's Literary Club, which had visited Wilson in early 1882, continued its efforts by circulating throughout the province a petition for the admission of women to University College. 'The exclusion of women from University College,' the petition read, 'is unlawful and unjust and has no basis in the Charter of the College.' Moreover, it argued, 'we regard the exclusion of women as students from University College as an insult to the sex and a wrong to the individual and to society.' The following September, a motion to admit women applicants for that academic year was brought before the university senate by William Houston, who had been elected to the body the previous year. The motion was rejected. Wilson noted in his diary: 'Posted to-day letters to five lady applicants demanding admission to the College. I say very decidedly No!'

Wilson was not in fact opposed to the higher education of women. What he opposed was co-educational classes. He had himself organized classes for women over an eight-year period commencing in the 1860s. Like many other educators, he favoured separate colleges for women, such as those at Oxford and Cambridge and at Harvard and Columbia. Other universities, such as London, Cornell, and Oberlin (the first one to be so in the United States) were co-educational. The first Canadian university to admit a woman was Mount Allison in New Brunswick in 1872. Victoria University in Cobourg had admitted a woman, Barbara Foote, in 1878, but she did not graduate. Emily Stowe's daughter, Augusta, received her medical degree from the Victoria medical school in 1883, and Nellie Greenwood her BSc degree from Victoria in 1884. It is Augusta Stowe who is said to have stated, 'The path of the female medical student is not one strewn with roses,' from which observation was drawn the title of the book celebrating the hundredth anniversary of women at the University of Toronto, *A Path Not Strewn with Roses*.

Like Wilson, William Dawson, the principal of McGill University, favoured a separation of the sexes and was able to achieve his objective in consequence of a $50,000 donation from Donald Smith, a wealthy Montreal businessman, who insisted on separation. Smith later donated more money, and before the turn of the century a separate college for women, Royal Victoria College, was built on the McGill campus. That is what Wilson wanted, and in order to block co-education he would use, according to his diary, 'the power of steady passive resistance.'

Wilson felt that the system of separate colleges 'under lady principals and other efficient oversight ... is the one best calculated to promote the refined culture and high intellectual development of women.' He was concerned about the 'physical differences that distinguish the sexes.' He was also concerned about the moral breakdown that might result from 'bringing scores of young men and women into intimate relations in the same institution at the excitable age of 18 to 22.' 'It is not in the lecture room that trouble is to be apprehended, or danger incurred,' he wrote. When a group of male students assured Wilson that women would be welcome at the University, Wilson replied, 'That's not what I fear, Gentlemen; what I fear is that your reception will be *too* cordial.' Furthermore, Wilson himself was concerned about delivering his classes in English literature to a mixed audience. He confided to his friend Dawson of McGill that it would be 'a painful ordeal to some; a source of mischievous jest to others.' He would have to avoid discussing Shakespeare's *Measure for Measure* or *Othello*.

On March 5, 1884, a motion was passed by the Ontario legislative assembly that 'in the opinion of this House provisions should be made for the admission of women to University College.' Houston had written to MPP John Gibson, a prize-winning 1863 graduate of Toronto, 'What is needed is a good man to take note of the matter in the House and, in my opinion you are just the man.' As a member of the university senate, Gibson had been the one to bring the motion allowing women to keep their scholarship money. Gibson, with the support of Richard Harcourt, an 1870 prize-winning graduate and a future minister of education, brought the motion, which had sufficient support in the assembly to make no vote necessary.

Houston would argue in the pages of the *Varsity* the following month that 'there is not the slightest ground for hoping that the Legislature of this Province will ever vote the money necessary to provide a college which will afford the same means of training for women as University College does for men.' He warned Wilson that 'the ladies have been advised that they have legal rights and some of them are not merely willing but ready to enforce them.'

In the meantime, however, new editors of the *Varsity* had been appointed, and the editorial view of the paper had changed diametrically. 'We are opposed,' it stated on March 15, 1884, 'to any system of co-education in college training ... The proximity and competition of the "softer sex" is rarely a spur to intellectual activity.' When criticized for its change in policy, the *Varsity* replied: 'We are sorry for this – sorry for all past errors of the *Varsity*. But we do not feel ourselves haunted by the ghosts of neglected and forgotten opinions, as we probably should.' The masthead was also changed in that year, from a male and female in academic dress on either side of the goddess of wisdom to the simple University of Toronto crest.

Wilson continued his 'passive resistance,' telling the minister of education, George Ross, and the premier, Oliver Mowat, that such a major change required legislation or at least an order in council. Throughout the summer of 1884, Wilson argued with Ross that the change was undesirable and that, in any event, University College did not have the physical facilities for women students. Wilson feared that Ross, later to be the premier of Ontario, did not appreciate his arguments, and noted in his diary that Ross was 'not a college man,' but 'an old school teacher and school inspector.'

Several women applied for admission and sent in their fees in September 1884. The money was returned, with the registrar stating, 'As no change has been made with respect to the admission of students to University College, I have the honour to remit to you the amount – $20 – which you sent me.' One applicant, Eliza Balmer, according to one of her classmates, Nellie Spence, was 'the leader in the prolonged agitation.' She was, wrote Spence, 'a little fair-haired, slightly built maiden, with deep blue eyes and a delicately moulded face.' Balmer, who had won a scholarship in modern languages and general proficiency, was determined to attend classes, whatever Wilson's view. In 1883, she had appealed to Andrew Stevenson, a recent graduate and a former editor of the *Varsity*, to ask the professor of philosophy, Paxton Young, if he would allow her to attend his lectures. Young supported co-education and agreed, stating that 'he would do nothing but accept her there just as he did the other students.' According to Stevenson, President Wilson was told that he would have 'the onus

Eliza May Balmer, said to be 'the leader in the prolonged agitation' for the admission of women, a graduate of University College in 1886.

Letitia Salter, the first 'Lady Superintendent' of women students at University College.

of ordering her out.' It is, uncertain, however, whether she actually attended the classes.

As it turned out, the Mowat government passed an order in council on October 2, 1884 supporting the earlier resolution and authorized the minister of education 'to confer with the President of University College, in order to make such arrangements as may be necessary in that behalf.' Wilson noted in his diary that the government had bowed to newspaper pressure to 'show backbone.' He had commented in his diary shortly after his earlier meeting with Mowat, 'It is to him a trifle, of no *political* moment; and in which the opinion of a girl outweighs the judgment of experience.'

Classes for all students, male and female, were put off for a week. During the week, the private room of the lecturer in German, William Van der Smissen, was fitted up as a waiting room for the women students, and a 'Lady Superintendent,' Letitia Salter, was quickly hired for $500 a year, at the government's expense (she would remain in that position until 1916, when she retired at age 67). On October 6, 1884, three students – probably Eliza Balmer, Ella Gardiner, and

Three of the women who graduated from University College in 1885, members of the first graduating class that included women: from left to right, Margaret Langley, May Bell Bald, and Ella Gardiner. Two daughters of the *Globe* publisher George Brown, Margaret and Catherine, also graduated in 1885, but their pictures were not included in the composite.

Nellie Spence, though the documents do not make it clear – officially attended lectures at University College. Eight other women would join them over the course of the year. At the beginning, according to Ella Gardiner, they were forbidden to stand at the bulletin boards in the halls, the notices being sent to them in their waiting room. Furthermore, they were not allowed to use the reading room or even consult the library catalogues. Wilson clearly was determined to limit contact between male and female students in the college.

Women also could not join clubs without the president's permission. The 1886–7 Year Book – the first such publication – shows only one woman as an officer or a member of the 'committee' of a club. That person was Henrietta Charles, who was a vice-president of the Modern Language Club. In 1889, the University College Literary and Scientific Society, which Daniel Wilson had helped found in 1854, rejected the inclusion of women in the society. Two years later, the women formed their own organization, the Women's Literary Society, to promote literary work among the women and to encourage public speaking. The society also planned to promote physical training for women by pressing the University to provide a gymnasium or recreation ground for women.

Women would not get their own gymnasium until the Benson Building was constructed, almost eighty years later, in 1959. But they did obtain a playing field, at the corner of Queen's Park and Bloor Street, for the 'Ladies Tennis Club,' founded in 1893, and the use of the East Hall of University College for

Annesley Hall, the Victoria College women's residence, opened in 1905. Picture taken between 1905 and 1910.

the 'Women's Fencing Club,' founded in 1895. Wilson would not permit co-educational sports activities, but after his death in 1892 a number of co-educational sports events began to take place, such as mixed doubles in tennis; and there were recreational ice-skating rinks from 1896 and a co-educational golf club in 1898. The golf club obtained permission to play throughout the university property, and within a year a thirteen-hole course ranged over the northern end of the University. Wilson would not have been pleased. Clara Benson, after whom the 1959 women's gymnasium would be named, was a member of both the golf and the tennis club as an undergraduate in the 1890s.

Five women graduated from U of T in the spring of 1885. Three of them were among the group of women who had attended lectures in 1884–5, including Ella Gardiner, who later became principal of Albert College in Belleville. The other two graduates were the Brown sisters, who had chosen to complete their education with private tutors and after graduation returned with their family to Scotland. Eliza Balmer graduated the following year and later taught at Harbord Collegiate. Nellie Spence, also in the first class, graduated in 1889 and became head of English and history at Parkdale Collegiate. Henrietta Charles, who had passed the entrance exams in 1879, did not graduate until 1888, having interrupted her studies to teach in Ottawa. She later taught mathematics at Humberside Collegiate. All three remained single. Both Balmer and Spence became members of the university senate, and in 1937, Spence received an honorary doctorate from the University. Teaching, particularly the teaching of modern languages and English in high schools, would be the path chosen by many of the early women graduates. By the beginning of the First World War, 87 per cent of the students studying modern languages and 64 per cent of those studying English at University College were women. The number of women attending the University increased significantly over the years. By 1892, there were more than a hundred in arts, and this number doubled over each of the next two decades.

No residences were provided for the women students. The men were able to use the west wing of University College. The women were forced to find lodgings in boarding houses on Bloor Street and in the Annex. The chancellor, Edward Blake, gave $1,000 for a residence in 1892, but it was never built. The first University College women's residence was not opened until 1905, when Queen's Hall (since then torn down), at the south-east corner of Queen's Park, was purchased by the University. At least three other buildings were acquired for University College women before Whitney Hall was built in 1931: the present University College Union building (then known as the University College Women's Union) on St George Street, in 1916; a building on the site of the eastern section of the present Royal Ontario Museum, in 1918; and a house on the site of the present Sidney Smith Hall, in 1919. Both Trinity and Victoria had residences for women before University College did. A small house on Euclid Avenue, not far from Trinity College's site on Queen Street, was rented in 1888 and designated 'St. Hilda's College.' It was originally intended to be a full women's college similar to those in Oxford and Cambridge, but that never happened. In 1903, Victoria University, with the help of money from the

Women's hockey. Photograph taken about 1910.

Massey family, opened Annesley Hall, on Queen's Park near Bloor Street, which still serves as a women's residence for Victoria.

As will be seen in a subsequent chapter, women were not admitted into U of T's faculty of medicine until 1906. Although there was no prohibition against women in engineering, the first woman to obtain a degree was Hildegarde E. Scott, in analytical and applied chemistry, in 1912. Only six women had been admitted to engineering by 1923. Among them was Esther Hill, who graduated from architecture (then part of engineering) in 1920. She was the daughter of Jennie Stork, who had been in the first class at University College. Another early graduate, in 1927, was Elsie Gregory MacGill, the first woman to graduate from electrical engineering, who later became an important aeronautical engineer. She was the daughter of Helen Gregory, who in 1886 had been one of the first two women to graduate from Trinity College. As with Emily Stowe and her daughter, Augusta Stowe-Gullen, pioneering seemed to run in the family.

After their admission in 1884, women students became an increasingly important part of university life. It would be another three-quarters of a century, however, before more than a handful of women would become tenured members of the faculty.

PART TWO

FEDERATION

chapter ten

1883

FEDERATION

In 1883, the University of Toronto's vice-chancellor, William Mulock, gave a commencement address that once again opened up the question of the relationship between the denominational colleges and the University. The part of the speech that attracted the most attention was a request by the University of Toronto for government assistance. Other universities, Mulock said, have their religious denominations to rely on, but the University of Toronto does not. It is 'our right,' he concluded, 'to lean on our only prop, the State; for this University and it alone, of all similar institutions, is the only one in this province that is controlled by the State.' Daniel Wilson, the president of University College, who had not been consulted before Mulock's speech, knew it would cause trouble. Wilson had been opposed to seeking further government support. With Trinity, Queen's, and Victoria 'all inevitably marshalled in opposition,' he wrote in his diary, 'it has always seemed to me the most short-sighted folly to dream of a legislative grant.' 'We may pay too dear for such a grant,' he noted in a later entry, 'but what appears to me more likely is that we shall come in for all the revived ill-will, miss the grant, and diminish our chances of sharing in private munificence.' The denominational colleges, as Wilson predicted, strongly opposed special financial treatment for the University of Toronto.

It will be recalled that Mulock as a student had participated in the St Lawrence Hall rally in 1863 that helped preserve the University from the claims of the denominational colleges. Twenty years later, however, he recognized that

Vice-chancellor William Mulock.
Picture taken about 1880.

some form of federation was desirable. He had been elected vice-chancellor in
1881 after the death of Chief Justice Thomas Moss. Indeed, he had campaigned
strongly for the position. Daniel Wilson had run against him and lost, by 11
votes to 4. Relations between the two were not good. Wilson noted in his diary
that Mulock, whom he referred to as the 'Mule,' was 'devoid of the instincts of a
gentleman.'

Mulock had enormous power. As vice-chancellor, he was head of the board
of management that had been created out of the finance committee of the senate
by order in council in 1878. Moreover, Chancellor Blake was busy in Ottawa as
leader of the opposition and so tended to leave most matters to Mulock. Wilson
was suspicious of Mulock's motives, thinking that Mulock sometimes adopted
positions that would enhance his career as a Liberal politician. They had not
clashed on the question of women, because Mulock agreed with Wilson's position that a separate college for women should be built. Women did not have the
vote, but Methodists, who now made up the largest religious denomination in
the province and were supporters of Victoria, did.

Mulock's platform in the campaign for the vice-chancellorship had included,
he later said, the establishment of 'friendly relations and co-operation with the
various other great educational institutions of the province.' Late in 1883, he

Samuel Nelles, the president of Victoria. Photograph from the 1880s.

Nathanael Burwash, the successor to Nelles as president of Victoria in 1887. Photograph taken in 1894.

communicated with Victoria through a friend who was on the governing body of both the University of Toronto and Victoria, suggesting that there was need for some action that would bring the colleges together and justify an increase in government assistance for an enlarged university. The principal of Victoria, Samuel Nelles, and the dean of divinity, Nathanael Burwash, met with Mulock, and later they discussed the issue with the principal of Queen's, the Reverend George Grant, and the provost of Trinity, the Reverend Charles Body.

Nelles and Burwash both supported the concept of federation. Victoria was in debt and could not afford a good science program. A university, Nelles said, could no longer function with 'a single professor for all the natural sciences and with a laboratory something similar to an ordinary blacksmith shop ... Every sect cannot have a genuine university.' Burwash, who would succeed Nelles as principal, took the same position. He had been the professor of natural science at Victoria, from which he had graduated with the Prince of Wales Medal in 1859, before switching to the study of divinity. Neither wanted Victoria to be simply a theological college as Knox was for the Presbyterians or Wycliffe for the 'low church' Anglicans. Wilson had a long meeting with Nelles, at the latter's request, and noted in his diary: 'It is desirable to encourage them if rational terms can be agreed on ... I think I see my way to confederation on a just and sound basis, if the politicians – including our own Chancellor and Vice-Chancellor – don't sell us for their own party purposes.' George Ross, the minister of education, called a conference for July 24, 1884, to which he invited all the colleges, including the theological colleges. Wilson, who attended, noted: 'When all are agreed on what they mean by confederation, it will be time enough to say what we think of the plan. Meanwhile much talk and not a little sectarian bigotry.' A series of lengthy meetings was held in December 1884 and led to an understanding, which was to be taken to the various governing bodies of the universities and colleges. After one of these long meetings, Wilson noted in his diary, 'More and more convinced that the scheme is neither more nor less than a revival of the old attempt of the Methodists to lay their hands on the University endowment.' And after another meeting a week later, he wrote: 'Day of weary College affiliation conference ... I wish it were possible to get a decent retiring allowance and be rid of political and clerical tricksters alike. But I must hold on, and hold them off. I did it before; why not now?'

The understanding that had been worked out was based on a scheme proposed by Burwash that the arts colleges, including University College, would teach a range of subjects in the humanities and that the University would be responsible for the scientific subjects. This scheme adopted the division-of-powers approach familiar to Canadians under the British North America Act of 1867. It would allow the University, in Burwash's words, to be 'organized on the German principle for the promotion of higher learning,' and the colleges to be 'organized on the English basis for a broad liberal culture.' Another proposed division was that the University handle the honours and the colleges the pass courses. That, however, would give the colleges an inferior status, so the subject-matter division was chosen.

A clear distinction between the humanities and the sciences in fact was not adopted in the understanding of 1884. Ethics, for example, was to be a college subject, whereas philosophy was to be a university subject. That may simply have been because the philosophy professor Paxton Young had the confidence of University College and all the denominational colleges. Although French and English were given to the colleges, Italian and Spanish were given to the University. That was because Victoria did not have a professor of Italian or

Spanish and because there was insufficient student interest to warrant hiring college staff in those fields. No college so far had a professor of political science, so this field was given to the University. Ancient history stayed in the colleges, but medieval and modern history went to the University. Modern history apparently was given to the University at Wilson's insistence. Wilson would occupy that chair, and he probably wanted to be a university and not a college professor. Moreover, Wilson was of the opinion that the more university professors there were who were sympathetic to University College, the greater the chances of blocking Victoria's ambitions, which he described as a 'Methodist grab.'

Wilson believed that Victoria wanted to oust University College from its building and have it relocated elsewhere, possibly in the downtown Upper Canada College site or even back in the old parliament buildings on Front Street. Stewart Wallace, who wrote the 1927 history of the University, described this belief as 'a figment of Wilson's imagination,' but in fact there was substance to it, as C.B. Sissons, the historian of Victoria University, later acknowledged. In 1884 – before the December understanding – Nelles had suggested in separate letters to Minister of Education Ross and Vice-chancellor Mulock that 'the main building,' that is, University College, be used for the university professoriate, telling Mulock that 'the University work should be carried on in the present main building and the government should provide other suitable accommodation for U.C.' James Loudon, the professor of mathematics and physics and a future president of the University, states in his unpublished memoirs that Mulock was prepared to assent to Nelles' plan. 'I ridiculed the proposition,' Loudon wrote, 'going to the length of telling Mulock that he was crazy, and he dropped it. Nelles, who also sounded me on the matter, also dropped it.' In the end, the University College building was used both for University College and for some of the university professors.

The agreement reached in late December 1884 was placed before the various university bodies. The senate of the University of Toronto accepted the proposal without amendment, as did the University College council. Queen's, however, rejected it. The proposal did not provide for any compensation for the college's moving to Toronto, and Queen's had recently built a major, $70,000 arts building. 'It is simply a bare invitation to the colleges,' stated Principal Grant in a convocation address, 'to throw aside their charters, associations, dignity, local strength; to uproot themselves at their own expense, and move to Toronto.'

Knox College on Spadina Crescent, completed in 1875; date of photograph unknown.
Note the horse-drawn streetcar. The Spadina streetcar line was electrified in 1892.

Moreover, Queen's wished to continue to serve the needs of eastern Ontario. 'There is nothing in it for Queen's,' he remarked.

Trinity also was unprepared to join the University, particularly when it became clear that the government would not compensate it for the move. As we have seen, Trinity had an impressive building on Queen Street, in the west end of Toronto, and in the fall of 1884 it had opened a fine new Gothic chapel. It would not enter into federation until after the turn of the century, and it would not physically move from Queen Street until its present building was constructed in 1925.

The ecclesiastical colleges of Knox and Wycliffe, however, were happy to continue their association with the University. Both formally affiliated with the University in 1885 and were satisfied to continue focusing on ecclesiastical training. Knox had had a long association with the University and encouraged its students – who at times constituted a significant proportion of University College students – to take degrees at the University while studying for divinity degrees at Knox. The college was located physically close to the University, having opened, in 1875, the still-standing churchlike structure on a crescent in the middle of Spadina Avenue north of College Street. In 1915, it moved even closer – to a prominent position on what would later be called King's College Circle. Wycliffe had been founded in 1877 by low church Anglicans who wanted 'to combat the Catholic heresies allegedly promoted by Trinity.' In 1882, it was established on university land near College Street. In 1890, it chose the closer link of federation with the University, and in 1891 it moved to its present location on Hoskin Avenue.

Another denominational college, however, the Toronto Baptist College, rejected federation in favour of becoming an independent arts and theological college. Its building on Bloor Street on land purchased from the University (now the Royal Conservatory of Music) had been made possible in 1881 by the generosity of the Toronto businessman William McMaster, who provided $100,000 for what became known as McMaster Hall, and an annual contribution of $14,500 a year. Although the college participated in the federation discussions, it had serious concerns about the form of federation. The college, for example, was worried by the prospect of leaving the teaching of biology to the university professoriate. The college wanted 'scientific teaching,' according to Wilson's diary entry in July 1884, 'to be put under a theological censorship fully as admirable as that of the Dominicans in Florence in Galileo's time.' Ramsay Wright, as we know, was a strong believer in Darwin's theory of natural selection. Wilson noted in his diary in March 1887 that A. Russell Wallace, a Darwinian invited to give a series of lectures at the University, 'is driving the Baptists into setting up a University of their own ... The very name Darwin is to most of them like a red rag to a bull; and the greater their ignorance the more pronounced their dogmatism.'

Later in 1887, legislation was introduced to unite the Baptist theological college with a Baptist arts college in Woodstock. The supporters of an independent Baptist university knew they could count on further support from William McMaster, and three weeks after the bill was introduced, he drew up a new will leaving virtually his entire estate to the new Baptist institution, McMaster University. He died suddenly the following spring, and the princely sum of close to $1 million came to the institution. A movement by some prominent Baptists to thwart independence and join the University of Toronto was decisively defeated by the Baptist Convention of 1888, which passed a motion that McMaster University 'be organized and developed as a permanently independ-

Postcard of McMaster University on Bloor Street. Date uncertain.

ent school of learning, with the Lordship of Christ as the controlling principle.' In 1912, the university purchased a large block of land on Avenue Road north of Eglinton, but owing to the war it did not proceed with its plans to relocate there. The question of federation would continue to be raised from time to time, and in 1930 it was finally laid to rest when McMaster University physically moved to Hamilton, Ontario.

St Michael's College, which had affiliated with the University in 1881, wanted to maintain its relationship with the University. The college had worked out an arrangement in 1881 whereby its students could take a university degree through University College, with St Michael's taking responsibility for teaching and examining in the sensitive subjects of history and philosophy. It wanted to continue the arrangement. The course in philosophy at University College, wrote the Roman Catholic archbishop of Toronto to the superior of the college in 1884, was 'highly tinged with scepticism,' and the course in history was 'used to belittle the work of the Catholic Church and to insinuate the fatality of

John Teefy, a graduate of University College in 1871, who became a teacher and later the superior of St Michael's College. Picture taken about 1883.

events, which will be calculated to utterly destroy free will.' St Michael's, he went on, should forbid students 'to expose their eternal salvation by attending lectures' in these subjects at any non-Catholic institution.

Affiliation in 1881 had been promoted by Father John Teefy, who had graduated with the silver medal in mathematics from University College in 1871, was later ordained as a Basilian priest, and taught at St Michael's College. In 1889, he would become the superior of the college. His proposal for affiliation was taken up quickly by Mulock, who, as we have seen, was promoting closer relations with the denominational colleges. Teefy had high ambitions for the college. He wanted to create 'a great Catholic university bearing the same relation to modern times that the University of Salamanca did to medieval,' but he recognized that the affiliation arrangement was the 'best attainable' at the time. It would not be until the 1920s, with the coming to Toronto of Etienne Gilson and Jacques Maritain and the founding of the Institute of Mediaeval Studies, later called the Pontifical Institute, that St Michael's would approach the stature Teefy had desired for it. The college federated with the University in 1890, but without any change in its character as primarily a theological college.

Until 1910, undergraduate degrees continued to be taken through University College. Only nine St Michael's students received BAs between 1881 and 1910.

❧

Nelles and Burwash of Victoria University at first had been in favour of leaving Cobourg for the University of Toronto. Nelles stated in his 1885 convocation address that he would 'regard it as a calamity to the country should the measure finally fail of going into effect.' The decision was left to the Methodist Conference, which was to meet in September 1886 in Toronto. Premier Mowat had made the move to Toronto somewhat more palatable by indicating that there would be a measure of financial support. 'If, for the present,' he wrote, 'Victoria alone should come in, the Government will not be deterred from taking the steps necessary to bring the scheme into practical operation.' During the course of the year, however, Nelles and Burwash turned against the scheme. For four days, the Conference's debate raged in the Methodists' Metropolitan Church in the presence of such dignitaries as Sir John A. Macdonald, Mowat, Ross, and Blake. In the end, the concept of federation was approved by a vote of 138 to 113. All the Victoria faculty, including Nelles and Burwash, voted against federation.

The government introduced legislation in April 1887 to allow federation, and it was passed with the support of both parties later that month. The legislation would not be proclaimed in force, however, until after Victoria indicated its support. It was a complicated bill with eighty-seven sections, which produced a new University of Toronto Act. The University would continue to be headed by a chancellor and a vice-chancellor, with Edward Blake and William Mulock still occupying those positions. Wilson would continue as president of University College. In 1890, he would become the president of the new university council, described below. It was not until 1901 that legislation would reinstate the position of president of the University. Still, Wilson is now almost invariably considered the University's second president, not just the president of University College.

Subject areas were divided between the colleges and the University along the lines of the understanding of 1884. A transfer of subjects between the colleges and the University would require the unanimous consent of the senate. That was, in effect, the veto against change of subject areas that Victoria had sought but Wilson had strongly opposed. Moreover, three years after entering federation, the federated colleges could leave the University at will and once again confer their own degrees. The legislation continued – even intensified – government control of the University. In particular, the faculty members continued to hold their positions at the pleasure of the government, and the lieutenant governor, as visitor – in effect, the provincial government – had to consent to every act of the senate.

The University College president, Wilson, had played a major role in the drafting of the legislation. He thought he had fooled Victoria by establishing a new university council, which would consist of all the university professors, with the president of University College as president of the council. He arranged to have all the University College professors, except Hutton, the professor of classics, become university professors. 'If my "University Council" escapes unscathed I shall be content,' he wrote in his diary, 'but that all depends on the Victoria men failing to discover my aim.' In fact, they probably did not much care about the university council, which had authority only over student societies and associations and controlled the officers and servants of the University. The important body was the senate, and Victoria, like the other partners in the federation, would by legislation have its own representation on that body. The result of Wilson's tactics was to weaken University College. Indeed, that seemed to be his deliberate aim. 'Our policy,' he wrote in his diary shortly after the legislation was passed, 'is to sink the College as much as possible, and develop the University with its Council and Faculty.'

Would Victoria, in fact, choose to move to Toronto and enter into federation? The Act of 1887 would not be proclaimed in force until Victoria agreed to move to Toronto. Nelles had died following a brief illness a few months after the legislation had been enacted, and Burwash, unanimously selected by the board as the new principal, would now be the one primarily involved in any move to Toronto. The relocation would be costly, even though the government had offered a site in the north-east corner of the university grounds at a token rent of a dollar a year. The college had also been offered the site that Trinity now occupies, but fortunately for Victoria, the former was chosen, which turned out to have valuable commercial potential on the now fashionable Bloor Street. In late 1888, the Victoria board decided to go ahead with federation and the move to Toronto. It adopted the plans that had been prepared by the architect

W.G. Storm. Storm, it will be recalled, had worked with Cumberland more than thirty years earlier in designing University College.

Strong opposition to the move continued. The Victoria senate rejected the board's decision. The Victoria Alumni Association was also against federation, as was the town of Cobourg, which did not want Victoria to leave and promised it $25,000 plus yearly grants if it stayed. Cobourg brought a lawsuit, claiming that it was illegal for Victoria to move. Pamphlets were circulated for and against the move. One pamphlet argued that 'Cobourg is a much more desirable place for the residence of youth, in pursuing their student work – especially of youth who may not resist the temptations or afford the expense of a large city – than Toronto.' Furthermore, it went on, Cobourg 'is a notably healthy town – not subject to the effects of the doubtful water and bad drainage for which Toronto has become notorious.' The pamphlet set out government statistics showing that the death rate in Toronto was more than double that in Cobourg. It was a well-known fact that Taddle Creek had been so polluted it had had to be covered over. Disease was widespread. (Even in Cobourg, four of Burwash's children had died of diphtheria in one week in 1889.)

Not only did Cobourg offer Victoria money to stay, but Hart Massey, the head of the farm implement company that earlier had had its headquarters near there, offered the college $250,000 if it would consent to remain as an independent institution in Cobourg. In September 1889, however, Victoria received $200,000 from the will of William Gooderham. He had made his money in railways, having declined a role in the family's distillery business. The money was given on the condition that Victoria move to Toronto. Gooderham had favoured an independent college not in federation on an 11-acre site on the high ground just west of the present Casa Loma, but acceptance of the concept was not made a condition of the bequest. The sudden windfall made the move to Toronto considerably easier. As it turned out, the college would have not only the Gooderham money, but also $200,000 from the will of Hart Massey, who died in 1896. The Cobourg lawsuit was settled during the summer of 1890, and in September the Methodist Conference once again voted for federation, this time with a more decisive vote – 165 to 83 in favour. Victoria's senate then reversed its earlier vote against the move, and the provincial government was notified that Victoria now accepted federation.

On November 12, 1890, the act of 1887 allowing federation was proclaimed in force. In spite of continuing problems over the years in the relationship

Victoria University, looking north-east, about 1900.

between the federated colleges and the University, most observers would agree with historian Stewart Wallace's assessment that the federation act 'must be regarded as a wise and statesmanlike measure.' But as Northrop Frye, Victoria University's most illustrious academic, later observed, the colleges 'sacrificed some crucial areas in the humanities themselves,' such as philosophy and history, and were excluded from the whole area of the social sciences.

The formal opening of the new Victoria College building took place two years later, on October 25, 1892, in its chapel. Although Burwash had favoured constructing a group of buildings, the decision was made to erect a single structure on the slightly elevated rise in the land, where the main building now stands. Storm, who had died suddenly that summer, had produced an impressive Romanesque revival structure, borrowing heavily from the major American architect Henry Hobson Richardson in the use of arches, coloured bands, ornaments, and a cast-iron skeleton and staircases.

The churchlike 'Old Vic' building, with its red sandstone and grey lime-stone, looks south to the new legislative building, which had been completed earlier that year. Hart Massey donated $40,000 on the occasion of the opening of the college to endow a new chair. His descendants would later donate other important buildings to the University, including, for Victoria alone, Annesley Hall, the women's residence built in 1903, and Burwash Hall, the Gothic men's residence and dining hall completed in 1913. When a minister was called upon to read the scripture lesson during the opening ceremonies in 1892, no Bible was at hand. 'It's a strange Methodist College without a Bible on the platform,' noted the chairman of the meeting.

chapter eleven

1887

MORE NEW PROFESSORS

Following federation, there were, as anticipated, a number of additions to the teaching staff of the University and of University College. Enrolment was increasing. In 1887, the University conferred 117 degrees; in 1891, not counting Victoria College, more than 200 degrees; and in 1904, more than 400. It had been expected that the government would help pay for the new staff – the appointments, of course, were all to be made by the government – but as Daniel Wilson wrote in his journal, the University did not 'see the colour of the government's money.' The funding for two of the positions, one in English, came from the city of Toronto as part of a settlement given to the University following a dispute over the city's default of its lease of Queen's Park.

There were intense disputes over a number of important appointments in the faculty of arts, particularly in political science, English, and philosophy. Nationalists at first simply wanted the appointments to go to Canadians – they had been opposed, for example, to going to England for a classicist – but later wanted appointments restricted to Toronto graduates. 'Canada for Canadians' was not good enough; it should be 'Toronto for Torontonians.' To a great extent, the promoters of Toronto graduates, such as physicist James Loudon and Vice-chancellor William Mulock, succeeded in achieving their aim. Between 1889 and 1911, as the *University of Toronto Monthly* later disapprovingly pointed out, there were 72 permanent appointments in the University and in University College, and of these, 54 – or 75 per cent – were Toronto graduates. At Yale

'Varsity Base Ball Club, 1887.'

University, in contrast, the *Monthly* observed, the number of 'home products' was only 44 per cent.

Recent graduates were often selected to fill temporary positions as instructors and lecturers, and these assignments often ripened into full-time positions, with the active support of the 'Toronto for Torontonians' contingent. When Daniel Wilson, the president of University College, wanted to hire a new chair of English in the early 1880s in order to cut down on his heavy teaching responsibilities, he resisted a temporary appointment, noting in his diary, 'Rather than having a temporary appointment at $800 as proposed with the chances of some incompetent slipping in by the side door, I shall hold on at all risks and do the work myself.' (Wilson had hoped to hire a Maritimer, Jacob Gould Schurman, who was subsequently hired by Cornell.) The following year, however, after Wilson had suffered a severe attack of pleurisy, the University followed its usual practice and hired a recent graduate, David Keys, as his assistant.

The same hiring pattern was followed with respect to the languages. Forneri's chair in modern languages had been taken over by a number of lecturers, most of them Toronto graduates, who later became full professors. William Henry Fraser, for example, was appointed – without a graduate degree – as a lecturer in Italian and Spanish in 1887. An 1880 gold medallist in modern languages, he was made a lecturer after teaching high school and eventually became a full professor in 1901. His research was in teaching methodology and not in literature. John Squair, a medallist in modern languages in 1883, had a similar career. Both concentrated on preparing high school texts – Fraser and Squair on French grammar was used widely for generations of students. They also had very heavy teaching loads and often gave as many as twenty lectures a week.

The splitting of disciplines occurred in many fields. In 1887, for example, mathematics and physics was split, with James Loudon taking physics and Alfred Baker mathematics. Baker had graduated with a gold medal from Toronto in 1869 and had taught high school. When Loudon was appointed a professor in 1875, Baker was appointed the tutor in the department, and in 1887, the professor of mathematics. He had no post-graduate degree and 'was not a research mathematician.' There appears, however, to have been no controversy over his appointment. Indeed, there was not even a competition for the position. He remained as head of the department until 1919. Others in the department, however, such as J.C. Fields, had strong research interests. Fields is today well known for the Fields Medal (it figured prominently in the 1998 movie *Good Will Hunting*) and the Fields Institute, now situated at the University of Toronto. He was a gold medallist in mathematics from Toronto and went on to do graduate work at Johns Hopkins University, where he received a PhD in 1887. He later spent ten years engaged in research in Europe, principally in Paris, Berlin, and Göttingen, before returning to join the Toronto faculty in 1902 and becoming a full professor in 1914. He was an outstanding researcher and advocate for science, and his celebrated book, *Theory of the Algebraic Functions of a Complex Variable*, won him many honours, including membership in the Royal Society of London.

In contrast, there was considerable concern over the appointment of the professor of political science. In the early 1880s, a senate committee had recommended a chair in political science. Such a position, it was felt, would make

William Ashley, the first professor of
political economy at the University,
appointed in 1888.

James Mavor, who succeeded Ashley as the
professor of political economy in 1892.
Photograph taken about 1905.

possible the study of the social and economic problems of industrial society. Wilson, however, was anxious and wrote to Chancellor Edward Blake that he viewed such an appointment 'with apprehension for fear of the introduction of party politics.' He was particularly worried that William Houston would be appointed to the chair, a person he referred to in his journal as 'the gorilla,' and who he claimed was 'devoid of the elements that go to the making of a gentleman.' Houston, who, as we have seen, played a central role in the admission of women, started a political science club at the University in 1885 and served as its president. He desperately wanted a position at the University for himself and lobbied for positions in political economy, law, English, and perhaps other fields, all without success.

It was inevitable that a political economy chair would eventually be created. The act creating federation had specifically mentioned such a chair. An advertisement was placed in the London *Athenaeum* in early 1888. A number of candidates applied, including Houston. Wilson suggested to the minister of education that J.W. Bell, an 1877 Toronto graduate with a PhD in political economy from Leipzig University and at the time a professor at the University of Colorado, be appointed. The minister, however, was 'inclined to prefer Mr. Ashley' of Oxford. Premier Mowat and Chancellor Blake, who were in England to argue a case before the Privy Council, interviewed Ashley, and in June, Mowat announced Ashley's appointment. Wilson was pleased. It was, he wrote, 'a selection from which I hope for excellent results in all ways.' The Toronto *World*, however, took the expected position that it was a 'mistake in passing Canadians over.'

The 28-year-old William Ashley was indeed an excellent appointment – a first-rate teacher and scholar, who would become even more distinguished. In 1888, he had published the well-received *Introduction to English Economic History and Theory*. A Balliol student of the philosopher T.H. Green and a disciple of Arnold Toynbee, he rejected laissez-faire economics that assumed fixed abstract laws of economic behaviour. He espoused 'evolutionary socialism,' openly supported organized labour, and believed that the state had a major role to play in improving society. His view was that political scientists and their students should engage in empirical research into modern social problems, so he began a series of such studies, *Toronto University Studies in Political Science*. Ashley was a great success. Blake reported that he was favourably received even by the bankers of Toronto. Unfortunately, he was lured away by Harvard in 1892 for a chair in economic history, and later moved to Birmingham University. His influence on developments at Toronto continued, however. He more or less selected his successor, James Mavor, who continued with the program Ashley had developed. Moreover, when Toronto established a diploma in commerce in 1901, it turned to Ashley's school of commerce in the newly created Birmingham University, with its liberal arts curriculum, for its model.

In October 1892, James Mavor was appointed professor of political economy. Until the turn of the century, he was the only regular full-time instructor in the department. The 38-year-old Mavor had been teaching at a new college connected with Glasgow University. Ashley, who had gone to England to seek his own replacement, strongly supported him, saying that it was 'an almost unhoped-for opportunity to get a really first rate Economist.' That type of endorsement trumped the petition signed by Toronto graduates to obtain a Canadian-born scholar. Mavor remained head of the department of political economy at

W.J. Alexander, professor of English at University College, appointed in 1889. From the 1905 arts graduation picture.

Toronto until 1924. There is no doubt that he was one of the most colourful figures at the University, with – to quote the Royal Society of Canada obituary – 'his loveable oddities, his amiable asperities, his unyielding devotion to principle, his genius for friendship, his magnetism, and his wit.'

In the 1880s, Mavor had been a journalist studying and writing about slum life in Glasgow. He became a Marxist, but in 1884, along with William Morris, he left the Social Democratic Federation and formed the Socialist League. He continued his move from left to right over the years, and after 1905 he was a major crusader against the public ownership of utilities. His circle of friends and acquaintances was extremely wide. He corresponded with Leo Tolstoy, George Bernard Shaw, the Webbs, and the anarchist Peter Kropotkin. Kropotkin even stayed with Mavor for several weeks on a visit to Toronto, and people seemed to see a physical resemblance between the two. Mavor was an accomplished scholar who produced more than twenty books and reports. His monumental *Economic History of Russia*, published in 1914, ran to half a million words. He also wrote reports for the British, Canadian, and Ontario governments on a range of economic issues. In 1900, for example, he produced a report for the federal government on immigration to Canada from Europe and a report for the Ontario government on workers' compensation. These commissioned studies increased his wealth to such an extent that he amassed a library of 30,000 volumes and became one of the founders of what is now the Art Gallery of Ontario. When Mavor died, Pelham Edgar, a distinguished professor of English at Victoria, wrote that 'no professor had ever done more towards enlarging the boundaries of University life and to relieve it from the imputation of cloistral aloofness and academic pedantry.'

It was not always smooth sailing for Mavor. President James Loudon disliked his manner and his role in supporting the student strike of 1895, and told the minister of education that Mavor was 'a charlatan, an impostor, and a disgrace to the University.' He was resented by the nationalists. Ten years later, there was discussion about removing him from his position. Edmund Walker, a financier and supporter of the University, is reported to have said in 1905 that 'probably the first act of the new governing body ... will be to dismiss Professor Mavor.' No such step was taken, however, and subsequently Mavor generally was regarded as an eccentric but valuable member of the faculty. He is indirectly remembered today through his daughter, Dora Mavor Moore, whose name graces a set of annual Canadian drama awards, and her son Mavor Moore, a graduate of University College, who has been actively involved in almost all aspects of the theatre.

In the year following Ashley's appointment in 1888, a professor of English, William John Alexander, was selected. What was chosen, writes Heather Murray in her study of the appointment, 'was both a candidate and a disciplinary direction.' Alexander would be a major force in the University and in English studies in Canada throughout the thirty-seven years that he was head of the English department at University College. A future head of the department, A.S.P. Woodhouse, was his student, as was Pelham Edgar, who would be head of English at Victoria. Alexander was responsible for a shift from philological and rhetorical study to literary studies. He 'wrote comparatively little,' but was known as a great teacher, 'perhaps the greatest this University has seen,' according to Woodhouse. Claude Bissell, later a member of the English department and president of the University, was taken by his high school teacher to hear Alexander's last public lecture in 1926. Bissell later wrote that he had 'never heard poetry read more movingly and more sensitively.'

Alexander's appointment was controversial in its day. There were several other candidates. Not surprisingly, William Houston applied for the chair. The *Varsity* supported Charles G.D. Roberts, the literary figure then teaching in the Maritimes, pointing out that he was a Canadian and 'our foremost littérateur.' Wilson was responsible for the application by a scholar of Anglo-Saxon from an English college that would later become Manchester University. The government had deliberately not advertised outside Canada, hoping thereby to limit applications to Canadians or to persons personally contacted. Another candidate was David Keys, who, as we have seen, was a lecturer at University College. Keys wrote in his application that he had been doing a job 'for which three men are thought necessary.' His candidacy was undermined by his rival Houston, who, according to Wilson's journal, 'employed all the unscrupulous tactics of a skilled ward politician in the detraction of his opponents – especially for Keys.' One candidate who did not apply was Jacob Schurman, the Canadian then teaching at Cornell, even though he was encouraged to do so, with the suggestion that he would succeed Wilson as president. Schurman became president of Cornell a few years later.

Alexander's credentials were first class in all respects but one. He had had only one year at the University of Toronto, having completed his BA with an important scholarship at the University of London, so he was not a Toronto graduate. He took his PhD at the recently opened Johns Hopkins University, where he studied classics and other literatures; his thesis on Greek literature was published in 1883 in the *American Journal of Philology*. He then spent a year in Germany studying German literature, and he returned to Canada as the professor of English literature at Dalhousie University. The benefactor of the Dalhousie chair held by Alexander offered him an additional $1,000 a year in salary if Alexander did not pursue the Toronto application. He allowed Alexander to visit Toronto before making his choice. 'I hesitated about rejecting Mr. Munro's offer for an utter uncertainty,' Alexander later reminisced, but after visiting Toronto over Christmas, 1888, and meeting with Wilson, Mowat, and Ross, he decided to do so. 'I got along excellently with Sir Daniel,' Alexander stated. 'He told me before I left that all his influence should be in my favour ... I determined to take the risk and refuse Mr. Munro's offer.' Alexander took steps to improve his chances by arranging to have some of his lectures on Browning published quickly, and was even able to arrange an advance review in the *Dominion Illustrated* magazine. His testimonials from the president and some of the leading scholars at Johns Hopkins were excellent. Finally, he had one more ad-

James Hume, appointed professor of ethics
and the history of philosophy in 1889.
Picture taken about 1890.

vantage – his brother-in-law was the increasingly important financier and general manager of the Bank of Commerce, Edmund Walker. 'The appointment has been made,' the Toronto *World* wrote, 'and surely the Minister of Education, Sir Daniel Wilson and the Bank of Commerce knew what they were doing.' The appointment was announced at the end of January 1889, and Wilson noted in his diary that 'the Minister had not the moral courage to entertain the thought of an Englishman; so I believe we have got the best man available.' Even the *Varsity* now conceded that the government had 'chosen the best man available.'

The following month, the philosopher Paxton Young suffered a stroke and died. 'His loss, both to the College and myself, will be very great,' Wilson wrote in his diary the day of the stroke. 'He was to have dined with me to-day.' An invitation for applications for the position that had thus opened up was published widely – in the *Athenaeum* in England, in the *Nation* in the United States, and of course in Canada. There were twenty-two applications. The nationalists, particularly those who wanted Young's replacement to be a Toronto graduate, became even more active than in the previous appointments. They and their principal spokesman, James Loudon, had their candidate, James Gibson Hume, who

President Daniel Wilson. Picture taken about 1890.

had graduated from Toronto in 1887 with the gold medal in both philosophy and classics.

Hume was at Harvard at the time, having spent a year at Johns Hopkins. He had not yet published. But he had been a favourite student of Paxton Young, and many wanted Young's philosophy to be perpetuated through Hume. The day before the deadline, Hume applied for the position. Shortly thereafter, thirty-one recent graduates sent a letter supporting him for the position. Hume had taken a course at Harvard from the famous psychologist William James, who wrote a letter to the minister of education saying that Hume was 'one of the 3 ablest men I have had as students in the 18 years in which I have taught at Harvard.' Hume did not include this letter in his testimonials, however, because James also said that Hume was 'somewhat of an unknown quantity,' and that he, James, would favour one of the other candidates if he were making the selection.

President Wilson took the same view as James. He wrote in his diary that Hume was 'a young graduate of undoubted ability.' 'But,' he went on, 'the idea, at such a crisis, of putting a raw inexperienced youth into the chair of Mental and Moral Philosophy shows to what lengths such folly [that is, the nationalists] can go.' Wilson favoured an American, James Mark Baldwin. Born in South Carolina, Baldwin had graduated from Princeton in 1884 and then spent a year in Germany, where his work included research at W.M. Wundt's famous laboratory in Leipzig. He completed his doctorate at Princeton. Baldwin's recommendations were excellent. At the time, he was teaching at a small Presbyterian college in Illinois and heard about the Toronto position from his friend at Princeton, James McCurdy, who was teaching Oriental languages at Toronto. Baldwin had recently completed his successful *Handbook of Psychology* and had published four significant articles. Until the 1920s, psychology belonged to the department of philosophy.

Baldwin and Hume were the two leading candidates for the position. Baldwin's appointment was supported by the presidents of Knox and Wycliffe, who were worried that Hume 'would merely give forth a weakened echo of Dr. Young's teaching.' They were asked by the government to outline why Baldwin should be hired, and Loudon was asked to reply to their points on behalf of Hume. Mowat was leaning towards Baldwin, but he was having trouble with members of his cabinet, such as the Toronto graduate John Gibson, who strongly supported Hume. In September 1889, more than thirty-five graduates, including Galbraith of engineering, Squair of French, Macallum of biology, Keys of English, and W.F. McLean of the *World* newspaper, approached Mowat in favour of Hume. The newspapers were full of letters and comments about the contest. An editorial in the *World* stated that Americans 'prefer the speculation of trade to the speculation of philosophy. And yet it is proposed to bring a young American from Princeton to teach us this very subject.'

On October 19, 1889, the cabinet announced that two chairs would be created, one for Baldwin, to be called the chair of logic and metaphysics, and the other for Hume, in ethics and the history of philosophy, after his return from further study in Germany. 'The agony is over,' Wilson wrote in his diary, 'the Minister was bent on a miserable makeshift arrangement.' Wilson had recommended that the government should simply hold out the prospect of a chair for Hume 'if his future career confirms his promise thus far.' 'And now,' wrote Wilson, 'I hope my colleagues will be considerate enough to live forever, or at least till I have shuffled off the mortal coil of presidency or of life.' Baldwin, the first American to be appointed to the Toronto faculty, came to Toronto the next month. The 28-year-old Baldwin was a great success. He was a superb teacher and attracted large classes.

Baldwin also established the first psychology lab in the British Empire. Like Ashley, he was interested in the inductive approach to knowledge. 'Facts are sacred,' he stated in his inaugural address in January 1890, 'lead to where they will. Do they interfere with our views of life? Then our views of life are wrong. Do they conflict with authority? Then authority must go, be it authority customarily considered even more sacred.' Darwinism would not stop at the human brain, though many in his audience, including Wilson, thought it should. Baldwin published much, including the results of experiments he conducted with his young daughters. In one experiment he recorded over two thousand observations of which hand his daughter used to reach for objects. These experiments were later published in an influential book, *Mental Development in the Child and the Race.*

Unfortunately, Baldwin was soon being tempted by an offer to return to Princeton. He was frustrated by the lack of funds for a demonstrator for his lab. Baldwin was lecturing eight hours a week and spending twelve hours a week demonstrating in the lab. He had wanted someone trained by Wundt, but Hume, who was now back, insisted that the person be a Toronto graduate. Moreover, the University College fire that occurred the month after his inaugural lecture naturally had disrupted Baldwin's work. President Wilson was worried about the Princeton offer after Ashley's departure for Harvard. 'If we should lose the two in one year,' he wrote, 'it would be worse than the fire.'

This was to be the 76-year-old Wilson's second-last entry in his diary. His health and his eyesight were failing. Three days later, on June 29, 1892, he wrote his last entry: 'Took the final step. Saw Dr. Reeve and got him to make a careful examination of my eyes, with a view to a report. Wrote out my resignation of the Presidency, and placed it in the hands of my good friend Dr. Hoskin, who undertakes to negotiate the whole matter with [Mowat].' Wilson became bedridden within a few days, gave directions during conscious moments as to his funeral and the preparation of the index to a new edition of one of his books, and died on August 5.

Baldwin left for Princeton in the summer of 1893. He was becoming one of the finest and best-known psychologists in North America. The direction he gave to the department at Toronto continued for many decades. His psychological laboratory was taken over by the demonstrator he had finally been permitted to hire, August Kirschmann, a Leipzig-trained psychologist who became an important experimental psychologist. Another assistant, Fred Tracy, took up Baldwin's interest in child psychology.

As for Hume, he was considered a disaster. John Slater, the head of philosophy in the 1970s, has studied the record of the controversy over his appointment, including Loudon's part in securing it, and writes, 'Much of Loudon's argumentation is little better than shameful, and, it must be said, did lasting harm to the Philosophy Department, since it succeeded in placing Hume in a position of authority for the next 37 years.' Slater concludes that Hume's philosophy was 'obscure' and that 'he was just competent as a teacher.' Hume was forced to retire at age 65, when almost everyone else in his position was granted an extension. His retirement was not noted in the *University of Toronto Monthly*.

But in general, the new appointments in the humanities and social sciences were good ones and set the course for the University for many years.

chapter twelve

1887

MEDICINE

The 1887 Act permitted the establishment of a 'teaching faculty' of medicine at the University. A few months after its passage, the new faculty came into being. Two decades later, it was recognized as one of the best medical schools on the continent.

After the closing of the medical school in 1853, the University had continued to set examinations and grant medical degrees, even though it no longer offered a teaching program. The teaching was left to the proprietary schools in the city. These schools did not have the power to grant degrees, and those of their students who wanted degrees – most were content to practise, as they were entitled to do, without a university degree – had to obtain them through a university. The University of Toronto kept raising its standards, so fewer and fewer students took a Toronto degree. In 1883, for example, only ten degrees were granted in medicine by the University of Toronto.

There were three proprietary medical schools in the city of Toronto in the 1880s: Trinity Medical College, the Toronto School of Medicine, and the Woman's Medical College; together they had more than 500 students. The Victoria medical school in Toronto, started by John Rolph in the 1850s, had closed its doors in 1874, and its faculty and students had transferred to the Toronto School of Medicine, which had purchased Victoria's building on Sackville Street opposite the Toronto General Hospital (then on the site of the present Regent Park) in the east end of the city. Both buildings have been torn

The Woman's Medical College; the building still stands on Sumach Street.
From the college's 1891–2 calendar.

down. Trinity's building – still standing as the Trinity Mews condominiums at
40 Spruce Street – was also in the same area. So was the Woman's Medical
College, established in 1883 at the urging of Emily Stowe. This college was
linked to Trinity University, and its enlarged 1890 building is also still standing,
at 291 Sumach Street. Women would not be admitted to the new University of
Toronto medical school until 1906.

Since 1853, when the medical teaching faculty had been closed down, there
had been agitation to re-establish the faculty at the University. Most major
American universities had medical schools. Unlike the Law Society, the medical
licensing body in Ontario had no interest in running a professional school. One
of the strongest advocates of a faculty at the University was William Aikins,
the dean of the Toronto School of Medicine, who had been a member of the
University of Toronto senate between 1862 and 1880, and who hoped that if a
faculty were established his staff would become its instructors. He believed in the
value of scientific research and had been instrumental in founding the *Canadian
Journal of Medical Science*. Vice-chancellor Mulock also was a proponent of a
teaching faculty, as was Ramsay Wright, the natural science professor. So was

William Aikins, the first dean of the resurrected U of T medical school, 1887–93.

Walter Geikie, dean of the Trinity medical school, who resisted a merger with the University of Toronto.

President Wilson, but he was not involved in the discussions that led to the re-emergence of the faculty. Mulock kept him out of the picture, regarding him – correctly – as the president of University College only and not the president of the University.

The proprietary schools in Toronto in fact were considered reasonably good ones, but they had one major disadvantage: they did not have the financial resources for the first-class scientific work that was increasingly required in medicine. Medicine was slowly moving away from medicine as an 'art' to medicine as a 'science,' and that meant laboratories, equipment, and staff – great expenses for the proprietary schools, which depended entirely on student fees. Philanthropists were not eager to give money to private for-profit institutions, and the government had stopped granting money to them in 1868 (at the same time that it stopped granting money to the denominational colleges). Many students who wanted a more scientific medical education were attending schools outside the province, such as Michigan and McGill. The great medical educator William Osler, for example, as a student had left the Toronto School of Medicine after two years to study at McGill.

Although the cost of scientific work was probably the primary factor that drove the Toronto School of Medicine to seek to become the faculty of the University of Toronto, there were other reasons for the move. The school was having trouble preparing its students for the increasingly scientific University of Toronto medical exams. In addition, its students would no longer be able to take their medical degrees through Victoria University, because, with federation, Victoria would be giving up its right to grant non-theological degrees. Furthermore, the Toronto School of Medicine was about to be faced with a potentially very strong additional competitor, a faculty of medicine at the University of Toronto. It is not surprising, therefore, that the Toronto School of Medicine was keen to join the University of Toronto.

Trinity Medical College was also offered the chance to join the University of Toronto, but declined. Although technically separate from Trinity College, it felt a strong allegiance to it. Moreover, its dean, Walter Geikie, who had played a key role in re-establishing the Trinity medical school in 1871, was not as enamoured of the new scientific focus and Ramsay Wright's 'frogology' as was Aikins. Geikie strongly opposed the section of the 1887 Act that had permitted the University of Toronto to establish a medical school. He had written to Premier Mowat, 'Ontario has now an abundance of good medical schools, and why add more?'

The University of Toronto made arrangements to use the Toronto School of Medicine's building and established a faculty of medicine with 29 members, drawn from both the Toronto School of Medicine and the University of Toronto. Ramsay Wright became the professor of biology, A.B. Macallum a lecturer in physiology, and W.H. Pike and William Ellis professors of chemistry and applied chemistry respectively. The new faculty officially opened on October 6, 1887. The opening, wrote Wilson, 'went off exceedingly well,' though the lieutenant governor, according to Wilson, did not attend 'lest he should offend Trinity College.' Aikins was elected dean by the teaching staff.

It was a relatively strong faculty. Aikins, for example, had built up an excellent reputation as a surgeon and had developed some important new medical procedures, such as a system for circulating cold water through inflamed joints by rubber tubes, and a new technique for amputation above the knee. Wilson noted in his diary that at an 1891 convocation, at which women made up the majority of the audience, Aikins gave 'a charming disquisition on amputation at the thigh.' Aikins was also the first surgeon in Canada to adopt Lister's methods of preventing infections during surgery, though it was said that he 'was

The Biology Building on Queen's Park Crescent, officially opened in 1889. It was
demolished in 1966 to make way for the Medical Sciences Building.

known to park his scalpel in his teeth to free his hands while operating.' Another
important surgeon was Alexander Primrose, a future dean of medicine. The
famous Toronto surgeon William Gallie, who entered medical school in 1899,
later described Primrose as 'superb.' 'I made up my mind,' Gallie wrote, 'that
some day I would work under him, and I did.' From the founding of the faculty,
surgery has been one of Toronto's strengths. Aikins, for example, trained George
Peters, whom Gallie called 'the best surgeon I ever knew,' and F.N.G. Starr, who
became a prominent surgeon at the Hospital for Sick Children. As contemplated
by the 1887 agreement, a complete review of the part-time professors was to take
place every five years. After a thorough review in 1892, a number of professors
were dropped, including Dean Aikins' brother, and full-time salaried professors of anatomy and pathology were appointed.

Shortly after the school was opened, the University made plans to expand its
program in biology and to house it in a new building on the site of the present
medical school. This would further enhance Toronto's growing reputation in
biology under Ramsay Wright. Wright espoused the German tradition, and
stated that 'the university has a higher function than the education of its own
undergraduates, namely the advancement as well as the diffusion of learning.'
The government gave funds for construction in return for having taken the

A.B. Macallum, professor of physiology.
Picture taken about 1900.

university land in Queen's Park for the legislative buildings, which were about to be constructed. The Biology Building was opened officially in December 1889. Four professors from the United States spoke, one from Harvard, one from Michigan, and two from Johns Hopkins, an indication of both the importance of Johns Hopkins in scientific research and the increasingly important link between Johns Hopkins and Toronto. Ramsay Wright had sent some of his best students there. One reason for the rapid success of the medical schools of both Johns Hopkins and Toronto was that they were new schools able to establish a serious scientific focus and were not as burdened with a conservative past as were the established medical schools, such as Harvard and Michigan.

One of Ramsay Wright's students who went to Johns Hopkins was Archibald Byron Macallum. His middle name, 'Byron,' was apparently invented by him when he first came to the University and was asked his middle name. He chose Byron, after his favourite poet. Macallum received his BA from Toronto in 1880 and completed his PhD at Hopkins in 1888. In 1889, he received his medical degree from Toronto, and in 1890 he was appointed a lecturer in physiology in the medical school, and the following year, a professor. His later biological work received international acclaim, particularly his studies of the kidneys, showing that animals and therefore humans had their evolutionary origins in the ocean.

He was the first Toronto graduate to be elected a fellow of the Royal Society of London. Macallum and others present at the opening of the Biology Building believed that the future of medicine lay in science. One of the Johns Hopkins speakers, the pathologist William Welch, lectured on tuberculosis, and William Osler, who just previously had moved to Johns Hopkins, discussed recent scientific work on malaria.

By the time the Biology Building was open, plans were being made to enlarge it. The government supported the plans, but what the government did not know was that the attic of the extension was to be used by the medical school for the dissection of cadavers. When the plans for the building were sent to the minister of education, there was no indication of the use that would be made of those rooms. The medical faculty wanted dissection at the University, and Ramsay Wright considered the dissecting of humans simply an extension of the dissection he practised on frogs and other species. Cambridge University and other universities had combined the two activities.

The matter was publicly exposed by Walter Geikie, the dean of Trinity Medical College, who argued that this was using university and therefore government money for the medical school, which, he said, was contrary to government policy. It had been understood when the medical school was established at the University that it should be self-supporting. The minister of education, George Ross, agreed, and the matter was temporarily smoothed over by having the faculty of medicine rent the space from the University – thus, in President Wilson's words, upsetting 'our Machiavellian Doctor.' Geikie kept up his attack, however, and wrote publicly about what Wilson referred to in his diary as this 'underhand proceeding.' Wilson replied to Geikie, but said nothing about the possible deception, telling Chancellor Blake privately that 'Dr. Geikie's statement could not be contradicted, so I said nothing about it.' Mulock publicly took full responsibility for the non-disclosure, saying that he did not want to make public that the rooms would be used for dissection because residents around Queen's Park would complain about the danger of infection from such use.

Mulock had reason to fear that the neighbours, perhaps stirred up by Geikie, would cause problems. They had already been successful in preventing the building of a hospital on university grounds. Lectures in basic sciences were at the time given in the Biology Building, but clinical work, for the most part, had to be done at the Toronto General Hospital, a few miles away. The faculty had wanted a hospital close to the University. The Hospital for Sick Children was close, but of course was open only to children. A wealthy businessman, Senator John Macdonald (not Sir John A.), was prepared to give $40,000 for a hospital on university grounds and would leave another $60,000 in his will. It had been the wish of his dying daughter that he fund such an institution. The Park Hospital – named after its location in what was then called the University Park – would be erected and maintained by the University on the north side of College Street, facing McCaul Street. The idea of a university-controlled hospital was much discussed in medical circles at the time. Johns Hopkins University, for example, was about to open such a hospital.

The University of Toronto purchased most of the required land from Wycliffe College for $60,000 and gave it an acre of land on Hoskin Avenue, where Wycliffe College now stands. Long-term leases for several lots on College Street were arranged. When the neighbours who rented property from the University on College Street and Queen's Park heard of the plan, some were very agitated. Moreover, many members of the university community, including the University College Alumni Association, felt that it was wrong to use university land for a hospital and that the property should be restored to the University. In the end, the plan proved abortive, partly because of the opposition, but mainly because Macdonald had died and his will had been declared invalid; there was therefore no money for a hospital. Wilson recorded his regret in his diary, saying that the hospital 'promised to be a valuable adjunct to our restored medical faculty.' The Toronto General Hospital would not move to its present site on the south side of College Street until 1913.

The Biology Building and Park Hospital issues were raised in a very bitter debate in the university senate in the spring of 1892. James Loudon, William Houston, and W.F. McLean, the editor of the *World*, led the attack on Mulock, stating that both actions had been carried out without the knowledge of the government, the board of trustees, or the senate. Mulock, they said, had deceived the university community with his underhand methods, and a motion to censure him was introduced. Nathanael Burwash of Victoria and Father John Teefy of St Michael's moved an amendment, however, that expressed 'appreciation' of Mulock's actions and 'continued confidence' in him. The amendment was carried 29 to 6. Loudon was one of the six dissenters. Wilson voted in Mulock's favour even though 'he had small claim on me for my courtesy.' A senate committee was later set up, at Mulock's suggestion, to hear evidence on the matter.

Before the committee could begin hearing evidence, Daniel Wilson died, and in September 1892, Loudon was appointed president. He was supported by the nationalists and, according to a public statement by Chancellor Edward Blake, was the only person considered for the job. In Loudon's opinion, Blake's support was probably responsible for his immediate appointment. Vice-chancellor Mulock had strongly opposed it – they had clashed on a number of issues, including the Park Hospital. Wilson had predicted that Loudon would be appointed; he wrote in his diary in June 1892 that the manner in which Loudon – whom he usually described in his diary as 'the Mole' – 'has deserted his old ally and bosom friend [Mulock], as his fortune declined, and turned to worship the rising sun – the Chancellor – is scandalous. A pair of old shoes [that is, Wilson's presidency] is the prize.'

President Loudon was a member of the senate committee dealing with the allegations against Mulock concerning the Biology Building and the Park Hospital. It was chaired by Justice (later the chief justice) Glenholme Falconbridge. Rather than take a less confrontational approach as Wilson probably would have done, Loudon entered into the hearing with both fists, vigorously cross-examining witnesses and impugning the integrity of Mulock and others, such as Ramsay Wright. On one of the votes, it was Loudon and Houston against the rest of the nine-person committee. As Stewart Wallace wrote in his 1927 history, 'compromise was a word not found in his vocabulary.' Falconbridge's committee found that there was no evidence of 'misstatement or misrepresentation' and that Mulock's conduct throughout was 'disinterested and honourable.' Loudon would, however, have to work with the vice-chancellor for eight more years, until Mulock resigned in 1900. The president had shown the same poor judgment he had shown with respect to the appointment of Hume as the professor of philosophy.

The number of medical students was increasing, and the physical facilities at the University and the building on Sackville Street were proving inadequate. Plans were made to build a medical school on university grounds, and a white-brick Renaissance-style building was constructed just south of the library on the site of the present medical building. A unit system recently developed at Harvard medical school was adopted that allowed the interior to be reconfigured as the use of the building changed. The official opening was on October 1, 1903. Dean R.A. Reeve presided, though he was suffering from influenza, with a temperature of 104°F, and had to cling to the lectern for support. As at the opening of

The medical school, King's College Circle, completed in 1903, demolished in the late 1960s to make way for the Medical Sciences Building.

the Biology Building in 1889, Drs Welch and Osler from Johns Hopkins took part. Osler paid tribute to 'the great work which Professor Ramsay Wright had done for the cause of scientific medical education in Ontario.' He had equally high praise for Macallum, who, he said, 'has carried the name of this University to every nook and corner of the globe.' 'How much you owe to him in connection with the new building,' he went on, 'I need scarcely mention in this audience.' Macallum, however, has now been almost forgotten in the University of Toronto. A movement in the 1980s to name the present Medical Sciences Building after him was unsuccessful.

The event celebrated not only the opening of the medical building, but also the merger of Trinity Medical College with Toronto's faculty of medicine. Beginning in early 1900, Trinity's new provost, the Reverend Thomas Macklem, a Cambridge-trained Canadian, had urged that steps be taken towards federation. That Trinity would move towards federation had been the understanding between Macklem and the governing body when he accepted the position of provost. He had told the *Globe* at the time of his appointment that 'the time has come when neither the University of Toronto nor Trinity University can afford to stand aloof from one another.' The University of Toronto medical school quickly established a committee to discuss amalgamation. Dean Geikie of Trinity Medical College, however, remained uninterested. Nevertheless, planning for the amalgamation of both the universities and their medical schools went ahead.

Shortly before the new medical building officially opened in 1903, Trinity Medical College rejoined Trinity and then was merged with Toronto's medical school. The Toronto medical faculty would now number 87 persons. A merger with the University of Toronto had not been a certainty. Some at Trinity wanted to keep their independence and to erect their own new medical building. The danger in rejecting amalgamation, however, was that the Toronto General Hospital might physically move closer to the University, thereby leaving the Trinity medical school isolated. The whole medical faculty transferred to Toronto except Geikie, who had resigned in protest during the summer. 'I could not,' he wrote Macklem, 'be a party to ... sending the faculty of which I have so long been a member over the Niagara Falls of Amalgamation.'

Trinity College itself, after 'long-drawn and bitter' discussions – to quote Macklem – had passed a resolution agreeing to federation at the end of July 1903. One important concession made by the University of Toronto was to permit Trinity to continue to provide religious instruction to its students. The clause of the University of Toronto Act prohibiting religious tests was amended to this end. The amendment allowed for the introduction of religious knowledge – or 'RK' as it was usually called – as a college subject. There was still, however, strong opposition to federation. The final Trinity vote in favour was only 121 to 73. A court injunction was sought by some of the dissenters, but eventually was dismissed. Trinity College officially joined the University as a federated college on October 1, 1904. The government would not provide compensation for Trinity's Queen Street site, however and it would be twenty years before the college would move physically to the University.

Trinity College provost Thomas Macklem (with cap), who helped bring about the merger of the
Trinity Medical College with the U of T medical school in 1903 and the federation of Trinity
College with the University of Toronto in 1904. To the right of Macklem is the philosopher
George Brett, a future dean of the graduate school, and in front of him is William Jones,
the bursar of the college.

The Trinity-linked Woman's Medical College was not included in the plans. It continued to operate a separate college and a separate hospital. The women's medical school wanted to establish a separate college for women medical students at the University and to continue to have its own professors (then consisting of 6 women and 5 men), who would become University of Toronto professors. Dr Augusta Stowe-Gullen would be the dean. But the proposal was rejected by the University, and women students instead were admitted to the university medical faculty, following the report of the 1906 Royal Commission on the University. The women's medical school thereupon was closed. The hospital remained and eventually became Women's College Hospital.

chapter thirteen

1889

LAW, DENTISTRY,
AND OTHER PROFESSIONS

The government approved the re-establishment of a 'teaching faculty' of law in 1889, as the 1887 Act had contemplated. An earlier faculty of law, along with a faculty of medicine, had been closed in 1853. The University continued to conduct examinations and offer degrees in law, but very few students took the optional LLB degree because they would still have to pass all the Law Society examinations and article with a lawyer for three years in order to practise law.

Over the years, there had been considerable dissatisfaction with the failure of the University to offer instruction in law and with the inadequate legal education offered by the Law Society. American universities, such as Harvard, Columbia, and Michigan, had established large, full-time, three-year post-graduate programs, and Dalhousie recently had established a similar one, whereas the Law Society of Upper Canada simply offered voluntary lectures. 'The necessity for some organized system of legal education in this Province,' the *Varsity* stated in 1886, 'must be apparent to any person who takes the trouble to consider the matter.' 'The most feasible method of establishing an efficient system of legal education in this Province,' it went on to say, 'is to bring about a union of purpose and of forces between the University and the Law Society.'

In early June 1887, the registrar of the University sent a letter to the Law Society stating that 'at a meeting of the Senate of the University of Toronto, held May 27th, it was resolved that the Senate should invite the Law Society of Upper Canada to co-operate with it in considering the question of the establishment of a Teaching Faculty in law in the University.' Vice-chancellor William Mulock had grand ambitions for the faculty. 'I see our way clearly,' he wrote to the minister of education, George Ross, 'to the establishment at once of the best Law Faculty on this continent.' He wanted Ross to hold off from appointing a political science professor so that the money could be used for law professors who could handle the work of a political scientist.

A joint committee was set up by the Law Society and the university senate, which reported in early 1888, recommending a four-year undergraduate course leading to an LLB degree, to be run jointly by the Law Society and the University. The University would be responsible for the first two years, and the Law Society for the latter two. No articling would take place during the first period, and during the second there would be two years of articling, coupled with practical lectures. By this route, the length of time it would take to become a lawyer would be reduced from seven (four years for a BA and three in articling) to four years. Alternatively, without a university degree it would take five years under articles.

The Law Society set up a committee of benchers (governors) to study the proposal and to get input from the other universities and the county law associations. Not surprisingly, the other universities did not like the concept. As the *Canada Law Journal* stated, 'there is in the minds of some who discuss it a tinge of jealousy of Toronto University.' Principal George Grant of Queen's thought the Law Society should in all cases require a university degree before the study of law. 'The great mass of candidates,' he wrote, 'will always prefer a short course, no matter how bad it may be. If a man can get a University Degree and the Degree of Barrister-at-law, and admission as a solicitor in four years, how many will take the present course of seven years?' Trinity was also worried about the effect of the scheme on its arts program. Many lawyers were unhappy with the possibility that the articling period would be shortened. Students were a form of cheap labour, even though they had never been quite as valuable after the introduction of shorthand and the typewriter. In addition, lawyers outside Toronto did not want a Toronto-centred school that would deprive them of articling students – whether run by the University or the Law Society.

A further committee was established by the benchers to study legal education, and this time the committee recommended that the Law Society 'reorganise' its own school and appoint a full-time president. 'It is not desirable,' the committee stated, 'to enter into any arrangement with any University for the education of students, nor to shorten in any way the period of study or service of students.' In January 1889, the Law Society approved the committee's report, and a month later the new law school, Osgoode Hall Law School, was officially established. Many of the benchers wanted to maintain the legal profession's control over legal education 'and to justify its claim to general professional autonomy.' Students would spend three years articling and at the same time attend lectures in the morning and late afternoons during the academic year. Those without a university degree – about half had degrees – would spend an extra two years articling. One change made by the benchers, however, was to substitute for the words 'it is not desirable' the words 'it is not expedient at present.' The amendment passed by a single vote. The door, therefore, was left slightly ajar.

On January 10, 1889, a week after the Law Society vote, an order in council was approved, permitting the establishment of the new faculty at the University and appointing two part-time professors. One was a judge, William Proudfoot, who in the 1840s had articled for William Hume Blake, the first professor of law in King's College, and who was about to retire from the bench because of his poor hearing. President Wilson sat beside him at a meeting two weeks before his retirement and noted in his diary, 'Justice Proudfoot, our new professor of law, sat next to me, just back from a winter in Italy; so deaf that he hears nothing except what is directly addressed to himself.' Proudfoot taught Roman law and English legal history, but as the writer of his entry in the *Dictionary of Canadian Biography* states, his interest in Roman law was 'more the result of antiquarianism and pretensions to scholarly elegance' than a 'commitment to constructive cross-pollination between civil law and the common law.' Proudfoot remained a professor until 1900. The second professor was David Mills, who had graduated from the University of Michigan law school in 1867. He lectured effectively in constitutional and international law, in spite of the fact that he lived and practised in London, Ontario. In 1897, he became the federal minister of justice, and eventually he resigned his professorship.

At the turn of the century, the government appointed two replacement part-time professors. One was A.H.F. Lefroy, an Oxford-educated Canadian, whom legal historian R.C.B. Risk has called the 'leading common-law scholar in Canada in the late 19th and early 20th centuries.' Lefroy remained a professor until his death in 1919, and published four major books and more than thirty substantial articles. The second professor, James McGregor Young, was a

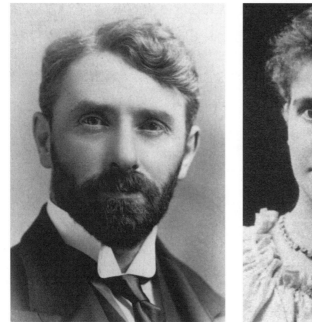

Lyman Duff, a law graduate who later became the chief justice of Canada. Picture taken at about the time he left a small-town practice in Fergus, Ontario, for British Columbia.

Clara Brett Martin, another early law graduate, who became the first woman barrister in the British Empire.

Toronto graduate of 1884 who also lectured at Osgoode Hall Law School. He resigned in 1913 to concentrate on the practice of law. In 1889, the government had also appointed a number of honorary and unpaid lecturers including Edward and Samuel Blake, D'Alton McCarthy, and B.B. Osler, who were among the very best lawyers in Canada and were the founders of some of Canada's major law firms. Unfortunately, most of the lectures were never delivered, and the scheme for honorary lecturers, which looked good on paper, was abandoned after a few years.

The university law course attracted only a handful of LLB students each year – the graduates included Chief Justice Lyman Duff, Prime Minister Mackenzie King, and Clara Brett Martin, the first woman barrister in the British Empire. Many arts students, however, took individual law courses as part of their BA. In 1903, an LLM was introduced. The LLB program could not compete with Osgoode Hall Law School, and Toronto therefore had a very small undergraduate body in comparison with the hundreds at Osgoode Hall Law

School. The University's LLB graduates still had to spend three years at Osgoode before they could practise. The 1906 royal commission recommended that arrangements be made with the Law Society to avoid duplication of work, but once again the Law Society was not interested. There was continuing tension between those who advocated the teaching of law as an academic discipline and those who advocated practical on-the-job training. It was not until 1957 that the Law Society would give up its monopoly on professional legal education in the province.

Other professions, however, such as dentistry and pharmacy, valued their association with the University. As the historians of education R.D. Gidney and W.P.J. Millar state, 'in social terms lawyers had the least to gain from a university professional school and would be the least tainted by establishing one of their own, independent of the universities.' Dentists, however, were eager to improve their status and prestige. Many dentists, for example, found it embarrassing that 8-by-12 foot advertisements emphasizing cheap dentistry could be found on all major roads entering Toronto. A university affiliation would certainly make dentistry seem more of a learned profession, just as would the decision taken by the college of dentistry to make Latin an entrance requirement.

The Royal College of Dental Surgeons of Ontario had been running its own school since 1875. In 1888, it affiliated with the University. Some of the science courses could now be taught by the University. The college still ran the dentistry program, which increased in length from two to three years in 1890 and was responsible for all aspects of the college, including the awarding of licences to practise; but a student could also take the prescribed university exams and be awarded a doctor of dental surgery degree. In 1889, 25 students received the degree, the first such awarded in Canada. Subsequently, Trinity College, not to be outdone by Toronto, also started awarding degrees in dentistry. Not everyone was happy with the result, however. One medical doctor wrote to the *Ontario Medical Journal* that dentists 'are no more entitled to the doctorate than barbers.'

The college of dentistry moved closer to the University, opening a new dental school in 1896 on the south side of College Street, east of University Avenue. J.B. Wilmott, who had been primarily responsible for bringing about the affiliation, had become dean of the college in 1893. At the opening ceremony, he asked, 'Is dentistry a speciality of medicine or is it not?' 'Dentistry,' he assured the audience, 'was one of the first specialties of medicine ... Early in the Christian era it had its foundation.' In 1903, the length of the course was

The dentistry building, on the north side of College Street at Huron Street,
now the building of the faculty of architecture.

increased from three to four years. The college was forced once again to move to
a new location when, in 1907, its property was purchased by the Toronto
General Hospital, which planned to move from its east-end location to a site
closer to the University. In 1910, the college of dentistry opened a five-storey
building on the north-east corner of College and Huron streets, now occupied
by the faculty of architecture. One can still see clearly the word 'Infirmary' above
the Huron Street entrance, and – though they are difficult to make out – the
words 'Royal College of Dental Surgeons' over the College Street entrance.
The college had 200 students with accommodation for 350. The college and the
profession would have liked to become a faculty of the University at that time,
but the change would not come about until 1925, when the faculty of dentistry
was established, and the University purchased the building and its equipment
for just under half a million dollars. Thenceforth, all examinations would be
conducted by the University. Two years later, the University established a graduate research degree, a master of science in dentistry.

Pharmacy followed the same pattern as dentistry, though its development was much delayed. The Ontario College of Pharmacy (now Pharmacists) was not established until 1882, seven years after dentistry's first course. Pharmacy offered fourteen weeks of classes on a voluntary basis. It affiliated with the University in 1892, and 22 bachelor of pharmacy degrees were awarded in 1895. The program was lengthened to two years in 1927. The minimum standard for accredited pharmacy schools in the United States was set at four years in 1931, but the college in Ontario became a four-year program only in the late 1940s. Dentistry, in contrast, had become a four-year program in 1903. Pharmacy was established as a faculty in the University in 1953. It did not physically move to the campus until 1963, one reason for the delay being that the college had built an impressive three-storey building on Gerrard Street East in 1887 and had opened a larger building next door in 1941 (the latter is still standing). In one respect, pharmacy was in advance of dentistry. The first woman to become a dentist was licensed in 1893, but women had been pharmacists even before Confederation. The editor of the *Canadian Pharmaceutical Journal* wrote complacently in 1872 that 'however proficient a female may become in any avocation, she seldom becomes attached to it to such a degree that she will not desert it for the charms of the domestic hearth.'

The Ontario Agricultural College affiliated with the University of Toronto in 1887, and its two-year diploma became a University of Toronto diploma. The college had been founded in 1874 on a 550-acre farm the government had purchased near Guelph. In 1888, students who had taken a new three-year course – there were five students that year – were able to obtain a Toronto bachelor of science of agriculture degree (BSA). As with dentistry and pharmacy, the University only examined the students and granted diplomas and degrees. The graduates – or at least their families – were less concerned with being regarded as belonging to a profession than with gaining practical skills. Some were not pleased with the change in name from school to college. The *Globe* stated in 1903: 'We see no reason why the title, "School of Agriculture" should have been changed. The less fuss there is about the institution the better our practical minded farmers would like it.'

The University was not responsible for the funding or administration of the Ontario Agricultural College – that was the responsibility of the Ontario government. Its establishment and operation were therefore similar to those of the

The pharmacy building, on Gerrard Street East, constructed in 1887 and since then demolished; pharmacy did not move to the campus until 1963.

The Ontario Agricultural College, Guelph, in 1893. The laboratory building on the right burned down in 1896. The building on the left, now called Johnston Hall, contained, and still contains, a residence and the administrative offices of the Ontario Agricultural College, now part of the University of Guelph.

School of Practical Science. As with engineering, however, there was a long association with the University. Toronto degrees would continue to be awarded until 1964, when the college became the University of Guelph. An article in the *University of Toronto Monthly* in 1903 claimed that the agricultural college was the 'best all-round equipped institution of its kind in the world.' At that time, it had increased the length of the course to four years, and it had a staff of 22 and more than 700 students, many of them from outside Ontario. Thirteen of its graduates were professors in American agricultural colleges. Just after the turn of the century, it received two large gifts, one from the industrialist Chester Massey for the building of a library and one from the tobacco baron Sir William Macdonald of Montreal for the establishment of a domestic science school for women.

A veterinary college would also become part of the University of Guelph in 1964. The Ontario Veterinary College began in Toronto in 1862 with a series of lectures given by Professor George Buckland of the University of Toronto and

Andrew Smith, a recently graduated Scottish veterinary surgeon. The college, which was the first accredited college of its type in North America, affiliated with the University of Toronto in 1897 and relocated to Guelph in 1922.

❧

The late nineteenth century saw a large number of professional schools – with the exception of the law school – prosper through their association with the University of Toronto. With the addition of the faculty of medicine and the School of Practical Science, it was clear that Toronto was becoming much more than an arts and science college.

chapter fourteen

1890

———— ❧ ————

THE FIRE AND
NEW CONSTRUCTION

On Friday evening, February 14, 1890 – Valentine's Day – much of University College was destroyed by fire. The news was immediately telegraphed to Edward Blake, the University's chancellor, in Ottawa. Blake received the report while addressing parliament. 'The great institution,' he interrupted his speech to tell the House, 'the crown and glory, I may be permitted to say, of the educational institutions of our country is at the moment in flames; and ... is now, so far as its material fabric goes, a ruin tottering to the ground.' President Wilson wrote in his diary the next day: 'A frightful calamity. Last evening I looked on while our beautiful university building was helplessly devoured by the flames. It is terrible. Thirty-three thousand carefully selected volumes have vanished. The work of a lifetime is swept away in a single night.'

On that Friday evening, at 8 o'clock, around 3,000 people were to take part in the annual *conversazione*, organized by the University College Literary and Scientific Society. There were to be concerts and literary readings, scientific exhibits, and demonstrations – one display was to show the embryonic development of the chick – and 'promenading' to two bands. Shortly before 7 o'clock, two college servants were carrying a tray of lit kerosene lamps from the basement to the upper floors to illuminate the rooms and the exhibits. Electricity was not then used for lighting in University College. While they were climbing the staircase at the south-east end of the building, the tray fell. Burning kerosene soon ignited the wooden staircase and spread to the upper library in the east

Program for the annual University College *conversazione*, Friday, February 14, 1890.

wing of the building. The city's entire fire brigade responded to the alarm – the city had only two engines at the time – but could do little. There was only one hydrant, and the water pressure was insufficient to send water to the upper storeys. The brisk wind from the north-west would have made it difficult to stop the fire even if there had been adequate pressure. But the wind also prevented the fire from damaging most of the west part of the college. By 10 o'clock the fire was under control, and by 11 o'clock it was largely out. Fortunately, there were no casualties.

The entire eastern section of the building was gutted. The interior of the central tower had collapsed, and the great bell had plunged to the ground and shattered. The massive oak doors to the college were destroyed. All the books in the library, with the exception of about a hundred that had been saved, were burned, including Audubon's *Birds of America*, a good copy of which is now worth about $10 million. Daniel Wilson's archaeological collection and Professor Chapman's mineral specimens were lost. Wilson also lost all his lecture notes. What is now called West Hall was then a museum. There was time to remove

University College the morning after the fire, Saturday, February 15, 1890.

most of the exhibits, including many of Professor Hincks' stuffed birds. The fire did not touch Professor Loudon's physics lab in the roundhouse, nor did it affect the residence wing. The stained-glass window on the west staircase was not damaged, and the ceramic tiles in the central atrium also survived. The exterior, including the elaborate carving around the front doors, was not visibly damaged.

'Varsity in Ruins,' headlined the *Globe*. The police had to hold back crowds of curious onlookers. On Sunday morning, according to one newspaper, 50,000 persons turned up to view the damage. The board of trustees, a university body responsible for financial matters, met on Saturday to assess the situation. They received a report from the university architect, David Dick, and the board member and engineer Casimir Gzowski. 'The walls are sound,' they reported, 'and admit of roofing in and restoring.' They estimated the cost, excluding

Edward Blake, the chancellor of the
University. Photograph taken about 1880.

library books, at about $260,000. Unfortunately, the University had only $90,000
of insurance on the building. The provincial cabinet happened to be meeting at
that very time. The board of directors obtained permission to meet with them
and received a favourable response from Premier Mowat and the provincial
treasurer. Legislation was quickly introduced to give the University $160,000 to
supplement the insurance money it would receive. The federal government
turned down a request for help, as did the city of Toronto. The province of
Quebec, however, promised $10,000.

A week after the fire, Wilson was feeling reasonably confident, and wrote in
his diary that the college would be returned to 'its old beauty and [would be]
internally vastly more convenient and suitable than before.' Almost no classes
were cancelled. Knox and Wycliffe colleges offered space for classes, and the
recently opened Biology Building was also made available. The School of Practical Science was asked to provide space but – to Wilson's annoyance – Galbraith,
who had recently become the principal of the reconstituted school, would not
give permission until he had discussed the matter with the minister of education.
SPS, though now officially affiliated with the University, was still controlled
directly by the government.

Blake returned to Toronto and took an active role in the events following the fire. He would not contest a seat in the 1891 federal election, and, until he left Canada in late 1892 to take a safe Irish seat in the British House of Commons, he devoted much of his time to university affairs. The architect David Dick was commissioned to prepare plans for the rebuilding. He had recently completed the new Biology Building and had earlier supervised the construction of St Andrew's Presbyterian Church on King Street. W.G. Storm, who had worked with Cumberland in designing University College in the 1850s and still had the original plans, would have liked to be entrusted with the task of reconstruction, but, probably because at that time he was working on the design for Victoria College, his being involved was not looked on with favour.

A decision was made not to include the university library or convocation hall in the rebuilt University College. Space was required for other purposes, and neither a library nor a hall large enough to meet future needs could be accommodated within its walls. The old library – now called East Hall – was to be used for a reading and retiring room for women students. Some had wanted to use whatever space was available for separate classrooms for women, but that did not come about. James Baldwin obtained four rooms for his psychology labs, but not the funds sufficient for running them. New decorative features were added, including the amusing round gargoyles in what is now known as West Hall and the well-known dragon on the newel post on the east staircase. An ugly smoke-stack, added after the original building was constructed, had been damaged in the fire and was not replaced. New water mains were placed on the campus. By October 1891, the building was sufficiently complete for the university convocation to be held in the old library. 'We are on the whole gainers,' Wilson noted in his diary on February 14, 1892, exactly two years after the fire. 'Even the beauty of the fine building has been increased by getting rid of the abominable engine-house and chimney stalk.'

A new library and books to fill it were needed. Wilson valued the collection at $150,000, but there was only $50,000 insurance money available. A plea for books was sent to potential donors throughout the world. A high-powered committee was established in Great Britain, which included the prime minister, Lord Salisbury, the archbishop of Canterbury, the vice-chancellors of Oxford and Cambridge and several other universities, and literary figures such as Lord Tennyson. Donors in Britain sent some 20,000 books, including, for example, sets of chemical publications bearing the bookplates of Cavendish and the works of the Brownings donated by their son. Tennyson presented a set of his work in eleven volumes. Queen Victoria donated a book on royal residences. More than 10,000 volumes came from Germany. The University of Marburg alone gave more than 1,000 volumes. Donors in the United States also sent 10,000 books. Columbia University allowed the University to choose from 3,000 duplicates.

By the end of 1892, more than 40,000 volumes had been received. According to Robert Blackburn, the chief librarian of the University from 1954 to 1981 and the author of the official history of the library, the collection was now 'richer as well as larger.' The books were temporarily stored in the School of Practical Science, whose space had recently trebled in size. When a new library building opened in 1893, there were 55,000 items on the shelves. The collection still remained the second largest in Canada after the parliamentary library in Ottawa. But it was far smaller than that of many American university libraries. Harvard's collection was at least seven times, and Yale's four times, as large.

David Dick also designed the new university library building, which still stands on the east side of King's College Circle. The architect visited many American universities then constructing new libraries, which, like Toronto's, would serve their universities until after the Second World War. The building was isolated from other structures to make it as fireproof as possible. The stacks were made of cast iron and the floors of massive sections of glass, which allowed light to penetrate from floor to floor.

The library stacks were designed to contain 120,000 volumes, and the reading room to accommodate 200 students at large oak desks. The room was divided into two – half for men and half for women. A private telephone system rather than the usual speaking tubes was installed for the librarians, and electricity for lighting, which meant the library could be open in the evenings. Its hours were 9 to 5 during the day and 7 to 10:30 in the evening. The building itself was generally shaped like a medieval church. Its front doorway was copied from a twelfth-century Scottish abbey that Wilson had illustrated in one of his early books. There was to have been a slim teardrop-shaped dome, similar to one being constructed for then Sacré-Coeur church in Paris, but it was abandoned for financial reasons, and the tower above the doorway is 6 feet lower than originally planned. The library was in full operation in January 1893.

The space available soon proved inadequate. In 1898, a third tier was added to the stacks, and by 1910 a five-storey extension to the stacks eastward into the ravine had been completed. Victoria College's separate collection was also grow-

The university library on King's College Circle, opened in 1892.

ing – by 1906 it had nearly 20,000 volumes – and in 1910 it was moved to the new Birge-Carnegie library (named after the principal donors, the industrialists Andrew Carnegie of Pittsburgh and Cyrus Birge of Hamilton) at Queen's Park Crescent and Charles Street, the first building on the campus to use the so-called collegiate Gothic style, subsequently used for Hart House, Knox College, and a number of other buildings.

One of the key questions to be decided was whether or not a new classification system should be introduced. The old catalogue ledgers, with their pasted slips placed alphabetically in broad categories, had been destroyed in the fire. The *Varsity* had complained about the system before the fire, stating that 'no one will assent, or even in the ravings of a febrile delirium imagine that the ponderous and heavy-headed scrap-books which encumber the reading room are any fit substitute for what is needed.' The library committee at first recommended the Dewey Decimal system, but in the end decided to keep a modified version of the system President McCaul had instituted in his King's College days. The card catalogues would be alphabetical for both authors and subjects, and the books on the shelves would be alphabetical in very broad categories – H for history and HCan for Canadian history, for example. Toronto's idiosyncratic cataloguing system gradually became a nightmare for librarians and for most users. But a new cataloguing system – the Library of Congress system – was not introduced until 1959, after Claude Bissell became president.

Dick designed two other buildings in the 1890s – both red-brick structures – a chemistry building and a gymnasium, neither of which is still standing. The gymnasium, with a swimming pool, bowling alley, and other facilities, was constructed in the early 1890s and served as the men's athletic facility until it was taken down in 1912 to build Hart House. Committee rooms for student activities were added later, and a football playing field was laid out close to what became Varsity Stadium several years later. The old Moss Hall had formerly been used for athletics and student activities, but it had been torn down in 1888 to build the new Biology Building.

In 1891, a committee to lobby for a new gymnasium had been established under the auspices of the University College student society, the 'Lit,' which received a promise of $25,000 from the senate. When the students returned to the University in the fall of 1892, they discovered that part of the foundation for the building had been dug north of University College and thus interfered with their outdoor playing field. The University agreed to move the building farther east if the students paid for the move, which they did with both money and their own physical labour. The Lit unsuccessfully tried to take over the administration of the new facility, but a separate university-wide athletic directorate of students and faculty was chosen to run it instead. The membership was fixed at $4 a year, and rules were established to prohibit smoking and to require the wearing of rubber-soled shoes on the gymnasium floor. University College women had to make do with space in the area of the former library of the college, and Victoria College women used the basement of their college for athletics. The 100-by-50-foot main room of the university gymnasium was also used for convocations and other events until Convocation Hall was erected in 1906.

Dick's utilitarian two-storey chemistry building was completed in 1895 near College Street, just north of the eastern part of the present Wallberg Building. Its 300-seat lecture room was the largest in the University and was used for arts and medical students. Engineering faculty and students would now have the School of Practical Science building to themselves. The chemistry professor, W.H. Pike, made little personal use of the laboratory space, however. The history of the chemistry department notes, 'One might infer from his slim output of published work that he lacked either skill or interest in experimental research.' He published altogether four papers, three of which were based on work done in Germany related to his PhD thesis. He did become rich from land speculation, however, having purchased and developed about 100 acres near Yonge and Davisville for a subdivision. Residents of Toronto (the author lives in the area) often have wondered why one street in the area is named Merton and another Balliol (pronounced 'Balloil' by many local residents). The answer is that before coming to Canada, Pike had been a fellow of Merton College and likely had a particular fondness for Balliol, where he may have conducted some of his laboratory demonstrations.

Pike nevertheless was able to inspire students to follow a research career. Five of his students, including W. Lash Miller, did post-graduate work in Leipzig, and one at Heidelberg. Of the six who went to Germany, four ended their careers as distinguished professors of chemistry, Miller at Toronto and the others at Michigan, California, and Stanford. Lash Miller became a demonstrator in chemistry in 1890 and a lecturer in 1894 and expected that he would replace Pike, who resigned in 1899 and returned to England. There were numerous applicants for the professorship, including two who were later knighted and a very young future Nobel laureate, Frederick Soddy, who had graduated from Oxford the previous year. The appointment, however, went to William Lang, a graduate of Glasgow, without an earned doctorate. He appears to have been a poor choice. 'The problem,' according to the historian of the chemistry department, 'was that he lacked research experience ... Much of his work published before 1900 appears to be rather trivial.' His later publications were also unimpressive. Lash Miller was upset and took steps to leave Toronto – he even went so far as to rent a house at Cornell – but in the end he stayed and was made an associate professor and head of the sub-department of physical chemistry. Lang, feeling trapped in Toronto, tried to get an appointment in England without success and eventually, in 1920, was forced by the president and the board of governors to resign. Lash Miller then became the head of the department.

The 1890 fire, though a 'frightful calamity' in President Wilson's words, turned out to be less catastrophic than first thought. Not only was University College rebuilt and improved, but the University acquired a new library and chemistry building.

chapter fifteen

1895

⸘⸙

THE STRIKE

On Friday afternoon, February 15, 1895, the 'largest mass meeting in the history of the University' was held in Wardell's Hall, since then demolished, a large hall on the west side of Spadina Avenue, half a block south of College Street. The hall was often used for religious and political meetings. A large sign greeted those entering the building: Gentlemen Will Please Not Spit on the Floor. Seven hundred students attended, including a hundred women. The immediate cause of the demonstration was the dismissal by the government of the popular University College professor of Latin, William Dale, which had been publicly announced earlier in the day. The news of his firing had galvanized the student body. William Lyon Mackenzie King – called 'Billy' by his classmates – a member of the class of '95 and a future prime minister of Canada, noted in his diary, 'I was that excited that I could not keep still, my blood fairly boiled. I scarcely ate any lunch.'

A motion was introduced at the meeting by the 'rather solemn, moon faced' 'Billy' King to 'abstain from attendance at lectures at University College until a proper investigation be granted by the provincial government into the difficulties existing in the University.' The journalist Hector Charlesworth, who was covering the meeting for the *World*, later wrote that King 'electrified his hearers by his denunciation of the age-old cult of tyranny,' just as his grandfather William Lyon Mackenzie had done as one of the leaders of the 1837 rebellion. The motion was seconded by Tom Greenwood, also a member of the class of

Tom Greenwood, left, and 'Billy' (William Lyon Mackenzie) King, two of the leaders of the 1895 strike; from the 1895 composite of the graduates in arts. Daniel Wilson had died in 1892, but he was president for the first year of the class of 1895 and therefore appears in the picture.

'95, who went on to achieve fame as secretary for Ireland in Lloyd George's United Kingdom cabinet in the aftermath of the Irish uprising. Another leader who spoke was James Tucker, the 'frail, but thoughtful and soft-spoken' editor of the *Varsity*. The secretary of the meeting was Bruce Macdonald, who would later become chairman of the board of governors of the University. The motion passed with five dissenting votes. A second motion to abstain from lectures until Dale was reinstated or the dismissal reconsidered was passed unanimously.

The strike was confined to University College. Chancellor Burwash had summoned some of Victoria's political science students and 'counselled abstention.' They took his advice. The boycott of classes was successful. George Wrong, the professor of history, wrote to his father-in-law, Edward Blake, then a member of parliament in England, that only one student turned up at one of his lectures: 'My lecture was in the big West Hall that will seat 600 and to lecture to one man in that huge place was certainly ridiculous.'

The causes of the strike are complex. On the one hand, the strike may have been owing to the presence of a surprisingly large number of future politicians at University College. (Thomas White, later a federal minister of finance, was also in the class of '95, and George Henry, a future premier of Ontario, was in the class of '96.) On the other hand, the strike and the drama surrounding it may have helped steer these students into politics. It was in the month of February 1895, for example, that King first noted, 'My ambition may carry me into political life.' There was hostility between the students and the administration in the years leading up to the strike. One must go back to 1892 in order to understand the tension between the classes of '95 and '96 on the one hand and the administration of the University on the other.

In October 1892, just as in previous years, there was a physical 'hazing' by the sophomores (the class of '95) of the freshmen (the class of '96). The faculty tried to stop the action by turning a fire hose on the students. James Loudon, who had become president of the University just a few weeks before, actually manned the hose. (Presidents, it is safe to advise, should not turn fire hoses on students.) The university council decreed that any repetition of the hazing would lead to expulsion. One of the leaders of the strike and another future politician, Arthur Chisholm, later reminisced in the U of T *Monthly*: 'Obviously

George Wrong, appointed lecturer in history in 1892 and professor of history in 1894. The latter appointment was a cause of the events leading to the student strike of 1895.

William Dale, professor of Latin, was fired by the government on February 15, 1895.

no student can wrest a fire hose from the hands of a president and turn it on his sacrosanct person. It is academic suicide ... By pardonable oversight we had neglected to cut the hose.' There was now a 'feud between '95 and the faculty as a whole ... For a couple of years the pot simmered. And in our final year came the blow-off.' King also was having his own troubles with the administration. In 1893, he had taken part in one of the Hallowe'en pranks that were part of student life – he and others tore down an old shed beside the college – and was fined $15. He at first refused to pay, but did so when told he would be unable to write his exams until the fine was paid.

It was the appointment of George Wrong as professor of history in 1894 that actually started the pot boiling. When Daniel Wilson died in August 1892, a replacement to teach history was required for the 1892–3 academic year. Wrong applied for the position. He had graduated in theology from Wycliffe College in 1883, had become an Anglican priest in 1886, and had taught church history at Wycliffe since 1883. The government had decided to seek a lecturer at $800 a year. Wrong, who was at Oxford over the summer, had assumed that a professor was being sought. He was not interested in being a lecturer at $800 a year since his salary at Wycliffe was $1,800. In late September, however, he was offered and accepted the position as lecturer at $1,500 a year on the understanding that he could apply for the professorship the following year. His salary created great turmoil among the other lecturers, who were paid only $800 and had a legitimate claim to more. Dale, who was seven years older than Wrong, was still a lecturer at $800 a year. He had graduated in 1871 with the gold medal in classics, had received his MA in 1873, and before returning to the University in 1884 had been paid more than $2,000 as principal of a high school in Quebec. He was not happy to learn of Wrong's $1,500.

One question that has been debated extensively over the years is whether Wrong's father-in-law, Chancellor Edward Blake, exercised any influence over the appointment. The relationship could not possibly be ignored. The principal of Wycliffe College, J.P. Sheraton, for example, wrote a confidential note to George Ross, the minister of education, saying that Wrong 'has written to me that it is his intention to apply for the Chair of Modern History in the University of Toronto.' His very next sentence is 'Mr. Wrong is a son-in-law of the Hon. Edward Blake.' Another confidential letter from a political supporter advised the government not to appoint Wrong because doing so would inevitably lead to an attack on Blake. Clearly the relationship would have had some influence on the appointment, both for and against, but the important question is whether Blake himself acted improperly. He certainly came at least close to the line.

Blake wrote to Ross, the minister of education, on July 27, 1892 from England, where he had just been elected as an Irish member of the British parliament. He was, he wrote, 'sorry indeed to hear' that Sir Daniel Wilson was 'in all probability gone.' Wilson was, in fact, on that exact date selecting his pallbearers and the inscription on his tombstone, and he died several weeks later. Two appointments would therefore be necessary – a new president and a professor of history. As to the former, Blake, as we have seen, supported Loudon, stating, 'I believe the proper nomination to be that of Professor Loudon ... I believe he will, if appointed do good work for the University.' He then turned to the history chair. While claiming to stay out of the selection, he managed to convey his view that Wrong would be a good appointment: 'I am debarred from taking any part in the choice for the chair by the circumstance that my son-in-law Professor Wrong of Wycliffe College, who has made History his speciality for some years and is now at Oxford engaged on its study, has informed me that he intends to apply for the Chair.' The promotional part of the sentence was certainly not necessary.

There were other candidates for the lecturer's position. Once again, William Houston applied unsuccessfully. One strong candidate, however, was Charles Stuart. He had graduated from Toronto in 1891 with double honours in classics and political economy and had then gone to Columbia University on a fellowship. When Wilson had been unable to complete his lectures in history in the winter of 1892, he had asked Stuart to return to lecture on his behalf. Ross left for England around the beginning of September 1892 (his health apparently was not good) and wrote a memo to the acting minister of education, William Harcourt, in which he expressed his preference for Stuart: 'I would like very much that you would consider C.A. Stuart's application very carefully before rejecting him. He has been a brilliant student, indeed more so perhaps than any other graduate of the University; has done more work under the able direction of the Professors of Columbia University, New York and was selected by the late Sir Daniel Wilson as the best qualified graduate to take up the work of his own department during his illness.'

Blake met personally with Harcourt in mid-September 1892 to discuss a number of appointments, the history appointment still not having been decided. Harcourt later acknowledged that the question of the history appointment was raised briefly by Blake, who had said, 'As to that I can say nothing, as Mr. Wrong is my son-in-law.' How exactly Blake phrased his comment we will never know. The appointment went to Wrong, who turned out to be a good choice. During his thirty-five-year career at the University he was successful in building a strong history department and in promoting the study of Canadian history. He was the founding editor of the *Canadian Historical Review*, the creator of the Champlain Society, and, in the words of Brian McKillop, 'the doyen of Ontario's historians.' Although he published many books and articles, 'it is not as a research historian that Wrong deserves to be remembered,' writes historian Robert Bothwell. How Stuart would have done as an academic no one can say, because he turned to the law and became a highly respected chief justice of Alberta and the chancellor of the University of Alberta from its founding in 1906 until his death in 1924.

Two years later, in September 1894, Wrong was appointed the professor of history at $2,500 a year. The existing government and university records do not show whether other candidates applied for the position or indeed whether there was a true competition. They do indicate, however, that if there was a competition, there was only about a month in which other candidates could apply. Coincidentally, Blake was back in Toronto at the time. Soon after the appointment, the *Varsity* raised the issue, referring to the rumours of nepotism in the appointment for both the lectureship and the professorship, and stating that 'though several applications were received, only one was actually considered and it took but fifteen minutes to make the appointment.' 'Is this true?' the paper asked. The following week – the *Varsity* was then a weekly run by undergraduates – the paper attacked unnamed professors in certain named departments 'who don't earn one tenth of the money they draw annually. Some are too indolent to earn it; some too ignorant of their work; others know their work but are too slovenly and unsystematic to be able to impart their knowledge ... If the University is intended as a Home for the Helpless let the fact be known.' Strong language.

The editor of the *Varsity*, James Tucker, a member of the class of '95 and considered by some of his classmates 'the outstanding man of our year,' kept up the attack, assisted by other members of the *Varsity* staff such as King, who wrote in his diary in mid-November, 'We are having quite a time re Wrong apptmt. etc.' One reason King disliked Wrong is that King, it seems, had asked Wrong to re-mark one of his history papers, and Wrong had done so and lowered the mark. On another paper, King got a mark of 65 from Wrong, which killed his chances for a renewal of his scholarship.

It is likely that behind-the-scenes support for the attack was being given by Dale and other members of the staff who lived in the University College students' residence, such as A.T. DeLury, who later became head of mathematics, and F.B.R. Hellems, Dale's assistant, who would resign in protest when Dale was fired. The evidence suggests that Vice-chancellor William Mulock was also acting behind the scenes. Mulock resented Blake's control of the affairs of the University following the fire of 1890 and, as previously described, Loudon's attempt to humiliate him with respect to the medical faculty. Contrary to the wishes of the government, Mulock wanted to be chancellor, a position he would obtain many years later. Tucker had contact with Mulock during the course of the controversy, and King's diary shows that on at least ten occasions King met

James Tucker, the editor of the *Varsity*, was suspended from lectures and never graduated from the University.

Joseph Montgomery, another editor of the *Varsity*, was prepared to apologize. He graduated and became a corporate lawyer.

with Mulock. Loudon and others clearly believed that Mulock was the 'guiding but invisible hand,' to quote Loudon's memoirs.

A further issue creating controversy was the cancellation by the university council in early 1895 of an advertised debate involving two workers' advocates that had been organized by the Political Science Association. The designated speakers, apart from their political views, had unorthodox religious views, one of them being an agnostic. Tom Greenwood, the president of the association, arranged to have the meeting take place off campus. Once again, the *Varsity*, with strong student backing at a mass meeting, attacked this 'most truly regrettable state of affairs': 'No other society about the University has ever been required to ... submit its programme to the council for approval before applying for an assembly room.' The university council, it said, 'should act on some manifestly honest principle.' Moreover, the *Varsity* committed the sin of stating that some members of the council were religious 'sceptics.' The *Varsity*'s current editor, Joseph Montgomery, was ordered by the council to apologize. He was prepared to do so, but the editorial board would not hear of it. Tucker was then brought back as editor. The issues, Tucker wrote in the next number, had to do with freedom of the press and freedom of assembly. He would not apologize. On Wednesday, January 29, 1895, the university council suspended him from attending lectures. 'Rather would we leave the University without a degree,' Tucker wrote, 'than surrender the principle for which we have been contending.'

The following week, the *Globe* published a remarkable letter to the editor from Dale, which inflamed both the government and the university professoriate. He had tried to publish it anonymously, but the editor refused publication without Dale's name. It appeared on the front page of the paper. Wrong wrote to Blake in England, 'It is the letter of a madman.' 'I have,' Dale wrote, 'read the testimonials which Mr. Wrong took the trouble to print and I should imagine that no chair in the University was ever filled on such slight grounds as those testimonials afford.' He then turned to the 'deep seated troubles of the University.' 'If during the next ten years,' he continued, 'the character of professorial appointments continues to be what it has been during the last ten years, the professoriate of the University will have lost the respect both of students and public, and the results to learning will be most disastrous.'

King was ecstatic, and wrote in his diary, 'Dale publishes a splendid letter in today's Globe siding with the boys and pitching in Wrong's apptmt.' The government and most of the professors in the University were outraged. Ramsay Wright and W.H. Pike told Loudon they would not sit on the same council as Dale and demanded that something be done. The government moved quickly. Loudon was summoned to meet with the cabinet on Monday and was informed 'they had decided to dismiss Professor Dale.' But first, according to Loudon's memoirs, 'they desired a letter from me on the matter. This I agreed to furnish.' Loudon produced the letter on Wednesday, and the following day Dale was summoned to a cabinet meeting and asked to resign. He refused to do so, and on Friday, February 15 his dismissal was announced officially. This announcement gave rise to the previously described mass meeting that afternoon, the strike vote, and the boycott of classes.

There was much discussion between the students and the university administration. On Wednesday afternoon, February 20, another mass meeting was held at Wardell's Hall, and a motion by Greenwood, seconded by King, was passed that

The Varsity

TORONTO, *February 20th, 1895.*

Published weekly by the Students of the University of Toronto. Annual subscription, $1. For advertising rates apply to the Chairman of the Business Board. Address all communications for publication to the Editor-in-Chief.

JAS. A. TUCKER, Editor-in-Chief.

EDWARD GILLIS, Chairman of Business Board.

Business Board.—Miss Fraser,'95 ; W. A. MacKinnon, 97 ; C. W. Macpherson, School of Practical Science ; W. Thom, '95, W. H. Libby, '98, Medicine.

Editorial Board.—J. Montgomery, '95 ; J. R. Perry, '96 ; Miss E. Durand, '95 ; W. Shotwell, '97 ; V. G. Smith, School of Practical Science; E. T. Kellam, '95, H. L. Heath, '97, Medicine.

Assistant Editors.—J. L. Murray, '95 ; C. P. Megan, 95 ; W. B. Hendry, '95 ; H. A. Clark, '95 ; W. L. M. King, '95 ; P. J. Robinson, '96 ; A. R. Clute, '96 ; C. H. Clegg, '97.

" *Suffer yourself to be blamed, imprisoned, condemned ; suffer yourself to be hanged ; but publish your opinions ; it is not a right, it is a duty.*"

THE WEEK'S EVENTS.

THE appearance of THE VARSITY this week is an adequate representation of the feelings of those who love the University most. We mourn all high ideals and every glorious hope that toil and self-denial have set up in half a century of hard-earned progress. For what has all the effort of the past come to—the effort of those who loved alma mater and hoped one day to see a great university stand on Toronto's historic soil ? Here, in this year of grace 1895, we behold the University torn by dissension—rent in twain by the fatuous policy of selfish, small-minded men. And the tragic aspect of the matter is that he who would dare speak out, must be willing to sacrifice himself before the blind hatred of those who are determined to *rule* though the heavens fall !

It is needless for us to recount the dire doings of the past week. Prof. Dale, admittedly one of the ablest men in the University, respected and revered by his students, loyal to the University as any man who ever trod her courts, honoured again and again by her alumni, dares to express an opinion adverse to the current policy of those who have secured control, and is hounded out of his position ! Other professors may write letters to the press. Their opinions are on the right side, you know, and the publication of letters is a good and proper thing ! But Prof. Dale is not so fortunate. He is constrained to say what he thinks, and his thoughts do not happen to coincide with the thoughts of certain gentlemen. They wound them—they

The *Varsity* of February 20, 1895.

students should return to lectures pending negotiations to appoint a commission. A committee of fourteen students, including three women, negotiated with the administration. On Friday, Loudon sent the government a recommendation for a commission of inquiry, which the government accepted. The students returned to classes.

Loudon continued to have problems with the students. The evening of the day the strike was called off was the *conversazione*, the first that had been held since the fire in 1890. Promenading, that is, walking with a partner to music, was part of the program, but the students preferred dancing. (Dancing was not officially permitted at the college until the following year, when polkas and waltzes were on the program. At Victoria, dancing was not allowed until 1926.) The Toronto *Star* described Loudon's undignified attempt to stop it: 'The president evidently anticipated [dancing] and was on hand at once to prevent it. He was successful in each room in which he was, but when he entered the East Hall the dancing began in the West, and when he returned to the West it was resumed in the East ... The dancing was kept up at intervals until nearly three o'clock.' As the journalist Charlesworth later put it, Loudon tended to adopt 'school-master methods suitable to boys in lower grades.'

A five-person commission of inquiry was established by the government with Chief Justice Thomas Taylor of Manitoba, a former member of the university senate, as its chair. Hearings were held from April 8 to 23. The report, dated April 27, 1895, rejected the students' complaints, though it found 'there was a want of tact in dealing with the students at certain points during these troubles.' The commission found that the *Varsity* articles 'were offensive, and entirely beyond the line of fair comment,' that the students had 'put forward a wholly untenable claim that they had the right to select outside lecturers to deliver lectures and addresses within the University,' and that there was 'no foundation for any charge, or even suspicion' that Blake had used his influence in Wrong's appointment. With respect to Dale, they stated, 'It is impossible to see how any other course could have been pursued towards him.' According to Stewart Wallace in his history, it was 'a distinct triumph for the University authorities.' King, however, noted in his diary that it was 'rather a whitewashing affair.'

The hearing clearly harmed Loudon, in spite of its findings in his favour. The students had directed their attack against him, arguing publicly that there was 'a feeling that President Loudon is unworthy of belief ... that in approaching him the student feels that he is approaching one who is lying in wait to entrap him.' Loudon continued to believe that Mulock was behind the students and was paying their lawyer, W.R. Riddell. According to Loudon's memoirs, Riddell's final statement at the inquiry had been that 'though they had not proven anything against me [Loudon], they had done enough to destroy my future usefulness.' Moreover, important members of the senate were losing patience with Loudon. 'I think it is unfortunate,' Edmund Walker wrote to Blake, 'that he sees intrigue against himself in everything done by the students or by his opponents in the Senate.'

The outstanding class of '95 went their separate ways. King turned down a fellowship to Chicago, expecting to get a fellowship in political economy at Toronto, which he never received. He spent the next year obtaining his LLB from Toronto and then went to Chicago and subsequently to Harvard to study with Ashley. Within a few years, Mulock, at the time the minister of labour in Laurier's government, brought him in as his deputy. Greenwood, who had had acting experience, went to England to try his hand in that profession, but then turned to law and politics. Chisholm went to British Columbia, after briefly practising law in Ontario, and became a journalist and novelist while maintaining his interest in politics. He continued to marvel at King's success, and wrote to another member of the class in 1925: 'Who in hell would have thought that Billy King would have done what he has done. It really makes a man doubt a lot of things.' Montgomery, the *Varsity* editor who had been prepared to apologize, became a corporate lawyer.

Tucker, who had been barred from classes, tried to write the final exams but was not allowed to do so. He completed his work the following year at Stanford University, probably financed by Mulock. A few years later, he applied to receive a Toronto degree, but was refused. He became the assistant editor of *Saturday Night* magazine, but died at the age of 31 in 1903. His friends published a volume of his poetry after his death. Chisholm suggested on the occasion of the class's thirtieth anniversary of graduation that there should be some memorial in Tucker's memory. 'He was a damned good man,' he wrote to a classmate, 'and got a rotten deal all around, not forgetting the one he got from the inscrutable Providence which cut him off just when he was beginning to find himself.' When Viscount Greenwood received an honorary degree from the University of Toronto in 1938, he observed that during the ceremony 'his mind was full of thought of a dead comrade in that revolt,' and that 'if post-mortem degrees were ever granted by universities, Tucker should have one from Toronto.' As for Professor Dale, he never found a permanent teaching position. He took up farming, became the mayor of St Marys, and did some sessional lecturing at McMaster and Queen's universities. Several years after his dismissal, he was elected by the graduates as a member of the University of Toronto senate.

The women students were criticized for their role in the strike. Theirs was called 'unladylike behaviour.' Women, said the *Mail and Empire*, were 'in many instances more extreme in their partisanship even than the young men.' Where would it end? Edward Blake's brother, Samuel Blake, who was counsel for the University at the royal commission, wrote to Premier Mowat that the 'class of young ladies seeking entrance differs very much from what we used to have ten years ago.' 'Unless something be done in the way of preserving order, discipline, and propriety,' he went on, 'possibly, there may be scandals arising from co-education.' But the women, as historian Sara Burke has observed, were simply 'exhibiting a new confidence, a sense of ease in their surroundings.' Sir Daniel Wilson had noted in his diary in 1890 that in his entertaining of the students, 'the young ladies are much more at their ease [than the male students], don't care for portfolios, albums, etc. Prefer talking to one another and are much more easy to entertain.' Shortly after the strike, however, the University introduced more stringent regulations, prohibiting men and women from living in the same boarding house unless they were related, and stating that women students were

The University College residence, with the cloisters in front. The residence was
closed down in 1899.

subject to the 'supervision of the Lady Superintendent whose directions as to
conduct are to be observed.' Ross, the minister of education, would have gone
further and prevented co-educational meetings of undergraduates after 6 o'clock
in the evening.

The strike probably helped contribute to the closing down of the residence in
University College in 1899. There had been earlier attempts to close it. Many
thought it had been responsible for much of the student agitation. Dale and
other staff members who supported the students lived in the residence. Some
argued that the residence – a 'pocket nobility' – ran student life in the college.
Moreover, the residence was losing money, and the space was needed for other

purposes. Fraternities were starting to emerge and could house students. Alpha Delta Phi had established the first fraternity residence for students in 1893. Two other fraternities, both still active in Toronto, had been established in Toronto even earlier, Zeta Psi in 1879 (two of Edward Blake's sons were members) and Kappa Alpha (Mackenzie King's fraternity) in 1892, but neither of these had residence facilities until later. The University actively encouraged fraternities during the late 1890s and early 1900s. In 1901, for example, the University gave Kappa Alpha a long-term lease of the land now occupied by Massey College at a dollar a year, and also gave the fraternity a loan for the construction of a house at favourable interest rates. The college council earlier had sold the residence furniture to the fraternity. Fraternities were becoming a significant part of university life. It would not be until 1960, after a black woman student was denied entry to a sorority, that the University formally would dissociate itself from fraternities and sororities.

The larger issues raised by the strike, such as the freedom of the student press and the right of student groups to control who could address them on campus, seemed to suffer a setback, but in reality they made students more aware of their potential power. In the future, the editors of the *Varsity* would look back at the strike in order to find the courage to challenge authority. In the first issue the following year, the paper referred to Tucker as 'a man worthy to be held up as an example,' called the royal commission a 'farce,' repeated the charge that Loudon 'has entirely failed to win and keep the respect or confidence of the Undergraduates,' and concluded that 'nothing has been altered.' There was also a recognition by many that a university-wide student association was needed. *Acta Victoriana*, the Victoria student paper, pointed out in the middle of the controversy that 'there was no organized body universally recognized as having power to act for the undergraduates as a whole.' Such a body would not be created until 1900, however, and in 1913 it would be renamed the Students' Administrative Council.

Academic freedom for faculty members was certainly not advanced by the events, and as Michiel Horn has argued in his recent book on academic freedom in Canada, some of the questions raised by the firing of Dale 'are still unanswered.' It is clear that a faculty member can now criticize his or her own university, but, Horn asks, can one go as far as Dale and criticize 'the teaching abilities or scholarly attainments of one's colleagues as an exercise of one's academic freedom?'

The strike made people aware of the danger of giving the government the power to appoint. Dale had rightly argued in his fateful letter to the *Globe* that appointments should be in the hands of an independent body. Goldwin Smith, the former Regius Professor of History at Oxford, living in splendour at the Grange in Toronto, had been asked by the commission of inquiry for advice and had recommended that the government not have direct control of the University. The University, he argued, should be in the hands of an independent board of governors or trustees who would be responsible for overseeing its affairs. Smith would later be a key participant in the royal commission of 1906, which would make just such a recommendation.

PART THREE

ASPIRATIONS

chapter sixteen

1897

GRADUATE STUDIES

Despite the difficulties encountered by President Loudon throughout his administration, he could claim success on one important front: the introduction of the PhD degree in 1897. Loudon had proposed such a degree fifteen years earlier, and though it had been accepted by the senate, no regulations implementing it had been established. In 1896, however, a motion by A.B. Macallum of physiology, seconded by W.J. Alexander of English, was passed to set up a committee to study the feasibility of offering the degree – the earlier senate approval had never been revoked. A year later, regulations were approved by the senate, again on Macallum's motion. 'The chief credit for this step,' Loudon later observed, was 'due to Professor A.B. Macallum.'

Doctorates were already being awarded in medicine (MD – though almost all physicians were content with the lesser qualification, the MB) and dentistry (DDS), but these were professional degrees, unlike the PhD, which was a research degree requiring a thesis. Macallum and Alexander, both of whom had PhDs from Johns Hopkins University, wanted the PhD to be a research degree based on a written thesis. It is not clear, however, that Loudon saw the PhD in the same way. The 1883 proposal he had put forward permitted the awarding of the degree by either thesis or examination.

Master of arts degrees had had a long history at the University. They had been awarded from the first convocation of King's College and had been continued by the University of Toronto. But the degree was not highly regarded. No

James Mavor's note on William Lyon Mackenzie King's MA thesis on the International Typographical Union: 'Pass A very competent paper. The only drawback is that there are no references to authorities. The Reports of the various organisations ought at least to have been referred to. J.M.'.

special courses were provided, nor was residence at the University required. In the early period, the thesis was actually written in an examination hall 'without reference to books, or to other aids.' In as late as 1900, the *Varsity* complained about 'giving a graduate the title of M.A. for work done entirely in absentia, and on the submitting of a thesis which he can construct in from one to three months, without even having done any original research worthy of mention.' Mackenzie King's MA, received from the University of Toronto in 1897, fitted the *Varsity*'s description. King produced a forty-five-page double-spaced thesis on the International Typographical Union. It can be found in the University Archives and contains James Mavor's revealing comments: 'A very competent paper. The only drawback is that there are no references to authorities.' The requirements were tightened in 1903, but it would not be until 1910 that a year's residence would be required for the degree.

One reason for Toronto to introduce the PhD was so that its graduates would not have to go outside Canada for doctoral work. Students had been travelling to Germany for many years, particularly to study chemistry. Five of Professor W.H. Pike's students, including Lash Miller, had studied in Germany, four of them at Leipzig. But students went there to study in other fields as well.

The professor of English, W.J. Alexander, for example, had done post-graduate work at the University of Berlin, and the philosophy professor J.G. Hume had received his PhD from Freiburg University.

Beginning in the late 1870s, however, most Canadian students went to the United States for their post-graduate training, and, unlike those who studied in Germany, many stayed there. This was a cause of concern for some. A professor of modern languages at Trinity, A.H. Young, for example, using language reminiscent of that used in the 1820s by John Strachan in arguing for the establishment of King's College, argued that it did not matter whether such students stayed there or returned to Canada. 'In the one case,' Young wrote, 'they are lost to their native land; in the other they propagate views which, if not hostile to England, are at least far from being friendly to her.' The loss to the United States can best be illustrated by the three (of five) Saunders brothers, who had graduated from Toronto and then received their doctorates from Johns Hopkins. One brother, Arthur, became the professor of chemistry at Hamilton College in New York, and another, Frederick, the chair of physics at Harvard. The third brother, Charles Saunders – later, Sir Charles – joined his father at the experimental farm in Ottawa and became famous as the developer of Marquis wheat.

McGill did not introduce the PhD degree until 1906, and though Queen's had provided for earned doctorates since 1889, none was awarded before the turn of the century. Moreover, students at that time could not receive a PhD in England. Advanced degrees (such as the LLD) were normally awarded in England five years after graduation and were granted for original work of a very high standard. Such degrees were not within reach of recent Toronto graduates, who could not afford to spend the required length of time in England. Students who went to England after graduation usually received just an additional bachelor's degree. PhDs were not introduced in England until towards the end of the First World War, in part to attract American students who formerly would have gone to Germany for graduate work, and also to divert Canadian and other students from the United States. But even if English universities had offered PhDs, very few scholarships were available that would enable students to go to England. When Charles Cochrane, who became one of Toronto's great classical scholars, wanted to study in Oxford just after the turn of the century, businessmen took up a collection in order to send him there. Students went increasingly to the United States, where scholarship money was readily available.

Research doctorates had been awarded by Yale since 1860 and by Harvard and other major institutions since the 1870s, but it was not until Johns Hopkins University – based on the German model – was established in Baltimore in 1878 that research doctorates became a major force in academic life in the United States. More than 500 PhDs were awarded by Johns Hopkins from its founding until 1900, with Toronto graduates receiving 19 of them. Toronto, by contrast, would have a total of only 40 PhDs from 1897 until 1921. Half the Canadians who attended Johns Hopkins – a large majority of whom received financial assistance from that university – were Toronto graduates. There were so many good Toronto graduates that President Daniel Gilman of Johns Hopkins wrote to Daniel Wilson: 'We have such a noteworthy succession of your graduates among us that I should much like to see their Alma Mater.' Some returned to teach at Toronto: in addition to Macallum in physiology and Alexander in English, there were Pelham Edgar in French and, later, English and J.C. Fields in mathematics. Ironically, Fields was probably attracted to Johns Hopkins because of the reputation of J.J. Sylvester, who, it will be recalled, had applied unsuccessfully for a position at King's College in 1843.

Toronto graduates also went to the newly established University of Chicago (founded in 1892) and to Clark University in Massachusetts (founded 1889), which was restricted to graduate students. In fact, more Toronto students went to Chicago than to Johns Hopkins, though far fewer obtained their PhDs there. Between 1892 and 1900, 39 Toronto graduates had gone to Chicago. At least two of those involved in the strike, Mackenzie King and F.B.R. Hellems, studied there. (Hellems went on to become professor of classics and dean of arts and science at the University of Colorado, where the present arts and science building is named after him.) Students went also to Harvard, Cornell, Princeton, Pennsylvania, and other institutions. In the 1890s, forty-six American universities awarded the PhD degree. The University of Toronto's research aspirations and the knowledge that most major universities in the United States offered the degree were strong inducements to the University to establish the doctorate at Toronto.

There had been determined opposition to its establishment at Toronto, which helps explain why there was a delay. The *Varsity*, for example, summed up the main concern – lack of resources – when it opposed the doctorate by recording 'its earnest protest against the University attempting to dabble in postgraduate courses until she is doing her undergraduate work thoroughly, and has energy and money to spare.' 'The professors,' it pointed out, 'are already as much overworked as they are underpaid.' Toronto, it added, should not 'sneeze, every time Johns Hopkins or Leipzig or Chicago take snuff.' These thoughts would have been shared by many members of the faculty, a high proportion of whom, like their counterparts at Oxford and Cambridge, did not have earned doctorates. In 1906, for example, only 3 out of 15 staff members at Victoria College had research doctorates, and only 1 out of 29 in the faculty of applied science and engineering. The minister of education, George Ross, was not a supporter of post-graduate degrees. Besides, a number of key persons were not at all alarmed about Canadian students studying abroad. 'Had I a son,' President Wilson told a university convocation in 1886, 'I should assuredly, when his undergraduate course was completed, send him abroad to seek among the scholars of other lands that breadth of culture which no single university fully supplies.'

The 1897 regulations provided for a PhD in arts or sciences after two years of residence, one of which could be spent at another university. (This was not changed to a three-year residency until 1910.) The doctorate was restricted to University of Toronto graduates until 1905. It required of a candidate a 'thesis on some topic in his major subject embodying the results of an original investigation conducted by himself.' At first, only seven departments were prepared to offer the degree – four science departments, Oriental languages and literature, philosophy, and political science. Mathematics did not offer the degree until after Fields came in 1902. All the doctoral fields were university subjects except 'Orientals,' as it was commonly called, which was a college subject. It offered the degree because James McCurdy of University College, who had a Princeton PhD, appears to have wanted to supervise doctoral students. Indeed, after the chemist Lash Miller, McCurdy supervised the greatest number of doctorates during the period up to the end of the First World War.

Surprisingly, the professor of English, W.J. Alexander, was not prepared to offer doctoral programs, even though he had seconded Macallum's motion to institute the degree. He was fully occupied, it seems, with the undergraduate program. During the academic year 1903–4, for example, he and associate professor David Keys, with whatever assistance they could get for $200, had to read more than 1,500 essays. George Wrong of history was clearly not interested in a Johns Hopkins–style degree. In 1923, Wrong declared that 'the American training is directed towards producing a learned treatise, while the Oxford training aims at the understanding of a subject.' The first PhDs in the department of history were not awarded until 1925.

There was no faculty or school of graduate studies, as there was in most American universities that offered the degree. The individual departments were responsible for setting standards under the overall supervision of an ad hoc committee appointed by the senate. It was not until 1915 that a board of graduate studies was established. Throughout most of this period, Macallum chaired the senate committee and, later, the board. A separate school of graduate studies, though advocated by the senate over the years, was not established in the University until 1922.

Between 1897 and 1915, a total of 35 PhDs were awarded by the University. This figure includes a degree awarded in 1912 to James Mavor based on his massive work on Russian economic history, and one in the same year to the professor of German at University College, William Van der Smissen, also based on published work. By looking at some of the other PhDs awarded and the persons who supervised their work, one can get a partial picture of who was engaged in research at the University during the period. Not only are almost all the supervisors noteworthy, but so are most of the recipients of the degree.

Not surprisingly, the first student to receive a PhD degree was one of Macallum's, Frederick Scott, who completed his thesis on nerve cells in 1899. He could not be awarded the degree, however, until a hundred printed copies of the thesis had been deposited. The university librarian required the copies in order to have something to exchange for other publications with other libraries. The fact that the paper had appeared in the *Transactions of the Canadian Institute* was not good enough. Fortunately, a new series, *University of Toronto Studies*, had just been instituted by the university librarian, and Scott was able to reprint the text of his thesis in that series and so receive his degree in early 1900. The rule about the hundred copies was subsequently changed to permit as a substitute a letter from the editor of a reputable journal stating that the work had been accepted for publication. Scott's work at the University of Toronto and in post-doctoral research in London and Berlin on the chemical transmission of signals from one nerve cell to another turned out to be very important in neurobiology, but its significance was not recognized until the 1960s, fifteen years after his death. His academic career was spent at the University of Minnesota, where he is credited with helping transform the medical school into a first-class institution.

The second PhD was awarded to John McLennan in physics, a person who, along with Macallum, ranks as one of the most important scientists in the history of the University. When he died in 1935, his Royal Society of London

U of T's first PhD was completed by Frederick Scott in physiology, under the supervision of A.B. Macallum, in 1900. Scott is shown in his 1897 arts graduation photograph.

W. Lash Miller, professor of chemistry. Photograph taken in 1924.

Physicist John McLennan, centre with bow tie, and other post-graduate students at Cambridge University in 1898–9, under the supervision of Sir J.J. Thomson, seated to the right of McLennan.

obituary referred to him as 'the acknowledged leader of Science in Canada.' He graduated at the head of his class at Toronto in the physics division and was immediately appointed an assistant demonstrator. With some difficulty, he managed to go to Cambridge and to work during 1898 and 1899 with Sir J.J. Thomson in the Cavendish Laboratory. His work there led to the publication in the *Transactions of the Royal Society of London* of his paper 'Electrical Conductivity in Gases Traversed by Cathode Rays,' which was translated into German by the great Wilhelm Ostwald of Leipzig. It was the basis for the awarding of a doctorate by Toronto. Loudon supported the granting of the doctorate, but claimed no credit for supervising McLennan's work. Loudon did not supervise any PhD students. McLennan's real supervisor was J.J. Thomson. Subsequently, McLennan supervised probably more PhD candidates than anyone else in the University up to the Second World War. One of his most distinguished students was E.F. Burton, who would later develop the electron microscope and become head of physics at the University of Toronto. McLennan and Burton have been recognized in the University in the name of the physics building, the McLennan Physical Laboratories, and of its main tower, the Burton Tower.

The third PhD awarded – to William Parks in 1900 – was supervised by the head of geology, Arthur Coleman, who in 1910 also became a fellow of the Royal Society of London. He would replace Macallum as chair of the board of graduate studies during the First World War. Coleman had been a student at Victoria College and had taught science there until Victoria moved to Toronto in 1892. His doctorate was from Breslau University in Germany, where his mentor at Victoria, Eugene Haanel, had received his doctorate many years earlier. Haanel was not taken on by the University of Toronto, but a position was created for Coleman at the School of Practical Science. In 1901, he was transferred to the faculty of arts as the professor of geology, his research speciality being evidences of glaciation. Parks spent forty-three years at the University, having become head of geology when Coleman retired in 1922. He was also the director of the museum of palaeontology at the Royal Ontario Museum from 1915 to 1936 and himself collected many of the dinosaur specimens at the museum.

The person who supervised the greatest number of PhD candidates during this early period was William Lash Miller, who had received his PhD in Germany. Lash Miller supervised six persons up to 1916, three of whom ended up in the United States, one teaching at Wisconsin, one teaching at Utah, and one

Chemist Clara Benson, left, faculty of household science, 1906–45, received a PhD at U of T in 1903; photograph taken in 1899, when she received her BA. Benson and the principal of household science, Annie Laird, right, were the first women professors at the University. Photograph of Laird taken about 1930.

The household science building at the corner of Bloor Street and Queen's Park, completed in 1912. The gates were subsequently moved to form the entryway to Philosopher's Walk at Bloor Street.

becoming assistant director of the General Electric Research Laboratories in Schenectady, New York. Another of his PhDs, R.E. DeLury, the brother of the mathematician A.T. DeLury, left the University after his doctorate to become the head of solar physics at the Dominion Observatory in Ottawa. Another, Maitland Boswell, joined the faculty of applied science and engineering and headed its school of engineering research. The chemistry building at the University was named after Lash Miller.

Miller also supervised Clara Benson, who received her PhD in 1903 for work published in the *Journal of Physical Chemistry*. She shared the honour of being the first woman to receive a PhD from the University with Emma Baker, who received a doctorate in psychology under August Kirschmann. Research positions for women chemists were not easy to find and, like many women chemists at the time, Clara Benson began her teaching in a household science school. She joined the School of Household Science, which had been started by Lillian Massey Treble, a daughter of Hart Massey (after whom Hart House would later be named.) The school had evolved from Lillian Massey's cooking classes to a school training teachers of household science. Degrees in household science (BHS) were first offered by the University in 1902.

Chancellor Burwash of Victoria had proposed the establishment of the household science degree to the senate. To Burwash, the course 'would help a young woman to put every department of the home of which she should become mistress on a thoroughly scientific basis.' 'This is the first course,' he wrote the minister of education, 'for a true woman's life in our university.' A 'true woman,' many then thought, should remain in the home. Clara Benson did not agree. In 1902, she had signed a petition organized by the Women's Alumnae Association of University College questioning the introduction of such a course in the University. Nevertheless, faced with limited job opportunities, she became a demonstrator in food chemistry the following year. The appointment required her to switch from physical chemistry to physiological chemistry. A.B. Macallum now became her mentor and coached her in her new discipline. When the teaching of food chemistry was transferred to the medical building, she became a lecturer in Macallum's department of physiology, the first woman in the University above the rank of demonstrator.

In 1906, following the report of the royal commission, the faculty of household science was established. Benson became an associate professor of physiological chemistry in the new faculty. She and the principal, Annie Laird,

were the first women professors at the University. But Benson publicly acknowledged her place in the hierarchy existing at the time by stating in an article in the
U of T *Monthly* in 1907 that the household science program could be an
'unqualified success ... under the direction of able men.' In 1912, an impressive
neoclassical building, still standing at the corner of Queen's Park and Bloor
Street (now the home of Ontario's Ombudsman and Club Monaco), was erected
with additional funds amounting to half a million dollars from Lillian Massey
Treble. Benson continued her research in food science. Her research record was
sufficiently strong to earn her a listing in *American Men of Science*! By 1928, 30
women had received PhDs from the University of Toronto, 28 of them in the
sciences.

The establishment of the PhD degree was a crucial step towards the University of Toronto's becoming a significant research institution. A very small group
of excellent professors, particularly in the sciences, were engaged in important
research and in training a group of PhD recipients who in their turn would
improve the research record of the University. There was still a long way to go,
however.

chapter seventeen

1901

⁓

THE TURN OF THE CENTURY AND THE RISE OF THE ALUMNI ASSOCIATION

The *Varsity* expressed a mood of optimism as Canada entered the twentieth century. In its last issue of 1900, the paper predicted that the year would be 'the beginning of what is likely to prove a new era in the history of the University.' No official New Year's celebrations took place at the University – it was, after all, the Christmas vacation – though it is likely the bells of St Basil's, and perhaps the bells of Knox and Wycliffe, were rung, as were most church bells in the city. Celebrations, however, took place at the recently opened Toronto City Hall. After the twelve strokes of midnight, there were twenty more for the new century.

The first issue of the *Varsity* in the new century referred to a 'revived spirit in university life' and foresaw 'brighter days in store.' Financially, things could not get much worse. There were large annual deficits. By 1901, the deficit amounted to over $30,000. The total university income during the previous four years had been, on average, under $125,000 a year, and the government contributed annually only $7,000 of that amount. In contrast, American public universities, as President James Loudon (like most future presidents) pointed out, were funded much more generously. The University of Michigan, with state financial support, spent about $500,000 annually, and the University of California more than $300,000. Governmental support of at least $50,000 a year, Loudon argued, was needed by the University of Toronto.

The new force in the fight for improved resources for the University would

President James Loudon. Photograph taken before 1906.

be its graduates. Many persons would have remembered that it was the graduates who had saved the University in the 1860s from the designs of the denominational colleges. Perhaps they could turn things around again. 'All eyes are turned on [them],' the *Varsity* noted, 'who, ten thousand strong, must bear the brunt of the battle.' Loudon expressed the same view: 'There is no doubt that the influence of the alumni will count for much. The clear duty of the alumni at this juncture is to help in putting the case before the people, and in bringing influence to bear individually and collectively on public opinion.'

The University of Toronto Alumni Association had been formed in April 1900, with Loudon a key agent in its establishment. The University historian Stewart Wallace called the formation of the association 'the greatest constructive feat of his administration.' It is, however, a rather odd story. In January 1900, Loudon had received a visit from Samuel Blake, the brother of Chancellor Edward Blake and a close confidant of William Ross's Liberal government. According to Loudon's unpublished memoirs, Samuel Blake told him that the government had decided that he, Loudon, was to be removed to make way for 'a man like Seth Low [of Columbia] or Principal Grant [of Queen's].' Loudon was naturally distressed and immediately wrote to Chancellor Edward Blake in England, complaining about the 'spirit of secrecy, and one might also say of conspiracy which has characterized this affair.' But before Chancellor Blake received Loudon's letter, the University received Blake's 'irrevocable' letter of resignation, which was to be 'acted on *immediately*.' 'The counsel I failed to get from Mr. Edward Blake,' Loudon wrote in his memoirs, 'I received from my wife, who on [Blake's] resignation being received, advised me forthwith to appeal to the graduates and form an Alumni Association.' Fortunately for the University, Loudon took his wife's advice. Such, then, are the curious origins of the Alumni Association.

Other important forces helped bring the organization into being. Toronto graduates living in Ottawa, where many worked for the federal government, had formed a strong local group in 1894 and wanted a wider association of graduates. The *Varsity* also gave its strong support to the formation of such an organization. The existing bodies were not proving effective. The statutory 'Convocation' of all Toronto graduates met very infrequently – it elected the chancellor, for example – and was not a substitute for an organized alumni association. The University College Alumni Association, formed in 1892, had ceased to function after William Dale, the driving force behind the organization, was dismissed, his dismissal having led to the student strike of 1895. Women alumnae of University College had been meeting for a number of years to promote a residence for women, without success. What was needed was a body to unite all graduates. The model often cited was the University of Michigan Alumni Association. The president of the Ottawa association, Otto Klotz, an astronomer with the federal government, had graduated from Michigan after spending a year at Toronto.

With the active support of the Ottawa alumni, who sent out a circular calling for a university-wide body, an organizational meeting was planned for the Easter break in April 1900, at a time when the Ontario Teachers Association, which included a large number of Toronto alumni, was meeting in Toronto. More than 200 persons met on a rainy April evening in the chemistry lecture hall, the largest meeting hall on the campus. Loudon took the chair and was joined on the platform by Chancellor Nathanael Burwash of Victoria, Father John Teefy of St Michael's, and Otto Klotz. The meeting agreed to form an association. Loudon was elected honorary president, R.A. Reeve president. Reeve was a good choice, being the dean of medicine, a graduate of University College, and, of importance to Victoria, a Methodist. Moreover, he had an interest in putting pressure on the government for a new medical building and in thwarting the Trinity medical dean Walter Geikie's attempts to block Toronto's medical ambitions. The secretary of the association was the physicist John McLennan, who was both effective and full of 'contagious enthusiasm' – and moreover wanted a physics building. McLennan remained as secretary until 1908 and succeeded A.B. Macallum as president in 1913. A number of women were elected to the council, including Gertrude Lawler, a prize-winning graduate of University College and the head of English at Harbord Collegiate, and Louise Nelles Starr, a graduate of Victoria and the daughter of a former chancellor of Victoria, Samuel Nelles.

The association cast a wide net. It included graduates and others who had attended 'a whole session' at the University, as well as current members of the teaching staff and governing body. It also included undergraduates. The members were organized on the basis of local branches. By the end of the first year of operation, there were 17 branches. McLennan attended twelve of the organizational meetings. In the summer of 1903, Loudon and McLennan travelled to the west coast to meet alumni. They were surprised at the number of Toronto graduates in the west. In Edmonton, for example, where they expected to find perhaps half a dozen, they met with thirty-five. McLennan used the occasion to promote graduate studies wherever he went, hoping that westerners would come to Toronto rather than go to the United States. By June 1904, there were 33 branches, 23 of them in Ontario.

In its first year, the association instituted the annual gathering of alumni at the June graduation exercises. Four hundred alumni attended a banquet in the gymnasium the night before graduation, June 1900. The new chancellor, Chief Justice William Meredith, welcomed the graduates, noting that the energetic secretary of the association, McLennan, would receive his PhD the following day. A garden party was held on the front campus after the graduation, and a moonlight boat cruise on Lake Ontario in the evening. No doubt sitting through convocation in the examination hall of the School of Practical Science brought home to the alumni the idea that a proper convocation hall was required to replace the one that had been destroyed in the fire. That first year also saw the appearance of the *University of Toronto Monthly*. The first editor, assisted, of course, by the ubiquitous McLennan, was Professor I.H. Cameron, a medical graduate who had replaced Dean William Aikins in 1897 as the professor of surgery. One rule established from the beginning was that all articles had to be signed. The University – and particularly Loudon – had had enough of unsigned attacks in the press. Within a couple of years a paid editor was hired, and the *Monthly* continued in more or less the same form until after the Second World War, when it was incorporated into the new *Varsity Graduate*.

The first real test of the strength of the new organization came in early 1901, when the association lent its support to the University's plea for more funding for science and engineering. What was needed, the University had argued, was general support for engineering and the sciences and a new building. Loudon complained that the government was starving Toronto, the state university, while indirectly generously supporting Queen's, a denominational university. Queen's had secured government support for its science program by calling it a 'school of mining and engineering.' Principal Grant, Loudon complained, 'is willing to take down the Presbyterian sign from the front door and put it at a side entrance.'

Toronto's engineering school needed greater financial support. The School of Practical Science (SPS) had affiliated with the University in 1889 and, in effect, dissociated itself from University College. Federation had transferred the science professors to the university professoriate, so the connection with UC was not needed. The change gave SPS more control over its affairs, which were now run by Principal John Galbraith and the engineering faculty rather than by University College professors. At about the same time, the government more than doubled the space in the red-brick 'Skulehouse' by building a large addition to the east. The main entrance to the building now faced Queen's Park, which still controlled SPS's budget, rather than University College, as it had until then. Enrolment kept growing, and though new faculty members were added in the 1890s, they were insufficient to meet the needs of the school. In 1892, an optional four-year degree program (BASc) was introduced by the addition of an extra year to the existing three-year diploma course.

In 1888, there were only 70 regular engineering students. Ten years later there were 200 students, by 1905 there would be more than 500, and by 1908, more than 700. In twenty years, therefore, there was a tenfold growth in the number of engineering students. This reflected the need for engineers in North America and the fact that a greater proportion of engineers were attending university. In the 1880s, Galbraith had done virtually all the teaching in engineering, with the sciences handled by University College. Additions to the faculty in the early 1890s, to assist Galbraith, included two recent graduates, Charles Wright, later the head of the department of architecture, and Thomas Rosebrugh, later the head of electrical engineering, who was appointed a demonstrator in the new engineering laboratory. Arthur Coleman, the distinguished geologist, who had been at Victoria College in Cobourg, joined the SPS faculty when Victoria moved to Toronto. He later transferred to the faculty of arts while continuing his association with engineering. New departments were established in the 1890s, including a combined department of mechanical and electrical engineering. But the facilities and the faculty could not keep up with the increasing demand for engineers.

SPS still looked to the government for its funding. In 1900, however, it allied itself more closely with the University when it officially became the faculty of applied science of the University. Principal Galbraith explained the advantages of the new arrangement at a dinner given in his honour. 'The result,' he said, 'is that the University gains without expense a fully equipped faculty of Applied Science and in this respect puts itself on an equality with the other great universities of the continent: while on the other hand the School gains public recognition of the fact that its work is of equal rank and dignity with that of the ancient faculties of Arts, Medicine and Law.' Galbraith also hoped that with faculty status the salaries of engineering professors, which lagged behind those of their counterparts in arts, would be increased. The new faculty was still separately funded by the government. SPS would not be integrated financially into the University until 1906.

One reason for the increasing demand for engineers was the opening up of Northern Ontario, sometimes referred to as the 'New Ontario.' 'The development of New Ontario,' the historian H.V. Nelles has written, 'was a joint public and private venture, a provincial equivalent to the opening of the west.' Scientists and engineers would be required so that the potential wealth could be capitalized on. The *Globe* had predicted in 1900 that 'the wealth in the forest, in mineral deposits, in the wasted energy of great waterfalls ... is certain to be developed as the world's demands and discoveries of science make such development remunerative.' Sometimes, however, the hyperbole was extreme. One writer proclaimed that Moose Factory on James Bay would become 'the new Chicago of the North.'

The Alumni Association made an appointment to see Premier Ross to back

The Mining Building on College Street, shortly after its opening in 1904; the engineering
building (SPS) can be seen in the background to the right.

the University's case for support for science and engineering. On March 13,
1901, 300 graduates from eighteen Ontario counties took part in the meeting to
press the claims of the University. Samuel Blake did not want Loudon to attend,
claiming that his presence would be 'like the historical red flag,' but Loudon did
take part. Some non-graduates joined the delegation, including the head of the
iron and steel works at Sault Ste Marie, who argued that 'industrial progress
depended upon efficient scientific teaching at the University.' Corporations in
the Sault were not able to find qualified Canadians to head their departments.
The *World* described the meeting as 'probably the most influential deputation
that has ever gathered at the Parliament Buildings.'

The previous week, a group of 200 engineering students had personally
delivered a persuasive petition to the government outlining why funds were
required. The petition was probably organized by the class of 1901, the first class
of the new century, which felt a special attachment to the University. (It was that
engineering class and the 1901 class in arts who donated the two guns in front of
Hart House that face the legislative buildings so threateningly. The guns, taken
from the bottom of Nova Scotia's Louisbourg harbour, had belonged to a French

vessel sunk by General Wolfe in 1758.) No member of the teaching staff accompanied the students, though representatives of such bodies as the Toronto Board of Trade and the Canadian Manufacturers' Association attended. The present facilities, the petition stated, were inadequate: 'very poor light and ventilation in the drafting rooms,' inadequate equipment in all departments, room for only twenty students in the library, and a teacher-student ratio double that of other engineering colleges. The petition then stressed the potential economic advantages to the province of an improved faculty. 'The importance of the undeveloped water-power of Ontario,' the petition stated, 'cannot be over-emphasized.' 'The future of Ontario,' it went on, 'depends largely upon the successful development of her mineral and forest wealth.' It ended by noting the growing strength of nations, presumably Germany and the United States, 'who have paid close attention to scientific study.' The premier listened but said 'he could make no promises.'

Premier Ross was worried about the political consequences of giving too much support to the University, considered by many the home of an elite group. 'I think that the University question is the most dangerous one we have taken up this session,' he wrote to a cabinet colleague in 1901. 'Although our followers will stand by us, I am quite uneasy as to the effect upon the country.' But the work of the alumni and students was having its effect.

Ross was also being pushed by the leader of the Conservatives, James Whitney. The evening before the alumni meeting with Ross, Whitney gave a major address in the legislature. The Conservatives, he said, would give greater financial support to the University. They would not allow it to 'remain suspended between heaven and earth, like the coffin of Mohammed.' University finances, Whitney stated, should be 'put on a sound, stable, and permanent footing,' and the University, he suggested, should be given an annual payment from the provincial succession duties. If the province does not do something, he predicted, 'our young men will go elsewhere for higher education.' Ross was convinced that Whitney was 'very much under Chancellor Meredith's influence' and was trying 'to outbid us for the support of the Alumni of Toronto.' Sir William Meredith was no doubt playing a role behind the scenes. He had been Whitney's mentor and predecessor as leader of the Conservatives in Ontario.

Exactly a week after the alumni meeting with Ross, a bill was introduced by the government that went a considerable way towards responding to the University's requests. The government would pay each year all the salaries and other costs of the science departments, with the exception of biology. This would initially amount to an additional $25,000 a year to the University. The University would also get a new building at a cost of about $200,000 on the north side of College Street for the university departments of mineralogy and geology and for the extension of SPS.

This new building would be called the Chemistry and Mining Building and, later, the Mining Building. The building, which was opened in 1904, more than doubled the space available to engineering. Several years later, even more space opened up when a building for the treatment of ores – later named for H.E.T. Haultain – was added directly north of the new mining building. Haultain became a professor of mining in 1910 after having had extensive practical mining experience. He had graduated in 1889 and been the first student president of the Engineering Society. In the 1920s, he would instigate the engineers' 'Iron Ring' ceremony. The construction of the Mining Building required that the former Wycliffe College building be torn down. The newly created University of Toronto Press, at that time primarily a printer, had to move from the old Wycliffe building to a small nearby cottage, one of its many locations over the years.

Whitney claimed that the government had not gone far enough. It should have undertaken, for example, to pay for the biology department as well, and should have provided for overall support of the University through succession duties. But the new Alumni Association was pleased. The bill was clearly a result of its influence. The faculty also was delighted. The legislation freed up money and space for other purposes. On the day the bill received royal assent (April 15, 1901) – perhaps coincidentally – the first faculty club was created and given quarters in the dean's house of the former University College residence.

The Alumni Association had further success in the promotion of the construction of the present Convocation Hall. The initial plan was to raise $25,000 from the alumni to build a hall in memory of those who had fallen in the Fenian raids and in the Boer War, but the plans kept expanding. If the alumni could raise $50,000, the government agreed to contribute another $50,000. The sum was raised – Goldwin Smith of the Grange gave the final $5,000 – and the cornerstone of the present Convocation Hall was laid in June 1904. The building, designed by Darling and Pearson, who had just completed a magnificent residence for the businessman Joseph Flavelle in Queen's Park, now the faculty of law, was modelled on the Sorbonne theatre in Paris and was intended to seat

The sod-turning ceremony for Convocation Hall, 1904: John Hoskin, chairman of the board, with spade; R.A. Reeve, president of the Alumni Association and dean of the faculty of medicine, holding wheelbarrow; and John McLennan, professor of physics and secretary of the association, with the large hat, on the left of the group.

Convocation Hall, completed in 1906.

2,000 people. It would require two years, and further government support, before the hall could be used.

The Alumni Association had another major success – helping to obtain a physics building for the University. Physics was housed in University College in what is now the Croft Chapter House and in several rooms in the cloisters in what had been the residence. The space was clearly inadequate. Physics had less than 10,000 square feet of space compared with over 30,000 for chemistry. Moreover, its facilities did not even approach the fine building and equipment provided by the philanthropist William Macdonald for McGill University, where Ernest Rutherford, who had come to McGill in 1898, was engaged in his path-breaking research. The University approved plans for a building just south of the site where Convocation Hall was being erected. Again, Darling and Pearson, the university architects, prepared a design. The government, however, was not particularly interested in financing yet another building. It hoped – with Galbraith's approval – that if SPS taught physics to its own engineering students, there would be less need for new facilities. SPS thereupon hired its own physics lecturer, much to the annoyance of Loudon and others. But that did not answer the need for a physics building.

Early in 1904, the Alumni Association once more came to Loudon's aid and sought an interview with the premier. Ross was reluctant to meet them, but the alumni executive said that if Ross persisted in his refusal, they 'would rent Massey Hall and invite the premier to meet the deputation there.' Three hundred alumni met with the premier at Queen's Park on March 23, 1904 – the same number that had met with him three years earlier. The action once again was backed by a student petition, with 1,400 signatures. The alumni reminded Ross that 'the next election might turn on the treatment accorded to the University and its alumni.' A little more than six months later the government announced that it would pay for the new physics building at a cost of $180,000. The announcement, the *Monthly* stated, 'came as a veritable surprise.'

The government was in the midst of an election campaign and perhaps agreed with the alumni that the grant would help their chances. In January 1905, however, after more than thirty years of Liberal rule in Ontario, the Conservatives formed the new government, with 69 seats to the Liberals' 29. Whitney was now premier of Ontario.

chapter eighteen

1905

WHITNEY AND THE
ROYAL COMMISSION

On May 17, 1905, a few months after he was sworn in as premier, James Whitney introduced a bill that removed the existing university deficit and generously provided for future funding. The bill, he said to prolonged applause in the legislature, would 'remove for the future the possibility and probability of any of those annual deficits which have been the cause of a great deal of worry, anxiety, and annoyance to the Government and the Legislature, and also to those in control of the University.' Whitney repeated the words he had used as leader of the opposition in 1901, that the University should be 'put on a sound, stable, and permanent footing.' Rather than being 'suspended between heaven and earth,' as Whitney had complained at the time, the University was now moving towards heaven.

Money was provided for finishing the construction of Convocation Hall and the physics building, both of which were proving costlier than originally anticipated. The government would not only cover the operating expenditures for the year but consider using the provincial succession duty (that is, taxes on the estates of deceased persons) in future years to assist the University. The total immediate direct grants to the University approached half a million dollars. In addition, $30,000 a year was promised for the next thirty years, which would allow the University to borrow money for future construction. 'Posterity,' Whitney said, 'ought to bear its fair share of the burden.'

The proposed legislation contemplated the building of a men's residence for

King's College Circle, showing, from left to right, the library, the medical school, and the engineering building. Photograph taken between 1903, when the medical building was opened, and 1913, when the Toronto General Hospital was built. Note the smog and the dominance in the skyline of the new city hall, completed in 1899.

about 180 students and an extension to the women's residence, Queen's Hall, which had just opened, as well as a museum for the School of Practical Science. Moreover, up to a quarter of a million dollars could be raised by the University to enable the Toronto General Hospital to erect a new building on a site more accessible to the medical faculty and its students than the hospital near the Don River. Finally, Whitney raised the possibility that during the summer recess the government might appoint a royal commission 'to acquire information for the purpose of informing itself as to the best manner of changing the entire administration of the affairs of the University.' The 1905 act was quickly enacted and received royal assent at the end of May. Samuel Blake, a diehard Liberal but also a strong supporter of the University, wrote to Whitney, the Conservative premier, saying that 'in your first session you have done more [for the University] than has been done at least in 10 years past by the former government.'

Devonshire Place men's residence, opened in 1907, looking north, in 1924.
Note Varsity Stadium to the north, the meteorological building on Bloor Street,
opened in 1909 and now the office of student admissions and awards, and Casa Loma,
at the top of the picture, opened in 1914.

Construction was started on a men's residence, Devonshire House, at the corner of Hoskin Avenue and Devonshire Place, which would be open to students of all faculties. The building, renovated in the 1990s to serve as the Munk Centre for International Studies and the John W. Graham library for Trinity, was originally meant to form a quadrangle. To provide additional space for buildings, the University was given permission to close up the north–south street, Devonshire Place, and to compensate those whose property would be affected. Premier Whitney's wealthy brother, the businessman E.C. Whitney, pledged $40,000 for the east house of the quadrangle if funds for the other three sides were promised. A group of wealthy benefactors, which included Samuel Blake and Joseph Flavelle, gave funds for the north house and the government offered money for the south house, but funds to complete the quadrangle were not forthcoming. E.C. Whitney, however, was sufficiently pleased with the result of his challenge that he fulfilled his pledge, and Devonshire House was constructed with only three sides and opened in 1907. (The premier's brother later bequeathed more than $300,000 to the University, which enabled the women's residence for University College to be built in the early 1930s at the south-east corner of Hoskin and St George. Whitney Hall is therefore named after him and not, as many believe, the premier.) The University also built, in 1904, an addition to the women's residence, Queen's Hall, on the east side of Queen's Park, which had been Mayor W.H. Howland's home (since then demolished for the construction of government buildings).

❧

During the summer of 1905, Premier Whitney set about forming a royal commission. It was to be his own commission, not that of his minister of education. He wanted Goldwin Smith to chair it. Smith was a highly respected intellectual, and his views on the desirability of separating the University from government control, which he had expressed to the commission of inquiry set up after the 1895 strike, coincided with Whitney's own. The 82-year-old Smith declined to serve as chair but agreed to be a member. Smith had been appointed the Regius Professor of History at Oxford in 1858 – the year before University College was completed – having earlier served as assistant secretary of a royal commission set up to investigate the British educational system. For several years in the late 1860s, he taught history at the newly opened Cornell University, but then he moved to Toronto, where he met and married the wealthy widow of the former Toronto mayor William Boulton. All the meetings of the commission would take place in Smith's elegant residence, the Grange.

The premier then turned to the 47-year-old Joseph Flavelle to serve as chair. Flavelle, unlike Smith, had humble beginnings, in Peterborough, Ontario, where the family name was pronounced 'Flavvle.' He left school at 17 and took a job in a flour and feed store, where his father had sometimes worked, and the following year he bought the store. He moved to Toronto in 1887 and was enormously successful in business – in meat packing, merchandising, and finance. His residence, 'Holwood House,' on Queen's Park rivalled the Grange in grandeur. Unlike the custom at the Grange, however, liquor was not served at the Flavelle home, which may have been one reason (Smith's age might have been another) why the meetings of the commission were held at the Grange.

From 1898, Flavelle had been involved in various academic matters – as a member of the board of Victoria, as chair of the Toronto General Hospital, and as a member of the board of trustees of the University, which had responsibility for its finances. He would be a member of the board of governors of the University for more than thirty years. 'I was amazed at [his] grasp of University affairs,' his fellow commissioner the Reverend Bruce Macdonald later stated; and Canon Henry John Cody, another commissioner, observed that Flavelle had 'a mind of marvellous clarity.' Flavelle was a supporter of Whitney, both financially and through Flavelle's daily paper, the *News*. One of his employees at the paper, A.H.U. Colquhoun, a graduate of McGill, was made secretary and a member of the commission. Privately, Flavelle expressed the view that it was 'a curious anomaly' for a businessman to chair the commission.

Another self-made millionaire, the 58-year-old Byron Edmund Walker, was appointed to the commission – in spite of his being both a Liberal and an agnostic. Walker, who in 1910 would become chair of the board of governors and later would become chancellor of the University, had left school in Hamilton at age 12 to enter his uncle's *bureau de change* business. At age 20, he joined the Bank of Commerce as a clerk, and subsequently he was transferred to New York City. There, he took advantage of the opportunities offered by the city's cultural treasurers, including the Metropolitan Museum of Art. He returned from New York to Canada in 1886 to become general manager of the bank, and in 1907 he became its president. He lived in one of the grand houses on the east side of St George (since then demolished and now the site of the business school), from which he witnessed the 1890 fire; later he stated that after the fire he 'realized for the first time that the university was the most important institution in Canada apart from the government itself.' Walker accepted Chancellor Edward Blake's request for financial expertise and became a member of the University's board of trustees and senate.

Over the years, Walker played an extremely important role in the intellectual and cultural life of Canada, and particularly of Toronto – in his many roles at the University and as one of the founders of the Royal Ontario Museum, the Art Gallery of Toronto (now the Art Gallery of Ontario), the National Gallery in Ottawa, and the Champlain Society. He also served as president of the Royal Canadian Institute, as honorary president of the Mendelssohn Choir, and as one of the promoters of a reference library for the city. He was an expert on Robert Browning's poetry and an amateur but expert geologist and palaeontologist. In 1911, he was elected a member of the Royal Society of Canada. Given the choice, Walker said, he would have preferred to be an academic. Relatively few persons ever connected with the University have been as gifted as Walker.

The chancellor of the University, Sir William Meredith, who had been Whitney's mentor and predecessor as leader of the Conservatives, was also asked to be a member of the commission. A graduate of the University, he had been appointed chief justice of the Common Pleas Division of Ontario in 1894. He would play a major role in the drafting of the subsequent legislation. Two other alumni were chosen, Canon Henry John Cody, a prize-winning University College graduate of 1889, who was the popular rector of St Paul's Anglican Church on Bloor Street, east of Yonge, and the Reverend Bruce Macdonald, a member of the famous University College class of 1895 and the head of St Andrew's boys' school. Both were ministers, Cody having graduated from Wycliffe College and Macdonald from Knox. Cody would go on to become chair of the board of governors and then president of the University, and Macdonald would become chair of the board when Cody became president.

Whitney announced the membership of the royal commission on October 2, 1905. Hours before the announcement, Loudon – in yet one more example of bad timing and poor judgment – sent Whitney a letter suggesting that Whitney set up a small 'committee' consisting of Loudon, Chancellor Meredith, and Goldwin Smith to study and report on the issues. His advice was ignored because he was part of the problem. The first meeting of the commission took place two days later in the office of the minister of education, the medical doctor R.A. Pyne, who would hold the office for the next thirteen years. Whitney, however, was present and was in control.

The commission met seventy-seven times in Goldwin Smith's elegant dining room, sometimes to hear witnesses, sometimes to discuss and formulate ideas, and sometimes to negotiate with interested parties. They met for three hours a day every weekday when they were not travelling, alternating between afternoon and evening meetings. The members of the commission visited universities in the United States. Flavelle, for example, visited universities in the west, including Chicago and Wisconsin, and in the east, including Harvard, Yale, and Princeton. No one visited England, however, or other Canadian universities. In a break with the past, the University of London model seems to have had virtually no influence on proposals for the University's reform.

Flavelle kept Whitney informed of their progress. He had a meeting with Whitney in January 1906 and followed it up with what he said were his 'present

Members of the 1906 Royal Commission on the University, meeting at the Grange, Goldwin Smith's home: from left to right, Reverend Bruce Macdonald, Canon Henry Cody, Chancellor William Meredith, Joseph Flavelle (chairman), A.H.U. Colquhoun, Goldwin Smith, and Edmund Walker.

views,' though it is likely they represented the tentative views of the commission. The full commission met with the cabinet at the beginning of March to outline their conclusions. The document was finalized a month later and signed on April 4 at a dinner at the Grange. Whitney introduced the report in the legislature on May 2, 1906, with all the members of the commission seated on the floor of the chamber. The content of the report came as no surprise, however, having been published by the *World* in early March. Two aggressive reporters had fooled a young employee of the printers, who was delivering a number of copies of the draft to Meredith's home on University Avenue, into putting down his package for a moment. They extracted a copy of the draft, which became headline news the following day in the *World*. Charges of theft were brought, but it is not clear whether there were convictions.

The report was well received by the press. The *Globe* called it a 'permanently valuable document,' and the *World* predicted that Toronto 'can become the centre of higher education, not only for the province, but for the Dominion.' The government accepted the report and, with two exceptions, introduced the draft legislation the commission had included with its report. The government decided to increase the size of the board of governors to 20 members from the commission's 15 and also turned down the commission's proposal that a million acres of land in northern Ontario be given to the University as an endowment. Otherwise, the legislation, with minor changes, was enacted exactly as the commission had recommended.

The crucial part of the report and the new legislation was removal of the government's direct control of the University and substitution of a board of governors. 'To administer the affairs of a State university by a political government,' the commission observed, 'occupied with different matters, constantly changing its party character, and gifted with no special talent for the management of universities, has not commended itself to a practical and progressive people.' No parallel to it, the commission found, 'exists either in Great Britain or in North America.' The commission therefore recommended that the board should 'possess the general oversight and financial control now vested in the State.' Richard Harcourt, now the opposition education critic, wanted the government to continue to approve appointments, but Whitney said that 'he would not intentionally inject poison into the Bill.' With the government's large majority, opposition amendments were easily defeated. The University Act, 1906 received royal assent on May 14, 1906.

The report was obviously strongly influenced by the businessmen on the commission. The board of governors would be like a corporate board of directors, appointed by the government – in effect, the shareholders – and removable at the pleasure of the government. The workers, that is the faculty members and the administrative staff, were excluded from membership on the board. Only the president would be a member. This was the pattern throughout North America, though in some universities the board itself would appoint new members, and in some the alumni would elect members to the board. The alumni had requested the right to elect some of the members of the board, but with the exception of the election of the chancellor, the request was not granted. The result was a significant reversal of the gains made by the alumni in 1873 for a significant role in the governance of the University.

A reconstituted senate would be responsible for purely academic matters. Deans and heads of colleges were members of the senate, but the ordinary faculty member's role was diminished by the rule that alumni could not, as they formerly could, choose a member of the staff as their representative. The faculty members, however, did play the major role in the faculty councils, in which all staff above the rank of lecturer were members. The legislation brought in a new council for the faculty of arts, with the president of the University as its chair.

The board, like a corporate board, would be responsible for selecting the president, specifically referred to by the commission as 'the chief executive officer.' The commission wanted a strong presidential office. The president would be relieved of all teaching duties. 'Instead of centralized responsibility,' the report had noted, 'we have had divided authority.' It therefore reduced the role of the chancellor to a mainly ceremonial one and eliminated entirely the position of vice-chancellor. All appointments, promotions, and dismissals were now to be made by the board, but only on the recommendation of the president. Victoria had recommended a form of cabinet that would advise the president, to be made up of the deans and principals, but the recommendation was rejected by the commission. The deans and principals, however, would handle discipline in the University through a body called the Caput. The bicameral structure of a board and a senate brought in by the commission lasted for two-thirds of a century. Moreover, it influenced the structure of the new universities founded in the west and elsewhere. It was not until 1972 that a new University of Toronto Act merged the two bodies into one unicameral governing council.

The commission also encouraged the creation of a larger, more diverse university – what today we would call a multiversity. Engineering would become a faculty in the University – the faculty of applied science and engineering – and would no longer be funded directly by the government. The budget for medicine would also be the responsibility of the University. The old but often circumvented policy that taxpayers' money should not be used for medical education would no longer apply. This measure gave further potential to an already strong medical school. The commission had been asked to recommend the establishment of a women's faculty of medicine, but instead negotiated the acceptance of women into the faculty of medicine. The commission tried to create a university faculty of law in conjunction with the Law Society of Upper Canada, but, as in the past, the Law Society was unwilling to give up its monopoly on legal education.

Technical education was supported by the commission. The Canadian Manufacturers' Association had argued in its brief that Canada's 'immense and varied natural resources are largely undeveloped.' 'In addition to a cultural course of studies,' the brief argued, 'the country also demands a training for its young men and women that will best aid the people in exploiting their varied natural wealth ... The needs of the country warrant the inauguration of a still more extended policy of technical training such as is called for by the great and varied development of our Province and of the Dominion.' The commission accepted 'practically all' of the Manufacturers' Association brief, stating: 'Canada must train her own sons to be her captains of industry. The agricultural, mineral and forest wealth and the water power of this Province call for a practical capacity and a specialized knowledge which only a modern university can supply.' The report therefore recommended increasing practical training. There were to be new faculties of forestry, education, and household science. The existing 'mutually satisfactory and beneficial' relationship with the Ontario Agricultural College would continue, and the relationship with the college would be enhanced by providing for the awarding of degrees and a new building in close proximity to the University. The commission gave science an equal place with culture in the University. It concluded its report by stating, 'We could do no more than provide a home for culture and science under the same academical roof, uniting them as far as possible, yet leaving each in its way untrammelled by the union.'

No change was recommended with respect to the colleges, even though the commission felt that the 'division of subjects is an illogical arrangement.' 'The commission,' it stated, 'does not desire to interfere with it, since it is part of the existing understanding between the University and the federated bodies.' Flavelle would have strengthened the colleges by transferring to them certain subjects such as philosophy and modern history, but the commission did not want to change a system that appeared to be working well. The University, it reported, has, 'by apparent chance, hit upon a system which, if properly and loyally worked, provides a combination of strong personal influence on students with the broad outlook and widened sympathies that come from membership in a great University.'

The commission had made considerable efforts to negotiate an arrangement that would bring Trinity from its site on Queen Street West to the downtown campus. (Trinity, it will be recalled, had federated with the University of Toronto in 1904, following the merger of Trinity Medical College with Toronto's faculty of medicine.) In the end, however, members of the commission could not agree on how much land would be provided for Trinity and how a new building would be financed. The commission felt that Trinity's demand for space was excessive. Moreover, Trinity had no inclination to sell its property at that time, being confident that the value would increase in the near future. The whole matter was therefore left to future negotiations by the new board of governors. Flavelle blamed himself for the failure, writing in a letter to Whitney that 'he had failed in leadership at a critical time.' Immediately after the release of the report, Trinity set up a committee to conduct negotiations when the new university board was established. An attempt was made to persuade Andrew Carnegie, who was in Toronto in connection with his gift of the proposed reference library on College Street, to assist financially, but nothing came of it. In the meantime, the existing arrangement to have separate duplicate lectures at Trinity was continued.

The land available, the commission recognized, was 'decidedly limited,' so 'the policy of the University should be to continue to acquire as much land as possible in the vicinity of Queen's Park.' The university lands did not then include the two sides of St George Street, and much of the land it did own had been rented on long-term leases to private persons. The commission stated that the new board 'should consider some comprehensive plan for the disposition and use' of its property and recommended that a superintendent of buildings and grounds be appointed. Fortunately, the commission rejected the submission of C.H.C. Wright, the professor of architecture, that 'a large tract of land should be secured as near the city limits as possible, and the Applied Science Faculty moved there immediately.' 'Ultimately,' Wright told the commission, 'the whole University will be forced to move, on account of the growth of the city.' Ebeneezer Howard's book on planning, *Garden Cities of Tomorrow*, had just been published, and Wright was probably caught up in the new schemes to keep homes and schools away from the pollution of factories.

The commission wanted to protect from development the Taddle Creek watercourse, which extended from Bloor Street down to the Biology Building. The creek itself, it will be recalled, had been brought underground in the 1880s. The University had considered locating the new household science building on a site just east of Wycliffe College on Hoskin Avenue. 'It seems scarcely fitting that any portion of this fine piece of land should be filled in and used for buildings,' the commission wrote, no doubt influenced by its chair, Joseph Flavelle, whose new residence looked over the ravine. It should be used, the commission recommended, for a botanical garden. Such a garden, in fact, was developed.

The commission said little about graduate work. There was no mention of a faculty or school of graduate studies. Nor did it say anything about the desirability of graduate fellowships to attract graduate students, which had been urged by some academics, including Professor James McCurdy of Oriental studies, who had pointed out that Chicago offered 70 such fellowships and Cornell 40, whereas Toronto had fewer than 10. The commissioners' view of research and graduate studies seemed to be that such endeavours exist more to assist industry than to develop basic knowledge. They recommended an addition to the university library, however, which had shelf space for only another three years, and a major addition was completed by 1910. No doubt at the urging of Walker, a museum was recommended. 'One of the necessary features of a great modern University,' the commission wrote, 'is a properly equipped Museum.' 'A site [should] be selected in the University grounds adjacent to a public thoroughfare and sufficient in area to permit of extending the buildings in the distant future.'

To pay for all this increased activity, the University would have to be properly funded by the province, as American public universities in such states as Wisconsin, Minnesota, and Michigan were by their governments. Funding, they concluded, should be linked to succession duties. 'This is a tax,' the commission argued, 'which grows in some relation to the growth of the Province and therefore to the growth of the University requirements.' During the previous six years, the tax on average had brought in the substantial sum of about $400,000 a year. But the commission had a problem. Goldwin Smith was violently against this form of taxation, and most likely others on the commission shared his opposition to it. In consequence of these strong feelings, before agreement could be reached in the commission, careful drafting of the report was required. The report acknowledged, 'This is a tax which has aroused much opposition and which may be subject to change in the future.' Moreover, it did not state that the University would receive a specified percentage of the tax, but rather 'a sum equal to a certain percentage of the revenues from succession duties,' without spelling out what that percentage would be.

The government accepted the proposal and set out in the legislation that an amount equal to one-half the succession duties (averaging the previous three years) be given to the University, and that if the amount was more than the University required for the year, it be added to the endowment. Unfortunately for the University, just before Whitney died in 1914, a cap of $500,000 a year was put on the amount the University could receive. Goldwin Smith never forgave the province for imposing succession duties. He told his fellow commissioner Bruce Macdonald that because of the duty he was planning to leave his money to Cornell University, not to the University of Toronto. Smith died in 1910; his wealthy wife had died the year before, leaving her money to him, and he left the bulk of his consequently large estate to Cornell University – about $700,000.

All the members of the commission received honorary degrees from the University for their work. The 1906 Act was certainly 'among the most important pieces of provincial legislation in the history of higher education in Ontario.' Whitney's biographer is correct in stating that Whitney 'may well have been the greatest friend the institution has ever had.'

⤫

Both the commission and the government agreed that Loudon was not the person to lead the University into the new era. The commission, Loudon complained in his memoirs, had only one session with him. Even before the report was released, Flavelle had written to Whitney, saying that Loudon should be replaced. 'The capacity to incorporate a new spirit into the University body, the wisdom with which it is done,' Flavelle wrote, 'are wanting in president Loudon.' Whitney met with Loudon and promised him a pension equivalent to his full salary if he resigned at the end of June, after the new board was in place. Loudon, then 65, agreed. He had been worried about whether he would get a decent pension and moreover was having heart problems. It was understood that if he resigned, the commission would not rake up past problems and he could retire with some dignity.

The new board took office on June 15, 1906. All the members of the commission were appointed to the board, with the exception of Cody, who had an academic appointment at Wycliffe and was therefore ineligible, and Colquhoun, who by then had become deputy minister of education. Goldwin Smith was reluctant to accept the appointment, but finally was persuaded that his presence would play an important role in giving credibility to the new structure. The board also included Whitney's brother, E.C. Whitney, Samuel Blake, Chester Massey, and the editor of the *Globe*, J.A. Macdonald. It was a strong board. The chair of the previous board of trustees, John Hoskin – one of the founders of the law firm of Osler, Hoskin and Harcourt, and after whom Hoskin Avenue is named – was appointed chair of the new board.

A unanimous board asked Loudon to remain in office until a new president was appointed. He agreed, but set forth a number of conditions. He wanted a higher salary and wanted the registrar of the University, James Brebner, with

Maurice Hutton, the principal of
University College, and in 1906–7 the
acting president of the University.
Photograph from the 1903 *Torontonensis*.

whom he had had several conflicts, either fired or given a leave of absence. The
board was not prepared to change Brebner's status – he remained registrar until
1929 – and accepted Loudon's resignation. The principal of University College,
Maurice Hutton, who said he would not be a candidate for president, was
appointed acting president. In the summer of 1906, the 65-year-old Loudon left
with his family for a holiday in Prince Edward Island, where, he wrote to George
Wrong, 'he was learning the rudiments of golf.' He continued to live in his house
on St George Street, on the site of the future Whitney Hall residence. He died in
1916, having just completed a rough draft of his disjointed, self-serving memoirs, which continually blamed others for the problems he had faced.

Edmund Walker was chosen by the board to chair the search committee for a
new president.

chapter nineteen

1907

~~~

ROBERT FALCONER CHOSEN

On April 25, 1907, Robert Falconer was asked by the new board of governors to be the fourth president of the University of Toronto. He was not their first choice, but he was an excellent one as things turned out. He remained in office until his retirement in 1932.

The search had begun at least a year earlier. Many wanted the 58-year-old Canadian doctor William Osler, then a professor at Oxford, to become president. During the summer, Premier Whitney had asked Osler if he would be interested. He could not officially offer him the position because the 1906 Act had given the power of appointing the president to the board, which in June had set up a search committee with Edmund Walker as its chair. The committee included Joseph Flavelle and Goldwin Smith, who had served with Walker on the royal commission. Many in the University, such as physiologist A.B. Macallum, urged Osler to take the job, but Osler declined, saying, 'I have no executive gifts, and I am 15 years too old.'

Flavelle had had doubts about selecting a person like Osler. He wanted 'a man young enough to earn distinction by his efforts yet to be put forth.' Someone like Osler, he told Goldwin Smith, would have 'passed the period when struggle gives pleasure and the appetite for accomplishment ... must of necessity have lost its keenness.' In any event, he preferred a humanist. 'The struggle for the culture subjects (in the commercial and practical community) to hold their own in the University,' he wrote, 'seems to call for a president whose interests have been on the culture rather than the scientific side.' The committee sympathized with this approach. The names of the scientists, such as Ramsay Wright, Macallum, and Ernest Rutherford of McGill, were set aside, even though Wright appeared to have the support of the faculty. 'He is considered not just the best of the local men,' the acting president Maurice Hutton reported, but in the faculty's opinion it 'would be safer to appoint him than go afield.' The committee, however, preferred an outside appointment. It would be 'more difficult for a member of the Faculty,' Walker wrote, 'than for a new man to carry out the view of the new Board of Governors.' For this reason, Hutton himself, who had been doing an excellent job, was rejected. In any event, Goldwin Smith observed, 'he looks old and could scarcely be a new start.'

Being Canadian would clearly be an asset. The Canadian president of Cornell, Jacob Schurman, was highly regarded in educational circles throughout North America. It will be recalled that Daniel Wilson had tried to recruit him for the chair of English in the 1880s, but the board of management had been willing to pay only for a lecturer. Schurman had spent two days with the royal commission in the fall of 1905, giving the members advice and also an opportunity to look him over. He was not willing, however, to let his name be considered. 'I could not under any circumstances consider it,' he wrote in 1906. 'I am bound to Cornell by ties of affection and of interest in my work and I will never leave it to take a place in another university.' Other Canadians teaching in the United States were suggested by various American university presidents canvassed by Walker.

Members of the royal commission were also suggested. William Houston recommended Chancellor William Meredith. George Wrong wanted Edmund Walker. The future premier of Ontario, Howard Ferguson, supported his former roommate at University College, Canon Cody. (Cody had been living with Stephen Leacock, but when Cody's parents met Leacock, they told their son to get a new roommate – which he did.) The Reverend Bruce Macdonald, who was also on the list, states in his unpublished memoirs that St Michael's College was concerned about Cody because 'he was in the habit of occasionally fulminating from his pulpit against the Roman Catholic Church.'

The committee had no end of names – there were at least ninety on their list. Even the governor general had put forward a name (the Canadian secretary of the Rhodes Trust), and Mackenzie King suggested a non-Canadian teaching at the University of Michigan. The board, however, still wanted Osler. His brother,

President Falconer in 1910.

the board member E.B. Osler, informed his colleagues that Dr Osler would return to Canada in late December 1906 for their mother's hundredth birthday, and that he would arrange to have Osler meet with the board. A lunch was held at Walker's residence. Bruce Macdonald remembers that Samuel Blake had been 'imbibing too freely of the wines that were served' and 'took it upon himself to invite Sir William Osler to accept the presidency.' The embarrassment was passed over, and Osler said he would think about it. On the last day of the year, Osler informed John Hoskin, the chair of the board, that he could not accept the position, stating that 'neither by training nor disposition am I adapted to it.'

The members of the committee were discouraged. Goldwin Smith warned Walker, 'Unless we proceed soon to the election of a President of the University we shall be in danger of losing our power of choice,' meaning that the government would appoint the president, as it had in the past. A full board of governors met on February 7, 1907. Walker had prepared a report on the candidates. For the first time, a new name was on the list, that of the Reverend Robert Alexander Falconer, the principal of Pine Hill Presbyterian College in Halifax. A board member and editor of the *Globe*, the Reverend J.A. Macdonald, had written to Walker in late January, describing Falconer, whom he had met on earlier occasions and had just seen in Halifax, in glowing terms.

Falconer, then just under 40, was not unknown in Toronto. He had written an article on church union for Flavelle's paper, the *News*, and on the basis of his impressive scholarship had been offered the chair of New Testament literature by Knox College, with the promise of succession to the principalship. Falconer had grown up in Trinidad, where his father was a minister, and had won one of the prestigious Gilchrist scholarships to study at Edinburgh University, where after four years he received his degree in arts, with a specialization in classics. He then entered Edinburgh's divinity school, where he received his divinity degree in 1892. He spent several summers studying in Germany. He was appointed to teach New Testament literature at Pine Hill in 1892, published a number of books and articles, and contributed to some of the great biblical dictionaries then being prepared. In 1902, Edinburgh awarded him an LLD, based on his scholarship, and in 1904 he was unanimously endorsed as principal of Pine Hill.

The list Walker submitted to the board contained only four names: Falconer, Cody, Dr A. Ross Hill, a Canadian who was the dean of the teachers' college of the University of Missouri, and Michael Sadler, a British educational reformer at Manchester, who later became vice-chancellor of Leeds University. Sadler's name was at the top of the list. The board asked Dr Osler to interview him in England. Osler was impressed and thought there was a good chance Sadler would accept. In the meantime, the press published the news that Sadler was the board's choice, which helped stimulate opposition to the appointment of a non-Canadian. 'Nativism,' Goldwin Smith observed, 'has not shown up very well in the person of Dr Loudon.' Sadler, however, turned down the offer.

Falconer had been placed second on the board's list, and he became more desirable the longer the process took and the more they heard about him. The premier of Nova Scotia described him as 'a man of striking personality and one who is continually growing in intellectual development.' Walker was probably equally if not more impressed by a letter he had asked for from the Bank of Commerce's representative in the Maritimes, who said that Falconer was 'easily the educational leader in the Maritime Provinces' and referred specifically to 'his moral force and large sympathy.' Like the premier, he made the point that Falconer 'will go on growing.'

Falconer was leaving for Europe on Tuesday, April 9. However, it would be just possible for him to go to Toronto, meet with the board on Monday, and still catch the ship leaving from Boston on Tuesday. Falconer met the members of the board at a luncheon at Walker's home and at other times during the day. He told Walker that he would accept only if he had the unanimous approval of the board. The board subsequently met informally to discuss the presidency. No doubt the discussion centred on the question of the wisdom of appointing a clergyman. E.C. Whitney wrote to his brother, 'I think he is a pretty good man,' though his being a minister was 'a distinct handicap.' Flavelle said that he was at first strongly against appointing a clergyman, but then concluded that because of Falconer's liberal views he would prove acceptable to the denominational colleges. St Michael's would have taken note of the fact that Falconer had received an honorary degree from St Francis Xavier, a Catholic college. On Thursday, April 25, the board agreed to offer the position to Falconer. Walker sent a two-word telegram to Naples, Italy: 'Unanimous. Reply.' Falconer arrived in Naples the following day and immediately accepted, subject to the agreement of the Pine Hill board. He cut his trip short and returned to Canada.

Not everyone was thrilled with the appointment. George Wrong told Walker that he had 'heard him preach once and he struck me as colourless and commonplace' (he later changed his view), and the secretary of the Rhodes Trust, George Parkin, who had been a candidate, thought it was 'a rather serious leap in the dark.' But William Osler probably expressed the general view when he stated that Falconer could become 'a great president.' Falconer arrived in Toronto in June 1907 and started learning the intricacies of a major university. His inaugural address would be in September.

❧

Hutton had been an effective acting president, who fulfilled his duties, in the words of Stewart Wallace, with 'dignity and acceptability.' It was during his tenure that the faculty of household science and the faculty of education were created, and the School of Practical Science began functioning as the faculty of applied science and engineering within the University. The royal commission had recommended the establishment of all three of these faculties.

The royal commission had also recommended a school of forestry. Loudon had argued for its establishment for several years, particularly when it appeared that Queen's was trying to establish such a school in Kingston. In 1903, Toronto had approved a three-year degree, but there was no money to hire a professor. In the spring of 1907, however, while Hutton was acting president, the University created the faculty of forestry, with a staff of three. Bernhard Fernow, who was born and trained in Germany before coming to the United States, was appointed dean. He had been chief of the forestry division of the United States Department of Agriculture and in 1897 became dean of the faculty of forestry at Cornell, the first such school in North America. He was known as 'the creator of modern forestry in the United States.' The number of students slowly increased. By 1914 there were 51 students enrolled in a four-year program. In 1925, the faculty took possession of the red-brick Georgian building – like many other campus build-ings, designed by Darling and Pearson – on the east side of St George Street. It had been built on the site of the present Galbraith Building, but in 1958 was moved, on steel rollers, 200 feet north to accommodate the new engineering building.

Hutton also assisted in bringing St Michael's College directly into the University. It is a somewhat complicated story. The royal commission of 1906 had dealt with St Michael's simply as a theological college, which for the most part it was. Between 1881, when it became affiliated with the University, and 1910, when it was formally admitted as a federated college, only some ten St Michael's students in total received degrees from the University of Toronto. Certain members of the royal commission, such as Goldwin Smith and William Meredith, were noted for their anti-Catholic views and may have wanted to keep St Michael's as primarily a theological college. Some members of the St Michael's community also probably wanted to keep it that way, thinking that their first objective was to produce priests. But the youngest member of the St Michael's staff, Father Henry Carr, wanted to bring St Michael's more directly into the University. He almost single-handedly changed the St Michael's high school curriculum to make students eligible for admission to the University. Before that, the high school had been modelled on European classical lines, which may not have been a problem for its many American students, who returned to the United States for further study, but which barred Canadian students, who did not have the necessary junior matriculation qualifications, from entering the University of Toronto.

Some time after the royal commission report and before the passage of the 1906 Act, a crucial addition was made to the bill. A section was tacked on that allowed the board of governors to establish future arts colleges, provided that any new college was established and maintained 'to the satisfaction of the Board.' The section does not specifically mention St Michael's, but it was clearly directed at the college. 'How this amendment came about,' writes the college historian Father Lawrence Shook, 'is not quite clear.' It appears likely that Father Carr helped engineer it, with the support of Premier Whitney, who had open-minded views on Catholicism.

Father Henry Carr, the superior of
St Michael's College, 1915–25, and the
founding president of the Institute of
Mediaeval Studies, 1929–36.
Photograph taken about 1905.

It is also likely that Hutton had played an important role as acting president and, more important, as principal of University College. Father Carr was a recent graduate of University College – he received his degree in 1903 – and was one of Hutton's favourite honour classics students. Hutton allowed St Michael's students to register in University College in the fall of 1906, while taking their college subjects at St Michael's. The first class graduating from St Michael's was therefore in 1910 – with University College degrees. Later that year, St Michael's College was approved by the board as an arts college. The first class graduating from St Michael's without the assistance of University College was in 1911. That year, the university arts calendar for the first time contained the name of St Michael's on its cover along with those of the three other arts colleges. In 1912, the two women's Catholic colleges, St Joseph's and Loretto, affiliated with St Michael's College, and their students were able to take University of Toronto degrees through St Michael's. It was not a co-educational program, however. The women's colleges taught the college subjects. The sisters first gave their lectures in St Michael's in 1952, and St Michael's was finally co-educational only when Carr Hall opened in 1954. St Joseph's did not move to the campus until 1926, when it obtained the Christie (of biscuit fame) grand residence at the north-east corner of Queen's Park and Wellesley Street. Loretto College would not move to its present location as a residence on the north side of St Mary Street until 1959.

Falconer's installation procession on September 26, 1907. Prime Minister Sir Wilfrid Laurier is in the light and dark academic gown and is preceded by John Hoskin, the chairman of the board, and Premier James Whitney, facing the camera; Robert Falconer is at the front right of the procession.

Father Carr, who became president of St Michael's in 1915, had ambitious plans for the college. In a letter to President Falconer the following year, he stated that in 'a comparatively short time' St Michael's College could be made 'the greatest Catholic education centre in the world.'

※

Falconer's inauguration took place in Convocation Hall on a clear fall day in late September 1907. Prime Minister Wilfrid Laurier and Premier Whitney were there, as were representatives of universities from across North America – all in their resplendent robes. Fourteen honorary LLDs were awarded, four of them in absentia. The 80-year-old Canadian engineer Sir Sandford Fleming received particularly warm applause when he received his. No woman, however, received a degree. It would not be until 1919 that a woman, Edith Rayside, would be so recognized. She was given an honorary master of household science degree (and not a doctorate), in recognition of her nursing work during the war. Also missing was the fine Quebec-built Casavant organ, which would not be installed until 1911. It is still used, having been totally reconditioned in 1979–80.

President Falconer gave an impressive and important address. 'The University of Toronto,' he stated at the outset, 'is a great university.' The ideas expressed in his speech were those he strove to implement over the next twenty-five years. He stressed the central position of arts in a university. This was a shift from the royal commission's view that culture and science had an equal place 'under the same academical roof.' 'A university,' he reminded those advocating practical education, 'is not a technical school.' Another departure from the report of the royal commission was his emphasis on research and graduate work. 'There must be,' he said, 'an increase in post-graduate courses and research.' The University of Toronto, he went on, 'should occupy more and more a national position ... by attracting graduates from every part of Canada ... The true university is a centre for both instruction and research for the impartation of knowledge already gained, and for the extension of the boundaries of knowledge.'

It was a fine speech that would appeal to the academic staff, particularly when Falconer said that professors' salaries should be raised and that academic freedom should be protected. His expressed view that the University 'does not belong to any privileged class' would appeal to the ordinary citizen. The press gave its approval. Falconer was unhappy with one aspect of the arrangements for the inauguration, which probably escaped the attention of almost all those in attendance. The first six rows of Convocation Hall had been reserved for dignitaries. The next morning Falconer wrote to Hoskin, the chairman of the board, complaining that this was inconsistent with 'bringing the University close to the people.' 'If there is any institution in Toronto that should not attempt to make class distinction,' he stated, 'it is the University.' No doubt the letter took Hoskin and his fellow governors by surprise.

There was considerable debate in academic circles throughout the world at that time as to the proper function of a university. Was it to be culture, scholarship, or service, or some combination of the three? As his biographer, James Greenlee, shows, Falconer embraced all three concepts. Falconer, Greenlee writes, was, 'perhaps, the most outspoken and influential Canadian champion of the many-faceted but organically integrated university.' In his inauguration address, Falconer stressed not only culture and scholarship but also service. 'I believe,' he said, 'that the nation should look to the universities for distinct help in the present social conditions.' 'It must cause concern to thinking people,' he

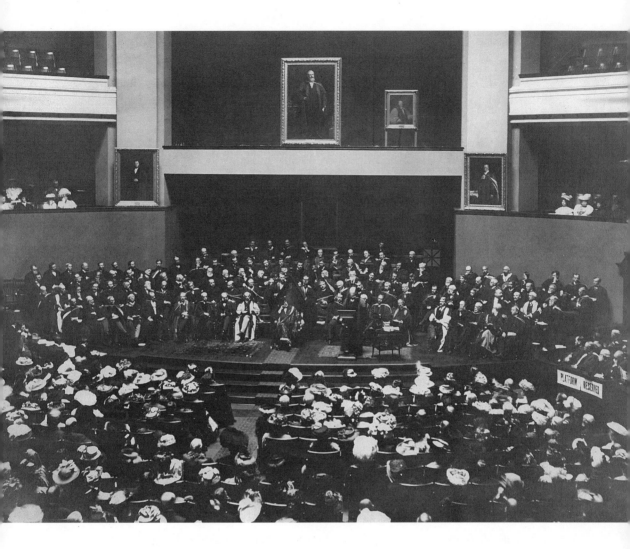

Falconer's installation address in Convocation Hall. Chancellor William Meredith is seated
in the centre, with Prime Minister Laurier to the left and Premier Whitney to the right;
Robert Borden, the future prime minister, is in the front row, five persons from the right.

went on, 'that there is such an indifference on the part of the well-to-do to take up the burdens of civic and political life; that we all suffer so much from the antagonism between employer and employed, and that the contrasts of wealth and poverty in our rapidly growing cities are so manifest.'

Concern about 'service' manifested itself in various ways during the coming years. In the summer of 1910, for example, the University opened a settlement house on Adelaide Street West, with Falconer as president. Interest had been growing in the settlement house movement that had originated in the 1880s at Toynbee Hall, an Oxford-linked house in the east end of London, and that later took root in Chicago at Hull House, which was connected with the University of Chicago. In 1906, James Mavor, the professor of political economy, had surveyed slum conditions among working people in Toronto, and various groups, particularly women's organizations, had taken steps to help improve conditions in the poorer areas of the city. Women were not at first included in the University Settlement House, and thus was overlooked, in historian Sara Burke's words, 'the long-standing commitment of university women to neighbourhood work.' The following year, however, they were permitted to participate.

The money to found the University Settlement House was provided by the YMCA, which had been raising funds for a new building on the campus. Its funds were no longer needed for that purpose, however, because the Massey family had announced in March 1910 that the family would build a student centre, Hart House, which would also address the YMCA's needs. The activities at the Settlement House at first were mainly athletic and were conducted by university athletes. According to its first pamphlet, the Settlement House would 'bring the university students into direct contact with those living amidst the unfortunate social conditions of our modern cities and thus broaden the one and elevate the other.' The activities of the Settlement House have changed over the years and now include educational courses, a music school, and a day-care centre. Its location has also changed: since 1926, it has been in Grange Park, facing what was Goldwin Smith's residence. The University of Toronto no longer has an official relationship with the University Settlement House, though many of the directors (including this writer) have helped to maintain the University of Toronto connection.

In a Sunday sermon in Convocation Hall shortly after the Settlement House opened, Falconer urged his listeners to 'find the highest good by serving your fellows through your intellect, your wealth, your position, or whatever talent

The first board of directors of the University Settlement House, about 1910, with the founder and chairman of the board, Robert Falconer, front row far right.

you may possess.' Falconer often 'preached' in Convocation Hall, though he was less willing to preach in churches. He later recalled that when he came to Toronto, it 'was more than hinted to me that I should be wise in keeping out of pulpits.' Another illustration of Falconer's concern for service was his interest in outreach programs, such as had been developed at the University of Wisconsin. In 1910, he visited a number of midwestern universities to study their extension and correspondence schemes. After the war, he would put these ideas into practice.

Falconer's outreach ideas were also manifested in his desire to offer places in the University to students from China. In 1909, he persuaded the board to admit ten Chinese students to free places every two years. Toronto graduates serving as missionaries with the YMCA in China had urged Falconer to take this step. There had been a long history of University of Toronto involvement with China. President Daniel Wilson had chaired the farewell meeting in 1888 when the first large missionary group left for China. Missionaries were being sent from almost all the denominational colleges connected with the University. Most of the Canadian medical missionaries in China, including a large contingent of women, had graduated from the University of Toronto or one if its affiliated medical colleges. In addition to having a humanitarian interest, Falconer wanted the returning Chinese students to look upon the British Empire rather than the United States as the model for their reforms and the object of their loyalty. American universities were opening their doors to Chinese students, but Canada feared 'cheap immigrant labour.' There had been riots in Vancouver over immigration from China in 1907 – and the government had imposed the notorious head tax of $500 on all Chinese immigrants. This regulation applied also to Chinese students who would be returning to China. Falconer tried to persuade Mackenzie King, the minister of labour, to exempt such students, but the head tax continued to apply to them until 1917.

It was Falconer's love of the British Empire that, in part, motivated many of his actions, such as his desire to instil British ideas in the Chinese students in Canada. This concern was taken a step further in 1910 with a plan to establish an Oxbridge-style university in China. Falconer was chairman of the Canadian committee, but the plan was abandoned in 1912 because the funds raised were inadequate. The empire also influenced his campaign to have British universities provide a PhD degree so that Canadian students would not be forced to attend universities in Germany and the United States. A two-year doctorate was not introduced in Britain, however, until after the First World War.

Falconer's inauguration address had nailed his program to the University's coat of arms. He would spend the next twenty-five years trying to implement it.

chapter twenty

1908

FALCONER'S EARLY YEARS

Falconer's inauguration was a great success. 'Yesterday's most important event in Canadian life,' a *Globe* editorial said the next day, opened 'a new era in the history of a great University.' That era commenced the day after the installation with the formal opening of the new physics building. The former president, James Loudon, observing that the University's 'Golden Age' had just begun, described the growth of physics in the University, and John McLennan, the head of the department, gave a lantern-slide presentation on how the building would be used. The new facility, said the head of physics at McGill, was 'excelled by none on this continent.' There was one important shortcoming, however. The recently created sub-department of astrophysics, headed by C.A. Chant, did not have an adequate observatory.

The old government-run magnetic observatory, located between the new physics building and the School of Practical Science on what is now the entrance road from College Street, was inadequate from many points of view. The smoke in the city made observation of the heavens difficult. Moreover, the building could no longer be used as a magnetic observatory because the electrification of streetcars on College Street in the 1890s had made accurate magnetic reading difficult. The observatory could still be used for weather analysis, but the University wanted the land on which it stood for a proper entranceway to the University – now King's College Road. In exchange for the land, the University

The old observatory, now the offices of the Students' Administrative Council; it was moved from its site south-east of Convocation Hall to its present location and given a somewhat different configuration. University College is in the background, and the now dismantled 'temporary' building that had been constructed for the bookstore after the Second World War can be seen on the left.

gave the federal government a site at the corner of Bloor Street and Devonshire Place for a new and larger meteorological building, which today serves as the office of admissions for the University. The old observatory was relocated east of University College, where it was initially used by engineering students for earth measurements. It is used today as offices for the Students' Administrative Council.

Loudon had tried to get a site for an observatory for the University in the years before he retired. He had in mind a site on a hill on the north side of Kingston Road in the east end of the city, but nothing came of the idea. Chant, however, kept up the campaign. In the meantime, he used the roof of the physics building, with his various small telescopes. He was also allowed limited access to the government telescope that had been moved to the meteorological building on Bloor Street. Chant, who has been described as 'undoubtedly the single most important figure' in the history of astronomy at Toronto, graduated in maths and physics in 1890 and then joined the staff of the physics department; later, he obtained a PhD from Harvard. In 1918, he would head the separate department of astronomy, and he would remain its head until 1935. He was the first editor of the *Journal of the Royal Astronomical Society of Canada*, begun in 1907, and he continued as its editor for the next fifty years. He had an enormous influence on astronomy in Canada. 'Until quite recently,' states a book on astronomy published in 1988, 'the story of the training of professional astronomers in Canada is simply the history of the Department of Astronomy, University of Toronto.'

Chant, with the support of Falconer and the board, had his eye on a site in Forest Hill Village on the east side of Bathurst Street, just north of the bridge. The city had purchased the land in 1911 for an isolation hospital, but the nearby landowners in Forest Hill Village, and even those in Wychwood farther south, had objected. The land was therefore available for other uses. At the end of the war, an agreement was finally reached with the city, but Chant could not interest any wealthy person in financing the construction of an observatory. In the spring of 1921, he gave a lecture on a faint comet (Winnecke's comet), which a British astronomer had calculated had some chance of hitting the earth. A large crowd came to hear him in the physics building. Fortunately, the comet missed the earth by 10 million miles. Also fortunately, one of the persons in the audience who spoke to Chant after the lecture was a wealthy amateur astronomer, David Dunlap. Dunlap's wife would later honour the memory of her husband by donating the funds for the University's David Dunlap Observatory in Richmond Hill. When it opened in 1935, its 74-inch telescope was the second largest in the world.

❧

Falconer faced a number of difficult challenges in his early years. About a month after his installation, a delegation of ministers from various denominations came to him to complain that University College should not be teaching theology in its Oriental studies department. This, they said, was contrary to the act of federation. Of greater concern to them was their belief that the so-called higher criticism, involving a non-literal interpretation of the Bible, was being used in

Thomas Eakin, professor of Oriental studies at University College, who became involved in a controversy in 1907 over the teaching of the Bible in his classes.

the teaching. Their principal target was Thomas Eakin, a Presbyterian minister who had received his doctorate under Professor J.F. McCurdy and lectured on the English Bible at University College. Falconer was unsympathetic to their point of view and refused their request that he bring the matter before the board of governors, saying he was 'satisfied with things as they were being taught.' Falconer himself was an exponent of the higher criticism and had faced just such a barrage when appointed to Pine Hill. But the Eakin matter continued to be the subject of controversy for the next two years.

A member of the board, Samuel Blake, took up the cause of the delegation. In late 1908, he wrote several letters to the chairman of the board of governors, John Hoskin, raising the same issues as the earlier delegation. Hoskin, like Falconer, took the position that the Bible could not be ignored in teaching at a university. 'A properly equipped University,' he wrote, 'should take some cognizance of literature which is ranked with the most important any nation has given to man.' Blake replied that taking 'cognizance' of the Bible should not be used 'as an opportunity to assail the authenticity of the Bible ... and to introduce the idea among students that large portions of the Bible, accepted by many as God's Word, are mere myths and allegories.' 'Even the question of the "Virgin birth" of our Lord,' Blake stated, 'has been discussed in the classes of this department.' Blake said he knew of 'nothing that is to-day of such moment to our dominion as the defence of the Bible.' He predicted dire consequences if nothing was done. 'The infidel attacks in our colleges made upon the Word of God,' he wrote, 'may shake the foundation of law and order and bring upon us a reign of lawlessness and anarchy.' The issue had the potential to create a Canadian version of the well-known Scopes 'monkey' trial of 1925 in the United States.

The University successfully defused the crisis. The board set up a committee, under the chairmanship of the Reverend Bruce Macdonald, to investigate the allegations. A number of those who had served with him on the 1906 royal commission were also members, including Meredith, Flavelle, and Walker. Falconer and Father John Teefy, of St Michael's College, were also appointed. The committee took evidence in the library of Osgoode Hall in February and March 1909. Meredith suggested during the hearing that 'if certain things give offence,' a provincial university should 'avoid touching them.' Walker disagreed, stating that 'we are entitled to use all proper criticism for the purpose of getting at the truth,' and Falconer commented that if the University tried not to offend people, 'you would have to go through the whole University and cut out probably fifty per cent of the work.' The committee reported in late 1909 that University College was indeed entitled to study the Bible in its various courses, such as ethics and ancient history as well as Oriental studies. 'To exclude all discussion of the Bible and the literary, historical, linguistic, and ethical sides thereof,' the committee stated in its report, 'would be to exclude from the Arts Course of the College an important literary work, an important historical work, an important help to the study of languages, and the greatest code of Ethics known to the world.'

This was the first attack on academic freedom that Falconer had to face. Over the years, there would be many more. The report, in historian Michiel Horn's words, was 'a victory of sorts for academic freedom.' It was not a complete victory because there were still restrictions on what professors could say. 'Discussions of the books and narratives of the Bible,' the committee stated, 'may take place without entering upon the domain of Theology contrary to the statute.' The controversy showed, however, that the new governing structure did not fall apart during its first crisis. As Falconer's biographer, James Greenlee, has argued, the true significance of the episode was that the board supported the president and the government stayed out of the controversy. It was, Falconer wrote to his best friend, Walter Murray, the president of the University of Saskatchewan, a 'hurricane' that 'knocked our hats off.'

While the hearings were taking place, a similar controversy was erupting at Victoria College. The Reverend George Jackson, who taught the English Bible at Victoria, had given a public lecture questioning the authenticity of the early chapters of Genesis, claiming that they 'contain not history but tradition.' This approach was too much for Dr Albert Carman, the general superintendent of the Methodist Church and the chairman of the board of Victoria. Many wanted Jackson fired, but Nathanael Burwash and the board held firm. Burwash took a relatively liberal view of religion. It was, after all, Burwash who had chosen the words inscribed above the door of Victoria: The Truth Shall Make You Free.

Another controversy Falconer had to deal with during his first few years in office was that over a college for women. In November 1907, George Wrong, the head of history, introduced a motion in the senate 'that a committee be appointed to enquire into and report upon the feasibility of establishing a separate college for women in the University.' The senate agreed, and Wrong was made chairman of the committee. It will be recalled that Wrong's predecessor as professor of history, Daniel Wilson, had unsuccessfully argued for such a college in the early 1880s. Wrong's arguments, however, were somewhat different from Wilson's. He expressed no concern about the danger of close contact between the sexes, as Wilson had. Instead, one of his arguments was that the colleges were becoming increasingly overcrowded – there were more than 1,000 students at University College alone – and that having a separate college for women would obviously reduce the numbers. At that time, the three arts colleges had almost 5,000 women students.

Wrong also thought that having their own college would be beneficial for women students. There were women's colleges in Oxford and Cambridge and at Harvard and McGill. Co-education, he believed, had the effect of creating a state of affairs in which certain courses, such as modern languages, were dominated by women and other courses, such as political science, were dominated by men. 'Neither sex,' he wrote, 'likes the predominance of the other in its chosen sphere of labor.' This, he believed, would not tend to happen in a women's college. Wrong also wanted to prepare women for their role as homemakers. He observed in private documents that in the 'vast majority' of cases, a woman's 'lot in life is to be that of a wife and mother,' and that 'the chief problem of women's education is to fit her for this sphere.' He wanted to introduce new courses in arts related specifically to 'good housekeeping.' In an article in the U of T *Monthly*, he referred to 'women's special needs.' The faculty of household science had been established in 1906, but it was not attracting very many degree students – generally fewer than ten annually in its first few years of operation.

Another institution for women, the Margaret Eaton School of Literature and Expression, had been established in 1901, with the help of Burwash, Wrong, and other faculty members, though it had no official affiliation with the University. Falconer gave a lecture on Greek sculpture at the school the year after he arrived. The moving force behind the school was Emma Scott Raff, who gave voice training to theological students at Victoria College and physical education classes at its Annesley Hall residence. The University's support of the school, observes the English literature scholar Heather Murray, may have been given because the school was thought to be a prototype for a women's college. Founded on principles integrating voice and movement established by the Frenchman François Delsarte, the Margaret Eaton School combined work in the gymnasium, knowledge of literature, and vocal expression. Its calendar stated that it was to provide 'professional and practical education for women.'

Margaret Eaton, the wife of the department store owner Timothy Eaton, had dreamed of becoming an actress and had taken classes at an earlier version of the school. She later persuaded her husband to donate money to construct a building for the school. A Greek revival building, known in Toronto as 'the Greek Temple,' was built on the west side of what is now Bay Street, just south of Bloor Street. It opened in 1907 and was torn down in 1924 when the street was widened. The school survived as a school of physical exercise on Yonge Street and in 1941 was merged with the University of Toronto's School of Physical and Health Education (PHE), established the previous year.

The senate committee's one-page report on a separate college for women was finalized in the spring of 1909. It recommended the establishment of a separate college. In April, such a college was approved by the senate by a large majority – 28 votes to 8. Women's groups reacted strongly against the proposal. The University Women's Club, having earlier expressed cautious approval, was now strongly opposed to the idea. The women undergraduates of University College also rejected the report. So did the United Alumnae of University College, Victoria,

Mabel Cartwright, the principal of
St Hilda's College and dean of women
from 1903 to 1936.

Trinity, and Medicine, which had been formed in response to the Wrong report. 'As far as we have been able to discover,' they wrote to the senate, 'all the women ... are opposed to the establishment of a College for Women.'

'We are not,' the alumnae said, 'dissatisfied with the measure of co-education which exists' at the University. A separate women's college, they argued, would lead to inferior teaching. The better teachers would teach in the men's colleges, as was happening at certain American universities. Women clustered in modern languages, they pointed out, because there were high school jobs in that field. Mabel Cartwright, the head of Trinity's St. Hilda's College, wrote in the U of T *Monthly* that there existed a 'prejudice ... that women may safely teach modern languages, but not classics or mathematics.' She also noted that the alumnae tended to mistrust 'special courses' for women. The United Alumnae met later in May with Falconer, Hutton, and Wrong. Wrong did not continue to push the issue, saying that 'if the women were not in favor of the College, that was the end of it.' The question of a separate college was now effectively dead. The senate, however, introduced household science as a course option in the arts program for the 1909–10 academic year.

The lobbying by the alumnae had played a central role in the rejection of Wrong's report. Having the president's secretary, Annie Patterson, as a member

Women and men were kept separate in the biology laboratory in 1924.

of the alumnae committee facilitated the committee's access to the president's office. She had been at the centre in the rejection of Wrong's report by the alumnae. A graduate in political science from University College in 1899, she had been Loudon's secretary and later would become President Cody's secretary, before retiring in 1940 after forty years' service to the University. She was noted for keeping people from having the easy access to the president that she herself obviously enjoyed. She probably influenced other university matters during her long career.

The alumnae now turned their attention to other issues that had come up while they were warding off the threat of a women's college. Why were there not more women faculty members, the alumnae asked? The only women of professorial rank in the faculty were in household science. Reports were prepared on these and other subjects. 'Is not co-education incomplete,' Mabel Cartwright wrote, 'unless women have some share in teaching as well as in learning?' 'The greatest drawback to the present system,' the *Saint Hilda's Chronicle* argued, 'is that the intellectual life of the women students is entirely controlled and directed by men.' Furthermore, should there not be a dean of women for the University as a whole? Why would the University establish a special school connected with the faculty of education that excluded women? Why were there no women on the senate?

The United Alumnae succeeded in effecting a change in only one of these areas, the election of women senators. Candidates were nominated by each of the alumnae associations. Three women senators were elected in 1911. Dr Augusta Stowe-Gullen, who had earlier hoped to be dean of a medical college for women at the University, was elected by the medical alumni. Another senator was Gertrude Lawler, who was head of the English department at Harbord Collegiate. She had graduated from University College in 1890 with a number of gold medals and was one of the first women to be awarded an MA. In 1927, she was awarded an honorary LLD by the University. The third to be elected was Charlotte Ross, also a UC graduate, who taught literature and rhetoric at the Margaret Eaton School for twenty years and then became head of English at Havergal College.

❦

Falconer faced yet other challenges in the early years. There was the problem of rapidly increasing enrolment: the student body had grown from well under 2,000 in 1901 to over 4,000 by 1910. Toronto was by far the largest university in Canada: McGill had 2,500 students, Queen's 1,500, and Dalhousie fewer than 500. Over the next four years, the province raised the requirement for junior matriculation (the equivalent of what would later be called grade 12) to an average mark of 60 per cent, whereupon enrolment levelled off. The question was raised by Falconer and others as to whether or not the first year of university should be transferred to the high schools, and senior matriculation (the equivalent of the later grade 13), which at the time allowed students to enter the second year of university, be required for entrance to the University of Toronto. An ordinary general degree would then take three years and an honours degree four. Such a change would also free up faculty members to devote more time to graduate work. Senior matriculation, however, would not become a requirement for all applicants to the University of Toronto until 1931.

Along with the problem of increased enrolment was growing financial concern at the University. The 1905 bonanza did not last. Inflation started to become a serious problem in 1909, and succession duties yielded less than anticipated. By 1910, the University was experiencing a $40,000 deficit. Moreover, in 1914, as noted earlier, the University's succession duty income was limited to $500,000. The University once more would have to go cap in hand to ask for yearly grants from the government.

One imaginative scheme to add funds to the University was Falconer's application to the federal government in 1913 for an endowment for a Canadian studies program to celebrate the centenary of Sir John A. Macdonald's birth. He asked Prime Minister Borden for $600,000 for new chairs in Canadian history, geography, and earth sciences and for a new department of sociology to study social problems such as immigration, town planning, and criminology. Unfortunately, the application was turned down, but, as Greenlee states, it was all part of 'Falconer's quest to build a national university.'

Staffing also had its problems. In spite of increases, salaries were still sufficiently low that it was difficult to recruit the most desirable candidates. 'Students of good academic attainments,' Falconer wrote in 1913, 'are unwilling to enter upon a career which begins at a low scale and advances very slowly.' Moreover, the retirement benefits were not generous, despite the Carnegie Corporation's having provided some form of supplementary retirement benefit for academics at non-sectarian institutions who had reached the age of 70. In order to come within the Carnegie scheme, Victoria College changed its governing structure to reduce the dominance of the Methodist Conference and to eliminate the requirement that half the board be ministers.

The 1906 Act gave Falconer the responsibility of recommending appointments for approval by the board. He took a direct interest in every appointment, and often travelled to other cities or abroad to interview candidates. He gave priority, writes Greenlee, 'to native sons who had completed their studies in Britain.' Both George Wrong of history and James Mavor of political economy also were particularly keen on persons who had studied in Britain. In 1911, for example, a junior appointment was needed in political economy. Mavor drew up a list of four possible candidates from Britain. A member of his department, Godfrey Lloyd, was in England for the summer and assisted in gathering information. The first three persons on the list were not interested in coming to Canada. Should they choose the fourth person, Gilbert Jackson, who had only a second-class standing at Cambridge, or a new prospect, L. Bernstein Naymier of

Oxford, later known as Louis Namier? The master of Balliol, A.L. Smith, described Namier as 'the ablest man we have had in economics and history for some years.' Others, however, were worried about Namier's spoken English. He had arrived in England from Poland some five years earlier. Lloyd reported that the two candidates were 'evenly balanced' but felt that Jackson was 'the safer choice.' Mavor agreed, and wrote to Falconer that Namier 'appears to be a brilliant Jew' who has 'the misfortune to have the Jewish characteristic of indistinct articulation strongly developed.' Falconer recommended Jackson, who accepted the position.

A position then opened in history. One of Wrong's colleagues, Kenneth Bell, who had also been in England for the summer, had decided to remain there for family reasons and wrote enthusiastically to Wrong about Namier. He 'is the man for the place,' Bell said. The other candidate, Hodder Williams, also from Oxford, Bell went on, 'will never set the Thames on fire, but Naymier will ... I don't want a colourless or second-rate successor.' Some of the correspondence is missing from the file, such as Walker's opinion, for which Falconer had asked, but a copy of Flavelle's assessment is contained in Flavelle's personal papers. Flavelle did not like the idea of appointing a 'second class honor man [Williams] for an important position.' 'Nor,' he went on, 'do I like the choice of a Polish Jew as an interpreter of history ... who by his broken accent constantly proclaims it.' Despite these views, he favoured giving Namier a one-year appointment, provided that there was no obligation to retain him beyond the year. In the copy of Flavelle's letter a section is crossed out and presumably was not included in what was sent to Falconer. It reads, 'Certainly the appointment would be a most interesting one and might give the University a man whose brilliance would bring to it much honor in later years.' The other candidate, Hodder Williams, was appointed and, as Bell had predicted, did not set the Thames on fire, but, as we know now, Namier did, in becoming one of England's finest historians. As far as can be determined, a Jew was not appointed to the position of lecturer or to any higher position at the University of Toronto until Jacob Finkelman was appointed a lecturer in the law faculty in 1930.

chapter twenty-one

1908

⁓

EDUCATION, MEDICINE, AND THE MUSEUM

The Canadian economy was flourishing. 'From the turn of the century until the outbreak of the First World War,' states a standard history of the period, 'Canada experienced the greatest economic boom in its history.' In the pre-war years, with the help of provincial capital grants, several important new structures were built on or close to the campus.

Engineering continued to expand as a result of the growing need for engineers. The country needs 'leaders,' Falconer wrote, 'in opening up new country by railways, in constructing large works, in developing mines.' Many of these leaders would come out of engineering. A new building, the thermodynamics and hydraulics building – now hidden between the medical school and the mining building – was opened in 1909 for mechanical engineering, to be used for steam, gas, and hydraulic work. It opened up space for the expansion of other activities, such as electrical engineering, in the main engineering building. Engineering was increased from a three- to a four-year program. The engineering faculty now had facilities that were more or less adequate. It was also developing some of its distinctive student traditions: the engineers' yell, the *Toike Oike* newspaper, and the miniature cannon that was – and still is – brought out from time to time.

⁓

The faculty of education, opened at the corner of Bloor Street and Spadina Avenue in 1910;
additions were later made to both ends of the building.

The faculty of education opened its three-storey red-brick building at the corner
of Bloor Street and Spadina Avenue in 1910. The faculty had been established in
late 1906 on the recommendation of the royal commission. The commission's
members had visited faculties of education at Columbia and Chicago, and it
concluded that the teaching of education 'is best performed where the theory
and practice can be made to supplement each other,' and that a university was
the place where that could be done best. A model school would also fit in with
the needs of the city of Toronto, which required a new high school in what was
then still the northern end of the city. Moreover, such a school would be able to
'conduct educational experiments.' As it happened, the superintendent of education, John Seath, held the same view and had urged his minister to transfer the
Ontario Normal School in Hamilton to the University of Toronto. It was
difficult to attract students to Hamilton, and consequently there was a shortage
of high school teachers in the province. The first education students were
admitted to the new faculty of education in October 1907. While the building
was being constructed, the West Hall of University College and other locations
were used for lectures, and various city schools were used for practice teaching.

Property was then acquired on Bloor Street between Spadina and Huron. Plans were drawn up for 200 teachers and a large model school of more than 1,000 students. The school would be for both primary and secondary students – both boys and girls – and would include a technical school. For that reason, it was given a pluralized name – University of Toronto Schools (UTS). As it turned out, however, the funding for the school was limited, and a decision was made to eliminate the technical school and to include only a secondary school and the higher grades of a primary school – and also to teach only boys. The United Alumnae were incensed. 'We feel very strongly,' they wrote Falconer, 'that the girls of Toronto should not be placed at a disadvantage by being excluded from what is to be the leading Secondary School.' Dr Helen MacMurchy, a noted woman doctor – the first woman to intern at the Toronto General Hospital – wrote to the president that it was shocking for the University to have a school where 'no girls need apply – no women are appointed as teachers – and no university student in the Faculty of Education can learn there how to teach girls, because there are no girls there to teach.' Falconer wrote that 'if the school is successful, we hope that we may be able to extend it before very long' to include women. Women were not admitted to UTS until 1973, however, almost seventy years later.

William Pakenham, who was strongly favoured by the government, was selected as the first dean of the faculty. He was a graduate of the University, having received a BA in the early 1890s. Although the University had not given instruction in education, it had allowed persons to take examinations for education degrees. Pakenham had taught in various schools in the province and at the time of his appointment was principal of the Toronto Technical High School. He would remain dean until 1934. The first principal of UTS, H.J. Crawford, who had been principal of Riverdale High School, would serve until 1922.

In 1917, the superintendent of education, John Seath, prepared a report on the faculties of education at both the University of Toronto and Queen's University. Queen's was not attracting enough students. Toronto also had problems. It did not have enough teachers for the number of education students, and it had inadequate facilities. There was, for example, no gymnasium connected with the model school. Moreover, there were disagreements over the length of the spring term for education students. The government wanted it extended into late June – the same as in the government's normal schools and the schools in which practice teaching was done. The University resisted, arguing that long summers were needed to allow the students to work on farms and in factories during the war, but finally agreed when the minister threatened to withdraw financial support.

In 1919, however, the government passed legislation allowing it to close both the Toronto and the Queen's faculties of education and to establish the government's own school. Falconer protested about 'this most retrograde step.' How could the government be more efficient than the University? Moreover, having staff and students interact with others in the University broadened their outlook. Furthermore, staff were hired on the basis that they would be part of the University, and if the faculty separated from the University they would not be eligible for the Carnegie pension scheme. A compromise was reached. The faculty would be renamed the Ontario College of Education (OCE) and be funded separately by the province, but it would continue to be administered as part of the University, and its degree would be subject to the authority of the senate. The Queen's school, however, would be shut down and its students transferred to Toronto.

OCE would train only secondary school teachers, though students could take an option allowing them to teach primary school. All students would require a university arts degree before being admitted. Pakenham remained the dean, and the faculty remained the same except that one member of the Queen's faculty was added to the Toronto staff. All appointments by the University and courses of study for OCE would require the approval of the government. This hybrid system, whereby OCE served two masters, lasted until 1966, when OCE once again became the college of education of the University. It became the faculty of education in 1972.

On June 19, 1913, another major building that would play an important role in the University, the Toronto General Hospital, officially was declared open. 'The thirty thousand visitors to Toronto General Hospital that day,' historian Michael Bliss has written, 'saw the most modern, best equipped hospital in Canada, one of the best in the world.' Planning for the building, on the south side of College Street between University Avenue and Elizabeth Street, had started almost ten years earlier when Joseph Flavelle was made chairman of the hospital's board of trustees. The hospital was then on Gerrard Street, near the Don River, and the University and Flavelle wanted it closer to the University. The possibility of a

Governor General Lord Minto and Lady Minto stayed in Flavelle's house shortly after
it was completed in 1903. They are seen here leaving for the races. The house is now
occupied by the faculty of law.

move had been brought to the fore because Cawthra Mulock, Sir William
Mulock's extremely wealthy son, had promised $100,000 for an out-patient
building for the hospital, and most thought that it would be wise to build it as
part of a new complex. In 1905, legislation was passed by the new Whitney
government to permit the University to contribute $300,000 for a hospital, and
for the city to donate $200,000 to purchase a site for it.

Unlike the education building, for which the plans kept contracting, those
for the hospital kept expanding – from 400 beds at a cost of $1,300,000 to 670
beds at a cost of $3,450,000. Flavelle was primarily responsible for raising the
funds. He was able to get the city to increase its grant substantially, and the
University to double its grant to $600,000. He gave $100,000 himself and put
pressure on other wealthy Torontonians, such as Chester Massey, E.B. Osler, and
George Cox, to contribute major sums. When Flavelle went to see John Eaton,
the son of Timothy Eaton, and showed him the plans for the surgical wards,
Eaton, according to Flavelle, said: 'Do you know what you are showing me? You
are showing me the wards of the surgical wing of the hospital which will be
erected in memory of my father.' His eventual donation was more than $350,000.

College Street buildings of the Toronto General Hospital, opened in June 1913.

Eight acres – roughly the present site of the hospital – of mainly slum housing in the area known as 'the ward' were purchased or expropriated, no doubt to the satisfaction of the owners of the grand houses on University Avenue. The original plan was to leave standing the dental building on College Street, but its space was needed, and dentistry was forced to move to a building on the corner of College and Huron streets. TGH would therefore extend from University Avenue to Elizabeth Street, with the Hospital for Sick Children, built on College Street in 1892, on the other side of Elizabeth Street. Once again, Darling and Pearson were chosen as the architects. They used – at extra cost – beige-coloured hardened brick in the construction of the four-storey main building and its three-storey wings, arguing that red brick would make the building look like a factory and white brick make it look cold and uninviting. Other buildings were constructed on University Avenue, just south of the main building, including the Cawthra Mulock out-patient building, and the Shields emergency building, named after two philanthropic sisters. A private patients' pavilion and an obstetrics building were also erected.

The University paid for a pathology building, south-west of the main hospital building, for the department headed by the distinguished pathologist J.J. Mackenzie. Mackenzie was a Ramsay Wright protégé. Having graduated in natural sciences in 1886, he engaged in post-graduate work in Leipzig and Berlin and then returned to Toronto to take his medical degree. In 1900, he was appointed to the chair of pathology. Another Wright protégé, A.B. Macallum, later noted that Mackenzie, 'because of his previous training in biology, physiology and bacteriology, qualified him, as few pathologists of the time have been, to understand and deal with the more intricate as well as profound factors in the problems of disease.' The medical school was able to attract other major researchers, including T.G. Brodie, a British physiologist, with whom Mackenzie published significant papers on the physiology and pathology of the kidney. Brodie, like Macallum, was a fellow of the prestigious Royal Society of London, as was another recruit, J.B. Leathes, appointed professor of chemical pathology in 1909. Leathes returned to England in 1914. Thus, before the war there were three fellows of the Royal Society of London in the medical school, whereas in other parts of the University only the mathematician Fields and the geologist Coleman were fellows. The physicist McLennan would join the group in 1915.

Ernest Jones, later to be Sigmund Freud's biographer, was also at the University and the Toronto General Hospital during this period. He had worked not only with Freud but also with Jung, Kraepelin, and Alzheimer and came as an assistant professor in 1909 highly recommended by William Osler. Jones' correspondence with his mentor, Freud, details the problems he faced in Toronto despite the support of C.K. Clarke, the professor of psychiatry and dean of medicine. Jones certainly did not think much of Toronto or Torontonians. 'Music is rare here,' he wrote Freud, 'and there is not a picture gallery in the country.' As for the people, they are, he wrote, 'naïve, childish and hold the simplest views of the problems of life. They care for nothing except money-making and sport, they chew gum ... They are horror struck with me because I don't know the date of the King's birthday, for they take their loyalty like everything else in dead seriousness.'

Jones lectured in psychiatry at the University and reported to Freud that 'two hundred innocent youths are being severely inoculated with psychoanalytic doctrines.' His psychoanalytic approach, however, was not making him very popular. There is, he wrote to Freud, 'a strong prejudice in Toronto against me on account of the stress I lay on sexual matters.' Complaints were made to President Falconer that Jones should be dismissed so that he could 'no longer pervert and deprave the youth of Toronto.' He was accused of recommending masturbation and sending young men to prostitutes. His home had to be guarded by detectives. Furthermore, his wife was unhappy and threatened suicide if they did not return to England. He announced that he was leaving, but Chancellor William Meredith, whose daughter he had treated successfully, and Clarke, who had just become superintendent of the TGH, a position he was to fill along with that of dean of medicine, came to his defence. In 1911, Jones was

Ernest Jones, psychoanalyst, as a young
doctor; he later would be Sigmund Freud's
biographer.

appointed an associate professor of psychiatry as well as head of a special unit in
neurology at TGH. Nevertheless, he stayed in Canada only two more years.

The University in 1913 had a first-class hospital building to match its
medical school. One problem that needed tackling, however, was the reorganization of the clinical staff of the hospital. A major step had been taken in 1908,
when the board of trustees of the hospital acted upon the unanimous report of a
special committee on reorganization, which had been meeting for a year. The
committee and the trustees wanted only one head for each of the departments,
such as medicine and surgery. This was the Johns Hopkins model. They also
wanted age limits for heads of departments – 55 for surgery and 60 for medicine,
though there would be the possibility of extension. Flavelle and the other
businessmen on the board of trustees wanted strong executive leadership, just as
the royal commissioners had wanted such leadership in the president of the
University. The result was that some of the older, senior clinical professors at the
University lost their status. In surgery, for example, the new head of the department was an associate professor, who was assisted by two other associate professors. The three full professors of surgery were passed by in favour of younger
men. There were loud complaints – well publicized in the press – by these
professors, who were supported by the former president, Loudon. Loudon wrote
to the premier that it had always been his understanding that the University not
the hospital would make the appointments, but the hospital trustees insisted it

was their responsibility. The trustees argued that ultimate responsibility for patient care was theirs.

Flavelle was upset by these 'mischievous and troublesome' professors. Falconer, who had attended many of the meetings of the special committee, was also concerned. 'It is unfortunate,' he wrote to Flavelle, 'that the troubles of a great University should have to be dragged into the public light. Our dignity demands that we should work this out ourselves.' A compromise was reached. Instead of one head of the departments of medicine and surgery, there would be three for medicine and four for surgery. The agreement between the University and TGH was enshrined in legislation in 1911, and not until after the Great War was it established that there would be a single head for each department. Appointments by the TGH board would be made on the recommendation of a joint committee of the hospital trustees and the university governors. The age limits, however, were maintained. So was a clause stating that all positions were open to women, which for many years was honoured more in the breach than in the observance. When overtures to join TGH were made in 1917 by Women's College Hospital, then on Rusholme Road in the west end of the city, the TGH board was not much interested, particularly because WCH would not accept that the TGH heads of departments would automatically be the heads of the WCH departments. In the late 1920s, two houses were purchased by WCH on Grenville Street and Surrey Place for an out-patient clinic, and in 1935 the first wing of the present hospital was opened.

❧

In March 1914 – a little less than a year after the opening of the Toronto General Hospital – the west wing of the Royal Ontario Museum was formally opened. The three-storey Byzantine-style building of buff-coloured brick and terracotta was located beside Philosopher's Walk, with its entrance on Bloor Street. 'With its unique colouring and its isolation from other buildings,' writes the historian of the ROM, Lovat Dickson, 'the new museum had about it the air of a temple.' The governor general, the Duke of Connaught, having been led to the entrance by two columns of UTS military cadets, opened the building.

Many people were influential in the establishment of the museum. The most important was undoubtedly Edmund Walker, who had dreamed of a museum for the city from his days in New York, when he had developed a deep affection

Postcard showing the Royal Ontario Museum, opened in 1914.

for the Metropolitan and other New York museums. He was also an avid collector of art and fossils. In 1904, he had donated to the University his important collection of invertebrate fossils, which he had begun as a boy, along with related library material. As a member of the royal commission of 1906, he had made sure that its report contained a strong recommendation for a university museum. 'One of the necessary features of a great modern University,' the commission had written, 'is a properly equipped museum.' It recommended that 'a site be selected in the university grounds adjacent to a public thoroughfare and sufficient in area to permit of extending the building in the distant future, that a museum on a reasonable scale be planned, and in such a manner as to be built in units, and that a sufficient number of units to accommodate conveniently the museum material now owned by the University of Toronto be built as early as possible.'

Museum collections had been scattered throughout the University. Victoria had brought its museum from Cobourg and, with more graduates becoming missionaries, was adding to its collection. All the theological colleges, the royal commission pointed out, 'may be large contributors in the future.' Nobody at the time raised questions about the propriety of taking valuable objects from other countries and other cultures. There had been museums in University College, but only a portion of the natural science collection, built up by Hincks and others, had been saved from the fire. It was relocated in the new Biology Building and kept growing. Lady Casimir Gzowski, for example, gave 166 mounted Canadian birds brought together by her late husband; Flavelle donated funds for 23 mounted mammals; and the distiller Hiram Walker and Sons gave funds for a fine series of birds of paradise. Daniel Wilson's ethnographic collection and the geology and mineral collections had been destroyed in the fire, but new ethnology material was being kept in the tower of University College. With the increasing interest in mining, both the geology and the mineralogy collections had been rebuilt and were housed in the new Mining Building. Engineering, however, was running short of space, and though an addition had been planned to the building to house the collections, many thought it would be better for these and other collections to be part of a larger museum that would be readily accessible to the public. One of the key arguments in favour of a provincially supported museum was that it would help the economic development of the province – citizens, for example, would gain knowledge of minerals, and artisans would benefit from seeing artefacts fashioned in earlier times.

Charles Currelly also played an important role in creating the museum. He had graduated from Victoria College in 1898 and was headed for the ministry, but through James Mavor's influence became interested in political science. Armed with Mavor's introduction to the anarchist Peter Kropotkin, Currelly went to England to gather material for a thesis on anarchism. Once again, he was diverted from his goal. By chance, he had met Sir Flinders Petrie of the University of London, who was about to return to Egypt to continue his excavations and invited Currelly to join him. Currelly was interested in archaeology, having been on digs with W.A. Parks during his student days. Kropotkin advised him to seize the opportunity. Currelly was never diverted again. He now became, in the words of Northrop Frye, who edited Currelly's autobiography, 'a cultural missionary.'

Burwash and Walker, whose sons were Currelly's close friends, became interested in Currelly's work in Egypt. They both asked Currelly to collect objects for them – in Burwash's case, objects that would be part of Victoria's collection and would shed light on Christianity, and in Walker's case, scarabs and other Egyptian objects for Walker's own personal collection. In 1905, Currelly returned on a visit to Toronto and talked with Walker. He told Walker about his hopes for a museum for the University. Walker replied that 'for twenty years this has been a dream of mine, and it is a terrible grief to me to say that it is impossible ... Objects are now so dear that it is utterly out of the question.' Currelly showed him some objects he had brought back and mentioned the relatively modest prices he had paid. Walker promised to bring the question of hiring Currelly before the University's board of trustees. References arrived. A Cambridge expert wrote to say that if it were up to him, Currelly would be the head of the great Fitzwilliam Museum in Cambridge. In the summer of 1906, the University offered to hire Currelly as the University's 'official collector' with a salary of $1,000 a year and $1,500 for purchases, sums that increased over the years.

In 1909, Walker and a delegation from the University went to see Premier Whitney. The board had already planned to acquire all the land from Taddle Creek to Queen's Park and wanted $50,000 with which to start construction. Darling and Pearson had prepared plans for an H-shaped building, with one side of the H being on Queen's Park and the other beside Taddle Creek. Construction would begin with the latter. The government initially gave sufficient funds to build the basement of the building, which, covered with tar paper, would serve as storage for the objects Currelly was sending back. In 1912, the government passed an act creating the Royal Ontario Museum, the cost of the initial structure to be shared equally by the government and the University; it was to be maintained and governed jointly by the University and the government. Walker was elected chairman of the board of trustees. The first board included a woman, Mrs H.D. Warren, who had become chair of the board of directors of the Dominion Rubber Company after her husband died and was a significant supporter of the museum. Another major benefactor in this early period, Sigmund Samuel, was appointed a trustee in 1921. He was probably the first Jew to serve on the board of such a major public institution in Toronto.

The museum consisted of five separate museums, each reporting to the board of trustees of the museum. The directors of each of the museums had university appointments. There was no desire to create the old system of government appointments under which the University had suffered in the past. For all practical academic purposes, the museum was part of the University. Currelly was made an associate professor of industrial art, later changed to archaeology. His division, which included ethnography, was given the first and second floors of the building to house its extensive holdings. In his years abroad, he had collected important Egyptian and Near Eastern objects. On one trip to England, he had acquired an important group of Chinese artefacts, the beginnings of the museum's major Chinese collection. On his honeymoon in 1909, he acquired the foundation of the museum's West Asian collection. Private individuals contributed various objects. Henry Pellatt, the owner of Casa Loma, for example, gave medieval arms and armour, and E.B. Osler presented the museum with important Paul Kane paintings of Indian life.

The director of the geology museum, Arthur Coleman, who was also head of the university department of geology (as well as dean of the faculty of arts), was relegated to the basement. The geology collection specialized in ores, many of which were donated by mining companies – nickel from Sudbury and silver from Cobalt. Coleman's presidential address to the Geological Society of America, on 'the permanency of continents,' expressed his opposition to the idea of 'continental drift,' a concept successfully promoted many years later by the Toronto geophysicist Tuzo Wilson.

The mineralogy museum was directed by Thomas Walker, a Queen's graduate with a doctorate from Leipzig who had spent a number of years working on the Geological Survey of India. He later won the Royal Society of Canada's prestigious Flavelle Medal for outstanding work in science. Mineralogy, it seems, had been made a separate department in the University because Coleman and Walker could not get along, and the separation was carried over to the museum. The two departments in the University were eventually reunited in 1944 as the department of geological sciences.

B.A. Bensley, who became head of zoology after Ramsay Wright retired, was director of the natural sciences division. Bensley had graduated from Toronto in 1896 and had completed his doctorate at Columbia with a thesis on the evolution of the kangaroo and other marsupials. Like a number of other Toronto academics, he spent his summers at Go Home Bay in Georgian Bay. His older brother, who had preceded him in the department, had conveniently created a federally financed biological station close to Go Home Bay, which B.A. Bensley directed after his brother left for a distinguished career at the University of Chicago. In 1915, Bensley published a book on the fish of Georgian Bay. Not surprisingly, collections of fish were added to the museum. So were collections of insects, because Edmund Walker's son, E.M. Walker, who had joined the department in 1906 (and became its head after Bensley died in 1934), had a special interest in entomology. Walker became one of Canada's most eminent entomologists, also winning the Royal Society's Flavelle Medal.

Madeleine Fritz, later a professor of geology at U of T, during a geological field expedition in the early 1920s.

Palaeontology – the study of fossils and evidence of life in the past – was under the direction of Coleman's colleague in geology and his first PhD student, W.A. Parks. Parks became chair of geology on Coleman's retirement in 1922 and was made a fellow of the Royal Society of London in 1934. His early interest had been geology – he published a five-volume work on the building stones of Canada – but later he turned to invertebrate fossils and finally to vertebrate fossils. He is best known for his work on dinosaurs. His PhD student Madeleine Fritz, later curator of the collection and a professor of geology, claimed in 1939, on the twenty-fifth anniversary of the founding of the museum, that the ROM contained 'the second best collection of dinosaurs in the world.' In 1942, Fritz became the second woman to be elected a fellow of the Royal Society of Canada. The first – Alice Wilson in 1938 – was, coincidentally, also a palaeontologist. A graduate of the University of Toronto and for a few years an assistant in the mineralogy department, Wilson built her reputation with the Geological Survey of Canada.

Although others had previously collected dinosaur bones for the museum, it was Parks who first collected whole skeletons. In 1918, he made his first trip to the Red Deer River in Alberta, the deep gorges of which helped expose the specimens. From this first trip, he brought back a complete skeleton of a duck-billed dinosaur, *Kritosaurus incurvimanus* – over 65 million years old, but then thought to be only 3 million years old – the first of its kind in the possession of a Canadian institution. It is still on display in the museum. On his second expedition, he obtained a hooded duck-billed dinosaur, which is also still on display and is easily recognized as one of only two dinosaurs standing on their hind legs. At the time it was mounted, it was believed, wrongly, that this species of dinosaur travelled on two legs. It has been left in its original mount, according to the assistant director of the section in 1999, to show schoolchildren and other visitors that sometimes scientists get things wrong.

❦

By 1914, Falconer had experienced seven good years. He had weathered a few storms. New buildings had been constructed, and new institutions created. Enrolment had increased, and admission standards had been raised. Some excellent staff had been recruited. Sadly, however, the lean years were about to begin.

PART FOUR

TURBULENCE

chapter twenty-two

1914

THE GREAT WAR

On August 4, 1914, the Great War began. President Falconer was still on a visit to Europe. When he and his wife finally were able to find passage back to Canada in early September, he was interviewed by a *Globe* reporter. 'There was not even a whisper of war,' he stated, 'everything seemed to be going on in a normal way, even in Hamburg.' The outbreak of war may have caught Falconer by surprise, but the potential for war clearly had been there. In his inaugural address in 1907, for example, Falconer had warned that there were 'here and there symptoms that may cause the patriot to fear lest not many hours of our day will have passed before heavy clouds gather.' The storm had now burst.

Falconer's opening address to the student body in September 1914 described the conflict in moral terms. 'This is the greatest of moral struggles,' he said. 'Are there to be democracies ... or will force tower arrogantly above freedom and enslave intellect?' 'The struggle,' he went on, 'had to come. It is well to have it decided one way or other finally, for our own sakes and for our children's.' Growing numbers of students enlisted. Even before Falconer had returned to Canada, about 250 Toronto graduates and undergraduates had left for England. The first University of Toronto person to die in combat was the Trinity student R.E. Mackenzie Richards, who was killed near Ypres, in France, on November 13, 1914. By the spring of 1915, nearly 500 undergraduates, 700 graduates, and 70 faculty members were on active service. In February 1915, a special convocation was held to grant degrees to nearly 50 of those students who were about to leave for overseas.

Most men who did not at first join the active force joined the Canadian Officers Training Corps (COTC), which had been started at the University just after the war began. On October 21, shortly after Ottawa's official recognition of the University of Toronto's contingent, classes were cancelled to allow students to hear an appeal from President Falconer for recruits for the COTC. Within twenty-four hours, more than 500 students had enrolled in the corps, and by early December, 1,800 men were drilling under the overall command of Professor W.R. Lang, the head of chemistry. Classes and laboratories ended every afternoon at 4 o'clock to permit their attendance. One participant recalls marching through vacant farm land north of St Clair Avenue. Later, they drilled in the incomplete Great Hall of Hart House and used the unfinished theatre as a rifle range. Sets resembling a ruined Belgian village, painted by Lieutenant Lawren Harris (later of the Group of Seven), were used on the range.

There was strong pressure on the students to join. An engineering student wrote home to his mother that 'with the President and profs and fellows all urging you to join I could scarcely do otherwise.' One parent complained to Falconer that he could not 'quite understand why you, the President of the great University, should take upon yourself to be the Recruiting Officer in General ... Leave this matter to the boys and their parents.' Lester Pearson, a future prime minister of Canada, joined a Victoria company that was led by Vincent Massey, then a lecturer in history and dean of Burwash Hall. 'I believed, of course, in the justice of our cause,' Pearson wrote in his memoirs, 'but above all, I was young and adventurous, anxious not to be left out of the response of youth to such a challenge, or to lag behind the others and have a white feather [signifying cowardice] pinned on me.' Another history lecturer, E.J. Kylie, trained a company of Trinity, Wycliffe, and St Michael's students. He died in the spring of 1916 in an accident while training at Owen Sound. The University College COTC instructors included F.C.A. Jeanneret of the French department and Malcolm Wallace of the English department, both of whom would become principals of University College.

The number of male students on the campus kept dropping, though female enrolment stayed about the same. In medicine, however, both the number and the proportion of women increased considerably. Over 1,200 male students had joined the active force by the end of the 1916 academic year. At the start of the war, men had outnumbered women at Victoria College by three to one, but two years later there were more women than men. The strictly male engineering courses had had about 600 students before the war, but there were fewer than 200 in 1916–17. The number of women in junior academic positions in the University increased from 15 at the start of the war to 60 at its conclusion. Throughout the University, classes ended a month early so that students – male and female – could work on the farms and in munitions factories. Falconer wrote about the 'quietness' and 'loneliness' of the campus. Intercollegiate sports were suspended, though intramural sports, including football, with its interfaculty Mulock Cup competition, continued. Official evening dances were discontinued. Afternoon dances, however, were permitted.

Later in the war, the campus became more active as a training ground for the British Royal Flying Corps. Tents to accommodate the airmen sprang up on the back campus and in front of Victoria College. They took over most of the old SPS building and a large part of the physically built but as yet unopened Hart House. Canada did not have an air force during the war, and Canadians – and Americans – who wished to enter that service joined the Royal Flying Corps. The 20-year-old American novelist William Faulkner trained on the Toronto campus, and shared a room with four other cadets on the second floor of Wycliffe College. Some of the lectures to the airmen were given by members of the engineering faculty. After conscription was legislated in 1917 and in spite of the heavy casualties at the front, the mood of the campus apparently improved. Conscription removed the uncertainty among the students. They 'definitely know what part they are to play in the great struggle,' the *Globe* observed. An unnamed professor was quoted as saying that 'they go around whistling now.'

The number of casualties was enormous. Over 6,000 persons connected with the University – graduate, undergraduate, and staff – served in the active service. About 10 per cent of that number – more than 600 persons – died. Even a partial list of the sons of figures met in earlier chapters tells how everyone on campus would have been affected by the deaths. The former president, James Loudon, lost a son; so did Chancellor Meredith and the former vice-chancellor Charles Moss; and so did George Wrong, W.H. Van der Smissen, the professor of German, and Dr Alexander Primrose, later the dean of medicine. The U of T *Monthly* contained lists of those killed, wounded, or captured. The *Monthly* of November 1918, for example, contains a list of casualties between June and October 1918. That one list contains the following number of University College students who graduated during the war or would have graduated if they had not enlisted: 6 killed from the class of 1915, 4 from the class of 1916, 6 from

Sopwith Camel aircraft in front of University College in 1918.

the class of 1917, and 4 from the class of 1918. The numbers of wounded, gassed, or captured would have been at least as great. The high number of casualties during that five-month period of 1918 was the result of the German spring offensive, which was blocked by the Allies, and the later Allied break-through, starting with the Amiens offensive, which eventually resulted in the Armistice of November 11, 1918. The university contingents had not been kept together as a fighting force, and personnel were assigned where they were needed, normally to the infantry. They became, in effect, 'enlisted footsoldiers' and experienced some of the fiercest battles in the war.

Some of the persons who will figure in later chapters were wounded in battle. Among them were Frank Underhill and Harold Innis. Underhill, who enlisted

Harold Innis, top left, later a professor of political economy, was wounded at Vimy Ridge.
Frank Underhill, middle, later a professor of history, was wounded on the Somme front.
Norman Bethune, top right, who had enlisted in 1914, part way through medical school, was
wounded and returned to Canada, and graduated in 1916. John McCrae, bottom left, the
author of 'In Flanders Fields,' died on active service in 1918. Thain MacDowell, bottom right,
won a Victoria Cross for his actions in capturing two German machine guns.

in September 1915, was wounded in March 1918 by shrapnel in his leg during the German spring offensive on the Somme front and spent a number of months recuperating in England. He rejoined his regiment with the rank of lieutenant and played a part in the victory at the Somme in September 1918. Innis, who would later come to Underhill's defence when Underhill was threatened with dismissal for making anti-war statements, enlisted after graduating from McMaster University in May 1916. On July 7, 1917, Innis and other signallers were on a reconnaissance mission on the then Allied-occupied Vimy Ridge. A German shell exploded behind them, and he was wounded in the leg. The University of Toronto Archives contains a shrapnel-damaged notebook that was in his hip pocket when he was injured and that may have saved his life. Innis returned to England to recuperate at the Canadian hospital at Basingstoke. While there, to the great benefit of future scholarship in Canada, he read such economic classics as Alfred Marshall's *Principles of Economics*.

Vimy Ridge was the scene of great devastation and great heroism. It was there that Major Thain MacDowell, who had played football for Varsity, won the Victoria Cross. With two other soldiers, he captured two German machine guns and chased one of the German survivors down a tunnel, where he was confronted by seventy-seven German soldiers. MacDowell convinced them they were surrounded by a large force, and so brought about their surrender.

Many of the University's casualties occurred at Ypres. Norman Bethune, a medical student, with one year to go before completion of his degree, enlisted in early September 1914 and served as a stretcher bearer in an army medical corps. He was wounded by shrapnel in the second battle of Ypres in 1915 and spent three months in a British military hospital. Bethune returned to Canada to complete his medical degree and then re-enlisted as a surgeon in the Royal Navy. Many others succumbed to disease. A Toronto medical graduate, the gold medallist John McCrae, the author of the well-known poem 'In Flanders Fields,' did not survive the war. In January 1918, he died on active service in France of meningitis and double pneumonia.

The Canadian hospital at Basingstoke, where Innis recuperated, was a University of Toronto endeavour. In February 1915, the University offered to provide a 1,000-bed base hospital. It was first located in Salonika, in northern Greece, at the request of the Serbian government, whose soldiers were involved in heavy trench warfare against the Germans. The hospital, known as No. 4 General Hospital, was originally staffed by 38 officers, including at least one

Doctors Duncan Graham, centre, and J.J. Mackenzie, right, in a tent at No. 4 General Hospital
in Salonika in 1914. Pathologist Cyril Imrie is on the left.

woman doctor, Harriet Cockburn, and 73 nurses, almost all of whom were
drawn from the Toronto hospitals connected with the University. In addition,
more than 200 soldiers, many of whom were Toronto undergraduates, worked at
the hospital. Private Lester Pearson was one of them. He had what he considered
a 'cushy job' looking after the stores. He also led his unit's hockey team to the
championship of the Macedonian front.

The hospital became a scientific centre for the district. It had two of Toronto's leading medical scientists, J.J. Mackenzie, the professor of pathology, and
Duncan Graham, who would later become the first Sir John and Lady Eaton
Professor of Medicine at the University. A team of top surgeons included Drs
Alexander Primrose, who would become dean of medicine, and F.N.G. Starr,
later the professor of clinical surgery. The hospital, which would eventually grow
to 2,000 beds, was supported by the military, but also by fund-raising in Canada
and by bandages, bed linens, and other supplies prepared by the University
Women's Hospital Supply Association. The association was headed by Lady
Sophie Falconer and consisted primarily of faculty wives, who were assisted by

undergraduate women. After two years of excellent work in Salonika, the hospital was reconstituted in Basingstoke, England.

⚜

A different loss experienced at the University during the war was the loss of German culture, scholarship, and language. The study of German became optional for all specialist courses except chemistry. J.G. Hume, the head of philosophy, announced in 1915 that he was 'replacing the two philosophy courses in the curriculum in which German works were read.' The rejection of German ideas continued long past the war. 'At no point in the next half-century,' writes Brian McKillop, 'would German or Austrian scholarship influence the Ontario professoriate as it had in the years since the 1870s.'

The strong anti-German feeling manifested itself in a desire to rid the University of professors with German roots. Two teachers of German, Paul Mueller and Bonno Tapper, and a professor of Oriental languages, Immanuel Benzinger, were forced to leave the University of Toronto. All three had been born in Germany, and none had yet become a Canadian citizen. Tapper had graduated from the University of Chicago and intended to take out American citizenship if the Toronto position was not made permanent. Benzinger had recently joined the Toronto faculty, after more than ten years teaching and doing research in Palestine. He had returned to Germany during the summer of 1914 to bring his family to Canada. The war intervened, however, and though he was able to return to Canada, his wife remained in Germany and his son was drafted into the German army. Mueller had the strongest case for sympathetic treatment. He had been in Canada for years and was a graduate of the University of Toronto. His German citizenship had lapsed, and he was not liable for conscription in the German army, but neither had he taken out Canadian citizenship.

Demands were made in the press that all three be fired. The Toronto *Telegram* said in late 1914 that the university officials who let them remain should be prosecuted for trading with the enemy. 'If we cannot get university professors of British blood,' a provincial member of parliament said, 'then let us close the universities.' Falconer would not take action against them, however, and told the press that 'they have done nothing that should arouse any suspicion that they are injurious alien enemies.' Many on the board of governors wanted them dismissed. Falconer, along with other board members, including Walker and Flavelle, wanted them to stay. A compromise was reached after a two-day board meeting in November 1914. All three would be given leaves of absence with full pay until the end of the academic year. Board member E.B. Osler was angry and spoke of resigning. 'I cannot see why we should be paying Germans salaries here,' he wrote, 'when thousands of the young men of Britain are being killed by Germans at the front.' Falconer tried to work out exchanges with American universities to assist the three members on leave and to help in the University's teaching program, but without success.

Tapper almost immediately returned to the University of Chicago to do further post-graduate work, and Benzinger also went to the United States, where he found a teaching position in a small college. Mueller remained in Toronto and secured a position at McMaster University on Bloor Street. His key to University College was taken back from him. He wanted to return to the University of Toronto, having been given Canadian citizenship in 1915, but the board would not have him. As Michiel Horn has observed, 'Amidst the clash of arms and the conflict of ideas, academic freedom was a losing cause.' Falconer had his dissent specifically recorded in the minutes of the board. The University, however, still needed German teachers. Special classes in French and German were being given to some soldiers who were going to the front. Fortunately for the University, Barker Fairley, who turned out to be 'one of the foremost Goethe scholars in the English-speaking world' and who had recently come from England to join the faculty at Alberta, was hired. He would add great distinction to modern languages at the University.

⋘∾⋙

The war demonstrated that Canada lacked significant scientific research capacity, particularly in comparison with Germany and the United States. The annual budget of the Massachusetts Institute of Technology exceeded that of all the faculties of applied science in Canada together. The University of Toronto biochemistry professor A.B. Macallum estimated that during the war Canada had 'not many more than 50 pure research men all told.' The total sum spent by the federal government for university research from 1912 to 1915 had been less than $300,000. In response to this concern, an Advisory Council for Scientific and Industrial Research – the predecessor of the National Research Council of Canada – was established in 1916 by the federal government to help promote scientific research. Macallum was made its full-time chairman. Where would the scientific work be done? President Falconer and the committee member John McLennan of the physics department, along with others, wanted government work to be done at or close by the existing laboratories in the universities, but the government and Macallum, who had moved to Ottawa, favoured centralizing the laboratories in Ottawa – a measure that would help solve the problem of choosing which individual universities would receive support. But such a decision would certainly weaken the research potential of the universities. Shortly after the war, the federal government approved the creation of central laboratories in Ottawa. In the meantime, some help was given to research at the universities by the institution of scholarships and fellowships for persons who had shown capacity for scientific research.

Nevertheless, there was considerable research activity on the campus during the war. The faculty of engineering for the first time engaged in organized industrial research. This was something that the royal commission of 1906 had recommended and that the Canadian Manufacturers' Association had advocated for many years. In June 1916, Dean W.H. Ellis – Galbraith had died a month before the war began – argued in *Applied Science*, the organ of the University's Engineering Society, that 'if we are to rise to the supreme demands of the present crisis and its unique opportunities, we must take some definite step forward in the direction of the encouragement and organization of industrial research.' He proposed the foundation of a School of Engineering Research. The school, within the faculty, was established in the spring of 1917, with $5,000 allocated by the board of governors from a special provincial grant for research.

Individual engineering professors, however, contributed directly to the war effort, mainly in relation to munitions. Using the strength of materials laboratory, engineers tested the steel casings of shells, and chemical engineers tested chemical explosives. J. Watson Bain, for example, worked on picric acid, used in the manufacture of explosives. Some staff members inspected finished shells and the shrapnel within them. Others within the University also worked on explosives. Clara Benson, for example, applied her knowledge of chemistry to the chemistry of explosives.

In 1918, the faculty of engineering procured the first wind tunnel in Canada, which allowed the testing of aircraft by simulating flight without risk to the pilot – but only up to about 60 miles an hour. The board of governors had given funds to allow J.H. Parkin to build a complete aerodynamics laboratory, includ-

John McLennan's official pass for work with the British Admiralty in 1918.

ing a wind tunnel, in the thermodynamics building. Engineering graduates had already played key roles in the development of flight in Canada. A graduate of 1906, Casey Baldwin, had conducted the first flight by a British subject in a powered aircraft, on March 12, 1908, over a lake in New York state. The first powered flight in Canada was by J.A.D. McCurdy, an engineering graduate of 1907, on February 23, 1909, in the 'Silver Dart' in Nova Scotia. Both Baldwin and McCurdy were associated with Alexander Graham Bell's research group in the Maritimes. After the war, Parkin, who was in charge of aeronautical research in the University, was able to build a new free-standing wind tunnel, paid for by the federal government, in a separate building just south of the thermodynamics building. The new tunnel would more than double the speed of the old tunnel. In 1928, the first course in aeronautical engineering – within the department of mechanical engineering – was introduced.

John McLennan and others from the physics department were particularly active in aiding the war effort. In 1915, McLennan was asked by the British Admiralty to determine the potential quantity of helium available from natural gas in Canada. Helium was desired for the navy's lighter-than-air ships, then using the potentially explosive hydrogen. Subsequently he was asked to produce quantities of helium. McLennan and some of his colleagues, including E.F. Burton, set up a plant and were producing some helium when the Americans entered the war and, owing to their greater resources, were able to produce the necessary quantities more quickly. In fact, the war was over before any helium could be used in military operations. McLennan's knowledge of helium, however, bore fruit in his new interest in liquid helium, which could be produced only at very low temperatures. It led to the department's long-standing interest and expertise in low temperature physics.

McLennan had a more direct effect on the war through his work for the British navy on anti-submarine devices. After spending the summer of 1917 doing research in England for the navy, he was asked to remain there on a full-time basis. He gathered a team of University of Toronto graduates to assist him. One simple but effective device they developed – using high school physics – was an electrified copper loop to be placed on the sea bed at the entrance to British harbours and other places, which could detect the presence of ships travelling above it because of the ships' magnetic characteristics. Another device was a fuse that would make sea mines more stable. A month after the war was over and when secrecy was less of a concern, he wrote in a letter that with the use of the loop 'we closed the Straits of Dover,' and that 'with a particular mine which I developed we got one cruiser, three destroyers, three mine-sweepers, two subs and a launch.' 'Our two methods of defence,' he wrote, 'have come to be recognized as of vital importance in meeting the sub for the future. They are now fully accepted by the Navy as standard devices.' After the war, he was asked by the Admiralty to take on the position of director of research for the navy. A large new research laboratory was to be part of the arrangement. McLennan would have taken the job, but, fortunately for Toronto, the British cabinet decided not to fund the laboratory, and in September 1919 he returned to the University.

The medical faculty also made very important contributions to the war effort, apart from the medical hospital in Salonika. The physiologist T.G. Brodie, for example, studied the physiological effects of wounds in the respiratory system. The surgeon Bruce Robertson, a member of the staff of the Hospital for Sick Children who served in France, to give another example, developed special techniques for blood transfusions. Robertson and other Canadians, such as the surgeons at the Canadian hospital in Salonika, used blood transfusions to a much greater extent than doctors from other countries, who routinely replaced

John FitzGerald, the founder of the
Connaught Laboratories, produced diphtheria
antitoxin in this barn behind a house at
145 Barton Avenue in Toronto in 1914.
Bill Fenton, who appears here, was the first
Connaught employee.

lost blood with saline solutions. Two influential articles in the *British Medical Journal* by Robertson, based on his and others' experiences with transfusions, changed attitudes towards their use. His articles, the *Journal* stated in an editorial, 'will convince the reader of the enormous value of the transfusion of blood in cases of severe hemorrhage.'

A particularly important contribution was made by the Connaught Laboratories. John FitzGerald was crucial in the development of the laboratories. He was a graduate of the faculty of medicine in 1903, and his early specialization was in psychiatry; after training at Johns Hopkins, he became a demonstrator in psychiatry at the University of Toronto. (Ernest Jones was a good friend of FitzGerald's and in 1910 gave him a complete set of Freud's works as a wedding present – 'a rather original little wedding present,' to use Jones' words.) FitzGerald's interests soon turned to bacteriology. He studied at Harvard and at the Pasteur Institutes in Paris and Brussels, and became an associate professor of bacteriology at the University of California at Berkeley. In 1913, he returned to Toronto as an associate professor of hygiene, the first full-time member of the department. He soon started producing the Pasteur anti-rabies vaccine and then turned to the production of a much-needed diphtheria antitoxin. The University was at first reluctant to become involved in a commercial venture, and FitzGerald at his own expense produced the antitoxin in a barn behind a house at

145 Barton Avenue in the Bloor and Bathurst area, where the four horses used in its production were kept. (The horses were unharmed by the process.) In May 1914, however, the University agreed to take over the work as part of the department of hygiene.

The laboratory became important during the war. FitzGerald argued that it would be 'a highly patriotic action for us to manufacture our own anti-tetanus toxins for the Canadian Expeditionary Forces.' Falconer was able to get $5,000 from the federal government. It was, he claimed, the first grant for laboratory work ever received by the University of Toronto from the federal government. Tetanus antitoxin as well as smallpox and typhoid vaccines were produced and given to the Canadian troops, as well as to many civilians. A member of the University of Toronto board of governors, Colonel A.E. Gooderham, who was chairman of the Red Cross, realized the potential for the laboratory and donated to the University a 50-acre farm and a laboratory north-west of the city, near the corner of Dufferin and Steeles, for the production of vaccines and antitoxins. The Ontario government contributed funds for future research. The formal opening took place in October 1917, when the facility was named after the former governor general, the Duke of Connaught. One of the guests at the opening was Simon Flexner of the Rockefeller Institute of Medical Research. The Rockefeller Foundation's interest in the new labs would lead to a major Rockefeller grant to establish the University's School of Hygiene in 1925, with FitzGerald as its head. The first phase of the fine red-brick and stone building on College Street was erected in 1927. In 1975, the building was appropriately named the FitzGerald Building.

FitzGerald and the professor of hygiene, John Amyot, both served overseas and helped organize for the Canadian army a system for treating and controlling contagious diseases. Amyot claimed that 'the preventive measures adopted by the Canadian Corps in France reversed the trend of more men dying from disease than from wounds.'

The University was also involved in helping the physical and mental rehabilitation of returned veterans. The psychologist E.A. Bott started a small clinic for what was called the 'functional re-education' of soldiers impaired by war disabilities, and 'in particular to remedy injuries to the nervous or muscular system received from wounds or shock.' His method was largely psychological, involving simple mechanical appliances that allowed the patient to register his progress and thus build up his self-confidence. J.J. Mackenzie, the professor of pathology,

The Red Cross Room in the university library, sometime during the war.

who had recently returned from Salonika, chaired a committee to supervise related work.

Bott's work was transferred to Hart House in 1917, and a course in physiotherapy was established in which 'functional re-education' and other forms of treatment, such as massage and electrotherapy, were taught. One of the returned veterans who learned to be a masseur was Donald McDougall, who had been blinded during the Battle of Flers-Courcelette. He went on to take a degree in history and became a Rhodes scholar and a distinguished professor of history at the University. Bott became head of the department of psychology in 1927, when it separated from philosophy to become its own department, a position he held with distinction for the next thirty years. It is a curious fact that Bott's doctoral thesis submitted during the war had been rejected by the philosophy department. His war work may have interfered with the thesis, but it is more likely, according to John Slater, the historian of the philosophy department, that George Brett of philosophy would not have approved a thesis on the pre-Socratics by a candidate who did not know Greek.

The faculty of engineering also contributed to the rehabilitation of veterans. H.E.T. Haultain of the department of mining was appointed vocational officer for Ontario for the Invalided Soldiers Commission. The commission was a large undertaking, with almost 400 people in its head office on Spadina Avenue. He and his colleagues organized two programs. One was to refit disabled soldiers for civilian occupations by instructing them in such fields as auto mechanics and applied electricity. They also trained more than 300 women as occupational therapists. The several-month course was conducted in the east end of the Mining Building, a stone's throw from the present facilities for occupational therapy on McCaul Street. The therapy was for veterans not yet able to take instruction in a trade and who faced long periods of convalescence. It consisted of crafts such as woodwork, bookbinding, and basketry. Helen LeVesconte, later the head of occupational therapy at the University, recalled the high numbers of injuries to the hand that required treatment, and the use of basketry. 'We all ridiculed basketry,' she said, 'we always have ... but when you come down to it, it was a very smart thing to introduce and nobody could ever have the face to say to you, "I can't do it."' The surgeon Alexander Primrose, who helped form the Ontario Society of Occupational Therapists shortly after the war, wrote that the work of the therapists helped shorten the patient's period of convalescence. Not only did their work help medically to improve function, but it is 'better for a patient to do some useful work than to leave him to brood over his troubles.' A two-year diploma course, established mainly to supply therapists for mental hospitals, was initiated at the University in 1926. Helen LeVesconte was a member of that first class.

'On November 11th,' 1918, the University's official *Roll of Service* volume records, 'the long agony was over. The buildings were closed, and for a day all gave themselves up to common rejoicing.'

chapter twenty-three

1919

POST WAR

On Armistice Day, 1919, one year after the end of the war, the foundation stone for a memorial tower was laid at the official opening of Hart House. The planning by the Alumni Association for a memorial honouring those who had served, and particularly those who had given their lives, had begun immediately after the end of the war. A tall Gothic tower visible from any point on the campus was to be constructed. A site immediately north of the main library on King's College Circle was selected, but the board of governors wanted to keep the land for the expansion of the library. Another site considered was one between Convocation Hall and Knox College, but the board wanted to keep that land for possible use as an administrative centre. So the decision was made to situate the building on its present site.

At 4 o'clock in the afternoon, the cornerstone for the tower was lowered into place, and the governor general, the Duke of Devonshire, carefully smoothed the mortar, telling the audience that 'through this Memorial, the great name and the great tradition established for the University by those who died will be handed down as long as the University endures.' A prayer was offered by Canon Cody of the board, and the 'Last Post' was blown by cavalry trumpeters. 'When the plaintive, haunting notes died away,' the *Monthly* noted, 'the audience, as if by common consent, remained still for some moments. It was a fitting close to the simple, impressive service.'

The tower, designed by Sproatt and Rolph, the architects of Hart House, was

Soldiers' Tower, November 11, 1924, after two minutes of silence.

not actually completed until 1924. The funds raised by the alumni were to be used not only for the memorial tower but also for scholarships and loans for the great number of returned veterans and the families of those who had not returned. It had been hoped that the federal government would assist the veterans with funds for education, but it refused to do so, saying that education was a provincial responsibility. 'We all foresee,' Prime Minister Robert Borden wrote to Falconer, 'a tremendous outcry and disturbance of public opinion if we should make general provision for assistance to students at universities and should fail to make the like provision for vocational training for assistance in embarking upon business enterprises, etc.' With no federal support, much of the money raised for the tower was needed for loans and scholarships. Half the students who wrote the entrance exam in engineering in 1919, for example, were ex-soldiers. By 1922, however, most of the demand for support had been met, and construction began. The planned 23-bell carillon was not put in place until 1927, the hundredth anniversary of the University. Since then, 28 more bells have been added, making a total today of 51 bells.

❧

The construction of Hart House – unique in North America – had been started before the war. The YMCA had planned to erect a new building, with the help of the Massey family. Vincent Massey, who was then an undergraduate at University College, persuaded his family that it would be desirable to combine the new YMCA and a desperately needed student centre in one building. Rather than having the Y and a student centre compete with each other, they could combine their work. In early 1910, a proposal to that effect was made to the University by the Massey Foundation, which controlled the funds left in a trust by Vincent's grandfather, Hart Massey. The land the foundation wanted for the new structure – the present site of Hart House – had been promised for new athletic facilities, and a gymnasium was therefore added to the plans. Construction began in 1911, and the walls and the roof were completed before the war.

Meant to cost $500,000, the building eventually cost close to $2 million. Vincent Massey worked closely with the architects, Sproatt and Rolph, in producing the prize-winning 'collegiate Gothic' structure, with its Credit Valley hammer-faced sandstone and smooth Indiana limestone. The architects had earlier been responsible for the Gothic Burwash Hall and residences at Victoria

Hart House, completed in 1919, and Soldiers' Tower, completed in 1924.

College. The construction was not easy. Hart House runs directly over the submerged Taddle Creek, and massive foundations were required for support. One of the myths connected with Hart House is that the theatre was added during construction when the Masseys saw that one of the arches to support the building looked like a proscenium arch. The theatre, however, is clearly shown in the plans drawn before construction started. One change that was made during construction was to designate what is now the upper gallery restaurant as a faculty club. Perhaps for that reason, it was thought desirable to have a staircase from the upper gallery to the Great Hall. The enclosed Gothic staircase can be seen at the south-west corner of the Great Hall. The craftsman responsible for painting a passage from Milton's oration *Areopagitica* around the wall of the Great Hall had already blocked out the spacing of the letters when the staircase was added. He did not want to change the spacing entirely, and as a result the letters are more compressed around the staircase than on the east wall.

Carved in stone at the entrance to the Great Hall is what is called the 'Founders' Prayer.' The prayer, wrote Ian Montagnes in 1969 on the fiftieth anniversary of the opening of the House, 'has served as a benchmark for five wardens. It remains the clearest and briefest statement of the aims and spirit which have infused the life of this institution.' It has continued to guide wardens. The prayer reads:

> The Prayer of the Founders is that Hart House, under the guidance of its Warden, may serve in the generations to come the highest interests of this University by drawing into a common fellowship the members of the several Colleges and Faculties, and by gathering into a true society the teacher and the student, the graduate and the undergraduate; further, that the members of Hart House may discover within its walls the true education that is to be found in good fellowship, in friendly disputation and debate, in the conversation of wise and earnest men, in music, pictures and the play, in the casual book, in sports and games and the mastery of the body; and lastly, that just as in the days of war this House was devoted to the training in arms of the young soldier, so, in the time of peace its halls may be dedicated to the task of arming youth with strength and suppleness of limb, with clarity of mind and depth of understanding, and with a spirit of true religion and high endeavour.

When Vincent Massey used the words 'common fellowship' he meant 'men.' Women were not admitted to Hart House on equal terms with men until 1972. The words 'common fellowship' have been considered elastic enough to include women. It is more difficult, though, to so consider the words 'conversation of wise and earnest men,' and in recent documents the word 'men' has been eliminated so that the prayer reads 'in the conversation of the wise and the earnest.' Moreover, 'true religion' in the Founders' Prayer originally meant Christianity, and possibly only Protestantism, yet it is now interpreted widely enough to permit Muslim prayer sessions to be conducted in the House. In the early days, other religious groups were not allowed official space for meetings.

In the early minutes of the committees of the House, certain issues kept arising. One was that of women. Some concessions were made. A number of designated concerts were open to women. At a meeting on February 18, 1921, it was decided that the fourth year University College class would be permitted to hold a dinner 'provided no ladies are present.' The following week a motion to delete the words 'provided no ladies are present' was passed, but the 'ladies' had to enter by the lower south-east door. Women's organizations were refused space. The women of the University of Toronto Swimming Club could not use the Hart House pool for club contests, and the Alumnae Association was refused

An Alumni gathering in the Great Hall, Hart House, sometime after 1928.

permission to hold a dinner in the House. Women faculty members could not use the faculty club while it was in Hart House. The University College Alumnae, however, were given permission to hold a dinner to raise funds to acquire their own premises. In 1922, University College women were able to purchase a large house – the Women's Union – on St George Street, south of Whitney Hall, for dining and meetings and other activities. The women in the University, however, never acquired a student union for all women students.

Another recurring issue for Hart House was smoking. At a meeting on

December 16, 1919, the house committee accepted the recommendation of the library committee that smoking be prohibited in the library, but would not accept a similar recommendation of the musical club. Smoking was prohibited also in the pool. The architects had written to Vincent Massey pleading for prohibition of smoking there, as 'butts are eventually lodged in the pool in some form or shape.'

The first warden of Hart House, Walter Bowles, stayed for two years and then turned to other pursuits, including radio broadcasting, and eventually became the CBC's newscast reader. He was replaced by Burgon Bickersteth, an Oxford graduate who had spent a number of years in western Canada as a lay member of a church mission. He would remain as warden until 1947. The various activities of Hart House were governed by committees made up of undergraduates, graduates, and faculty members. Professor Barker Fairley, for example, who was a painter and a friend of the Group of Seven, was the first chair of the art committee. Ernest MacMillan and Healey Willan were members of the music committee, and political economist Vincent Bladen and law professor Norman 'Larry' MacKenzie (later the president of the University of British Columbia) were members of the debates committee.

It was in these early years that the Sunday Evening Concerts were instituted and the Hart House String Quartet established. The quartet performed until the end of the Second World War, and the Sunday Concerts have continued to the present day. There were also impromptu recitals in the music room. A resolution was passed, however, in December 1919 'that all music of the kind known as "ragtime" be excluded from the piano.'

Paintings began to appear on the bare walls of the House. With Barker Fairley's advice, the art committee purchased two or three paintings a year. The first painting purchased was A.Y. Jackson's *Georgian Bay, November*. Other Group of Seven pictures acquired were by Arthur Lismer, Fred Varley, Lawren Harris, and J.E.H. MacDonald. George Wrong gave the House $5,000 as an endowment for art purchases in memory of his son, Harold, who was killed at the Battle of the Somme, and another son, Murray, who died at Oxford after the war. Some of the most important and memorable paintings in Hart House, including Tom Thomson's *Birches* and Lawren Harris's *Isolation Peak*, were purchased with these funds.

Hart House Theatre contributed to the cultural life both of the University and of the wider community. In a production of three one-act plays in November 1921, both Vincent Massey and his later well known brother, the actor Raymond Massey, had leading roles, the sets were designed by three members of the Group of Seven (Harris, Lismer, and MacDonald), and the music for one of the plays was composed and played by Healey Willan. During the academic year 1925–6, seventeen plays were produced. The University of Toronto was becoming the centre of cultural life in Toronto.

The first Hart House debate was held in 1924. Instead of using the American debating style of prepared speeches judged by a special panel, the House adopted a parliamentary style similar to that used at Oxford and Cambridge in which wit, repartee, and heckling were encouraged along with speeches from the floor. At the end of the debate, the persons present divided into those who supported the proposition debated and those who opposed it. The topic of the first debate was 'That this House views with confidence the formation of a Labour government in England and would welcome the development of a party of a similar character in Canada.' At the end of the debate, 184 supported the motion and 88 opposed it.

The most important debate of the 1920s was undoubtedly in 1927, when Prime Minister MacKenzie King was the principal speaker. He had visited the House several years earlier after a number of invitations to do so by Bickersteth. King had at first refused to come, according to Bickersteth, thinking he was unwelcome because of his role in the strike thirty years earlier. Bickersteth, however, reassured him that he would be warmly received. The motion for the debate was that the House supported the recent Imperial Conference favouring greater independence for the Dominions. More than 500 people squeezed into the debates room, which normally accommodated 350. Three hundred more were turned away. King's speech, wrote Bickersteth, 'was delivered with such keenness, vigour, charm, humour and real enjoyment that it was a huge success, listened to breathlessly by the packed House, who realized they were listening to the Prime Minister of Canada defend a proposed agreement which he had not even debated as yet at Ottawa.' The House divided 408 to 125 in favour of the prime minister.

∽❧∽

Trinity College's move to the University had also been delayed by the war. In 1909, the University had offered Trinity a free site – its present location – along

Trinity College moved from its Queen Street site to its present location on Hoskin Avenue in 1925; a quadrangle was completed during the Second World War, and Sir Giles Gilbert Scott's chapel in 1955.

Hoskin Avenue and a further site for its women's college, St Hilda's, on the west side of Devonshire Place. This offer was approved by Trinity, which thereupon sold its site on Queen Street to the city of Toronto for $625,000, retaining the right to continue to occupy the building for five years. The war intervened, however, and it was not until 1923 that the foundation stone of the present building was laid. In fact, two foundation stones were laid, one on top of the other. A month before the event, the original stone from the old building on Queen Street was discovered. The two stones can be seen today to the left of the main entrance. The ceremony resembled the one conducted by Bishop Strachan seventy-two years earlier. The silver trowel used by Strachan was used by the archbishop of Algoma, who repeated the words spoken by Strachan. The building, the archbishop said, would be 'a place of sound learning and religious education in accordance with the principles and usages of the Church of England in Canada.' The site was across the road from Wycliffe College, which also trained students for the Anglican ministry, but with a 'low church' emphasis. In 1910, Premier Whitney's wealthy brother, E.C. Whitney, had offered $200,000 if the divinity schools of Wycliffe and Trinity would agree to unite. The attempt had failed, and another one, in 1921, also failed.

There was not enough money to construct all of Trinity College – construction costs had risen enormously – so the college began with only that part of the building facing Hoskin Avenue. Darling and Pearson, who had designed most of the major buildings on the campus over the previous twenty years, designed a Gothic building to resemble the old college. During the summer of 1925, Trinity moved to its new site. Its students, unlike students at other colleges, continued to wear gowns to lectures and to meals, and to this day they continue to wear them to dinner. Enrolment was relatively low in comparison with University College and Victoria. In 1920–1, there had been only 97 men, including 16 divinity students, and 60 women, who could not then be divinity students. By the end of the decade, there were more than 300 students – still well below the number at UC or Victoria. Residences had not been constructed at that time. A number of houses – including Sir Edmund Walker's house on St George Street – were purchased for women's residences. St Hilda's was not built until 1937. A large six-storey luxury apartment building, renamed Trinity House, at the south-west corner of St George and Harbord, which had been built just after the turn of the century, was purchased for a men's residence. The dining hall and residences at Trinity were completed during the Second World War. Part of the library in the building on Hoskin Avenue had to be used initially as the chapel. The present chapel, the last work designed by the English architect Sir Giles Gilbert Scott, was completed in 1955.

The inflation that had affected construction costs at Trinity College affected the entire University. Enrolment was rising, and costs were increasing. Prices had nearly doubled between 1907 and 1915 and had doubled again by 1920. Salaries had not kept up with inflation and were becoming uncompetitive. A full professor at Toronto received $5,000, whereas full professors at Harvard, Yale, Columbia, and Michigan received about $8,000 Canadian. The professors' standard of living at Toronto had been declining. 'I could make my own bed and black my own boots quite well,' George Wrong wrote a friend in Oxford in the fall of 1919, 'but I am doubtful about cooking my own dinner!'

The yearly deficit also kept increasing. Each year, the University had asked the government to make up the deficit – the projected deficit reluctantly approved by William Hearst's Conservative government for 1920 was approaching $1 million. With the unexpected election of the United Farmers of Ontario government in October 1919, the future of the University was considerably less secure. Many members of the United Farmers viewed the University as an elite institution governed by an elite Toronto-based board. Premier E.C. Drury favoured having non-Toronto men on the board. 'Toronto has quite the village point of view,' he told the *Globe*. 'Its mind is isolated.' The government filled several vacancies with its own supporters. Moreover, the government was not in sympathy with the 25 per cent salary increase in the budget it inherited. After considerable negotiation, it approved an increase, but only for academic staff and based on merit, with a maximum increase of $500 per person.

In September 1920, Drury's government announced that a royal commission on university finances would be appointed. The members of the commission, to the surprise of many, were sympathetic to higher education. Canon Cody, its chair, had been a member of the royal commission of 1906 and was a member of the university's board of governors, as was the businessman T.A. Russell. The commission's report was very positive; it recommended a return to Whitney's scheme whereby an amount equal to half the succession duties would be given each year to the University of Toronto, and smaller maintenance grants would continue to be given to Queen's University and the University of Western Ontario. In 1914, it will be recalled, a cap of $500,000 had been placed on the amount that Toronto would receive from this source. If the commission's recommendation had been adopted, the University's financial problems would have been solved, because the amount collected for succession duties in the year 1920 was about $4 million and was expected to rise in future years. Unfortunately for the University, the government ignored the recommendation. The government, Drury told the *Globe*, had to ensure 'a sense of proportion between the needs of the universities and the crying needs of the Province.'

Another major recommendation that was to a great extent ignored was to give an outright grant of $1.5 million to the University for capital expenditures. But the government did give a grant of $500,000 for a new anatomy building, to be built just east of the old medical building. Funds for a new administration building – the present Simcoe Hall – were also provided, and the building was completed in 1923. This move allowed the University College Literary and Athletic Society to gain possession of the Junior Common Room, which had

In 1923, the president and other administrative officers moved from University College
to the newly constructed Simcoe Hall.

previously been administrative offices. In 1926, the Literary and Athletic Society
inscribed the names of its past officers in gold leaf on the walls of the JCR, a
practice that has continued to this day. No special money was promised for other
buildings recommended by the royal commission, such as an extension to the
Royal Ontario Museum and a women's gymnasium. The ROM extension would
not take place until the 1930s, and the women's gymnasium, the late 1950s.

⌘

In 1922, there was a further investigation into the affairs of the University, this
time by a select committee of the legislature. The issues involved were considered

of sufficient importance that the committee was chaired by Premier Drury himself and had as one of its members the leader of the opposition, Howard Ferguson. Fourteen meetings were held between October 1922 and January 1923. Falconer attended every sitting. The immediate cause of the hearings was the recurring issue of the organization of the medical departments at the Toronto General Hospital and the Hospital for Sick Children.

Towards the end of the war, the University had decided to institute a single academic and clinical head for the department of medicine and a single one for surgery, instead of the multiple heads for each department reluctantly permitted before the war. Sir John and Lady Eaton gave half a million dollars to endow a chair in both their names for the head of medicine, and the Rockefeller Foundation gave a million dollars to the University for a chair of surgery and for other purposes in the faculty of medicine. Duncan Graham, the bacteriologist who had served with J.J. Mackenzie in Salonika, though only 37 years old, was selected as the professor of medicine. He is said to have been the first full-time professor of medicine in the British Empire. Falconer informed him that 'very probably we shall be able to secure a change in the matter of medical services [in the hospitals] and have them under the direction of one man, at least we will attempt to secure this.' Graham, in fact, became the sole clinical head of medicine, and two years later Clarence Starr, the head of surgery at the Hospital for Sick Children, was selected as the single head of surgery for both the Sick Children's and the Toronto General Hospital. At about the same time, the department of paediatrics was reorganized, with Dr Alan Brown as its head. The clinical head was also the academic head of the teaching department in the faculty of medicine.

In the restructuring, certain doctors lost their hospital positions. Some had been persons who had served with distinction overseas, including Major-General J.T. Fotheringham, who was director general of army medical services. The administration of both the University and the hospital were attacked. Colonel Thomas Gibson, a lawyer who had been the assistant deputy minister of overseas forces and was closely involved with the Alumni Association, led the charge, saying that the present governing structure of the University was 'autocratic in the extreme.' Many graduates wanted the alumni to have greater power – by electing a number of the members of the board of governors and by giving the senate, on which graduates were already represented, greater authority over financial matters. 'The control of the University,' Gibson wrote, 'has been divorced not only from politics but also from those who are most directly interested in the University's welfare, namely, the graduate body and the staff.'

The select committee's unanimous report agreed with much of the criticism. The reorganization of the medical faculty, they stated, was 'illegal and unauthorized.' It should have been approved by the cabinet. Moreover, the reorganization, they said, showed a 'regrettable lack of consideration for those whose services were abruptly and irregularly terminated.' The committee recommended that the alumni should be given direct representation on the University's board of governors by being able to elect 8 of its 24 members. Decisions to construct new buildings and to accept major gifts should require the approval of the senate. This discussion foreshadowed that of the 1960s, in which similar criticism of the separation between the board and the senate eventually gave rise to the present unicameral governing structure.

Another issue that has contemporary resonance was the criticism of the gifts by Sir John Eaton and the Rockefeller Foundation. In each case, it was alleged – with some justification – that private donors were controlling the agenda of the University. Not only did the Eatons have a major say in the selection of the holder of the chair, but the gift stipulated that a committee be created to advise the president on the reorganization of the department of medicine. It was also a condition of both gifts that the board should not decrease the amount that had been spent in the two departments, a promise that owing to lack of funds caused the discontinuance of teaching honorariums to most of the clinical teaching staff in the hospitals. The Rockefeller grant required other changes, including improved physical facilities such as new anatomy laboratories and better pathological laboratories.

The legislative select committee recommended that henceforth gifts should not be accepted unless given unconditionally. No change was recommended in the system of funding the University. The cap on succession duties was to be continued, and each year the University would have to appeal to the government for additional support.

One aspect of the University that the select committee liked and wanted to encourage was the department of extension, which had been increasing its activities since its formal establishment as a department in 1920. Lectures outside the formal university structure had been given by the University's professors for decades, but never on a very systematic basis. Falconer deeply believed that Toronto had a role to play outside the ivory tower, and with the election of the United Farmers in 1919 there was a practical need to demonstrate its commitment. There were not only correspondence, summer, and other courses

Robert Falconer in his office in Simcoe Hall in 1929.

for teachers and bank employees, but also lectures for working men and women through the Workers Educational Association, which had been established at Toronto in 1918. Vincent Bladen notes in his memoirs that the classes for workers paid the lecturer a welcome $200 a year, but that the Bankers Association paid an even more welcome $400. After the election of the Farmers, free classes were given to farmers in rural settings. W.J. Dunlop, a teacher at UTS, was appointed full-time director of extension and publicity. The publicity from the extension work, Dunlop wrote, 'did a great deal to propagate the idea that the University is a democratic institution, anxious to serve all the people.' By 1923, there were more than 2,000 persons enrolled in extension courses. Later in the decade, courses were offered in Windsor and Fort William, and diploma courses in both occupational and physical therapy were offered through the extension department. By 1927, 3,000 persons were involved in extension courses.

The United Farmers government never had a chance to implement any of the select committee's recommendations. The day after the report was tabled, an election was called, and in 1923 a Conservative government under Howard Ferguson was elected. The government, Ferguson told the board chairman Edmund Walker, had no intention of implementing the report, even though Ferguson had signed it. The new government did ensure greater alumni representation, however, by enacting that in the future up to eight alumni representatives selected from a list prepared by the Alumni Association would be added to the board when vacancies occurred.

The University had survived the political challenges of the early post-war years. It was now in a position to benefit from a period of stability and a sympathetic provincial government during the rest of the 1920s.

chapter twenty-four

1922

⊷⊶⊷

RESEARCH AND
GRADUATE STUDIES

In early 1922, two important events took place at the University of Toronto: the discovery of insulin and the creation of the School of Graduate Studies. The former established Toronto's international reputation, and some would argue that the combination of the two was the turning point in Toronto's becoming the leading university in Canada. In any event, the University was now in contention with McGill for that honour.

⊷⊶⊷

The first successful injection of insulin was administered to an emaciated 14-year-old charity patient, Leonard Thompson, at the Toronto General Hospital on January 23, 1922. The full story of what led up to this event and its aftermath has been told by the University of Toronto historian Michael Bliss and will only be touched on here. The idea of using a hormone produced by the pancreas to control diabetes had been known for more than thirty years. Many researchers throughout the world had tried to extract such a substance, known as 'insulin' even before its actual 'discovery.' Some had come very close.

In the fall of 1920, Frederick Banting, a young doctor in London, Ontario, thought of a possible technique for extracting the substance from the pancreas of dogs. He went to see J.J. Macleod, the head of physiology at the University of Toronto, from which Banting had graduated in the class of 1917, to see if he could use Toronto facilities to work on his idea. Macleod, a highly respected European-trained Scotsman, had joined the University in 1918, having been a member of the faculty at Western Reserve University in Cleveland since 1903. He was quite willing to let Banting come, even though Banting had no postgraduate training or research experience. Banting had been a mediocre student in his two years as an undergraduate at Victoria College – he had to repeat his first year – and had been only an average student in medical school. (Until the Second World War, anyone with the necessary high school grades or their equivalent could enter medical school at Toronto.) Banting then served as an army surgeon in England and, later, in France, where he was wounded and received the Military Cross. After the war, he took a position at the Hospital for Sick Children with Clarence Starr, with whom he had worked overseas. Banting was not kept on at the Sick Children's, perhaps because he and the physician-in-chief of the hospital, Dr Alan Brown, disliked each other.

Banting came to Toronto in the summer of 1921 and was given facilities on the top floor of the medical school and the use of Macleod's two summer research assistants. The research assistants apparently flipped a coin to see who would start working with Banting. Charles Best won the toss. The other researcher, Clark Noble, was supposed to take over part-way through the summer, but the two later agreed to let Best continue with Banting, a decision that Noble, who became a general practitioner in Toronto, regretted for the rest of his life. The 21-year-old Best started his work with Banting the day after finishing his last exam in the honours program in physiology and biochemistry. Banting and Best worked assiduously over the summer, trying to extract insulin from dogs.

They continued their work in the fall with some involvement from Macleod and with help from a professor from the University of Alberta, James Collip. Collip, who had completed his PhD in 1916 under the supervision of A.B. Macallum, was on leave for the year to work with Macleod. Collip's task was 'to purify the pancreatic extract so that it might be quite safe for use in therapeutic trials.' It 'was only that which any well trained biochemist could be expected to contribute,' he later modestly stated. But his work was crucial to the success of the endeavour. It was Collip who, probably on the evening of January 19, 1922, purified the extract that was to be used. 'I experienced then and there all alone on the top floor of the old Pathology Building,' he later recalled, 'perhaps the greatest thrill it has ever been given me to realize.' The results of the second injection on January 23 in young Leonard Thompson were 'spectacular.'

Frederick Banting, right, and Charles Best on the roof of the medical building with one of the diabetic dogs used in their experiments with insulin. Picture thought to be from the summer of 1921, but dated April 1922 by Banting in his scrapbook.

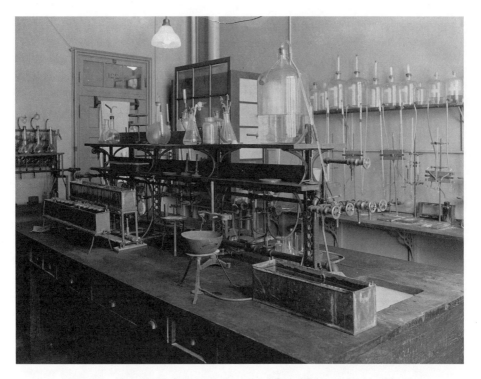

Banting and Best's laboratory on the second floor of the medical building.

On May 3, 1922, Macleod delivered a paper on the work to an important association of physicians in Washington, DC. Banting did not attend. It was greeted with a standing ovation. The paper had the names of the contributors in alphabetical order, starting with Banting, Best, and Collip and ending with Macleod and, finally, Clark Noble, who had been able to work on some later aspects of the discovery. In October 1923, it was announced that Banting and Macleod had been awarded the Nobel Prize in Medicine. Banting was incensed that he was to share the prize with Macleod and not with Best, and had to be dissuaded from turning it down. He was the first Canadian to win a Nobel prize. He split his share with Best, as did Macleod with Collip.

There has been considerable controversy over the years as to who should have received the prize. Bliss rightly takes the position that all four deserve credit for the discovery: 'Insulin emerged in 1921–22 as the result of collaboration among a number of researchers, directed by J.J.R. Macleod, who expanded upon and carried to triumphant success a project initiated by Banting with the help of Best. The single most important technical achievement was that made by Collip

J.J. Macleod, the head of physiology.

James Collip, physiologist, on leave from the
University of Alberta.

in the purification of the extract. On their own, Banting and Best would probably not have reached insulin.' In his 1922 annual report, President Falconer was diplomatically careful to give all four credit: 'This remarkable and now widely known discovery has been due to the persistent and imaginative efforts of Dr. Banting, together with Mr. Best and Dr. Collip, aided by others, chiefly in the Physiological Laboratory, in which Dr. Macleod put his wide knowledge and experience at their disposal.'

The discovery of insulin was, of course, of immense benefit to those suffering from diabetes. One patient, 6-year-old Ted Ryder, weighed only 26 pounds when he first received insulin in July 1922. In 1990 – in his seventies – he attended the ceremony at the University of Toronto at which a plaque was unveiled at the medical school celebrating the discovery of insulin.

Its discovery, however, was a mixed blessing for the University. Until 1941, when Banting was killed in a plane crash in Newfoundland on his way to England, much of the University's medical research was concentrated in his hands, and reportedly he was not a very good scientist. For the next eighteen years he tackled large problems, such as finding the cure for cancer, without success. If he could do it once, he and others thought, he could do it again. Money to support Banting poured into the University. The provincial government gave him $10,000 a year, including a salary of $5,000, for the Banting and Best Chair of Medical Research. The federal government gave him a lifetime annuity of $7,500. Sir William Mulock, who had helped establish the medical school in the 1880s and had just been appointed chief justice of Ontario – assisted by Canon Cody, who had succeeded Edmund Walker as chairman of the board of governors in 1923 – raised more than $500,000 to support the newly established Banting Research Foundation. In 1930, a building, named the Banting Institute, was opened on College Street opposite the Toronto General Hospital. Banting and his staff occupied the top floor of the five-storey building. Some of the researchers, of course, made significant contributions to medical research. 'Banting's only success at the University in these post-insulin years,' Bliss pointedly notes, 'was in continuing to blacken the reputation of J.J.R. Macleod.'

By 1927, Macleod had had enough – he and Banting apparently did not speak to each other – and decided to take a position as professor of physiology at his alma mater, the University of Aberdeen. Collip had returned to Alberta, and in 1928 he took a position at McGill, replacing Macallum, who had joined the McGill faculty in 1920, having completed his term at the National Research Council in Ottawa. Collip continued to do excellent work in endocrinology. Charles Best completed a medical degree at Toronto and went to the University of London for a doctorate, and then returned to teach and conduct research at Toronto. After Macleod left for Scotland in 1928, Best was appointed to the chair of physiology, where he continued to do good work. One of his early successes was in purifying the anticoagulant heparin, which was first used in clinical practice by the surgeon Gordon Murray at the Toronto General Hospital in 1935. Heparin made possible such later procedures as kidney dialysis and open-heart surgery. In 1950, the Best Institute was constructed beside and connected to the Banting Institute. The two buildings are now often referred to collectively as 'the Banting and Best.' Over the years, as Bliss has shown, Best continued to exaggerate his importance in the discovery of insulin, just as Banting had done before him.

On Banting's death in 1941, at the age of 49, Best was appointed to the chair of medical research at the University. For some time, relations between the two had not been good. Just before taking off on the flight across the Atlantic,

Banting is reported to have said: 'This mission is risky. If I don't come back and they give my Chair to that son-of-a bitch Best, I'll never rest in my grave.' Shortly before Banting's death, his good friend John FitzGerald died. FitzGerald had worked with the team to produce insulin. He had founded the School of Hygiene and was dean of medicine in the 1930s. Then, suffering from mental illness and having attempted suicide, he was sent to Connecticut for treatment and was given insulin shock treatments. After returning to Toronto and making another suicide attempt, he was admitted to the Toronto General Hospital, where he managed to hide a knife after a meal and to open an artery in his hip. Undetected by the staff, he bled to death.

A myth developed over the years that scientific medical research came to Toronto *because* of the discovery of insulin. The notion that an inexperienced researcher with an idea, aided by a young research assistant and using what was thought to be inadequate facilities, could come up with a major discovery appealed to the public. It appealed also to many medical practitioners who resented the control the scientific community had exercised over the practice of medicine at Toronto.

In fact, as shown in earlier chapters relating to developments in medicine, the myth is incorrect: the discovery was made *because* of the quality of the staff and facilities. After all, prior to 1922, the medical school and the Toronto General Hospital had developed some of the finest research facilities in the world. The opening of the new medical school building in 1903 and the Toronto General Hospital in 1912 contributed to the University's research potential. The Carnegie Corporation's famous Flexner Report on medical education in the United States and Canada concluded in 1910 that Toronto's laboratory facilities were 'among the best on the continent.' Persons with a sympathy for research, such as Duncan Graham, were appointed as heads of service at the Toronto General Hospital. Excellent researchers such as Macleod and J.P. McMurrich were attracted to Toronto, partly by the good facilities for research and animal quarters. The Connaught Laboratories under the direction of John FitzGerald were ready to assist researchers, and a new anatomy building was in the course of construction, under the guidance of McMurrich.

Scientific research at the University was in a sense held back by the discovery of insulin. In retrospect, says Charles Hollenberg, a former chair of medicine and head of the Banting and Best Diabetes Centre, the University of Toronto would probably have been better off if insulin had been discovered someplace else. Some of the research momentum that had been established was diverted and perhaps lost.

⚜

The establishment of the School of Graduate Studies in May 1922 owed much to J.P. McMurrich. He had become chair of the board of graduate studies in 1919 and had told Falconer before accepting the appointment, 'My endeavour will be to make the Department of Graduate Studies what it seems to me it ought to be, at least equal in rank to any of the other departments of the University.' In 1915, Macallum had brought graduate studies close to that goal by the creation of the board of graduate studies. From his new position as head of the National Research Council, he continued advocating the development of strong graduate schools at Toronto and McGill – 'like an American Graduate School of first rank.' The Cody royal commission of 1921 also advocated increased graduate work and research. 'The Great War,' the commission wrote, 'opened the eyes of the world to the possibility involved in scientific research. By applying the results of science to industry, agriculture and commerce, Germany grew rich and strong.' Charles Saunders, who had developed Marquis wheat, was used as an example of the value of graduate studies and research. 'Marquis Wheat,' one of the submissions to the commission had pointed out, 'has added tens of millions of dollars to the wealth of his native country.' The discovery of insulin the following year made the point even more dramatically, and one week after its discovery was officially announced, the board of governors approved a School of Graduate Studies. McMurrich later was appointed as its first dean.

Some would have gone further. Physicist J.C. McLennan had proposed a scheme in which the new body would be responsible for research as well as graduate studies. The Cody royal commission had made a similar proposal. The scheme, however, was rejected by the senate. When McMurrich retired in 1930, McLennan became dean of the graduate school and once again proposed that research and graduate studies be joined. Once again, his proposal was rejected. Other professors, such as M.C. Boswell of the School of Engineering Research, did not want a central body to control their research agenda. As one writer noted, 'Academic freedom and the liberty of departmental control could not lightly be sacrificed.' Shortly after the rejection of his scheme, McLennan

James Playfair McMurrich, professor of
anatomy, appointed in 1922 as the first dean
of the School of Graduate Studies.

announced his resignation as dean, and he retired to England at the age of 63.
He was succeeded by George Brett of philosophy, who would remain as dean
until his death in 1944.

The numbers of graduate students grew significantly. Only 1 PhD had been
awarded in 1906; in 1932 there were 23, and 131 registered for the degree.
Many of the students were from the west. President Falconer had strongly
advocated attracting such students, 'who will be living links to bind Canada
together.' If they did not come east, he argued, the western students would go to
universities such as Wisconsin and Chicago, and their links would be with the
United States. Graduate fellowships were therefore required to attract students.
Joseph Flavelle, E.B. Osler, and other businessmen, as well as various businesses
such as the Canadian Pacific Railway and Imperial Oil, donated fellowships –
more than 60 were awarded between 1921 and 1932 – primarily for non-
Toronto students. The fellowships were also restricted to students who were not
eligible for National Research Council awards, which had been established
during the war for promising science students in order to build up the country's
relatively poor research potential. Between 1918 and 1932, a total of 70 PhDs
were awarded to doctoral candidates at Toronto who had held National Research
Council awards. The physics department dominated the list of those awards that

went to the University of Toronto; it received 25 awards before 1932, with McLennan supervising 20 of the successful candidates. The next highest number of awards went to chemistry and biology, with 9 each.

The facilities for graduate students and for the dean and his staff, however, were poor. Students complained that they were in a 'somewhat anomalous position,' barred from undergraduate facilities and not members of the faculty. They were, they said, 'a nonentity in the life of the University.' The Graduate Students Union was formed to lobby for better facilities, including a hall of their own, with living accommodations. By 1927, all they had achieved was a common room in the library and a small residence for women graduate students. McMurrich, the dean, was confined to one room in the library, which he shared with the secretary of the school. 'It is exceedingly awkward,' he wrote to Falconer, 'to be interrupted continually by students coming to make inquiries when one is discussing matters concerning the policy, etc. of the School.' It would not be until 1964 that the graduate school would get adequate facilities. As this book was being completed, the first large graduate student residence built for that purpose was opened, at the corner of Spadina Avenue and Harbord Street.

The list of departments willing to take on doctoral students kept expanding. History and English were added, though the two departments were somewhat reluctant. As stated earlier, George Wrong did not think much of the American-style research-oriented PhD. 'If you wish to see an illustration of it,' he wrote to Falconer, 'look at the *History of the CPR* just issued by Innis of our Dept. of Pol. Econ. It is a sound piece of research but it is almost formless in respect to literary quality and the text is overburdened by footnotes to an absurd extent.' The first PhD in history was not awarded until 1925. Between 1915 and 1939, there were only 10 doctorates in history, 9 in English, and 4 in classics. Modern languages had even fewer, with German and French having 3 PhDs each and Italian and Spanish 1 each. (Beatrice Corrigan received her PhD in Italian in 1932 and later became a major force in Italian studies at the University.) But, though few in number, the recipients of Toronto's PhDs played a part in helping to tie the country together, as Falconer had hoped they would. In English, for example, R.K. Gordon, who received a PhD in 1920, taught at the University of Alberta and was head of its English department from 1937 until 1950. Two westerners, Earle Birney and Roy Daniells, completed their doctorates in English in 1936 and later joined the English department at the University of British Columbia, where the latter became the chair of the department in 1947.

The one area in the humanities that continued to attract many students was philosophy, which produced 33 doctorates from 1915 to 1939. In addition, 19 PhDs were awarded in psychology, which had formed its own department in 1927. George Brett's reputation as a major scholar probably helped attract students, as did his headship of the department of philosophy and deanship of the graduate school. The third volume of his acclaimed *History of Psychology* was published in 1921. He was also the founding editor of the *University of Toronto Quarterly*. He was perhaps, said one writer, 'the most learned man in the university.' There were 37 PhDs in philosophy during his deanship and Brett is said to have supervised 20 of them. Among the doctorates he supervised was that of Thomas Goudge, who became chair of the department in 1963.

The Institute of Mediaeval Studies at St Michael's College, which had been established in 1929 and was renamed the Pontifical Institute in 1939, also attracted numerous graduate students who took their degrees in philosophy through the graduate school. Father Henry Carr, the president of St Michael's, invariably had ambitious plans for the college. He brought to the college notable figures such as Sir Bertram Windle, an anthropologist and Catholic writer, W.P.M. Kennedy, then a professor of English literature, and the French philosophers Etienne Gilson and Jacques Maritain. Gilson, a Thomist philosopher from the University of Paris, had been a visiting professor at Harvard and came to St Michael's in 1928 to deliver some lectures. He had wanted to establish a medieval institute and found St Michael's to be the ideal location, physically and intellectually. 'There is the spot!' he wrote. 'The institute will be there or it will be nowhere!' For each of the next ten years – he could not return from France in 1939 because of the war – he spent a term at Toronto. He was aided by Father Carr, also a philosopher, and Father Gerard Phelan, who had started teaching at St Michael's in 1925, having received his PhD from the University of Louvain in Belgium a few years earlier. The Institute attracted scholars from around the world. A.C. Pegis, for example, came to the Institute from Fordham University, and did his doctoral work under Gilson, Phelan, and Maritain. Although never formally a constituent part of the University, the Institute clearly added an important dimension to Toronto's growing international reputation.

There were relatively few PhDs in the social sciences. From 1915 until 1939, only about 10 PhDs were awarded in political economy, which then included sociology. Two PhD graduates from 1938 had a particular influence on future graduate studies at the University. W.T. Easterbrook was head of the department

George Brett, professor of philosophy, the successor to John McLennan as dean of the graduate school in 1933 and dean until his death in 1944.

The French philosopher Etienne Gilson, the prime mover for the establishment of the Institute of Mediaeval Studies. Photograph taken in 1929.

The Institute, on the left, was renamed the Pontifical Institute of Mediaeval Studies in 1939; Teefy Hall is on the right.

from 1961 to 1970 and oversaw a major growth in graduate studies. Similarly, S.D. Clark, whose doctorate on the Canadian Manufacturers' Association was supervised by Harold Innis and Alexander Brady, became head of sociology when it was made a separate department in 1963. It is surprising that more doctorates were not awarded in political economy between the wars. Important scholars such as Innis, Alexander Brady, and W.P.M. Kennedy (who switched from English to history and then to political economy and would later switch to law) were hired in the early 1920s, and all had doctorates.

Perhaps the slow growth in the doctoral program in political economy was due to the demands of the undergraduate programs, which included commerce and finance. The number of undergraduate students in political economy kept increasing. E.J. Urwick became its head in 1927, after R.M. MacIver left for a distinguished career in sociology at Columbia University. Urwick, a 60-year-old Englishman, had come to Canada after retiring from his position as professor of social philosophy at the University of London, and earlier had been head of the London School of Sociology, the predecessor of the London School of Economics. Falconer, with MacIver's support, invited him to become the head of the department. Under his guidance, political economy became the largest academic department in the University, thereby forcing a move in 1933 to the larger quarters in McMaster Hall on Bloor Street, where the department remained until Sidney Smith Hall was built in the early 1960s.

Most of the doctorates between the wars were in science and medicine. Excellent research, which attracted large numbers of graduate students, was being done by persons we have already encountered, such as W.A. Parks in geology and B.A. Bensley, A.G. Huntsman, and E.M. Walker in zoology. When Bensley pointed out to Falconer shortly after the discovery of insulin that good work was also being done in other departments deserving of support, Falconer's reply was 'Ah, yes, but they do not have the same advertising value.' One of Walker's students in entomology, Carl Atwood, received his PhD in 1937 and joined the zoology department. (Atwood's son, Harold, would become a distinguished member of the same department and, like Macallum, later move to physiology in the faculty of medicine. Atwood's daughter Margaret, the acclaimed author, is one of the University's most illustrious graduates.) Two members of the department of botany had a significant number of graduate students. Herbert Jackson, who came from Purdue University, was a world authority on rust and fungi that attacked plants, and later was head of botany, attracted many graduate students. D.L. Bailey, also an expert on plant rust, came in 1928 from the Dominion Rust Research Laboratory. When he retired in 1964, some 50 plant pathologists had attained their PhDs under his guidance.

The basic sciences in medicine continued to produce good research and to attract numerous graduate students. Biochemistry produced 30 PhDs, physiology 20, and bacteriology 17. Banting does not appear to have supervised any doctoral students. Best did. There was relatively little experimental research in the clinical departments. The reputation of the medical school continued to be strong, however, in part because of the many standard texts produced. Among them were texts by persons already encountered, such as Macleod, McMurrich, and Best. Others that could be added were by William Boyd in pathology and J.C.B. Grant in anatomy. Post-graduate studies were available in some of the clinical departments, but not the PhD degree. Surgery established a master's in surgery, and diplomas were available in radiology and psychiatry. A diploma in public health had been introduced before the war.

There were other professional graduate degrees in the University. Education produced a very large number of DPaed degrees. The president's report for 1924–5, for example, states that there were 57 candidates for DPaed degrees compared with only 69 PhD candidates in the rest of the University, and 139 for MAs. Teachers obviously wanted to improve their qualifications for possible advancement in their profession. There were also master's degrees in other faculties, such as dentistry and forestry. Engineering had established a master of applied science degree in 1913, and most of the students taking the degree received funds to act as research assistants from the research funds given each year to the School of Engineering Research. A master of architecture – architecture was then part of engineering – was established in 1922, the year Eric Arthur arrived from England. He used funds from the School of Engineering Research to begin his inventory and analysis of historic architecture in Ontario. Chemical engineering was the first engineering department to offer the PhD, and 8 of the 12 PhDs awarded in engineering before the Second World War were in chemical engineering.

Physics was responsible for the most doctorates in the University between the wars; they were supervised principally by McLennan and, after he left in 1932, by E.F. Burton. There was a great amount of research productivity in the department, and McGill's pre-eminence in physics under Rutherford passed to Toronto. Elizabeth Allin, one of McLennan's PhD graduates – 3 of McLennan's women graduate students received doctorates – described his morning visits to see what progress had been made. 'Each morning,' she wrote, 'McLennan, accompanied by the head of the workshop, the glassblower, and often a junior staff member, visited the site of the experiment of each of his graduate students, to enquire what, if any, progress had been made, what difficulties had been encountered and how it was proposed to overcome these. The initial query was: "What's new". It was unwise to have nothing to discuss since this was regarded as evidence of lack of endeavour.' She obviously made good progress because she joined the department in 1930 and remained there until her retirement in 1970.

McLennan had a number of areas of research. One was spectroscopy, that is, the study of the spectra of atoms and molecules, on which he started work in 1910. One of the students who worked with him in this area was Harry Welsh, who received his PhD in 1936. Welsh himself would supervise about 65 PhD students, including Boris Stoicheff, who received his PhD in 1950 and at the time of writing continues to work on lasers in the physics department. A number of Stoicheff's own graduate students have positions in Toronto and across North America in physics, electrical engineering, and chemistry.

Another area of research for which Toronto became well known was 'low temperature physics,' which facilitates the study of atoms and other particles. Helium was important in achieving low temperatures. At the end of the Great War, McLennan had access to large quantities of helium gas, which he was producing for balloons and similar lighter-than-air vehicles. If liquid helium could be produced, it would be possible to create the desired low temperatures. In 1923, liquid helium was successfully produced by McLennan's team. He and his students could now study matter under conditions approaching absolute zero.

McLennan also had great success through the work of one of his former doctoral students, Gordon Shrum, in determining the composition of the 'green line' of the Northern Lights. The composition of all the other colours had been identified by other scientists, but this one could not be identified. By combining the two fields of spectroscopy and low temperature physics, the Toronto team was able to identify it. It turned out to be caused by oxygen rather than nitrogen, as others had thought. McLennan was awarded the Gold Medal of the Royal Society for the discovery. Shrum went on to head the department of physics at UBC from 1938 to 1961. The first PhD at UBC was in physics, and by the time Shrum left the department there were 84 graduate students in physics. At least one prominent scientist has claimed, according to Shrum's autobiography, that 'if McLennan had been more popular with other scientists at the time, he would probably have received a Nobel prize for the discovery' of the green line's composition. Although no faculty member of the physics department has received a Nobel prize as yet, three of its graduates have: Arthur Schawlow in 1981, Bertram Brockhouse in 1994, and Walter Kohn in 1998.

When McLennan left for England, Burton further enhanced the reputation of the department by constructing, with the help of a number of graduate students, the first practical electron microscope, a high resolution instrument using an electron beam, which allowed the study of substances not visible with ordinary microscopes. McLennan's legacy continued at Toronto and elsewhere. Burton and others took over McLennan's work on low temperature physics and superconductivity, and M.F. Crawford, another of McLennan's PhDs, became the leader in spectroscopy.

The chemistry department was less successful in leaving a legacy of important research, although prior to the Second World War, it had produced 34 doctorates – the second-highest number in the University. Lash Miller, the head of the department, was a dynamic, ambitious person, not unlike McLennan, with whom he did not get along. There were bad feelings between them in part because of an allegation in the early 1900s that McLennan unfairly had given a graduate fellowship to one of his own students. Miller was said to be the 'the most distinguished, the most colorful, and the best-known chemist in Canada.' When the Sterling Laboratory at Yale opened in 1923, Miller was selected as 'one of the seven greatest chemists of the world' who were invited to give addresses.

A serious problem, however, was that Miller did not believe in atomic theory. 'Don't get involved with those fellows ... in chemistry,' McLennan warned Shrum, 'they don't know atoms exist.' Miller had received two doctorates in Germany, one from Munich and a second from Ostwald's laboratory in Leipzig. Ostwald was a follower of what was called 'Gibbsian thermodynamics,' named after the renowned J. Willard Gibbs of Yale, who published in the 1870s and 1880s. Gibbs, Ostwald, and Miller were all prominent and outspoken sceptics concerning the reality of atoms and molecules. In 1912, however, Ostwald changed his view. Unfortunately, Miller and his successor as head of the department, F.B. Kenrick, did not. Moreover, they ensured that atomic theory was omitted from high school teaching in Ontario. As late as 1935, a text written by a University of Toronto professor and approved for use by the province made only passing reference to atomic theory. 'Chemistry students at the University of Toronto,' W.A.E. McBryde, a student of the history of chemistry, has written, 'learned their discipline virtually without benefit of an atomic theory, or the new ideas made possible by that theory concerning the structure of molecules or condensed matter, or concerning the influence of molecular structure on the speed or outcome of chemical reactions.' Miller's research over a twenty-year period was into 'the nutrient substances essential for the growth and reproduction of micro-organisms.' This 'holy grail,' McBryde wrote, 'represented an investment of time and effort too costly in proportion to the meagre and probably now inconsequential results that it yielded.' The failure to use atomic theory probably did not affect most graduates, who were otherwise very well trained, but it certainly affected research in the department. It was not until after the war and the appointment of a new head, Andrew Gordon, that the 'chemistry department began a gradual process of renewal and expansion' to reach the strong position it occupies today.

⁓

In 1927, the University celebrated the hundredth anniversary of its founding. There was a feeling of pride in the strength of the University and optimism about its future. Insulin had been discovered. Major studies had been published. A year after the celebrations, Falconer, still enthusiastic, wrote to Premier Howard Ferguson, 'Evidence of the esteem in which the University … is held was shown at the celebrations of the Centenary a year ago, to which 250 delegates came from all over the civilised world.'

chapter twenty-five

1926

GOOD YEARS

The second half of the 1920s brought good years to the University of Toronto. Premier Howard Ferguson's Conservatives treated the University well. The situation was helped by the fact that Canon Cody, the chairman of the board of governors, had very close relations with the government. Cody's good friend and college roommate, Ferguson, had appointed him to the position in 1923, after Sir Edmund Walker stepped down. Some thought Cody's influence with the provincial government was greater than that of any cabinet minister. The economy was performing well – between 1926 and 1929 the gross national product increased by 20 per cent, while prices generally declined. Between 1925 and 1930, the annual grant to the University was increased from a little over $1,500,000 to over $2 million, and it seemed likely that the University would continue to thrive. Ferguson was re-elected in 1929 with a landslide victory, which Cody helped bring about by an important supportive radio address the night before the election. In the same month as the election victory, however, the stock market crashed, signalling the onset of a worldwide depression.

But in the second half of the decade, the University was full of optimism. It was still basking in the glow of the Nobel prize, for insulin. The graduate school was attracting students from across the country. The sciences, particularly under the influence of physicist John McLennan, were adding lustre to the University, and the social sciences, with such names as Urwick, MacIver, and that of the young Harold Innis, were gaining in stature.

Convocation, June 1925.

Furthermore, the humanities were very strong in both teaching and scholarship, a strength the coming depression would not seriously affect. Although three prominent department heads who had joined the faculty in the 1880s retired during the second half of the 1920s – W.J. Alexander in English in 1926, George Wrong in history in 1927, and Maurice Hutton in classics in 1928 – all three departments remained vibrant.

Alexander had had a profound effect on the teaching of English at the University. His student the Renaissance scholar Malcolm Wallace – the principal of University College from 1928 until 1944 – replaced him as head of English at University College. In 1928, another Toronto graduate, the seventeenth-century specialist A.S.P. Woodhouse, was appointed after serving five years at the University of Manitoba. He would become head of the University College department in 1944 and would exert a major influence on English studies at the University until his retirement in 1964. In his autobiography, *Halfway up Parnassus*, Claude Bissell notes that the department was 'at the height of its powers' when he came to University College in 1930. 'I suspect,' he wrote, 'that rarely on this continent has there been assembled in one place a group of teachers of such diverse and splendid power.' He mentions, among others, the Toronto graduate E.K. Brown, who later became a professor of English at the University of Chicago, Mossie May Kirkwood, who later would move to Trinity College to become head of St Hilda's College, and his PhD supervisor, Herbert Davis, an Oxford-trained Englishman, who became head of English at Cornell. Bissell followed him there, and thus received in 1940 a Cornell rather than a Toronto doctorate.

Alexander's influence was felt also at Victoria, where his student Oscar Pelham Edgar was head of the department, which included the poet E.J. Pratt. Kathleen Coburn and Northrop Frye studied under Pelham Edgar, and both have given him credit for influencing their careers. Coburn writes about Pelham Edgar's fourth year course on English Romantic poetry in the spring of 1928. He introduced the class to Coleridge, she says in her autobiography, *In Pursuit of Coleridge*, and 'to the whole business of the imagination, for me a first glimmering notion, the first articulation of something felt but never expressed. A turning point.' The English department, she says, was not 'prepared to take on a thesis dealing with Coleridge's philosophical ideas. Would I not switch to Wordsworth?' She wanted Coleridge. Fortunately, the philosopher and graduate school dean George Brett was interested in the functioning of the imagination and was prepared to supervise her post-graduate work. She later discovered, deciphered, and, in 1949, published Coleridge's notebooks, the research for which she is best known. The husband-and-wife team of Robin and Heather Jackson, both members of the English department, have now completed a number of volumes in the projected thirty-volume series of the *Collected Works of Samuel Taylor Coleridge*, of which Coburn was the general editor.

Similarly, Northrop Frye was influenced by Pelham Edgar. Frye wrote a paper in 1932–3 on William Blake for Pelham Edgar's eighteenth-century course, and, in Frye's words, he 'was hooked.' He dedicated his great work on Blake, *Fearful Symmetry*, published in 1947, to Pelham Edgar. Perhaps no one at the University of Toronto has cast a longer shadow than Frye, who died in 1991. At present, the University of Toronto Press is publishing his collected works, predicted to number thirty-five volumes. His notebooks are being deciphered by a team of scholars, just as Coleridge's were by Coburn.

Other departments in the humanities, such as modern languages (with, for example, Barker Fairley and Hermann Boeschenstein in German, Dana Rouillard and Robert Finch in French, and Emilio Goggio and Milton Buchanan in Italian and Spanish) and Near Eastern studies (William Taylor, T.J. Meek, and F.V. Winnett) were also a source of pride for the University. Classics was particularly noteworthy. Few classics departments in North America could rival the combined strength of the college classics departments. At Victoria College, there was Eric Havelock, appointed in 1929, who became a professor of classics at Harvard after the war and later the chair of the Harvard and, still later, the Yale classics departments. He is noted for his 'bold remapping of early Greek intellectual history' and, in line with work being done by Innis, theories of communication. At Trinity, George Grube – like Havelock, a Cambridge graduate – was appointed in 1928 and, like Havelock, published widely on Greek philosophers. Also like Havelock, he was involved in various left-wing controversies, as we will see in the next chapter. University College had two distinguished classicists during this period, Gilbert Norwood – another Cambridge classicist – who came in 1928 as Hutton's successor, and Charles Cochrane – an Oxford graduate – whose great work, *Christianity and Classical Culture*, was published in 1940.

Wrong was succeeded in 1927 as head of history by Chester Martin, who had been at Manitoba for the previous twenty years and would remain as head at Toronto until 1953. Like Wrong's, his interest was in Canadian history. A Rhodes scholar from the Maritimes, he published *Empire and Commonwealth: Studies in Governance and Self-Government in Canada* in 1929. Other Oxford-trained historians were appointed, including Donald Creighton, Frank Underhill, and Donald McDougall, a Rhodes scholar who had lost his sight serving overseas during the war. The historians continued to look to Oxford, just as the classicists tended to look to Cambridge. Openings had developed at Toronto because a number of historians had entered the foreign service. Canada's more independent policy after the war required the acquisition of talent in foreign affairs. Toronto became a breeding ground for public servants. George Wrong's son, Hume, and Lester Pearson both joined the Department of External Affairs. W.P.M. Kennedy had advised Pearson that his future was in government and not in the academic world, where he would have to compete with scholars such as Creighton and Innis.

An exception to the stream of Oxford historians was George Brown, who had a Chicago PhD. Brown took over the running of the *Canadian Historical Review* in 1930 and would later become editor at the University of Toronto Press. He also had the distinction of writing what may still be the best-selling book by any Toronto academic. His *Building the Canadian Nation*, written for high school use, sold more than 600,000 copies. The librarian Stewart Wallace, whose text *A First Book of Canadian History* sold a little more than 500,000 copies, is the runner up. (Neither, however, could touch the University of Toronto alumnus Charles Gordon, a Presbyterian minister, who wrote under the name Ralph Connor. Some claim that the total sales of his books during his lifetime reached 30 million copies. His *Sky Pilot*, published in 1899, alone sold over a million copies.) Brown's sales can be contrasted with the 1930 publication of Innis' *Fur Trade in Canada*, which sold only 136 copies in its first year, but has since then become a classic and, over the years and through more than one edition, has sold many copies.

W.P.M. Kennedy left the department of history in 1926 for political economy, with which he had been associated for a number of years as a special lecturer on federal institutions. MacIver, the head of political economy, wanted to develop the law side of the department, and the head of history, George Wrong, was upset – according to Father E.J. McCorkell, who had taught with Kennedy at St Michael's – that Kennedy had married one of his history students. Kennedy was not, in fact, a lawyer and had no legal training. His interest in the intricacies of constitutional law stemmed from his early study of sixteenth-century ecclesiastical history. As the political scientist Alexander Brady has written, 'His earlier explorations in ecclesiastical law and institutions exhibited the special bent of his mind, which in Canada found in the constitution a new and fascinating theme.' Kennedy was an 'impressive scholar.' By the end of the 1920s, he had written ten books. He was also a sparkling teacher. J.J. Robinette, one of Canada's greatest lawyers, who was taught by Kennedy in the 1920s, recalled that 'Kennedy was one of those brilliant Irishmen who could dazzle you ... a performer as much as a teacher.'

A number of lawyers were appointed to political economy. N.A.M. ('Larry') MacKenzie, a Maritimer who would become an accomplished international law scholar and, later, the president of UNB and then UBC, was hired in 1926, and the following year an honours program in law was introduced in political economy. Kennedy kept expanding the scope of the program. At first, the law portion was introduced only after second year, and then after first year. A department of law was established under the wing of political economy in 1930, which would become an independent School of Law in 1941. These programs

W.P.M. Kennedy, dean of law.

Jacob Finkelman, appointed a lecturer in law
in 1930 and an assistant professor in 1934.
He was the first Jew to be appointed to
the full-time professoriate at the
University of Toronto.

attracted some of the best students in the University. Apart from Robinette, there were G. Arthur Martin, thought by many to be Canada's greatest criminal lawyer, William Howland and Charles Dubin, both distinguished chief justices of Ontario, Sydney Robins, later the treasurer of the Law Society and a member of the Ontario Court of Appeal, Moffat Hancock, who joined the faculty and later became a noted professor of law at Stanford University, Bora Laskin, the chief justice of Canada, and many more. Their later success was disproportionate to their relatively small number. Perhaps they were inspired by Kennedy's view that legal education should 'create a body of citizens endowed with an insight into law as the basic social science, and capable of making those examinations into its workings as will redeem it from being a mere trade and technique and ... make it the finest of all instruments in the service of mankind.'

Jacob Finkelman, who had graduated from the honour law program, was appointed a lecturer in 1930. Kennedy pressed Falconer to appoint him, saying, 'Our opinion of him coincides with that of Dean Sidney Smith [of Dalhousie law school] that he is a man of first class mind.' He noted that Finkelman 'is a

Hebrew' and added, 'As far as I am concerned this is no objection.' Nor would it have been to Falconer, says his biographer James Greenlee, noting that Falconer 'was among the least anti-Semitic types of his generation.' Before he was appointed, however, according to Finkelman's later recollection, he had to meet the head of political economy, the dean of arts, and the dean of the graduate school, as well as Cody, the chairman of the board. After his appointment, Larry MacKenzie asked him if he was 'surprised at the number of people you saw before you were appointed to the staff of the university.' 'No, I wasn't,' Finkelman replied, 'I assumed that an appointment to the staff of the university is a very important thing and that you would have to go through seeing, being interviewed by various people.' 'Nonsense,' said MacKenzie, 'Kennedy wanted to make sure that anyone who had anything to do with your appointment knew that you were Jewish ... that when he recommended promotion, you would get the promotion and there would be no difficulty about that.' In 1934, Finkelman was promoted to assistant professor, without difficulty. Finkelman was the first Jew appointed to a full-time position at the University.

⸎

The 1920s were good years for sports and culture at the University. During the decade, writes Bruce Kidd, an Olympic runner and now dean of the faculty of physical education and health, 'U of T athletes – both men and women – captured virtually every honour they sought.' The men won Allan and Grey Cup championships in hockey and football, Olympic medals in hockey and rowing, and intercollegiate championships in every sport in which there was competition. The women won the very first intercollegiate championships ever held in Canada – in basketball and hockey – and, according to Kidd, 'contributed significantly to the legitimation of energetic sport for women in the community.' Kidd observed that not only were they excellent athletes, but 'some of the most prominent student athletes went on to distinguished careers in medicine, law, journalism, and the public service.' Hockey, football, and, to a lesser extent, rowing were the most popular spectator sports at the time.

There is no question that the men's hockey teams produced in the 1920s were outstanding. They won every intercollegiate title from 1920 until 1929. In 1921, they won the Allan Cup as the best amateur team in Canada, defeating Brandon, Manitoba. In 1925, the Varsity team was again in the Allan Cup finals, but lost to Port Arthur. Virtually the same players made up the 1926 Varsity team, and it was expected they would easily capture the intercollegiate title against Queen's and McGill – which they did – and possibly win another Allan Cup. At the end of the season, their intercollegiate dominance was demonstrated once again – in total they had scored 42 goals and allowed only 13. Toronto then played against the American intercollegiate champions, Dartmouth, at the new Madison Square Garden, easily winning the international intercollegiate title 6–1.

The Toronto team once again would face Port Arthur for the Allan Cup. Joseph 'Stonewall' Sullivan, a member of U of T's Sports Hall of Fame, was goalie. A medical student, he later became a distinguished ear, nose, and throat specialist, a member of the University of Toronto board of governors, and, in 1957, a member of the Canadian Senate. Captain Lou Hudson, Hugh Plaxton, 'Red' Porter, and Dave Trottier were leading scorers for Toronto. It would be the best of three games. The first two were played in Montreal. Port Arthur won the first, and Toronto the second. The final game was played in Toronto at the Mutual Street Arena – Varsity Arena would not be completed until later that year. Plaxton scored a goal within the first fifteen seconds. At the end of the first period, Varsity was ahead 3–0. At the end of regulation time, however, the teams were tied 3–3, and still tied after three ten-minute overtime periods. There would have to be another deciding game. Once again, the game ended in a tie – 2–2 – but with four minutes left in the second overtime period, Port Arthur beat Sullivan and won the cup. 'It was,' said *Torontonensis*, 'the greatest Championship series ever played in Canada.'

Most of the members of the team graduated that year and formed themselves into the Varsity Grads, which competed in the 1928 Olympics in St Moritz, Switzerland. The team, writes the historian of sports T.A. Reed, was 'probably the most powerful hockey aggregation that ever wore the "Blue and White."' Observers called them 'the greatest hockey team ever seen in Europe.' It easily won the gold medal. No other team in the finals came close. It beat Sweden 11–0, Switzerland 13–0, and Great Britain 14–0. It was during the Olympics that goalie Sullivan received the nickname 'Stonewall.' At a dinner at Hart House on their return, the head of the Canadian Olympic Committee said that when he was in Europe, people would ask him, 'Is this the same university which has produced Dr. Banting?'

Although women had played interfaculty hockey at the University since 1901,

The 'Varsity Grads' Olympic hockey team, undefeated at the Winter Olympics,
St Moritz, 1928.

The women's intercollegiate hockey team, 1926. Marion Hilliard, later a well-known medical
doctor at Women's College Hospital, is second from the right.

the first intercollegiate game was in 1922, when McGill challenged Toronto to a match to be played following the women's intercollegiate basketball tournament. (The women's basketball team dominated intercollegiate basketball in the 1920s, winning 7 of the 10 championships.) The hockey game was played in Toronto at the Mutual Street Arena – and Toronto won. Queen's then joined the league, but McGill dropped out. So future championship matches were between Toronto and Queen's. The 1925 match was in Kingston, and Toronto won 1–0. Marion Hilliard, an original inductee into the University's Sports Hall of Fame, scored the winning goal after a scramble in front of the Queen's net. Hilliard, who had played on all the teams since 1922 and was also the University's women's tennis champion, was in first year medicine, having graduated from Victoria College the previous year. Her later career in medicine brought her fame as head of obstetrics and gynaecology at Women's College Hospital and the author of a best-selling book, *A Woman Doctor Looks at Love and Life.* The hockey games were played aggressively and allowed body checking. Thora McIlroy, the goalie, later recalled: 'We had arm and leg pads and, as the goalie on the team, I wore a chest protector. That was about it. We had no dressing rooms, no showers, no face masks and no indoor ice.' The 1925 team also won the Ontario Ladies Hockey League – without suffering a loss. Toronto won all but one of the championship matches for the rest of the decade. Queen's dropped out in 1934–5, however, and intercollegiate women's hockey would not be resumed until after the war.

Men's rowing was also a prominent sport in the 1920s. The Varsity eight-oared crew won a silver medal in the 1924 Olympics in Paris. Much of the credit for the success of rowing during this period was due to T.R. 'Tommy' Loudon – the son of the physicist W.J. Loudon. His great-uncle, also Tommy Loudon – a brother of President James Loudon – had been a champion rower, but lost the Canadian individual sculling championship to the great Ned Hanlan in 1873. A University team was first successfully organized in 1897, coached by Hanlan. While he was an engineering student, Tommy Loudon's small size – he weighed only 135 pounds – prevented him from competing, but in 1904 he was asked to cox the Argonaut Rowing Club's senior heavyweight eight, which he did for the next ten years. After the war, when he had become a professor of engineering, he coached the re-established team, made up mainly of returned veterans. Loudon himself had been wounded at Passchendaele. His knowledge of mechanics helped him to adopt a scientific approach to rowing. He even designed a boat

The Varsity eight-man crew, practising on the Toronto waterfront in May 1924, shortly before participating in the Paris Olympics. Note that the Toronto Harbour Commission building on the far right is directly on the waterfront, and that the then tallest building in Toronto is the twenty-one-storey building still standing on the north-east corner of King and Yonge streets that at the time was the Royal Bank building.

that could handle the swells of Lake Ontario more effectively. The crew Loudon coached, made up of students, alumni, and a biology professor, Alan Coventry, won the Royal Canadian Henley Regatta in St Catharines for the four-year period from 1920 to 1923. The 1924 team did not compete at Henley because it had already been chosen to represent Canada at the Olympics.

The final Olympic race took place on July 17 on the Seine outside Paris. 'Fighting their way from the back of the field,' writes sports historian Patrick Okens, 'they passed first the Italians and, by the thousand meter mark, the British eight. The Yale crew was, however, in a class by itself and although the Varsity men extended their lead on the other boats, they were unable to catch up.' One of the members of the crew, R.S. Hunter, later wrote, 'Yale was a great crew but they were not 15 3/5th seconds better than we should have been.' Perhaps, as some said, it was dysentery, possibly caused by drinking tap water. The Americans had brought their own water to Europe.

Rowing continued to attract great interest in Canada. McGill organized a team and for the next ten years, starting in 1926, competed against Toronto in an Oxford and Cambridge–style event. McGill won the first race on the Lachine

Canal in Montreal and the second on the Toronto waterfront. Most of the future races were on the Lachine Canal on the same weekend as the McGill Redmen and Toronto Blues football game. Toronto won all the subsequent races, until McGill's club was disbanded in 1936. Rowing would not appear again as an intercollegiate sport until the 1960s. Women's rowing at Varsity would not appear until the 1970s and would produce such competitors as the Olympic medal winners Kay Worthington and Emma Robinson.

One of the more powerful members of the Olympic rowing team was medical student Warren Snyder. He was also a star rugby football player who played for seven seasons with the Blues – from 1920 to 1926. The 1920 team – coached by Hamilton ('Laddie') Cassels, who later became the solicitor of the University – defeated the Argos 16–3 for the Grey Cup. From 1922 to 1925, however, Queen's was the intercollegiate champion. In 1926, Toronto had a potentially winning team, which contained four future U of T Sports Hall of Fame members, including Snyder. One was the scholarship winner Donald Carrick, who was also an Olympic boxer and the Canadian amateur golfing champion. He would be the runner-up to Lionel Conacher for the Canadian male athlete of the half century. Another was 'Hec' Crighton, who later rewrote the amateur football rule book and refereed a record 16 Grey Cup games. In 1925, Chrighton had captained Varsity's junior team, coached by Lester Pearson. Interest in the 1926 team was high. There were long line-ups for season tickets. Varsity Stadium had been enlarged in 1924 to seat 19,000 persons. (The rowing coach, Tommy Loudon, a structural engineer, had designed the new bleachers, just as he would later design the new Varsity Arena.)

Toronto defeated Queen's for the intercollegiate championship in late November 1926 before a 'record-breaking, noisy, jostling crowd' at Varsity Stadium. Toronto would now meet the Ottawa Senators on December 4 at Varsity Stadium for the Grey Cup. The temperature hovered around 0°F (about –18°C). The field, the *Globe* reported, was 'coated with snow with a gale of biting wind prevailing from the north.' The ball was a 'cake of ice.' Foster Hewitt, who broadcast the game from the roof of the stadium, 'was bundled in an aviator's helmet, sweaters, coat and overshoes, and he had two oil stoves beside him.' 'At the end of the game,' he said, 'I was positively frozen. I couldn't move.' It was too cold for cheerleaders or bands. The game, however, went on. The outcome was in doubt until the final play. Toronto lost 10–7. There has been, the *Globe* reported the next day, 'much better but not more thrilling football.'

The 1920s were clearly golden years for men's athletics. Interest in intercollegiate sports would continue during the depression, with football games attracting as many as 20,000 spectators. Football star Warren Stevens – he threw the first touchdown pass in Canadian Grey Cup history – would be appointed full-time director of men's athletics in 1932 and would coach senior football, basketball, and hockey. Stevens was instrumental in establishing the School of Physical and Health Education in 1940, the first such degree program in the Commonwealth. He would remain a dominant figure in men's athletics until his retirement in 1970. The new athletic centre built in 1979 is named after him.

~❧~

The cultural life of the University also improved in the 1920s. To a great extent, this expansion was due to Hart House, with its art, music, and drama. It was also due in part to one key addition to the university community – Ernest MacMillan. In 1926, he conducted Bach's *St Matthew Passion* in Convocation Hall for the first time – the composer and faculty member Healy Willan played the continuo parts on the organ – a performance that would be repeated annually for many years. In the same year, MacMillan became head of the Toronto Conservatory of Music, and several months later he was appointed dean of the faculty of music, after the death of A.S. Vogt, who also had held both positions. The University had taken over the conservatory – the largest in the British Empire and one of several affiliated with the University – in 1919 and at about the same time had established a faculty of music, which shared the conservatory building on the south-west corner of College Street and University Avenue. The conservatory would handle diplomas, and the faculty would be responsible for academic degrees.

MacMillan would have a remarkable career as dean of the faculty until 1952, when he was succeeded by Boyd Neel. He would also be the permanent conductor of the Toronto Symphony Orchestra for twenty-five years as well as of the Toronto Mendelssohn Choir for fifteen. He had been a child prodigy; he had played the organ at Massey Hall at the age of 10. Before the war, he had been assistant organist at Convocation Hall while a history student at the University. In the summer of 1914, he had gone to the Wagner festival in Bayreuth, Germany, but the outbreak of war forced him to spend the next four years in a civilian internment camp. His biographer, Ezra Schabas, later the principal of

Ernest MacMillan, in 1926, shortly after his appointment as dean of the faculty of music and head of the Toronto Conservatory of Music.

the conservatory, has described MacMillan's active musical life in the 4,000-man prison camp, Ruhleben, which included thirteen performances of *The Mikado*, the music of which had to be reconstructed from memory. MacMillan also received an earned Oxford doctorate for the secular oratorio he composed in the camp – *England: An Ode*, based on a Swinburne poem. The work was performed by the Mendelssohn Choir at Massey Hall in 1921.

As principal of the conservatory, MacMillan organized a choir to sing with the conservatory orchestra. At the inaugural concert in 1928, he conducted Mozart's *Requiem*. He also introduced opera at the conservatory: Humperdinck's *Hansel and Gretel* at the Regent Theatre in 1928 and Purcell's *Dido and Aeneas* the following year at Hart House Theatre. Opera, however, would be a victim of the depression. In 1929, he organized a rival to the Hart House String Quartet, the Conservatory String Quartet, which included the later Toronto Symphony Orchestra concertmaster Eli Spivak. It will be recalled that during his time in Toronto before the war, the psychiatrist Ernest Jones had complained to Sigmund

Women undergraduates in front of University College, 1928.

Freud, 'Music is rare here.' If he had remained in Toronto, what would he have said now?

The historian Brian McKillop has carefully combed the *Varsity* and other sources to help determine whether University of Toronto students in the 1920s were like those depicted in some of F. Scott Fitzgerald's novels. He concludes that they were not, and that academic life 'reflected a reality significantly removed from that of flappers and gin flasks.' Indeed, there seemed to be less drinking than shortly after the war. Students, he argues, 'were neither morally out of control nor in revolt against a meaningless past.' As historian Paul Axelrod states, 'Student Life in the 1920s was more frequently characterized by seriousness, morality, intimacy, and compliance with authority,' although 'the degree of deference ... could be easily overstated.'

Two controversies involving the *Varsity* illustrate this lack of deference in some segments of the student population. In 1929, the *Varsity* editor had written an editorial on 'petting' after a clergyman had condemned it at a Student Christian Movement meeting in Hart House. 'It is not for undergraduates to contradict a man whose experience of the world has been so much greater than their own,' the editor, L.J. Ryan, wrote, 'but in the light of our close connection with the younger generation who are thus accused of debasing their souls, we should like to attempt an explanation of our generation and of its actions.' 'Petting as an institution,' the editorial stated irreverently, 'has come to be recognized by all who are not wilfully blind to existing conditions.' The board of governors was incensed and, according to the *Varsity*, wanted the editor fired. The Students' Administrative Council eventually dismissed Ryan. A few years later, in 1931, another editor, Andrew Allan, made the mistake of claiming that 'practical atheism' was prominent on the campus. He was suspended by SAC, and the university disciplinary body, the Caput, suspended the *Varsity* for the remainder of the year. The administration tried to keep a fairly tight rein on the public expression of students' opinions, just as they would on the public expression of controversial opinions by members of the faculty, as we will see in the next chapter.

Nevertheless, the University in the late 1920s and early 1930s was a remarkable institution. Claude Bissell called the University he attended in the early 1930s a 'great good place' – from the title of a Henry James short story about an ideal world. The University attracted and inspired an excellent group of students. Out of 18 Rhodes scholarships awarded to Ontario students between 1928 and 1936, 16 were to University of Toronto students. Many of the names are still well known – the academics Moffat Woodside and Gordon Skilling, the writer Lionel Gelber, the politician E.B. Jolliffe, the Commonwealth secretary Arnold Smith, and the diplomat and provost of Trinity College George Ignatieff.

chapter twenty-six

1931

⁂

DEPRESSING TIMES

In January 1931, 68 University of Toronto professors sent a public letter to the press, protesting against the action of the Toronto police commission in preventing a group called the Fellowship of Reconciliation from holding a public meeting. The police alleged that the organization was a communist front, a proposition the *Canadian Forum* said was 'so manifestly absurd that it will not be accepted by anyone of average intelligence.' The letter had been drafted by historian Frank Underhill and classicist Eric Havelock, and was signed by other leading members of the academic community, including Vincent Bladen, George Brett, Donald Creighton, Harold Innis, Chester Martin, E.J. Urwick, and Malcolm Wallace. They claimed that 'the right of free speech and free assembly is in danger of suppression in this city.' To restrict the right, they argued, 'as has been the tendency in Toronto for the last two years, is short-sighted, inexpedient and intolerable.' Few scientists signed. Physicist J.C. McLennan is reported to have told the press, 'We have no time to bother about free speech or papers signed by other professors.'

The *Varsity* backed the professors, referring to the 'blundering, arbitrary tactics of the police commissioners' and the 'thick skull of the ultra-conservative section of our community.' A student poll run by the *Varsity* favoured the professors by a margin of 5 to 1. (The *Varsity* editor, Andrew Allan, would be suspended the following month on another issue, the 'practical atheism' statement mentioned in the previous chapter.) Some members of the board of

Frank Underhill, upon receiving an honorary degree from the University of Toronto
in 1962 at age 72.

governors were incensed with the actions of the professors and asked Falconer to meet with a group of them to warn them of the danger to the University if they got involved in public controversies. Falconer reported to Canon Cody, the chairman of the board, that the six signatories he met with had undertaken 'to use their influence with the members of their staff to refrain from further discussions on this or other political matters.' The following week, the board publicly dissociated itself from the views of the 68 professors.

A few months later, Underhill wrote an article in the British *New Statesman and Nation* criticizing Prime Minister R.B. Bennett's handling of imperial relations. Falconer wrote to Underhill, cautioning him that such writing 'endangers the autonomy of the University.' Underhill responded that many professors had engaged in such public discussions in the past. Moreover, he argued, 'if professors at Toronto must keep their mouths shut in order to preserve the autonomy of the University, then that autonomy is already lost.' At the opening of the term in September 1931, Falconer warned the University community to be careful. 'Now, more than ever,' he said, 'skylarking on the ragged edge of folly irritates onlookers.'

Ten years earlier, Falconer had given a similar speech in Convocation Hall. A professor, he said, should be able 'to pursue and expound his investigations without being compelled to justify himself to those who differ from him.' But, he went on, academics were like judges, who should not serve particular parties. Professors should not get actively involved in party politics or 'burning political questions.' The issue at the time was R.M. MacIver's so-called ultra-socialistic teachings and his pro-labour book *Labour in the Changing World* (1919). The board member and wealthy St Catharines mining engineer Colonel Reuben Wells Leonard wanted MacIver fired. 'If we are to encourage in the University the teaching of one line of extreme, unusual or dangerous doctrine,' he wrote, 'why not encourage others, such as ... Lenine [*sic*] when Russia should get tired of him.' MacIver's professorship, he claimed, should be renamed the 'Chair of Political Anarchy and Social Chaos.' Far from being a radical, Falconer assured Leonard, MacIver was a 'steadying influence' on labour. Falconer was able to ward off possible support for Leonard's extreme position through his special Convocation Hall address.

In June 1931, the 64-year-old Falconer announced that he would retire at the end of the following academic year. He had been diagnosed with a severe heart disorder in June 1930 and later suffered a mild heart attack, but he wanted to complete twenty-five years as president before retiring. Canon Cody, an Anglican clergyman, was rumoured to be his replacement. 'If he does get the job,' Underhill wrote to a friend, 'I expect that those of us who are connected with the *Forum* will have to watch our step.'

Cody, in the eyes of many, was the 'obvious choice.' As we have seen, he was extremely well connected with the Conservative government in Ontario – a close friend of the new premier, George Henry, and his predecessor, Howard Ferguson, now the high commissioner in London. Cody had preached before the King and Queen in Buckingham Palace and was 'probably the most sought-after speaker in Canada' for addresses to service clubs and church organizations. He had friends everywhere. As his biographer, D.C. Masters, writes, Cody was 'a very humane person, highly regarded by the parishioners of St. Paul's and by the many other men and women with whom he came in contact.' He also had a 'phenomenal memory for names.'

One can easily see Cody's potential support in the University. The dean of engineering was a parishioner, as were other members of the faculty, and he was a friend of Brett, Burton, Kennedy, Innis, Urwick, Woodhouse, and many other influential professors. Not only was he chair of the board of governors, but his association with many of its members went back many years. He had served with Joseph Flavelle and Bruce Macdonald on the 1906 royal commission and with T.A. Russell on the 1922 commission. His recent chairmanship of the royal commission on the treatment of cancer by radium would likely have appealed to the scientific side of the University. What the editors of the 1931–2 *Varsity* might have said cannot be known, because the University's disciplinary body, the Caput, had closed the *Varsity* down in February, the second year in a row that the *Varsity* had been disciplined.

On the other hand, Cody would be 64 when he took office – only one year younger than Falconer – and his ties with the Conservatives were also a potential problem if they lost the next election, which they did in June 1934. Mitchell Hepburn's Liberals regarded Cody with suspicion. Moreover, he was not a scholar and had no post-graduate training, though he had taught at Wycliffe in his earlier years. There was also the issue of appointing a practising cleric to the position – his status had been considered a negative factor when Cody had been a candidate for the presidency in 1906.

Two other persons, Vincent Massey, most recently the ambassador to the United States, and R.C. Wallace, the president of the University of Alberta, were

Canon Henry Cody with Premier George Henry after the announcement of Cody's
appointment as president in October 1931.

apparently considered for the position, but neither was interviewed. (In 1936,
Wallace was appointed principal of Queen's University.) Massey, according to his
wife, would have liked the position and indirectly approached the board member Joseph Flavelle. 'Poor V[incent] had another blow the other day in a letter
from Rowell,' Massey's wife wrote her sister, adding, 'The latter had had a talk
with Sir Joseph Flavelle about the University of Toronto and V. succeeding there
– which between ourselves V.'s whole heart would love – a real job to do for
Young Canada – but Sir J. says Cody wants it and must evidently have it.'

On October 8, 1931, the board, without recorded dissent, voted in favour of
appointing Cody, who did not attend the meeting. Cody accepted the appointment the following day. 'What went on behind the scenes,' Masters writes, 'must
remain a matter for speculation.' We do know from the memoirs of the Reverend Bruce Macdonald, the vice-chairman of the board, who would be appointed
its chairman by the government in place of Cody, that although some members
of the board had thought a younger man than Cody was required, Macdonald
had pointed out to them that 'what the University needed at that time was a

period of consolidation and not one of creation.' That is roughly what they would get.

In the early 1980s, the professor of higher education Robin Harris tried to find out what the members of the university community of the time thought about Cody's appointment. He received more than a dozen replies to his requests for information. E. Horne Craigie of zoology, for example, gave a typical response: 'We accepted it simply as a *fait accompli* and regarded it definitely with apathy, certainly not with satisfaction.' Most of the respondents were too junior in the early 1930s to offer much that was helpful. The poet and academic Earle Birney, for example, replied that he was 'a feckless grad student unconcerned and uninformed about matters of university government other than the Dean of Men's rules about liquor, poker and women visitors at 73 St. George.' The distinguished classicist Eric Havelock probably got it right, in noting that 'Massey was talked of as an ideal candidate for the post, particularly I think in the colleges,' but that 'it was accepted widely that Cody was the ideal person to conciliate the Tory power structure and obtain the necessary funding.'

It is difficult to know whether a younger person, intent on 'creation' rather than 'consolidation,' would have done better than Cody in keeping up the momentum created by Falconer. Did Cody press the University's case as strongly as he should have, or did he hold back in the first few years so as not to embarrass his friend Premier George Henry? It may be that Cody did as well as anyone could have done in his first two years in office during the depth of the depression, but it is likely that the University suffered under Hepburn's Liberals more than it might have under a less political president. The annual assistance to the University of Toronto had been more than $2 million in both 1930 and 1931, and it had gone down somewhat to about $1,800,000 by 1934. In 1934, however, the Liberals dramatically reduced the grant by another $600,000. This reduction occurred at the same time the province was starting to recover from the depression and while the grants to Queen's and Western remained constant. When Cody was appointed, Mitchell Hepburn, the Liberal leader, had warned the University in a speech in the legislature that Cody was 'partisan in his political leanings,' and that 'if he retained the political partisanship which he manifested for so many years, it would be ill days for the University of Toronto.' The very day his appointment was announced, Cody had had dinner with the Conservative premier and posed for pictures with him – as the one reproduced in this chapter shows.

The sharp reduction in the grant in 1935 meant that tuition fees had to rise. The basic fee in arts went from $75 to $130 that year, causing a number of students to drop out of university. Faculty salaries had already been reduced, as had administrative expenses. Very few departments now had secretaries. The office in University College had one secretary and shared another with the registrar's office. Research funds allotted by the University were reduced in 1933–4 from $80,000 to $29,000 and remained at that figure throughout Cody's presidency. Various alumni organizations and other bodies, such as the Students' Administrative Council, arranged loans for needy students. 'Most students,' wrote the social historian Paul Axelrod, 'came from modest middle class ... families.' There were relatively few entrance scholarships. Reuben Wells Leonard had set up a trust in 1923 with generous funds for scholarships restricted to white, Protestant, British subjects, a restriction that would be declared against public policy by the Ontario Court of Appeal in 1990. Percy Hermant of Imperial Optical, the father of Sydney Hermant, who graduated in 1935 and would later be a member of the board, donated scholarship funds without any restrictions except that the student maintain first-class honours. Edward Safarian, for example, the future dean of the graduate school, whose father had emigrated from Turkey before the First World War, received a Hermant scholarship in 1942. Without it, he says, he would not have attended university. There were apparently no admission quotas on race or religion, though it should be noted that in the 1930s the central administration kept a running tally of the number of Jews at the University. In a private letter, Cody said it was because 'a small group of Hebrew race' were entering university without adequate funds rather than staying out, as he put it, 'until he can earn money sufficient to pay his way.' 'This has always been the way in which the people of our stock have acted in the past,' he added.

The number of students attending the University remained relatively stable during the 1930s. Enrolment in 1932–3 was over 8,000, the highest it had ever been, even though senior matriculation had become a requirement for all degree courses in 1931–2. A university education was thought to be a help in getting a job and, in any event, was better than being unemployed. Students, understandably, tended to enter courses that offered greater possibility of employment after graduation. Some courses, such as commerce and finance and engineering, did well in the early stages of the depression, but enrolment in them dropped after 1932. About two-thirds of the first year female and half of the first year male students in the University in 1935 came from families with professional or business backgrounds. Relatively few students were politically active during the depression, though they were heavily involved in religious organizations such as the Student Christian Movement. 'The bleak economic climate did not rouse much protest,' stated Axelrod. 'If anything it had the reverse effect ... It made most students more cautious.'

Women students continued to represent just under 40 per cent of the total, though the proportion varied from faculty to faculty and from course to course. In Victoria College and University College, women made up some 50 per cent by the end of the decade, but there were very few women in medicine, law, commerce, engineering, or dentistry. (Future president George Connell's mother was one of the very few women in dentistry, and graduated along with her future husband in 1923.) 'Women,' observed Brian McKillop, 'studied subjects that had come to be associated with their sex, its social attributes, and its instincts.' So, apart from enrolling in arts, they entered occupational and physical therapy, and the numbers in those fields doubled. They also entered nursing, after the University set up a basic training program in a new School of Nursing. There were no men in nursing or in occupational or physical therapy in this period. Women also dominated the department of social service, which would become the School of Social Work in 1941. Women had constituted the majority of students at the Ontario College of Education in the 1920s, but in the 1930s more men – many of whom had lost their jobs in industry or business – wanted to get jobs in teaching, and as a result the proportion of women declined to about 40 per cent.

The depression affected the development of new programs. Those that were established looked to outside sources for support. As in the past, the Rockefeller and Carnegie foundations played a significant role in encouraging change and innovation in the University. The School of Nursing, for example, was established in 1933 with the support of the Rockefeller Foundation. There had previously been diploma courses for graduate nurses – public health nursing in the School of Hygiene and an extension course for administrators – but the school was to be the first basic training course for nurses in the University. The Rockefeller Foundation's initial offer, in 1930, had been conditional on the University's or the government's contributing a comparable sum, particularly in the form of a building. The University, however, did not have the funds, and the government was reluctant to promise support. Kathleen Russell, the director of public health nursing at the University, who would head the School of Nursing, kept pressing for a commitment. 'It makes a sorry tale,' she wrote to Falconer in late 1931, 'to consider the millions that have been spent upon medicine and to compare with this, the utter impossibility of getting any attention to an offer of help for nursing.' A building on Queen's Park Crescent was eventually provided, and the new program was established with a yearly grant of $17,500 from Rockefeller. In 1939, the foundation gave the University $250,000 as a permanent endowment for the school. The first degree program was established in 1942.

Also new during these years was a program in fine art, the introduction of which had been recommended almost thirty years earlier by the royal commission of 1906. A Toronto businessman had promised $50,000 in the 1920s to endow a chair, but Falconer could not find a suitable candidate, and, owing to the depression, the offer was withdrawn. The Carnegie Foundation then provided the initial support that enabled the University in 1934 to hire John Alford – a Cambridge graduate and student of culture – as its first professor of fine art. Peter Brieger, a refugee from Germany who had received his PhD in medieval studies from Breslau and was working at the Courtauld Institute in London, was added to the faculty in 1936, again with the help of Carnegie money. Other staff were brought in, including the artist Charles Comfort, who was in charge of studio work, and several courses were offered in conjunction with the School of Architecture, then still part of the faculty of engineering. In 1946, the department of fine art was amalgamated with the department of archaeology to become the department of art and archeology.

Both the Carnegie and the Rockefeller foundations assisted in establishing a program in Chinese studies at the University under Bishop William C. White, who joined the faculty in 1934 as associate professor of Chinese archaeology and keeper of the Royal Ontario Museum's Chinese collection. (Until the 1960s, the ROM was an integral part of the University.) The Carnegie Foundation helped pay White's salary for a number of years, and the Rockefeller Foundation assisted with the maintenance of the Chinese library collection of the more than 40,000 books White had purchased in China for the museum. The ROM already had a fine collection of important objects obtained for it in the early twenties by a fur merchant and collector of artefacts in China, George Crofts. Crofts laid the foundation for the museum's extraordinary Chinese collection. He had, for example, obtained the 'Ming tomb,' now in the large gallery facing Bloor Street,

William C. White, bishop in Honan, China, sometime before his appointment in 1934 as associate professor of Chinese archaeology and keeper of the Royal Ontario Museum's Chinese collection.

with its two camels, which many readers may remember climbing on as children when the tomb was outside the building. He also obtained the two stone lions now on Bloor Street, each of which weighs 17 tons, and the large bronze Buddha and bell at the west end of the Currelly Court.

White's contributions to the museum were of equal importance. In 1897, after graduating from Wycliffe College, White had been sent as a Church of England missionary to China and had become the bishop in Honan, in north-central China, one of the last areas opened to Western influence. He developed an interest in archaeology after he saw an inscription on an abandoned synagogue in Kaifeng, the capital of Honan. The inscription date, 1489, described the construction of the synagogue many centuries earlier. On a leave in 1924, White went to see Charles Currelly at the ROM. They had attended the University of Toronto at about the same time. Crofts had recently died, and Currelly agreed that Bishop White would now collect material from China for the museum.

For the next ten years, White collected thousands of objects, notably early bronzes, as well as the valuable library previously mentioned. Some of his colleagues in China, states his biographer L.C. Walmsley, 'claimed that White's enthusiasm for Chinese archaeology ... came to surpass even his interest in religion.' Greatly exceeding his budget, he took advantage of civil turmoil in China to obtain some of the finest Chinese objects in the world. One of these is the large mural on the north wall of the 'Bishop White Gallery.' The mural, dated 1298, which depicts a Buddha in paradise, had been in a Buddhist temple in northern China. The priests, fearing that it would be looted by war lords, carefully cut it into sixty-three sections, which they hid. Because of famine, however, they were forced to sell it, their only valuable possession. White was able to purchase the mural and sent it to the ROM, where it was painstakingly restored to its original grandeur. The cost was borne by Sir Joseph Flavelle. White had reported to Currelly that with 'the present nationalistic feeling in China' he would have only a limited time in which to acquire objects before the Chinese government put an end to their exportation. Currelly, who had acquired objects in similar circumstances in the Middle East twenty years earlier, replied that 'there is need to make hay while the sun shines.' Bishop White left China in 1934. There is no evidence that museum officials or the museum board were particularly concerned about the ethics of acquiring valuable treasures in these circumstances.

White had kept up a relationship over the years with Canon Cody – who had taught him at Wycliffe College – and proposed to Cody that the University establish a program of Chinese studies. Such a school was eventually established in the University in 1943, with White as its director. He published a number of books on the collection, including a three-volume work, *Chinese Jews*. He did not, however, adjust particularly well to the academic world. Not only did he have no training as a scholar or an archaeologist, he was not used to the give and take of the academic world. L.C. Walmsley, who taught in the program under White and succeeded him as director, wrote in his biography of White that 'anyone who questioned his opinion presented a threat.' Another colleague stated that he 'remained at heart a medieval bishop.' White retired in 1948, and the school became the department of East Asiatic studies, later renamed East Asian studies. In 1947, the Chinese scholar Dr C.C. Shih had joined the department. Shih may well have been the first 'visible minority' faculty member at the University.

The collection of Chinese and other objects had completely outgrown the

An addition to the Royal Ontario Museum on Queen's Park, opened in 1933.

original building, and it was to be housed in a major addition to the museum that would triple the space available. The planning for the addition, which would front on Queen's Park, and its approval by the board of the museum and the government had taken place before the depression started. Nevertheless, the province allowed construction to proceed, as a make-work project. No machinery was permitted, only pickaxes, shovels, and horse-drawn wagons, and only Ontario building products could be used. The new addition was opened in 1933.

The building was so constructed that four large totem poles – or crest poles as they are now called by museum officials – that had been brought from British Columbia could be placed in the two main open staircase wells in the building. One of the totem poles – a memorial pole erected by the Nisga'a Eagle Chief, Sagawen – is over 80 feet (24.5 metres) tall and reaches from below the floor of the basement to a cupola above the ceiling of the third floor. At the time, it was the tallest and finest example of its kind in existence. It had been collected by Marius Barbeau, an ethnologist who worked with the National Museum. The red cedar totem pole had been carved by the expert craftsman Oyai about sixty years earlier and was, according to Barbeau, designed to be 'the tallest of its kind ... for all time.' It honoured the memory of a deceased relative of its owner. Barbeau had first seen it in 1927 on the bank of the lower Nass River in British Columbia, close to the Alaskan border. Both Charles Currelly and Tom McIlwraith, the keeper of ethnology, were eager to buy it for the museum, in spite of their general lack of funds. McIlwraith had been appointed a lecturer at the University in 1925 after extensive work on the Bella Coola Indians of British Columbia, the results of which were eventually published in two volumes in 1948. In 1936, he would be appointed professor of anthropology and head of the newly created department of anthropology, a position he would hold until his retirement in 1963.

Barbeau approached the owner of the pole, an aged chief named Mountain, and told him what an honour it would be for Mountain to have the totem pole on display in Toronto. 'Give me the tombstone of Governor Douglas' (the first governor of British Columbia), Mountain replied, 'and I will give you the totem pole of my grand-uncle.' Barbeau withdrew, and after Mountain died the following year, he purchased the object from his nephews for $600. Barbeau later wrote that he thought it would have 'tumbled to the ground and decayed.' The pole was larger than any pole previously seen. It had to be cut in three sections in order for the Canadian National Railway to transport it to Toronto. 'I don't see how we can house it,' McIlwraith wrote Barbeau at the time, 'but we will find some way.' They did, and it can now be seen on the north side of the museum between the gold-domed rotunda and the Currelly Gallery.

Another addition to the faculty during the depression was Griffith Taylor, who was hired in 1935 to set up the new department of geography. James Mavor had advocated hiring a geographer in the early 1920s, and Harold Innis kept up the campaign. The department thus emerged from political economy rather than from geology, the usual route in universities. Innis hoped to hire a Canadian, but a suitable candidate could not be found. He thereupon proposed the name of Griffith Taylor, who had established the first geography department in Australia and was teaching at the University of Chicago. Taylor had grown up in Australia, studied at Cambridge, and received his doctorate from the University of Sydney, where he taught until coming to Chicago. He had been the chief

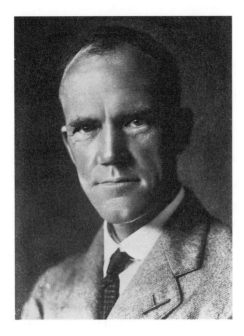

Griffith Taylor, appointed in 1935 to head the
new department of geography.

geologist on Captain Scott's ill-fated expedition to the Antarctic in 1911–12.
Unlike Scott, Taylor returned from the expedition and wrote a book about his
experiences. Taylor was a controversial figure. The unpopularity of his views in
Australia probably made it uncomfortable for him to remain there. Not only was
he against the 'White Australia' policy, believing that intermarriage with Chinese
immigrants would strengthen Australia 'biologically,' but he also predicted that
Australia's population growth would be far less than the official estimates.

Although Taylor was more than prepared to come to Toronto, the depression
made it difficult for the University to find enough money to come close to
matching his Chicago salary. In 1935, however, the Ontario Department of
Education agreed to share part of the cost if he would also teach geography at the
Ontario College of Education. At Taylor's insistence, the University established
an independent department of geography in the faculty of arts. He rented a
magnificent house at 110 Forest Hill Road for $75 a month – the depression had
certain advantages for those who had a little money – and later bought the house
for $15,000 (about twice his yearly salary). 'It's the nicest house and surrounding
of any of the faculty,' he wrote in 1936. He remained head of geography until 1951. Taylor was a productive scholar, the author of 20 books and some
200 articles over the course of his career. He was almost as controversial in Canada

as he had been in Australia. His interest was in relating populations to their material environment and in showing how the environment influences history. This was 'cultural geography' as distinguished from the more traditional physical geography. In one of his books, *Our Evolving Civilization*, published by the University of Toronto Press in 1946, he predicted that Canada could have a population exceeding 100 million persons, a view that may have helped to widen Canada's doors to immigration after the war. He also predicted in a *Chatelaine* article in 1945 that Alberta could be 'the industrial and financial centre of Canada, and rival London as the political centre of the British Empire.' The Alberta government enthusiastically republished the article. He was right about Australia's relatively small population growth. Time will tell about Canada.

Only a few major private donations came to the University during the depression. The largest gift by far was a bequest in 1933 from Miss Ida Wallberg, who left $1 million to the University for an engineering building to be called 'The Wallberg Memorial Building' as a memorial to her brother, Emil Andrew Wallberg, who had died in 1929, never having married, and had left his estate to his sister. Neither Miss Wallberg nor her brother was a graduate of the University of Toronto. Emil Wallberg had been born in Sweden, emigrated to the United States at an early age, and received his engineering education in Illinois. He moved to Canada in 1892, where he practised as an engineer and became president of several large companies, including Canada Wire and Cable. The start of construction of the Wallberg Building, at the corner of College and St George streets, was delayed, however, because the University did not have the additional resources needed for its completion. Funds would not become available until after the war.

A second major donation during the depression – also from a woman – was from Jessie Dunlap for an observatory in honour of her late husband, David Dunlap. Again, neither the donor nor the person honoured was a University of Toronto graduate. It will be recalled that, in 1921, David Dunlap, an amateur astronomer, had met C.A. Chant, the head of astronomy. A good relationship began to develop between Chant and the very wealthy Dunlap, who had made his fortune as a lawyer and mining promoter in Northern Ontario. Dunlap, however, died in 1924. A few years later, Chant sent a note to Mrs Dunlap reminding her of her husband's possible interest in assisting the department and boldly asking if she 'would be willing to consider the question of providing the observatory – or, if not the entire observatory, the great telescope – as a memorial

Members of the astronomy department in 1962, with the David Dunlap Observatory in the background: from left to right, S. Van den Bergh, Helen Hogg, D.A. MacRae, Ruth Northcott, J.D. Fernie, and J.F. Heard (director).

to Mr. Dunlap.' She expressed interest in the project, and in 1927 Chant visited her at her elegant home in Rosedale – 93 Highland Avenue, coincidentally to be purchased by the University in 1956 from a subsequent owner to serve as the official residence for presidents of the University. The money for the observatory was promised, but could not be given until her husband's estate was finally probated a number of years later.

In 1927, Chant and Mrs Dunlap examined various sites, and eventually they chose a large block of land on a gentle rise near Richmond Hill, 25 kilometres north of the campus, which Chant had picked out from the contour lines on a government map. 'This is the place,' she said to Chant, and instructed her lawyer to purchase the property. The observatory officially opened in 1935 on Chant's seventieth birthday and the date of his retirement from the University.

Mrs Dunlap was given an honorary degree. The 74-inch (1.88-metre) telescope was the second largest in the world, after one at the Mount Wilson Observatory in California, and was – and still is – the largest in Canada. The separate administration building has three domes, two of which contain smaller telescopes. The first director, R.K. Young, was a Toronto graduate who received his PhD from the University of California, having worked there at the Lick Observatory. He brought in a number of talented astronomers, such as Frank Hogg, a Toronto graduate, who received Harvard's first PhD in astronomy and later became head of astronomy at Toronto. His wife, Helen Hogg, an American, who received her PhD at Harvard, where she met and worked with her future husband, also did important research at the Dunlap Observatory, finding pulsating stars in globular star clusters of the Milky Way. She did not start teaching until 1941. After her husband died in 1951, she took over his column on stargazing in the Toronto *Star*, which she continued on a weekly basis for the next thirty years. She became a full professor in 1957 and officially retired in 1976. The University's 24-inch telescope in Chile, opened in 1971 – the Richmond Hill observatory was having problems caused by the development of the surrounding area – was named after her. In 1998, the observatory in Chile was moved piece by piece to Argentina, but the telescope is still named the Helen Sawyer Hogg Telescope.

❧

This chapter began with a discussion of academic freedom. It will end on the same subject. It is well to note, however, the observation made by Michiel Horn in his recent book *Academic Freedom in Canada* that by 'focusing on a small minority of professors and on controversy and conflict, a history of academic freedom distorts the reality of academic life. In the midst of depression and budgetary distress, Canadian universities were mostly tranquil.' But not for Frank Underhill. At the close of the decade, an attempt was made to fire him.

The Trinity classics professor George Grube had given a speech at a Co-operative Commonwealth Federation (CCF) convention in April 1939. He was quoted by the *Globe and Mail* as saying that any war that would come in Europe at that time would 'have nothing to do with democracy.' Premier Hepburn and others attacked Grube in the legislature. The leader of the opposition Conservatives, George Drew, used the occasion to attack Underhill for words that he had published four years earlier in a report prepared for the Canadian Institute of International Affairs and that had been reprinted recently. Underhill had written, 'We must therefore make it clear to the world, and especially to Great Britain, that the poppies blooming in Flanders fields have no further interest for us.' Hepburn said the statement 'smacks of rank sedition.' A Liberal MPP introduced a motion of dismissal, saying that Grube and Underhill were 'rats who are trying to scuttle our ship of state.' Cody summoned Underhill and informed him that the board of governors was thinking of firing him. Underhill described the meeting to a friend, saying, 'Cody was terribly worked up … and told me it would all depend on how I behaved before the governors whether I came out of the business safely.'

Cody had been concerned throughout his presidency about Underhill's activities. Not only did Cody dislike Underhill's left-wing views, for which he 'had a low tolerance,' but he disliked Underhill's attacks on the British Empire, an institution for which Cody had the highest regard. In the summer of 1933, for example, Underhill had given a speech at the annual Couchiching Conference near Orillia in which he had said that 'Canada's economic interests lay with the United States, not with the British Empire.' In the fall of that year, Underhill gave a similar lecture under the auspices of the University's extension department. Cody made sure that Underhill gave no more extension lectures. We will 'give him one more chance,' Cody wrote to the chairman of the board, Bruce Macdonald, 'with a warning that if he does not restrain his tongue from insolent remarks the welfare of the University will require his removal.' The following summer, Underhill once again spoke at the Couchiching Conference, saying that the British Empire should be assigned 'to the scrap heap,' and that 'we went into war blindly because we swallowed the British propaganda about democracy.' He had a knack for the vivid image. The retired George Wrong, who had served as his mentor, warned him that he had to be careful or he might lose his job. Wrong was particularly concerned about Underhill's 'deplorable' mode of expressing his ideas. Underhill promised Cody that he would make no more public speeches for a year. He continued, however, to write anonymous pieces for the *Canadian Forum*.

Cody did not want professors publicly discussing controversial topics. Cody himself, however, often openly discussed such subjects. In the summer of 1933, for example, he had been in Italy, from which he returned praising aspects of Mussolini's regime. Mussolini, he said, was 'a very efficient man, who had a plan and the necessary faith in it to carry it out.' In a speech in Convocation Hall several months later, he spoke favourably of the Italian fascists. 'Canadians are inclined to emphasize too strongly the "rights" of the individual and the "duties" of the government,' Cody said, 'rather than to recognize that the government has rights and the individual has duties toward it.' 'Cody's infatuation with fascism in the very year of the destruction of the German Reichstag,' Brian McKillop later wrote, 'should not particularly shock us. What should be of concern, however, is how convenient it was that he managed to remain so oblivious to the clear political implications of speeches he delivered as university president in the very days when he carried out a campaign to halt the political activities of his professoriate.' When Italy entered the war, it should be noted, Cody returned the decoration he had received in 1936 from the Italian government.

Underhill's involvement with socialism also concerned Cody and the board. Cody was not particularly concerned with communism at the University during this period. A student poll conducted in 1935 reported that only 128 of the more than 4,000 students who participated would vote for a communist candidate in the coming federal election. 'I don't know anyone who is a communist,' Cody told the *Globe and Mail* in 1935. But he did know a lot of socialists at the University. Many, such as Grube at Trinity and Havelock at Victoria, were at colleges over which the University had no disciplinary jurisdiction. 'The chief sponsors of socialism in this part of the country,' Cody wrote privately, 'are members of the staff of Victoria College.' Much of Cody's focus was therefore on Underhill. In 1931, Underhill and Frank Scott of McGill were primarily responsible for bringing about the League for Social Reconstruction, organized along the lines of the English Fabian Society. It was primarily members of the League from the University of Toronto – Underhill, Harry Cassidy of the department of social science, and Joseph Parkinson of political economy – who provided the draft for what became the Regina Manifesto of the CCF party. There was never an official connection between the League and the CCF, so members of the faculty were able to produce the League document, *Social Planning for Canada*, in 1935, but Underhill, Havelock, and Cassidy were forced by the University to resign their executive positions in the CCF clubs with which they were associated.

On April 19, 1939, the board of governors held a special meeting to consider whether Underhill should be fired for his 'Flanders fields' statement. Senior people in the University, such as Dean of Arts Sam Beatty, Harold Innis, who had become head of political economy in 1937, W.P.M. Kennedy, and Chester Martin, appeared at the meeting to support Underhill. More than a thousand students signed a petition in favour of Underhill and Grube. Underhill had sent a letter – 'contrite in tone' – explaining the circumstances of the publication and indicating that he had meant no disrespect for those who lost their lives in Flanders. He himself had been wounded in the war. 'I shall do my best in future,' he assured the board, 'to behave as reasonable men would expect a professor to behave.' Moreover, Cody reported, some senior professors were discussing setting up a method of investigating controversial public statements by members of the faculty (it was never set up). The issue was deferred to a subsequent meeting of the board. Cody recommended in June 1939 that in the circumstances 'the Board take no further action at present.' Eugene Forsey and Leonard Marsh at McGill were not as fortunate in similar circumstances. Both lost their jobs. About a year after the outbreak of war, however, as will be seen in the next chapter, Underhill would once again be under threat of dismissal.

chapter twenty-seven

1939

THE SECOND WORLD WAR

Canada entered the war on September 10, 1939. 'Last year we began the year under the shadow of a threatening war,' President Cody told the incoming class. 'For the time the cloud was lifted, a respite was given. Today the storm has broken upon us.' In early September – a week after Britain had declared war – Cody demanded that Canada join her, stating that 'our gratitude to the Motherland from whom we sprang demands it.' The strong attachment to Great Britain had been evident at the University the previous May, when the King and Queen had visited the campus. Twelve thousand people thronged the grounds in front of Hart House to catch a glimpse of the royal couple. The U of T *Monthly* described the scene as the motorcade approached from Queen's Park: 'The excitement was scarcely to be endured. And then around the bend appeared the Queen, a lovely, gracious figure in blue, smiling and making her characteristic little gesture of greeting in answer to the cheers of the great assemblage.'

Whereas the students had been under pressure during the First World War, this time they were not immediately urged to enlist. The chief of defence staff, General A.G.L. McNaughton, had told the universities that the students could 'serve their country in a most valuable way by continuing their university training until graduation.' There was, he stated, the 'possibility of the present war extending over a very long period and the need for ... large numbers of well trained men in all branches of pure and applied science, including medicine, dentistry and agriculture.' After June 1940, all single males between 21 and 45

King George VI and Queen Elizabeth leaving Hart House, May 22, 1939. Some members of the Hart House staff are on the right.

had to register for service, but university students who joined the Canadian Officers Training Corps (COTC) could remain at university until they graduated, provided they were making satisfactory progress. Even before registration was compulsory, large numbers joined the COTC – in 1938–9 there had been only 327 members in the corps, but by the end of September 1939 there were 1,800 (including 500 graduates).

Some activities were curtailed because of the war. Intercollegiate athletic schedules were cancelled, though exhibition games took place. The University of Toronto rugger team, for example, which had been intercollegiate champion before the war, arranged games with various RCAF teams. Interfaculty competitions, however, increased during this period. Hart House reluctantly suspended its debates, and the number of dances was reduced. The medical students' annual production, 'Daffydil,' was cancelled. The sombre tone of the campus resembled that during the First World War.

The number of students and alumni who died in the war totalled 557, somewhat fewer than the number who died in the First World War. Their names are listed on the memorial tablet under Soldiers' Tower. The numbers who served in the forces was substantially higher – more than 10,000, compared to

J.K. Macalister, left, was a Rhodes scholar executed by the Nazis at Buchenwald in 1944; Douglas LePan, right, later the principal of University College and a two-time winner of the governor general's award for literature, served in the Canadian army in Italy. In 1995, LePan published a long verse drama about Macalister, *Macalister, or Dying in the Dark.*

about 6,000 in the first war. Well over half those who died had served in the RCAF, including Pilot Officer Gregory Maher, a recent engineering graduate, who was the first University of Toronto person to be killed – in a bomber crash at Trenton on November 29, 1939.

Two former Rhodes scholars died. One of the two, George Cartwright, had won a Rhodes to Oxford in 1929. The Memorial Book for the Second World War records :

F/O George Stevenson CARTWRIGHT 425 Sqn RCAF – Trinity College, BA 1929. Killed in an air operation over Hamburg, Germany, 9, November 1942. Buried in Dishforth Cemetery, Yorkshire, England.

The other Rhodes scholar was John Kenneth Macalister. He had graduated from University College in honour law in 1937 and was studying at Oxford on the outbreak of war. When it was clear that Larry MacKenzie of the law faculty was to be confirmed as president of the University of New Brunswick in the summer of 1940, Dean W.P.M. Kennedy wrote to Macalister offering him a position as a lecturer. Macalister, who had earlier expressed an interest in an appointment, cabled back immediately: 'IN ARMY SINCE YESTERDAY SORRY MANY THANKS – MACALISTER.' He had joined the Canadian infantry, was assigned to British intelligence, and, along with Frank Pickersgill (a graduate of 1938 and the brother of the future cabinet minister Jack Pickersgill), was parachuted behind enemy lines in France in June 1943 to act as a secret agent. They were captured, tortured, and executed at Buchenwald concentration camp on September 14, 1944.

Women students and staff at the University of Toronto – as well as alumnae – participated in the war effort. It was not until the summer of 1941, however, that the army and air force set up their own women's corps. The navy corps was formed the following year. 'Of the approximately 9,000 women students who attended the University of Toronto during the Second War,' stated historians Nancy Kiefer and Ruth Pierson, 'only an estimated 325 enlisted in the armed forces of Canada,' including service in the medical corps of the three services. The largest proportion – 118 of the total – had studied physical and occupational therapy. Three University of Toronto women died on active service: physiotherapy graduate Jean Burgess Atkinson, former Trinity student Dorothy Britton, and occupational therapy graduate Mary Susannah McLaren. From the beginning of the war, voluntary war work had been carried out, initially organized by the Faculty Wives' Association. This developed into the Women's War Service Committee, with Barbara Cody, the president's wife, as its president. Women volunteered to take courses in first aid, motor mechanics, and sewing. The U of T *Monthly* of December 1942 noted that about 15,000 garments had been produced that year. The *Varsity*, like society at large, was against any form of conscription for women, and stated in 1943 that women's 'best service in the interest of the war effort is to preserve the home.'

Women on the campus did organize a voluntary paramilitary service under the auspices of the Red Cross, which required three hours of training and drill every week. They received instruction in such courses as first aid and map reading, and in a motor mechanics course offered by the Ford Motor Company. In the fall of 1942, women were for the first time compelled to register for national service to work in war industries and essential services. In keeping with the change, the University's board of governors required all women in courses where there was not already training directly related to the war effort to contribute sixty hours a year to war work. Courses, such as those for hospital nursing aides, civilian defence, and recreational leadership, were offered. Kiefer and Pierson drew the conclusion from their study of women students and the war effort at the University of Toronto that 'the war service of female university students did not result in the breakdown of sexual stereotypes or of the sexual division of labour ... The programs that the women helped to establish worked against them in the end, for those programs reinforced their inferior status and popular conceptions of femininity.'

The threat of war had been building up for most of the 1930s. 'Here is a bid for world power,' Cody stated shortly before Canada entered the war. 'One race, one blood is seeking to dominate not only a continent, but a world.' Ever since Hitler had gained power in 1933, Jews and others persecuted by the Nazis had been trying to find safety in other lands. The tragic drama of the ship, the *St Louis*, that had more than 900 Jewish refugees aboard, unfolded in the spring of 1939. No country would allow them refuge. A number of prominent persons in the University, including former president Robert Falconer, University College principal Malcolm Wallace, and historian George Wrong, joined others in sending a telegram to Ottawa, urging Mackenzie King to offer sanctuary to the passengers. Ottawa refused to help. 'The line must be drawn somewhere,' stated F.C. Blair, the head of the immigration service in Ottawa. Falconer continued to urge the admission of refugees. A week before he died in 1943, he gave a radio address as honorary chairman of the National Committee on Refugees, urging Canadians to sign a petition asking that Canada open its doors to refugees from Hitler's persecution. President Cody also had advocated a more open policy.

From 1933 to 1939, only some 5,000 refugees – Jews and non-Jews – were admitted to Canada. 'Of all the immigration countries in the world,' historians Irving Abella and Harold Troper have written, 'Canada had by far the worst record toward Jewish refugees.' 'By 1939,' they wrote, 'an unofficial, unholy triumvirate had been forged, with the Immigration Branch, the cabinet and to a lesser degree, the Department of External Affairs opposing the admission to Canada of refugees in general and Jewish refugees in particular.' Michiel Horn concludes that the total number of refugees appointed to academic positions in Canada between 1933 and 1945 'barely exceeded twenty.' The government, supported by the Conference of Canadian Universities, would not grant immigration permits if there was a Canadian who could fill the position concerned. Moreover, it was argued, the universities did not have the funds to hire staff.

When the future Nobel laureate Gerhard Herzberg lost his position as a

Economic historian Karl Helleiner
fled his native Austria in 1939.
Picture taken in 1958.

physicist at a German university in 1935 because he had a Jewish wife, he explored the possibility of coming to the University of Toronto. He was turned down twice, even though on the second occasion he had a good prospect of obtaining a Carnegie grant that would pay his salary for two years. Carnegie grants required that a university applying for funds had to show that there was 'a reasonable possibility of providing a permanent position for the scholar.' The University could not promise Herzberg a permanent position. He was given a temporary non-immigrant position at the University of Saskatchewan, however. When Herzberg applied two years later to become a permanent immigrant, the immigration department wanted assurance that he was not 'displacing any Canadian resident.' In the end, Herzberg was permitted to stay because of his 'unusual qualifications.'

The University of Toronto appointed approximately ten refugee academics – about half of all those hired in Canada. Some, such as Peter Brieger of the department of fine art and D.B. Haurwitz of the physics department – both Jewish – came with Carnegie money. Haurwitz had been promised a position as a meteorologist with the federal government when his Carnegie money ran out. The economic historian Karl Helleiner fled his native Austria in 1939 with his wife, who was of Jewish origin. He refused the Nazis' demand that he divorce his wife, and the couple became servants in England. He came to Canada late in

1939 by virtue of a fellowship given by the Canadian Society for the Protection of Science and Learning and joined Innis' department of political economy in 1940. (His son, Gerry Helleiner, later became an equally distinguished professor in the same department. His other two sons became heads of academic departments at other Canadian universities – Fred in geography at Trent and Chris in biochemistry at Dalhousie.)

Frederick Banting, who at an earlier time had expressed anti-Semitic sentiments – he is reported to have said in the 1920s, 'If I'd known so many Jews had diabetes I don't think I'd ever have gone into it' – was able to bring two Jewish scientists to his medical laboratories. Bruno Mendel came in 1937 to investigate the causes of cancer. He received no salary and brought with him his own laboratory and enough money to finance his research. Hermann Fischer, an organic chemist and the son of a Nobel laureate, was appointed in 1937 after Cody, moreover, was able to raise private funds to support him for ten years. Cody, who had advocated a more open policy on refugees, had to convince Ottawa that 'there is no one in Canada who could take the work we are expecting Fischer to accomplish.' Fischer left Toronto after the war and later became chair of biochemistry at the University of California, Berkeley. Donald Fraser, of the department of hygiene and preventive medicine of the School of Hygiene and the Connaught Laboratories, also helped bring a number of scientists to the University, including Robert Schnitzer from the Robert Koch Institute in Berlin and Carl von Seemann from the University of Munich, both of whom worked in the field of chemotherapeutics. Schnitzer, until forced to leave Germany in 1938, had also been chief of the department of chemotherapy of the giant German pharmaceutical company I.G. Farben, and had directed the testing of all their new chemotherapeutic products.

The department of mathematics was also able to hire a number of Jewish refugee scientists. Sam Beatty, who became head of mathematics in 1934, was eager to build up the strength of the department. Richard Brauer joined it in 1935. He had left his university position in Germany in 1933 for the United States, and had ended up at Princeton's Institute for Advanced Study. A Royal Society of Canada publication described him as 'undoubtedly one of the really great mathematicians of our generation.' From 1937 to 1940, the department produced 10 PhDs, 6 of which were supervised by Brauer. The theoretical physicist Leopold Infeld came to the University of Toronto in 1938 to join J.L. Synge, the chair of applied mathematics. Infeld had left Poland in 1933 and after

Barbara Keyfitz, a mathematics student, in 1965, pointing to the plaque in the mathematics department showing Toronto winners of the William Lowell Putnam Mathematical Competition for North American undergraduate students. Note the name of a future president, R.J. Birgeneau, in 1962.

working with Max Born in Cambridge had accepted a fellowship from Princeton, where he had collaborated with Einstein on producing the popular *Evolution of Physics*.

Within a few short years, mathematics became an outstanding department. H.S.M. Coxeter from Cambridge, who joined the faculty in 1936, published ten books, and unlike Brauer, Synge, and Infeld, remained in Toronto for his entire career. Described in the 1970s as 'Canada's most distinguished mathematician,' he gave the University great strength in geometry, just as Brauer did in algebra. It was certainly not an inbred faculty. (It would continue to welcome outsiders. After the war, it hired a number of outstanding mathematicians, such as Hans Heilbronn, Abraham Robinson, and Peter Scherk, who had fled from Nazism before the war and had taken positions in other universities.) In 1938, the teaching staff produced the first winner of the prestigious Putnam Mathematical Competition, open to undergraduate teams from across North America. It could not compete the following year because the school with the winning team set the problems for the next competition. It won again in 1940 and in the next two competitions in which it was eligible to compete. Coxeter has written, 'Toronto has never given special training to Putnam candidates.' The team members in the early years included later staff members such as A.J. Coleman, D.A.S. Fraser, and George Duff (a future chair of the department). It is likely that other departments might have benefited to the same extent as mathematics if they had been able to add to the faculty some of the extraordinary refugee talent that was available.

Another group of refugees came to Canada because of the war – persons who had been sent from England as enemy aliens. These 'accidental immigrants' had been rounded up after the start of the war and interned in England. During the difficult summer of 1940, over 2,500 men were sent to internment camps in Canada. The German Jews obviously were not Nazi sympathizers, and beginning in early 1941, individuals were released in order to assist the war effort or to attend university. The majority of persons who had been university students in England returned there, but many of university age stayed in Canada. The first group of 23 students were admitted to the University of Toronto without difficulty for the 1941–2 academic year, but in the summer of 1942 several influential persons expressed concern about admitting more former internees.

For the year 1942–3, a group of 16 internees and 2 Japanese Canadians from western Canada wanted to study at a university. Cody was enthusiastically in favour of admitting them, but the board of governors was opposed. Both the Students' Administrative Council and the university senate protested against their exclusion. The board finally backed down in late 1942, after the minister of defence gave them a way out by stating that the released internees could take military training. Some on the board had argued that they would have a competitive advantage over students who had to take military training. The board also permitted the registration of 2 Japanese Canadian students who had been relocated under emergency powers from the west coast, Mr M.S. Yoshioka and Miss T. Nikaido. Both became students at Victoria, where the former studied in preparation for becoming a United Church minister, like his father.

The interned students who attended university in Canada were an extraordinary group who have enriched academic life throughout North America. A

Two U of T professors who had been interned as so-called enemy aliens: the philosopher
Emil Fackenheim, on the left (picture taken in 1979), and the Spanish and Portuguese scholar
Kurt Levy (picture taken in 1958).

number of students entered the maths and physics program at the University of
Toronto. One of these, Walter Kohn, a 1998 Nobel prize winner in chemistry
from the University of California, has described how the chair of mathematics,
Sam Beatty, tutored the group until they caught up. 'He was an exceptional
human being,' Kohn said. Another internee was Emil Fackenheim, the philosopher and student of the Holocaust. He had received his ordination as a rabbi in
Berlin in 1939 and, in his words, 'got out of Germany on May 12, 1939, one
week or so ahead of the Gestapo.' He pursued graduate studies at Aberdeen, and
then was interned and sent to a camp in Sherbrooke, Quebec. After his release in
late 1941, he went to see George Brett, the dean of the graduate school, saying
that he had no academic degree, just a rabbinical diploma, but that Aberdeen
had admitted him to their PhD program. 'What is good enough for Aberdeen,'
Brett replied, 'is good enough for us.' Fackenheim completed his doctoral thesis
on medieval Arabic philosophy and several years later became a member of the
philosophy department. Yet another internee was Gregory Baum, who later
became a well-known Roman Catholic theologian at St Michael's College.
Before they could be released from the detention camps, students had to receive

permission from F.C. Blair, the director of immigration. Blair questioned the motive of one student, saying, 'We are not very well satisfied as to his being a student for any other purpose than getting out of the Camp.' The student was Kurt Levy, who completed his doctorate at Toronto and later became head of the department of Spanish and Portuguese. He had made it out of Germany just in time. 'It was July 23, 1939,' he later recalled, 'and I got one of the last trains out, so to speak, before the war started six weeks later.' He credits Hardolph Wasteneys, the head of biochemistry at Toronto, as being instrumental in getting him released from the camp.

During the desperate summer of 1940, Frank Underhill was once again the subject of great controversy. France had fallen, the USSR still had a non-aggression pact with Germany, and the Battle of Britain was about to be fought. Canada and the United States had just established the Permanent Joint Board on Defence. At the annual Couchiching Conference on public affairs in August, Underhill told the audience what was obvious to almost everyone at the conference: that Canada now had 'two loyalties, the old one to the British connection ... and the new one to North America involving common action with the States.' 'The relative importance of Britain,' he went on, 'is going to sink no matter what happens.' Again, not very controversial. But then he added, 'We can no longer put all our eggs in the British basket.' Perhaps the image of not putting eggs in the British basket in Britain's hour of greatest need had the same impact on readers of the news reports as had the controversial statement reported the previous year that Canada was not interested in 'the poppies blooming in Flanders fields.' Underhill continued to have a way of creating verbal images. Brendan O'Brien, a former treasurer of the Law Society of Upper Canada, still vividly recalls Underhill telling his class in the late 1920s that 'the British flag should be made of wool so that it could shrink with the British Empire.'

The former prime minister Arthur Meighen, an 1896 graduate, privately urged the minister of justice to intern Underhill. The board of governors unanimously wanted Underhill fired. But under the 1906 Act this could not be done without the president's recommendation. Cody vacillated over the nine-month period during which the controversy raged. Principal Malcolm Wallace of University College had warned Cody that a recommendation for dismissal would split the University. At first, Cody recommended that no action be taken, but then at a special board meeting in December 1940 he changed his mind and told the board that 'viewing [Underhill's] record as a whole, I believe it is in the best interests of the University that his services be dispensed with; and I so recommend.' The board was obviously pleased, but delayed taking action until the provincial government's view could be heard. The minister of education agreed with the board's position.

A delegation of members of the board met with Underhill and urged him to resign, promising him a year's salary and the pension money that had been contributed by the University. Underhill refused. The dean of arts, Sam Beatty, led a delegation of senior professors, who urged Cody not to dismiss Underhill. Harold Innis – like Underhill, a wounded veteran of the First World War – told Cody 'to remember that any returned man who has faced the continual dangers of modern warfare has a point of view fundamentally different from anyone who has not.' A petition supporting Underhill, organized by the history student Ken McNaught and signed by third and fourth year history students, was sent to Cody. Another, signed by 258 former students of Underhill, including the future University of Toronto professors Claude Bissell, Douglas LePan, Albert Rose, and Gordon Skilling, was also sent.

The final decision was to be made at a meeting of the board in June 1941. In the meantime, a number of persons expressed concern about the effect of a dismissal on relations with the United States. Hugh Keenleyside, the Canadian secretary of the Permanent Joint Board on Defence, sent a telegram saying that a dismissal would have 'most severe repercussions ... and add to our difficulties abroad.' The associate minister of defence in Ottawa called the Ontario premier, Mitchell Hepburn, and informed him of the government's concern, which was passed on to Cody and the board. The board put the matter over to a subsequent meeting. Cody did not know what to do and , according to his biographer, D.C. Masters, 'seriously contemplated his own resignation.' In the end, Cody did not recommend dismissal. Nevertheless, the board passed a motion that Underhill's services 'be dispensed with' – an ineffective resolution without the president's concurrence. 'What saved me,' Underhill correctly observed in a letter to Larry MacKenzie, 'was chiefly the argument that it would look terrible in the U.S. just now for a professor to be fired for his pro-American sentiments.'

The outcome, writes Michiel Horn, was 'a qualified victory at best.' Although Underhill was not fired, his ordeal did not encourage the exercise of academic freedom. He himself was determined to stay out of the public spotlight in the future. When Bora Laskin was hired by the faculty of law in September

1940 to replace Larry MacKenzie after J.K. Macalister could not accept the appointment, W.P.M. Kennedy wrote to Cody, 'I have told him – as indeed I tell *all* those whom I recommend to you for appointment – that his duties are to teach law, not to make any public statements – oral or written – on political or public questions.'

Kennedy also took the extraordinary step, he informed Cody, of making Laskin 'declare unequivocally' in front of witnesses that 'he has no connection – public or private, expressly or implicitly – with organized or unorganized Communism.' The USSR was not yet an ally, and earlier that month a research fellow in geophysics had been arrested (and subsequently convicted) of possessing communist pamphlets. The attitude to communism changed, however, after the Soviet Union entered the war. A Canadian-Soviet fellowship organization was established in 1943 at an overflow rally in Maple Leaf Gardens, with Sir Ellsworth Flavelle – Joseph Flavelle's son – elected as president. The same year, the Toronto Symphony Orchestra under Sir Ernest MacMillan performed Shostakovich's Fifth Symphony and a fanfare composed by John Weinzweig, *Salute to the USSR*.

❧

As the war continued, the campus took on the appearance of a military camp. Many students were in uniform, and special courses were given for military personnel and others. In the summer of 1941, for example, 500 members of the RCAF, many of whom lived and ate in Hart House, were given a three-month training course as radar technicians. Overall enrolment at the University went down slightly, from about 8,000 in 1938–9 to under 7,000 in 1943–4, and then rose with the return of the first group of veterans. Enrolment in engineering increased, while that in the faculty of arts decreased. In 1943, students in courses that would not directly aid the war effort could avoid conscription only if they were in the top half of the class at the final examinations – a strong incentive for application to one's studies. Some, including the principals of McGill and Queen's and the *Globe and Mail*, advocated that the arts faculty be curtailed or closed, but Harold Innis, George Brett, A.S.P. Woodhouse, and others helped block such a move. It was a close call, and it resulted in the formation at the end of 1943 at a meeting in Hart House of the Humanities Research Council.

❧

A tank in front of University College during the Second World War.

Students in uniform in the Hart House Library, 1942.

The numbers applying to medicine greatly exceeded the capacity to train them, and in 1942 – for the very first time at the University of Toronto medical school – a method of limiting enrolment was devised. In 1941, 210 students had applied, whereas in earlier years there normally had been only about 140 applications. The following year there were more than 350 applications for 150 places. A new admission system was therefore instituted in 1942. Until then, as the historians R.D. Gidney and W.P.J. Millar have shown, completing senior matriculation would assure one a place in first year medicine at the provincial university. Students were subsequently weeded out in their first and second years. The number who advanced to third year usually bore an 'uncanny correspondence' to the number of clinical places available. Unlike the situation at a number of other medical schools in Canada, no 'formal mechanisms' had been used to limit enrolment at the University of Toronto. In 1932, for example, 27 per cent of the incoming class was Jewish.

In 1942, however, various subjective methods, including letters of reference and interviews, were employed to limit student numbers. Moreover, rural candidates were given special consideration. Geographical considerations were often used in American medical schools to limit the number of Jewish students, who tended to be concentrated in large urban centres such as New York City. At the time, the main teaching hospital in Toronto, the Toronto General Hospital, did not accept Jewish staff members and permitted only one Jewish intern a year, and it would be surprising if this attitude was not reflected also in the new discretionary admission practices of the faculty of medicine. Indeed, the medical faculty's admission committee specifically refers in its minutes to 'the serious problem' of Jews in the medical school, and notes 'the almost vitriolic criticism from parents and others on ... the large number of jews.' It appears reasonably clear from both the anecdotal and the statistical evidence available that discriminatory practices prevailed for a period of time – at least a dozen years – after the new policy was introduced. Discrimination against women is even clearer, because in 1965 the University told the Royal Commission on the Status of Women that it had discriminated against women but no longer did so.

⚬⚬

Because so many faculty members had left the University to serve in the military or been seconded to work in Ottawa or elsewhere, teaching the still substantial number of students posed a problem. 'We are finding it very difficult,' Cody wrote to a friend in the fall of 1941, 'to hold enough members of the staff to carry on the work of teaching efficiently.' Almost 200 members of the academic staff were in the armed forces by the autumn of 1942. The psychologist E.A. Bott reported in 1941 that three of his colleagues had applied for leave, and there were more leaves to come, including his own to do special work in England for the Royal Air Force. The following year, Eli Burton, the head of physics, noted that four of his colleagues had been seconded to the military. Fortunately, a number of female physicists were available, three of whom – Elizabeth Allin, Kathleen Crossley, and Florence Quinlan – became assistant professors. The latter two did not have doctorates and did not rise above this rank. Allin, who had received her doctorate under McLennan, became a full professor in 1963 and retired in 1972.

Of the academics who had gone to Ottawa, some joined the National Research Council or another government organization. Brough Macpherson, for example, was seconded to the Wartime Information Bureau, Joseph Parkinson to the Wartime Prices and Trade Board, and Wynne Plumptre to the Department of Finance. (Plumptre would not return to the University until 1965, when he was appointed the first principal of Scarborough College.) Vincent Bladen writes that, as a result of the many departures, his teaching load was overwhelming – it included giving an introductory economics course to 600 engineers.

A serious shortage of engineering professors developed. A number of engineers were seconded to Research Enterprises Limited, a crown corporation set up early in the war and located in Leaside, then a suburb of Toronto. The corporation produced radar and other scientific equipment. It was headed by Colonel Eric Phillips, an engineering graduate and successful businessman who later would play a dominant role in the University as chairman of the board of governors. Civil engineering professor T.R. Loudon, to pick another example, became the chief technical officer for flight research in Ottawa, responsible for testing aircraft used by the RCAF. At the University, he had been in charge of aerodynamics and airplane stress analysis and had lectured on the theory of flight. The faculty at first brought in practising engineers as part-time instructors, but this arrangement did not work out. Permission was granted for the 1943–4 academic year to defer the military service of some of the faculty's own graduates so that they could work as instructors.

The University of Toronto made a major research contribution to the war effort. Most of Canada's research was coordinated by the National Research Council at Ottawa, which had been established during the First World War. Its single, well-equipped laboratory on Sussex Drive in Ottawa, which had been opened in 1932, had 300 professional staff by 1939, and by the end of the war the NRC operated 22 establishments, including 8 new permanent research centres, and a staff of about 3,000. Most of the war research was done in government laboratories, but some was assigned to the universities, particularly work relating to chemistry. British and American scientists worked on the same projects as Canadian scientists – one laboratory at MIT, for example, which worked on radar, employed over 1,000 scientists – so it is difficult to sort out the exact importance of the contributions made by the various participants, including that of the University of Toronto, to the Allied victory.

The University, for instance, did some work on radar development, but its main contribution in that area was in training technicians and offering expertise to Research Enterprises Limited, which manufactured nearly 9,000 radar sets for the Canadian and British navies. The one area in which Toronto does not appear to have made much of a contribution was in the development of the atomic bomb. Atomic research in Canada during the war was concentrated in a special laboratory at the University of Montreal, the core of which had been transferred from Cambridge.

One crucial weapon Toronto did help develop was the proximity fuse, which would allow an anti-aircraft shell to destroy a plane without a direct hit. The British, who had secretly been working on such a device, shared their expertise with Canada and the United States in 1940. The task of working on the project in Canada was assigned by the NRC to a team at the University of Toronto, headed by the physicist Arnold Pitt, a Canadian who had studied in the United States and had joined the faculty in 1927. The fuse consisted of a very small radio transmitter in the cone of a shell that could detect proximity to an object. Once it did so, the shell would explode. Pitt's team produced a number of important innovations, one of which was the development of a radio tube that could withstand the impact of the launching of the shell. C.C. ('Kelly') Gotlieb, later the head of computer science at the University, joined the group after graduation in 1942 and did research on the ability of the radio to withstand shock. This research was considered so significant that he and others were flown 'VIP' to England in a Lancaster bomber to test the fuses on British guns. A particularly important innovation for the effectiveness of the fuse related to the battery that powered the radio. Ordinary batteries had a short shelf life. The Toronto team developed a system whereby the liquid electrolyte was kept separate in a glass container, which would shatter when the shell was fired but would still have time to power the radio.

The Americans, who had taken over the principal role in the development of the fuse, did not want the device used in situations in which it could fall into enemy hands, but it was used against Japanese kamikaze bombers and in England against the V-1 flying bomb attacks that began in 1944. In the latter case, the fuse, combined with radar, resulted by the sixth week of operation in three-quarters of the rockets being destroyed in the air. 'It is possible that without the Canadian contribution,' C.P. Stacey, the official historian of Canada's war policies, wrote, 'the shells that beat the German flying bomb offensive against England in 1944 would not have been available in time.'

George Wright and others in the chemistry department, including Andrew Gordon, who became the head of chemistry in 1944, did valuable work on a number of projects involving shell propellants and explosives. Wright, an organic chemist who had come from the United States in 1936, was also in charge of distributing grants for the many projects involving explosives conducted at Canadian universities. He was noted for his eccentricities and, according to one of his colleagues, 'drove his team ruthlessly.' Until the Second World War, TNT was used for explosives. Wright helped develop a more powerful explosive, RDX. It had been known about since the First World War. The problem was that it was unstable. Wright and his colleagues at the University worked on improving its stability and testing various methods of production. A senior official with the Department of Munitions and Supply was shocked, however, to discover that Wright was conducting some of the experiments using this unstable substance in the elevator shaft of the old chemistry building. 'He and his whole group would probably have been blown to pieces,' the official reported. By early 1943, RDX was being mass-produced in the United States for use by the American forces. Wright also conducted research on propellants, one of which – DINA – was used by the Canadian and US navies. After the war, he was awarded the US Medal of Freedom for his contributions.

Excellent research was also done in the medical field. Dr Arthur Ham, for example, did work on burn dressings, and the Connaught Laboratories produced large quantities of the new wonder drug penicillin. The Connaught Laboratories expanded from a staff of about 250 in 1939 to almost 1,000 in

1944, and the old Knox College on Spadina Circle was purchased for the production of the antibiotic. Charles Best and others, including Jessie Ridout, who had recently completed a PhD in physiology and was one of several women connected with the School of Hygiene, worked on finding a whole-blood replacement for military use. 'It was possible,' Best stated, 'to demonstrate very quickly that serum was as effective as whole blood in the treatment of shock and hemorrhage in experimental animals.' In the fall of 1939, he obtained blood from staff in the School of Hygiene and 300 student volunteers throughout the University, and by freezing and concentrating the blood – the first experiment in blood derivatives in Canada – he was able to produce dried human blood serum, or plasma. The work was carried out in both the School of Hygiene, now the FitzGerald Building, and the Connaught Laboratories. By the summer of 1941, they were producing 5,000 bottles of blood serum a week. In the last year of the war, the project received almost a million blood donations.

Physiologist Donald Solandt, who from 1941 headed the department of physiological hygiene in the School of Hygiene, undertook research on vision and hearing and related biophysical matters. One project on shock was undertaken jointly with Jeanne Manery, who had received her PhD in biology from the University in 1935. Solandt was awarded the Medal of Freedom by the US government for his work, particularly his contributions to the study of night vision. He died at the age of 48. His equally brilliant brother, Omond Solandt, also a medical graduate of Toronto, became the first head of the Defence Research Board and later would become chancellor of the University.

The University of Toronto led Canada's efforts in aviation medicine. Frederick Banting and others in the Banting Institute, such as Edward Hall, who later became dean of medicine and president of the University of Western Ontario, had started working on aviation medicine before the war. They were later joined by a number of American scientists. The team investigated the physiological problems caused by high speeds and high altitudes. High speeds, particularly in aerial dives and dog fights, produced blindness and then unconsciousness, as blood was drawn from the eyes and the brain by the effects of accentuated gravity.

Two devices were built by Banting's group at the Eglinton Hunt Club on Avenue Road north of Eglinton Avenue – a decompression chamber to study the effects of high altitudes and an accelerator to test the effects of speed. The decompression chamber, completed in 1941, was the first in North America,

Frederick Banting died in a plane
crash in 1941.

Wilbur Franks invented the world's first anti-gravity suit. Picture taken in 1962.

though Germany had at least eighty such chambers. Banting was the first to test it, and obtained the equivalent of a height of 25,000 feet at a temperature of –59°F. Banting tended to be somewhat reckless. Still suffering from the effects of the mustard gas he had tested on himself, in a confused state in the chamber he wanted to increase the decompression on that first experiment, but the staff wisely said no. One result of their work was an improved oxygen mask.

Physiologist Wilbur Franks, a cancer researcher in Banting's laboratory, developed an idea that resulted in the world's first anti-gravity suit. Franks had noted in his cancer research that his test tubes often broke when subjected to severe centrifugal force. He had solved the problem by first inserting them in larger and stronger liquid-filled bottles. The same idea, Franks thought, could be employed for pilots, who could wear water-filled outer suits. Mice who would otherwise have died survived when spun in water-filled condoms (presumably with their heads out of the water). A large centrifuge – the most advanced in the world – was built with the help of the department of electrical engineering for experimenting with the concept. It worked, and the so-called 'anti-G suit' was first used in 1942 by carrier-based Royal Navy aircraft in the amphibious landing in North Africa. 'Our planes,' a contemporary report stated, 'performed feats of aerobatics deemed impossible without the pilots blacking-out.' The present suit used by astronauts is a direct descendant of Franks' flying suit.

Most readers will be surprised to learn that the University of Toronto played a significant role in chemical and biological warfare during the war. Banting was convinced that Germany would use such weapons. In a 1937 memo to General McNaughton, then head of the NRC, Banting had written that 'undoubtedly the next development in war will be the utilization of epidemic disease as a means of destroying an enemy.' Plague bacilli, for example, could be delivered 'by means of rats harbouring infected fleas.' Shells, he went on, could contain 'bacteria such as gas gangrene, tetanus and rabies ... so that even a scratch would be deadly.' The University of Toronto, with the government's and President Cody's blessings, became heavily engaged in both chemical and biological warfare research.

Most scientists at the time did not have serious ethical qualms about the work. 'Biological warfare research,' wrote historian Donald Avery, 'was viewed as a viable option for most scientists during the Second World War.' Research had to be conducted so that effective vaccines and protective devices could be produced to counter the enemy's use of these weapons. Italy had used chemical weapons in Ethiopia, and it had been reported that Japan had used them against Chinese troops. Moreover, a potential retaliatory capability would make their use by the enemy less likely. Both Churchill and Roosevelt threatened such a response. As it turned out, Germany did not use such weapons against the Allied forces, though it had, for example, over 10,000 tons of nerve gas available in charged munitions, and it clearly had no qualms about using gas to kill civilians in its death camps.

Many people in the University were involved in the activity. H.M. Barrett of the department of physiological hygiene and Andrew Gordon and others in the department of chemistry, for example, worked on chemical warfare. In 1941, Barrett became superintendent of research at the 2,000-square mile Suffield Experimental Station in Alberta, where various weapons were tested. Members of Banting's team at the department of medical research, as well as persons at the School of Hygiene and the Connaught Laboratories, worked on biological warfare. James Craigie, for example, experimented with parrot fever and typhus, and Donald Fraser with typhoid and salmonella poisoning. The salmonella poisoning work, according to one writer, 'appears to be the first-ever attempt among English-speaking nations to cultivate a bacterial agent specifically for use against humans.'

Banting had spearheaded the biological research, and after his death in a plane crash in early 1941 there was less enthusiasm for it. The School of Hygiene and the Connaught Laboratories understandably were more comfortable working on penicillin, plasma, and sulpha drugs – drugs designed to save lives, not destroy them. The official history of the School of Hygiene and the Connaught Laboratories stresses Fraser's involvement in the development of the TABT vaccine and Craigie's work on the typhus vaccine – for which he was awarded a US Medal of Freedom – and not the possible aggressive use of destructive biological weapons.

＊

Canada's wartime experience drew it closer to the United States. Frank Underhill turned out to be right. Canada would no longer be putting all her 'eggs in the British basket.' Canada was now tied militarily to the United States. It purchased large quantities of military equipment from American suppliers, thus departing from the British Imperial principle of similarity of equipment. Moreover, American research and manufacturing had for the most part taken over the development of advanced weapons and equipment. Canadian universities would contribute to their development, though not to the same extent as American universities, where 'the war brought about fundamental changes in the relationship between science and government.' Finally, the link with British universities continued to weaken because of the close contacts made during the war between Canadian and American scientists. Indeed, the rapid and extensive shift in emphasis on all fronts from Britain to the United States probably surprised even Underhill.

PART FIVE

GROWTH

chapter twenty-eight

1944

CHANGING THE GUARD

Enrolment in universities soared at the end of the war. The federal government, reversing the position it had taken after the First World War, took responsibility for the post-secondary education of veterans. An announcement to this effect had been made as early as 1941, so the universities were not caught by surprise. All who had served were promised free tuition and a living allowance – $60 a month for single and $80 for married persons, with a further allowance for dependants. In addition, universities were given $150 a year for each veteran. At the end of the war, enrolment at the University of Toronto was about 7,000 – the same as it had been at the beginning of the war. In 1946–7, however, it was over 17,000, an increase of 10,000 students. About half the total number were veterans. Toronto took about a quarter of all of the veterans in Canada who went on to university.

There were serious doubts in the minds of many as to whether President Cody was the right person to oversee the anticipated increase in numbers. The Conservative premier George Drew, who had been elected in August 1943, was certainly one of the doubters. Drew did not like Cody. He had attacked Cody while in opposition on the issue of the admission of 'enemy aliens' to the University and continued with various attacks after he became premier. Relations could not have been helped by a 'private and confidential' letter Cody had sent to his friend the former premier George Henry in 1943, which was subsequently passed on by Henry to Drew, comparing Drew to Hitler on the issue of 'enemy aliens.'

Cody turned 76 in 1944 – he was almost twice the age of the principal of McGill, Cyril James. His health was deteriorating. For a number of years he had suffered from ulcers, and he was becoming hard of hearing. 'No one spoke clearly any more, everyone mumbled,' Cody complained to Dr Ian Urquhart, the head of the University Health Service, in 1942. 'Mr. President,' Urquhart informed him, 'you are getting just a little bit deaf.' Urquhart also discovered that Cody had diabetes, which was treated with a special diet and insulin. Some time later, Cody told him of a strange experience he had just had. He had been at Hart House to give a speech. 'What worried him,' Urquhart was to write, 'was that he did not remember much about the event. He really did not know whether or not he had made a speech – and if he had, he had no recollection of what he had said.' Urquhart phoned the dean of medicine, W.E. Gallie, who had been at the event, to ask him whether Cody had made a speech. Dr Gallie assured him that Cody 'had made an excellent speech.' Urquhart concluded that Cody was having an insulin reaction. Many members of the board were aware of Cody's problems. 'It has been quite clear to most of us,' the board member and medical doctor Herbert Bruce wrote in 1944, 'that Dr. Cody could not continue very long as he has been slipping badly.' Bruce Macdonald, the chairman of the board, recalled telling Cody that he 'must contemplate resignation.'

Herbert Bruce and several other influential members of the board wanted Vincent Massey, then Canada's high commissioner in London, to succeed Cody as president. The matter was raised with Massey in early 1944 on a visit Massey made to Canada. He would make an 'ideal president,' they thought. Massey told Bruce he would consider the idea and get back to him. Before Massey had replied, however, other events intervened. It is not known whether Massey would have accepted an offer of the presidency of the University if it had been made. His biographer, Claude Bissell, thinks that 'most likely' he would not, but one wonders, considering that he later toyed with becoming master of Balliol College in Oxford.

Cody had thought up a plan that would prolong his presidency for at least a few more years. His scheme was first revealed at a typically poorly attended meeting of the board on March 9, 1944 – only 7 out of 22 members attended. Macdonald, the chair of the board, heard about the plan on the day of the meeting. Cody's idea was rather ingenious. University College needed a new principal because Malcolm Wallace was about to retire. Sidney Smith, who had been president of the University of Manitoba for the previous ten years, would

President Cody with Sidney Smith, the principal of University College and assistant to the president, in 1944 or 1945.

become the new principal, with the right to succeed Cody as president. In the meantime, the 47-year-old Smith would be executive assistant to the president. The board passed a resolution authorizing Cody 'to make inquiries concerning a possible successor to Professor M.W. Wallace ... keeping in mind someone who might later succeed to the office of President.'

Cody wrote to Smith to sound him out on the idea. 'I am seventy-five years old,' Cody wrote, 'and in the natural course of nature ought not to carry my present burden of responsibility too long ... You are the man who in my opinion can best carry on the tremendous and growing work of this University.' They had known each other for a number of years through their work on the National Conference of Canadian Universities. Smith had succeeded Cody as president of the association in 1942. How long Cody hoped to continue is not clear, but probably for at least a couple of years, considering that Cody told Smith that he wanted to 'have a hand in the building programme that we shall carry out immediately after the war, and in the general rehabilitation of returning students.' That could be some years away.

The members of the board who had not attended the meeting were caught off guard. Herbert Bruce wrote to Massey saying that the idea of Smith as president 'came as a great surprise to me as it did to nearly all of the members of the Board.' It was one thing to appoint a principal of University College and another to appoint a president. The Massey supporters were not pleased with Cody's actions. At the next meeting of the board, the reference in the minutes of the earlier meeting to the possibility of the person's succeeding to the office of president was deleted. Not only were a number of board members interested in Massey, but another name was now quietly being promoted, that of Lester Pearson. 'I have just learned from a good authority,' Cody wrote to his friend Howard Ferguson, 'that the Victoria people are working up a lobby to secure the Presidency for one of their own graduates, L.B. Pearson, now minister-councillor of the Canadian Embassy in Washington ... He is an able man, but I should think not as suited for academic administration as Smith.'

Cody's plan had, however, a momentum that was hard to stop. Smith had an excellent reputation in Manitoba. W.L. Morton later wrote in his history of the University of Manitoba that Smith's 'deft administrative touch, his geniality in all personal matters, the firmness and legal exactness in all matters of business, had made him indeed a reconciler of irreconcilables, a model administrator president.' George Drew said that the decision was for the Toronto board, but that he himself thought Smith would make a good president, a view probably shared by members of his cabinet. A graduate of Dalhousie law school, Smith had taught at Osgoode Hall Law School from 1925 to 1929 before becoming dean of Dalhousie Law School and then president of the University of Manitoba. Drew and some of the other lawyers in the cabinet – the treasurer, Leslie Frost, the attorney general, Leslie Blackwell, and the planning and development minister, Dana Porter – would probably have known Smith by reputation, if not personally, when he was in Toronto. All members of the cabinet would have known that Smith might have been the leader of the federal Conservative party in 1942 if he had not withdrawn in favour of Premier John Bracken of Manitoba.

The board approved the plan on April 27, 1944. Its resolution included the words 'with the promise of succession to the Presidency of the University in due time.' The offer of a salary of $10,500 included $1,500 for expenses. It also included a fine house, which had been set aside for the president beside the museum on the site of the present McLaughlin Planetarium and which was being used as a women's residence. Falconer had lived there, but Cody had preferred to stay in his home on Jarvis Street, where he had lived since before the turn of the century. Smith's appointment took effect as of July 1, 1944.

Drew's idea of 'in due time' was far shorter than Cody's. Almost immediately after Smith came to Toronto in the late summer of 1944, Drew started putting pressure on Cody to resign. In September, Drew told Cody and Macdonald in general terms that he wanted the board to give 'serious consideration ... to the future prospects of the University, particularly in view of the heavy obligations which will be laid upon it following the conclusion of the War.' He was 'not convinced that the University was prepared to meet the new conditions.' Macdonald and the board offered to tender their resignations, but Drew said this was not what he had in mind. He clearly wanted Cody to go, but had no power to fire him.

Cody was being pushed by Drew, but he was also being pulled by the vacancy created by the death on October 1, 1944 of Sir William Mulock, the 100-year-old chancellor. Mulock had been around the University for a long, long time. He had entered the first year class at University College in 1859, the same year that University College was opened. In 1943 – eighty-four years later – he had, as chancellor, granted a degree to his great-grandson, William J. Mulock. The complex drama that was played out concerning his replacement as chancellor is not easily described in a few paragraphs. Cody and others had not expected Mulock to run again for chancellor, and shortly after Smith had been selected eventually to succeed him, Cody wrote to Massey saying he would do everything he could to promote Massey as the next chancellor. 'I have long desired to see you elected as Chancellor of your Alma Mater,' Cody wrote, 'and I shall gladly use whatever influence I possess to bring that to pass.' But then Mulock decided he wanted to die in office. Massey, who had let his name stand for chancellor, withdrew it. Nobody wanted to oppose the venerable Mulock.

After Mulock died, Cody changed his tune. He would no longer support Massey. He wanted the job for himself, since it would keep him on the campus and in a prestigious office for another four years. He knew that the senate, which was to make the decision, would easily elect him. Massey would not dare run against him in such circumstances. Massey's supporters failed in their efforts to have the procedure changed so that the chancellor would be elected by all the graduates of the University, a procedure that might have favoured Massey.

President Cody and members of the U of T Alumni Association at the reading of a citation celebrating Chancellor William Mulock, probably on the occasion of his hundredth birthday in 1944.

Cody – the only candidate – was acclaimed chancellor by the senate for a four-year term in November 1944. Massey could not understand why Cody had offered to support him the previous spring. One likely explanation is that Cody thought at the time that he might remain as president for a number of years and would become chancellor after Massey's term was up. It was becoming increasingly clear, however, that he could not stay on much longer as president. Mulock's death gave him both a convenient exit and a re-entry. Cody finally resigned as president as of June 30, 1945.

Massey's supporters were angry. 'It is clear that Dr. Cody is moving heaven and earth to receive the appointment,' Drew had written to Massey in October 1944. 'It seems that Dr. Cody has come to look upon Toronto University as his own private property to be dealt with according to his own wishes.' Smith could not have been pleased to have Cody as a member of the board offering unsolicited advice. A move was made by the Massey supporters to change the method of selecting the chancellor. In 1947, an act was passed that took the power of selection out of the hands of the senate and gave it to a committee made up of members of the board, of the senate, and of the alumni. It also reduced the chancellor's period of office from four to three years. Of immediate importance was the fact that the three-year period applied deliberately and retroactively to Cody. 'The purpose,' Cody's biographer has written, 'appeared to be to get rid of Cody.'

Cody's supporters were now furious. Both Cody and Massey accepted nominations, and Cody actively campaigned for re-election. Massey, however, was selected by the committee. The board quickly approved the selection, but the senate refused to accept it. Among those who led the fight in the senate on Cody's behalf were Sydney Hermant, a businessman and later vice-chair of the governing council, and E.A. Macdonald, the general secretary-treasurer of the Students' Administrative Council, who was very loyal to Cody and over the years had kept Cody informed of events on the campus. Macdonald reported to Cody after one difficult senate meeting that 'Sydney Hermant was magnificent.' The university solicitor, Hamilton Cassels, gave an opinion that the senate could not reject Massey's nomination. Cecil Augustus 'Caesar' Wright of Osgoode Hall Law School gave an opposite opinion. Smith pleaded with the senate to elect Massey. In the end, Massey was elected by the senate in a secret ballot and was installed as chancellor in November 1947. Canon Cody did not attend.

Drew was also anxious to bring greater dynamism to the board. In October 1944, Eric Phillips was appointed a member by the government. Within a few months, the 72-year-old Bruce Macdonald had resigned as chairman, and the 52-year-old Phillips took over – a position he would hold until 1964. A 1914 graduate in chemical engineering from the University, he was a veteran of the First World War and had won a Military Cross for 'conspicuous gallantry.' He had been in Europe intending to further his studies in chemical engineering in Germany when the war broke out. He joined the British army and became one of its youngest lieutenant-colonels. Between the wars, he had established a successful glass manufacturing plant in Oshawa, and during the Second World War he had been the 'dollar-a-year' head of Research Enterprises Limited, which had successfully and rapidly produced precision instruments and optical devices, such as bombsights and radar sets. In 1945, he became one of the key figures in Argus Corporation, a holding company that controlled a number of major

Colonel Eric Phillips, the chairman of the board of governors, and Chancellor Vincent Massey.
Picture taken during Massey's term as chancellor, 1947–53.

enterprises, including Massey-Ferguson. He had a reputation in the business world,' Claude Bissell later wrote, 'for brilliance and ruthlessness, a combination that carried him to the top.' Phillips worked closely with Smith and with his successor, Bissell. 'Phillips had a powerful and incisive mind,' Bissell wrote. 'His opinions were expressed with a deceptive sense of tentativeness, and always with great urbanity and style. Few could resist the combination of toughness, intelligence, and charm.' Phillips collected art and read widely, particularly history. When he died, Bissell recorded in his diary, 'I had a sense of great warmth for Eric: he had been affectionate, almost father-like toward me.' In many ways, Phillips was to play a role in the University similar to that of Edmund Walker earlier in the century.

Within a few years, Phillips and Drew were able to entice several other talented individuals into joining the board. A key appointment was that of Henry Borden, a corporate lawyer (the founder of the law firm of Borden Ladner

Gervais) and president of Brazilian Traction (later Edper Brascan). Like Smith and Phillips, he had roots in the Maritimes. A McGill and Dalhousie graduate, he had been a Rhodes scholar. Like Phillips, he had been a 'dollar-a year' man in Ottawa during the war, where he served as chairman of the Wartime Industries Control Board. He served as vice-chairman of the University of Toronto board and would take over as chairman when Phillips resigned in 1964. O.D. Vaughan, an engineering graduate and the vice-president of Eaton's, was also appointed. He in his turn would become chairman of the board, after Borden – the second-last chairman before the new governing structure was established in 1972. The appointments between 1944 and 1946 accordingly had a profound effect on the future development of the University. Other men – there were no women – appointed in this period included the lawyers Beverley Matthews and Arthur Kelly, Edward Johnson, who was general manager of the Metropolitan Opera, and the accountant Walter Gordon, who would later serve as head of the Royal Commission on Canada's Economic Prospects and minister of finance in Pearson's government.

The board therefore had considerable administrative expertise. The central administration was restructured by Smith, Phillips, and Borden. Cody had had basically one assistant, his secretary, Agnes MacGillivray, a 1916 graduate of University College. She had taken over after the retirement in 1940 of Annie Patterson, who had served four presidents over a period of forty years. Miss MacGillivray in her turn also would serve four presidents, before retiring in 1963. 'It is no exaggeration to say,' Phillips stated, 'there was practically no trace of any organized plan for the administration.' For the first time, organization charts appeared in Simcoe Hall.

The board brought in a comptroller. The new officer did not report to the president, however, but rather to the board. Smith, it seems, was comfortable with the arrangement, having lived with a similar system at the University of Manitoba after a financial scandal forced its board to take more direct responsibility. This 'dual system of administration,' however, created a clear separation between academic and financial matters. The chief accountant and the superintendent of buildings as well as the various business officers throughout the University were under the authority of the comptroller (later designated a vice-president) and therefore under the authority of the board. The first comptroller was Arnold Gaine, who had been Phillips' comptroller at Research Enterprises Limited. The president was therefore 'stripped of a good deal of authority,' to quote Claude Bissell, who operated under the procedure when he was appointed assistant to the president in 1948 and later when he became president. The system did not change until Phillips resigned and was replaced by Henry Borden in 1964. Bissell describes in a diary entry in January 1965 a meeting with Borden at which he asked him whether there was 'any corporation in Canada (or the world) where a subordinate officer would be responsible directly to the Board.' Borden could not think of one, 'at least in the area of policy,' and the system was changed. Thereafter, the vice-president of administration reported to Bissell. During the previous twenty years, however, the board had controlled much of the growth of the University, for good and ill.

⌘

The first large group of veterans appeared in 1945. 'We will not treat you as a peculiar group, to be segregated,' Smith told them in his welcoming address. Nevertheless, it was recognized that many would have problems, so a special advisory bureau offering psychiatric and other assistance was set up to assist veterans. Furthermore, a placement service was established to help students get jobs after graduation. Both facilities continued after the veterans had left the University.

In general, the veterans were a no-nonsense body. They took their studies seriously. The *Varsity* reported that in the 1945–6 academic year, ex-service students had a failure rate of about 12 per cent, less than half the average failure rate at the University during the previous three years. 'They are less apt to think of examinations as the thing to be constantly in mind, and more likely to be concerned with developing a real acquaintance with their work, for its own sake,' Sam Beatty, the dean of arts, reported in 1948. Their maturity and life experiences made classes more exciting for the non-veteran students. Raids on UC's Whitney Hall women's residence by Victoria and Trinity freshmen were reported in the *Varsity* in September 1947, but by this time few veterans were freshmen. The veterans, however, may well have been the spur for the nine new applications for cocktail licences on the north side of Bloor Street between St George and Avenue Road. Phillips wrote to Drew saying that their presence would 'constitute a most undesirable situation ... The two cocktail bars now in existence provide sufficient facilities without any additions.'

The increase in enrolment was the result primarily of an increase in the number of male students. The percentage of women at the University declined from about 45 per cent in 1944–5 to 27.5 per cent in 1950–1. After the war, as Alison Prentice and her colleagues have written, 'women were expected to return to their primary sphere of activity – the home.' Marriage rates soared. For women aged 15 to 19, the rate more than doubled what it had been before the war. Not only did more women marry, but they married earlier and had more children. The result, of course, was the post-war 'baby boom,' which would hit the universities twenty years later. Most women who did enter the University went into traditionally female courses, as they had before the war.

Finding classrooms to accommodate the large numbers was difficult. Some courses were given in Convocation Hall, and a number of temporary structures were built, including the huts later used for physical and occupational therapy students on the site of the present Massey College, and the bookstore beside the old observatory. Engineering, in particular, needed additional space. Many veterans wanted to become engineers. Of 1,000 air force personnel discharged in the first quarter of 1945 who had chosen to attend the University of Toronto, one-half chose engineering. The post-war period brought an economic boom and a continuing need for engineers. The anticipated recession had not materialized, and, as the economist K.J. Rea has written, 'the economy operated at high levels of employment and, even after the removal of controls, without serious inflation through the remainder of the 1940s.'

The engineers could not be accommodated in their existing facilities on the downtown campus. The solution was to take over a very large munitions plant in Ajax, Ontario – about 25 miles east of Toronto. During the war the plant, built at a cost of $12 million, had filled more than 40 million shells. The property, owned by the federal government, consisted of over 4,000 acres, with more than 100 buildings and 600 wartime houses. The reconstruction minister C.D. Howe agreed to lease it to the University for a nominal rent, but then discovered that Prime Minister Mackenzie King, without telling Howe, had promised it to the RCAF for storing surplus planes. Phillips, Borden, and probably Smith went to Ottawa to try to persuade the government that there were many places in which planes could be stored, but only one place close to Toronto that would meet the needs of the University. Besides, the academic year was only about a month away, and other arrangements could not be made. The government agreed.

Within a year of opening, well over 3,000 first and second year students were studying engineering at Ajax, a self-contained community that also included a

The Wallberg Memorial Building, for chemical engineering and the department of chemistry, officially opened in late 1949.

student centre, 'Hart House Ajax.' The federal government later offered to sell the property at a low price to the University. 'It seems to me,' Howe wrote to Phillips, 'that you will be driven out of the city eventually, and I doubt if there is any more suitable location than the one you have.' The engineering dean, C.R. Young, thought the faculty 'in the course of the next 20 years [would] have a very definite interest in making use of some of the facilities' at Ajax. The University, however, declined the government's offer.

By the end of the decade, the engineering students were back on the main campus. In the meantime, a number of new engineering facilities had been constructed. It helped to have an engineer as chairman of the board. A new mechanical engineering building was finally constructed fronting on King's College Road, and the Wallberg Memorial Building was completed on College Street. The Wallberg Building, which cost four times the sum left by Miss Wallberg in the 1930s, was shared by chemical engineering and the department of chemistry. In 1949, a research-minded dean, Kenneth Tupper, was brought in from his position with the National Research Council's atomic energy project at Chalk River. A 1929 engineering graduate, he had spent his entire career at the NRC working on exciting projects such as jet propulsion and atomic energy.

Tupper's expertise on aspects of atomic energy was probably a factor in his appointment. The previous dean, C.R. Young, had been worried that Toronto 'was losing ground in research on atomic energy' to other universities. Tupper's inaugural address focused on atomic power. It was, he said, limited by the 'scarcity of fissile atoms in the earth's crust.' It may be, he speculated, that in the future we might turn to 'the nuclei of hydrogen atoms, using a material which we might get from sea water by the millions of tons.' Three years later, the Americans exploded a hydrogen bomb.

Tupper, however, did not find the deanship very satisfying. He told Smith in 1954 that he was 'frustrated ... listening to a lot of chatter without much decision.' All he could do, he complained, was 'push the canoe up the stream just a short distance.' He left to become a consulting engineer and later returned to the National Research Council to become its vice-president. Smith wrote to Phillips suggesting that Roland McLaughlin, who had received his PhD in chemistry in 1926, be appointed. 'Roly has done admirably as Head of the Department of Chemical Engineering; he has built up a good staff, and he has developed a graduate programme.' Phillips, who took a strong interest in chemical engineering, approved. McLaughlin continued as head of the department while serving as dean. Tupper, Smith said, had 'contributed much to the development of the Faculty, more than he realizes.' During his deanship, professors with doctorates and strong research backgrounds, such as James Ham, Howard Rapson, and Allen Yen, were appointed. Ham became head of electrical engineering, dean of the faculty, and later the president of the University. Rapson established the faculty's productive Pulp and Paper Centre, and Yen did path-breaking work in electrical engineering by developing an instrument that became a major tool in astronomical studies.

The Institute of Aerospace Studies perhaps best illustrates the growing interest in research in engineering in the late 1940s. It also illustrates the continuing involvement of the University in defence work during the cold war. The report of the Royal Commission on Espionage in June 1946 – following the Gouzenko revelations – changed the public's and the government's perception of the Soviet Union. The Defence Research Board was created to continue the defence research work that had been engaged in by the government during the war. Much of the research would continue to be done by Canadian universities, though they never became as heavily involved in defence work as many American universities. 'The military-driven technologies of the cold war,' wrote the

American historian Stuart Leslie, 'defined the critical problems for the postwar generation of American scientists and engineers.' Moreover, as the Toronto philosopher Ian Hacking has written, 'it is not just the weapons ... that are being funded, but the world of mind and technique in which the weapons are devised.' President Smith was aware of the danger of too great an involvement. 'Practical, applied research,' he said, 'is an important public service which universities should not refuse to perform, but at the same time they must remember their more important duty to the lonely scholar whose inexplicable interest in a seemingly trivial question may lead to real advances on the frontiers of the subject.'

Aerospace Studies – then called the Institute for Aerophysics – was established in 1949 as a result of the drive and determination of Gordon Patterson. He had been hired by the University in 1946 to become professor and head of aeronautical engineering. A University of Alberta graduate, he had first come to Toronto in the early 1930s to pursue graduate work in aeronautical engineering. His Alberta degree in engineering physics, however, was not recognized by the faculty, and in any event, J.H. Parkin, who could have supervised his work, had left for the National Research Council. As a result, Patterson – fortunately as it turned out – did his work in the physics department under Eli Burton in association with the applied mathematicians J.L. Synge and H.A. McTaggart. He studied atomic physics and fluid mechanics, two subjects crucial to an understanding of supersonic flight. After receiving his PhD, he worked at Farnborough, England, and using its wind tunnel contributed to the improvement of the duct cooling systems of the Spitfire and Hurricane aircraft. During the war, he worked at the Jet Propulsion Laboratory in California and later with the well-known mathematician John von Neumann at Princeton. Patterson had developed an international reputation on problems connected with supersonic flight and was being courted by a number of institutions. He was therefore able to negotiate the establishment of a separate department of aeronautical engineering in the faculty of engineering, which would not simply be part of the department of civil engineering.

Omond Solandt, the head of the newly established Defence Research Board, and J.C. Mackenzie of the National Research Council were interested in supporting Patterson's work. 'A University,' Solandt wrote to Smith, 'cannot be expected to do effective research in a field such as Supersonics without substantial Government support because the equipment required is so expensive.' The

Gordon Patterson became head of aeronautical engineering in 1946. Photograph taken before the move from Downsview airport to the Dufferin Street site in 1959.

University was also eager to establish an institute to be headed by Patterson because it felt that Toronto had not been sharing in some of the major government research projects to the extent that other Canadian universities had. Many potential graduate students showed an interest in working in the institute. At least 30 Toronto engineering students in the fourth year wanted to do postgraduate work in the field, and there was great interest from other parts of the country. Moreover, Smith was sure that if Toronto did not get support, Patterson would leave. In 1949, with substantial government support, the Institute for Aerophysics was created.

An engine test shed at Downsview airport was given by the government, along with $250,000 for renovation costs and $100,000 for expenses for the next three years. (The institute would not move to its present site on Dufferin Street until 1959.) The facility was to be opened officially on September 26, 1950. The minister of defence and other dignitaries were invited to attend. Patterson had developed the supersonic wind tunnel with the help of two graduate students, Irvine Glass, who joined the institute that same year as a research associate and went on to an illustrious career in aerospace studies at the University, and Gerald Bull, who went on to an infamous career – he was assassinated in Brussels in 1990 because of his work on the development of a 'super gun' for Saddam Hussein. The night before the opening, however, the supersonic wind tunnel, designed to operate at three times the speed of sound, was still not working. 'I recall,' Patterson wrote, 'that Dean K.F. Tupper dropped into the laboratory that evening to see how matters were proceeding and promptly rolled up his sleeves to help.' At 3 o'clock on the morning of the opening it finally 'ran supersonic.' The next day the tunnel worked, but only after the button was pushed a second time.

The institute was responsible for research, and the department of aeronautical engineering for teaching. Before the establishment of the department, aeronautics was taught as one of the upper year options available to students in the engineering science course (then called engineering physics). Patterson claims that his experience in not being able to combine engineering and physics was in part responsible for the engineering physics course, which had begun in 1933 with 12 students and now, with approximately 500 students, is considered one of the jewels of the engineering faculty. Ben Etkin, later the dean of engineering, had been an early graduate of the course and joined the engineering faculty as a lecturer in 1942. He would be one of many who would enhance the reputation of the institute. Patterson wrote that Etkin's 'exceptional versatility in the field of flight dynamics, covering the spectrum from ground cushion vehicles to space-craft, soon became well known through his two books.' 'At first,' wrote Etkin, 'graduate students were not assigned to individual supervisors, but somewhat on the principle of a commune, all students were the responsibility of all staff. Morale was high and the atmosphere was creative.' Research grants were obtained from Canadian and American sources. There was little, if any, discussion of whether engaging in research that was covered by strict rules of secrecy, security clearances, and restrictions on publication was desirable. It seemed natural to continue the type of government-sponsored research work that had been done during the war.

Computer science was another area in which there was substantial government support. In the year following the end of the war, a committee was established at the University that included, among others, mathematicians Sam Beatty and B.A. Griffith and electrical engineer V.G. Smith. In the summer of 1946, a group of professors toured American research centres to examine emerging computing equipment. A computation centre was subsequently set up at the University with a five-year grant of $40,000 a year, half from the National Research Council and half from the Defence Research Board. C.C. ('Kelly') Gotlieb, who had recently completed his PhD in physics, became acting head of the centre and later its director. The 27-year-old Gotlieb – he looked even younger than his age – was interested in large-scale computations as a result of his work with Arnold Pitt on the proximity fuse during the war. The computation centre wanted to build its own computer. The NRC, however, rejected the University's request for funds to build a mechanical relay-based computer. The future was correctly thought to be in electronic machines, and money was given to the University to begin work on one. Smith hired two graduate students, physicist Josef Kates and electrical engineer Alfred Ratz, to design a machine, named UTEC (University of Toronto Electronic Computer). (Kates later became head of the Science Council of Canada and chancellor of the University of Waterloo.) The team, along with others, started with a small pilot model and eventually received $300,000 from the government agencies to build an operating computer based on the UTEC prototype.

In the meantime, a machine that had been built in England by Ferranti for the British Atomic Energy Authority became available when the newly elected Conservatives replaced the Labour government and cancelled all contracts over

UTEC, a computer developed by the University of Toronto. Photograph, taken about 1950, shows three of its principal developers: from left to right, R.F. Johnston, Josef Kates, and Leonard Casciato.

£100,000. The Ferranti machine was the first one commercially produced by this company and was based on a machine it had built for Manchester University. The Canadian Atomic Energy Commission, which had immediate need of a high-speed computer, urged the University to use its $300,000 grant to purchase the Ferranti, but the University said no. 'We met as a committee and said "thanks but no thanks,"' Gotlieb recalls, adding, 'We have the connections, and we think we can make UTEC into a big machine.' The Ferranti at Manchester was slower than UTEC and was not very reliable. The government, however, promised a further $150,000 to develop UTEC if the University purchased the Ferranti. The offer was too good to turn down. In the meantime, work continued on UTEC. The Ferranti machine arrived in 1952 and was named Ferut (Ferranti University of Toronto) by Beatrice (Trixie) Worsley, who had been one of the earliest members of the UTEC team, had gone on to Cambridge for a doctorate in physics, and then had returned to the centre. After Ferut arrived, however, UTEC was 'simply left to wither away.' 'Although time has dulled the sharpness of the pain,' an historian of the project wrote in 1994, 'several of the development team still feel let down by the fact that such a project was cut off just when it was beginning to show promise.'

Ferut, which filled a large room and contained hundreds of vacuum tubes, was the first electronic computer in Canada and only the second commercially sold computer in the world, the first being Remington Rand's UNIVAC for the US Bureau of Census the previous year. It was installed in the recently completed Burton Wing of the old physics building (now the Sandford Fleming Building). Gotlieb spent several months at Manchester working with the computer science pioneer Alan Turing and others to understand the machine they had just purchased. Patterson Hume of physics, with the assistance of a visitor from Manchester, Christopher Strachey, devised a new operating system, an improvement on the one used at Manchester, and Hume and Worsley created software that enabled scientists to program their own applications without using the complicated Ferut machine code. Hume had received his doctorate in spectroscopy from Toronto in 1949 and became interested in computers because of the great number of calculations required in his work – wave-function calculations for complex atoms. By September 1952, the machine was able to play checkers at a computer conference held in Toronto. One of the first major tasks of the new computer was to provide Ontario Hydro with computations on the effect of the planned St Lawrence Seaway on water levels.

The Ferut computer was in operation at the University until 1958, when it was replaced by an IBM 650 machine, which, though no more powerful than Ferut, offered a much wider software base and easier maintenance. In the early 1960s, a transistorized IBM 7090 – five hundred times faster than the previous machines – was installed, the first and for several years the only large-scale computer in Canada. In 1964, a graduate department of computer science was established, the first in Canada, and later, a regular arts and science department, which now ranks 'among the top ten research departments in North America.'

chapter twenty-nine

1950

'EASY STREET'

It was good to be a student in the 1950s. By 1950, almost all the veterans had graduated, and overcrowding was no longer a serious problem. It would be more than a dozen years before the first wave of baby boomers would appear on campus. The economy was strong, and there was relatively little unemployment. Employers were desperate for university graduates, particularly if they were men. Anyone could go on to law school, with whatever marks. Moreover, the public expected that the 'good times' would continue. There was neither the seriousness of the post-war veterans, nor the intensity of the students of the 1960s. This was the apolitical, silent generation of students who attended football games, spent hours each day playing bridge, and were not particularly worried about their future.

During this period, the Students' Administrative Council concentrated on student activities, such as running dances, organizing 'snow queen' contests, and producing various publications such as the *Varsity* and the university year book *Torontonensis*. The *Varsity* editors, including Wendy Michener and Peter Gzowski, produced lively and controversial issues. In March 1952, the *Varsity* editor Barbara Browne, the news editor Ian Montagnes, and all senior staff members resigned when SAC suspended publication of the *Varsity* following a 'gag' issue containing part of Sidney Smith's last annual report, in which he had complained about the lack of proper training in English at the high school level and stated a need for remedial English instruction. The *Varsity* simply substituted the word 'sex' for the word 'English' in the story, and the rest followed. Although

University of Toronto cheerleaders, about 1953.

Varsity staff members Peter Gzowski, left, and Michael Cassidy in 1956. Gzowski became the editor-in-chief the following year.

'standards have been stiffened,' the *Varsity* reported, more or less using Smith's exact words, there was a high failure rate in an examination 'designed to test the student's knowledge of punctuation, range, and ability,' and the result was 'frustration and a weakening of confidence.' 'I have no faith,' Smith is quoted as saying, 'that teaching in technique will provide a magic cure. The saving virtues must be scholarship and a passion for the subject.' The University's disciplinary body found the material 'in shockingly bad taste.' This was one of the great controversies of the decade. It would probably pass unnoticed today.

For the most part, SAC was not involved in wider issues until the late 1950s, when it investigated ways of combating discrimination on the campus, an issue that had arisen in 1959 when a black woman student was denied entry into a sorority. This type of social concern intensified in the 1960s.

In many respects, the 1950s were like the 1880s and 1890s, enlivened by drinking and student pranks, particularly surrounding initiations. The *Varsity* is full of stories about clashes between various student bodies and run-ins with the police. In 1951, for example, Trinity frosh were sent on a scavenger hunt, one item to be obtained being a streetcar advertising sign. Seventeen students were arrested for causing damage to the property of the TTC. A month later, some students, allegedly engineers, painted the word 'Skule' on arts buildings throughout the campus. Principal F.C.A. Jeanneret of University College said that he could not remember 'a worse case of vandalism in all my years at the University.' In 1953, women frosh from Victoria were taken by bus to the stockyards in the west end of the city, heavily sprayed with perfume, and, after each had had one shoe removed, required to find their way back to Vic on their own. In the course of the event, eight windows of the bus were broken. When Hal Jackman was sworn in as the University's thirtieth chancellor in 1997, he reminisced about 'swiping' the chancellor's chair in the early 1950s to be used for the annual picture of Burwash Hall students. 'I don't want you to think that I spent all my university days doing this kind of thing,' he said, 'although it did seem to take quite a bit of time.'

And so it continued throughout the decade. A three-hour battle between Trinity and Wycliffe students ended in a bonfire and the arrival of three fire trucks. The next year, UC students dumped eighteen cans of garbage over Trinity's front steps. One of the perpetrators was quoted as saying, 'We felt it was time one of the Arts Colleges did something.' Football weekends gave rise to a number of stories – a thirty-minute melee around the goal posts at a Varsity-

The initiation of first year engineering students in 1959; cleaning up parks and beaches replaced earlier hijinks. Note that the two tallest buildings in Toronto in 1959 were the Royal York Hotel, far left, and the Bank of Commerce building.

Queen's game in Kingston in which five Queen's students were injured, and a train trip from a McGill game in which windows were broken and silverware stolen. A particularly serious incident occurred in the fall of 1954, when hundreds of engineering frosh, to the accompaniment of the engineering cannon and the Lady Godiva Memorial Band, were sent on a 'tour' of the campus. They entered UC looking for material that could form part of a later auction. In the course of the raid, the UC registrar, Professor W.J. McAndrew, was injured. 'Any question of retaliation,' UC Lit president Marty Friedland was quoted as saying, self-righteously, would be 'as juvenile as the entire incident itself.' It was a sobering experience for everyone. The constitution of the engineering society was suspended for several months, and the society was fined $4,000. Shortly after the event, however, many engineering students were commended for taking part in the clean-up after Hurricane Hazel. By 1957, part of the engineers' initiation activity involved cleaning up debris in High Park.

The 1950s rival the 1920s for the best intercollegiate teams and the greatest spectator interest in intercollegiate sports. The football team, coached by Bob Masterson, was by far the most popular, with an average attendance of over 25,000 at each game in 1950. The stadium had been renovated that year to increase its capacity: concrete stands had been built on the west side, and the concrete stands on the other side had been extended to form a U-shaped stadium. A league record was established on October 21, 1950, when 26,764 persons watched Western beat Varsity 41 to 6. One of the co-captains that year was Fraser Mustard – 'Moose' Mustard according to *Torontonensis* – later the dean of medicine at McMaster and from 1982 the founding head of the Canadian Institute for Advanced Research. He had been on the championship team in 1948, and in 1949 he was judged by his teammates the 'most worthy' player on the team. A pre-season injury sidelined him in 1950, and his team-mate John Evans, later the founding dean at McMaster medical school and still later the president of the University of Toronto, took over as captain on the field, while Mustard continued as captain from behind the bench.

The team did not win the championship in 1950, but it did in 1951, with Evans – the only two-time winner of the George Biggs trophy as the best male athlete in the University with respect to 'leadership, sportsmanship and perform-ance' – as captain. The 1951 team included Steve Onyschuk, who later played professionally for Hamilton, and Bill Bewley, who played for Calgary and Montreal. It also included Roy McMurtry, the current chief justice of Ontario. The senior team won the championship again in 1954 with the help of John Sopinka, who later became a justice of the Supreme Court of Canada, and again in 1958. The rough and tumble of football and the ability to bounce back after losses seemed to help one rise in later life.

Rowing, which had been a major sport in the 1920s, had been dropped from intercollegiate competition and did not reappear until the 1960s. This was in part because there was no 'Tommy' Loudon to promote it, but it also reflected a continuing move away from British towards American sports and culture. Bas-ketball had taken its place as a major sport at the University. Warren Stevens, who had captained both the football and the basketball teams at Syracuse University, had been appointed director of athletics in 1932, and he promoted basketball at the University. Because basketball was played in the Hart House gymnasium, large crowds could not be accommodated. Still, there was great interest in the sport, and it was the University's most popular interfaculty

Steve Onyschuk in 1955, leading Toronto to an 11–9 victory over Queen's. The future Supreme Court of Canada judge John Sopinka scored the winning touchdown.

George Stulac on the intermediate basketball team in 1954; in 1956 he would compete in the Olympics in both basketball and track and field.

activity – leaving aside the hijinks described earlier. In the mid-1950s, there were 140 men's basketball teams participating – almost half the total number of men's interfaculty teams in all sports. Coached by John McManus, the intercollegiate team won the championship in 1957–8, its first title in eighteen years. George Stulac, one of the most versatile athletes ever to compete for Toronto, was a member of that team. Stulac also played intercollegiate football and competed in track and field as well as swimming, in which he established a number of intercollegiate records. He competed in the 1956 Olympics in Melbourne in both basketball and track and field. Another outstanding basketball star was W.A. 'Pete' Potter, who played nine seasons on the basketball team, starting in 1952. He continued to play after graduating in arts and while studying dentistry, and won the Biggs trophy in 1960. Alan Eagleson was the manager of the basketball team in 1956–7. His move to hockey did not come until later.

Hockey spectators filled Varsity Arena. Varsity won the intercollegiate championship in 1950–1, and won again in the years 1954 to 1959. The 1954–5 team, coached by Jack Kennedy, had three players who made the intercollegiate all-star team – Dave Reid, who led the league in scoring, Paul Knox, who was second in scoring, and medical student Dave 'Red' Stephen, a defenceman who played from 1951 to 1959 and was the captain for four of those years. The 1954–5 team, *Torontonensis* wrote, was 'perhaps the best ever to represent the University of Toronto including the well-known Varsity Grads,' which had been undefeated and unscored against in the 1928 Olympics. The team applied to represent Canada in the 1956 Olympics, but was not selected. Tom Watt, who coached the Toronto Maple Leafs in the 1990s, played for Varsity in the late 1950s and coached the team from 1965 to 1979. During those fifteen years, Toronto won 11 Ontario and 9 Canadian university titles, including 5 Canadian titles in a row.

Women's teams were also successful in the 1950s. The women's intercollegiate basketball team won three of the four intercollegiate titles from 1950 to 1954. Two members of the team in those years became members of the U of T Sports Hall of Fame, Sallie Wallace and Mary Macdonald. Wallace, who played from 1951 to 1957, was named the outstanding women's intercollegiate basketball player for three of those years. Mary Macdonald played on two of the championship basketball teams and also participated in intercollegiate archery and volleyball. Mary Foster, who also became a member of the Hall of Fame, played on the championship basketball team of 1957, as well as participating in

The women's intercollegiate basketball champions, 1952–3; Captain Sallie Wallace is in the front row centre, and Mary Macdonald is in the back row, third from left.

badminton and softball. Women's hockey began the decade with a winning intercollegiate team, but then intercollegiate women's hockey was discontinued. It began again in 1960–1, with the help of Mary Foster, who coached the team from 1960 to 1963 and won three league titles.

Women's athletics continued to suffer from a lack of adequate facilities. Although President Cody had announced in the late 1930s that a women's athletic building would soon be constructed, nothing was done during his tenure in office. In the 1950s, however, Sidney Smith and the board approved a plan to build a women's gymnasium behind the present Falconer Hall – on the west side of Queen's Park south of the Royal Ontario Museum. Falconer Hall, then called Wymilwood, had been built by the financier E.R. Wood at the turn of the century and given to Victoria in 1925 as a women's residence and social centre. In 1949, the University, which owned the land, obtained the building from Victoria in exchange for giving up the University's ownership of various properties east of Queen's Park that had been leased to Victoria. It turned out to be a very good deal for Victoria, which obtained the land south of the old college building, where the E.J. Pratt Library and Northrop Frye Hall now stand, as well as money for the construction of a new student centre, which took the name

Wymilwood, to be built east of Queen's Park, and a women's residence, Margaret Addison Hall. At the same time, the University sold to Victoria its ownership of eight lots on Bloor Street, east of the Lillian Massey Building, for $240,000. The Colonnade commercial and residential complex sits on part of this property and now pays a large sum each year in rent to Victoria University

The new women's athletic facility was announced by Sidney Smith in 1952, and the planning was started. 'It will not be just another Hart House,' the women's athletic director, Zerada Slack, told the *Varsity*. 'There will be, at times, mixed badminton and mixed swimming – but not nude,' she added. The servants' quarters and coach house were demolished to make way for the new structure, but then Premier Leslie Frost entered the picture. (He had taken over as premier in 1949 after George Drew became leader of the federal Conservative party.) Frost had been shown the plans by Sidney Smith and strongly objected to having a gymnasium on the approach from the north to the legislative buildings. The board dutifully changed its mind. At some point in the future, the board chairman, Eric Phillips, told the women's alumnae associations, all three houses south of the museum, including Flavelle House, would be torn down and replaced by a grand building comparable to the museum. The north-west corner of Devonshire and Hoskin – the present site of Massey College – was offered instead for the gymnasium, but was found to be too small for the purpose. Plans were then made for a building at the corner of Harbord and Huron streets. In 1959, the Benson Building was officially opened for women's athletics. Women, however, still had no access to a students' union. There had been discussions in the early 1950s about building one on the lawn south-east of Hart House for both men and women, but because of competing academic priorities the board was against it. 'Of all the projects related to new buildings at the University,' Phillips stated, 'I feel that the [student union] is the most unrealistic.'

❧

Hart House continued to be the focal point of cultural and athletic activities – for men, at least. After the intense crowding in the years after the war, the House now had adequate room for its many activities. Warden Burgon Bickersteth had returned to England a few years after the war, and Nicholas Ignatieff, the eldest son of the minister of education in the last Czarist cabinet and the brother of the diplomat George Ignatieff, was chosen as warden. Vincent Massey and Bickersteth had wanted the philosopher George Grant to be warden, but the board was unwilling to appoint a person who had been a conscientious objector during the war, even one who had served in a civil capacity in London during that difficult period.

Women slowly gained limited entry to certain Hart House activities. However, they could not attend the debates that flourished in the 1950s, such as the 1950 debate with Prime Minister Louis St Laurent as the honorary visitor, the 1956 Lester Pearson debate, or the 1957 Senator John F. Kennedy debate. Starting in 1952, they could come as guests to Sunday evening and Wednesday 'five o'clock' concerts. They would therefore have missed hearing Glenn Gould the previous academic year, but would have heard Lois Marshall sing in the 1952–3 season. Most Sunday evening concerts attracted audiences of more than 500. Women were also entitled to visit Hart House's art gallery, but only on Wednesday afternoons.

One show in the gallery, in 1955, containing nude drawings by Graham Coughtry and Michael Snow, attracted great media attention after the mayor-elect of Toronto, Nathan Phillips, accompanied by the media, made a special trip to Hart House to view the pictures. It was art of a kind which 'a young man or woman of impressionable age should not see,' he declared, and he asked that the pictures be taken down. The ensuing publicity increased attendance tenfold, according to the chairman of the exhibition committee, Alex Gigeroff. It proved, said the *Varsity*, that 'four-star, triple-plated, gold-spangled 19th century pompous bigotry is still firmly entrenched in Ontario.' The *Varsity* had a field day later that year over the threat by the Lord's Day Alliance to prosecute Hart House for charging admission to the Hart House Orchestra's special Sunday evening concerts. The Lord's Day Act specified that only certain sporting events could charge admission on Sunday. 'Evidently,' said Boyd Neel, the conductor of the orchestra, 'you can play baseball in Toronto on Sundays but you can't play Beethoven.' The concerts took place. In the 1950s, much of the cultural life of the city continued to be centred at the University.

One significant innovation was made in 1954 by Warden Joseph McCulley, who had been appointed in 1952 after Ignatieff died suddenly. The former billiard room in the basement was transformed into the co-educational Arbor Room. The first permanent women students' washroom was installed in Hart House, and a new outside entrance was constructed in the south wall of the building. President Smith and Chancellor Beatty and their wives cut the ceremo-

Joseph McCulley, the warden of Hart House. Photograph taken in 1965.

nial tape, and roses were given to the first two hundred women to enter the room. Women could not enter until 3 o'clock in the afternoon, however; until then it was reserved for men. They could also come as guests to the 150-acre Hart House farm in the Caledon Hills, purchased in 1949. Warden McCulley, who had been head of Pickering College and then deputy commissioner of penitentiaries, wanted to keep the House itself as essentially a male preserve. So did Vincent Massey, then the governor general of Canada. It was not until the appointment of a new warden, Arnold Wilkinson, and after Massey's death that women became full members of the House. President Claude Bissell recorded in his diary in 1968 'the possibility now, with Vincent Massey's death, of opening

Donald Sutherland, fourth from right, in the 1956 Hart House production of
Molière's *School for Wives*.

Hart House to women.' He appointed a committee, which so recommended, and on January 27, 1972 the university board of governors approved a recommendation that women be admitted to the House on the same terms as male students.

Women had always taken part in Hart House Theatre, which was administered separately from Hart House. The theatre, used only sporadically since 1937, was revived after the war. Robert Gill, an American actor with academic credentials, was brought in to run the program for students. The theatre would in large measure be used for student productions, unlike in the pre-war years, when it was used mainly by amateur and semi-professional actors. The first production in 1947 was Shaw's *Saint Joan*, with Charmion King in the title role. 'Her performance of Joan,' the *Globe and Mail* critic wrote the following morning, 'is a luminous portrayal, instinct with an inner fire of truth and spiritual beauty, and exquisite in its shadings of emotion and execution.' 'We used to sell out pretty well every performance' of the student productions, said the theatre manager Jimmy Hozack. When Gill died in 1974, a memorial service in the theatre included a reading of *Saint Joan* by some of those who had taken part in the first production – Charmion King, David Gardner, Donald and Murray Davis, and Eric House. Every year in the 1950s, Gill would stage four student productions. In the 1949–50 season, for example, he put on Robertson Davies' *Fortune My Foe*, Shakespeare's *Othello*, Molnar's *The Guardsman*, and an adaptation of Dostoyevsky's *Crime and Punishment*. About 350 persons auditioned for the 70 parts in the four plays, with women outnumbering men three to one. Many now well known actors and directors in addition to those in *Saint Joan* worked under Gill's direction, including Frances Hyland, Leon Major, Kate Reid, and Donald Sutherland. Many who worked with him went on to Stratford when it opened in 1953. The drama scholar Ann Saddlemyer calls Gill 'one of the most significant figures in the development of Canadian theatre.' In 1966, the new Graduate Centre for the Study of Drama took over the theatre, and in 1987 the centre's activities were transferred to the new Robert Gill Theatre in the Koffler Student Centre.

In the 1950s, the campus gradually began to take on an international flavour. There were many new Canadians, almost exclusively from Europe. There were very few members of visible minority groups among the students, as a glance through any issue of *Torontonensis* for those years shows. It was extremely difficult for persons from developing countries to immigrate to Canada. Until 1956, immigration from Asia, Africa, and the Caribbean was limited to the spouses and children of persons already citizens of Canada. In that year, the government permitted very small quotas from Commonwealth countries. The 1962 government regulations sought to eliminate discrimination based on colour, race, and creed. It was not until 1967, however, as was observed by Ninette Kelley and Michael Trebilcock in their study of Canadian immigration policy, that the 'regulations finally removed all explicit traces of racial discrimination from Canada's immigration laws.'

The number of students coming from developing countries on student visas was increasing, but the total was still very low, compared to today's. The Toronto branch of FROS – Friendly Relations with Overseas Students – estimated in 1950–1 that there were only about 60 Asian, 20 African, and 20 West Indian students at the University. In total, there were only about 250 visa students in the early 1950s, compared to more than 2,000 today. In the early 1980s, the number was over 4,000, but later it decreased, when foreign students began to be charged higher fees.

Kay Riddell, the director of the International Student Centre, housed in Cumberland House on St George Street. Photograph from 1965.

FROS played a crucial role in making foreign students feel welcome and in bringing them into closer contact with Canadian students. Along with World University Service of Canada, which held seminars and arranged study tours abroad, it helped create greater understanding and links among students at an international level. FROS was started on the campus in 1951 by a Toronto graduate, Catherine Steele, then the educational director of the Royal Ontario Museum and later the principal of Havergal College. The Toronto graduate Kay Riddell was appointed executive director. She had returned to Toronto in 1951 after the sudden death of her husband, the permanent head of the Canadian delegation to the United Nations. With Sidney Smith's support, space was provided in the Lillian Massey Building at the corner of Bloor Street and Avenue Road. Helen Frye, Northrop's wife, became the first volunteer typist. Many members of the faculty and staff contributed to the work of the organization. John Wevers of Near Eastern studies, James Ham of engineering, Jarvis McCurdy of philosophy, and Michael Powicke of history successively chaired the organization after Catherine Steele's tenure. Ham met his wife, Mary Augustine, while both were working for the organization.

During the course of its first fourteen years, FROS had nine temporary homes. Finally, in 1966, Cumberland House on St George Street – named after its builder and owner, the architect Frederic Cumberland, who had also designed University College – became the permanent home of the organization, renamed the International Student Centre. The building had been slated to be torn down to make room for the Galbraith engineering building, but fortunately someone thought of moving the forestry building on rollers to the north; enough space was thereby provided for the engineering building, and Cumberland's magnificent home was saved. It was restored by Eric Arthur with funds provided by the Rotary clubs of Toronto.

The cold war brought East European students to the University. Bosko Loncarevic, for example, escaped by boat from Yugoslavia in the early 1950s and became a student in engineering physics. He recalls first entering the office of FROS and saying: 'I am an overseas student. Are you going to be friendly?' The following year, a number of talented Yugoslavian water-polo players – among them Dick Glumac and Marijan 'Bibi' Stipetic – defected, enrolled in engineering at the University of Toronto, and helped it win the intercollegiate water-polo title in 1953–4. (The author was a member of that winning team, but rarely got wet during games.) The crushed Hungarian Revolution in 1956 also brought a number of students to the University, including students and staff from the school of mines of Sopron University, the most advanced engineering school in Hungary. Sopron students had both taken a leading part in organizing the demonstration that led to the uprising and been involved in the uprising itself. In January 1957, 91 students, 7 staff members, and 22 dependants from Sopron arrived in Toronto. The University and various industries, along with the federal and provincial governments, provided financial assistance.

Canadian universities, including the University of Toronto, did not experience the hysteria over communism that developed on American campuses. Mathematician Chandler Davis, for example, who came to the University of Toronto in 1962 with his wife, historian Natalie Zemon Davis, had been fired from the University of Michigan in 1953 for refusing to give information to the

House Un-American Activities Committee and was imprisoned and blacklisted from permanent university employment in the United States. 'This constant absorption with how one is going to live,' Natalie Davis wrote a friend at the time, 'instead of living and acting is a great waste, and takes one's mind off scientific work and humanistic political concerns that go beyond one's own problems. I am quite fed up.'

No anti-communist witch-hunt took place at Canadian universities, mainly because, as Michiel Horn has observed, there was 'a lack of real or apprehended witches to be hunted.' President Cody at the University of Toronto had been more than unsympathetic to the hiring of communists. Smith shared Cody's concern over the threat of communism. Smith took the possibility of war very seriously. In 1951, he wrote to the warden of Hart House, saying that the board of the Royal Ontario Museum had discussed the 'awful contingency of the outbreak of war, and the placing of some invaluable objects in a more secure setting.' 'Tentative arrangements have been made with the Provincial government under which they could be put in a government building in Lindsay,' Smith wrote, suggesting that Hart House should plan to remove its valuable Lee collection of medieval and Renaissance objects (donated by Viscount and Viscountess Lee of Fareham to the Massey Foundation in 1940) to a safe place in the event of war.

'Without a doubt,' Smith wrote to the president of the University of Alberta in 1947, 'the Canadian Communists have a well-formulated and long-term policy with respect to establishing cells within universities.' There were, he wrote, 'only two avowed Communists,' and 'to date they have been very discreet, and have discussed public affairs in an academic and abstract fashion. They are not personally active in the organization within or beyond the University.' The following year, Chancellor Vincent Massey assured a correspondent that 'no member of our teaching staff is a Communist.' 'There are,' he went on, 'now and then a few undergraduates who profess this pernicious doctrine, but to exclude them from the University on those grounds would be in itself an imitation of Soviet methods.' 'Out of a student body of over 16,000,' Smith wrote to a fellow university president in 1949, the communist club 'can muster only 37 members.' The number '37' is suspiciously precise. Smith likely was kept informed by the Canadian security service of communist activities on the campus. In 1957, the *Varsity* reported that there were apparently no student communist activities on the campus that year.

Leopold Infeld, right, with Albert Einstein. Date of photograph uncertain.

The one case at the University of Toronto that came anywhere close to approaching the hysteria like that developing in the United States was that of the refugee scientist Leopold Infeld. As mentioned in an earlier chapter, he had come to Canada to join the department of applied mathematics (it really should have been called 'theoretical physics') after working with Albert Einstein in Princeton. Einstein wrote that Infeld 'was one of the most remarkable men with whom I had the pleasure to work.' Infeld was a valued member of the faculty who brought great prestige to the University. He supervised the work of several students who later gained recognition, such as Walter Kohn, the winner of a Nobel Prize for Chemistry in 1998. He also helped bring Ursula Franklin, later an outstanding metallurgist and educator, to the University as a post-doctoral student after the war. On his appointment as a full professor in 1948, Smith praised his 'splendid work for the University.' He visited Poland in the summer of 1949 and wanted to spend part of the academic year 1950–1 there. Samuel Beatty, the head of mathematics, supported the leave, and Smith was sympathetic. Infeld had not had a leave since coming to Canada. But then George Drew, the leader of the opposition Conservatives in Ottawa, discovered that Infeld had been to Poland the previous summer and planned to go again. Drew told the House of Commons that Infeld would be going back to Poland 'armed with certain atomic knowledge ... gained during two years' association with Dr. Einstein in the United States, and from several years' activity in the fields of mathematics and physics at the University of Toronto.'

Beatty assured Smith, 'There is no chance whatever that he would attempt to pass over scientific secrets to the Soviet masters of Poland,' but Smith, who had been in touch with Ottawa, preferred that he not go, stating that Ottawa thought 'the company that Professor Infeld keeps in Poland' was 'questionable and indeed dangerous.' Smith assured Infeld that no one had suggested he was a communist. 'My past is comparatively clean,' Infeld had written Einstein in 1949, and then added, 'although, as you well know, I am left of Louis XIVth.' (He had been involved, along with Barker Fairley of the German department, in a number of left-wing causes, such as helping found the Canadian Soviet Friendship Society in 1941, and in collecting money for those charged after the Gouzenko revelations.) Infeld said he would not go if Ottawa prohibited his going, as long as he could get into the United States during his leave. But Ottawa was unwilling to issue a prohibition, though preferring that he not go. By chance, a reason for denying Infeld leave suddenly appeared. One of the few members of the staff of applied mathematics, A.F.C. Stevenson, had resigned, and Infeld was now needed in the coming year, particularly for graduate teaching. Infeld, who had already left for Europe, was told he must return in September. Infeld resigned. Smith was relieved because now he did not have to fire him. 'I was praying that we would receive a final refusal to return,' Smith wrote to Eric Phillips. 'We are well rid of him.'

Infeld became head of the Institute of Theoretical Physics in Warsaw. He lost his Canadian citizenship, and a special order in council later removed citizenship from his two children. Infeld died in 1968. The citizenship of his children was subsequently restored, however. The daughter of Infeld's next-door neighbour in Toronto, Louise Starkman, had been a childhood friend of Infeld's son, Eryk, and later in life established contact with him. She took up his father's cause. In 1994, the secretary of the governing council, Jack Dimond, and the chair of the academic board, the historian Michael Marrus, examined the case. They concluded that Infeld's wish to go to Poland centred on 'his desire to contribute to the rebuilding of the Polish academic community, which had been devastated during the Second World War,' and that he should have been granted leave when he applied. They pointed out, however, that Beatty and Smith had legitimate staffing concerns at the time Infeld's leave request was finally dealt with. It had been delayed because of Drew's attack, and in the meantime Stevenson had resigned. Perhaps most important, they observed that there is 'no evidence of any University defense of Infeld as a colleague whose character was under unfair public attack.' The climate at the University was such that those who should have spoken out did not.

In June 1994, President Robert Prichard wrote to Eryk Infeld, a professor in the Institute for Nuclear Studies in Warsaw, asking for his permission 'to designate Professor Leopold Infeld, posthumously, Professor Emeritus of the University of Toronto.' Eryk and his sister, Joan, accepted the gesture on behalf of their father, stating that the 'family always believed that there was still an important injustice waiting to be rectified by the University of Toronto. Now this is no longer the case.'

chapter thirty

1955

❧

PLANNING FOR GROWTH

By 1955, it was clear that the number of students attending university would increase dramatically. The 'baby boom' would hit the universities at the end of the decade. Edward Sheffield of the Dominion Bureau of Statistics presented a paper at the annual meeting of the National Conference of Canadian Universities in 1955, predicting at least 'a doubling of enrolment in Canada from the present total of approximately 67,000 within ten years.' The Ontario government's predictions coincided with Sheffield's. In 1956, the NCCU set up a committee under Claude Bissell, who had recently become president of Carleton University in Ottawa, to publicize Sheffield's findings.

Sidney Smith had warned about the pending crisis in higher education. In 1954, he had written an article for *Saturday Night* magazine pointing to a growing enrolment in high schools that would soon hit the universities. It was not, he argued, a 'bulge,' like that represented by the returning veterans after the war, but a new level of enrolment – a new 'plateau' – that would continue into the future. In the fall of 1956, he set up a powerful senate committee – called the Plateau Committee – to explore what the University of Toronto should do. Chaired by the mathematician Gilbert de B. Robinson, the committee produced its own statistical predictions. The numbers of persons seeking to attend the University of Toronto, it predicted, would be even higher than the Canadian or Ontario average. Large urban centres already had a higher university participation rate. Whereas 7 per cent of persons in Ontario in the age group 18 to 21

Aerial view of the campus in 1949, before expansion. With a few exceptions, the University did not extend west of St George Street. The labels are on the original photograph.

attended university, the figure for the Toronto area was already 11 per cent and was 'rapidly rising.' The committee reported to the senate in June 1956 that its best estimate of possible future enrolment at the University was of an increase from about 12,000 to somewhere between 21,000 and 25,000. 'We are now in a position,' Smith wrote to the board chairman Eric Phillips, perhaps not realizing the appropriateness of his language, 'to do some concrete planning.'

The Plateau Committee's twelve-page report set the stage for future planning. The University should be prepared to double its enrolment to 24,000, but, the committee emphasized, 'under no circumstances should the registration of the whole University be allowed to increase beyond' that. The existing residences should be expanded, and 'two new colleges' should be established on the campus, each with a residence to accommodate 500 students. To meet enrolment demands, the committee also recommended that 'one or more new colleges should be established immediately on the outskirts of the metropolitan area.' They would initially be 'integral parts of the University of Toronto, but could in time become independent institutions.' New staff, of course, would be required, and the committee wisely recommended that departments be allowed to hire at a gradual pace – 10 per cent a year over the next ten years – and not be forced to wait until the need was overwhelming. To wait would make it 'harder to recruit and harder to retain staff.' The committee also recommended that building priorities be established as soon as possible, but nothing was said in the report about an overall planning process.

A planning committee had been set up by the board of governors in 1948, before the enrolment crisis developed. Eric Arthur of the School of Architecture had complained the previous year about the University's planning process, and as a result the board established the planning committee, with Arthur as its chair; it included two others associated with the School of Architecture, James Murray and Anthony Adamson. 'Only a plan of future growth,' Arthur had written in 1947 to A.D. LePan, the superintendent of buildings, 'will determine which way and how we should grow.' The southern part of the campus, he stated, is now 'an agglomeration of buildings in defiance of the most elementary rules of light and air ... The land coverage ... must be 90 per cent ... One gets the impression that the University is building in lower Manhattan.' He complained also about the new temporary bookstore 'butchering' the lawn beside the old observatory: 'I believe the building to be of a temporary nature, but as has been proved many times, there is nothing so permanent as the temporary building.'

The building was eventually taken down fifty years later. A committee, Arthur argued, could produce a master plan for the next twenty-five years. 'It would surely be of prime importance,' he wrote, 'to be able to say of a projected building, "This is the site," rather than "Where can we put it?"'

The planning committee's report of 1949 confirmed the ideas contained in an earlier survey done by the planner James Murray that the campus should move west. Murray had concluded that the campus should not extend north because of 'the serious barrier of heavily traveled Bloor Street,' coupled with the expense of purchasing properties in the area to the north. Murray's guiding principle was that it should take no longer than ten minutes to walk from one part of the campus to another – the time allowed between lectures. It took ten minutes, walking briskly, to go from Bloor to College Street. 'A circle with its centre just south of Hart House and a diameter stretching from College Street to Bloor Street,' he noted, 'extends east as far as Burwash Hall and west as far as Spadina.' The campus should therefore extend to Spadina Avenue. Indeed, some buildings were already located west of St George Street, such as the education and dentistry buildings and several student residences. St George Street, which was about to be widened, he conceded would create a 'traffic hazard, but pedestrian overpasses or underpasses could solve this.' Eric Arthur's committee fleshed out Murray's ideas, stating that the buildings on the west campus should be 'grouped about a series of green areas from which vehicular traffic is excluded.'

Faced with the need to expand, the board could not make up its mind on the direction the campus should go. Some members of the board, including the influential chairman of the property committee, O.D. Vaughan, wanted the University to expand to the south. 'I feel sure that O.D. still feels that we should go south,' Smith wrote to Phillips in March 1956, 'but in placing the Heating Plant and the School of Nursing west of St George Street we have, in effect, made the decision to go west.' Moreover, circumstances required that the University purchase another large property in the area. The owners of 74 St George Street, a house across from Knox College, were proposing to build a large apartment building on the site. The property committee, Smith wrote, 'agreed, that we must step in to prevent a big apartment house going into the middle of our westward expansion.' 'Whatever happens west of St George,' he went on, 'we are all of the opinion that we must hold St George Street ... Once we get a big apartment block there, then we would have a problem in finding money for expropriation.' Phillips agreed, and the University expropriated the property, as it then had the power to do, and quietly started buying up other properties, including a number of fraternity houses on the west side of St George and other properties farther west. So that the identity of the purchaser would remain unknown, some of the properties were bought in the name of employees of the superintendent's office. By the end of 1956, the government had approved the designation of a west campus for university purposes, and the expropriation of the remaining properties west of St George Street and north of Harbord Street took place.

How would the west campus be developed? Eric Arthur's planning committee expressed the view in its report that it no longer had a useful role to play and recommended that future planning be done by a committee more directly under the control of the board. In addition, Professor Arthur may have thought he would have difficulty working with some of the large architectural firms in the city, who believed he was responsible for forcing an international competition for Toronto's new city hall. Three of these firms, Marani and Morris, Mathers and Haldenby, and Shore and Moffat, without a competition, had been given a contract to design a new city hall for Toronto. They produced a design in late 1955 that was attacked by a number of senior students in architecture and their design instructor, R.H. Grooms, as 'colourless and inhuman piles of stone.' The students and Grooms continued the attack, taking part in a radio broadcast in which Grooms said the design was 'twenty to thirty years *at least* behind the times.' The architects, he repeated, had produced 'a dehumanized pile of stone.' 'That sums up pretty well my views ... It does not say anything to the citizens of Toronto,' added the architecture student Peter Richardson, who later left architecture for theology and still later became principal of University College. The critics of the design, favoured competitions for major public buildings, as had been recommended a few years earlier by the Massey Commission. In the end, the voters of Toronto rejected the design, and a competition was held in which the Finnish architect Viljo Revell's design was selected. The University had therefore played no small role in giving the city one of its most recognizable landmarks.

Many in the architectural establishment were sure that Eric Arthur was behind all this. It was well known that he favoured holding competitions and had written a document for the Massey Commission to that effect. Furthermore, he was later appointed professional adviser for the city hall competition. The

The board of governors member Neil McKinnon of the Canadian Bank of Commerce, centre,
who co-chaired the 'National Campaign' in 1959, points to the westward expansion of the
University. He is flanked by the president of the Students' Administrative Council, Vince Kelly,
and its vice-president, Adrienne Poy, later Clarkson, now governor general of Canada.

The architect Eric Arthur with the dragon (a bird's head, lion's body, and serpent's tail) at the bottom of the east stairway of University College. In the 1980s, Arthur would act as the principal consultant on the extensive renovations to the college. Picture taken in 1970.

evidence suggests, however, that he was not directly behind the scuttling of the original design, though his ideas surely played a role in stirring things up. The competition for the city hall had important consequences for the University and the city. It brought to Toronto several architects who had taken part in the competition, such as John Andrews, who later designed Scarborough College, and Macy DuBois, who would design New College. Both had been graduate students in architecture at Harvard and were finalists in the competition. Others came to Toronto because of the newly recognized potential for exciting work in the city, such as Jack Diamond, who would design Innis College and the Earth Sciences Centre, Eberhard Zeidler, who would design the Rotman School of Management, and Ron Thom, who would design Massey College.

The decision to hold a competition for the new city hall thus helped change the face of Toronto and the University. It also probably affected the 59-year-old Eric Arthur's chance of becoming head of the School of Architecture when H.H. Madill retired in 1957. Arthur later said he had heard that the committee advising the president had been told by Smith that 'he would be prepared to consider any name except mine.' Smith, it seems, took the view that the school needed 'a much younger man, preferably someone not at present connected with the school.' Peter Richardson, however, maintains that Arthur should have been appointed, but he 'was blackballed and did not get the deanship that everyone believed he deserved.' Instead, the University went outside the faculty to hire Thomas Howarth from the University of Manchester.

The board of governors set up an advisory planning committee in 1956 that did not include Eric Arthur but did include a colleague he respected, Gordon Stephenson, the professor of town and regional planning in the School of Architecture. Stephenson was an Englishman who had worked with LeCorbusier in Paris before the war and had helped prepare the Greater London Plan and the new town of Stevenage after the war. The committee hired Howard Chapman, who had graduated from Toronto in 1948 and then worked for a year in Arthur's architectural firm. He was the son of Alfred Chapman, the designer of several major buildings on the campus, including Knox College and the extension of the Royal Ontario Museum. He had also designed the Toronto Reference Library on College Street before the First World War. Howard Chapman would be responsible for the sensitive conversion of the library building into the Koffler Centre in the 1980s.

The committee worked for almost a year under the chairmanship of the board member William Osbourne, a Toronto engineering graduate and the head of a large industrial company in Galt, Ontario. It included three other board members along with Moffat Woodside, the dean of arts, and Roland McLaughlin, the dean of engineering. The committee produced a report on September 12, 1957, which, had it been implemented, would have produced a 'west campus' that actually looked and felt like a campus.

First and foremost, as in the earlier Arthur report, the committee would have eliminated all the streets (including Russell, Huron, and Willcocks) on the 33-acre new campus south of Harbord Street and extending to Spadina Avenue, and barred vehicles from the area. The campus would have been 'reserved for pedestrian use only.' Deliveries would take place via underground routes from the main city streets. Parking would be confined to lots on Spadina Avenue, which would provide a buffer from the then contemplated Spadina Expressway. Moreover, the plan provided for two large playing fields in the middle of the campus, between the residences and athletic buildings on the west and the academic buildings on or close to St George Street. One or more major faculties or divisions, they advocated, should move to the west campus, one of which should be the faculty of arts. Arts, which was expected to grow by more than 100 per cent, particularly in the non-college subjects, would therefore have a number of departments clustered together rather than spread around the campus. Although the committee was asked to plan 'for the next twelve years,' it wisely 'tried to keep in mind the requirements of a great university several generations hence.' It did not, however, make any proposals with respect to St George Street itself, nor did it attempt to save any of the houses in the area. The preservation of fine older buildings was not a serious concern at the time.

The committee made detailed proposals for the University as a whole, most of which were implemented. University College, it argued, should have a north wing, which would complete the quadrangle. A centrally located arts building should be built on the west side of St George Street. Buildings for chemistry, physics, and zoology should be constructed close by. Engineering, which, it predicted, would expand by about 75 per cent, should get a new building fronting on the east side of St George. A new psychiatric institute should be constructed. And so on.

But some of its ideas did not come to pass in the way the planning committee had thought. An athletic building, for example, was to be constructed on the west campus; it would free up the north wing of Hart House for a students' union. A students' union was never built. The faculty should have a new club, but should temporarily occupy the expropriated former Primrose Club on Willcocks Street. The faculty club is still there. Law should get a new home on the west campus – it was then at Glendon Hall in the north end of the city. In fact, it took over Flavelle House on Queen's Park. Pharmacy should move into the old dental building after dentistry moved to its new facility on Elm Street, and architecture should get a new building. Instead, architecture took over the dental building, and pharmacy got its own building. Medicine, which then had some 825 students (225 in the pre-medical and 600 in the medical years) should not expand significantly, so new construction would not be necessary. If additional space were required for medical students, the committee concluded, it 'should be provided in some centre other than Toronto.' Ten years later, however, Toronto greatly expanded its medical facilities.

Changes in the location of individual buildings of course can be expected as circumstances change. The key question, however, is why the planning committee's general conception of the west campus was abandoned. Cost appears to have been the main consideration. The overall cost of implementing the plan would be over $50 million, not including the cost of the land, which would be about $10 million, or the $8 million for the projects already in progress. Howard Chapman recalls Phillips telling him: 'It's a dream. It's good to dream.' Two years earlier, Smith had told the government that the University of Toronto's estimate of capital costs over the next ten years would be in the $12 million, not the $50 million, range.

The new estimate would have come as a shock to Premier Leslie Frost and his treasurer, Dana Porter. The government was faced with additional demands from other Ontario universities – McMaster University had partially freed itself from its religious ties and was now eligible for funding, and Carleton University had recently been established. There was a pressing need to create new universities. The University of Waterloo, for example, was founded in 1957. Phillips wrote to Smith during the summer of 1957 that although he was 'much in sympathy' with the closing of the roads and the two playing fields, his feeling was that 'no such luxury will be accepted by the Government.' These were the two crucial aspects of the plan. 'It is my feeling,' Phillips wrote, 'that the layout as a whole should be based on the complete absence of playing fields from this area, and that such open space as is involved in the over-all plan should be limited to what I call "quadrangles."' The plan was thereafter effectively emascu-

Sidney Smith addressing a conference in 1957, shortly after leaving the University to become minister of external affairs.

lated. New buildings were built using the existing street pattern, and cars were not excluded.

The planning committee's report was dated September 12, 1957, the very date Sidney Smith officially resigned and left the University in order to take up his new position as minister of external affairs. Prime Minister John Diefenbaker had invited the 60-year-old Smith to join the cabinet at the beginning of September, and it appears likely that Smith wanted the report of the planning committee, of which he was an *ex officio* member, to be completed before he left Toronto. He was sworn in as minister of external affairs the next day. Smith had grown weary of academic administration – he had been a university president for more than thirty years – and wanted a new challenge. Chancellor F.C.A. Jeanneret, with whom he had discussed the offer, later wrote that 'some of us had known for some time that he felt that he had done all he could for the University of Toronto, and felt that a change would be good for all concerned.' Smith had thought about resigning the previous year. In early 1956, he had written to the board chairman Phillips, expressing 'serious doubts' about whether he would be able to tackle the new challenge with the 'vigour' he had been able give to the post-war challenge. 'If these serious doubts persist,' he wrote, 'I feel that I should recommend to the Board that they should look for a man who has the vigour and vision that will be so necessary for the progress of the University in what will be, perhaps, the most severe testing period in its history.' Whether he would have been able to find a way to implement the concepts in the planning report if he had remained in office is uncertain. The acting president, Moffat Woodside, who had been dean of arts, did not have stature enough to prevent the powerful board of governors from moving away from the central ideas in the planning report.

It is not easy to characterize Smith or his achievements as president. In addressing the senate after his departure, his friend Caesar Wright, the dean of law, said that 'most members of this body would not hesitate' to describe him as a 'great' university president. That was also Eric Phillips' view. Others saw him differently. Eric Arthur, for example, said that 'everything about him was super-ficial and jovial, you know, always the back slapper. I don't know into what fraternity of Lions or Elks I'd put him, but in one of those he'd find his spiritual home.' Wright, on the other hand, who knew him well, described him as 'a complete extrovert on the surface but actually deeply introspective,' and Phillips referred to his 'complicated simplicity.' Bissell wrote: 'He belonged to no stere-otype. He was something at once more simple and more complex: a highly intelligent man with a flexible point of view.' 'His success,' according to Bissell, 'was based not so much on mastery of detail as on skill in choosing his associates, his emphasis on basic principles, and his driving concern for harmony and strength.' Towards the end of 1957, Smith was having problems coping with his new position in Ottawa. Lester Pearson was not an easy act to follow as minister of external affairs. Bissell, then at Carleton in Ottawa, wrote in his diary about some of Smith's 'weaknesses not generally recognized: a constitutional inability to be direct in a public situation ... and a strong attraction to the platitude and the repetitive.' He also included in the list 'an unnatural respect for the man of affairs ... illustrated time and time again in the Board of Governors when he was almost servile before the business man.' Bissell himself would meet the 'business man' head on ten years later.

Shortly after Smith left for Ottawa, Caesar Wright told the senate that a small group of colleagues had asked Smith 'what he considered to be the

Historian Donald Creighton leading a small seminar, probably in the 1950s.

outstanding achievements of his tenure of office at Toronto.' Without hesitation, Smith listed four items: the new general course in arts, the raising of academic salaries, the reorganization of the School of Graduate Studies, and the resolution of the issue of legal education. The first three will be discussed in this chapter, and legal education in the next.

The new general course was important because it raised the standard for admission to the University as well as the standards within the University. Prior to the introduction of the general course in 1951–2, anyone having nine credits – at least 50 per cent standing in each subject – from grade 13 could get into the so-called pass arts course. (The requirement of graduation from grade 13 had been established in 1931.) About a quarter of the students entering the first year of the pass course failed to get clear standing at the end of the year, and, not surprisingly, the lower the high school record, the greater the failure rate. Students in the course were in large classes and had fewer opportunities for individual instruction and less personal contact with instructors than those in the honours courses. A committee under the historian Edgar McInnis was established in 1947 to investigate what should be done.

The committee recommended that admission standards be raised for a new general course so that four of the applicant's high school marks be at least third-class standing – a far cry, of course, from later standards. Rather than being allowed to take whatever subjects they wanted in the pass course, students now would be required to take courses within major subject categories in first year and then choose a subject of concentration in the second and third years. They were also required to have an average of 60 per cent in the subject of concentration, rather than the 50 per cent required in other subjects. The old pass course would be buried with what the committee called its 'stigma of inferiority.' The report did not question the desirability of continuing the four-year honours courses, which required much greater specialization and had higher internal standards as well as higher entrance standards. That questioning would come twenty years later.

Smith also raised faculty salaries, which had become dangerously low. Edgar McInnis, for example, had been appointed in 1928 as Lester Pearson's replacement in the history department. An expert on international affairs, he left the University in 1952 to become president of the Canadian Institute for International Affairs at a salary of $12,000 a year, with a generous expense allowance – much higher than the $6,200 he was making at the University, without an expense allowance. The discrepancy between the two amounts illustrates how inadequate were the salaries paid to university professors after the war. The cost of living had increased significantly, but academic salaries had not increased accordingly. Before the war, a professor's salary was equal to about two-thirds of the salary of a doctor or lawyer, but by the late 1940s it had fallen to about half.

The Committee of Teaching Staff, which had been formed in June 1939 by Sam Beatty, Barker Fairley, Harold Innis, and F.C.A. Jeanneret, passed a resolution at the annual meeting of 1950, unanimously declaring that it was 'urgent, in view of the continued and unabated rise in the cost of living, that there be an increase in salaries commensurate with that rise.' The chair of the committee, the geophysicist Tuzo Wilson, argued that 'if salaries do not rise ... the morale and efficiency of the staff will be seriously affected.' Wilson arranged a meeting of the Committee of Teaching Staff, the president, and the board members Eric Phillips, Henry Borden, and Walter Gordon. Several weeks later, Smith announced that the floor for lecturers had been raised by 40 per cent, but for full professors by only 12 per cent. Two years later, the salary scale was raised once again, with the floor for lecturers increased from $2,000 to $3,100 and for full professors from $5,500 to $7,200. Salaries were becoming more realistic – from 1953 to 1959 the rate of inflation averaged only a little over 1 per cent a year.

The faculty committee, renamed the Association of Teaching Staff (ATS) in

1954, continued to press for increased salaries and better benefits. A more comprehensive amalgamated pension and group insurance scheme was brought in by the University in 1955. Smith continued to seek higher salaries in order to make Toronto competitive with American universities. He attended the annual meetings of the teaching staff, a precedent that would be followed by presidents for the next twenty years. In 1957, he announced another very significant rise in salary levels. Over the next three years, the scale for lecturers was to be raised by 57 per cent and for full professors by 50 per cent. This may have been the high point for University of Toronto salaries in comparison with American salaries. The Canadian dollar was then worth more than the American. Caesar Wright told the senate in November 1957 that salaries at the University were now 'certainly on a parity with the highest salaries in the United States.' And at a staff meeting in early 1958 to honour Smith, Thomas Goudge of philosophy noted in his remarks that 'between 1945 and 1957 five major salary increases ... were implemented in this university,' so that salaries were now 'in line with those of institutions of commensurate status on the North American continent.' Goudge pointed out, however, that university professors 'have not begun to share in the enlargement of real income which has been made available to Canadians.' He then announced that the faculty had established an award in the School of Graduate Studies to be known as the Sidney Smith Open Fellowship, and he also presented Smith with a silver cigarette box for his desk at his new job.

Smith had taken a strong interest in graduate studies, so this award in his honour was certainly appropriate. Shortly after being appointed president, he had asked Harold Innis, the head of political economy, to chair a committee to examine ways of strengthening the school. The committee met for nine months and visited fifteen American graduate schools, plus McGill in Canada. In the spring of 1947, it presented its report, which was accepted by the senate and the board. The timing was designed to coincide with the appointment of a new dean of the graduate school. George Brett had died in 1944, and Andrew Hunter, the professor of pathological chemistry, had been appointed by Cody for a three-year term – he was 67 years old when appointed – which would give Smith the opportunity to select a new dean.

The report recommended a number of significant changes to the graduate school, all designed to centralize and strengthen it. The graduate school was to be divided into two divisions with a senior academic as the head of each division. F.C.A. Jeanneret, the head of the French department at University College, was appointed chair of the humanities and social sciences division, and Andrew Gordon, the head of chemistry, was chair of the scientific division. This arrangement would take considerable pressure off the dean, who no longer had to chair all PhD orals. There was concern in the graduate school about the standards in the college departments, and the solution was for the president to select one person to chair a university-wide graduate department for each discipline, rather than allow each college department head to chair its graduate faculty members. In the university departments, the head of the undergraduate department was – until 1956 – also head of the graduate department.

Innis' committee recommended further that there be better library resources, increased funding for faculty research, greater subsidization of publications through the University of Toronto Press, and more funding of graduate students. The committee also recommended that the graduate school acquire new premises or at least be able to take over the whole of the building it occupied jointly with the Women's Health Service on the site of the present Massey College. The committee felt uncomfortable about what it referred to as 'the ignominious or ludicrous joint tenancy recorded on the name-plate above the door.' Moreover, it recommended that 'a beginning should be made towards providing graduate residences ... a matter of great importance in a graduate school where so many students come as complete strangers from other universities.' Finally, the new dean could continue as head of his or her department, but would have relief from teaching and assistance in handling administrative matters.

The position was tailor-made for Harold Innis, who was eager to have the job. It appears, however, that he had not let Smith know, and Smith was courting the English professor E.K. Brown, then at the University of Chicago, whom Smith had known at the University of Manitoba. When Innis heard about the possibility of Brown's becoming dean, he wrote to Smith that it would be a mistake, and that if Brown were appointed he would 'cease to have much interest in the possibilities of the graduate school.' Two weeks later, Innis sent a letter to Smith resigning from the University, not the first time he had taken such action. He claimed it was because of the 'hostility of the humanities to the social sciences' that had been expressed at the senate meeting approving his committee's report, but it was surely the fact that he had not been asked to be dean. 'I have come to feel,' he wrote to Smith, 'that the best interests of the school and of the University would be served by my resignation.' Smith was taken by surprise and sent a long cable to Innis, who was then out of the

Sketch of political economist Harold Innis,
date uncertain.

province, pleading with him to stay – 'You cannot leave me – need you beyond words.' Smith asked if he had said something inadvertently to cause Innis' letter and threatened to resign himself if Innis left. A few days later, he met with Innis and offered him the deanship on very generous terms. The University could not afford to lose Innis. Smith then wrote to Brown, who had been delaying his decision on whether to move from Chicago to Toronto, saying that 'there is a nearly unanimous opinion among my colleagues ... that we should make an appointment from the staff of the university, and the name that was suggested on all sides was that of Harold Innis.' Thus Innis became dean of the graduate school.

One feels some sympathy with Smith over this incident. There is no evidence that Innis had ever indicated to Smith or anyone else in the University that he wanted the job. Indeed, Smith would probably have thought Innis would shy away from a heavy administrative position, which would cut into his research and other activities. Nobody in Canada had a better international reputation as a scholar than Innis. By 1947, according to his biographer, Donald Creighton, Innis 'had reached the pinnacle of his influence and authority in Canadian university life. He had become Canada's senior academic statesman.' He was president of the Royal Society of Canada, had recently sat on two royal commissions, had received very attractive offers from such places as Chicago, and had embarked on path-breaking work in communications, a subject he had turned to during the war. Bissell, who became chair of the humanities and social science division of the graduate school after Jeanneret became principal of University College in 1957, worked with Innis and has written that 'no academic carried with him more unmistakably the mark of greatness.' Why would Innis want to combine the headship of political economy with deanship of the graduate school? But the fact is that he did.

As graduate dean, Innis was able to continue his scholarship. He published three major books on communications between 1950 and 1952, including *The Bias of Communication*, in which he noted, for example, that 'as modern developments in communication have made for greater realism they have made for greater possibilities of delusion.' His work influenced Marshall McLuhan and others. 'By directing attention to the bias or distorting power of the dominant imagery and technology of any culture,' McLuhan later wrote, 'he showed us how to understand cultures.'

Innis pressed the central administration of the University for additional funding for graduate work. The thirty-seven institutions that made up the Association of American Universities, he pointed out, had an average of $100,000 a year for graduate fellowships, whereas Toronto had less than $25,000, mainly for the sciences. Over a four-year period, only 138 students out of the more than 5,000 who enrolled in the graduate school held fellowships. He raised other questions about what was happening at the University. He was concerned, for example, about the concentration of undergraduate students from the Toronto area. It was becoming a streetcar university. The graduate students were also predominantly from Ontario, and almost half were from Toronto. In earlier periods, the majority of students had come from outside Toronto. Just before the First World War, for example, about two-thirds of the students were from outside Toronto, and in the 1880s the proportion of those from outside had been even higher.

He was also concerned about the role of the colleges, which were losing their importance because students were less interested in the college subjects than in the university subjects and the professional courses. Innis had suggested earlier to President Cody that University College could be revitalized by bringing in the social sciences. In the fall of 1951, Smith formed a high-powered committee to examine the humanities and asked Innis to head it.

The humanities committee had held three meetings when Innis became ill. In January 1952, he felt pain in his back while walking from the University to his home on Dunvegan Road. He was diagnosed with prostate cancer, and in May he underwent surgery. He kept working from his home, meeting on graduate school matters with Andrew Gordon and Jack Sword, the graduate school secretary. Innis was also preparing his presidential address for the American Economic Association meeting in December. He died on November 8, 1952 at the age of 58. The *American Economic Review* published a rough draft of his intended speech. His wife, Mary Quayle Innis, an economic historian and literary author who in 1955 became dean of women at University College, published a collection of his essays and supervised the reissue of some of his books. Andrew Gordon became dean of the graduate school and continued to follow the path laid out by Innis. Moffat Woodside was appointed chair of Innis' humanities committee, which reported in early 1954 that its members could not reach agreement. The position of the colleges would not change for another twenty years. One suspects that if Harold Innis had lived, a consensus somehow might have emerged in the committee.

chapter thirty-one

1958

FINANCING EXPANSION

About two weeks after Sidney Smith left office, Eric Phillips, the chairman of the board, telephoned Claude Bissell, the president of Carleton University, and asked whether he would let his name stand for the presidency. Phillips obviously favoured Bissell over the acting president, Moffat Woodside, or another serious contender, Edgar Steacie, the president of the National Research Council. The board had appointed a committee from among its own members to select Smith's successor. Phillips, according to Bissell's recollection, told him that 'at the proper time I shall take your name to the committee, I will get unanimous support and the discussion will end.' Henry Borden later recalled that the decision was 'pretty well a decision by Colonel Phillips as chairman.' Bissell, however, did not immediately agree to accept the position. Several days later, Phillips phoned again and asked, 'What is going on in that vast mind of yours?' Bissell was wavering, as his diary shows, but within a week he phoned Phillips to say that if he received a call from Toronto he would accept. Bissell was appointed by the board on December 12, 1957. He would not return to the University until the end of the academic year, however. Bissell had concluded, he stated in his memoirs, that the University of Toronto 'was certainly the strongest Canadian university by the only criterion that mattered – the international distinction of the academic staff.' 'With a number of changes,' he went on, 'it could easily become a great university.'

One of the probable inducements for Bissell to return was the elegant new

Just after the address given by Claude Bissell, right, upon his installation as president in
November 1958, with Eric Phillips, chairman of the board of governors, on the left,
and Chancellor Samuel Beatty in the middle.

presidential house, which had been acquired the previous year, at 93 Highland
Avenue in Rosedale, a house that earlier had belonged to David Dunlap – after
whom the observatory north of Toronto was named. Smith had written to
Phillips the day after he and his wife had first visited the house, saying that he
had not 'seen any house so well designed for a presidential residence ... In the
centre of the house there is a large living room, with several doors that provide
the maximum in circulation for entertaining large groups.' The University,
Smith said, could buy the whole property with its 340-foot frontage and sell
building lots on 220 feet. Fortunately, the property, which is in constant use for
university functions, was kept intact.

Over a two-day period in October, 1958, the 42-year-old Claude Bissell was
installed as the eighth president of the University. The brilliant blue presidential
gown was placed over his shoulders by Principal F.C.A. Jeanneret of University
College and Dean J.A. MacFarlane of medicine, and the cap was presented by
Dean R.R. McLaughlin of engineering. The installation, Bissell recorded in his
journal, was 'a great success,' which brought him a 'sense of relief.' In part, this
was because he had been suffering from nosebleeds and had had a 'stubbornly
assertive fear' that one would occur during his speech. The University of Toronto, he told the audience in Convocation Hall, was 'the custodian of the

excellent,' with a 'tradition of vigorous individualism.' Those in the audience probably felt the same confidence in the future of the University as had those attending Robert Falconer's installation fifty years earlier. After his speech, students in the top balcony sang the Toronto song, 'The Blue and White' ('Old Toronto mother ever dear ...'). Bissell's delighted reaction was captured in his favourite academic picture, reproduced in this chapter.

One of Bissell's first tasks on assuming office was a fund-raising campaign. Alumni had given generously in the past – to construct Convocation Hall at the beginning of the century and Soldiers' Tower after the Great War – but there had never been a successful campaign at the University of Toronto aimed at the general public. Cody had started a $5 million campaign in 1944, towards the end of his tenure as president, but after it was launched, the federal government changed the income tax regulations, with the effect of discouraging corporate donations. Cody complained to Ottawa that McGill had just raised $5 million in its campaign and that it was unfair not to permit Toronto to do the same. The government regulations were not substantially changed, however, and the campaign was a failure. President Sidney Smith had also undertaken a campaign in 1948, but it too was unsuccessful and was abandoned discreetly. It was, however, partly responsible for Morley Callaghan's nostalgic novel *The Varsity Story*, which the board had encouraged him to write.

Eric Phillips had been chairman of the board during the Cody campaign and was probably not keen on another campaign and the possibility of another failure. Smith, however, had urged him to launch one, as did Bissell shortly after his appointment. 'It is important for Toronto to have a campaign,' Bissell wrote from Ottawa, 'if only to dramatize her situation and to demonstrate that the university is far too important to be left entirely to the state.' It was not good for universities, he believed, to be too dependent upon governments. Moreover, the University of British Columbia had recently mounted a successful campaign for $8 million.

In October 1958, the board agreed to launch the 'National Fund' campaign for $12.6 million, even though their expert advisers warned them that their case was 'weak' on account of the public's perception that higher education was a government responsibility. Both Bissell and Phillips had wanted E.P. Taylor, the president of the holding company Argus Corporation, to head the campaign, but he declined. They turned to two board members, Neil McKinnon, the president of the Canadian Bank of Commerce, and Wallace McCutcheon, the vice-president and managing director of Argus, to serve as co-chairs. (In the post-war years, the University of Toronto drew heavily upon the personnel of the Argus Corporation, with Phillips, McCutcheon, and James Duncan being key members of the university board.) McCutcheon had graduated from Victoria College in maths and physics. McKinnon, like many bankers of his generation and his Bank of Commerce predecessor, Sir Edmund Walker, had not gone to university.

The campaign was launched in the spring of 1959, with the full support of the federated universities, which were to share in the proceeds. Five hundred corporate canvassers attended a fund-raising meeting at the King Edward Hotel. The board members personally contributed almost half a million dollars, as did the staff, said to be 'the largest staff contribution ever recorded in North America.' Bissell worked hard to make the campaign a success. 'I am anxious that the campaign, by its success,' he wrote in his diary, 'and by intense (but discreet) publicity establish Toronto as *The Canadian University*.' The campaign generated a great amount of favourable publicity. One *Globe and Mail* headline in 1959, for example, read, 'Bissell Proposes Scholars Be Lured Home from U.S.' Toronto, the story said, was encouraging senior scholars to return to Canada to help train the teachers who would soon be needed. The campaign was more than successful. Within about a year, over $15 million had been raised.

Buildings that had been designated as recipients of the money started to appear, including, on the east side of St George Street, engineering's Galbraith Building, and on the west side, the Ramsay Wright Zoological Laboratories, the Lash Miller Chemical Laboratories, and the McLennan Physical Laboratories, with its Burton Tower. The cornerstone of the arts building, named after Sidney Smith, who had died suddenly of a heart attack the previous year, was laid in October 1960, and the building was opened a year later. The reaction to John Parkin's design was mixed. 'There are lively reactions to the building,' Bissell wrote to W.A. Mackintosh, the principal of Queen's, who would speak at the opening, 'ranging all the way from the enthusiastic to the hysterically critical.' 'I find,' Bissell added, 'that the attitude depends upon the kind of quarters from which the individual came.' The historians were unhappy because they had been forced to give up their comfortable quarters in Flavelle House, which would be occupied by the faculty of law. Moreover, Sidney Smith Hall was uncomfortable in warm weather because the low-cost air conditioning system was not adequate for a building with so much glass. There were even problems with the bust of

Architect's sketch of the proposed physics building, looking east towards St George Street, with Sidney Smith Hall on the far left. Note the planned green space and the absence of roads and vehicles.

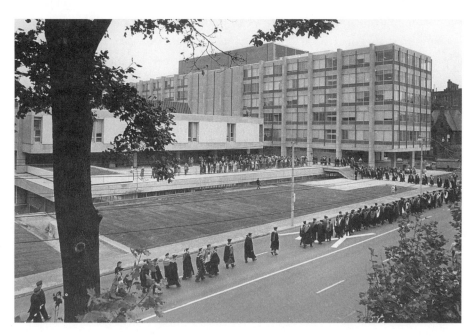

The official opening of Sidney Smith Hall, October 14, 1960.

Sidney Smith that was to have been placed in the lobby of the building. The members of the board did not think it a good likeness of Smith, and Bissell had the sad task of telling the artist that her work was rejected. There is still no bust of Smith in the building.

New buildings were also constructed by the colleges. The north section of the University College quadrangle was completed. Victoria College built a new residence for women, named after its first dean of women, Margaret Addison. St Michael's College built the five-storey Loretto College women's residence on St Mary Street and a new library, the John Kelly Library, on St Joseph Street. Trinity completed the Chapel, designed by Sir Giles Gilbert Scott, enlarged St Hilda's by constructing the Mossie Waddington Kirkwood Wing, and also built a new academic building, the Gerald Larkin Building, on Devonshire Place. At no period in the University's history had so much building taken place in so short a time.

The University of Toronto was now one of many universities in Ontario competing for funds. The close personal relationship existing between Eric Phillips and Premiers George Drew and Leslie Frost was still important, but less so than in the past. In a five-page letter to Frost in 1960, Phillips complained that the University was not getting the support it needed. Recent provincial grants, he wrote, left the University with a shortfall of about $8 million. That made it difficult to hire the staff that soon would be needed. The gradual accumulation of faculty members that had been advocated by the Plateau Committee, therefore, did not take place, and as a result massive hiring was required in the mid-sixties. Moreover, the University's position was particularly difficult because it could not predict from year to year what the government's allocation would be. In the early 1950s, Phillips had worked out with Frost the idea of three-year plans. Multi-year planning, however, was abandoned in 1958, when the province instituted the Committee on University Affairs (CUA), made up mainly of civil servants who would advise the government on what the grants to universities should be each year. Phillips was not pleased with this decision. He liked the former cosy arrangement with the premier. But for the most part those days were over.

In the early 1960s, the presidents of Ontario universities organized themselves into a new body, the Committee of Presidents of Provincially Assisted Universities of Ontario. They did so at the urging of the now expanded CUA and were asked by it to study the higher education needs of Ontario. The universities had the research resources that the CUA lacked. What the CUA had succeeded in doing, writes historian Paul Axelrod, 'was to turn the responsibility of planning back to the universities themselves.' The result was the 1963 Deutsch report, named for John Deutsch, the principal of Queen's University. The report recommended two new liberal arts colleges in metropolitan Toronto – in addition to the already existing York University – and a system of community colleges. Both these recommendations would be implemented. In 1964, the government for the first time established a Department of University Affairs, with its own minister and an increasing number of staff. The relationship between the Ontario government and the universities was now big business.

A significant and historic change in the University's relationship with the provincial government occurred in 1967, when a formula was introduced for the funding of Ontario universities. Formula funding had been recommended by the Commission on the Financing of Higher Education set up by the National Conference of Canadian Universities and headed by Toronto's Vincent Bladen, which had been established following discussions with the CUA and the NCCU. An arts student in a three-year program, for example, would be worth one basic income unit (BIU), and a PhD student would be worth six units. Thus, a research-intensive university, such as the University of Toronto, which could attract graduate students, would in theory receive a greater slice of the pie. The scheme sounded reasonable, but it would cause increased competition for students and unwarranted expansion of graduate programs throughout the Ontario system, and in some cases a lowering of standards. As the size of the provincial pie for universities over the years tended to be fixed, more students in the university system meant less money for each BIU. At the same time, the ability to raise student fees was restricted. Moreover, the weight given to graduate programs did not adequately take into account what would prove to be the indirect costs of research. Formula financing, as it was called, did tend to keep the provincial government at arm's length from the universities – like the recommendations of the royal commission of 1906, fifty years earlier – but it created serious financial problems for the University of Toronto.

❧

The federal government too was assisting Canadian universities, as the Massey Commission on National Development in the Arts, Letters, and Sciences had

Members of the Massey Commission on National Development in the Arts, Letters, and Sciences, 1951: Vincent Massey, in the centre; Arthur Surveyor, a Montreal consulting engineer, on the left; Norman Mackenzie, University of British Columbia, on the right; Hilda Neatby, University of Saskatchewan, directly behind; and G.H. Lévesque, Laval University, beside her.

recommended in 1951. The commission had been set up in part to find something for Vincent Massey to do. 'He is somewhat restless,' Lester Pearson told Prime Minister Mackenzie King's private secretary, Jack Pickersgill, 'and does not find the Chancellorship of the University much of an outlet for his energies.' At first, Massey had not felt that the commission's mandate was wide enough to cover federal aid to the universities, which were in desperate need of assistance. The federal grants given to the universities after the war to assist them in coping with the influx of veterans were drying up as the veterans left the universities. The universities, as well as the commission member Larry MacKenzie, the president of the University of British Columbia, urged the commission and the government to continue federal support.

In the fall of 1950, Prime Minister Louis St Laurent had given his blessing to such a move in an address he delivered upon receiving an honorary degree from the University of Toronto. With Chancellor Massey presiding, St Laurent stated, 'Many of us recognize increasingly that some means must be found to ensure our universities the financial capacity to perform the many services which are required in the interest of the whole nation.' 'The Massey Commission,' he hoped, would 'be able to help us find a proper solution to that difficult problem.' It had done so. Universities, the commission decided, were part of its mandate to protect Canadian culture, which was being overwhelmed by American influences. Universities were 'nurseries of a truly Canadian civilization and culture' and were 'facing a financial crisis so great as to threaten their future usefulness.' Direct federal support to universities – over $7 million in 1951–2 – had begun almost immediately. 'It recognizes and emphasizes,' President Smith told the *Varsity*, that 'the nation as a whole has a stake in the welfare of our institutions of higher learning.' The University of Toronto received almost $1 million from the federal government in 1951. Once again, the desire to decrease the influence of American ideas helped shape the development of the University of Toronto.

The federal direct grants kept increasing in amount. From an initial sum of 50 cents per capita, they rose to $5 in 1965–6. The Bladen Commission on the Financing of Higher Education had recommended the $5 per capita figure, and had also recommended that it continue to increase by $1 each year. The federal grants therefore rose from $7 million in 1951–2 to some $100 million in 1966–7. The program, noted the U of T economist David Stager, 'clearly was an essential element in Canadian university financing at a critical stage in the development of higher education.' A shift took place in 1966, however, following a federal-provincial conference. Education, many argued, was a provincial responsibility. Instead of direct support to the universities, the federal government would now give grants to the provinces for universities equal to half their cost. The universities were still being generously treated by the federal government. Ten years later, however, the system would change again. As the historian of education Glen Jones has noted, the 'arrangement had become quite expensive and the government sought ways of controlling the level of its involvement.' The federal grants were capped and were no longer conditional on the money's being spent by the provinces on education. Instead, the money could be spent on highways or anything else if a province wished.

The Massey Commission had helped the universities in other ways. It had recommended the establishment of scholarships and bursaries for post-graduate work in the humanities, the social sciences, and law, as well as of fellowships for 'advanced study' in those areas. A council to administer these and other programs was also proposed. The implementation of these recommendations would be delayed for a number of years. In 1956, however, the government had had a windfall: it was to receive $100 million in succession duties from the estates of two wealthy Maritimers, Izaak Killam and Sir James Dunn. Prime Minister St Laurent announced that the Canada Council would be set up with half that sum, and that the other half would be used for capital grants for university expansion, administered by the Canada Council.

∞

A major capital grant would be given by the Canada Council to the University of Toronto to assist in the construction of the new faculty of music building. When Bissell was appointed, one of his goals was 'to bring Music more firmly and obviously into the university.' At the time, the faculty was located in two old houses beside the Royal Conservatory of Music at the corner of College Street and University Avenue. In 1953, Boyd Neel, who had succeeded Sir Ernest MacMillan as head of both the conservatory and the faculty, was determined to get a new building. 'I well remember thinking,' he wrote in his memoirs, 'that if I ever did take the job my first aim would be to get a new building and separate the Faculty of the University of Toronto from the conservatory.' Neel later went to see every member of the board of governors, but as Bissell states, the board generally was 'not noticeably tender to the arts.' The fact that Sidney Smith was tone deaf would not have assisted Neel's case. It took Neel seven years to achieve his objective. As it turned out, the province wanted the conservatory property for an expansion of its hydroelectric headquarters. The University received $3 million for the property, which the Canada Council matched under its new capital grants program. There was now enough money to build a fine home for the faculty of music behind Falconer Hall and at the same time to renovate part of the old McMaster Hall on Bloor Street for the conservatory. The Bloor Street building had become available because a number of departments located there had moved into the new Sidney Smith Hall on St George Street.

Neel insisted that the new building contain an opera theatre, and it was difficult for the board to say no given the unexpected funds that had been received. Under the guidance of Arnold Walter and Nicholas Goldschmidt, both of whom had left Europe as refugees before the war, the conservatory opera school had produced some great singers, such as Lois Marshall, Jon Vickers, and

Boyd Neel, left, with Ettore Mazzoleni, centre, and Arnold Walter in the MacMillan Theatre
of the faculty of music, in 1963. The official opening of the building, named after
Edward Johnson, who had been the general manager of the Metropolitan Opera
in New York, took place the following year.

Teresa Stratas. When Stratas first auditioned for a place at the school, she knew nothing classical and sang 'Smoke Gets in Your Eyes.' Walter was impressed and assigned her to a former Metropolitan Opera soprano, Irene Jessner, a teacher at the school. The opera school's first full-length production had been Smetana's *The Bartered Bride*, performed in 1947 at Eaton Auditorium. The new opera theatre was a success. Neel was pleased with its acoustics. 'One of the most exciting moments of my life,' Neel wrote, was when he 'heard the first sounds of Britten's *Albert Herring* arising from the pit at rehearsal. It was a tense moment, because acoustics are so unpredictable, and I wondered – yes or no? – and it was yes!'

The relationship then existing between the faculty and the conservatory is not easy to describe or understand – even for deans of music. When John Beckwith succeeded Boyd Neel as dean in 1970, he asked President Bissell: 'What was I now dean of? Was it the Conservatory, the faculty, or both?' Bissell's reply, according to Beckwith, was 'It's a good question.' Boyd Neel had described it as a 'crazy set-up.' The relationship between the two bodies, with its various tensions and misunderstandings, could form the basis of a long Mozart-like comic opera. The faculty gave academic degrees, and the conservatory gave diplomas for performance, mainly in piano. When Neel first came, he was surprised to discover that 'ninety per cent of the students learned only the piano.' Among these students was the renowned pianist Glenn Gould, who studied under Alberto Guerrero. In 1990, after a series of reports over a period of two decades, the conservatory was separated from the faculty and would no longer be an official part of the University. Indeed, the University transferred to the conservatory the deed to McMaster Hall and the land on which it sits.

Although the music building was in use before March 1964, the official opening did not take place until that month. Guests arriving for the opening took their places to organ music by Charles Peaker, and the academic procession was accompanied by fanfares from the faculty's brass choir, conducted by Ezra Schabas. Sir Ernest MacMillan's work *England: An Ode*, which he had composed while interned in Germany during the First World War, was performed, with MacMillan conducting, as was a dramatic symphony, *Esther*, by Godfrey Ridout, conducted by Ettore Mazzoleni. Many other distinguished composers were on the faculty, such as Beckwith, Oskar Morawetz, and John Weinzweig, and their work just as appropriately could have been performed that day. The faculty has continued to have many well-known names in the field of music. 'No other division of this University,' Beckwith would state in 1995, 'houses as many members of the Order of Canada.'

The opening took place in the 800-seat theatre, named after MacMillan. The building itself was named after Edward Johnson, a member of the board of governors of the University who had died in 1959. He had been a celebrated opera tenor and later became general manager of the Metropolitan Opera. His son-in-law also happened to be the former premier, George Drew. 'Why,' asked the philosopher Francis Sparshott, who writes on aesthetics and the performing arts, 'did they name the music building after the opera man, and name the opera theatre after the music man?' Beckwith agrees that 'the naming of the building may have been inappropriate,' but in view of Johnson's contributions to the board and to music, 'some gesture of the sort *was* deserved.'

❧

Other faculties also benefited from outside financial support. Metropolitan Toronto provided funds earmarked for a building for the School of Social Work and a building for the School of Business. Both had been housed in the McMaster building. The business school moved to Cumberland House on St George Street in the early 1960s to make way for the conservatory, the first of its several moves, while awaiting a new building. Social work, however, stayed in McMaster Hall. In 1970, both divisions moved into a renovated office building, the former Texaco building, on the north-west corner of Bloor Street and Bedford Road, which the University had recently purchased.

The business school had been established in 1950 as the Institute of Business Administration within the graduate school, following the report of yet another committee chaired by Harold Innis. Sidney Smith seemed to call on Innis to chair all the significant university committees during this period. The report, drafted by the vice-chair of the committee, Vincent Bladen, had recommended that the institute not be part of the department of political economy, which was then 'as large as some universities and ... too unwieldy to carry on the interdepartmental and outside activities envisaged in graduate business.' Bladen was made director, but resigned in 1953 to become chair of political economy after Innis died. The University of Western Ontario, which had established a business school in 1949, complained to Premier Frost that the new Toronto program was a 'wasteful duplication.' Smith was summoned to the premier's office and in defence pointed out that the Toronto program, unlike that at Western, would not use the Harvard case study method and would appeal to part-time students. Frost apparently was satisfied.

The institute was not particularly successful in attracting full-time master's students. There were only about 20 full-time students in each of the two years, Bladen recalled, but there were 'several hundred degree candidates working at night.' After Bladen left, however, the institute 'gradually began to curtail the night work.' The institute's research record was weak. Warren Main, who became director in 1960, claimed that 'the amount of research and the amount of writing was abysmally low.' He was one of only two persons in the institute with a doctorate – a U of T degree, begun under Innis. Bladen had been keeping an eye on the institute, and in 1958 he wrote to the incoming president Claude Bissell that it was 'falling apart.' 'There are eleven members of the staff,' he wrote. 'Three have resigned, a fourth is on the verge, and I gather from what I observe and hear that the morale of the group is pretty low.' 'They need a strong guiding hand,' he concluded, 'and that soon.'

The University was unable to find an acceptable outside candidate and turned to Warren Main, who had joined the faculty from the University of Saskatchewan in 1953. The name was changed to the School of Business. Part-time degrees were eliminated, and the name of the degree was changed from a master of commerce to a master of business administration. Main was not able, however, to develop a close relationship with the business community. He told Bissell of his concern over his 'failure to communicate with business.' This, he said, was 'accentuated by the rise of York's school under the aggressive [James] Gillies.' Bissell's diary shows that in 1959 he had met with Gillies – a Canadian then teaching at the University of California – as a possible candidate for the directorship at Toronto and was 'impressed by him.' Main had been a member of the search committee that had proposed Gillies as director, but Gillies, who had excellent academic credentials, was apparently not acceptable to the other members of the faculty. Whether Gillies would have come if asked is not clear. He later maintained he had been 'uninterested' in the position.

Bissell urged Main to concentrate on research and to develop a PhD program, since 'this was the area in which we could assert superiority.' A doctoral program was introduced in 1969. The school under Main stressed research by the faculty and by the students. 'We are giving our students exposure to courses which emphasize research,' he told the *Varsity News* in 1966, and added, 'and

Warren Main, seated, succeeded Vincent Bladen as the director of the Institute of
Business Administration in 1960. The photograph, taken in 1963, also shows
Donald Forster of the department of political economy.

that essential tool of research, the computer.' Unlike their counterparts in the
1950s, the vast majority of the faculty members now had doctorates. A report
prepared in 1971, from a committee chaired by the acting director John Crispo,
pointed out that 'the faculty had grown to 22 full-time members, of whom 18
had PhDs from a broad cross-section of outstanding universities.' The school
also had a new home. Main saw that the Texaco building on Bloor Street was for
sale and alerted Simcoe Hall, and the building was purchased quickly. The
University, the report stated, now 'has a firm foundation upon which to build a
leading school.' The board of governors of the University agreed, and resolved
that 'further development of the school of business should receive a high
priority.'

In 1972, the School of Business became the faculty of management studies,

Harry Cassidy became the director of the
School of Social Work in 1945.

with Crispo, an outspoken professor of industrial relations who had received his
PhD from the Massachusetts Institute of Technology, as its first dean. The
faculty has continued to be noted for its strong research and the academic
quality of its student body. At the end of the 1990s, there were around
50 students in its PhD program. Its finance division has a particularly strong
international reputation, with scholars such as Myron Gordon in corporate
finance and John Hull in financial derivatives. A $3 million donation from
Sandra and Joseph Rotman – he graduated from the school with an MCom in
1960 – assisted in providing a new building on St George Street. A further
contribution of $15 million by the Rotmans in 1996, which was matched by the
University, has given the faculty – now named the Rotman School of Management – a greater ability to hire and keep its faculty.

The School of Social Work also moved into the former Texaco building in
1970 and also became a faculty in 1972. The school had been established as a
separate professional school in 1941, having previously been the department of
social science in the faculty of arts, and before that the department of social
service. Towards the end of the Second World War, the University looked for a
new director. President Cody invited Harry Cassidy, who had taught at the
University in the late 1920s and early 1930s and was then a productive scholar
and the founding director of the school of social welfare at Berkeley, to accept
the position. Cassidy wanted to return to Canada to play a role in the anticipated post-war expansion in social welfare policy. 'What is needed,' he had

written to Prime Minister Mackenzie King, 'is a bold program for research and planning in this field.'

Harold Innis, however, was strongly opposed to Cassidy's appointment. In the early 1930s, Cassidy had been associated with Frank Underhill and others in the League for Social Reconstruction and had helped draft the CCF's Regina Manifesto. University professors, according to Innis, should be involved in detached scholarship, not the advocacy and 'present-mindedness' that Cassidy represented. Academics should not become 'a standing surplus labour pool to meet the varying demands of government.' 'To buy universities,' Innis believed, 'was to destroy them and with them the civilization for which they stand.' Serving governments, however, was exactly what Cassidy was advocating; he told Cody that 'faculty members should be equipped to serve governments through making surveys, serving as advisors, and undertaking research projects.' Innis tried to persuade Cody to appoint Agnes McGregor as director. She had graduated with a certificate from the department of social service in 1916, had joined the department as a secretary, and had risen to become assistant director and an associate professor. She was the one constant in an ever-changing department. Innis advised Cody that 'her appointment should be made without consulting her' because 'if she is consulted she will advise against' it, but if made, 'she will be pleased.' In 1945, Cassidy was selected, and Innis resigned as chairman of the school's governing body.

Cassidy was an ambitious, dynamic, aggressive director. 'When that man Cassidy comes through the door,' Smith is reported to have stated, 'I feel like ducking under my desk.' Cassidy introduced a one-year post-graduate bachelor of social work degree, a two-year master's degree with a major research component, and the country's first doctoral program in social work. He increased the number of students and faculty members and stressed research. During his period as director, wrote John Graham in his history of social work at the University, 'the school went through the most significant era of transition' it would ever go through. The number of faculty members quadrupled, and the number of students more than doubled. Many of the faculty appointments had a research focus. They included Albert Rose, who later would become dean of the faculty, Humphrey Carver, who would become head of the Canadian Mortgage and Housing Corporation, Elisabeth Wallace, who would become a professor of political economy at the University, and Murray Ross, who would replace Claude Bissell as Smith's vice-president and go on to be founding president of

York University. Cassidy seems to have had his way in most things, and Smith's desire to duck when he came in is understandable. Cassidy did not succeed, however, in changing the school's name to the school of 'social welfare,' the name he favoured, nor did he get the major research grant he had sought for the school. He died of cancer in 1951. On his deathbed, he dictated a letter to the staff: 'I am going down hill very rapidly and I will not see you again ... Chick, I am sure, will be a fine director.'

Charles 'Chick' Hendry was director for the next eighteen years. Some of the research momentum built up by Cassidy was unfortunately lost. Many of the scholars, as noted above, moved on to more senior positions elsewhere. There was increasing tension and division between the policy side of the department and the service side, which included the case work and group work teachers. Most social work students were interested in the service side. Such tension is found in most professional schools. Hendry, whose roots were in camping and the YMCA but who also had an interest in policy issues, tried to keep a balance between the two groups. Another tension was that between the women members of the faculty – about half the faculty – who tended to be case workers and group workers with MSW degrees, and the policy members of the faculty, who were mainly higher-paid men with doctorates. During this period, concludes John Graham, the school 'always seemed to fall short of its potential.'

As in virtually all other faculties at the University during the 1960s, the number of students and faculty members grew. The BSW degree was dropped in 1965, and the thesis requirement for the MSW in 1967. Between 1960 and 1965, the faculty increased from 20 to 30 members, and it had reached 35 by 1972. A number of those appointed, such as the British criminologist John Spencer and the sociologist Ben Schlesinger, were particularly productive scholars. Hendry was also able to raise over $200,000 for the Harry Cassidy Memorial Research Fund, which helped bring in visiting professors and assisted in the publication of numerous scholarly works, such as Albert Rose's *Regent Park*, Murray Ross's *Community Organization*, and Ben Schlesinger's *One-Parent Family*. In 1964, the school hired two black academics – Don Meeks as an assistant professor and John Gandy as a lecturer. Meeks was likely the first black person to be given a tenure-stream appointment at the University. Daniel Hill, later head of the Ontario Human Rights Commission, and B.A. McFarlane, later a professor of sociology at Carleton, both had been hired several years earlier, but both were one-year appointments.

Albert Rose became director in 1969 and dean in 1972, when the school became a faculty. He had been a gold medallist from the department of political economy at the University and had received his doctorate in the United States. On his death in 1996, Allan Irving of the faculty, who had completed his doctorate under Rose, made the statement that the faculty had 'lost its most prominent and accomplished scholar.' The 1970s and 1980s were somewhat difficult times for the faculty, whose budget and complement decreased. By 1989, the number of full-time faculty members had dropped from 35 in 1972 to only 22. With the appointment that year of Heather Munroe-Blum, an epidemiologist from McMaster University with a background in social work, the fortunes of the school would turn.

Unlike the money for the homes for music, business, and social work, the money for the faculty of law's new home in Flavelle House, just south of the music building, would come directly from the University's fund-raising activity. The building was officially opened in the fall of 1962. The route to Flavelle House had been circuitous and filled with obstacles. Law had occupied a number of buildings over the years, most recently Glendon Hall, the estate in north Toronto given to the University by the financier E.R. Wood, and before that, Cumberland House on St George Street. The faculty had felt isolated at Glendon and wanted to return to the campus. Bissell supported the move, and told Eric Phillips that 'it would give the Faculty a central position on the campus.' 'Moreover,' he added, 'it has Caesar Wright's apparently enthusiastic support, which, as you realize, is no small matter.' A library, designed by Vincent Massey's son, Hart Massey, with classrooms underneath, and a separate but connected moot court building were constructed.

From the moment of his arrival at the University, Sidney Smith had shown interest in establishing a professional law school. Smith had been dean of such a school at Dalhousie before becoming president of the University of Manitoba, which also had a professional law school. 'There should be established in Ontario,' he wrote, 'a Law School that would rank first in Canada, and be among the leading schools of the North American continent.' W.P.M. Kennedy's law school was an English-style undergraduate program that had grown from a special program in the department of political economy into a separate department in the faculty of arts and then into a separate division. But it was an undergraduate program, not a professional law school. Osgoode Hall Law School, run by the Law Society of Upper Canada, was the only professional school in Ontario and would not tolerate competition for students. Graduates of Kennedy's school had to enter first year at Osgoode. Smith and his friend Caesar Wright, then a professor at Osgoode, discussed ways of changing Kennedy's school into a professional school. Smith and Wright had known each other since the 1920s, when both taught at Osgoode. Smith knew of Wright's brilliance: he had graduated with gold medals from the University of Western Ontario, had stood first in all three years at Osgoode, and after only one year at Harvard Law School was given a doctorate at the age of 22. In 1946, Smith had offered Wright the deanship, but Wright felt the time was not right.

In 1949, however, his opportunity to move to the University came. The Law Society had produced a reactionary report on the Osgoode program that would further have reduced its academic component. The two years of full-time study that preceded a year of articling and a year of mixed articling and lectures would be replaced by more articling, with a lecture at the beginning and the end of each day. This was too much for Wright, who had recently been appointed dean of Osgoode. He resigned as dean, giving his grievance a large measure of publicity. 'Students working in offices all day just become parrots,' he told the *Globe and Mail*. 'They can't explore a legal problem. They just accept it.' The Law Society did not back down, and Wright and three of his colleagues resigned. Wright, John Willis, and Bora Laskin then were invited to join the University of Toronto faculty, with Wright as dean. Laskin had moved from the University to Osgoode in 1945. Many members of the Law Society and others believed the controversy had been engineered by Smith and Wright. At around the time of the resignations, Smith told the dean of the McGill law school, 'For your ear, we are ready to take on our staff Wright, Laskin and Willis.'

Toronto now had a very strong faculty, to which Jim Milner from Dalhousie and the German-trained international and comparative lawyer Wolfgang Friedmann were added. Some from Kennedy's school, such as Eugene Labrie, continued under Wright's leadership. A three-year, second-entry LLB program was instituted. Wright, Laskin, Willis, Milner, and Smith were all Harvard trained. It would certainly be American ideas and teaching methods that would guide the direction of the faculty in the future. In spite of the fact that the Osgoode faculty had been left with almost no full-time teachers, it was able to

Three law professors who resigned from Osgoode Hall Law School in 1949 and joined the
faculty of law at the University of Toronto: from left to right, John Willis, Bora Laskin,
and Cecil (Caesar) Wright, who became dean.

continue to attract almost all the students who wanted to practise law in Ontario
because it would take a year longer to become a lawyer if one went to the
university law school. Very few students therefore attended the University's
school. One board member wrote to Premier Frost saying that something must
be done because the faculty 'at present almost equals in number its students.'
John Willis left for practice, explaining to Wright that 'just two years after it
started up as a professional school, the School of Law is to all intents and
purposes dead.' Wright had won the battle, but seemed to have lost the war.

The Law Society ignored the University's request for recognition of its
program. It took a year and a half for the treasurer of the Law Society, Cyril
Carson, to respond to a letter from Henry Borden, the chairman of the board of
governor's legal education committee. Borden was certainly not used to such
treatment. Premier Leslie Frost, however, was not prepared to help the University. Eric Phillips had a long discussion with him on legal education and reported

to Smith, 'He is definitely anti-Wright and has the impression that you have been taken into camp by Caesar Wright and have unwittingly become the vehicle to make articulate Caesar's hatred of Osgoode.' A peaceful demonstration by some 45 law students in front of Osgoode Hall, asking for the elimination of the final year at Osgoode for Toronto graduates, brought publicity but no positive response from the Law Society. One unnamed demonstrator told the press that the present arrangement was 'giving Toronto lawyers the equivalent of slave labour.' 'Surely the practising lawyers of Ontario,' stated the treasurer, Carson, 'are best able to judge the period required for service under articles before Call to the Bar.'

In 1955, the Law Society changed its tune. It was now interested in sharing legal education with the universities. What caused the change of heart were the projections about the growth in numbers that would hit the universities and Osgoode Hall Law School the following decade. It appeared that some 1,500 persons would want to attend law school in Ontario. Osgoode was prepared to expand its school on Queen Street from the existing 900 students and did build a new wing, but it could not take all the potential students. Queen's University wanted to establish a law school, but insisted on equality with Osgoode: it should not, it insisted, take longer to qualify for the bar by going to a university law school than by going to Osgoode. Wright worked closely with Alex Corry of Queen's in the negotiations. The final details were worked out over two days in early 1957 by Corry and two benchers, Park Jamieson and John Arnup. Wright was not there. 'To be quite frank,' Principal Mackintosh of Queen's wrote Smith, 'I do not think Caesar Wright would help at this stage.' He might have upset the apple cart. The solution adopted was to make the course offered by the law schools, including Osgoode, a three-year course, followed by a year of articling and a six-month practical bar admission course. Wright was 'incredulous but ecstatic.' The proposal was unanimously approved by the Law Society benchers on February 14, 1957 – a Valentine's Day present for those in the University of Toronto Law School (including the author), who would therefore save a year. After the move to Flavelle House in 1962, the number of law students at the University rose to about 400.

Wright resigned effective June 30, 1967. Not only was his health failing, but he felt pressure to resign because a university committee under Dr Reginald Haist had recently brought in a report recommending that deans be limited to a seven-year initial appointment. At that point, Wright had been dean for eighteen years. According to Bissell's diary, Wright seemed 'quite happy at the prospect of a sabbatical and a return as professor.' He died suddenly at the age of 62 a few months later. Convocation Hall was packed for his funeral. The Law Society, which was to have given him an honorary degree later in the spring of 1967, noted, 'He has rightly been called the architect of legal education in Ontario.'

In 1972, Martin Friedland, who had been a student and a teacher at the faculty, took over from Ronald Macdonald, Wright's successor as dean. In the same year, two outstanding scholars, Michael Trebilcock and Ernest Weinrib, were appointed, both of whom subsequently became University Professors. They joined such accomplished law teachers as Frank Iacobucci, a future justice of the Supreme Court of Canada, and Stephen Waddams. It was also the year that an enthusiastic young student named Rob Prichard entered first year law. He came with an MBA from the University of Chicago, following study at Swarthmore College in Pennsylvania. His accomplishments at the law school were so remarkable that in his third year he was given an appointment to the faculty, to take effect after he had completed his graduate studies at Yale. Under Friedland's deanship, the faculty deliberately moved more directly into the University, by increasing the amount of interdisciplinary work and placing a greater emphasis on scholarship. A succession of future deans – Frank Iacobucci, Rob Prichard, Bob Sharpe, and Ron Daniels – would appear to have brought the school to the position dreamed of by Sidney Smith: 'a Law School that would rank first in Canada and be among the leading schools of the North American continent.'

chapter thirty-two

1960

❦

NEW COLLEGES

In the fall of 1960, York University – which initially was affiliated with the University of Toronto – admitted its first class of about 75 students. An agreement had been worked out between Toronto and the York board for an affiliation that would last not less than four years and not more than eight. During this period, students would have to meet Toronto's admission standards for the general course and write Toronto examinations. Faculty appointments had to be approved by the president of the University of Toronto. Toronto gave York the temporary use of Falconer Hall, $500,000 from its campaign funds, and Glendon Hall, which the law school was about to vacate when it returned to the downtown campus.

The idea of another university in the Toronto area had been suggested in a number of earlier reports and had been promoted by a group from the YMCA and a business group headed by former air vice-marshal Wilfred Curtis, a senior executive with the aircraft company A.V. Roe. It was unclear, however, what direction the new university would take. In the fall of 1958, Bissell wrote to Eric Phillips, the chairman of the Toronto board, suggesting the possibility that York become another non-sectarian college at the University of Toronto. 'It would be a federated college,' Bissell said, 'in the sense that it would have its own Board of Trustees and would manage its own financial affairs.'

The York board, however, had grander plans. Some members thought of having an engineering and a medical school as well as an arts and science college.

York University's temporary quarters in Falconer Hall at the University of Toronto in
September 1960, with President Murray Ross on the right and Robert Winters,
the chairman of York's board, on the left, flanking Ann Dalziel and Gary Caldwell,
members of the first class, which had 76 students.

In the spring of 1959, a bill was enacted by the Ontario legislature authorizing
the creation of York University. With Bissell's support, the York board selected
Murray Ross, Bissell's vice-president, as York's first president. Ross, a professor of
sociology in the School of Social Work, had also been Sidney Smith's vice-
president after Bissell went to Carleton. According to Bissell, Ross had been
chosen as vice-president over more experienced candidates because Smith wanted
to work with a fellow Cape Bretoner. As vice-president to Bissell, Ross had
helped draw up the affiliation agreement with York and had impressed the
members of York's organizing group.

During the course of the next year, Curtis and Ross brought onto the board a
number of prominent businessmen, such as the mining executive Robert Winters. According to Ross' memoirs, Eric Phillips, whose support was probably
essential if the province was to finance the new university, told him that 'York
can't go ahead with Wilf Curtis as chairman ... Who of the new people would
you suggest?' 'Perhaps Bob Winters,' Ross replied. 'I'll call you back in half an

hour,' Phillips said. Phillips got Frost's approval – even though Winters was a Liberal – and then persuaded Winters to take the job. Curtis became chancellor of the new university. York made a number of impressive appointments in the early years: Edgar McInnis, an historian who had left U of T in the early 1950s to become president of the Canadian Institute for International Affairs, and two U of T professors who became deans of arts and science at York, the geographer George Tatham and the historian John Saywell.

It soon became clear that York's original idea of a small arts and science college on the site of Glendon Hall's 86 acres could not accommodate all the additional students requiring places in the Toronto area. 'If York is to be of major assistance to us in handling student enrolment,' Bissell wrote to Phillips in 1961, 'then it must be prepared to accept in the vicinity of 10,000 students, say by 1970.' This projection would require a large campus elsewhere, and Bissell and Phillips thought they should lease Glendon to York only until it could develop a new and larger campus. Toronto had an interest in keeping Glendon because the departments of botany and forestry felt they had a legitimate claim to the use of the property. Nevertheless, it was given to York, but on the condition that it continue to be used for academic purposes. The government and the York board also realized that the new university had to expand, and in 1961 the province gave York about 500 acres of land at the corner of Steeles Avenue and Keele Street in the north-west section of Metropolitan Toronto. Ross predicted there would be 15,000 students by 1980.

Relations between the two universities were not particularly close. Ross felt that Toronto treated York as 'a kind of junior branch,' and York was suspicious of Toronto's motives. When senior administrators from the two institutions met in late 1962 to discuss the future development of professional education, Bissell recorded in his diary that the session was 'useless,' and that the York representatives acted like 'a group of virgins, nervous about our advances.' Ross stated in his autobiography that about that time 'there was an increased determination on the part of our board to make York both independent of, and competitive with, the University of Toronto.' In 1965, the affiliation was terminated, and York became completely independent of the University of Toronto.

❧

At the University of Toronto, new residences would be required to accommodate the anticipated increase in the number of students. The federated colleges were

Architect's model of New College, 1963.

expanding their residence facilities, but they could not meet the expected demand. The University's original plan was to construct large low-cost residences on the west campus along Spadina Avenue. Bissell was concerned, however, as he later noted in his memoirs, about the board's view that the residences 'must be designed so as to contain as many bodies as possible in as little space as possible.' He was 'determined to fight the proposals for faceless dormitories.' Residence students who were in arts, like all arts students, would have to belong to a college – that was the Toronto system. The students who could not be accommodated in the federated colleges would therefore end up in University College, in numbers – perhaps 4,000 students – that would destroy the college as a community. Bissell set up a committee that recommended – as he knew it would – that enrolment at University College be limited to about 2,000 students. The solution was therefore to go back to the Plateau Committee's idea that two additional colleges be built on the campus.

In the fall of 1964, the cornerstone of the first phase of a new undergraduate college – appropriately called New College – was laid at the corner of Willcocks and Huron streets on the west campus. It was, Bissell said at the ceremony, a 'new chapter in the history of the University of Toronto.' It would be the first college directly under the control of the University constructed since University College was built in the 1850s. Bissell also commented on its 'fresh and imaginative' serpentine design. Meant to accommodate 1,800 students, with nearly 600 in residence, it admitted the first students in 1962. Henry Borden, who had taken over from Eric Phillips as chairman of the board, officially opened the building.

The chemist Frank Wetmore had been selected as the first principal, but he died of a heart attack in 1963, and the physicist Donald Ivey became principal and took part in the official opening. One feature of the new college was that it was to include students from the professional faculties, as would the second undergraduate college to be planned, Innis College. Because of New College's proximity to the science buildings and the fact that the first principals came from science backgrounds, the college has proved attractive to science and engineering students.

❧

Innis College did not proceed as quickly or as smoothly as had New College. Indeed, the sod-turning ceremony did not take place until the fall of 1973, even though the college had officially come into being on July 1, 1964. At Vincent Massey's urging, the board had chosen to name the college for Innis rather than Falconer. In 1963, English professor Robin Harris was chosen as its first principal, and the college, housed in the 'temporary' bookstore beside the old observatory, admitted its first students in the fall of 1964. At one point, the college was to have been housed in the second phase of New College, but neither New nor Innis wanted that. The second half of New College, which owing to inflation cost twice as much as the first phase, became a New College residence for women. Plans were prepared for a large new complex for Innis. The architect Hart Massey produced an award-winning design for a $12 million structure for 1,500 students at St George and Sussex streets. The development would have included two residential towers – one for men and one for women – with the college quadrangle between the towers.

The Ontario government, however, had been cutting back on capital contributions to universities, and the board insisted that Innis' plans be reduced. Harris complained to Bissell that 'the importance of Innis College in the developing plan of the University of Toronto has been forgotten.' Political scientist Peter Russell had become acting principal in 1968–9, when Harris took a sabbatical leave, and Russell called an emergency meeting of the Innis council.

Turning the sod for Innis College, 1973. From right to left, Principal Peter Russell, Sheldon Sinukoff, president of the Innis College Student Society, Robin Harris, the founding principal, and President John Evans.

It was, Russell wrote, 'possibly the most critical moment in the College's history.' The council passed a resolution that permanent facilities were imperative and that Innis would not take any more first year students until the college had adequate support from the University. If nothing was done, therefore, Innis College would cease to exist at the end of four years. The tactic helped put the college at the top of the University's list of capital priorities. Federal housing funds, however, were becoming more difficult to obtain, and the scale of the college, now to be designed by Diamond and Myers, was severely reduced. It would not include a residence at this stage and would be limited to 750 students.

In the meantime, the college was developing a unique personality. Students, for example, played an active role in the governance of the college and were the first in the University to be regular members of a college council – 5 of the 25-member Innis council were students. The college offered interdisciplinary courses and took an interest in contemporary media, such as modern art and film. Harold Innis, whose later work involved the relationship between communication and technology, probably would have been pleased. Peter Russell, who took over from Robin Harris as principal in 1971, has observed: 'Although Harold Innis was a social conservative and would have been very ill at ease in the rather bohemian environment of the College that takes his name, the intellectual character of Innis College does reflect some of his own iconoclastic character. He would certainly have applauded the College's commitment to be a multi-media house of learning, and understood its strong commitment to film.' The distinctive character of Innis College, to which a residence was added on the east side of St George Street in 1994, continued under subsequent principals – William Saywell, who went on to be president of Simon Fraser University, Dennis Duffy, John Browne, and Frank Cunningham.

❧

York University and the two new colleges on the St George campus would not be able to satisfy the expected demand for places in the Toronto region. In 1962, the committee of Ontario presidents recommended – as had the Plateau Committee's report in 1956 – that two new colleges on the outskirts of Toronto be established by the University of Toronto. The board, with the encouragement of the government, purchased two large blocks of land – a 200-acre site in Scarborough about 20 miles (30 kilometres) east of the main campus, and a 150-acre site on the Credit River in Mississauga, 20 miles west of the campus. (The main campus was known as the 'Queen's Park campus,' but within a few years, after the west campus became an established fact, the main campus came to be known as the 'St George campus,' an indication of how the centre of the campus had shifted.) A planning committee under the psychologist Carl Williams, the director of extension at the University, recommended that Scarborough be built first. The government and Eric Phillips wanted quick action so that students could be admitted by the fall of 1965. The two colleges were to be like other colleges in the Toronto system, though it was envisioned that they would gradually achieve greater autonomy.

Carl Williams became the first principal of Scarborough in 1963 as well as vice-president for planning of the two suburban colleges. Three members of the School of Architecture were asked to plan the Scarborough site – John Andrews, the head of design at the school, landscape architect Michael Hough, and

Map, prepared in the 1960s, showing the location of Scarborough and Erindale colleges.

Carl Williams, here lecturing on psychology on a CBC program in 1957, became the first
principal of Scarborough College and vice-president for planning of the two suburban
colleges in 1963.

Aerial view of Scarborough College, September 1966.

planner Michael Hugo-Brunt. The team, in fact, went further than their man-date and actually designed a building. Bissell and Williams and, perhaps more important, Phillips were delighted with the design, and in the spring of 1964 the sod was turned by the minister of education and U of T graduate William Davis. The imposing concrete structure was placed dramatically on a ridge overlooking the heavily wooded valley of Highland Creek below. Bissell recorded in his diary following his first visit in the spring of 1965 that he was 'immensely impressed by the way in which the building had been planned for human beings.' The *Architectural Forum* gave it a rave review, stating that 'the visitor succumbs most willingly to the sheer power of the whole, to Andrews' ingenious blending of light, form and space into a single experience.' Not everyone was thrilled, however. Some members of the board regarded it as 'conspicuous waste.'

Having established Scarborough College, Williams moved on to take charge of the planning of Erindale. Wynne Plumptre, who had taught in the depart-ment of political economy before the war and then become a senior federal official in the Department of External Affairs and then in Finance, was invited to return to Toronto to take responsibility for one of the new colleges. Although his inclination at first was towards Erindale, in 1965 he accepted the position of principal of Scarborough College. Williams tried to get the name changed to 'University of Toronto, Scarborough' or 'University of Toronto at Scarborough,' feeling that the use of the term 'college' hindered recruitment because it connoted 'a small, isolated, exclusively undergraduate institution.' Simcoe Hall, however, did not accept such a change. It would not be until the 1990s that Scarborough adopted the name 'University of Toronto at Scarborough' and Erindale College became 'University of Toronto at Mississauga.' Erindale was the name of an historic village just south of the college. The name 'Mississauga College' had been suggested when the land was first acquired, because the Mississauga Indians had once inhabited the area. Indeed, the site of Erindale along with other lands along the Credit River had been purchased by the Crown from the band shortly after Upper Canada was established so that lands could be provided for retired veterans of the British army.

One distinctive feature of Scarborough College was the plan to make widespread use of television for teaching purposes. This was not an afterthought but was built into the design of the college. 'Scarborough was planned as a TV college,' the sociologist John Lee has written, 'in a way which at that time was original in North America.' Carl Williams had promoted the use of television in the extension program, and the first dean at Scarborough, the zoologist William Beckel, had successfully used the medium in his own teaching. Half the classes were to be taught using videotaped lectures. Expensive production facilities were incorporated into the building. The use of television, it was thought, would save money and help ease the problem of finding enough staff members to teach the courses.

The television experiment failed, however. Students – particularly students in the second half of the 1960s – were not willing to accept either the lack of interaction with lecturers or what in most cases were second-rate productions compared to what they were seeing on television at home. 'The first outbreak on the Berkeley campus,' Plumptre noted in retrospect, 'took place while the Scarborough TV centre was being constructed; and the whole thrust of the new educational objectives and desires ran contrary to the concept of mechanized, standardized instruction.' Moreover, the use of TV did not save money. It might have, if the college had had the 5,000 students planned for, but there were fewer than 2,000 in 1970, and the cost of production was higher than the savings on live lecturers. The production facilities were ultimately turned over to other uses.

Economist Wynne Plumptre succeeded Williams as principal of Scarborough College in 1965;
Plumptre is shown here in 1972 with Scarborough's television production facilities.

Fortunately, however, the conduits buried in the concrete that carried the television cables were perfect for the cables for the computers now widely used in the classrooms and other rooms at Scarborough.

Scarborough College experienced another problem. Many members of the staff felt themselves under the thumb of the St George campus, particularly owing to the control exercised by the downtown departments, which made the hiring and promotion decisions. Plumptre wrote to Bissell in the spring of 1970 asking for 'a fundamental review of the position and prospects of Scarborough College.' 'All our affairs,' he wrote, 'are apparently to remain under detailed supervision from the St George Campus. Yet, if we are to survive as a vigorous alternative to the St George Campus, attracting both good faculty and good students, it is clearly essential that we should be distinctive and, in the measure required, autonomous.' 'I now believe,' Plumptre concluded, 'that the College should, over a short period of years, become an independent university ... Its primary function would be the undergraduate teaching function.'

Many faculty members also wanted complete independence, including the philosopher Bill Graham (much later the president of the University of Toronto Faculty Association). The then dean of the college, political scientist John Colman, did not hold such extreme views, but agreed that something had to be done. 'The pull of the St George campus,' he wrote to Bissell, 'will always be too great, in such circumstance, for good undergraduates, for graduate students and for faculty ... Many Scarborough College faculty are absentee members now: this will become the established pattern.' Scarborough will not have a dedicated faculty, he went on, 'unless appointments are to a clear entity that is capable of stimulating, receiving and rewarding loyalty.'

Bissell set up a university-wide thirty-member committee, headed by the University of Toronto geographer Kenneth Hare, that included senior administrators from the St George campus and representatives of the dissidents. (It tells us something about the campus in 1970 that there was not one woman on the committee.) Hare had excellent academic credentials and also wide administrative experience, including a period as master of Birkbeck College in the University of London. The terms of reference were 'to consider the status of Scarborough College, and make recommendations for its future.' 'By all reports,' Bissell recorded in his diary, it was 'the most acrimonious and personally venomous committee in the recent history of the University.' Some wanted an autonomous college – to be named the 'University of Southern Ontario' – while others valued their association with the University, particularly their involvement in the graduate school. The committee member R.C. Roeder, the chair of physical sciences at the college, told the committee that the physical scientists 'consider appointment to the graduate faculty as essential to the development of their careers,' and that if such appointment was not possible, many would leave the college.

In April 1971, twenty-six members of the committee, including Plumptre and Colman, signed a report recommending greater autonomy for the college. The recommendation, the report stated, was 'not a consensus, but a prospective course of action.' Henceforth, it would be Scarborough College that determined the need for new faculty and that would have the majority of members on hiring and tenure committees, not the departments on the St George campus. The Scarborough College council quickly endorsed the report, and Bissell accepted the Hare compromise between the status quo and separation. He recorded in his diary his conviction that 'more autonomy for the colleges, particularly Scarborough, was both healthy and inevitable, and that insistence upon St George control would be bad both for the central campus and for the satellites.' In 1972, academic appointment procedures were passed implementing the Hare report. Principal Ralph Campbell, a former Rhodes scholar who would later become president of the University of Manitoba, took over from Plumptre in 1972 and was succeeded in 1976 by psychologist Joan Foley, who became the first woman principal of a college and who later would serve as provost of the University. Together, they helped bring a greater sense of purpose back to the college.

The diversity that many had expected did not come about at Scarborough, except in one significant respect – the development of co-op programs. The first such program was established in the 1970s in public administration. It was followed in the 1980s by co-op programs in international development studies and arts administration, and in the 1990s by programs in computer science and environmental science. Such programs are now seen as a distinctive feature of Scarborough.

The principal of Erindale College, the geophysicist J. Tuzo Wilson, did not agree with the committee's report – at least with respect to Erindale. 'As the only representative of Erindale College on the committee,' he wrote in an addendum to the report, 'I wish to make it clear that no one at Erindale College has ever indicated any desire to follow the same path.' 'There are difficulties and complications in operating a university on more than one campus,' he stated, 'but in our experience these can be overcome and the advantages of a close association with the St George campus greatly outweigh the disadvantages.' The Erindale College council had taken the same view and in early 1971 voted 45 to 0 in favour of remaining 'fully integrated within the Faculty of Arts and Science of the University of Toronto.' This relationship has continued. Political scientist Paul Fox, the principal from 1976 to 1986, has written that 'there was never any doubt at Erindale about its continuing affiliation.' 'In fact,' he added, 'I don't recall there ever being even any significant discussion of the issue.'

The morale of the Erindale faculty, it seems, was higher than that of their colleagues at Scarborough. They complained less and seemed to share a common vision for the future of the college. In fact, a good doctoral thesis could be written about the differences between these two colleges created at about the

Erindale College, 1971.

same time. Perhaps the thesis would begin with the physical facilities. Scarborough was located in a dramatic structure that seemed to call for great drama. Moreover, it probably raised expectations that what would take place inside would be as exciting as the building itself. The same might have occurred at Erindale. John Andrews and his team had prepared an imaginative plan for Erindale, but various delays, including protests against the expropriation of additional properties and financial concerns, put off its implementation.

Erindale started life with a 'preliminary' building to greet the first class that entered in 1967. The building was to be used for non-academic purposes once the campus was developed, but it has continued in use for academic purposes and is today known as the North Building. The makeshift quarters may have had a positive effect on the students. Tennys Hanson, a student in the early 1970s and the campaign director at the University of Toronto in the 1990s, has recalled: 'What I quickly learned was that the structures were less relevant than the people. Erindale wasn't about buildings. Erindale was all about the people.'

The striking South Building, designed by Raymond Moriyama, was not officially opened until 1973.

A more important consideration in accounting for the relative contentment at Erindale was that J. Tuzo Wilson, a very distinguished geophysicist noted for his contribution to earth plate tectonics who would become president of the Royal Society of Canada in 1972, had been chosen in 1967 as principal of Erindale. Bissell had approached Wilson three years earlier about becoming a principal of one of the new colleges, but nothing came of his proposal at the time. The opportunity offered itself again, however, when Carl Williams, who had started the college, was selected as president of the University of Western Ontario. Wilson was a scientist, a product of the University, and had both knowledge of and attachment to the main campus; Plumptre was to a considerable extent an outsider.

From the very beginning, it was thought that science would be important at Erindale. Early documents, for example, mention the significance of the new Sheridan Research Park, which was being constructed nearby. As at Scarborough, the scientists valued their connection with the St George campus and its graduate school. Wilson was able to attract some excellent scientists to the campus. Their laboratories and graduate students were there, so they were content to spend time on the campus. While this was also true in life sciences at Scarborough, it was less so in the physical sciences.

Among the scientists in the early days was the geophysicist David Strangway, who had been head of geophysical research for the American space agency NASA. He was an expert in the magnetic properties of minerals and continued his work with NASA by analysing moon rocks at Erindale. On one occasion, 3,000 people lined up to see the samples. Strangway would become provost of the University and, for one year, its president, before moving on to become president of the University of British Columbia. Two future University Professors (a designation given to only about 25 persons at any one time in the University) taught at Erindale – Mitchell Winnick of chemistry and Fergus Craik of psychology.

Erindale also became part of the local community. This was one of Principal Paul Fox's goals. The Mississauga Symphony used the Meeting Place in the South Building for its concerts, and Mississauga mayor Hazel McCallion came to almost every public event. Student residences – row housing instead of big

Moon rock display at Erindale College, September 1969. From left to right,
Associate Dean Irving Spiegel, geophysicist David Strangway, Principal J. Tuzo Wilson,
and Dean E.A. Robinson.

apartments – were built, and gave the students a greater presence on the campus
in the evenings than they would otherwise have had. Residences for Erindale had
been recommended because of the negative effect of the lack of residence space
at Scarborough, which had not built its first residence until 1973, nine years
after the first students arrived.

Both Erindale and Scarborough have been fertile breeding grounds for
university administrators. From the Erindale campus – to give only three examples – Marsha Chandler became chair of political science and then dean of arts
and science; Martin Moscovits, chair of chemistry; and Betty Roots, chair of
zoology. (Roots supervised the astronaut Roberta Bondar's doctorate in neuro-
chemistry at Erindale. Bondar would be the first Toronto graduate and the first
Canadian woman in space.) Among the many administrators who started their
Toronto careers at Scarborough were economist Jon Cohen, who became dean
of graduate studies; Peter Richardson of religious studies, who became principal

of University College; and philosopher Paul Gooch, who became a vice-provost at Simcoe Hall and in 2001 the president of Victoria University. At Victoria, Gooch joined David Cook, who had been a political scientist at Erindale and then at Scarborough and a vice-provost at Simcoe Hall before becoming principal of Victoria College in 2000. There has thus been considerable mobility among the three campuses.

By the end of the 1980s, Erindale and Scarborough each were approaching some 4,000 full-time students. In the year 2000, as will be noted later, they were poised to increase their size and range of activities.

PART SIX

EXPANDING HORIZONS

chapter thirty-three

1962

❦

GRADUATE STUDIES: FROM MASSEY COLLEGE TO THE ROBARTS LIBRARY

The year 1962 was particularly important in the history of the University. It was the year the foundations were put in place for the future growth of graduate studies. In the spring, the cornerstone of Massey College was laid, the University's first, and still its only, graduate college. The year also saw the promise by the provincial government of extensive scholarships for graduate work, the acceptance of the millionth book for the library, and the determination to build a new humanities and social science library. It was also the year that Ernest Sirluck, who shared Claude Bissell's ideas about the importance of graduate studies and the need for a major research library, came back to the University.

❦

The Massey College cornerstone was laid by Prince Philip in May 1962. It was a visible statement that Toronto took graduate studies seriously. The Massey Foundation had offered the college as a gift to the University in 1959. It would be, Vincent Massey said, for male graduate students – to be called 'junior fellows' – 'of special promise.' There was some concern among members of the University's board of governors about the elite nature of the institution, and the one woman member of the board, the publisher Irene Clarke, along with others in the University, objected to its being restricted to men. Nevertheless, the gift was accepted quickly. Eric Phillips stated that he had 'never been one to look a

Vincent Massey and Claude Bissell with a model of Massey College, September 1963.

gift horse in the teeth,' adding that 'this is a pretty big horse.' As usual, Phillips' main concern was finances: 'We must preserve from the very start our principle that our financial obligations must be known and they must be limited.' It turned out to be wise advice, because within two years the cost of the building had doubled from the original estimate. Vincent Massey was apparently unconcerned. After all, the cost of Hart House had also doubled fifty years earlier. Some members of the board were worried that the college would be too independent, but that fear was alleviated by making the president and the dean of the graduate school senior fellows of the college, and it was the senior fellows who would run the college. Moreover, the head of the college – to be called 'the master' – would be selected by the senior fellows but appointed by the University's board of governors.

The college was to be located at the corner of Hoskin Avenue and Devonshire Place. Massey's son, the architect Hart Massey, wanted a 'modern treatment'; Vincent Massey, however, was 'determinedly traditionalist.' The Vancouver architect Ron Thom managed to satisfy both father and son while creating a universally acclaimed building. The college has the feel of a traditional English college, with its inner courtyard and grand dining hall, but is also strikingly modern in design. As with Hart House, Vincent Massey was 'concerned with every detail.' The playwright and novelist Robertson Davies, then publisher of the *Peterborough Examiner*, was appointed as the first master. He had been the choice of both Vincent Massey and Bissell. 'I would strongly support Davies if he is willing to let his name stand,' Bissell wrote to Phillips. 'He is the leading Canadian man of letters, with an international reputation, and he would bring great distinction to the post.'

The college opened in the fall of 1963. The first group of senior fellows included distinguished scholars such as William Dobson of Chinese studies and Robert Finch of the French department, members of the Massey family such as actor Raymond Massey and architects Hart and Geoffrey Massey, and young academics such as political scientist James Eayrs and chemist John Polanyi. (Polanyi's Nobel prize, awarded in 1986, is permanently on display in the college.) The initial meeting of the senior fellows had taken place in 1961 in one of Toronto's private clubs, with Davies wearing an academic gown and thereby setting a formal tone for future official meetings and dinners.

In 1966, Vincent Massey arranged for most of the remaining money left in the Massey Foundation (a little over a million dollars) to be given to the college

Robertson Davies, the founding master of Massey College, date uncertain.

as an endowment. Some Massey relatives thought Vincent had gone too far, and there was talk of a lawsuit to get the money back, but in the end no action was taken. Vincent Massey died in 1967. Davies remained as master until 1980, elegantly presiding over the college while teaching at Trinity College and continuing his literary pursuits – all three volumes of his *Deptford Trilogy* were written while he was master. Later masters have continued the literary tradition: the computer scientist Patterson Hume, who had written, directed, and acted in the annual Arts and Letters Club spring review; Ann Saddlemyer, a head of the drama centre at the University; and John Fraser, the noted journalist and author. Most important, the college has provided a desirable physical and intellectual home for about 60 resident and 50 non-resident graduate students each year – including women as of 1974. Students are able to meet informally with faculty members and others associated with the college, including some half a dozen journalists selected each year as Southam Fellows.

❧

The establishment of Massey College portended other significant developments in graduate studies at the University. The dean of the graduate school, Andrew Gordon, was to retire in 1963, and Bissell had been concerned about the selection of his successor. 'Finding a successor to Gordon,' he wrote to his friend Ernest Sirluck, a professor of English at the University of Chicago, who had previously taught with Bissell at University College, 'is, I think, my crucial administrative problem.' Would Sirluck be interested in the position? Bissell knew Sirluck as both forceful and articulate. When he first met Sirluck, who had come to Toronto in 1940 from the University of Manitoba to do graduate work, Bissell had recorded in his diary that Sirluck had 'an argument on every subject and a theory on most.' The year before the graduate school offer, Bissell had wanted Sirluck to take over from A.S.P. Woodhouse – like Sirluck, a Milton scholar – as chair of English at University College. To Bissell, having Sirluck as dean of the graduate school was more important. The school, he wrote, 'is the fighting edge of the University, upon which its scholarly reputation principally depends.' Chicago had a first-class graduate school. In his autobiography, Sirluck describes his discussions with Bissell: 'We talked far into the night, stimulating each other's sense of the possible until we were both seized of a vision of the U of T transformed by research, graduate study, and new disciplines into a university of international quality.'

Sirluck accepted the position and returned to the University in June 1962, with the promise of being Gordon's successor as dean of the graduate school. In the meantime, he would be the graduate school's associate dean of humanities and social sciences. Sirluck was the first Jew to be appointed to a senior position at the University. He was invited to join the York Club, where many university meetings were held. According to his autobiography, he accepted and was to be notified of the next vacancy. Some time later, he wrote, he was lunching at the club as Bissell's guest when the chairman of the club's membership committee started chatting with him. 'What is your background? Norwegian?' Sirluck was asked. 'No,' Sirluck replied, 'Russian Jewish.' After that, Sirluck noted, 'I never heard from the club about my election to membership.'

The previously discussed special committee on the higher-education needs of Ontario, chaired by John Deutsch and set up by the Ontario university presidents, had advocated strengthening the graduate schools in the province to meet the expected demand for university teachers. There were 2,000 academics in the province in 1962–3, and it was predicted that some 8,000 would be needed by 1975–6. For most, a doctorate would be required. The government accepted the recommendation that graduate fellowships be established to encourage students to undertake post-graduate work in Ontario. The fellowships, which would pay $2,000 for twelve months' study at an Ontario institution, would be limited mainly to the humanities and social sciences. The sciences were more easily able to generate assistance through funds provided by the federal granting agencies. Twenty per cent of the students awarded fellowships could come from outside the province. In the first year of operation, 1963–4, Toronto's full-time graduate enrolment increased from 1,225 students to 1,645, and by the 1965–6 academic year it was over 2,000. The University was also benefiting from the recently introduced Commonwealth and Canada Council scholarship programs. Moreover, a significant portion of the US-funded Woodrow Wilson fellows – in 1962, Toronto graduates ranked third after Harvard and Yale in the number awarded – chose to study at Toronto.

Unfortunately, the University could not provide residences for most of the students. Massey College could take only about 60 students. Sirluck tried to obtain a graduate residence and graduate centre on the east side of St George Street, without success. An apartment building at the south-east corner of St George and Bloor streets was purchased, however, and in 1968 a large apartment building on Charles Street was acquired for graduate and also undergraduate married students. The School of Graduate Studies had to leave its home in order to make way for Massey College and was for a time housed in the 'temporary' bookstore beside the old observatory. It then moved to a grand old house at 65 St George Street, and eventually also took over 63 St George, which in the previous century had been the home of Sir John A. Macdonald and, later, Sir Oliver Mowat. The graduate school still occupies these two buildings.

Under Sirluck, the graduate school slowly exerted greater influence within the University. Although, theoretically, the graduate school could control graduate school appointments and could select the heads of graduate departments, in fact, as both Innis and Gordon had found, this power was strongly resisted by the departments in arts and science and the professional schools. Moreover, the dean did not have much budgetary clout. The faculty members in the under-graduate departments were almost automatically the faculty members in the graduate school, and the heads of undergraduate departments almost invariably assumed the position of head of the graduate department. A breakthrough was made in 1966, when Mary White from Trinity became head of the graduate department of classics, even though she was not the head of an undergraduate department. It was a breakthrough in another respect as well: she was the first woman to head a graduate department at the University. The graduate school also wanted to be involved in senior appointments, and though this was ac-cepted in arts and science, it was resisted by the professional faculties. Bissell and Sirluck felt that the solution was to set up a university-wide presidential commit-tee to examine and make recommendations on 'the academic, administrative and financial structure of the School of Graduate Studies.'

A very powerful committee was established in 1964, with Bora Laskin as its chair. The eleven-person committee, which Bissell later described as 'the strong-est internal committee in the history of the University,' included such persons as Northrop Frye, John Polanyi, economist Harry Eastman, engineer William Winegard, physicist Archie Hallett, and Sirluck. It met for almost two years. The committee was to stress the importance of graduate studies in Canada. 'Such studies,' its report concluded, 'must be relied upon to establish the country's intellectual horizons.' The committee had held more than forty meetings and visited more than thirty universities in the United States and Europe. In late 1965, it was able to produce a unanimous report. 'The auguries for such a consensus were quite poor when the inquiry began,' the report – written mainly by Laskin – stated. Some had wanted a stronger centralized graduate school, while others wanted the departments to control graduate studies. In the end, the members adopted a centralist version. The graduate school would have greater control over appointments to graduate departments and in the selection of senior academics. This version did not go as far as the University of Chicago system, in which there was a division between undergraduate and graduate faculty. Whether or not the members of the committee were aware of it, the result reflected Laskin's constitutional views. He was a strong centralist in the Canadian federal system. Indeed, in one Supreme Court of Canada constitu-tional case on which he sat many years later, his colleague Justice Brian Dickson referred to Laskin's views as 'blind centralism.'

The anticipated strong negative reaction to the report by the heads of

The Laskin Committee on Graduate Studies, meeting in the senate chamber on the day
the report was signed, December 1965. From left to right, front row: Northrop Frye,
Frances Ireland (secretary of the committee), Bora Laskin, Ernest Sirluck; second row:
A.C.H. Hallett, John Polanyi, William Winegard, Robert McRae, Charles Hanes,
Harry Eastman, John Cairns, and Kenneth Fisher.

departments did not take place. Perhaps that was because Laskin, who in the
meantime had become a judge of the Ontario Court of Appeal, gave a masterful
defence of the report. The dean of arts and science, Vincent Bladen, backed off
from an expected confrontation, and after various committees had studied the
issues, the Laskin report was approved. The centralized graduate school had
four divisions, rather than the previous two, and a much smaller council was
instituted.

Other Ontario universities were establishing graduate programs, spurred on
by their apparent prestige and by the funding incentives under the anticipated
formula financing system. The University of Toronto wanted this increase to be
controlled to ensure that new programs were of a high quality. The other
universities, however, were suspicious of the University of Toronto's motives.
After all, they argued, Toronto already had numerous graduate programs. A
commission was set up jointly by the provincial Committee on University
Affairs and the committee of Ontario presidents to study graduate programs.
The minister of education, Bill Davis, strongly supported coordination, stating
that 'of the many areas of higher education that require planning, the most

important is that of graduate studies.' The commission, chaired by the president of the University of Saskatchewan, John Spinks, reported in 1966 that there had to be closer cooperation among the Ontario universities and recommended that an appraisal system for new programs be established. It went further, however, and advocated a University of Ontario, along the lines of the University of California. This recommendation alarmed the newer universities. A system of appraisals organized by the universities themselves seemed to them a better alternative than being swallowed up in a province-wide system that would be dominated by the University of Toronto. The new appraisal system came into operation in early 1967.

❧

The largest number of graduate students in the University of Toronto before long was to be found in the Ontario Institute for Studies in Education (OISE). The institute had been established in 1965 by the Ontario government with its own board of governors and degree-granting powers. It had emerged out of an earlier proposal for an institute for curriculum development and research promoted by Robin Harris. Bill Davis had seized upon the idea and wanted to expand the concept. Graduate studies in education in Ontario were almost nonexistent. Almost all Ontario residents who wanted to do graduate work in education went to Alberta or the United States.

The Ontario College of Education (OCE), however, was not happy with the creation of OISE. The dean of the college, D.F. Dadson, complained to Davis that its establishment as an independent institution would mean a 'diminished role' for OCE and suggested that the proposed institute be set up within the college. Both Bissell and Sirluck, however, were content to have the institute separate from OCE. 'There are important merits in the proposal,' Sirluck advised Bissell. 'It has not been possible to organize educational research adequately from the present institutional bases.' But it could not be completely separate, he went on, because 'persons of the academic calibre needed to perform the graduate instruction and supervision and the academic research and theoretical study will not commit themselves to an Institute which does not give them membership in a university.' The University of Toronto, he warned, could not drive 'too hard a bargain,' however, because 'there are universities that would leap to close with [Davis] on almost any terms.'

The Ontario Institute for Studies in Education (OISE) was established in 1965, and the building on Bloor Street was completed in 1970; the building on the right is now the home of the faculty of social work.

An affiliation agreement was worked out with Toronto in 1966. All graduate degrees would be recommended by the graduate school at the University, and OISE's graduate faculty members would have to be approved individually as members of the University's graduate school. Students would have to meet the University's admission requirements, and graduate courses be approved by the graduate school. Furthermore, all doctorates would have to be research degrees, as had been established as university policy following the Laskin report. In exchange for affiliation, OISE would suspend the right to award its own degrees. These understandings gave the University – in theory – a great measure of control over OISE's academic programs. Moreover, the University was given representation on the OISE board – at first, both Sirluck and Moffat Woodside. Robert Jackson, who had headed OCE's department of educational research and was highly respected by the government, became the first director of the institute, and George Flower, the head of the graduate program at OCE, became head of the graduate department of educational theory. Justice Laskin was appointed chair of the board.

Bora Laskin, then of the court of appeal of Ontario, became the first chair of the OISE board; here he congratulates his son John, later of the same court, on his graduation from law school in June 1969.

In 1970, after occupying temporary quarters, OISE moved into its present twelve-storey building on the north side of Bloor Street, constructed specifically for OISE. By the end of the decade, there were about 150 academic and 500 non-academic staff members. Some areas, such as cognitive science with the psychologists Carl Bereiter and David Olson, and women's studies with Paula Caplan, Margrit Eichler, Alison Prentice, and Dorothy Smith, became well known and well respected. Relations with the University, however, were not always smooth. Sirluck and others in the graduate school saw their role as maintaining standards. 'Woodside and I,' Sirluck stated in his memoirs, 'tried never to miss meetings, since OISE had a tremendous budget and a predilection for wild schemes, not all of which we were able to stop. It hired staff at a bewildering rate, brought in students on extremely fat fellowships and proposed dissertation topics ranging from the respectable to the laughable.'

The friction continued through the 1970s, and some at OISE wanted to break away from what they considered the University's stifling control over their activities. This was a repeat of the Scarborough College scenario. The University, after a series of reports, wanted either integration with the faculty of education (it ceased to be called OCE in 1972) or disaffiliation. In the early 1980s, a university task group headed by zoologist David Mettrick recommended that the agreement with OISE be terminated. 'There are two major flaws in the present arrangement,' Mettrick told the council of the School of Graduate Studies: 'The first is that it's completely unmanageable and there's absolute unanimity on that. The second is that it separates graduate work in education from what's being done at the undergraduate level.' An attempt to merge the two institutions in the mid-1980s was unsuccessful.

It was not until 1996 that OISE and the faculty of education were joined together. The NDP government wanted the merger to take place, and OISE no longer had the will to mount a campaign to oppose it, as it had done in the 1980s. The original OISE faculty members, who had been inspired by the idealism of the 1960s, had for the most part retired or were close to retirement. The marriage would certainly give new life to the faculty of education. Dean Dadson had been right: the creation of OISE had given it a 'diminished role.' Michael Fullan, the dean of the faculty of education, now became head of both institutions. He had been a professor of sociology at OISE from 1968 until 1987 before being appointed dean of education and so had an understanding of the institutional culture of OISE, which probably made the merger more palatable to many at OISE. One benefit of the merger for OISE is that it is now less vulnerable to closure. As the OISE educational theorist Michael Skolnik has written, 'In an era of contraction and penury when the government is looking for things to cut or cut out, it is best not to be too conspicuous.' The then acting director of OISE, Angela Hildyard, stated on the eve of the merger that the two bodies 'have the potential to rise to new heights.'

❦

It was accepted by the early 1960s that the university library system had to expand in order to provide library facilities for the expected increase in the number of graduate students. A separate research library for the humanities and social sciences was a high priority for Bissell – an 'obsession,' he confessed in one of his annual reports. A committee, chaired by Harold Innis, had reported in 1947 that the library needed 'the most radical and extensive improvements.' It then had fewer than 500,000 books and was ranked thirty-sixth among university libraries in North America. The opening of the Sigmund Samuel wing of the library in 1954 helped, but it was clear that Toronto could not build a major graduate school without greater library resources. Book purchases increased, and in 1962 the library celebrated the acquisition of its millionth item, a sixteenth-century French royal patent, donated by the recently established Varsity Fund. American alumni contributed a 1632 edition of Shakespeare's works to start the next million books.

The colleges and departments were also building their collections, which, together with the university library, brought the total to about two million books, twice as many as any other university library in Canada. The colleges planned extensive expansions. Victoria College opened the E.J. Pratt Library in 1961, and University College completed its quadrangle with the Laidlaw Library a few years later. Trinity was able to obtain more space for its library when the Larkin academic building was opened. St Michael's made temporary arrangements for more library space in Carr Hall and at the end of the decade opened its new library on St Joseph Street, later to be named after Father John Kelly, a former long-serving and respected president of St Michael's. By 1965, the University of Toronto was ranked eleventh in North America in library holdings.

In the early 1960s, the board of governors allocated $10 million for university library facilities. The original plan was to expand the existing library complex by building into the hollow behind the library, replacing the old library, built in the 1890s, with a seven-storey tower, and building a new science library on the site of the old engineering building. At about this time, Ernest Sirluck came to the University. He had been involved in planning the new University of Chicago library and advised that with land becoming more expensive in the city, the University should plan for the next fifty years, rather than adopt a twenty-five-year horizon. But where would the new library go? Some still advocated the site of the old library. At one point, people were eyeing the back campus on Hoskin Avenue. Others liked the west campus, but the federated colleges were opposed to situating the library too far away.

The University had not originally planned a major expansion north of Harbord Street, but this now seemed the only reasonable possibility for a major library. The province was sympathetic, and the machinery for acquiring the present site of the Robarts Library and other land north of Harbord was put in place. The firm of Mathers and Haldenby, which had extensive experience in library design – it had been responsible for the Sigmund Samuel and Laidlaw libraries as well as the National Library in Ottawa – was asked to prepare plans. But A.S. Mathers, who was in charge of the design, died suddenly, and his son, who had taken over the design, was thought too inexperienced to handle such a major assignment on his own, so a New York firm was brought in – it had recently produced two widely admired university libraries, one at Cornell and the other at Brown.

The New York firm offered a number of designs, one of them in the form of a triangle, that would provide a window for each of the private carrels. The board approved the triangular form. The library itself would have a rare book library and the university archives in one wing, and a library science school, which would be relocated from the Ontario College of Education, in the other. In 1964, librarian Brian Land became director of the school, which was expected to grow from 100 to 400 students. Of course, the cost of the project kept rising – from $10 million to $20 million and then to $40 million – but Henry Borden, the chairman of the board, was apparently not alarmed, having recognized the need for the library. The University still had $1.5 million remaining in its Canada Council account, and the province would pay for the rest.

But then in 1966 came the report of the Spinks Commission, on graduate studies, and the library was almost lost. The commission had made a plea for greater library resources, stating that 'the library is the heart of the University.' Understandably, it called for greater cooperation among the Ontario university libraries. 'We therefore recommend in the strongest terms,' the commissioners stated in the text of their report, 'that an Ontario Provincial Universities Library system be established.' In the summary of the recommendations, however, the word 'system' was left out, and as the University's chief librarian at the time, Robert Blackburn, has written, 'those who read only the summary, as busy people are inclined to do, saw only that a "Provincial University Library" was proposed.'

A number of other universities rather liked the idea of a provincial library on neutral territory, one that would not be dominated by Toronto, though this was not what the Spinks Commission had in mind. The Conservative premier John Robarts toyed with the idea of a provincial library as a centennial project, but then, fortunately for Toronto, chose the Ontario Science Centre instead. The government, however, was interested in having the Toronto library also serve

The Robarts Library, nearing completion in 1972.

provincial needs. Bissell was quite happy to oblige, and three more floors were added to the plans. It would now be a sixteen-storey building, including two underground floors. When Blackburn asked the New York architect Dan Toan how the extra floors would affect his design, he replied that it would 'improve the hell out of it.'

Construction of the building began in 1968. As with the building of University College in the nineteenth century, no official ceremony was held so that further controversy would be avoided. There had been and continued to be vocal opposition from local residents and citizens' groups opposed to what often came to be called 'Fort Book.' Moreover, as will be discussed later, undergraduate students successfully protested against being denied access to the library stacks. The library was officially opened in 1973 at a cost of over $40 million. Blackburn, writing in 1989, said it was 'still the largest academic library building in the world.' Each side of the equilateral triangle is 330 feet long – the length of a

Canadian football field from goal post to goal post – and it can provide space for 4,000 persons at any one time. At the time of its opening in 1971, the School of Library Science – to be constituted a faculty the following year – was one of the two or three largest in North America. That year, a PhD program was added to its two-year master of library science program.

The interior of the rare book library is one of the most spectacular sights in the University, with its six-storey open interior and floor-to-ceiling shelving. It was named the Thomas Fisher Library after the great-grandfather of Sidney and Charles Fisher, who had donated their collections of books to the library, the former his Shakespearean collection and the latter his books on modern British writers. The tower jutting out from the top of the Fisher Library – originally planned as a bell tower – is strictly decorative, designed to give visual balance to the structure. It could have been lost in an attempt to save costs, but the chairman of the building committee, O.D. Vaughan, liked it and approved the $10,000 needed for its construction. A clock had also been planned, but then, as Richard Landon, the head of the Fisher Library, observed, 'Someone realized that it would be possible to see it from only one spot on St George Street.'

In 1971, at O.D. Vaughan's last meeting as chairman of the board, the main library was named after the recently resigned premier, John Robarts. It probably should have been named the Bissell library, but the board was in no mood to name it after the person who, as will be seen, was primarily responsible for getting rid of the board of governors. Still, it was the province that put up the money, and the library is designed to serve provincial needs. Bissell graciously says in his memoirs that the project 'went ahead with [Robarts'] support and could not have been built without it.' The library school building is named after Bissell.

By the end of the century, the Toronto library system contained over 8 million volumes. It ranks first in Canada and third among universities in North America, taking into account a number of factors such as total holdings, budget, and number of permanent staff. Moreover, most faculty members and students have come to like the Robarts, with its recently improved accessibility – one can now enter the building at street level and not have to climb a long flight of stairs. Bissell seems to have been right in his memoirs, published in 1974, when he predicted that the library 'would grow steadily in importance; it would be absorbed and proudly taken for granted.'

chapter thirty-four

1963

MULTIDISCIPLINARY ENDEAVOURS

The 1960s would see the creation of numerous multidisciplinary centres and institutes, especially in the humanities and social sciences. They were a means of integrating knowledge among the established disciplines. Such an approach was designed to assist in the understanding of the past and in the shedding of light on specific societal problems. The barriers between disciplines were slowly coming down, but owing to jealousy on the part of the traditional academic departments, their removal initially took place in the graduate school.

The decade would also see the rapid expansion of the activities of the University of Toronto Press, particularly with respect to large multidisciplinary editorial projects. The centres and institutes and the Press were both significant forces in the promotion of scholarship in the University and in the enhancement of its growing international reputation, which continued to be based primarily on the important work done by the traditional university departments. There were towering figures such as the historian Donald Creighton and the political theorist Brough Macpherson. The same was true in the sciences. Overall, the faculty of arts and science was the strongest in Canada and among those at the top in many fields in North America.

The centres and institutes gave a focus for multidisciplinary scholarship, and the Press provided a vehicle for its dissemination. But, as Marsh Jeanneret – he had become director of the Press in 1953, after a successful career in educational publishing – stated in 1961 on the Press' sixtieth anniversary: 'A university press does much more than disseminate the results of scholarly investigation, impor-

Marsh Jeanneret, director of the University of Toronto Press, right, and Hilary Marshall, sales manager, in 1976, displaying a number of books published by the Press with the assistance of a grant from the Mellon Foundation.

tant though that function is. It increases enormously the academic effectiveness of scholars whose works it publishes and of scholars who see in it the prospect for publication of work on which they are engaged.' 'Thus the learned press,' he went on, 'becomes a powerful catalyst in the programmes of research.'

☙

A number of the centres and institutes were created strictly as graduate departments, the first being the Centre for Medieval Studies, established in 1963, with the historian Bertie Wilkinson as its first director. Wilkinson, who had come from England before the war with an established record of scholarship, has been described as 'the pre-eminent medievalist in Canada of his generation.' The University of Toronto had great talent in medieval studies scattered around the University. It included Wilkinson and his younger colleagues Walter Goffart and Natalie Zemon Davis in history, Karl Helleiner in economics, G.M. Wickens and Roger Savory in Near Eastern studies, and John Leyerle in English, who would take over from Wilkinson as director in 1966. And, of course, there was immense strength in the Pontifical Institute of Mediaeval Studies, with scholars such as the French philosopher Etienne Gilson, Leonard Boyle (later the head of the Vatican library), J.A. Raftis, and Michael Sheehan, who would be joined in 1964 by James McConica, a future president of the Pontifical Institute and of St Michael's College. There were more than 50 medieval specialists at the University offering more than 150 courses. This gave Toronto the means, wrote Ernest Sirluck, 'to become the strongest force in medieval studies in North America.' It remains so to this day.

The second graduate centre established in the University was the Centre for Linguistics. Sirluck, along with others, particularly John Wevers of Near Eastern studies, had been a strong advocate for such a centre. Wevers had concentrated on linguistics in completing his doctorate in divinity at Princeton and was editor of the *Canadian Journal of Linguistics*. A number of departments, however, were generally not supportive. 'When I came to the U of T in 1951,' Wevers wrote, 'where language study was pervasive in the humanities, I found an unthinking prejudice against the study of linguistics, particularly in such entrenched departments as English, Classics and Near Eastern Studies.' Sirluck, however, was able to get the centre approved. He had written to Bissell, 'It will very soon be as impossible to maintain a good language and literature department without the presence of a modern linguistic activity as it now is to maintain a good physics department without taking account of nuclear fission.' Although a centre for linguistics was established in 1963, it had difficulty attracting a director. After one rejection, Sirluck wrote to Bissell, 'Everybody respects, admires, and loves us, but in linguistics we are so far behind that to come to us is to forfeit for some years their chance of pushing forward their own research.' It was not until 1966 that the centre was able to attract, towards the end of his career, the noted linguistic scholar Martin Joos from Wisconsin, who had earlier taught German at U of T, from 1938 to 1942. The centre was also able to hire H.A. Gleason, a major linguistic scholar from the Hartford Seminary in the United States.

In 1974, a department of linguistics was created in arts and science, and the graduate centre was closed. A number of the interdisciplinary centres established in the 1960s later became so accepted in the University that undergraduate departments in arts and science were subsequently formed. These departments had a graduate component and therefore made a graduate centre unnecessary. The history of the University can be seen as a study of the creation of new disciplines, and the changing nature of old ones.

Another graduate centre that became a department in arts and science was that in comparative literature. It had been established as a graduate program in 1969 under the chairmanship of Canada's foremost literary critic, Northrop Frye, with the active promotion of a number of other scholars, including Martin Mueller of the English department and Mario Valdés of Spanish. Frye remained as chair until 1971, when Cyrus Hamlin of the German department took over. Unfortunately, there was now little money available from the graduate school to support the program's activities. It was able, however, to bring in some of the major international figures in comparative literature as visiting professors, such as Paul Ricoeur of Paris and Hans-Georg Gadamer of Heidelberg, and to attract excellent students. The first doctorate was awarded in 1975 to Linda Hutcheon, now a recognized star of the English and comparative literature departments. (It should be noted that Frye, Valdés, and Hutcheon all have served as president of the Modern Language Association, the largest and probably the most influential humanities organization in the world.) In spite of good external appraisals, the graduate school could not find the money to support the program adequately, and, as a result, Mueller left for Northwestern and Valdés for Illinois. The University was able, however, to induce Valdés to return to head the program, which was then designated a centre. Money was found to make a number of cross-appointments, such as those of Hutcheon and Ted Chamberlin of English, and of Lubomir Dolezel of Slavic literature.

Northrop Frye, centre, with Prime Minister Lester Pearson on the right and the president of Victoria, A.B.B. Moore, in 1963.

Mario Valdés of the Spanish and Portuguese department and Linda Hutcheon of the English department, both former presidents of the Modern Language Association, the world's largest humanities organization. Photograph taken in 1994.

Still one more department that had its beginnings as a graduate centre is the computer science department. The centre was established in 1963 with Calvin 'Kelly' Gotlieb as its director. The University had just acquired its new $1 million IBM 7090 – federal money paid for about half the cost. It was a transistorized system 500 times faster than any computer the University then had. Among its first tasks was bringing space satellites back to earth. According to Gotlieb, it was, however, vastly less powerful, had far less memory, and was perhaps 100 times slower than the laptop used by this writer to write this history of the University. Other more powerful machines were later acquired by the University over the years, including various Cray computers located in the physics building. Computer hardware has now been dispersed throughout the University, and it is not easy to determine who has the most powerful computer. Richard Peltier, a physicist who looks at climate change and heads the University of Toronto's Physical Sciences Computer Network, says that his group's recently installed NEC SX5 is the most powerful computer system in the country outside the government laboratory at Dorval, Quebec. By the time this history has been published, there will likely be others to challenge Peltier's claim.

In 1964, the centre introduced Canada's first doctoral program in computer science. Gotlieb was in charge of both the growing academic and the computation services programs. In 1968, Thomas Hull, who had joined the centre from UBC in 1964, took over as director. It became a department in arts and science early in the 1970s. The number of faculty members and students has continued to grow. By the late 1990s, there were more than 450 undergraduates, about 100 doctoral students, and some 30 post-doctoral fellows. Two of computer science's present 35 faculty members, Stephen Cook and Geoffrey Hinton, were recently elected to the prestigious Royal Society of London. Cook, who won the Turing award, the world's highest honour for computer scientists, had come to Toronto from Berkeley in 1970 and the following year had published a celebrated paper on 'computational complexity.' Hinton's work is on artificial intelligence, one of the department's strongest divisions. Enrolment in computer science (and computer engineering) will double under a recently announced provincial government program designed to increase the number of graduates in these fields.

One interdisciplinary centre, the Centre for Culture and Technology, is unique. It was created in 1963 specifically to keep Marshall McLuhan at the University of Toronto and to provide a suitable base for the development of his ideas. McLuhan was building an international reputation and was being wooed

Marshall McLuhan conducting a seminar in 1973.

by American universities, the latest offer being an attractive one from the University of Pennsylvania. Bissell was a friend of McLuhan's and, unlike some others, valued his contributions to scholarship and to the world of ideas. He also seemed to appreciate the jokes McLuhan would occasionally send him. 'At this time of year,' McLuhan wrote to Bissell in December 1964, setting out a number of jokes, 'it is useful to use the story of the clerk at the toy counter who saw a woman curiously studying a toy and said to her: "Madam, I can recommend that toy. It will help your child to adjust to the modern world. You see, no matter how you put it together, it's wrong!"' It is not known whether Bissell ever used the joke.

Father John Kelly, the president of St Michael's College, where McLuhan had taught English since 1946, also wanted McLuhan, a convert to Roman Catholicism, to remain in Toronto. (McLuhan had applied to teach at University College in 1943 after completing his Cambridge doctorate, but A.S.P. Woodhouse was not impressed with McLuhan's interest in twentieth-century English literature. He later told academic administrators that McLuhan 'was not the sort of person we want at the University of Toronto.') Bissell's plan was to set up a graduate centre for McLuhan and give him a 50 per cent teaching load. Several years later, Toronto's other international star in the humanities, Northrop Frye, also was given a reduced teaching load to counter a generous offer from New York University. The device used in Frye's case was to appoint him in 1967 as Toronto's first University Professor, with a capital 'U' and a capital 'P' – an honour perhaps understood and valued only in the academic world.

The dean of the graduate school, chemist Andrew Gordon, would not consider supporting a graduate centre for McLuhan. Gordon was, wrote Bissell, 'the last person in the world to have any sympathy with McLuhan's unorthodox probes.' The solution was for the president to set up a centre outside the graduate school, which Ernest Sirluck would then bring before the graduate council the following year after he became graduate dean. This was done. Only one graduate course was offered by the centre in the 1960s, a course in media and society. McLuhan and the anthropologist Edmund Carpenter had started a similar interdisciplinary seminar in 1953, with the assistance of a major Ford Foundation grant, its first grant to any Canadian university. When the grant ran out, McLuhan asked that Ford fund a permanent centre, but he was turned down. The participants in that early seminar initially included economist Tom Easterbrook (McLuhan's best friend from his Manitoba days), psychologist Carl Williams, and architect Jacqueline Tyrwhitt. During those years, McLuhan and Carpenter published the provocative journal *Explorations*. The ideas developed helped McLuhan produce his major scholarly book, *The Gutenberg Galaxy*, in 1962 and his more popular book, *Understanding Media*, in 1964.

The new centre was approved by the board of governors in the fall of 1963, probably with much scepticism. 'This Fall I became the Director of a new Center at the University of Toronto for the Study of the Extensions of Man,' McLuhan wrote to an American interested in technology. 'All our culture and technology,' McLuhan went on to explain, 'are immediate extensions of our own bodies and senses and nervous systems. But each extension has quite distinct psychic and social consequences. We hope to study them all.' Because McLuhan's ideas owed much to Harold Innis, it was thought that the centre might be housed in the proposed Innis College. At that time, however, Innis College was to be two high-rise buildings, and its principal, Robin Harris, concluded that this structure would make it difficult to give the centre a separate identity. In 1968, a coach house behind some of the old houses on the east side of Queen's Park was given to McLuhan. From there, he could communicate with the 'global village.' McLuhan had spent the previous year at Fordham University and while there was operated on for a brain tumour. He was, Carpenter wrote Bissell, 'making an extraordinary recovery ... Toronto is getting back from Fordham something better than was sent ... Marshall may well have some great creative years ahead.'

Ten years later, McLuhan had a stroke that left him without speech, and he died on the last day of 1980. 'No academic of our generation was more widely known than Marshall McLuhan,' Bissell wrote in an obituary. McLuhan had officially retired from the University the previous June at age 67. What would happen to the centre? The dean of the graduate school, John Leyerle, set up a committee chaired by the assistant dean, E.A. McCulloch, which reported that the centre could not continue in its present form without McLuhan: 'Marshall McLuhan was the Centre, and the Centre was Marshall McLuhan.' It concluded that the centre should be converted into a program, to be named the McLuhan Program in Culture and Technology, which 'would serve to honour, preserve, and extend the work of Marshall McLuhan.' There was heated opposition to the apparently diminished role for the centre, including protests from such notable figures as Buckminster Fuller, Woody Allen, and Tom Wolfe, but the change was made. During the 1980s, the University's Connaught fund provided a significant three-year grant, but the program has had to search for secure funding since then. The McLuhan Program, now under the wing of the faculty of information studies, has broadened its scope 'to promote and extend the investigations of what is described as the "Toronto School of Communications" initiated by Harold Innis, Eric Havelock, Marshal McLuhan, and others, on the impact of technology on culture.' It is clear that McLuhan has had and continues to have an enormous impact. Neil Postman, the head of the media studies program at New York University, acknowledges McLuhan's importance to the NYU program: 'As of 1996, over one hundred of our students have earned PhDs and more than four hundred have earned MAs ... All of them know they are the children of Marshall McLuhan.'

Claude Bissell was also actively involved in setting up the drama centre, established in 1965. Hart House Theatre was struggling to make its way against competition from the growing number of commercial theatres in Toronto. Moreover, Bissell stated, 'the sixties was a philistine era, with students preferring rock concerts and political rallies to the theatre.' Robertson Davies, the master of Massey College, was asked by Bissell to advise him on the University's needs. Davies reported that changes had to be made to the theatre – the stage should be enlarged to give it some of the character of a thrust-stage, and a better system of lighting was required – and that a more academic program in drama should be instituted. 'The University,' Davies wrote, 'is in pretty much the position it held in 1935, so far as the theatre is concerned – respectable but unadventurous, and now losing ground.' Bissell agreed, though he thought the Hart House productions better than Davies thought them. Sirluck and Clifford Leech, the head of English at University College, were opposed to Davies' becoming director of the proposed new centre because he did not have a graduate degree or a body of published academic work. Several outside drama scholars were approached, but they declined, stressing the inadequacy of the theatre facilities at the University.

After two years of frustration, the University turned to a young Shakespearean scholar, Brian Parker of Trinity College, to head the centre. At the same time, Leon Major, who had been the director of the Neptune Theatre in Halifax and had been one of Gill's protégés in the 1950s, became the centre's theatre director. Robert Gill, who had not been well, would continue to direct some plays and would be a 'special lecturer in drama' in the graduate centre. Soon after arriving, Major took on the role of artistic director of the St Lawrence Centre in Toronto, and the following year (1970) he resigned from the University. The centre shifted to more academic pursuits. The University had a large number of graduate courses in drama in various departments and could mount a fine academic program. It was also able to design a small theatre in a former Russian Orthodox church on Glen Morris Street, in the shadow of the Robarts Library. The centre needed a place seating perhaps a hundred persons that was 'not too formally structured and capable of infinite transformations.' The church, Sir Tyrone Guthrie of the Stratford Festival declared, was 'perfect for the purpose.' In 1969, the centre put on some fifteen low-budget productions. Ann Saddlemyer, an expert on Anglo-Irish literature who had come to Toronto from the University of Victoria in 1971, took over from Parker as director in 1972. She had written her doctoral thesis on the Abbey Theatre in Dublin and had published widely on persons connected with the Abbey – W.B. Yeats, J.M. Synge, and Lady Augusta Gregory – and she continued the academic emphasis of the centre.

Other successful centres and institutes were established in the humanities, such as the Institute for the History of Science and Technology and the Centre for Reformation and Renaissance Studies. The renowned Galileo scholar Stillman Drake was associated with both centres. He had been in the world of finance in California and while travelling on the commuter train to and from work had tried his hand at translating Galileo's writings into English. That resulted in his early books on Galileo and his subsequent appointment to the University of Toronto in 1967. Drake retired in 1979, leaving to the University his impressive Galileo collection, now housed in the Fisher Library.

A number of centres and institutes were designed to shed light on specific societal problems. These included the Centre for Urban and Community Studies, the Centre for Industrial Relations, and the Institute for Policy Analysis. Only two of the numerous research and policy-oriented centres will be discussed here, the Centre of Criminology and the Centre for Russian and East European Studies.

The Centre of Criminology was created in 1963, with John Edwards as its director. The 1956 Fauteux royal commission on the parole system had recommended that universities become involved in the education and training of persons who could serve in the penal system, but nothing had yet been done in English Canada. The Ontario Department of the Attorney General and Department of Reform Institutions were interested in supporting a research institute, and the University of Toronto was prepared to have one. Deans Caesar Wright of law and John Hamilton of medicine thought that if Toronto did not take the initiative it would be established at Queen's or at some other Ontario university. John Edwards, an English-trained legal scholar then teaching at Dalhousie, was invited to become director. In its first year, the centre was part of the faculty of law. It became part of the graduate school the following year, 1964, and later had its own separate quarters in adjoining houses on Spadina Avenue.

From the beginning, Edwards insisted that the centre not be located in any one division or be restricted to certain disciplines. 'It was always an open question in my mind,' he has written, 'as to where the future contributions would originate.' He recalled that one of the first telephone calls he received as director was from a professor in the department of zoology. 'I asked him,' Edwards wrote, 'if he was quite sure that he wanted the Centre of Criminology.' 'Yes,' the zoologist replied, 'I have a problem concerning nature conservation and the use of criminal sanctions.' The call convinced Edwards that his concept was the correct one. In the early years, the centre attracted the active involvement of academics from a wide variety of disciplines apart from law, such as John Beattie of history, Tony Doob of psychology, Richard Ericson and Clifford Shearing of sociology, and Peter Russell and Peter Solomon of political science. Edwards also took the view that building up a multidisciplinary library collection was 'of the greatest significance' in creating a strong research centre. A number of foundations, such as Ford and Donner, assisted financially with the library and the research program, as did both the Ontario and the federal government. At various times, however, both levels of government tried to control the publication of the results of the research they were funding. Edwards, with the backing of the University, resisted all such efforts and succeeded in establishing what became the policy of the University in this area. Government sponsors, he argued, are entitled to comment on the research results and might delay publication for a short time, but should not have a veto on their publication. Financing was a continuing problem – as it was for every centre and institute in the late 1960s – and in 1971 an MA program in criminology that would attract regular government funding was established. A PhD program was added in 1989.

The cold war created a strong interest in Russian and East European studies, and in 1963 a centre under that name was established, with Gordon Skilling as its director. Skilling, a 1934 Rhodes scholar from Toronto, had returned to Toronto's political economy department in 1959 from his position at Dartmouth College. Before the Second World War, he had been working on his doctorate in Prague and broadcasting in English for the Czechoslovak Broadcasting Corporation when the Nazis entered the country. He later broadcast in Czech for the BBC and the CBC. Towards the end of the war, Toronto had started teaching night courses on the Russian language, a beginning that led to the formation of the Slavic studies department in 1949 – with the help of a substantial grant from the Rockefeller Foundation.

Skilling, then at Dartmouth, had sent Harold Innis a report in 1951, advising that a multidisciplinary centre was desirable at the University because of 'the significance of Russia, not only as a great power, but as a historic cultural region and as a distinctive social order.' 'These features,' he went on, 'make Russian civilization and Soviet society inherently worthy of study on a permanent basis, irrespective of current conflicts and their outcome.' At the beginning of the twentieth century, James Mavor, the chair of political economy, had taken a similar approach, but interest in Russian studies had decreased after his retirement. Innis had wanted to hire Skilling, and told Sidney Smith that Skilling 'has established a reputation as a scholar with his volume on Canadian Foreign Relations, and has the advantage of a thorough training in Political Science and a specialized training in Slavic Studies.'

Political scientists Cranford Pratt, left, and Gordon Skilling, in 1967.

The number of students interested in Slavic studies kept increasing, particularly after Sputnik was launched by the Soviets in 1957. Skilling set out a plan for a centre on his return to the University. Toronto had built up a large body of scholars interested in the field, including George Luckyj in Russian and Ukrainian literature, Edward McWhinney in Soviet law, Harold Nelson in Russian history, and Stephen Triantis in economic planning, and also including some younger scholars such as Ian Drummond in Soviet economics and Stephen Clarkson in Soviet government. By 1965, there would be some 35 specialists on Russia and Eastern Europe at the University. As with criminology, funding was obtained from major foundations, such as Ford and Mellon.

The centre stimulated research and publication and offered summer courses in Russian and exchange visits with the Soviet Union. The exchanges sometimes created problems, however, as in 1970, when a scholar from the Soviet Union at the University of Alberta, Boris Dotsenko, defected and took a temporary position in the mathematics department in Toronto. Bissell resisted Soviet pressure to fire him, and the Soviets withdrew their students from Toronto and cancelled the program. The previous year, a Toronto exchange student, Susan Solomon – now a professor of political science at U of T – had been arbitrarily apprehended and threatened by the Soviet security police for meeting with dissidents.

The break-up of the Soviet Union in the early 1990s has had an effect on Slavic language study. Ken Lantz, the chair of Slavic studies, notes that 'public interest in our field has declined now that Russia and the East Bloc are no longer seen as threats, which is reflected in student enrolments.' It is true, wrote Robert Johnson, a former director of the centre, that 'the end of the Cold War removed some of the earlier strategic motives for studying Russia and its neighbours, but it opened so many doors, inside and outside of academe, that the net effect was an increase rather than a decrease in interest in the region.' 'Older traditions and literatures,' he continued, 'were rediscovered; the old obstacles to travel, research, and archival access were mostly removed; and a host of new opportunities arose as a result of the economic and political transitions that have been launched.' The historian Harvey Dyck, for example, who directs the Mennonite studies program in the centre, wrote, 'Since 1990, I've personally been to Ukraine and Russia fifteen times for extended research stints. We've made exciting archival discoveries, including the rediscovery and microfilming of a very important Mennonite archive that had been confiscated by Soviet authorities in 1929.' Most students in the centre's master's program (established in 1991) spend a summer working in Russia or Eastern Europe on an internship. The interest in Russian and East European studies remains strong for both teaching and research.

⚬⚭⚬

The University of Toronto Press played – and has continued to play – a significant role in promoting scholarship in the humanities and social sciences at the University. By 1960, the Press had more than 500 books in print, ranked fifth among scholarly presses in North America, and issued more titles annually than any other Canadian publisher. Between 1957 and 1960, the Press published 300 new books.

Immediately after the war, a committee on the Press, consisting of Vincent Bladen, George Brown, and A.S.P. Woodhouse, had recommended that the University become 'a national leader in developing scholarship and letters.' Although the Press had published – and not just printed – books since 1911, its scholarly list was thin. By 1950, it had only about 100 books in print. President Sidney Smith encouraged the Press to become more active and personally chaired the scholarly publishing committee.

Until 1960, when McGill established its press, the U of T Press was the only English-language university press in Canada. Its mission was 'to serve the cause of scholars at the University of Toronto and throughout Canada,' and to this end it published, to choose only two examples, *The Vertical Mosaic* by John Porter of Carleton and *The Literary History of Canada* edited by Carl Klinck of Western Ontario. It also produced leading journals such as the *Canadian Historical Review*, the *University of Toronto Law Journal*, the *Canadian Journal of Mathematics*, and the *University of Toronto Quarterly*. Today it publishes more than 25 scholarly journals.

Important books by University of Toronto scholars published by the Press have included Harold Innis' *Bias of Communication*, McGregor Dawson's *Government of Canada*, Marshall McLuhan's *Gutenberg Galaxy*, Eric Arthur's *Toronto: No Mean City*, and James Eayrs' *In Defence of Canada*, to name just a few. Of course, many important books by University of Toronto scholars have been published by other presses. Donald Creighton's *Sir John A. Macdonald* and Maurice Careless' *Brown of the Globe* were published by Macmillan, to cite only two authors from one department. The Press has also developed technical skills in scientific publication and in design. It produced, for example, Yousuf Karsh's *Portraits of Greatness*, and historical atlases such as the geographer William Dean and the cartographer G.J. Matthews' *Economic Atlas of Ontario*, designed by Allan Fleming, which won the Leipzig prize in 1970 for 'the most beautiful book in the world.' Recent books such as those on the painter David Milne and the *Historical Atlas of Canada* have continued the tradition. The award-winning three-volume *Historical Atlas*, produced by Dean and Matthews and a team of workers over a twenty-five-year period, cost well over $7 million for research and production.

The Press was becoming increasingly important to the University of Toronto, and in 1958 a splendid new building was opened between Knox and University College, the last remaining open space on King's College Circle. The bookstore moved there from its temporary quarters on the other side of University College, and the editorial and administrative offices from Cumberland House (then called Baldwin House) on St George Street. In 1985, the Press moved the bookstore to the Koffler Centre (the former city of Toronto reference library), and in 1989 it moved its editorial and administrative offices to a building at

Yonge and St Mary streets. The former Press building was needed by the central administration for alumni and development purposes.

Almost every scholarly book loses money. In the case of the University of Toronto Press, scholarly publishing is cross-subsidized by other Press operations, such as the bookstore, the printing plant, and a reference division that publishes books such as the *Canadian Who's Who*. The Press became a separate non-profit corporation in 1992 but is still controlled by the University. Like other Canadian publishers, it receives government block grants and subsidies for individual titles from the Social Sciences and Humanities Research Council. A number of foundations over the years have contributed to various projects, and the Ford and Mellon foundations have contributed to the Press' general scholarly publishing program, but the Press has not yet found a major benefactor – such as the Bollingen Foundation at Princeton University Press – to endow its general scholarly publishing program.

The Press' international reputation has come primarily from its major multidisciplinary projects. The first of these projects was the *Collected Works of John Stuart Mill*. The project had been promoted by a young Victoria College English professor, John ('Jack') Robson, who had completed his PhD on Mill in the mid-fifties at Toronto under A.S.P. Woodhouse. He had tried without success to interest at least one publisher in England in the idea of Mill's collected works, but was able to spark the interest of Woodhouse and F.E.L. Priestley of the English department of University College. Both the Press director, Marsh Jeanneret, and the editor Francess Halpenny, who had joined the Press in 1941, were receptive to the idea. In 1960, Priestley became general editor and Robson textual editor.

In the early planning of the project, it was thought there would be about 13 volumes. As it turned out, however, there were 33, the final volume published in 1991. Robson took over from Priestley as general editor in 1972, while continuing as textual editor. One important editorial decision was to use the last edition of a publication approved by Mill and not the first edition, as most collected works at the time would have done. 'It seemed a little silly,' Robson said, 'to think that Mill lost control of his senses as he revised *Principles of Political Economy*, making it into a worse and worse book.' Among those from the University who wrote introductions to individual volumes were Vincent Bladen of political economy, John Cairns of history, and Francis Sparshott of philosophy.

John Robson, professor in the department of English and editor of the *Collected Works of John Stuart Mill*, in 1973.

Although the Mill collected works was the first of the Press' major projects actually to produce a volume, the *Dictionary of Canadian Biography* – described by the critic Robert Fulford as 'the most ambitious project in the history of Canadian scholarship' – had been approved before the Mill project was undertaken. In 1952, a wealthy bird-seed manufacturer, James Nicholson, who had left school at an early age and never attended university, died and left his collection of *Punch* magazines and, more important, a residuary amount of some $350,000 to the University. The money was to be used for a series of volumes similar to the British *Dictionary of National Biography*. The bequest took Sidney Smith by surprise, but he was delighted because he knew that such a project had been one that the historian and honorary editor of the Press, George Brown, along with others, had hoped to undertake. The money would not be available, however, until after Nicholson's wife, Janie, died. For some time, it was felt that raising the matter with her would be indelicate. In the meantime, the Press and a committee under George Brown were eager to proceed with the project and started making plans for carrying it out. In early 1957, the University's vice-president of administration, Frank Stone, discussed the project with Mrs Nicholson and reported that she would be delighted to see the project begun during her lifetime. Arrangements were made to ensure that she would receive whatever income she might require from the estate.

Brown was appointed editor in 1959, and the project – with the bequest now worth about $1 million – was officially announced. The planning committee had made the decision – over the historian Donald Creighton's opposition – that the dictionary would not follow the British concept, according to which the entries would be alphabetical, but rather would have the volumes cover periods of time, and use an alphabetical format within each volume. This had the advantage of making the volumes useful from the start and of allowing persons interested in specific periods to purchase only those volumes of interest. The first volume was published in 1966. Unfortunately, George Brown died while the volume was in press. The 89-year-old Mrs Nicholson, however, was able to attend the ceremony, at which she was presented with a copy of the volume.

There was simultaneous publication of a French edition of the volume by Les Presses de l'université Laval. Jeanneret's father, the respected French scholar F.C.A. Jeanneret, had helped to arrange the founding of the *Dictionnaire biographique du Canada*. Its volumes are not translations of the English version; instead, an editorial team in Quebec works as an equal partner with the Toronto group to produce two editions of each volume, made up of texts originally written in either English or French and then translated. As might be expected, the first volume, covering individuals who died before 1700, was in large part the work of Quebec scholars. Francess Halpenny became general editor in 1969 and was succeeded by the York University historian Ramsay Cook in 1998. (At the same time, there have been a series of comparable Quebec-based Directeurs généraux adjoints.) Most of the volumes have been assisted by Canada Council and Social Science and Humanities Research Council funding. Volume 14, covering the decade from 1911 to 1920, was published in 1998. The volumes have been extremely helpful to this author in writing the history of the University of Toronto.

Perhaps Canada's greatest contribution to international scholarship in the humanities has been the Press' English translation of the collected works of Erasmus. The first volume of the series was published in 1974, and the eighty-ninth volume will likely appear about twenty years from now. The series has been described by the British historian Hugh Trevor-Roper in the *Times Literary Supplement* as 'a splendid enterprise: I cannot commend it enough.' It all started with a memo from the University of Toronto Press editor Ron Schoeffel to the managing editor Francess Halpenny in 1968 that began 'In case you haven't had your fair share of hare-brained ideas today ...' and then proposed a collection of the works of Erasmus in English – something never done before. Earlier that week, Schoeffel had tried to find an English translation of one of Erasmus' works, without success. The St Michael's English professor Richard Schoeck and the Italian scholar Beatrice Corrigan were the coordinating editors in the early years. Corrigan died in 1977, and James McConica was selected to replace her. He remains chairman of the editorial board. The members of the board and the contributing editors are drawn from universities throughout the world. The project, Robert Fulford has written, 'has given Canada's largest university the sort of place, within Renaissance studies, that it dreams of having in every field: it now stands firmly at the centre of a vast international web of research and learning.'

The University of Toronto Press now has approximately 300 books in print in medieval and Renaissance studies. The Erasmus series is its flagship, but there are others, one of them the *Records of Early English Drama*, directed by the English scholar Alexandra Johnston, encompassing records for Great Britain from the Middle Ages until 1642, when the Puritans closed the theatres. Johnston had completed her doctorate at Toronto on the portrayal of Christ in English biblical drama. She and a team of international scholars are searching out the records of theatrical performances county by county and city by city. Volume 14 of the series, for Dorset and Cornwall, was published in 1999. It should be noted that this project, like many of the others discussed in this chapter, has had significant financial assistance over the years from the Social Sciences and Humanities Research Council of Canada to support its skilled editorial staff. Like most of the others, however, it has also been leading a hand-to-mouth existence.

Another endeavour that will eventually be published by the University of Toronto Press is the *Dictionary of Old English*, which will include all known words in Old English used between about 700 AD and 1200 AD, when the *Oxford*

Alexandra Johnston, professor in the department of English and director of the *Records of Early English Drama*, right, and Sally-Beth MacLean, the project's executive editor, in 1997.

English Dictionary takes up the story. The dictionary was the vision of the former Rhodes scholar Angus Cameron, who joined the University in 1968. A plan was laid out in the early 1970s by Cameron and the Harvard-trained medievalist Roberta Frank, his colleague in the University College English department. Cameron assembled a team and worked on the computerized project until 1983, when he died of cancer at the age of 42. The project has continued under the direction of English scholar Antonette ('Toni') diPaolo Healey, a Toronto PhD recipient supervised by Cameron, who joined the project in 1978 after teaching at Yale. It publishes each letter on microfiche as completed. The team is now working on the letter 'F.' To the surprise of many, the most famous 'F-word' in the English language will not be in the dictionary; apparently it was first used in the fifteenth century.

chapter thirty-five

1966

ENGINEERING AND MEDICINE

The year 1966 saw the demolition of the old engineering building and the start of construction of the new Medical Sciences Building. Both acts were significant statements that the two largest professional faculties were entering new phases in their development. The old engineering building, completed in 1878 – a symbol of the past – was no longer physically useful for scientific work. Moreover, engineering had recently acquired the former physics building – to be renamed the Sandford Fleming Building – connected to the Galbraith Building, which had opened in 1961. In the same year that the engineering building was torn down, the faculty dropped surveying from its first year course. The once ubiquitous engineering student surveyors would become a far less familiar sight on the campus.

The key event in the change of prospects for the engineering faculty had been the almost fortuitous presentation by the Ford Foundation to the University in early 1963 of $2.3 million over five years for graduate work in engineering. Many American foundations had contributed generously to the University over the years, but – with the possible exception of the $1 million Rockefeller grant to medicine in the early 1920s – nothing had approached this donation in amount or created the same impact. The Ford Foundation had acquired over half a

Demolition, begun in 1966, of the old School of Practical Science (SPS) building.

billion dollars in 1956 and was starting to distribute large sums to a number of causes. The following year, the Russians launched Sputnik, the world's first space satellite. The United States was humiliated. The West, it was widely felt, was losing its pre-eminence in science and technology. Bissell recorded the general despair at the time: 'The Russian satellite has created general gloom, and now the dismal failure of the first American attempt to launch a counter-Sputnik has intensified the gloom.' The Ford Foundation decided that one of its major projects would be to assist engineering schools to develop their research activity and their graduate programs. MIT and Case Institute of Technology in Cleveland were each given close to $10 million in 1959.

Representatives of the Ford Foundation had made an unsolicited visit to the engineering faculty in 1958 and returned in early 1960, when they met with President Bissell, Dean R.R. McLaughlin, and various faculty members. There was general recognition in Canada that more engineers had to be trained. Employers were having difficulty finding engineers to fill positions. The following year, one of the Ford Foundation officials, Carl Borgmann, came to Toronto wanting to know 'how financial aid can best help in developing doctoral education in engineering at Toronto.' Over lunch at the York Club, Borgmann posed this question to McLaughlin: 'If the Ford foundation were to make you a grant of $1 million to $2 million over a four or five year period to promote graduate work, how would you propose to spend it?' McLaughlin replied that he would want some time to think about it. Two months later, McLaughlin sent a five-page document, developed by him and his department heads, asking for $2 million over a five-year period, to be divided evenly between persons and equipment. There should be, McLaughlin wrote, generous graduate fellowships – perhaps 25 a year – along with a number of research associates and visiting professors. About half the equipment budget would be used to move aerospace's supersonic wind tunnel and other equipment from the Downsview airport to its present site on Dufferin Street. The rest of the equipment funds would be divided among the other engineering divisions. Ford accepted the proposal and even added $325,000 to permit an addition to the Wallberg Building to accommodate the department of metallurgy.

The grant had the desired effect. The number of graduate students in engineering increased dramatically, from about 140 students in 1960 to more than 650 in 1970, including 250 doctoral students. (Today, there are more than 1,000 graduate students, almost 40 per cent of whom are pursuing doctorates.) Some of the other Canadian universities trying to develop graduate programs in engineering were concerned; one complained to McLaughlin that the effect of the Ford grant would be that 'a very large proportion of the cream of the graduate students will migrate to Toronto.' This was, of course, what Toronto was hoping for. The Ford money also stimulated research activity in the faculty. In 1960, the total amount of research funding in engineering was under half a million dollars, with a large proportion of that going to aerospace studies. At the end of the decade, however, after the Ford money had been spent, the research funding was approaching $3 million a year. Much of this was accounted for by the National Research Council's increasing willingness to fund applied research throughout Canada. The Ford money assisted the faculty to compete successfully for the new NRC money.

Although undergraduate enrolment was expected to expand dramatically in these years of growth, it did not, primarily because other engineering schools in the province had been created or expanded. By 1958, engineering schools at Carleton, McMaster, Ottawa, Waterloo, and Western had been added to those at Toronto and Queen's. Undergraduate enrolment at Toronto had been under 2,000 in the 1950s, and predictions were that it would rise to perhaps 4,000, but in fact by the end of the 1960s undergraduate enrolment was only about 2,200. There were very few women in this group. The total number of women students in the faculty in the 1950s had been less than 10 in any given year. By contrast, women students today comprise over 25 per cent of the class, and in one program, chemical engineering, the number has risen to more than 50 per cent.

To handle the increase in graduate enrolment, the number of engineering faculty members doubled during the 1960s – from some 75 in 1960 to some 150 at the end of the decade. The very heavy teaching loads experienced in the 1950s – sometimes amounting to 20 hours per week – were reduced. Faculty members now had more time for research. During the decade, the average number of publications per staff member of professorial rank nearly doubled. Faculty members were now expected to engage in research and not just professional practice. In the 1950s, wrote the historian of the engineering faculty, Richard White, 'there was plenty of talk about research, and plenty of urging that it be done, but the rhetoric seems to have exceeded the output.'

In 1965, James Ham, with a doctorate from MIT and a strong record of research, was appointed McLaughlin's successor as dean. The committee advising Bissell had reduced the list of candidates to five names. According to Vice-president Moffat Woodside's report to the president, the 62-year-old C.F. Morrison, the head of civil engineering, was considered too old; the 40-year-old metallurgist William Winegard, then assistant dean of the graduate school, 'although brilliant' was 'a little too young.' (Two years later, Winegard became president of the University of Guelph; he then went on to a successful political career, and became federal minister of science and technology in the early 1990s.) Gordon Patterson, the head of aerospace, Woodside reported, did not have a degree in engineering, and his 'interests have for years been detached from the Faculty as a whole.' Perhaps the same concern about selecting someone from aerospace influenced the selection of Ham over Ben Etkin. Moreover, Etkin had as yet had no major administrative experience. In 1967, he would head the increasingly important division of engineering science, from which he himself had graduated. The course – which was attracting about 20 per cent of the

James Ham, the dean of engineering, giving an address in 1967 entitled
'Forecasting Changes in Technology.'

engineering students – had originally been called engineering physics, but had
been renamed engineering science in 1962 after an option in chemistry had been
added. Etkin would succeed Ham as dean in 1973. Gordon Slemon, a Toronto
engineering graduate who had joined the faculty in 1955 after receiving his
doctorate at Imperial College, London, took over from Ham as head of electrical
engineering. He would later succeed Etkin as dean.

Many talented professors interested in research and publication were appointed in the 1960s. Another future dean, Michael Charles, was also appointed
during this period. He had taken an undergraduate degree from Imperial College and a doctorate in chemical engineering from the University of Alberta
before joining the Toronto faculty in 1964. Still another future dean was
electrical engineer Anastasios Venetsanopolous, whose undergraduate degree was
from the University of Athens, and who came to Toronto in 1968 after completing a doctorate at Yale. In electrical engineering, to mention other examples,
André Salama, an expert on micro-electronics, joined the department in 1967

after receiving his doctorate from UBC, and Adel Sedra, later the chair of the department and provost of the University, joined the faculty in 1969 after receiving his engineering degree from Cairo University and a doctorate from Toronto. Another outstanding electrical engineer appointed during this period was Murray Wonham, a McGill graduate with a Cambridge doctorate then teaching at Brown University. His work on mathematical systems theory has made possible the design of sophisticated and complex control systems, such as those used in communication networks and transportation systems, including space applications used by NASA. The New Zealander Michael Collins, whose specialty lay in preventing failures in reinforced concrete construction, joined the civil engineering department in 1969. He had earned his doctorate from the University of New South Wales and then taught at the University of Colorado. The Ford Foundation grant was clearly acting as an important catalyst for increasing the research potential of the faculty.

Aerophysics, which had been interested in space research for many years, continued to attract international attention. 'We were not Sputnikked into space research,' Bissell remarked in 1959 at the opening of the new facilities on Dufferin Street. There was so much space research going on that in 1963 the name of the institute was changed from Aerophysics to Aerospace. The institute's supersonic wind tunnel, Gordon Patterson had told the press in 1957, was the only one in the Western world that could duplicate the conditions of satellite flight. Work was being done, for example, by Irvine Glass for the US Air Force on measuring shock waves created by satellites, by Ben Etkin on the flight dynamics of space vehicles, and by Barry French and J.H. deLeeuw on upper atmosphere rare gases.

French's involvement in measurements by the Viking satellites of the upper Martian atmosphere helped shed light on why Mars does not have an atmosphere that can sustain life. His interest in detecting minute traces of gases later led to the development of equipment for detecting illicit drugs, pollution, and other substances on earth. Research at the institute continues today on such topics as space robotics. And work continues on other aspects of flight, such as the development of the world's first microwave-powered aircraft and the world's first manned mechanical bird – a plane that actually flaps its wings. Perhaps the institute's most dramatic involvement with the space age was its role in 1970 in assisting with the calculations that would allow the damaged Apollo 13 spacecraft to return safely to earth.

Another institute in the faculty of engineering, the Institute for Biomedical Electronics, was directly linked to the faculty of medicine. It was formed in 1962, with Norman Moody, the former head of electrical engineering at the University of Saskatchewan, as its first director. At Saskatchewan, Moody had developed a cardiac-output computer to measure the efficiency of the heart as a pump. 'Can one doubt,' Moody said, 'that the marriage of the two disciplines, of medicine and engineering, will produce people with a much deeper insight into the mysteries of nature and nature's living machines than can be obtained by separate studies in these fields?' The following year, E.L. Llewellyn Thomas, a medical doctor who had also trained as an engineer, joined the institute. Projects were developed through the institute on measuring blood flow in the liver, detecting cancerous tumors through gamma ray cameras, and creating biological adhesives.

The work of the institute expanded to encompass more than electrical engineering, and in the early 1970s it was renamed the Institute of Biomedical Engineering, without the word 'electronics.' The institute has continued to evolve. Hans Kunov, an engineer who joined the group in 1967, recalled that in the early days 'we were measuring and recording physiological activities and constructing systems that could help in therapy and rehabilitation.' 'Later,' he observed, 'the engineers became involved in modeling the complex living systems, and the understanding of fundamental physiological processes. In the 1990s, we are beginning to design living systems themselves.' The chemical engineer Michael Sefton, for example, the present director of the institute, now called Biomaterials and Biomedical Engineering, is working with others on the development of synthetic hearts and pancreases.

❧

The faculty of medicine was also transformed in the 1960s. In the summer of 1963, the board of governors set up a special committee on the future development of the faculty, which issued a comprehensive but discouraging report in May 1964. The committee, chaired by John Hamilton, the dean of medicine since 1961 and before that the head of pathology, included two influential members of the board of governors, Senators Wallace McCutcheon and Joseph Sullivan. The secretary of the eight-person committee and the person primarily responsible for writing the report was John Evans, a Toronto medical graduate and former Rhodes scholar. He had recently been appointed a Markle scholar and had returned from Harvard Medical School to the University to engage in research on cardiac diseases. Dean Hamilton, who had received his medical degree from Toronto in the 1930s, had written to Bissell in the spring of 1963, stating that the medical school was 'slipping badly into a secondary position' compared to McGill. Toronto, according to Bissell, was 'the home of the high powered specialist and the skilled practitioner' and not a university 'that nurtured academic medicine.' It continued to be well known as the source of many of the standard medical texts used around the world, such as J.C.B. Grant's *Atlas of Anatomy*, Charles Best's textbook on physiology, Arthur Ham's on histology, and William Boyd's on pathology.

One 'high-powered' clinical specialty, for example, which continued to bring international recognition to Toronto, was surgery. W.E. Gallie, the chief of surgery at the Toronto General Hospital from 1929 until his retirement in 1947, had introduced the first comprehensive post-graduate training course for surgeons in Canada. He was able to continue as head of surgery while also acting as dean of medicine from 1936 until his retirement – the last person to be a part-time dean of medicine. Toronto surgeons had made a number of significant breakthroughs. Gordon Murray, for example, was the first to use the anticoagulant heparin, which had been studied by Charles Best in the mid-1930s and which permitted significant advances in cardiovascular surgery. Murray later developed the first artificial kidney in North America and was one of the first to operate on congenital heart diseases before heart/lung pumps were introduced. At the end of the war, the neurosurgeon Harry Botterell, working with the physiatrist Albin Jousse, developed rehabilitative techniques for treating persons with spinal injuries. W.G. Bigelow, who, like Botterell, had studied in the 'Gallie course' before the Second World War, found in the 1950s that lowering the patient's body temperature reduced the need for oxygen during operations and thus permitted such operations as open-heart surgery. Bigelow also led the team responsible for the first implantable cardiac pacemaker. In the 1960s, William Mustard, another Gallie graduate, was the first to transpose arteries in so-called blue babies, a procedure known as the 'Mustard operation.' The orthopaedic surgeon Robert Salter, still another graduate of the Gallie course, developed techniques that permitted surgical correction of congenitally deformed or diseased hips, one of which is called the 'Salter operation.' Many more such contributions could be named.

'No University in Canada other than the University of Toronto,' Hamilton's 1964 report concluded, 'has the potential to assume the role of leadership in academic medicine that is required in Canada during the next two decades.' Toronto, however, could not do so satisfactorily, it went on, 'unless the gross deficiencies in academic staff and facilities are remedied by an immediate and long term program of expansion and reorganization.' Medical expansion had not been contemplated in the national University of Toronto campaign launched in 1959. Only $2 million had been included for medicine in the campaign, and it would be exhausted simply by adding two floors to the Banting Institute – space that would be used primarily 'to improve and enlarge the deplorable quarters for experimental animals.'

'During the thirties,' the report stated, 'there is no doubt that the facilities of the faculty of Medicine were good and the educational programs advanced satisfactorily. Specialist training was well organized, most notably in general medicine and general surgery.' But the only new medical facility built by the University since the Banting Institute had opened in 1931 was the Best Institute, in 1953. Moreover, the University had relatively few full-time medical faculty members compared to leading American medical schools, in which the number of full-time staff had increased dramatically during the previous decade – some by 1,000 per cent. At Toronto, the increase had been only 20 per cent. There were only about 50 full-time clinicians at the University, including heads of departments. Post-graduate training leading to diplomas was offered in the clinical departments – indeed, it was estimated that 40 per cent of all specialists in Canada received some or all of their training in Toronto – but the University did not offer graduate academic degrees in clinical fields.

As with engineering, government funding for medical research in Canada (through what would become the Medical Research Council) was increasing significantly – from $500,000 in 1952 to about $7 million in 1964 – but the lack of facilities and full-time faculty meant that Toronto was unable to take full advantage of this funding. The result, the report concluded, was that 'the University of Toronto has failed to maintain its position on this continent let alone in Canada. The inadequacies of space have frustrated the development of research and the increasing demands of administrative duties and undergraduate and postgraduate teaching have markedly reduced the effectiveness of the existing staff and hindered the acquisition of new staff of high calibre.'

Moreover, the province was not training as many doctors as were required.

'The output of physicians from medical schools in Ontario,' the committee stated, 'is insufficient to meet the needs of the province with respect to both general and specialty practice.' New medical schools would have to be built in Ontario, including a second school in Metropolitan Toronto. From its very beginnings, York University had been looking at the possibility of a medical school. An alternative to a second medical school in Toronto, argued the committee, was an expansion of the Toronto medical school from 175 to 250 entering students each year. The cost would probably be less than the cost of establishing a new medical school. Furthermore, the existence of a new school in the Toronto area, it was argued, 'would mean competition with the University of Toronto for government and private support which might seriously interfere with the program of development for the Faculty' outlined in their report. 'Increased enrolment of up to 250 students in the entering class,' the committee stated, 'should be considered as a reasonable alternative to the development of a second independent school in Metropolitan Toronto.'

Several months after the release of the Hamilton report, in the spring of 1964, the federally appointed Hall Commission on Health Services reported that six new medical schools were required if Canada was to be in a position to support a proposed universal health care system. The Hall recommendations were endorsed by Ontario's Committee on University Affairs. In the meantime, the chairman of the University of Toronto's board of governors, Henry Borden, had been actively pursuing Toronto's expansion. The board quickly approved the Hamilton report, and Borden went to see Premier John Robarts to get his support for an expanded medical school and a new medical sciences building. When Robarts had invited Borden to replace the ailing Phillips as chairman of the board earlier that year, Borden, according to his memoirs, had 'warned him that if he appointed me I would be a thorn in the side of the government until the medical side of things ... had been corrected and improved ... Frankly I wanted a much larger turn out of doctors, which meant more and highly complicated teaching and laboratory facilities.' Borden had become interested in the faculty of medicine when a close family member had been confined as a psychiatric patient in inadequate facilities. He had chaired a committee of the board that recommended a new university psychiatric hospital. 'I had a chat with P.M. [Robarts] yesterday afternoon and with the Minister this morning,' Borden wrote in the summer of 1964 to Bissell, then on vacation in Nova Scotia. 'The result is that I have a "green light" on the medical program.' At the end of

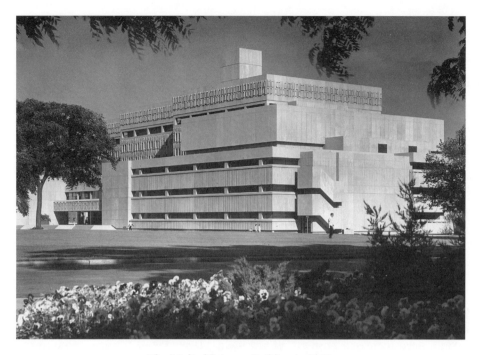

The Medical Sciences Building in 1969.

October 1964, Robarts announced support for expansion of the existing medical schools in the province, including Toronto's, and the creation of a new medical school at McMaster University in Hamilton. There would not be a second medical school in the immediate Toronto area.

A number of sites for a new medical sciences building had been explored in the Hamilton report. The ideal solution, the report observed, would be to construct a 'university hospital–medical school complex,' such as had been promoted by the University in the 1880s using the Johns Hopkins model, but the Hamilton committee had rejected the concept because of the many non-university hospitals in Toronto used for teaching. The committee favoured building a new complex south of College Street between McCaul and Henry streets. Less desirable would be a plan to keep the old medical building and to construct a high-rise building on the site of the former Botany Building at the north-west corner of College Street and University Avenue.

The board of governors decided not to expand south of College Street, and after the government approved $36 million for a new building and equipment, the decision was made to tear down the old medical, biology, and engineering buildings, which would have been expensive and difficult to renovate effectively, and to construct a new medical sciences building on the site where it now stands. The cornerstone was laid in 1967, and staff began to move into the building in late 1968, though the official opening would not take place until 1970. Borden was proud of the accomplishment, and stated in his memoirs that 'in spite of a nine months strike in the construction industry, the building was built, equipped and occupied some eighteen months ahead of schedule and at somewhat below the estimate of roughly forty million dollars.' The result, he wrote, 'helped to enable the University to maintain its accreditation as one of the top medical teaching centres on the continent.' 'I often think,' Borden added, 'how ironical it was that a McGill graduate should have had the opportunity to do this for its great rival, the University of Toronto, particularly in the field of medicine.'

Even before the release of the Hamilton report, Borden was working on another scheme – to acquire Sunnybrook Hospital, a 1,500-bed veterans' hospital in the north-eastern part of the city, as one of the University's teaching hospitals. If the University was to increase its intake of medical students, it would need increased hospital resources. In March 1964, Borden wrote to the minister of veterans' affairs, offering to take over Sunnybrook, the largest veterans' hospital in Canada. According to his memoirs, Borden was 'warmly comforted and encouraged' by his own doctor and a fellow Maritimer, Ian McDonald, the chief of staff at Sunnybrook. John Evans has said that McDonald was 'undoubtedly instrumental in the decisions about Sunnybrook Hospital being affiliated with the University and becoming a major teaching hospital ... It would have been extremely difficult for him to have attracted highly qualified faculty to teach and a resident staff to cope with the service load if the hospital was not a training facility.' Dean Hamilton was also interested in acquiring Sunnybrook, to have it as a teaching hospital and to prevent its forming the basis for a second medical school in the greater Toronto area.

Borden raised the matter with Robarts, he stated in his memoirs, 'while in a fishing boat with him ... and after telling him my reasons he immediately agreed and I went on from there.' In early 1965, Robarts announced that agreement had been reached between Ontario and the federal government to hand over Sunnybrook to the University for $1. This was the first – and still is the only – hospital controlled by the University. Indeed, it was the first so controlled by any university in Ontario. The teaching staff at Sunnybrook would be full-time members of the University. At about the same time, the University – with the

The University of Toronto took possession of Sunnybrook Hospital in 1967.

concurrence of the province – expropriated the adjoining Vaughan and McLean estates to ensure that there would be room for future expansion. 'This,' Bissell recorded in his diary, 'has been Henry Borden's obsession for months.' In October 1967, the University took possession of the hospital. With the expropriated land, the University now had about 180 acres at Sunnybrook – roughly the same amount of land that it had on the entire St George campus.

Bissell had not been closely involved in the decisions relating to the increase in the number of medical students, the new Medical Sciences Building, or the acquisition of Sunnybrook. These developments were all initiated and concluded by the board of governors, primarily by Borden, who claimed to have spent about half his time on university work while he was chairman. The board was kept informed and approved what was taking place, but the senate of the

University was not involved in the decisions. These were supposedly financial and not academic matters, though clearly they were both. Bissell's main concern was that the medical plans 'would set back my special project, the research library,' but, Bissell recalled, 'Borden recognized the library needs and at the crucial moments of decision when his opposition or his indifference would have killed the proposal, he came to my support.' According to Borden's memoirs, he and Bissell had 'talked things over and I agreed to support the idea of a large research library ... On his part, he agreed to give me full rein on the medical sciences side and this he did.'

The Hamilton report had raised the possibility of subdividing the 250 students in each year into three or more smaller groups, each affiliated with a teaching hospital. This was an idea John Evans had promoted. Evans and an informal group of other relatively young Toronto colleagues, which included the biochemists George Connell and Ronald Williams and the pathologist Fraser Mustard, had been developing ideas for a problem-based curriculum. It would be difficult, they thought, to introduce major changes applicable to the entire body of 250 students at one time. One solution was to divide the class into three or four groups and to allow some autonomy and experimentation in each division, as had occurred at the University of London medical schools. Besides, smaller units would reduce the impersonal nature of the learning experience. Evans prepared a memo, with Dean Hamilton's 'unqualified support,' that would have permitted the development at Sunnybrook Hospital of 'a smaller, more flexible undergraduate and graduate teaching college within the University of Toronto, with autonomy for the development of its own educational programme.'

Hamilton took Evans' ideas to the council of the faculty of medicine, where they were defeated. 'The chairs of the various clinical departments,' Evans later wrote, 'were opposed to the balkanization of the undergraduate program and the chairs of the basic science departments did not particularly favour the possibility that some basic scientists would move from their campus location out to laboratory facilities in some of the teaching hospitals.' The ideas would later take shape, however, at McMaster's new medical school. Evans left to become the first dean of the school, and Mustard joined him there the following year, and became dean when Evans returned to succeed Bissell as president of the University of Toronto in 1972. The McMaster problem-based learning program has now been widely adopted throughout North America, including at Harvard

Medical School. In the 1990s, it was introduced at Toronto, and, moreover, students were divided into groups, called academies, housed at specific hospitals. It had taken almost thirty years for the ideas of Evans and his colleagues to be accepted at the University of Toronto.

The sudden expansion of staff and facilities in the 1960s created problems for Hamilton, who had become vice-president for health sciences in 1966, and A.L. 'Laurie' Chute, who had succeeded Hamilton as dean. A graduate of Toronto in the same medical class as Hamilton, and with a doctorate in physiology from the University of London, Chute had been the head of paediatrics for fifteen years. The two had to face the growing-pains of an increase in enrolment, the development of the medical sciences complex, and the absorption of Sunnybrook Hospital. They also had to cope, according to Bissell's diary, with 'the growing resentment of the medical faculty against decision-making in the Board.' In addition, a new curriculum was introduced in 1969 that eliminated the two pre-medical years. Students now came from a wide variety of academic backgrounds. Moreover, the faculty had an unmanageable council of about 600 members. A smaller representative council was later put in place. Another change was to eliminate the quota on the admission of women. It had been in place for several decades before 1966, as the University acknowledged in 1968 in reply to a request for information from the Royal Commission on the Status of Women in Canada.

The most contentious issues, however, related to the relationship between the University and the teaching hospitals. Consultants from the New York–based Commonwealth Fund were asked to advise the University on university-hospital relations and reported in 1968 to a joint committee of the board and the medical faculty, chaired by Borden. Two of the consultants' recommendations in particular attracted considerable opposition: controlling physicians' fees and deciding which hospitals should be the principal teaching bodies. Hamilton reported back to the Commonwealth Fund on what transpired after their report had been delivered: 'One of your key recommendations, that the University should control the distribution of fees,' Hamilton wrote, 'has floundered.' 'This more than anything else,' Hamilton went on, 'seems to have stirred up the whole of the clinical staff, in that we have not even been able to discuss it rationally, with other than the clinical department heads, who are in agreement that these fees must be controlled, with ceilings on income, and that excess fees should be used for educational purposes.'

The other issue causing great concern was the concentration – leaving aside the specialty hospitals such as the Sick Children's and the Clarke Institute of Psychiatry – of training for medical students at the Toronto General and Toronto Western hospitals. The chairman of the Sunnybrook board, the businessman Budd Rieger, predicted that if Sunnybrook were no longer a teaching hospital, it would lose the majority of its full-time staff and the 'high level of patient care' would 'decline precipitously.' Both the hospital and Hamilton argued that the University had recruited staff for Sunnybrook on the understanding that it would be a teaching hospital. Renewed support for Sunnybrook, however, at a time of reduced funding for hospitals, worried the Toronto General and Toronto Western hospitals, who were concerned that funding for Sunnybrook would result in decreased funding for them. All this in turn greatly alarmed St Michael's Hospital. Dr Joseph Sullivan, a member of the board of both St Michael's and the University, wrote to Borden, 'I do not intend to sit idly by and see the great hospital of St Michael's under the Sisters of St Joseph be sacrificed on the funeral pyre for the benefit of Sunnybrook Hospital on account of the whims of Dean Chute and Dr Hamilton.' Sullivan had been the goalie on the famous team of Toronto graduates who competed in the 1928 Olympics, when the opposing teams failed to score a single goal. Characteristically, he was not about to lose this contest. In the end, all the teaching hospitals carried on as before. The complex and continuing drama of hospital-university relations, including hospital financing and restructuring, continues to this day.

When the Hamilton committee reported in 1964, there were five fully affiliated teaching hospitals: Toronto General, Toronto Western, St Michael's, Sick Children's, and the Toronto Psychiatric Hospital, soon to be relocated at College and Huron streets and named the Clarke Institute of Psychiatry after a former dean and head of psychiatry, C.K. Clarke. Other hospitals, such as Mount Sinai, Princess Margaret, Wellesley, and Women's College, played a lesser role as teaching hospitals.

Mount Sinai, however, gradually would become one of the University's major teaching hospitals. In 1962, Dean Hamilton and K.J.R. Wightman, the head of the university department of medicine, had arranged for the affiliation of Mount Sinai with the University and the teaching of undergraduate medical students in Mount Sinai's department of medicine and, shortly thereafter, pathology. In 1953, Mount Sinai had moved from a small hospital in the Yorkville area to a new 350-bed building on the north-west corner of University Avenue and Elm Street, primarily for Jewish doctors. Jews at that time were still almost completely excluded from interning or joining the teaching staff of the Toronto General Hospital. Only one Jewish doctor, Barnet Berris, had become an in-house doctor at the General. Berris had stood high in his graduating class but could not get an internship at the General or the Western, where he had applied, and went to the University of Minnesota instead. After Berris had had four years of specialty training there as an internist, the professor of medicine recommended him to R.F. Farquharson, the head of medicine at the General. The hospital board was opposed to his appointment, and apparently it was only after Farquharson threatened to resign that Berris was given an appointment – in 1950 – in the department of medicine. Berris remained there for fourteen years and in 1964 became chief of medicine at Mount Sinai. Staff doctors normally get daily referrals from other doctors in other departments in their hospital. When Berris was asked whether it was true that in his thirteen years at the General he had received a total of only 8 referrals, he replied: 'Not true. It was 6.'

By 1969, Mount Sinai was training medical students in at least seven departments and was planning a large new hospital beside the old one. A major addition to the existing hospital, as originally planned, could not be built because Taddle Creek flowed under the building. The hospital acquired land directly to the north, but in 1969 the government cut back on the capital funding of hospitals. Mount Sinai was permitted to proceed with its plans only after it promised not to ask for government assistance for the first two years of construction. In 1973, Queen Elizabeth officially opened Mount Sinai's new, now fully affiliated 600-bed hospital.

By the late 1960s, the faculty of medicine's research potential had significantly improved. The endocrinologist Irving Fritz, for example, succeeded Charles Best in 1968 as head of the Banting and Best Department of Medical Research. At the time, the department included Cecil Yip, a biochemist with a doctorate from Rockefeller University, who had joined the faculty in 1964 and would later serve as vice-dean of research. In 1969, David MacLennan from the University of Wisconsin – a specialist in muscle membrane biochemistry – joined the department. He would become a winner of a Gairdner award and a Killam prize and hold membership in the Royal Society of London. 'Within five years,' writes George Connell, the chair of the department of biochemistry during this period, Fritz 'had transformed the Banting and Best to one of the most effective in Canada, through selective pruning and recruiting.'

There were other success stories, but probably nothing that equalled those of the scientists associated with the Ontario Cancer Institute. The institute had opened new quarters in 1958 on Sherbourne Street, just north of the Wellesley Hospital. It treated cancer patients and also engaged in research, and became well known for both endeavours. The treatment part of the institute came to be known as Princess Margaret Hospital. Patients and clinicians preferred to be in a hospital rather than an institute, whereas for the scientists the opposite was true. The clinicians included, for example, Vera Peters, who had been involved in cancer treatment at the Toronto General and then at Princess Margaret since graduating from the Toronto medical school in 1934. She kept careful track of her patients and published a widely cited study of Hodgkin's disease, showing that radiation could help certain patients. Another study, using the 8,000 breast cancer patients she had treated between 1935 and 1960, showed that radiation and lumpectomies produced results comparable to those of radical mastectomies, without the same emotional and psychological damage.

Arthur Ham, the author of the leading textbook of histology and the prime proponent of a cancer institute, became the first head of its biology section, and Harold Johns, the head of its physics section. Johns had received his PhD in physics in 1939 from the University of Toronto and joined the physics department at the University of Saskatchewan, where he published extensively on the physics of radiology. He is known as the father of the 'cobalt bomb,' a radiation device that was cheaper, safer, and more powerful than radiation therapy and became widely used in the treatment of cancer. He joined the Ontario Cancer Institute in 1956 and was also made a professor in the physics department. The institute was able to attract excellent young – later to be eminent – research scientists, such as microbiologist Lou Siminovitch, physicist James Till, haematologist Ernest McCulloch, cell biologist Arthur Axelrod, and, in the 1970s, immunologist Tak Mak and molecular biologist Victor Ling. All six, along with Harold Johns, were later named University Professors, a designation that gave the institute a far higher concentration of such honour than any other part of the University. Like the centres and institutes described in the previous chapter, and the Institute of Biomedical Engineering described above, this was a true multidisciplinary enterprise.

Siminovitch had received his doctorate in physical chemistry from McGill and then spent six years at the Pasteur Institute in Paris working in the field of genetics. Four of the persons with whom he worked in Paris later won Nobel

(Top left) Cancer clinician and researcher Vera Peters, date uncertain.

(Top right) Medical biophysicist Harold Johns, in 1966, with the 'cobalt bomb'
radiation device he invented.

(Bottom left) Arthur Ham, head of biology of the Ontario Cancer Institute, in 1966.

(Bottom right) Geneticist Louis Siminovitch, about 1965.

prizes. 'I planned to work in Paris for two years,' he wrote, 'but remained for six. In the process, I learnt about the power of genetics as a discipline. I learnt, as well, the values of multidisciplinary approaches to biological problems.' He joined the Ontario Cancer Institute after working for several years at the Connaught Laboratories. Siminovitch had a very high opinion of Arthur Ham, whom he described as 'wise, erudite, understanding, giving, and intensely humanistic ... Dr Ham understood the role of basic science and the importance of multidisciplinary approaches to the development of understanding of the cancer problem.' The group worked well together and produced numerous significant papers. 'We had the intellectual engine of Lou Siminovitch,' reminisced McCulloch. 'We had just an absolutely magnificent, happy glorious time in which we were making discoveries ... We were playing in the big leagues ... but nobody was pressuring us.' He and physicist Till had a particularly close working relationship, and published more than 60 papers together.

In the years before 1958, it was not clear what the relationship would be between the Ontario Cancer Institute and the University. Some, such as Ham and Johns, had university appointments, but others did not. There was resistance by some in the University to creating the institute as a department in the faculty of arts and science, and an unrealistic concern about graduate students doing their work off campus. The solution adopted in 1958 was to give OCI a home in the faculty of medicine and to make it a department in the graduate school – the same solution that was later adopted for other multidisciplinary centres, such as linguistics, where there were objections from the established disciplines. Ham chaired the department until 1961, and Johns served as chair for the next ten years. The graduate department was given the name medical biophysics. Johns wanted the name to have as wide a scope for research as possible. From 3 full-time graduate students in 1957, it grew to about 40 in the late 1960s.

Not all the cancer research was being done in the faculty of medicine. Seminal work on the division of cells was quietly being conducted with a small budget by Yoshio Masui in the department of zoology. Trained at Kyoto University in Japan, he joined the faculty in 1969, and, working with frogs' eggs, he and his associates found the first protein factors that regulate cell divisions. In 1998, he was awarded the prestigious Lasker Medical Research Award. More than half the recent Lasker winners, it should be added, have gone on to win a Nobel prize.

Yoshio Masui, department of zoology, in 1991; his cellular research uses frogs' eggs.

Although much graduate work took place in the basic science departments in the faculty of medicine, there was no provision for graduate degrees in the clinical sciences. Jack Laidlaw of the department of medicine, with the support of Ernest McCulloch of medical biophysics, was primarily responsible for introducing a single graduate program in 1967 – the Institute of Medical Science (IMS) – for all the clinical departments. It would allow for the maintenance of more uniform standards and more interdisciplinary work than would be possible if each clinical department had obtained its own graduate component, assuming that such programs could have passed the various hurdles that had to be overcome before they could be funded by the government. Laidlaw, a medical doctor from U of T, received a PhD in biochemistry from the University of London in 1950. After further research at Harvard as a Markle scholar, he returned to Toronto and became director of the TGH's clinical investigation unit. He and McCulloch, whom he had met when they both worked at the Lister Institute in London, were unhappy with the system of post-graduate training in the clinical departments at Toronto. As McCulloch states, students 'were trained essentially on an apprenticeship mode ... They didn't really learn how to do research. There was no rigor involved and [Laidlaw] felt that the way to overcome that was to use the structure of a graduate program.' Dean Chute was a strong supporter, and Sirluck and Bissell welcomed the idea, in part as a way of bringing the medical faculty more directly into the University. They had a very high regard for Laidlaw. Indeed, Bissell had offered the medical deanship to Laidlaw the previous year, but he had turned it down.

Laidlaw was appointed as the first director of IMS, with McCulloch as graduate secretary. McCulloch would take over in 1975 after Laidlaw left to become chair of medicine at McMaster and later its dean of health sciences. The establishment of the institute coincided with the opening of the Medical Sciences Building, and the institute was given the top two floors to allocate to the clinical departments. It was anticipated that most of the students would be graduate MDs, and this was so in the early years, when there was a total of about 20 students a year. Today, there are more than 200 students – about half master's and half PhD students – and some 300 participating faculty members. Only about one-third of the students now have medical degrees. The institute was also responsible for introducing a joint MD/PhD program in the early 1980s – coordinated by Mel Silverman, who later became director of IMS – for students who wanted to do both degrees at the same time. 'There is no doubt,' stated George Connell, 'that the creation of the Institute was one of the most significant steps in the advancement of clinically-related research and graduate study at the University.'

The 1960s were important years for both engineering and medicine, and shaped their future direction. Both faculties expanded their research activities and graduate programs. Both ceased to be inward looking and hired talented faculty members from wherever they could be found. Symbolic of this approach was the hiring from McGill of the research-oriented Charles Hollenberg in 1970 as chair of medicine in the University and chief of medicine at Toronto General Hospital. Considering the historical reluctance to hire Jews at the hospital, the significance of Hollenberg's appointment cannot be overestimated. Before that, stated John Evans, 'you really had to be a white Anglo-Saxon Protestant,' and moreover, 'if you hadn't come up through the Toronto system it was very unlikely that you would be looked at for a job.' Hollenberg has said that some of the trustees of the Sir John and Lady Eaton chair did not want him to have the Eaton chair, which previously had gone automatically to the head of medicine. The members of the university board of governors, however, persuaded the trustees that to deny him the chair would be embarrassing to everyone concerned. Hollenberg got the chair, but – like Sirluck before him – did not receive membership in the York Club, which previously had come with the position. Hollenberg's appointment at Toronto was part of a general move of English-speaking doctors from Quebec in the early 1970s following the FLQ crisis. Two future Toronto medical deans, Arnold Aberman and Frederick Lowy, for example, left McGill at that time. Toronto was a direct beneficiary of the insecurity in Quebec.

PART SEVEN

———— ❧ ————

ADJUSTMENT

chapter thirty-six

1967

―――――――― ⊰⊱ ――――――――

STUDENT ACTIVISM

Unlike the apolitical 'silent generation' of students of the 1950s, students in the 1960s on the whole were vocal, active, and involved in a wide range of issues. Student leaders such as Bob Rae, a member of the Commission on University Government, established in 1968, and later the premier of Ontario, and Steven Langdon, the president of the Students' Administrative Council and later an NDP member of parliament, wanted to reform the University of Toronto in particular and universities generally. Others, such as Andrew Wernick, a member of the far-left Students for a Democratic Society (SDS) and now a professor of sociology at Trent University, and William Schabas, also a member of SDS and now director of the Irish Centre for Human Rights at the National University of Ireland, wanted more fundamental, radical changes in society and the universities. Bissell's strategy was to work closely with the former group and try to prevent their alignment with the more extreme students. The University of California at Berkeley had experienced a major disturbance in 1964, and universities throughout the world were anticipating problems. After meeting some student leaders in the spring of 1965, Bissell noted in his diary, 'There is an ugly undercurrent, deep and irrational.'

There were many reasons why students became politically active at universities throughout the world in the second half of the 1960s. The American civil rights movement played a part, as did – particularly in Canada – the nuclear disarmament campaign. But the Vietnam war was probably the most important

A protest against the Vietnam war in front of Convocation Hall in 1965, when Adlai Stevenson, the United States ambassador to the United Nations, received an honorary degree.

factor. 'No political event,' wrote Bob Rae in his autobiography, 'so galvanized opinion on the campus as the Vietnam war.' The universities, many activist students felt, were part of the so-called military-industrial complex that supported the war. The more extreme students wanted to 'liberate' the university from its influence. The many young men who came to Canada to avoid the American draft also contributed to the politically charged atmosphere at universities.

Many students during the decade rejected parental and other authority, and the universities were thought to be authoritarian institutions. The permissiveness that came with the birth control pill as well as the drug culture contributed to this defiance of authority. The 1960s saw the creation of Rochdale College on Bloor Street, a large high-rise self-governing student residence, officially unconnected with the University, but where many students and staff lived. Rochdale attempted alternative forms of teaching and learning, and some of the reform ideas concerning the University of Toronto emanated from the 'college.'

At the end of the decade, another lifestyle issue, sexual orientation, became the subject of discussion and active organization on the campus. In the fall of

1969, after the liberalization of the criminal code, the first gay and lesbian group in Toronto and on any Canadian campus – the University of Toronto Homophile Association – was formed. Jearld Moldenhauer, a research assistant in the faculty of medicine who would later establish the Glad Day Bookstore and help found the gay liberation magazine *The Body Politic*, placed a four-line classified advertisement in the *Varsity*, asking others to join in setting up an organization. The first meeting drew 16 people – 15 men and 1 woman. 'In little more than a year,' political science professor David Rayside has written, 'the group, under its first president Charlie Hill, a graduate student in art history and later a curator at the National Gallery of Canada, had established a significant community profile in and beyond the City of Toronto, challenging discrimination in law, in policing, and other arenas.' 'It was soon spawning,' Rayside went on to state, 'activist development beyond the campus.' Two decades later, Rayside himself would organize the Committee on Homophobia on the campus, and ten years after that he would help introduce a sexual diversity studies program at University College.

Students wanted changes that narrowed the division between students and faculty. Over the years, they would have considerable success in achieving their objectives. They gained a strong voice in decision making at most levels in the University, helped bring about changes in the curriculum and the evaluation of teaching performance, and changed the method of disciplining students. They freed the Students' Administrative Council from the supervision of the board of governors, and they even brought about the elimination of separate staff and student washrooms.

The first disruptive event at the University of Toronto did not occur until the fall of 1967 and involved protests against recruiting on campus by Dow Chemical Corporation, the manufacturers of the napalm being used in Vietnam. On the morning of November 20th, a group of students and faculty, with signs saying Down with Dow and Napalm Kills Babies, attempted to block the entrance to the University's recruiting centre by lying in front of the entrance – non-violent tactics successfully being used in the civil rights movement in the United States. Dow officials suspended interviews on campus. Although the University and the Toronto police stood by, no action was taken.

Faculty and students had focused their attention on Vietnam and other revolutionary movements two years earlier in a 'teach-in' entitled 'Revolution and Response.' Organized by a group led by Charles Hanly of the philosophy department, which included students who later came to be well known, such as the writers Matt Cohen and Michael Ignatieff, the historian Irving Abella, and Rosalie Silberman (a future justice, who met Abella while working on the teach-in and later married him), the program attracted so many participants that it had to move from Convocation Hall to Varsity Arena. Over 5,000 people took part in the various sessions, the largest being for the session on Vietnam. One of the participants, the American journalist Max Freedman, later wrote that it was 'a serious and responsible discussion worthy of a great university in its fairness and scholarship ... No university in the United States has matched the fairness of the University of Toronto in seeing that all sides of the discussion had an equal chance.' The next year, a teach-in on China also attracted large crowds, as did the one the following year on religion and morality.

⟨✑⟩

University governance became one of the central issues of the decade. In 1963, the Canadian Association of University Teachers and the Association of Universities and Colleges in Canada had set up a commission to look at the governance of universities. The Duff-Berdahl commission, named for the co-chairs, Sir James Duff, the former vice-chancellor of Durham University in England, and Robert Berdahl, a political scientist from San Francisco State College, did not report until 1966, however. It recommended that some faculty members, but not students, should be on boards of governors. It also approved the establishment of a body like Toronto's President's Council, which Bissell had set up in 1965 to advise him. The President's Council initially consisted of five elected faculty members, a number of senior administrators, and several members of the board of governors, but no students. It acted as a bridge between the senate and the board, but also could give guidance and direction to the president, guidance that would be increasingly needed over the next half-dozen tumultuous years.

Bissell wanted to go further than the Duff-Berdahl report. He wanted the board and the senate to merge into a unicameral body that would be able to deal with both academic and financial issues. The existing arrangement was one Bissell described as 'double innocence' – academic decisions were being made by the senate without their financial implications being known, and financial decisions were being made by the board without their academic effects being known. The students too were unhappy with the Duff-Berdahl report because it ignored their voice. Duff-Berdahl had stated that 'most young people to whom we talked were willing to concede that [student representation on the board] was not a feasible proposal.' Students at Toronto were, however, now demanding equality – known at the University as 'parity' – with faculty in decision-making bodies. Bissell wanted some form of commission to explore these issues. With the support of the President's Council, he proposed a commission, to be made up of two faculty members, two students, two administrators, two alumni, and two members of the board. The proposal was accepted by the board of governors. The students, however, rejected it. They wanted parity – four faculty members and four students, with the president and board members being non-voting participants. Some of the more radical students, such as Wernick, wanted no participation by students, fearing that the students would be co-opted by the establishment.

Langdon and Rae attended a meeting of the Association of Teaching Staff (ATS) to put forward the students' position – for a committee consisting of an equal number of faculty members and students. 'We convinced the faculty association,' wrote Rae, 'that the time had come to challenge all the existing structures,' including the administration. A motion for a more broadly based committee had been put forward to the meeting, which had the support of Bissell, the President's Council, and the ATS executive, but Kenneth McNaught, who several years earlier had had 'bitter experience' with the administration at United College in Winnipeg, where he was teaching, proposed an amendment urging the faculty to accept something comparable to the Langdon-Rae scheme. The amendment passed by about 90 votes to 50.

Bissell was devastated and wanted to resign the presidency, but was assured that he had not lost the confidence of the faculty, including McNaught, who had moved the amendment. This latest version concerning composition was reluctantly approved by the board of governors, and the Commission on University Government (known by the inelegant designation CUG) was established. Four faculty members – Ben Etkin of engineering, J.E. Hodgetts, the principal of Victoria College, Larry Lynch of philosophy, and J.S. Thompson of anatomy – were elected, as were four students – Stephen Grant, D'Arcy Martin, and Bob Rae, all undergraduate arts students, and Gary Webster, a graduate political science student. Webster had taught for two years in Nigeria before coming to Toronto and, according to Bissell, had 'the most hardened views, shaped, one

The Commission on University Government, 1967. With back to camera, Larry Lynch;
from left to right, left side, Bob Rae (with pipe), Gary Webster, Claude Bissell, J.S. Thompson,
Ben Etkin, and Robin Ross; right side, R.A. McKinlay, Robert Hicks, J.E. Hodgetts,
Stephen Grant, and D'Arcy Martin.

gathered, by his experience of colonialism in Africa.' Over 145 meetings were
held over the next year, and the report, written primarily by Lynch and Rae, was
published in 1970. The members of the committee had worked well together
and, as often happens in such cases, recommended the creation of a body that
generally reflected their own composition – a unicameral body that would
replace the board, the senate, and the President's Council. The governing council
would consist of 66 persons – 20 elected faculty members, 20 elected students,
20 lay members, and 6 *ex officio* members. The aftermath of the CUG report and
the establishment of a unicameral governing structure in 1972 will be discussed
in the next chapter.

Teaching and the curriculum were also matters of concern to students. The great influx of students had resulted in large classes and many newly minted professors with little or no teaching experience. Many undergraduates felt that the new emphasis on graduate training and research had left undergraduates as second-class citizens. Furthermore, students taking the 'general' arts and science course felt that professors concentrated their attention on students in the honours courses, and that general students were treated as even less than second class. Bissell concluded that 'in the current anti-elitist atmosphere, we couldn't continue a policy based on the slighting of half the student population in our largest faculty.' In the spring of 1966, he set up a presidential committee, under the chairmanship of political scientist Brough Macpherson, to examine undergraduate instruction in arts and science. The eight-member committee contained only one student, Frank Buck, a graduate student in economics. Nevertheless, student opinion was very influential. The vast majority of the more than 400 submissions were from students. The committee agreed with the concerns they expressed. 'We are disturbed,' they wrote in their report, published in the summer of 1967, 'by the evidence that a significant proportion of the lectures offered to undergraduates are simply bad, whether because the lecturer is inaudible, insufficiently articulate, obviously uninterested, or merely unaware of his faults.'

A number of solutions were proposed. There should be less reliance on lectures, and more time freed up for reading and reflection by the students. Teaching should be given greater weight in decisions concerning appointments and promotions. The evaluation of teaching performance, which had recently been introduced by the students, should be encouraged. One of the first evaluations of teachers had been organized by the department of political economy in the 1965–6 academic year, and a faculty-wide appraisal had been introduced by the Students' Administrative Council in 1966–7 for arts and science. The faculty, the committee stated, should cooperate in the preparation of the forms. And class time should be allotted to filling out the questionnaires. Such evaluations are now standard throughout the University.

The most radical and most controversial proposal by the Macpherson committee was to abolish the distinction between the honours programs and the general course. For almost a century, there had been a complete separation of the three-year general course and the four-year honours programs, with different admission and passing standards and, for the most part, separate courses for

Some members of the Macpherson committee set up in 1966 to examine undergraduate instruction in arts and science: left to right, Stanley Nyburg, Wim Kent, C.B. Macpherson, and graduate student Frank Buck, meeting in the Galbraith Building.

each. Slightly more than half the first year arts and science students entered the thirty or so honours programs, though the number of graduates from these programs was significantly less than half on account of the students who transferred to the general course after first year. Many members of the faculty were reluctant to abandon the honours programs, for which Toronto was well known. In general, the graduates of these programs received an excellent though specialized education, one that was highly regarded by employers and graduate programs.

It was not the quality of the honours programs that disturbed the committee, but what the programs did 'to the students who are not in them.' 'The non-specialist,' the committee wrote, 'cannot get the first-rate work in any subject: each department reserves that for its own specialist students.' 'The generalist,' the committee went on to state, 'is a second-class citizen, not because he is necessarily less capable but because he will not commit himself to high specialization.' The solution was to treat honours and general students the same. There would no longer be separate courses for each group. Students, if they wished, could specialize and take a four-year degree, but also had the option of graduating with a three-year general degree. This recommendation was consistent with the students' views that they should be given greater choice in selecting their courses and also with their complaint about 'the rigidity of the boundaries between the disciplines.' Greater student choice soon found its way into other faculties, including law and engineering. After extensive debate in the faculty of arts and science, a motion to abandon the honours system was adopted. The resulting unstructured nature of the arts and science program and the steps taken to overcome it will be discussed in later chapters.

In early January 1969, Bissell's executive assistant, political scientist Donald Forster, was able to write to a fellow academic, 'So far, of course, we have managed to avoid direct confrontations with our more activist student colleagues and have escaped the kinds of problems which have beset so many universities recently.' Within weeks, however, the University experienced the 'Clark Kerr affair,' described by Robin Ross, the vice-president who had primary responsibility for student activities, as 'our first real exposure to the tactics of the revolutionaries.' Kerr had been invited to Toronto by the University's American Studies Committee to give a public lecture at the museum. He had been president of the University of California during the troubles there in 1964, later had been fired by Governor Ronald Reagan for allegedly being soft in his dealings with students, and was opposed to the Vietnam war. He was, however, a proponent of the multiversity with its links to business, government, and the military and was thus a target of the far left. The University expected some problems. Pamphlets had been distributed before his talk, claiming that 'Bissell has invited Kerr up from the metropolis of the Empire to this colony to get advice on how to keep the natives down ... Come to confront Kerr at the Royal Ontario Museum ... Let's harass him until he leaves this *Canadian* campus. May the ghost of Mario Savio [a Berkeley student leader] rise to haunt him.'

As Bissell began his introduction, two students rushed onto the stage, presented Kerr with a bunch of artificial roses, and hung a chain of marshmallows around Bissell's neck. Part way through Kerr's speech, which was interrupted by 'jeers, shouts, and cynical laughter,' Andrew Wernick, according to Bissell's diary, 'grim and determined, walked up on the platform and moved towards Kerr.' Bissell gently pushed Wernick back, and immediately half a dozen

A motion to adjourn an unruly meeting of the subcommittee to examine the composition of
the University's disciplinary body, the Caput, at an open meeting in the debates room of
Hart House in September 1969. Facing the camera, at the table, from left to right:
Greg Kealey and Andrew Wernick, student activists who took over seats at the table,
Albert Abel, the chair of the subcommittee, and Claude Bissell; with backs to camera,
from left to right, F.E. Winter, Craig Brown, John Rist, and John Kelly.
The motion for adjournment was proposed by Michael Vaughan, standing at left.

of Wernick's supporters were on the stage. Bissell tried to establish order, saying, 'We have had enough fascism this evening,' but his remarks further enraged the protesters. Then two student members of CUG, Bob Rae and D'Arcy Martin, climbed onto the stage, and Rae suggested that Bissell give Wernick equal time. Bissell followed his advice. Wernick, according to Bissell, spoke with 'nervous ineffectiveness,' and Philip Resnick, the 'official student theoretician of the far left' and now a professor of political science at UBC, added his views. Kerr was then able to finish his speech. Bissell's diary noted that 'the extremists had demonstrated for all to see and hear' that they were 'childish' and 'desperate.' No charges were brought.

There were more serious incidents at other Canadian universities, particularly at Sir George Williams in Montreal, where the university's main computer was destroyed by student activists. Harvard and Cornell in the United States also saw violent events. The University of Toronto expected more trouble. Langdon had publicly predicted that there would be sit-ins in the coming academic year, 1969–70. The committee of Ontario university presidents published a paper suggesting that it might be necessary to use strong tactics to counter threatening student protests. This was followed by a similar statement by the Caput, the principal disciplinary body at the University. The Students' Administrative Council condemned the threat of strong action by the University and demanded that Bissell dissociate himself from both documents. He refused to do so, but committed the University to implementing the recently released report on discipline from a committee chaired by the economist Ralph Campbell. SAC gave Bissell a deadline of a week in which to repudiate the statements and called a mass meeting in Convocation Hall for noon on October 1, 1969. Implicit in the demand was a threat that Simcoe Hall would be occupied if Bissell's response was not acceptable. On the morning of the deadline date, the *Varsity* urged a sit-in.

Engineering and medical students, who had arrived at Convocation Hall early, occupied the front rows, and the president of the Engineering Society, Art McIlwain, was elected chair of the meeting. Ernest Sirluck states in his autobiography that he had 'telephoned a number of faculty members, including two engineering professors, and suggested that they and perhaps some of their students might like to attend the mass meeting to give the president some support.' Bissell entered a packed Convocation Hall. The audience cheered. Moderate law student Gus Abols, the SAC president, whispered to Bissell that there was not 'any doubt about where this audience, stands.' Marshall McLuhan gave his support by squatting at Bissell's feet below the lectern like a court jester. Bissell's response to the SAC demand was accepted as adequate by the audience, and Bissell left with the audience singing 'For He's a Jolly Good Fellow.' The immediate crisis had temporarily disappeared. Bissell was elated.

In March 1970, a crisis emerged over day-care facilities at the University. For a number of years, the University had been 'assisting' women's groups to find space for a day-care centre. A house slated to be torn down for the construction of Innis College had been taken over by a group of women who wanted the University to provide some $2,000 for renovations. No positive response from Simcoe Hall was forthcoming. Historian Jill Conway, soon to be a vice-president of the University, would write in her autobiography that 'nothing excited such volatile and irrational feelings among male faculty, administrators, and trustees

President Claude Bissell addressing one of the sit-ins during his presidency, probably the
day-care sit-in of 1970.

as the issue of providing day care on the University campus.' The supporters of day care, led by philosophy professor Lorenne Smith, demonstrated outside Simcoe Hall and demanded that Bissell speak to them. He refused, and the result was that the senate chamber in Simcoe Hall was occupied by the demonstrators, many of whom had brought their children. Banners hung out of the windows, one of which read, Infants of the World Unite, You Have Nothing to Lose but Your Diapers.

The demonstrators were soon joined by others, and that night approximately 200 people spent a congenial evening in the senate chamber. Forster reported to Bissell from Simcoe Hall that SAC had voted $500 for food for the occupants and that 'the chamber [was] heavy with the sweet smell of pot.' Bissell called a meeting of the President's Council for the next morning, which Lorenne Smith and historian Natalie Davis addressed, arguing for adequate day-care facilities on campus. After this one night's occupation, Bissell pledged to find the $2,000, and the latest crisis was over. Thus far, the Toronto police had not been called in. Documents had been prepared to obtain a court injunction to deal with those illegally occupying the senate chamber, but we will never know whether it would have been followed by police action if the injunction had not been obeyed. The involvement of children made the issue a difficult one. As Forster wrote a friend after the incident, 'I am sure that many of our police officers still are haunted by the image of three and four year olds leading the charge.'

The Toronto police were called in, however, to end a Simcoe Hall sit-in in 1972 over the issue of access to the library stacks in the as-yet-unopened Robarts Library. When the library was planned, it was assumed that faculty members, graduate students, and fourth year undergraduates would have access to the stacks, but not other students. The undergraduates, however, wanted equal access. Bob Spencer, the SAC president, wrote to Jack Sword, the acting president – following Bissell's resignation as of July 1, 1971 – pointing out 'the almost unanimous opposition of the student body' to the proposed stacks policy, an opposition that included the Students' Administrative Council and the Graduate Students Union. A petition containing 4,500 names was placed before the library council. Linda McQuaig, the co-editor of the *Varsity* and now a well-known author, presented 2,500 coupons that had been printed in the paper and that students had signed and returned. The students' position was in line with other demands for equality respecting such issues as the equal treatment of general and honours students. 'Books, like all other raw materials of education,' one pamphlet read, 'should be available to anyone who wants to use them.' A library council committee, chaired by English professor Peter Heyworth, continued to recommend limiting access, and this was approved at a meeting of the senate in the Medical Sciences Building on a Friday evening in March 1972 by a vote of 67 to 28.

After the vote, about 75 people left the meeting and forced their way into Simcoe Hall. They refused to leave the senate chamber until the senate had met again and granted open stack access to all undergraduates. On Sunday morning, about 25 protesters who remained in the building were evicted with the assistance of the Toronto police, who had to break through the door of the senate chamber to get in. Fourteen people were charged with criminal code trespass offences, including the SAC president, Spencer, and Thomas Walkom, a co-editor of the *Varsity* and now a writer for the *Toronto Star*; four others were charged with trespass along with more serious charges, such as assault. On Monday afternoon, a mass student rally in Convocation Hall was followed by another occupation of the senate chamber, this time by more that 500 people. Removing this number posed the significant risk that the violence would escalate. The occupation was abandoned the following day after extensive negotiations and after Acting President Sword said he would call another meeting of the senate and would personally support equal access to the stacks, subject to a daily quota to be set by the library administrators. The University also agreed to tell the crown attorney that it was not in the University's interest to proceed with the charges.

Sword sent a detailed letter to the university community explaining the problems the administration had faced. 'The calling of police to clear the building of six to eight hundred students,' he wrote, 'would have involved a very large number of police and the probability of serious violence and damage, and we would have borne the responsibility of using overwhelming force against our own students.' Nevertheless, the council of the faculty association condemned the administration's actions by a vote of 14 to 3. 'The reaction of conservative faculty against the administration,' Forster acknowledged, 'was quite bitter and left some wounds which will take time to heal.' As it turned out, the crown attorney agreed to drop the trespassing charges but proceeded with the more serious charges, which resulted in convictions in three cases.

The senate meeting a week later decided to refer the issue back to the Heyworth committee, with instructions that access be based on 'academic need' and 'on the widest possible scale consistent with the effective use of the resources and facilities of the library.' The revised rules of the Heyworth committee were subsequently approved by the senate. The incidents, recalled Vice-president Robin Ross in his memoirs, 'were the potentially most dangerous to the university among all the student demonstrations which took place' in his twenty-five years as a university administrator. When the library opened in 1973, it was decided by the library itself that upon application all students would be given stack passes. The result, Ross concluded a dozen years later, was that the system 'seems to have worked well and without the dire consequences forecast by the professional librarians.' The retired university librarian Robert Blackburn, however, was still not convinced, and has written in his memoirs, published in the early 1990s, 'In the long run, I think egalitarian access to the research stacks will be very expensive in terms of volumes mutilated or lost, and scholarship will be served less well than it might have been.'

⚬⚬⚬

The extreme left made one more major appearance on the University of Toronto stage. The occasion was a series of lectures to be given in March 1974 by the American political scientist Edward Banfield. His writings dealt with the problems of the urban poor, and some radical students considered his views racist. The week before Banfield's lectures a 'teach-in on racism,' which criticized Banfield's views, was held at the University. At Banfield's first lecture, he was harassed by the audience, but at the second, in the West Hall at University College, he was prevented from speaking. Two radical student leaders of the Students for a Democratic Society, Anthony Leah, a master's student in sociology, who had earlier been charged with trespass in the library stacks affair, and William Schabas, who was pursuing a doctorate in history and had been involved in the day-care sit-in, were subsequently charged with disciplinary offences. Leah and Schabas and others had taken over the platform and were determined to prevent Banfield from speaking. Stefan Dupré, the head of political economy who was chairing the meeting, later testified that someone had said, 'Banfield, you're not coming on stage ... You're going to get hurt, Banfield.' Dupré quickly adjourned the proceedings.

Many faculty members were outraged that steps had not been taken to ensure that Banfield could deliver his lectures. The University had been warned that there was likely to be trouble. Bill Nelson, the president of the faculty association, was particularly critical of the administration. 'I think it simply outrageous,' he told the *Bulletin*, 'that the administration of the University failed in its primary responsibility of protecting freedom of speech and assembly on the campus for academic purposes.' The faculty association unanimously endorsed a demand that President John Evans, who had assumed office two years earlier, 'issue an explicit statement of the right of free discussion,' and that the president 'accept responsibility for using all his lawful authority in future to secure such free discussion.' Forster, who invariably kept his ear close to the ground, advised Evans in a memo that 'Nelson and most militant members of the faculty association are still in a very nasty and belligerent mood,' and that the faculty generally agreed with Nelson's position, though not necessarily with the tone of his remarks. Jill Conway, the vice-president of internal affairs, who had the primary responsibility for such matters, conceded in her autobiography that she probably misjudged the situation. 'I had,' she wrote, 'mistakenly decided to work through the event using campus police, only to be outnumbered and outmaneuvered by the disrupters.'

With hindsight, it is perhaps easy to say that the Toronto police in addition to the campus police ought to have been on hand, but as Evans stated several days after the incident, 'there exists a strong feeling on the campus that Metropolitan Police should be called on the campus only as a last resort when serious danger to life or property exists.' A subsequent document from Simcoe Hall set out procedures to be followed in the event of future disruption. The disrupted meeting, it stated, should be postponed generally for up to twenty-four hours to give the University the opportunity to make arrangements 'for the meeting to take place in a suitable environment.' The environment would presumably be one in which the Toronto police were available.

The governing council resolved that the president should ask the Caput to deal with the disruption, and disciplinary charges were framed against Leah and Schabas. An unrepentant Schabas argued before the governing council that it was not he who should be charged, but those who had invited Banfield, and that Banfield's books should be removed from any required reading list. The Caput, made up of all the principals and deans in the University, was still the only body available to deal with disciplinary matters. Proposed new structures had not yet been brought in. Law professor Albert Abel had served as chair of the Caput for a number of years and would serve as chair of this hearing. The nineteen-day hearing, popularly known as 'the Albert Abel show,' was televised by a local station and closely followed by people inside and outside the University. Gavels are not used by Canadian judges, but Abel, then still an American citizen who had been a judge in the American navy during the war, constantly used his navy gavel. Those who watched the proceedings still carry a vivid picture of Abel banging his gavel on the table trying to restore order, and particularly remember the time Leah tried to take the gavel away from him.

Leah and Schabas defended themselves, with advice from civil rights lawyer Charles Roach. They had wanted the hearing to be put over until September, when there would be more students around to give them support, but Abel decided it should start in May. The number of Caput members attending, however, kept dwindling as conflicts and commitments caused various persons to leave. (For legal reasons, one could not participate in the final decision unless one had attended all meetings. This writer left at a very early stage of the proceedings.) At the end, there remained only 7 members of the tribunal, out of the 29 possible members of the Caput. They found both defendants guilty and suspended them from the University of Toronto, for three years in the case of Leah and four years in the case of Schabas.

The defendants appealed to the governing council. Some thought the sentences too severe, including Schabas' parents, Ezra and Ann Schabas – professors of music and of library science respectively – who, found them 'extraordinarily harsh. Two academic careers have been effectively destroyed.' In fact, Schabas, the grandson of the left-wing professor of German, Barker Fairley, went on to study law at the University of Montreal and is now a respected authority on criminal law who has written scholarly books on the death penalty and other human rights issues. The governing council – to the annoyance of some members of the Caput as well as of its secretary, Robin Ross – lowered the sentences to two years' suspension. Similar obstructions at Yale and Chicago, it was argued, had brought far less severe penalties. In the Chicago case, only a week after the Toronto episode, students had prevented Banfield from speaking and had been given suspended sentences.

The Banfield affair more or less ended a decade of student activism. Most of the students who had been involved continued to press for changes in society. 'Everyone I know who was active then is active now,' said the activist songwriter-musician Bob Bossin in 1980. Their activities at the University of Toronto had helped produce a number of significant changes in the governance of the

Zoologist Donald Chant, the founder of Pollution Probe, left, and other members of
the organization, at a ceremony in 1970 burying a time capsule on the south side of the
Robarts Library. The plaque reads, in part, 'We have buried here a record of man's folly on
the planet he's outgrown.'

university, in the curriculum, and in disciplinary procedures. In the process,
however, they had somewhat tarnished the image of the University in the eyes of
many members of the public, damage that would be reflected in the public
support of the institution. The University's measured responses had also engen-
dered a sense of uneasiness and even hostility in some members of the faculty
towards the administration. It would now be the faculty's turn to flex its muscles.

chapter thirty-seven

1971

❧

A NEW ACT

On July 23, 1971, Acting President Jack Sword sent a telegram to Claude Bissell, who was vacationing in Nova Scotia. 'Your thirteen year effort endorsed today,' it stated. 'Legislature approved third reading stop fifty member governing council twelve staff eight students stop warmest congratulations stop all well here.' The new act, which was to come into force on July 1, 1972, had adopted a unicameral system of one governing body, eliminating both the senate and the board of governors. It was the first – and is still the only – major English-speaking university in North America to do so.

Bissell had resigned as president as of June 30, 1971. He would then be 55 years old. For several years, according to his diary, he had wanted to leave office. In one entry in October 1969, for example, he had expressed a firm determination to resign at the end of that academic year – or earlier, if a successor was chosen – but the following day he changed his mind and decided to 'stay and fight through the changes.' Some members of the board were encouraging him to leave. Chairman Henry Borden, for example, thought that he should retire. Bissell had what he described in his diary in October 1969 as the 'cynical thought' that it was a plot: 'If the Board could wait out the year, then get rid of me, it could secure some compromise that would not strip it of power.' He would resign, he wrote the following year, 'as soon as there was a clear basis within the University for changes in the governing structure.'

The report of the Commission on University Government (CUG) had been released in October 1969. One of its principal recommendations – there were 107 in all – was to establish 'a sole governing authority with final control over all financial and academic matters within the University of Toronto, to be named the Governing Council.' The council, the commission proposed, would consist of 66 persons: 20 elected faculty members, 20 elected students, 20 lay members, and 6 others. The governing council would replace the senate and the board. Bissell had lost confidence in the board and its ability to govern the University. He and the commission had spoken of the 'double innocence' of the existing system. The board was innocent of academic matters, and the senate of financial matters. A single governing body, he and the commission concluded, could bring all parties together at the same table. There would be, Bissell stated, 'a representative body of final, indisputable authority.'

Most members of the board were opposed to the recommendations of the CUG report. Borden later reminisced that he 'didn't feel that there was any need for a fundamental change.' The 1906 royal commission, he believed, had 'produced an extraordinarily well thought out report and the statute that implemented it. I saw no reason to throw that all over. It had worked.' The board had had two observers on CUG, the businessmen Vacy Ash and Wallace McCutcheon, the latter of whom died during the commission's deliberations and was replaced by William Harris, a 38-year-old banking executive who had joined the board in 1968. The board member Sydney Hermant later said in an oral interview that the board 'gave it away by default.' 'The board wasn't even represented on CUG,' he went on. 'They allow two of their members to sit as observers – it was ridiculous.'

The board was in disarray. Some of its younger members, such as Harris and John Tory, supported the general principles of the CUG report, but most did not. Certainly, the new chairman of the board, the former Eaton's executive O.D. Vaughan, was opposed to change. The 73-year-old Vaughan, who had given long and devoted service to the University since being appointed to the board in 1945, was, according to Borden (who had resigned as chairman, but continued as a member of the board), 'not a good chairman.' 'I can recall,' Borden reminisced, 'being shocked, really, at the manner in which he conducted board meetings.' 'It was like having no chairman,' Hermant stated, adding, 'He's the only man I've ever seen fall asleep while conducting his own meeting – literally.' Whether a different chairman could have diverted the University and the government from the path towards unicameralism will never be known.

A programming committee was planned to organize a discussion that would determine the University's views on the report, and in October 1969 such a committee was set up by the president, with the concurrence of the major organizations on the campus. Martin Friedland, then a member of the President's Council, was chosen to chair the committee, which included the chairman of the faculty association and the presidents of the Students' Administrative Council and the Graduate Students' Union. During the course of the academic year, the committee organized and encouraged discussion within the University of the many difficult issues raised in the report. Debates were arranged on all three campuses, special sessions were conducted with the support staff and the alumni, and space was made available for comment in the pages of the *Bulletin* and the *Varsity*. The committee struggled to find a way of reaching some form of consensus within the University on the issues. How could this be done in such a complex institution? Bissell later wrote that the answer the programming committee proposed was 'both simple and bold ... to form a constitutional assembly, a broad and generous representation of the whole university, which would debate and vote on a series of specific resolutions that had emerged from the discussions of the preceding few months.'

A questionnaire, devised by the programming committee, was sent to the entire university community. It sought to determine the University's views on a number of issues, such as unicameralism, and to get its opinion on the desirability of setting up the assembly, which would become known as the University-wide Committee (UWC). There was widespread support within the University for holding an assembly at the end of the academic year, and the committee's determination to proceed was endorsed by the President's Council. Although the council of the faculty association did not want to take part in the meetings, it was outvoted at a general meeting of the association. Over a three-day period in early June 1970, the UWC met in a large room in the Ontario government's Macdonald Block. The UWC, wrote the vice-president and registrar Robin Ross, whose office helped organize the assembly, was 'the largest, boldest and most ambitious Presidential Advisory Committee ever struck or likely to be struck in the University of Toronto.'

The University-wide Committee was to be made up of 160 persons: 40 faculty members, 40 students, 40 academic and non-academic administrators, and 40·others, including 20 alumni representatives and 10 members of the board of governors. All members, except the board and *ex officio* members, were elected

Physicist Archie Hallett, chairing a session of the 146-person University-wide Committee in
June 1970, with members of the six-person steering committee in the background.

from carefully worked out constituencies. Understandably, the board did not
have its heart in the exercise and refused to take part, though several board
members attended as observers. The alumni, however, were fully engaged, just as
they had been actively involved with CUG and would be actively involved in
the later debates on the report. In the end, 146 persons officially took part in the
deliberations. The associate dean of arts and science, Archie Hallett, who had
been selected by the delegates, effectively chaired the meetings, which worked
through a series of resolutions prepared by a six-person steering committee
drawn from the elected members of the UWC. Was the UWC in favour of a
unicameral system? Yes, said the UWC decisively by a vote of 111 to 15. Was the
committee in favour of parity between faculty and students on the top governing
body? No, it said, by a narrow vote of 60 to 56. These votes led to the much-
debated question of the composition of a unicameral governing body.

Eleven models were in contention at the meeting, ten of which were slowly
eliminated in a series of votes. Political scientist Brough Macpherson had wanted

the faculty to constitute half the membership of the governing body. The faculty association, however, had not gone that far, but had advocated a model of 20 faculty members, 20 lay persons, 10 administrators, and 10 students. The students had advocated parity between students and faculty. Many members wanted a lay majority. And so on. The final vote resulted in a recommendation that the governing council be a 72-member body made up of 24 lay persons, 21 faculty members, 14 students, and a number of academic administrators and support staff. The students therefore would have two-thirds the number of faculty members.

One further crucial decision had to be made. In order to induce the faculty and student organizations to take part in the whole endeavour, one of the ground rules had been that either the faculty or the students by a majority vote could force a further meeting in the fall at which the decisions concerning the top governing structure could be revisited. If the fall meeting reaffirmed the earlier decisions, the result would simply be given to the president. The faculty was reasonably content with the compromise outcome of the UWC meeting, but a number of students were not. After discussion in their caucus, however, the students decided not to require a fall meeting, but stated that they unanimously 'deplore the outcome of these deliberations' and would come forward with 'a very strong minority report.' No such report, however, was ever prepared. In general, wrote Bissell, there was ' a sense of immense relief, even a note of jubilation at the outcome.'

Within days, Bissell received a letter from classicist John Rist, the chairman of the faculty association, suggesting quick action. 'I do not believe,' he wrote, 'that you will ever have a proposal which will command as wide support on the campus as that which is now miraculously available. In particular in carrying the proposals to Queen's Park *quickly* you will have stronger and more widespread backing from the faculty with more shades of political opinion than could possibly have been foreseen.' The major changes proposed by the UWC required provincial legislation. The President's Council also urged action and suggested that a joint committee of the President's Council and the board be established.

At the end of June 1970, the executive committee of the board of governors forwarded to the premier, John Robarts, the official summary of the proceedings of the University-wide Committee, stating that 'comments by the Board of Governors will follow.' The summer passed. At a board meeting in October 1970, a delegation consisting of the University College principal Hallett, the faculty of arts and science dean A.D. (Bert) Allen, and the engineering dean James Ham expressed concern over 'the apparent lack of progress in the matter of the revision of the University of Toronto Act.'

In late November 1970, a short document was publicly released by the board, stating that the 'majority of the members of the Board have strong convictions' that a bicameral model is preferable to the unicameral system. If, in spite of the board's view, a unicameral system were to be brought in, it argued, a much smaller council than that recommended by the University-wide Committee should be adopted – 'in no event to consist of more than 35 members.' Moreover, the board advised, the governing council should 'include an effective majority of Government appointees.' It also recommended that the cabinet appoint a full-time salaried non-academic person 'to share [with the president] overall university responsibilities and to act as chairman of the top governing body.' Bissell quickly reassured the academic community that he had not voted for the recommendations and had not changed his mind with respect to the desirability of the unicameral system. Vice-provost Donald Forster, writing to a friend, complained that the board 'had learned almost nothing from the recent ferment in the university.'

In the spring of 1971, the government – now led by William Davis – decided to go ahead with a new act along the lines proposed by the University-wide Committee. Board members William Harris and Malim Harding and President Bissell worked with the minister of university affairs, John White, and his officials to prepare the legislation. (Harris would succeed Vaughan as chair of the board at the end of June 1971, and Harding would become its vice-chair.) Two major departures from the conclusions of the UWC were introduced into the legislation, however, in line with the views of the board. Lay members, that is, those appointed by the government together with those elected by the alumni, would constitute a majority of the members of the governing council. Moreover, the council would be far smaller than the 72-member body recommended by the UWC. The bill introduced later that month had a 42-member council, but the legislation that was finally enacted increased it to 50 members.

The relative composition of faculty and students again became an issue in the legislature. The opposition Liberals and NDP demanded parity between the two groups. The bill, however, roughly maintained the composition that had been recommended by the University-wide Committee: students would have about two-thirds the number of faculty members. After second reading in July 1971, the bill was sent to the human resources committee of the legislature for detailed examination. During the eight days of hearings, students argued for parity, and faculty opposed it. Bissell, who was no longer president, made an appearance at the hearings, urging acceptance of the UWC ratios. Minister John White, however, was concerned because an election was looming and, for the first time in Ontario, 18-year-olds would be voting. At one stage, he proposed a compromise form of potential parity: 10 faculty members, 6 students, and 4 persons elected by faculty and students together. The faculty association was strongly opposed. This, the faculty association president James Conacher wrote to his colleagues in the University, was 'de facto parity' because in the voting for the four positions 'the students would outnumber the faculty 15 to 1.' In the end, after strong representations by the faculty and the board, the minister withdrew the proposal. Had it been put to the legislative committee, claimed Tim Reid, the Liberals' education critic, 'the committee would have unanimously adopted his proposal.' Amendments in the legislative assembly to bring about parity were defeated by the government majority. On July 23, 1971, the act was passed by the assembly.

❧

Bissell had announced his resignation in June 1970, after the results of the University-wide Committee had made it likely that the governance issue would be resolved. It was up to the board to make the arrangements to select his successor. In the past, the decision had been strictly one for the board, and in some cases, such as the appointment of Bissell, it had been made by the chairman and rubber-stamped by the board. There had never been a search committee involving persons outside the board, and O.D. Vaughan, the chairman, was not keen to have such a committee. The President's Council had asked the board not to determine procedures for the selection of the president until it had put forward a proposal, which it did put forward in October 1970. Vaughan eventually accepted the idea of a representative committee. Its 14 members would consist of 3 faculty members, 3 students, and 3 members of the board, plus 4 others, including Chancellor Omond Solandt as chairman. Elections for the positions were held early in 1971, and the first meeting took place in February. Don Forster observed privately at the time that 'most people think that the committee has a somewhat "conservative" slant,' and Bissell's diary records his 'great elation' that the committee contained no 'activist undergraduate.' Although Bissell was not on the committee, he was kept informed of its deliberations by the chair, Chancellor Solandt, and Bissell recorded these in his diary.

The committee eventually narrowed the choice to four names: A.W.R. (Fred) Carrothers, the president of the University of Calgary; John Evans, the dean of the McMaster medical school; James Ham, the dean of engineering; and Ernest Sirluck, the former dean of the graduate school and at the time the president of the University of Manitoba. Ham was the first to be dropped from the list. The three faculty members on the committee, James Conacher, Edward Safarian, and Stanley Schiff, strongly supported Sirluck, but, though initially tempted, he decided that in fairness to Manitoba he could not allow his name to be put forward. He did agree, however, to meet with the committee to discuss his experience at the University of Toronto, thinking he had made it clear that he was not a candidate. Nevertheless, his name was kept on the list. Solandt thought the choice was between Evans and Sirluck, and Don Forster thought it was between Carrothers and Sirluck. When news reports continued to include Sirluck's name, he told both the University of Toronto and the University of Manitoba that he was not a candidate. The choice was therefore between Carrothers and Evans. 'The former,' according to Bissell's diary, 'was thought to be the more experienced and dependable administrator. The latter had greater general appeal, and held out a larger promise.' The committee was evenly divided, but eventually chose Carrothers. 'It now remained to be seen,' Bissell wrote, 'whether Carrothers would accept.'

The board approved the recommendation, and O.D. Vaughan and Bill Harris flew to Calgary to discuss a possible contract. Carrothers and his wife then visited Toronto. 'It was doubtful,' Bissell recorded at the time, 'whether he would come ... He seemed a little overwhelmed (as well he might be) by the job.' Carrothers decided to negotiate the terms through a lawyer from London, Ontario, who had taught at Western when Carrothers had been dean of law there. Every time the persons negotiating for the board agreed to one of Carrothers' demands, another one was put on the table: an interest-free loan for a place in the country, a generous pension, a high salary, and so on. His lawyer now says that Carrothers in fact did not want the job, but did not want to turn it down; he wanted the board to be the one to break off negotiations. Carrothers was a westerner, a graduate of the University of British Columbia, and probably wanted to be president there. The executive committee, however, approved the terms and recommended the appointment to the board.

At the board meeting of June 24, 1971, a motion to accept the recommendation to appoint Carrothers was put by Sydney Hermant, who had been a member of the search committee, but Henry Borden, at his last meeting as a board member, moved an amendment rejecting Carrothers as president. He did not like the terms that had been negotiated – 'these conditions shocked me, truly shocked me,' he said years later in an oral interview – and particularly did not like the fact that Carrothers was negotiating through a lawyer. Borden had been a strong supporter of Evans. Himself a Rhodes scholar, Borden had written to the Rhodes selection committee to support Evans for the scholarship. The board agreed with Borden – it was 'just about unanimous,' he later recalled – and the offer was rescinded. Jack Sword stated shortly afterwards that Carrothers had told him that 'if the Board turned down his conditions, he would "drink to it."' The matter then went back to the search committee, which easily selected Evans, and the board unanimously approved offering him the job. Harris, now chairman of the board, drove to Hamilton to offer his friend Evans the position. Evans accepted. He would take up the position on July 1, 1972.

The appointment of the 42-year-old Evans was announced publicly towards the end of November 1971. 'I don't envy him the job he is taking on,' the acting vice-president and provost Don Forster wrote to a friend. 'Financial prospects for the next few years are quite bleak and morale at the University is going to be very low.' Moreover, Evans was 'almost an outsider,' to use Evans' own words. He knew the medical school well, but not the rest of the University. 'I didn't know the power structure,' he later said, 'the kind of constraints and forces' within the University. Still, the University had been a significant part of his life. He had been a student at the University of Toronto Schools before entering the U of T medical school, both his parents had graduated from U of T – his father had been president of the Victoria College alumni association, and his mother vice-president of the UC alumnae – and all six of his brothers and sisters had attended the University of Toronto.

His experience at McMaster had given him greater respect for the quality of some of the programs at other Ontario universities than was often accorded by Toronto administrators. Even before he took office, he went with Forster and the graduate school dean, Ed Safarian, to a number of other Ontario universities to make Toronto more aware of what was taking place throughout the system and

Acting President Jack Sword congratulates John Evans on the announcement of
Evans' presidency on November 23, 1971.

of how Toronto was regarded by other universities. Shortly after the visits,
Forster noted their 'more than grudging admiration for the quality of some of
our programmes,' but also their 'fear of our size and influence [and] doubt about
the recent quality of our "management" and direction.'

The installation took place at the end of September 1972 on the front campus –
the first time such an event had taken place out of doors. It was also the first time
the proceedings were presided over by a woman – Chancellor Pauline McGibbon,
a Victoria College graduate of 1933, who would later become lieutenant governor of Ontario. Between six and seven thousand people attended the ceremony,
under a clear sky. To no one's surprise, there were minor disruptions and a large
number of placards – in favour of 'free day care' and 'access to library stacks,' and
against 'racism' and 'repression of women.' At one point, graduate student Tony
Leah, who later would be involved in the Banfield matter, sprinted past the

guards and onto the platform and handed Evans a subpoena to appear at a trial the following week in connection with the day-care controversy.

Evans' speech carefully laid out the agenda he was to follow over the next six years. Directing his remarks to Premier Bill Davis, he asked for greater resources from the province and pleaded that these funds not be obtained by raising tuition fees. 'The combination of higher tuition fees and more limited bursary assistance,' Evans observed, 'will act as a serious deterrent to individuals from lower income groups, from large families, and from those families who have come recently to Ontario and who are least certain about the future.' Another theme was a restructuring of the role of the colleges. 'It seems to me highly desirable,' he stated, 'for the colleges to attempt to establish a distinctive educational flavour, and I recognize that this may be impossible to accomplish within the framework of the traditional college subjects.'

Still another concern was part-time students. Such students, he said, 'are in special need of linkages and interactions because of the shorter time they can spend on campus. We might well explore whether the college system can help to provide such linkages, either through a part-time students' college, or some part-time membership in existing colleges, or both.' Evans also anticipated that greater planning would be needed within the University. 'Planning,' he noted, 'that is, the definition of objectives, assignment of priorities, and devising of mechanisms for implementation, will be a major preoccupation for the next few years.' The new governing structure, he thought, would assist in implementing change. 'This gives us for the first time,' he noted, 'a body representative of all interests ... where spokesmen for different groups must, and do, listen to other voices and not just themselves – where there is a genuine attempt to reach conclusions through rational argument, not by political compromise.'

⁂

Little had been done to develop the structure of the governing council before Evans was appointed. The new president, it was felt, should help shape its development. Only the composition of the governing council and of the executive committee was spelled out in the legislation. In early 1972, before taking office, Evans had a series of meetings at the York Club with the board chairman, Harris, the vice-chairman, Harding, Acting President Sword, Provost Donald Forster, and the secretary of the board, David Claringbold. Harding would soon

John Evans and Malim Harding, chair of the governing council, at a council meeting
in April 1975.

become the first chair of the governing council, and Harris its vice-chair.
Elections were held in the spring for the various governing council positions.

Evans was also actively involved in recommending to the government possible appointments to the governing council. He was eager to have it more
representative of the wider community, and put forward suggestions, adopted by
the government, for representation, for example, from labour and the Italian
community. The new council first met on July 4, 1972. It had to develop rules of
procedure. The new act, Evans later stated, had 'erected a parliament without a
tradition, without a speaker, without rules.' It was sometimes an unruly, contentious body. 'If it lasts 50 years,' Evans predicted, 'it will have its rules and its
traditions and it will be more manageable.'

A decision was taken to create a number of executive positions and then to
match them with standing committees of the governing council. There would be
five vice-presidents and therefore five such committees. A vice-president of
internal affairs and an internal affairs committee were necessary because of the
continuing disruptions within the University and the desirability of paying close

The first group of alumni members of the governing council, 1972: from left to right, standing,
Graham Cotter, Ian Tate, James Joyce, William Broadhurst, Keith Hendrick,
and Walter MacNeill; seated, Patti Fleury and Gesta Abols.

attention to the needs of the student body. Historian Jill Conway, who had been involved in the day-care issue, was selected as the first vice-president of internal affairs. She was the first woman vice-president in the history of the University. 'John Evans was in the process of building his new administrative team,' she recalled in her memoirs, 'and, to my astonishment, he wanted my advice about it.' They discussed who would be a good appointment for the new internal affairs position. 'When, at our next meeting,' she stated, 'John Evans told me he thought I would be the best person for the job, I was utterly dumbfounded.' Three years later, Conway became president of Smith College, and Frank Iacobucci, the associate dean of law, took her place as vice-president. The chair of the governing council's internal affairs committee was engineering student Paul Cadario, who would be replaced the following year by Marnie Paikin from Hamilton, later to be chair of the governing council. Evans had become aware of her when he was at McMaster as a result of her dedicated and impressive community work.

There was also to be an external affairs vice-president and a matching governing council standing committee, but several years' experience suggested that the work of this committee would be more effective if merged with that of other committees, and it was dropped. Alex Rankin continued as vice-president of business affairs, and the publisher Gordon Fisher became the first chair of the business affairs committee. A new portfolio on planning and resources was created with Jack Sword and then George Connell as vice-president, and the businessman W.O. Twaits as chair of its standing committee.

The fifth committee was the academic affairs committee, chaired by classicist Ron Shepherd, with Don Forster as the vice-president and provost. This committee would turn out to be the most controversial. It had replaced the senate, which had been dominated by faculty members, but the faculty had very little numerical power on the academic affairs committee. Their relative weakness was owing to a combination of two rules that limited the number of faculty members who could be on any committee. One was the legislative requirement that there be a majority of governing council members on any committee that had authority to act for the council. The other was a rule brought in by the governing council itself that no estate could constitute a majority on any standing committee. This latter rule had been passed by the governing council by a single vote. The faculty was strongly opposed to the rule, which was just as vigorously supported by the student members of council. The result was that the number of faculty members taking part in the deliberations of the academic affairs committee was relatively small compared with their number on the earlier senate. There were only 12 faculty members, including academic administrators, on the 25-member academic affairs committee.

Academic administrators were also concerned about their role on the academic affairs committee. Whereas most had been members of the senate, they now had no official standing on the governing council or its committees. They could run for faculty positions on the council, and the president could appoint two persons to the council, but, in the eyes of the administrators, that was not enough. Principals, deans, and directors – the persons who knew most about the issues being discussed – were thus effectively left out of the decision-making process. A substitute body – weekly meetings of principals, deans, and directors – was established by the provost to ensure that their views could be heard, and that they could be kept informed of what was being contemplated by Simcoe Hall and the governing council and its committees. The president would participate in the discussions, though the meetings were chaired by the provost.

The last meeting of the President's Council, with its large component of faculty members, held in the governing council room in Simcoe Hall on May 24, 1972. Front row, from left to right: Malim Harding, Alex Rankin, Dorothy Robertson, Donald Forster, J.H. Sword, Robert Spencer, and Bernard Etkin; standing, from left to right: A.E. Safarian, Kurt Loeb, Harry Eastman, Robin Ross, J.B. Dunlop, A.L. Chute, J.D. Hamilton, and W.B. Harris.

The effect was to give administrators influence through the president and thus strengthen the power of Simcoe Hall. The perceived inadequacy of their representation on the academic affairs committee was a continuing source of concern to the faculty.

Fights over parity went on throughout the decade. The University of Toronto Act required that a review take place within two years after the coming into force of the legislation. A committee, once again chaired by Archie Hallett, began its review in late 1973 and reopened the question of the composition of the governing council. It brought forward a proposal to the council that the government be asked, among other matters, to change the composition of the governing council by increasing the number of students to 12, the same as for the faculty. The governing council rejected the proposal, but passed a resolution recommending narrowing the gap between the number of students and of faculty. The governing council debate on this issue, wrote Robin Ross, 'was one of the low points reached by the Council.' 'It was,' Don Forster wrote at the time, 'political horse-trading of the worst sort, the ultimate politicization of the university governing process ... The faculty are terribly unhappy and, if the government adopts the proposal, the drift to faculty trade unionism will only accelerate.' Bill Nelson, the president of the faculty association, urged the minister of colleges and universities, James Auld, to postpone action or widen the legislative review. In the latter case, Nelson stated, 'not only should there be very full discussion of the whole question of a unicameral governing structure within this University, but expert outside views should be solicited as well.' The governing council resolution was not acted upon by the government.

It was now the faculty's turn to put pressure on the governing council. In 1975, the faculty association wrote to the governing council chair Malim Harding, proposing that 'a majority of members on the Planning and Resources committee and no less than two thirds of the members of the Academic Affairs Committee should be drawn from the academic staff of the university.' The governing council examined the issue, but made no major changes. Agitation by the faculty continued, and in 1977 Evans proposed a five-year review. John B. Macdonald, a former president of the University of British Columbia and the executive director of the Council of Ontario Universities, completed his one-person report on 'the effectiveness of the Governing Council system' at the end of 1977. He concluded that the governing council was being too activist and was involving itself in details that were not of major significance to the University. The governing council should react to proposals by the administration and generally not initiate action. He also concluded that more delegation to the divisions was required. As to numbers, he thought it best that the University not engage in another debate on the composition of the governing council. 'Reopening the question of numbers,' he wrote, 'would plunge the University once again into a fruitless and damaging conflict.' The council accepted these views.

The shortage of faculty input in the process, Macdonald thought, could be handled by substantially increasing the number of faculty members in a much-enlarged new committee that would combine the academic affairs committee and the planning and resources committee. The proposed changes, which gave the faculty 33 seats out of 61 on the new committee, would therefore require abandoning the rule that no one estate could constitute a majority. Neither the council nor Simcoe Hall was willing to adopt the proposal. The council, however, did increase the size of the academic affairs committee so as to allow more faculty participation, and also permitted 7 principals and deans to be members of the committee, but without a vote. Major changes in the structure of the academic affairs committee would not come for another ten years.

Throughout the 1970s, the central administration became increasingly more powerful. Once every week, the vice-presidents and vice-provosts met with Evans in what became known as 'Simcoe Circle.' Bissell usually had met individually, not collectively, with his senior officials. 'Everyone looked forward to these weekly meetings,' wrote Jill Conway. 'The issues were endlessly fascinating, and the information absorbed invaluable, but the most enjoyable part was to listen to the President sum up, and provide the prescription for action, on the issue of the moment.' The senior officials in Simcoe Hall were the persons with whom Evans felt most comfortable. He had handpicked them. A great number of changes were initiated by the Evans administration. 'It is ironic,' observed Don Forster, 'that, while Evans' philosophical bias is towards a more consultative style of decision-making and greater decentralization of authority and responsibility, the kinds of demands he is putting on the system are inevitably concentrating power in few hands and those hands are in Simcoe Hall.'

Evans generally did not have the same relationship with the academic administrators that Bissell had had. Because of the relatively new Haist rules, named for the chair of the committee that developed them, the physiologist Reginald Haist, the appointment of divisional heads and chairs was no longer a presidential prerogative, subject to approval by the board. Deans and chairs were now recommended for limited-term appointments by committees with strong representation from their colleagues and would normally rejoin them as regular faculty members after completing their term. Considerable influence could be exerted by the president in the composition of the committees, and with respect to the selection of deans the committee recommendations could be rejected, but this was not likely to happen in many cases. Academic administrators, Evans stressed, generally did not, therefore, have the same loyalty to the president as administrators had had in the past. The Haist rules, Evans stated, 'seriously weakened the line between the president and the deans and the deans and their chairs in the system.' The Haist rules, he argued, have 'been seriously underplayed as the most important factor in changing the university.' One result has been that presidents have learned to use whatever techniques they could under the Haist rules to ensure that future deans would share the presidents' own plans and aspirations.

This then was the governing structure Evans faced as he tried to institute changes and cope with financial constraints and a growing sense of alienation among the faculty.

chapter thirty-eight

1975

⟨⟩

SLIDING DOWN PARNASSUS

In 1975, the salary and benefits committee of the University of Toronto Faculty Association (UTFA) demanded that salaries be increased by 25 per cent. Inflation had reduced the value of salaries, and the faculty was becoming more militant. They had seen the gains made by student activism in the 1960s. Moreover, most members of the faculty felt they had been effectively and unfairly cut out of their previous dominant role in the governance of the academic affairs of the University. UTFA, stated Bill Nelson in his history of the association, 'became the only major repository of faculty influence and very nearly the only voice of the faculty.' A growing group wanted the faculty to be certified as a bargaining unit under the Labour Relations Act, as was then happening at a number of other Canadian universities. Nelson, the president of the association between 1973 and 1976, seized every opportunity to build support for UTFA. The handling of the Banfield affair, Nelson wrote, 'enabled UTFA to hammer Simcoe Hall on an issue where we had whole-hearted faculty support. We were able to drive a wedge between many conservative faculty members and the administration they had habitually trusted.'

The administration was not able to meet UTFA's demand for a major salary increase, and offered 9 per cent instead. The government money that had been available during Bissell's tenure was no longer there. Ontario's yearly grant to its universities was not even keeping up with inflation. Federal transfer payments to the provinces, begun following the Massey Commission, no longer had to be used specifically for education. The Ontario government for some years had wanted to control university expenditures, which had grown between 1965 and 1969 from 1 per cent to about 10 per cent of the government's budget. 'We have reached the end of the line,' stated William Davis, the minister of education, in 1969, 'we cannot afford to increase to any significant degree the amounts being directed to universities in future years.' The Canadian public thought the cost of university education was too high, and a later minister of education, John White, wanted – to use his memorable phrase – 'more scholar for the dollar.' President Evans had received the message clearly in his first six months in office when the government imposed a province-wide freeze on all new capital expenditures, including the renovation of old buildings. 'The plain truth of the matter,' wrote Provost Donald Forster at the time, 'is that the government's reading of public opinion suggests a further squeezing of the universities which so far have been utterly hopeless in their attempts to influence that public opinion.'

Ontario was becoming less generous than other provinces. By the mid-1970s, the province ranked near the bottom in expenditures per student, and the University of Toronto ranked last among Ontario universities. Toronto suffered under formula financing because it had deliberately chosen not to expand enrolment in the 1970s as other universities had, and so received less from a fixed pot of money. Moreover, in the area in which Toronto had a clear advantage, graduate studies, the amount granted to the University for each student was cut, and new growth was frozen. Graduate studies were no longer a priority for the government. The hiring of academics across the country was decreasing, so there was less need for the training of new professors. Evans summed up the situation in a speech in late 1974 entitled 'Sliding down Parnassus,' in which he used medical terms: 'An operating squeeze put us on a reducing diet for 1971 and 1972; by 1973–74 the patient's ribs could be counted, and 1974–75 has brought on real malnutrition.' Administrative staff were being cut, and in many cases faculty members who had retired or resigned were not being replaced.

The faculty was teaching 20 per cent more students with the same complement of staff as at the beginning of the decade. 'For five successive years,' Robert Greene, the dean of arts and science, complained to the minister of colleges and universities in early 1977, 'the base budget of this Faculty has been reduced.' Jill Conway was discouraged because 'the job which had seemed such a chance to build a promising future had to be redefined with this sea change in the external environment.' 'The daily routine of meetings,' she wrote, 'was now filled with anguished discussions with heads of services about how to cut back staff, hours, facilities.' 'It's not a pleasant job to do nothing but cut back,' Don Forster wrote to a friend in late 1973. It is not surprising, therefore, that Forster found the decision to leave U of T to become president of Guelph 'surprisingly easy.' In spite of cutting costs, the University was incurring a deficit. The administrators at Simcoe Hall even explored the question of whether universities could declare bankruptcy. Evans thought the government would not allow that to happen, but did publicly speculate that if there were 'unmanageable deficits or serious internal disruption from labour unrest, a take-over and direct control by the Government is a possibility.'

The University of Toronto, along with other Canadian universities, was also suffering from a reduction in research funding from the federal granting agencies. Fortunately, the University had research funds available from the sale of the Connaught Laboratories to the Canada Development Corporation in the early 1970s. An offer to purchase Connaught had come without apparent warning in early 1972. The timing was good because the board of governors had been concerned about the future of Connaught, which required large amounts of capital to finance new products and exports. It agreed to sell Connaught for about $25 million, but on condition that insulin and other products the laboratories were then producing would continue to be available to the public at reasonable prices, that Connaught continue funding research at the University at the same level, and that the laboratories remain in Canadian hands. (This last condition turned out to be important in 1989, when the Canada Development Corporation wanted to sell Connaught to a French company, Institut Mérieux. In exchange for not insisting on the condition against the sale to a foreign company, President George Connell was able to negotiate substantial research support for the University for the next ten years.)

In the mid-1970s, this endowed fund was yielding about $2 million a year. The fund was – and still is – the largest pool of capital available for research that the University has ever achieved. It played and continues to play an important role in promoting research within the University. Modest grants for expenses are now given freely to junior faculty members, to help them establish research programs; to established scholars, to free up their time and so enable them to devote themselves to major projects; and to scholars, to assist them in starting innovative programs, particularly of an interdisciplinary nature. In the mid-

1970s, for example, the law and economics project in the faculty of law, headed by Michael Trebilcock, with the assistance of the then junior professor Robert Prichard, was initiated with a Connaught development grant. Another successful early project assisted by the Connaught fund was laser research by chemist John Polanyi and physicist Boris Stoicheff.

To ease the financial crisis, a $25 million fund-raising campaign – the 'Update' campaign – was undertaken in 1976. 'One of my great problems,' Evans later said, 'was stimulating the governing council to do a campaign ... There really weren't any people on the governing council of the old type who could go out and crack a campaign' – he was no doubt thinking of powerful figures like Wallace McCutcheon and Henry Borden. The council chairman, Malim Harding, a respected businessman, was not optimistic about the campaign's success. Colleagues on several boards of which Harding was a member had reacted negatively to the idea of a campaign, and other Canadian universities were having difficulty meeting their campaign objectives. St Clair Balfour, the chairman of the board of Southam Press, and W.O. Twaits, a former member of the governing council and the chairman of Imperial Oil, agreed to serve as co-chairmen, with Murray Koffler of Shoppers Drug Mart as vice-chairman.

The campaign was launched in the fall of 1976 by the comedians and U of T alumni Johnny Wayne and Frank Shuster. By the end of John Evans' tenure as president in June 1978, the University had received pledges of $21 million, including $1 million from Koffler for what became the Koffler Student Centre. Most of the campaign funds were to be used for renovations, including the comprehensive restoration of University College. Other funds went towards a new athletic centre and earth sciences building. Over the first three years of James Ham's presidency, another $16 million was raised in the Update campaign, making a total of about $36 million. In the anti-university climate of the times, the campaign was considered a success. But it did not solve the University's problems with its operating budget.

❦

Not only did the faculty association want larger salary increases, it also wanted to be able to negotiate with the administration over salaries and benefits. Simcoe Hall was willing to enter into discussions, but not into what UTFA sought – negotiations. Some, including the association president, Bill Nelson, thought

The Koffler Student Services Centre, formerly the Toronto Reference Library, opened in 1985 at College and St George streets.

that collective bargaining through certification under the Ontario Labour Relations Act was the best way to bring about this result. It was uncertain, however, whether the faculty would support the creation of a union. An UTFA survey in 1976 showed that the faculty supported 'a more formal process of collective bargaining' by a two-to-one majority, but opposed immediate certification by a similar majority. There was widespread support, however, for a voluntary agreement outside the Labour Relations Act. In 1976, political scientist Jean Smith became chair of the association's salary and benefits committee and relentlessly sought a voluntary agreement with the University. Smith – described by Nelson as 'a native Mississippian, soft-spoken and confidential in manner, but hard-edged underneath' – assembled a formidable team of twenty faculty members. They included Adrian Brook, the chair of chemistry, the former UFTA presidents Jim Conacher and Mike Uzumeri, sociologist Lorna Marsden, then vice-president of UTFA, and librarian Carole Moore.

The UTFA committee worked over the summer and produced a draft agreement, which was supported in a referendum by 70 per cent of the faculty members who voted. The draft dealt with a wide range of matters of interest to the faculty, such as a formal binding grievance procedure, leave policy, access to

Historian Bill Nelson, president of the University of Toronto Faculty Association, 1973–6. Photograph taken in 1971.

Political scientist Jean Smith became chair of UTFA's salary and benefits committee in 1976, and was later the president of the association. Photograph taken in 1981.

personnel files, and maternity leave benefits, and set out a formal system of salary negotiations including resolution, if necessary, by binding arbitration. It also incorporated the Haist rules on appointments and tenure, which had recently been revised by a committee chaired by Provost Forster to tighten up procedures and provide an appeal process.

In 1967, the board of governors had accepted the Haist committee's recommendations on tenure. For the first time, tenure was formally recognized by the University. It was defined as 'a continuing full-time appointment which the University has relinquished the freedom to terminate before the normal age of retirement except for cause,' and after following certain procedures. Tenure was to be recommended by faculty-dominated committees. Throughout the 1970s, many members of the faculty were worried about the possibility that tenure, so recently recognized, would be abolished or, more likely, be interpreted to permit the wholesale removal of faculty members for fiscal reasons. The Forster committee revising the Haist rules had included in them the possibility of reducing the faculty on economic grounds, but had made the hurdles so onerous that such reduction was unlikely ever to happen. So far, it never has.

The governing council authorized the administration to negotiate with Jean

Smith and members of his team. Simcoe Hall's group was chaired by environmentalist Donald Chant, the vice-president and provost who had replaced Don Forster, and included law professor Frank Iacobucci, who had succeeded Jill Conway as vice-president of internal affairs. Twenty-one meetings were held during the winter months between the UTFA negotiating committee and the Simcoe Hall team. In March 1977, the administration team produced an alternative draft that left many of the disputed matters in the hands of the governing council. With the support of the UTFA council, Smith broke off negotiations, and in another faculty referendum UTFA received an endorsement of its position by 87 per cent of the faculty members who voted. 'We feel that the Governing Council has been insincere in stringing us along,' commented Smith in the *Bulletin*. Marnie Paikin, the chair of the governing council, noted that the governing council 'is charged with the responsibility of overseeing the affairs of the University, setting its policies, goals, and priorities ... The proposals of the Faculty Association ... ask the Governing council voluntarily to surrender significant parts of this responsibility in favour of collective bargaining.'

Many administrators, however, were worried that failure to achieve an agreement would lead to certification. In subsequent negotiations, a memorandum of agreement was reached, and subsequently it was approved by UTFA and the governing council. It changed existing policy in a number of areas. It did not, however, accept UTFA's position on binding arbitration. That would have to wait for another day. Any salary award therefore could still be rejected by the governing council. Evans had been strongly opposed to binding arbitration. 'As long as the University accepts a responsibility for its financial affairs,' he had written to Chant and Iacobucci, 'it cannot delegate something of as far-reaching significance as salary settlements to someone who comes in for a short period of time to look at only one element of the total University picture.'

The agreement contained a list of policies, such as those relating to conflicts of interest and tenure procedures, that had not been changed. These came to be known as 'frozen policies' – policies that could now be amended only with the consent of the faculty association. The agreement, of course, limited the ability of the governing council to change them unilaterally. It did, however, block the movement towards certification. Either party after three years of operation could reject the agreement, but that has not happened. When the initial period was about to expire, Chant advised President Ham not to reject it because, in his view, 'the contract has served the interests of the University well, and it has been

Provost Frank Iacobucci addressing a hearing of the Bovey commission on the Ontario university system in the fall of 1984.

workable.' Rejection, Simcoe Hall knew, would probably lead to certification under the Labour Relations Act. The agreement still operates today.

Financial constraint helped bring about what Evans described as 'by far the most important single change' during his administration, that is, a major readjustment in the relationship between the University and the federated colleges. All three federated colleges – St Michael's, Trinity, and Victoria – were going into debt. The tuition fees they collected went only so far in meeting their expenses, and, because they were church-related institutions, the Ontario government gave them only partial formula funding. St Michael's had a further problem: it was no longer able to count on a continuing stream of low-cost priests and religious sisters to make up a large proportion of its faculty. In the early 1950s, the only non-religious lay members of the St Michael's faculty had been Marshall McLuhan and philosopher Larry Lynch.

Of at least equal importance to all the colleges and the University was the declining role of the colleges in the academic life of arts and science students. Most students now had little, if any, connection with their colleges. When Victoria College federated with the University of Toronto in 1889, it will be remembered, various subjects were assigned to the colleges and the rest to the University. The college subjects, all in the humanities, were becoming less popular among students than the sciences and the social sciences. This state of affairs had been a matter of concern for many years. Harold Innis, for example, had suggested to President Cody in the 1940s that the social sciences be transferred to University College. Innis' field, political economy, had not been given to the colleges at the time of federation because no one then was teaching the subject at the University of Toronto. Other courses, such as modern history, were given to the University because particular individuals – President Daniel Wilson in the case of history and George Paxton Young in the case of philosophy – wanted to be university professors. The breakdown did not make much sense then and made even less sense as the years went by.

Many people in the University were concerned about the students' lack of close identification with any one institution and their consequent feeling of anonymity. (This was less of a problem for Scarborough and Erindale, where students could more easily feel themselves part of their colleges.) The federated colleges had required their students to take a course in religious knowledge, which brought the students into some contact with the college, but the experience was not always a happy one, and the 'RK' requirement was discontinued in the early 1970s. Students in the old honours programs had been able to get to know their professors and fellow students, but the honours system had been eliminated in 1969, following the Macpherson report. The Macpherson committee had recognized the college problem, however, and had urged strongly that the colleges be given a greater academic role – in this they echoed a report from the late 1950s chaired by University College principal Moffat Woodside.

In 1974, the colleges on the St George campus and the University worked out a memorandum of understanding that dramatically altered the relationship between the University and the colleges. College subjects would all become university departments, paid for by the University. Staff for the new departments would no longer be hired by the colleges. In exchange, the colleges would be able to develop courses and programs that they themselves would teach. One of the stated objectives was 'to make it possible for most students in the Faculty of Arts and Science to spend the larger part of at least their early years, and as far as

The second memorandum of agreement with the colleges, signed in the summer of 1984.
From left to right, Goldwin French (Victoria), James McConica (St Michael's),
William Dunphy (St Michael's), St Clair Balfour (chair of the governing council),
President David Strangway, John Cole (Trinity), H.J. Sissons (Victoria),
and Kenneth Hare (Trinity).

possible of all their years, in courses and programmes taught in the College in which they have registered.'

In theory, it was an excellent scheme, but in the early period it failed to work well because the University's finances did not permit the hiring of new staff to develop the college programs. At the same time, many of the older faculty members in the colleges, who had been teaching the old college subjects, felt their colleges were losing their identity, so problems of morale were created. Moreover, money was not available to refurbish facilities outside the colleges to allow the faculty members of the new departments then housed in the colleges to have offices together in one location. As a result, space was not readily available within the colleges for the offices of cross-appointed faculty members. Space problems created a measure of disappointment and anxiety in the colleges. The classicists, for example, were eventually shunted off to the temporary structure beside University College. Furthermore, the newly created university departments were unhappy that they were not able to replace people who had left or retired. Arthur Kruger, the dean of arts and science, met with one of the disgruntled departments – the French department – and pointed out that

Toronto still had the largest French, English, and classics faculties in North America. Indeed, the three departments were probably the largest in the world.

Archie Hallett, the principal of University College, was particularly concerned about the pace of change. He had, recalled the university vice-provost who had helped negotiate the memorandum, Milton Israel, 'a grand vision for the revival of UC' and 'saw himself bringing back some past golden age when UC was *the* college.' The golden age did not arrive. Hallett called the memorandum the 'memorandum of misunderstanding,' and his frustration contributed to his decision to leave U of T for a position in Bermuda, where he had grown up.

Nevertheless, all the colleges started developing new programs, pulling together faculty from various departments in arts and science. Many of those programs continue to this day, such as the drama program in University College, literary studies at Victoria, the program in international relations at Trinity, Christianity and culture studies at St Michael's, women's studies at New College, cinema studies at Innis, and criminology at Woodsworth. Over the years, numerous programs have been added in new fields, including peace and conflict studies at University College, semiotics and communication theory at Victoria, and immunology at Trinity, to mention only a few examples. In addition, the colleges began to increase their offering of sections of the large university courses. These courses and programs are open to all students in arts and science, not just those in the college in which they are given.

Overall, however, the colleges still were not teaching a significant proportion of their registered students. Trinity College provost George Ignatieff pointed out in 1977 that fewer than 20 per cent of Trinity students were being taught in the college. Continuing dissatisfaction gave rise to further reviews, which eventually brought another memorandum in 1984 – a memorandum of 'agreement,' not just of understanding. The new memorandum gave the colleges a more pronounced role in academic work. They were to be brought into a closer relationship with the faculty of arts and science and were to have a potentially greater complement of faculty positions. In consultation with the appropriate departments, they could now make their own academic appointments at their own expense. Pia Kleber and Thomas Homer-Dixon, to give two examples from one college, were appointed by University College to the drama and the peace and conflict studies programs, respectively, and other appointments were made at other colleges.

The role of the colleges has continued to evolve. Another agreement, essentially similar to the 1984 document, was signed in 1990, and still another in 1998, the latter designed to last for at least ten years. The latest agreement has given the colleges an even stronger academic role. Procedures have been developed for the creation of new programs by the colleges not just with the faculty of arts and science but with other faculties and schools in the University. The agreement promises 'equitable compensation' for college programs, which in turn will be subject to periodic external review. As a result, the colleges are looking at new possibilities. Paul Perron, the principal of University College – to cite one example – is working on a program in health studies that will draw on faculty from a wide variety of disciplines, including community health, sociology, political science, and physical and health education. Furthermore, whole departments have now taken up quarters in colleges. The department of Spanish and Portuguese, for example, is now housed in Victoria College, and the departments of French, Italian, and Slavic studies in St Michael's.

Another important change made in the arts and science curriculum in the early 1980s was to give more structure to the students' choice of subjects. Other universities, such as Harvard and the University of California, Berkeley, had recently brought in a more structured curriculum. The freedom given to students to choose the courses they wanted as a result of the Macpherson report had meant that some chose a 'cafeteria-style' program, that is, a little bit of everything, the result often being a lack of 'any strong identification with other groups of students, with departments, or even with colleges.' Meanwhile, other students had concentrated too much on their area of specialization. A report by a committee chaired by Father John Kelly, the president of St Michael's College – adopted by the governing council after vigorous debate – tried to prevent both extremes. Arts and science students, whether in a three- or a four-year course, now had to have a greater degree of concentration, but also had to have breadth in other fields. The report had been opposed by Dean Arthur Kruger, who wanted even more structure, and by the students, who wanted less. 'In our opinion,' wrote the president of the Arts and Science Student Union, Tamara Baggs, 'students are, by and large, mature individuals capable of choosing their own curriculum programme.'

⚜

The 1970s also saw the creation of a new college – Woodsworth College – primarily for part-time students who were taking courses for academic credit.

Until Woodsworth was established in 1974, such students had been under the umbrella of the division of extension, which had operated successfully since President Falconer's day. Over the years, the extension division had offered courses at the University and in other locations throughout the province to teachers, factory workers, farmers, and bankers as well as to the general public.

The University has always taken its outreach activities seriously. It had, for example, presented a series of forty radio talks in 1932 over station CFRB, introduced by President Falconer. In the 1950s, the University developed several television series for the general public. Even before the first television stations were opened in Canada, the extension department had offered a course in television script-writing. At the time, a number of American universities owned public television stations, but the University of Toronto decided that such a step was unnecessary because of the existence of the CBC. The first series of ten half-hour TV programs, entitled *The Varsity Story*, was broadcast in 1953, using some of the University's best-known personalities. The psychologist William Blatz, for example, talked about the Institute of Child Study, the physicist John Satterly gave demonstrations involving liquid air, and the physiologist Charles Best discussed some of the work taking place at the Banting Institute. The next year Marshall McLuhan talked about his communication theories – probably his first active involvement with the new medium – and the anthropologist Ted Carpenter discussed circumcision rites in Africa. Apparently no member of the University's television committee had a TV set, so the committee asked Simcoe Hall to borrow one so that they could view the live productions. Other series followed, including a twelve-part one given by Carl Williams in the late 1950s on the psychology of learning, and another the following year by members of the physics department, planned by Patterson Hume and Donald Ivey. The University's interest, however, then turned to the use of television for teaching purposes within the University, which, as we saw earlier in the discussion of Scarborough College, proved unsuccessful.

During the 1960s, the number of part-time arts and science students kept growing, and they became increasingly unhappy with their treatment. They complained that they were regarded as second class, were not offered a full range of courses, and often had poor teachers. Students in the 1960s wanted more control over the selection of courses and the pace at which they completed their degrees. In 1968, the part-time student Norma Grindal and others formed the Association of Part-time Undergraduate Students (APUS), which became a

Physicists Donald Ivey and Patterson Hume on a 1958 CBC television series, 'Live and Learn.'

determined and effective lobby for change. A 1970 report by a committee chaired by John Colman of Scarborough College, which included the then APUS president, Joyce Denyer, recommended that part-time degree students be formally integrated into the arts and science colleges and that a seventh college be established, primarily for part-time students.

A more controversial recommendation by the committee was that the University discontinue its non-credit courses and close the extension division. Such courses, in the committee's view, should be 'organized by the communities that want them, for only then can the recipients of this type of education ensure that their needs are met.' The University, however, decided to keep the extension division and transfer the degree, certificate, and diploma courses to a new college, known colloquially as 'College X.' Evans did not want the University to give up the outreach aspects of the extension division: 'We are deeply conscious of our duty to serve many groups besides the regularly enrolled degree students – elderly people, for instance, and ethnic minorities newly arrived in Canada.' The division was maintained. Now called the School of Continuing Studies and located in a four-storey building on the west side of St George Street, it has continued to grow. It now offers more than 450 courses and a number of certification programs each year to about 15,000 persons at the University and at other places, such as the Art Gallery of Ontario and the Oakville public library. The courses range from its most popular, English as a second language, to others on dispute resolution and on the internet. The numbers 'are going way up,' says Mary Cone Barrie, the director of the school. 'Baby boomers in mid-life are letting their inner student out and the economy is demanding continual professional skill upgrading.'

In 1973, the University agreed to establish a new college for part-time students. Economist Arthur Kruger was selected as its first principal. He had taken an interest in the extension program over the years and recognized the problems encountered by persons of modest means or different backgrounds upon coming to University. He himself had worked almost full time during high school in his parents' store in Kensington Market and was the only one of his siblings to go to university. A name had to be chosen for the college and, with Kruger's support, a committee of what until then had been called 'College X' chose 'Woodsworth College.' J.S. Woodsworth, the first leader of the CCF (the predecessor of the NDP) party, 'had a very strong interest in broadening the educational opportunities for those who did not have a chance to obtain their education at the usual stage.'

For several years, Kruger would be the only academic member of the college. There was a deliberate decision not to build up a separate body of academics to teach part-time students, as had occurred at other institutions, such as Atkinson College at York University. The college would therefore be forced to draw into its teaching program academics from other parts of the University. A number of full-time staff, however, were available to counsel its students. Most divisions have had dedicated long-serving staff members, but few other divisions can compare with Woodsworth, where people such as Alex Waugh, Bill Bateman, and June Straker have developed programs and counselled students in the college from its founding. Off-campus sites were developed to make it easier for students to attend classes – Queen's Park, corporate board rooms, the General Motors plant in Oshawa, and Yorkdale shopping centre. Woodsworth also offers summer courses for credit at a number of locations around the world – at present, in Siena, Hong Kong, Jerusalem, and Guadalajara. Another innovation permits those over 65 to take courses for credit without the usual academic credentials.

In recent years, the number of full-time students at Woodsworth College has been increasing – at the same time that part-time enrolment has been decreasing. Many who start as part-time students switch to full-time status. Moreover, many of the students who begin in the college's part-time pre-university program, designed to prepare students who do not have the required academic credentials for university work, become full-time students in Woodsworth. There are now about 1,000 students a year in this program, and more than 10,000 have completed it successfully. Many of these students have been from visible minority communities.

Another similarly valuable program, called the Transitional Year Program, originally located at Innis College and designed to assist students in the transition to university studies, has operated since 1970 for some 50 to 60 full-time students a year. The one-year program had its roots in Toronto's African-Canadian community, and black students in some years have comprised up to half its student body, with First Nations students and single parents as other significant components. In recent years, as many as 80 per cent of the students have been recommended for admission to the faculty of arts and science at the University.

The facilities in Woodsworth College, housed in an old house at 119 St George Street, were inadequate, however, and Principal Peter Silcox initiated planning for additional space. For a number of years, each Woodsworth student donated $20 a year to a building fund, which by 1988 amounted to close to $1 million. The following year, the government announced that almost $5 million would be given for expansion and renovation of the college's facilities, and the new award-winning building, imaginatively combining some old houses on St George Street with the old drill hall, was officially opened in 1992. 'This expansion,' said the principal, Noah Meltz, 'is a tribute to the importance of part-time education.' A site at the south-east corner of Bloor and St George streets is about to be redeveloped as a residence for approximately one-third of the 1,000 or so full-time Woodsworth students. Woodsworth has clearly been a success story. Students who have taken advantage of the various Woodsworth programs range from the noted author Rohinton Mistry (BA, 1982) to Selma Plaut, who started taking courses for a degree in her eighties (hon. BA, 1990 – in

Architect's model of Woodsworth College on St George Street, officially opened in 1992.
The large house on the right and the old drill hall, behind and further to the right, were
incorporated into the new building. The house to the far left contains the media centre,
and the middle house is the Centre for Industrial Relations.

her hundredth year), and to the former police chief David Boothby (certificate
in criminology, 1981).

The creation of Woodsworth College was not particularly difficult. The closing
of two other divisions in the University, however, was. It is always less painful to
create new structures in universities than to close old ones. In 1973, the decision
was made by the governing council to discontinue the faculty of food sciences
and to transfer the members of its faculty to the School of Hygiene. Later the
same year, the School of Hygiene itself was closed down, and most of its staff
transferred to the faculty of medicine. Both the food sciences and the hygiene
division had been in the University since before the First World War. Hygiene
had been started in 1913, and food sciences in 1902 (then called household
science – a name that was not changed until 1962). Closing food sciences turned
out to be more difficult to accomplish than closing hygiene.

Claude Bissell had tried to discontinue food sciences in 1970. The faculty was not attracting very many students – it had a student-faculty ratio of five to one – and required funds to upgrade its laboratories. Many of its programs were duplicated in other parts of the University, and Guelph and other universities in the province offered similar programs. Simcoe Hall, however, did not anticipate the strong feelings of the alumni of the faculty. Eight hundred alumni responded to a questionnaire from their association and packed a mass meeting held in the gymnasium of the faculty's home in the Lillian Massey Building. One hundred and fifty people attended a senate meeting, at which the senate declined to take action to stop further enrolment. 'I began to wonder,' Bissell later wrote, 'whether, under the traditional governing structure, the university could radically change itself … I placed my hope in the single, representative body that was clearly emerging as the goal of structural reform.'

Evans had a strong interest in planning and rationalizing resources, so the food sciences issue was soon on the table of the governing council. The new governing structure did not make the task any easier, however. A series of reports was produced. The alumni kept up the attack, which included a protest by a great-niece of Lillian Massey, the faculty's original benefactor. In the meantime, the faculty had improved its curriculum, and enrolment was increasing. The decision to close it down was becoming more difficult. Nevertheless, in December 1973, the governing council – without dissent – decided not to enrol any more students in the faculty.

Evans, who had produced a report for the Rockefeller Foundation on schools of public health, and John Hamilton, the vice-provost of health sciences, wanted the School of Hygiene to be part of the faculty of medicine, as at the McMaster medical school and all other Canadian universities. With some exceptions, such as the epidemiologist Harding le Riche, there was, wrote Hamilton, 'very little communication between the School as a whole and the Faculty of Medicine.' Having public health in the medical faculty, it was hoped, might influence medicine to give more attention to the wider picture, to look at what is now referred to as 'population health,' rather than concentrating on the clinical treatment of individual patients.

Moreover, there were growing space problems in the School of Hygiene. A 1970 accreditation committee had criticized the deteriorating facilities. Furthermore, as with food sciences, there was considerable duplication of resources with other divisions of the University, including the faculty of medicine. Funding was

The FitzGerald Building on College Street, 1967.

also a concern after the sale of the Connaught Laboratories in 1972. Although Connaught had formally separated from the school in 1956, there was still a close relationship between the two institutions, including an infusion of funds from Connaught. This close relationship decreased, however, with the sale of Connaught, and the Connaught fund derived from its proceeds was now spread widely throughout the University. A more basic concern was the purpose of a school of hygiene. In earlier days, its primary mission was clear: to control and, if possible, eliminate infectious diseases. The School of Hygiene, wrote John Hamilton, has 'lost its principal objectives just as every other School of Public Health in North America has through the conquest of infectious disease.'

A 1974 report to the governing council by a committee chaired by philosopher Charles Hanly, which included John Hamilton and J.C. Laidlaw, the director of medicine's increasingly important Institute of Medical Science, recommended that a new division of community health be created in the faculty of medicine, and that most of the faculty in the School of Hygiene be transferred there. They would be joined in the new division by the faculty of medicine's own department of behavioural science. Others in the School of Hygiene, such as those in nutrition and food sciences and in microbiology, would go to the basic sciences division of medicine. The task force believed that 'the School of Hygiene has become more isolated, especially from the Faculty of Medicine, than it should be, if it is to help medicine and be helped by medicine, in the work of disease prevention and health promotion.' The report was accepted by the governing council. A number of changes were subsequently made. The new division in the faculty of medicine became the division of community health, and the name of the hygiene building was changed to the FitzGerald Building, after the founder of the school, John FitzGerald. Master's degrees, as recommended by the task force, were offered rather than diplomas, and the number of graduate students grew, so that by 1992 there were some 400 graduate students, the largest group in the life sciences division of the graduate school. Research funding increased; by 1992, it was double the annual operating cost of the division.

Many in the division, however, such as the public health specialist John Hastings and his successor as associate dean of the community health division, Eugene Vayda, still wanted an independent school of public health, like those that were regaining strength at Harvard, Yale, Johns Hopkins, and other American universities. The debate has continued over the years. Evans and George Connell, both of whom had been involved in the decision to close down hygiene, later wondered whether the merger really changed the outlook of the faculty of medicine towards a public health or preventive medicine approach, as they had hoped it would. In 1988, at the seventieth anniversary of the founding of the School of Hygiene, Evans half-seriously stated that 'instead of merging the School of Hygiene into the Faculty of Medicine, he should have merged the Faculty of Medicine into the School of Hygiene.'

A further restructuring of community health took place in 1997. The department of behavioural science and the department of preventive medicine and biostatistics were merged to form a new department of public health sciences, with psychologist Harvey Skinner as its first chair. Various programs within the University, such as the centre for health promotion and the occupational and environmental health unit are linked to the new department. Ten new tenure-stream appointments have been given to the department. It appears to have a promising future, particularly because the present dean of medicine, David Naylor, is both a physician and an epidemiologist. It is likely, however, that the University has not heard the last of the question of the proper place of public health in the University of Toronto.

❧

John Evans announced in September 1977 that he would leave office at the end of June 1978. He had decided not to seek another term – he had already extended his term for an extra year. It had not been an easy six years in office, coping with the poor financial picture and the faculty association's demands, dealing with student activism, trying to make the new governing structure work, and negotiating the restructuring of the colleges and several divisions. There was also the need to respond to the call to hire more Canadians, which had been provoked by the hiring of many non-Canadians to fill the numerous new positions created in the 1960s. The University even suffered a serious fire in 1977, when engineering's Sandford Fleming Building was gutted.

In the winter of 1978, the 48-year-old Evans decided to seek the nomination as Liberal candidate in a federal by-election in Rosedale made necessary by the resignation of the finance minister, Donald Macdonald. There was much speculation that Evans might end up as Pierre Trudeau's successor. He had been on the national stage as a member of the Pépin-Robarts National Unity Task Force and at a subsequent conference on confederation organized by the University. The Conservative candidate, however, was the popular former mayor of Toronto, David Crombie – Toronto's 'tiny perfect mayor' – who had won the last two Toronto mayoralty elections with about 85 per cent of the vote. Evans lost. For the next four years he headed the study of population health issues for the World Bank, and subsequently he became chair of the board of a number of major enterprises such as the *Toronto Star* and Alcan Aluminum. He has continued to be called on by the University of Toronto and by various governments and foundations for his expertise in medical and university affairs.

chapter thirty-nine

1980

⸎

FINANCIAL AND OTHER CONCERNS

Financial constraint continued – even intensified – after Evans left office. Federal transfer payments to the provinces were no longer legally required to be devoted to higher education. Ontario continued to rank last in provincial expenditure per student. By 1980, funding per student was 25 per cent below the average of all the provinces. The new president, James Ham, spent much of his five years in office cutting budgets. Drastic reductions were made to the budgets for library staff and acquisitions, for secretarial services, and for other administrative staff, as well as for equipment and supplies. Owing to these cuts, excellent faculty members were leaving the University. Relatively few new tenure-stream appointments were made. Ham estimated that in his five years as president there were in total only about 100 such appointments. The number of faculty positions was being reduced by attrition.

Funding was so poor during this period that a government report chaired by the deputy minister of education, Harry Fisher, recommended that some Ontario universities be closed. That did not happen, however, and all the Ontario universities continued to struggle with inadequate funding. Toronto was particularly hard hit. Not only was it not growing, but it had decided to reduce enrolment, and lower enrolment reduced its formula funding. Ham wanted the University to reduce its enrolment over the next fifteen years by at least one-sixth of its size in 1980, and become, in his words, 'an intellectually leaner and tougher place.' He also wanted the funding formula to be suspended. 'The University is at the edge of decline,' Ham told the governing council in 1979.

The dean of engineering, Bernard Etkin, places a cap on President James Ham's head at Ham's installation in September 1978. Paul Fox, the principal of Erindale, is to the left and behind, and Peter Richardson, the principal of University College, is directly behind.

Ham had been chosen in December 1977 by a fifteen-member search committee, headed by the chair of the governing council, Marnie Paikin. Five persons were interviewed: one external candidate, Arnold Naimark, the dean of medicine at the University of Manitoba and later its president; and four internal candidates, political scientist Stefan Dupré, who had recently been chair of the government's Ontario Council on University Affairs, economist Harry Eastman, the vice-president of research and planning, Chinese studies scholar William Saywell, the then principal of Innis College and later the president of Simon Fraser University, and Ham, the former dean of engineering and the then dean of the graduate school. The appointment of Ham was made by the governing council in early January 1978.

The 57-year-old Ham had been a serious contender from the beginning. He had broad experience throughout the University and was liked and respected. The appointment was well received. Jean Smith, the president of the faculty association, said that Ham 'combines a profound sense of the University community with a deep personal sensitivity,' and Joan Foley, the principal of Scarborough College, who had been on the search committee, referred to the 'incredible degree of respect in which Jim Ham is held by people in all areas of the University – he has their loyalty, trust and affection.' 'Only a person perceived throughout the University to be sensitive and utterly fair,' stated *The Graduate* magazine shortly after his appointment, 'would be acceptable as the hatchet man' for the necessary cuts that were coming.

He was attractive to the professional faculties and also to the humanities. In his installation address in late September 1978, he described the University using the image of concentric circles with humanities in the central ring. 'The humanities,' he stated, 'define the shape of civilization and help the individual find himself in his or her uniqueness.' Ham was often referred to as a 'philosopher-engineer.' As a student, he had taken part in a philosophy club that met in Hart House, and when he graduated in 1943 with top honours from electrical engineering, the *Torontonensis* entry stated that he 'thinks engineers make good philosophers.'

Ham's personal style was almost completely different from that of Evans. Evans gave 'incisive solutions'; Ham asked 'incisive questions.' Furthermore, observed *The Graduate*, 'he often spends a long time agonizing over decisions,' at times 'losing his listeners in a convoluted maze of abstractions.' Sometimes his speculations, such as those engaged in during a public musing about the closing of Scarborough and Erindale colleges, would get him into trouble. The then vice-principal of Erindale, the historian Desmond Morton, who would later become its principal, demanded a public apology. Principal Joan Foley demanded and received an undertaking from Ham that he would write to all students accepted into Scarborough, assuring them that the college 'offers excellent opportunities for undergraduate learning and that the University has a sustained commitment to its staff and students.' The very week of his appointment he was criticized by the *Globe and Mail* for stating in an interview that 'the university is not about vocation.' 'How can universities possibly *avoid* being "about vocation"?' the paper asked editorially. 'How can universities avoid participating in the real world?'

His administrative style also differed from that of Evans. After a year or two, he stopped the weekly meetings of senior Simcoe Hall officials that Evans had instituted and instead met with individual divisions to determine how they would plan for the bleak future facing the University. 'Rather than provide vigorous leadership in attempting, at least, to obtain acceptable funding for the university,' Bill Nelson, the former faculty association president, has written, 'he grimly accepted underfunding, immersed himself in detail, worked to achieve small economies, and tenaciously resisted increased expenditures.' 'I don't see any long-term relenting' on the part of the government, Ham said. Perhaps his fatalistic attitude towards financial hardship resulted from his growing up during the depression in a small Ontario farming community.

The faculty association did not want its members to be left behind in the fight for a proper share of declining resources. It was unhappy with the system of setting salaries under the memorandum of agreement, which permitted the governing council to reject an arbitrator's award. The association president, Michael Finlayson, said that the faculty wanted binding arbitration, not 'binding supplication.' The problem with the existing system, the association claimed, was that it tended to constrain an arbitrator's award. Knowing that the governing council could reject it, the arbitrator would likely produce an award thought to be acceptable to the council. In 1981, an arbitrator took into account the University's ability to pay and more or less accepted the administration's position. The faculty was angry that the award did not even meet the increase in the cost of living and was less than the percentage increase in funding given by the government to the University. In a referendum, the faculty approved the concept of binding arbitration by a majority of over 85 per cent of those voting.

In the spring of 1981, historian Harvey Dyck was elected president of the association, narrowly defeating electrical engineer Adel Sedra in the association's first contested election – by 18 votes out of nearly 1,000 cast. Sedra then joined with Dyck in seeking to force Ham to agree to binding arbitration – a process Ham opposed. But Dyck and the faculty association knew that Ham was even more opposed to the faculty's being certified as a union. Throughout the summer and fall, Dyck worked to create the impression that union certification was likely if the administration rejected binding arbitration. Dyck, who personally did not want certification, sought support for binding arbitration from all quarters. He persuaded the Students' Administrative Council to support the faculty's position and developed allies in the governing council.

The association gave the administration a deadline of December 8, 1981 for negotiating an agreement. If it was not met, a certification drive would be launched. Simcoe Hall took the threat seriously. Shortly before the deadline, Ham agreed to discuss binding arbitration and invited Dyck to meet with him to determine the process for the ensuing discussions. Dyck would not meet in Ham's office, however, and insisted on meeting with him as an equal on neutral territory. Ham suggested they meet in front of Simcoe Hall. They did, and walked around King's College Circle three or four times, discussing how to structure the subsequent negotiations. Ham later said that he found working with the association an 'immense personal strain.' Over the next nine days, Dyck and Sedra met with the vice-president of business affairs, Alex Pathy, and the vice-president of research and planning, David Nowlan, in a downtown hotel. On Monday evening, December 14, the four negotiators signed a two-year agreement, which was approved quickly by the faculty association.

It now had to be approved by the governing council. Here, there was strong opposition to the agreement. The president's position was on the line, however. 'If we fail to support this motion,' said St Clair Balfour, later the chair of the governing council, 'I am convinced that the President will resign.' Others were also convinced that that would be the outcome. The law dean, Frank Iacobucci, told the council that the alternative to binding arbitration 'is a process that none of us wants.' Others, however, stressed the fact that it was the job of the governing council to control salaries. 'Governing Council's central task is basic strategic budgetary decisions,' argued the Woodsworth principal, Peter Silcox, and unless it fulfilled that task it would be a 'useless body.' The vote narrowly upheld the agreement for binding arbitration by 23 votes to 20. Both the chair of the council, lawyer Terrence Wardrop, and the chancellor, George Ignatieff, neither of whom would normally have voted, cast their votes in favour of binding arbitration.

The faculty association now asked for a 30 per cent 'catch-up' increase in the cost of living component of salaries – in addition, there would be what is called a 'progress through the ranks' (PTR) component, based on merit. The administration refused to meet the demand, and binding arbitration under the arbitrator Kevin Burkett was undertaken. His award in June 1982 of an 18 per cent cost of living increase by the end of the following year included part of the 'catch-up' factor the association had asked for.

The University would now have to find an extra $14 million every year for faculty and staff salaries. Ham had pledged that he would not be party to an increase 'that would lead to disparities with salaries of administrative staff.' Budgets had to be cut further, and faculty hirings were frozen. The dismissal of faculty for fiscal reasons was even explored by a seventeen-member committee on institutional strategy under Provost David Strangway. The consequences of the arbitration award, said Ham, were 'traumatic.' He defended his decision to support binding arbitration by stating that 'my academic colleagues, almost to a man, urged me to proceed on the fateful track that led to binding arbitration.' Although one will never know whether the faculty would have voted for certification if the governing council had not accepted binding arbitration, it appears likely to this writer that if it had been rejected, the faculty today would be unionized. Moreover, without the salary increase the University would have continued to lose some of its best faculty members.

Even before the Burkett award was announced, Jim Ham had written to the chair of the governing council, Terrence Wardrop, that he would not let his name stand for a further term as president. He was in the fourth year of his term as president, and a twelve-person search committee had already been established. When a representative of the search committee had asked Ham if he might be interested, Ham – perhaps sensing the mood of the committee – had replied, 'No, not under any circumstances.' Clearly he would have had no regrets about his decision after the subsequent Burkett award.

❧

In spite of the financial difficulties, a number of significant physical changes to the University took place during his tenure. The athletic centre – to be used by both men and women – was opened officially in September 1979, and named after the long-time director of men's athletics, Warren Stevens. It contained excellent facilities – for example, an Olympic-size pool, a 200-metre indoor track, and twelve squash courts. A sod-turning event was avoided because local residents were opposed to what they called 'Fort Jock,' and Vice-president Frank Iacobucci advised the director of athletics, Bud Fraser, that 'a ceremony at this time would be seen by the local residents' associations as "rubbing salt in the wounds" and might even spark demonstrations.'

The reconstructed Sandford Fleming engineering building, which had been gutted by a fire in 1977, was opened officially in June 1982, with a provincial

The Earth Sciences Centre in the fall of 1989.

grant of almost $10 million, and a library for Scarborough College, named after Vincent Bladen, was built after the students raised $400,000 in a student levy. The former Toronto Reference Library at College and St George streets was acquired from the city, and construction started on its conversion into the Koffler Student Services Centre, which brought together, from around the campus, such services as health, housing, and career counselling, as well as the University of Toronto Press bookstore. It did not include space for student-run activities, however, such as the Students' Administrative Council or the *Varsity*.

Ham also received a commitment from the Ontario government for two-thirds of the approximately $40 million required for a new earth sciences building on the south-west campus, between Huron Street and Spadina Avenue. A limited campaign to raise the rest was undertaken by the Noranda executive Adam Zimmerman. The Earth Sciences Centre, which was to accommodate teaching and research programs in botany, forestry, geography, geology, and environmental studies, would not be opened officially until 1989. One project Ham wisely opposed was a non-University proposal for the construction of an immense domed stadium on the south side of Bloor Street to replace Varsity Stadium and other buildings. Premier Bill Davis had invited Ham to view the proposed site, which had the convenience of being adjacent to two subway lines. Ham told him it was 'impossible,' and the Skydome was subsequently built on its present site close to Lake Ontario.

President Ham can be credited also with reopening academic exchanges with China and other East Asian countries, including Korea and Japan. He and a number of colleagues made two trips to the Far East during his term and with the assistance of the government of the Republic of Korea established a fund of $500,000 to support Korean studies at the University. The University had been active in China during President Falconer's tenure, but the subsequent political situation there had made continuing involvement difficult. After the cultural revolution ended in the 1970s, however, China was eager for academic assistance, and Toronto, with its long relationship with China and its program in Chinese studies, and as the alma mater of Norman Bethune, was a welcome participant. In the early 1970s, the University established a joint program in modern Chinese studies with York University, and in 1980 it established a centre for South Asian studies.

The increasing number of Asian immigrants settling in the Toronto area and the resulting increase in the number of students of Asian background at the University were also factors in the growing interest in these areas. So-called visible minority immigrants to Canada rose from 10 per cent of all immigrants in 1962 to more than 50 per cent by the mid-1970s, and by the late 1990s visible minorities would comprise about one-third of the population of the greater Toronto area, with persons from Chinese and South Asian backgrounds making up about one-half of that number. A survey of undergraduates at the University in 1994 found that slightly under half considered themselves 'white.'

The search committee to find a replacement for Ham held its first meeting in early May 1982. It was the first presidential search committee at the University to use professional consultants to assist in gathering information. Between 75 and 100 names were assembled, and the committee interviewed 10 candidates, half from within the University itself and half from among Canadian university presidents. After thirty-four meetings, Donald Forster, the 48-year-old president of the University of Guelph, who had been a leading candidate from the beginning, was selected. His appointment was warmly welcomed

Donald Forster arriving at Hart House on January 21, 1983, the day after the announcement of his appointment as president.

within the University. The former presidents Ham, Evans, and Bissell all praised the appointment. Forster had been a success at Guelph. Moreover, he was well respected by the faculty association. He knew the University of Toronto, where he had been a student and a professor of political science and had served as provost and chair of the budget committee. He also knew the Ontario university system. There was a mood of optimism. He would take over on September 1, 1983. A large celebration dinner was planned for September 21. On August 8, Forster died of a heart attack. The University reacted with shock and great disappointment.

Provost David Strangway, who had been acting president since Ham left at the end of June 1983, was appointed president by the governing council until a new president took office. Another search committee was established in November 1983; it was chaired by the governing council chair, John Whitten, and included six members of the earlier committee. This time, the faculty association had considerable influence on who the faculty members of the committee would be. The committee interviewed fewer candidates – some internal and some

George Connell. Photograph taken while Connell was chair of biochemistry in the 1960s.

external – but in the end was not able to make a clear-cut choice. David Strangway, an excellent scientist who had been head of the geophysical aspects of the Apollo moon missions and later the chair of geology at the University, was interviewed for the job, but did not have the support of the committee. He was not popular with the faculty association, having chaired the report of the blue-ribbon committee on institutional strategy that Ham had appointed after the Burkett award. Its interim report in the spring of 1983 had been particularly hard-hitting – it recommended, for example, that two denials of promotion to full professor be a ground for dismissal – and was rejected by both the faculty association and the Canadian Association of University Teachers. Moreover, Strangway was considered a strong opponent of binding arbitration, which at the time was being renegotiated.

Many members of the committee wanted George Connell, the president of the University of Western Ontario, who had been chair of biochemistry at U of T and then an associate dean in the faculty of medicine and vice-president of research and planning. But he had recently taken a second term as president of Western and did not let his name stand. John Whitten told him that the committee was having difficulty, and indicated that if Connell met with the committee, there was every likelihood he would become president. The University of Toronto, Whitten argued, needed his experience and ability. Connell was torn, but decided that he would not let his name stand. He informed his wife, Sheila, who until then had tried not to influence his decision. 'You're crazy not to take it,' she said, 'the University of Toronto needs you.' The next day, Connell changed his mind and decided to meet with the committee. He was selected quickly and took office on October 1, 1984.

Strangway was disappointed. At a dinner in his honour, the chair of the governing council, St Clair Balfour, wished him 'new moons to conquer.' A game of musical chairs then ensued. George Pedersen, the president of the University of British Columbia, who had been interviewed as a candidate for president of U of T, became the president of Western, and Strangway's 'new moon' turned out to be the presidency of UBC.

⥈⥈

Before leaving office, Strangway appointed the University's first status of women officer, senior administrator Lois Reimer. There had been an equity commissioner in the 1970s, but the office had been closed down in 1981 for financial reasons. Strangway also provided money for research on the history of women at the University in preparation for the centenary celebrations of the admission of women to University College in 1884. Great interest in women's issues had developed throughout the 1970s and early 1980s. Women were first admitted to Hart House in 1972 and to Massey College in 1974. A number of women were appointed to senior positions in the University in the 1970s: Pauline McGibbon and then the medical doctor Eva Macdonald were the first two women chancellors; Jill Conway became the first vice-president; Joan Foley and then Alexandra Johnston were the first college principals; and Marnie Paikin was the first chair of the governing council. During this period, women's studies courses were first introduced. In 1971–2, two students, undergraduate Ceta Ramkhalawansingh and graduate student Kay Armatage, organized an interdisciplinary course on women, and in the same year a course on the history of women was presented by Jill Conway and Natalie Davis.

Women's studies seminar in Innis College, March 1975, led by Ceta Ramkhalawansingh, with back to camera.

When Conway became vice-president of internal affairs in the early 1970s, she helped correct anomalies in the salaries of women – a group that held only about 7 per cent of all full-time faculty positions. A further review and adjustment of women's salaries began in the latter part of the 1980s. Throughout the 1970s and 1980s, the University addressed a range of other issues of particular interest to women – maternity leave, day care, safety on campus, and sexual harassment. The sexual harassment officer handles about 250 cases a year. In one widely noted sexual harassment case in 1989, a male professor was banned from the athletic wing of Hart House for five years for harassing a female swimmer in the Hart House pool.

Conway and others also worked to increase the number of women faculty members. Over the next dozen years, the number increased, but it was still under 20 per cent of full-time faculty in the mid-1980s – even though women constituted about 50 per cent of the student body. Although indicative of long-standing inequity in the hiring of women, the slow increase was also, in part, the result of a low turnover of faculty and the various hiring freezes. The issue of the preferential hiring of women created considerable controversy in the late 1980s. The faculty association wanted women to be hired unless a male candidate was 'demonstrably better.' But many wanted hiring to be based strictly on merit. Historian Michael Marrus, for example, argued that 'candidates should be judged solely and exclusively on the basis of their academic performance and potential.' Others, such as chemist John Dove, argued in favour of more women professors to serve as role models. The issue was widely debated in the U of T *Bulletin*. In the end, Provost Joan Foley put forward a proposal that stressed the importance of women's inclusion as candidates in the hiring pool, and changed the criteria for selection so that a woman would be hired if she was 'essentially equal' to the male candidates. Marrus wrote to the *Bulletin* calling the new proposals 'reasoned and thoughtful.'

Reimer was kept busy with these and other issues, such as that of *Toike Oike*, the Engineering Society's humour publication, against which complaints that it was offensive to women had been made. The president of the Engineering Society, Luis Alegre, apologized to President Connell for one offensive edition, saying that in future all issues would be reviewed by the president of the society and that its aim was 'to create a publication that everyone will be able to take home and have their families read for enjoyment, and a good laugh!' Reimer sent a memo to Connell, saying: 'I am sure that we haven't seen the last outrageous TOIKE ... I shall try to encourage communication between the Engineering Society and some of the women's groups on campus, and see what might rub off.'

❧

Connell inherited a demoralized university when he arrived in October 1984. Funding continued to be a problem. The province refused to depart from its formula-funding scheme based on student numbers, which rewarded growth – in spite of a recommendation by a provincial commission under the business-man Edmund Bovey that some funding be allocated according to a university's success in getting federal research grants. That would have helped Toronto. Moreover, a negative report prepared for Simcoe Hall on the quality of student life at the University of Toronto greeted Connell upon his arrival. Students, the report stated, complained of inadequate classroom space, of poor campus food, and of feeling 'faceless, alienated and lonely.' One student said, 'It's like being a cedar chip on the bottom of the hamster cage.' Connell's installation address acknowledged problems at the University of Toronto. 'This university,' he said, 'in company with all others in Canada, from the Atlantic to the Pacific, is in a state which at best can be described as uncertain, at worst as perilous.' Nevertheless, he expressed hope of 'renewal.' 'The opportunities,' he told the Convocation Hall audience, 'are boundless and they are not beyond our reach.'

One issue had very recently been solved. The day before Connell's installation address in mid-November 1984, the administration had managed to avoid a serious crisis and yet another possible certification drive over binding arbitration. (At the time, about half the university faculties in Ontario were unionized.) The two-year agreement signed in 1982 had expired, and negotiations over the previous ten months had not brought a solution. The administration did not want a repeat of the Burkett award, and the faculty association did not want a return to the old system. Provost Frank Iacobucci presented a compromise formula: an arbitrator's award could be rejected by the governing council, but the following year an award would be binding.

The formula was accepted by the faculty association negotiators, and at 5 o'clock in the morning Iacobucci woke Connell to say that an agreement had been reached. 'I was never so happy to be woken at 5 a.m.,' Connell told a meeting of principals, deans, directors, and chairs the following day. The agreement was approved by the faculty association council the day before the installation and by the governing council a few days later. In all but one case over the next six years, the faculty association and the administration were able to settle their differences without arbitration. In the one case that led to arbitration, the relatively modest award was accepted by the governing council.

Connell was unhappy with the administrative structure he inherited at Toronto. It had borne the brunt of financial cuts. He wanted a civil service that would 'ensure some continuity from one presidential regime to the next.' In spite of financial constraints, Ham had not attempted a fund-raising campaign, and the organization that had been established for the earlier Update campaign was no longer in place. In order to work more closely with his vice-presidents and others, Connell moved from the elegant office on the second floor of Simcoe Hall overlooking King's College Circle, which previously had been occupied by President Falconer and all successive presidents, to a functional office on the ground floor overlooking a parking lot. The move was in keeping with Connell's low-key, self-effacing style. In contrast, his successor, President Robert Prichard, moved the office back to its original location, stating that moving the office was the one mistake Connell had made.

Connell also discovered that the University had been allowing its modest endowment to decrease in value by using all the income generated and not providing for inflation. Rules were brought in so that in the future only part of the increase in value could be paid out. The amount of the endowment was greatly increased after a deal was struck with the faculty association in 1987 that would acknowledge the University's right to control the surplus in the University's pension plan in exchange for the indexing of faculty pensions to meet 60 per cent of inflation, as well as make other improvements to the plan. The pension plan was overfunded, so the University did not have to contribute to the fund. For the next four years, the sum saved – over $100 million – was contributed to a special fund. It was this fund – later converted into an endowment fund – that would be used so effectively by President Prichard to provide the matching funds for donations for named professors and student scholarships. It would also be money that many active and retired faculty members believe should be used for further enhancing faculty pensions.

Connell also inherited an automated library system called UTLAS (University of Toronto Library Automation Systems) that, whatever its merit, was becoming a serious drain on university resources. About $12 million had been invested in a system that now needed further capital. One of Connell's first tasks was to sell the system to Thompson International for the modest sum of $1 million. Thompson would assume the University's liabilities, and the University would share in future profits. Financially, the University's investment never paid off, but it should be noted that its library and many other libraries in Canada still use the services of UTLAS and its successor companies.

Within a year of the sale of UTLAS, however, another commercial venture, this time one involving large-scale computation, was undertaken by the University. The provincial government provided $10 million to allow the University to acquire a Cray supercomputer. The cost of its operation would be financed by the sale of time to bodies outside the University. Many potential users within the University supported its acquisition. The associate chair of physics, George Luste, however, was one of a few faculty members to publicly criticize the assumption that the exercise was viable. The plan, he wrote, 'proposes a risky enterprise bordering on certain disaster.' Within a year of the acquisition of the computer, this risk was becoming apparent to some of those responsible for its commercial operation. The commercial and academic use was disappointing. 'The phrase "Son of UTLAS" has come to mind,' wrote the faculty association president, Fred Wilson, who demanded, on behalf of a unanimous council, an independent review of the Cray operation. The province put in another $8 million. The computer, however, continued to be a drain on university resources, and shortly after Prichard took office, he arranged for the termination of the University's involvement in the Cray project, just as Connell had done for UTLAS when he took office. Researchers could use supercomputers elsewhere, such as in Pittsburgh. More important, large-scale computation could now be done on smaller, less expensive computers. The Cray was removed from the computation centre in the physics building in June 1992.

❦

A series of complex issues had to be faced in Connell's first few years. Two of them reflected international concern about South Africa. The Hart House debates committee invited Glenn Babb, the South African ambassador to Canada, to participate in a debate in November 1985 on investment in South Africa. Owing to disruptions – one of the speakers from the floor threw the ceremonial mace at Babb, and others in the audience stomped and chanted – the debate had to be cancelled. 'The need to dissolve the Hart House debate before all sides of the divestment issue were heard,' wrote Brian Burchell for the Students' Administrative Council, 'was a shameful moment in the history of the University.'

After the Banfield incident in the early 1970s, the University had established procedures that required offering another invitation to a speaker whose talk had been disrupted. Connell supported the policy, stating that it 'has no qualifications. The right of freedom to speak is extended to everyone without reservation.' Not everyone agreed. Peter Rosenthal from the mathematics department along with a large group of professors sent a petition to Connell saying that 'no official representatives of the government of South Africa should be invited to speak at the University of Toronto until apartheid has been completely dismantled.' A group of law students, led by the future Ontario cabinet minister Tony Clement, and the Hart House debates committee, however, invited Babb to debate law professor William Graham at the law school on the issue of apartheid. The dean of the law school, Robert Prichard, welcomed those attending the debate, stressing the importance of free speech. Throughout, shouts of 'Jail Botha, free Mandela' were heard outside the moot court room. Protected by RCMP officers as well as by the Toronto police, the debate took place. The issue,

Law students demonstrating against a speech given in January 1986 by Glenn Babb, the South African ambassador to Canada.

stated the U of T *Magazine*, had created 'the most sustained, widespread, loudly publicized and acrimonious debate to visit the U of T campus in a decade.'

The other issue involving South Africa was whether the University should invest its endowment funds in companies that had dealings with that country. This question preceded the Babb affair, having first arisen during Strangway's presidency. Then, in 1984, Connell received a petition containing more than 1,000 names from a university committee asking for total divestiture by the University. Connell, however, took the position that 'the University as an institution' should not be 'committed to a particular political cause, no matter how worthy, no matter how overwhelming the majority of those supporting that cause.' When the matter came before the governing council, Connell proposed an amendment to a divestiture motion that provided for a case-by-case analysis of each company, as was then the practice in a number of leading American universities. The amended motion passed by 32 to 8, but the controversy continued. A group of faculty members publicly wrote that 'the clear will of the University community is to divest from South Africa,' and that 'if President Connell feels that he cannot represent this overwhelming opinion of the University community he should resign.' One meeting of the governing council was terminated because of a serious disruption over the issue by some 250 demonstrators. In the end, a commissioned report by historian Archie Thornton recommended complete divestiture of all securities in companies doing business in South Africa, a policy that was approved by the governing council.

Other issues had to do with the restructuring of academic units, never an easy task, as President Evans had discovered. A 1985 proposal for a merger of the Ontario Institute for Studies in Education (OISE) and the U of T's faculty of education, desired by the newly elected Liberal government under David Peterson, presented one such task. Bernard Shapiro, the director of OISE, and President Connell had been trying to establish a closer relationship between OISE and the faculty of education. Shapiro had been the provost at Western when Connell was its president, and they worked well together. Then, in October 1985 – to the surprise of both Shapiro and Connell – the treasurer of Ontario, Robert Nixon, announced in his first budget speech that 'as a step towards eliminating duplication in the public sector, the government will transfer the Ontario Institute for Studies in Education to the University of Toronto.'

Connell wrote to Shapiro, saying that 'the action of the government, while unexpected, offers to both our institutions a tremendous opportunity for future development.' The OISE faculty association, however, opposed the move and set up a fund to lobby members of the legislature. Other faculty organizations joined the protest, claiming improper government interference. The city of Toronto and others were against the move. The OISE board stopped negotiations with the University on the issue. Michael Fullan, OISE's assistant director, claimed that before the government announcement, he 'would have said that long term affiliation with the University was the desire of the majority of our faculty ... Each day the hearts and minds of more and more faculty are moving to non University of Toronto options.' One of the options proposed by the OISE board was to ask for a change in legislation to give OISE degree-granting powers, a prospect that did not appeal to the government. It would take another ten years before the merger with U of T's faculty of education would finally come about.

A further academic issue involved the closing of the faculty of architecture, proposed by Simcoe Hall in early 1986. The faculty, it was argued, suffered from deep and acrimonious divisions, had a poor scholarly record, and was housed in inadequate quarters. University resources were not available to improve the situation. Faculty, students, and the architecture profession joined ranks to oppose the closure. 'If someone could just pull all the divergent positions together and give it direction,' said the architect Eberhard Zeidler, 'it could survive.' Politicians, the faculty association, and many others joined in opposition. In the end, Simcoe Hall backed down and, adopting a face-saving device, converted the faculty into a school – as though that would change the situation. After an unfavourable review, the school discontinued its graduate program. The school continued to struggle. 'If I had known the extent of the problems here,' said the new dean, Anthony Eardley, 'wild horses wouldn't have got me to take this job.' He helped to bring a measure of calm to the faculty in his seven years as dean. Larry Richards, the director of the University of Waterloo's school of architecture, became the director in 1997 and breathed new life into the institution. Facilities were improved, new staff hired, graduate programs reinstituted, and the undergraduate program discontinued. In 1998, the school again became a faculty.

In general, then, it was 'more of the same' during the earlier years of Connell's presidency, the same internal squabbling and lack of adequate resources that had plagued Ham's administration. Then came Polanyi's Nobel prize and George Connell's document *Renewal 1987*.

PART EIGHT

RAISING THE SIGHTS

chapter forty

1986

⟨⟨⟨⟩⟩⟩

MOVING FORWARD

A turning point in the fortunes of the University was reached on Wednesday, October 15, 1986. This was the day the announcement was made that the 57-year-old John Polanyi had won the Nobel Prize in Chemistry for work done at the University of Toronto thirty years earlier. He had been awakened early in the morning by a wire service telling him the unexpected news. Polanyi had obtained his PhD from Manchester University, where his father, Michael Polanyi – a refugee from Nazi oppression – was a well-known professor of chemistry and philosopher of science. In 1956, after two years at the National Research Council in Ottawa and another two at Princeton University, the 27-year-old Polanyi had been appointed a lecturer in chemistry at the University of Toronto. He rose quickly through the ranks: he became a full professor at the age of 33, and in 1974 he was the first scientist to be named a University Professor.

President George Connell received the news later that morning at Simcoe Hall. When he could not reach Polanyi by telephone, he went to his house in Rosedale to congratulate him in person. He discovered Polanyi patiently explaining to a group of reporters the research that had brought him the prize. His research, Polanyi told them, had involved studying the infrared radiation produced by chemical reactions in the creation of molecules. The work eventually contributed to the development of chemical lasers. 'As a spin-off of the work we did,' he went on, 'we discovered that those chemical reactions formed vibrationally excited molecules and that you could put those molecules in a tube

John Polanyi in his study at home in 1985, the year before he won the Nobel Prize
for Chemistry.

and infrared radiation of very high intensity would come out. That's what's
called the chemical laser.' The dean of arts and science in the late 1950s, Vincent
Bladen, at the time had found the then substantial sum of $10,000 required for
the infrared spectrometer that Polanyi and his first graduate student, Ken
Cashion, needed for their work. 'You damn well see you win a Nobel prize,'
Bladen had told him.

By a happy coincidence, a large rally to seek greater funding had been
planned for the next day in Convocation Hall by Toronto-area post-secondary
institutions. The hall was packed, and between one and two thousand more
people heard the proceedings over loudspeakers outside the building. At the very

end of Connell's remarks, Polanyi entered the hall and received an exuberant two-minute standing ovation. He gave, in Connell's words, 'a quiet but intense and compelling defence of the academic enterprise.' The rally, Connell wrote in a memorandum prepared at the time, was 'a really electrifying and memorable experience. The impact on the crowd and on the politicians must have been immense.' That afternoon, Connell heard that the Ontario cabinet was likely to add $50 million to the funding of Ontario universities.

The federal government followed within weeks with a program that would match research funds given by the private sector. Polanyi, however, criticized the federal initiative, stating that 'the insistence on relating fundamental science – university-type science – to the needs of the marketplace ... has become short-sighted.' It had taken over a decade, he had pointed out repeatedly, for the practical applications of his own research to come to fruition. He observed that it was not by chance that the phrase is 'R and D' (research and development), not 'D and R.' When asked by reporters what his advice was to talented and ambitious Canadian scientists, he reluctantly replied, 'I would suggest they go abroad.'

Saturday, October 18 was 'U of T Day,' the annual campus-wide open house. 'There were,' Connell wrote, 'many thousands of visitors on the campus, and the prevailing mood was one of great cheerfulness and optimism. It was a fitting end to one of the most remarkable weeks in the history of the University.' The euphoria came at an opportune time. For the past several months, Connell had been working on a personal document to be entitled 'Renewal,' describing possible ways of bringing the University of Toronto out of its financial and psychological depression. He would now work with renewed vigour to finish the document.

❦

George Connell's discussion paper, *Renewal 1987*, was released in March 1987, after widespread consultation within the University community. Connell had actively worked on it for some ten months, prompted by his conviction that there was 'abundant evidence of the effects of financial attrition and a widely-shared view that the University is not achieving its full potential.' He had considered appointing a committee of distinguished persons from both inside and outside the University to prepare a report, but was persuaded that he himself

President George Connell at a news conference in March 1988 on the
1988–9 university budget.

should undertake the task. 'The University of Toronto,' he wrote, 'has legitimate
aspirations of greatness,' but before it could reach what he referred to as 'the
pinnacle of Parnassus,' there must be 'a consensus within the University about
the goals we should pursue and the pattern of conduct which will conform to
those goals.' *Renewal 1987* was written to help shape that consensus. The decade
and a half since 1970, he wrote, had been 'years of uncertainty ... No coherent
policies were framed to replace the concerted drive for expansion that characterized the 1960s.'

The University took his challenge seriously and engaged in a wide-ranging
discussion of the many issues raised by the paper. A positive mood was growing
on the campus, helped by the spotlight on the University as a result of Polanyi's
prize as well as by the publicity given a few months later to the discovery at the
University's astronomical observatory in Chile of a supernova by a young Toronto scientist, Ian Shelton. Named 'Supernova Shelton,' the discovery was
featured on the cover of *Time* magazine. The financial climate was slowly
changing. Polanyi publicly noted that one of Toronto's most talented scientists,

Winners and finalists for the University of Toronto National Scholars program, 1987.

the immunologist Tak Mak of the biophysics group, had resisted the lure of an American offer and had decided to remain in Toronto.

❦

Renewal 1987 argued that undergraduate education had to be improved. Toronto was losing excellent students to other universities, such as McGill, Queen's, and Waterloo. The residence facilities and student services were inadequate. A curricular structure for first year arts and science students – more than 70 per cent of undergraduates were in arts and science – was lacking. Classrooms were crowded. 'The more successful our efforts in improving undergraduate education,' Connell wrote, 'the more likely we are to gain public support for improved funding.'

Connell advocated in his document an end to the three-year arts and science degree, a policy that would be adopted at the end of Robert Prichard's term of office fifteen years later. He also wanted to increase the geographical diversity of the body of full-time undergraduate students, over two-thirds of whom came from the Toronto area, with only about 3 per cent from other provinces and 2 per cent from outside Canada. (In contrast, about 15 per cent of graduate

Teaching award winners, 1984–5: from left to right, Han-Ru Cho (physics),
Carol Rogerson (law), James Ham (engineering), Marta Horban-Carynnyk (French),
and Janice Stein (political science).

students were from outside Ontario.) As a symbolic step towards increasing the
number and academic quality of undergraduate students, including out-of-
province students, the University initiated the National Scholars program in
1987 for 6 or so students a year. The program over time was expanded to
20 scholarships a year.

Teaching was given greater emphasis throughout the University, and figured
more prominently in hiring, tenure, and promotion decisions. Instructional
development programs for faculty members and teaching assistants began to be
offered, for example, by the faculty association, the faculty of arts and science,
and the School of Continuing Studies. Woodsworth College later offered a
popular course on teaching effectiveness for PhD candidates. In 1989, Provost
Joan Foley appointed the French professor John Kirkness as her adviser on
undergraduate education. Arts and science and other divisions introduced awards
for outstanding instructors. A conscious attempt was made to link research and
teaching. Starting in 1994, a series of awards named after Northrop Frye have
been given to faculty members who successfully link teaching and research. One
of the first awards was given to the faculty of arts and science for developing a

course that allowed upper year students to work closely with a professor on a specific research project of particular interest to the professor.

Arts and science later introduced a policy that gave all first year students the option of taking one of their courses in a small group of about 20 students, a technique that had been used successfully in the faculty of law for the previous twenty years. 'No longer will new students sense that they have arrived at a large impersonal place,' predicted the dean of arts and science, Marsha Chandler, in 1994. 'Instead, the dominant feeling will be a sense of the range of opportunities – of being able to connect with faculty members and connect with other students.' Some courses continued to be given successfully to large numbers of students. In psychology, for example, Barney Gilmore and Martin Wall received rave reviews for their first year courses given in Convocation Hall. (The author's own most memorable undergraduate course was given to more than 250 students in the large hall of the old McMaster Hall by the economic historian Karl Helleiner.)

Graduate studies was also highlighted in *Renewal 1987*. Toronto's 'greatest distinction,' Connell wrote, 'is the strength and diversity of its graduate programs.' The number of master's students was almost double that in any other English-speaking university in Canada. The University had 66 doctoral programs, nearly 20 of which were not duplicated at any other Ontario university, and several of which were unique in Canada. It had about 3,000 doctoral students – about one-third of all doctoral students in Ontario. The next-highest enrolment at a Canadian university was at the University of Montreal, with fewer than 2,000 doctoral students, followed by McGill, with a few more than 1,200. The University, the report stated, 'has the capacity (given reasonable financial support) for more graduate students, particularly in the research streams' and recommended that Toronto consider increasing the number in the doctoral stream by perhaps 500 students.

A serious problem was graduate student funding. Most graduate students needed some financial support, and scholarship money was not adequate. This was particularly true for foreign students, who at the time Connell wrote his report had to pay over $6,000 a year for tuition, compared to about $1,300 for Canadians. Not only were the research grants that normally supported graduate students not keeping up with inflation, but their absolute value was decreasing. The University, in fact, tended to do well in the competition for sponsored research grants, but, as Connell observed in his report, because no provision was made for indirect costs, 'we cannot afford this success.' One solution would be to increase the endowment for scholarships, but this would have to be a long-term strategy. Another would be for governments to provide adequate overhead funding, as had recently been recommended by a federal study conducted by the former CBC president Albert Johnson, a professor of political science at the University at the time.

❧

Both the provincial and the federal government were receptive to the idea of increased funding in targeted areas of research based on 'excellence.' David Peterson's recently elected Liberal government in Ontario had promised in 1986 to 'support excellence through appropriate funding,' and Brian Mulroney's Conservative government in Ottawa had pledged that same year to support, 'with the provinces, a system of post-secondary education based on excellence.' Ottawa later announced 'an initiative that could provide a billion dollars in new funding for scientific research over the next five years,' and Ontario established seven 'Centres of Excellence' for Ontario universities that would cost about $200 million over five years.

Much of the increased government funding was tied to cooperation between universities and industry. An Ontario commission on the Ontario university system, chaired by the businessman Edmund Bovey, which included Fraser Mustard, the head of the Canadian Institute for Advanced Research, had recommended in 1984 that the government establish 'university-industry linkages and research relationships.' Both levels of government followed the commission's advice, and partnerships between universities and industries, including drug companies, became increasingly important, particularly in the faculties of engineering and medicine. A new position of vice-dean in charge of industrial collaboration was established in engineering, with the chair of chemical engineering and future dean Michael Charles as its first incumbent. By 1991, the National Science and Engineering Research Council (NSERC) had funded eleven industrial chairs in the faculty of engineering, all of which required participation by an industrial partner. Between 1980 and 1990, external research funding in the faculty had increased by more than 400 per cent.

Toronto did well in the competition for both the Ontario and the federal programs. Out of 7 Ontario Centres of Excellence, Toronto became, in 1987, a principal participant in 5: information technology, integrated manufacturing, materials research, space and terrestrial science, and laser and lightwave research. The last-mentioned centre was exclusively a U of T operation. In 1992, the five programs were renewed for a further five years. Under the Ontario program, over $10 million a year flowed to the University of Toronto for research, with a significant portion of that sum being for indirect overhead costs. Adel Sedra, the chair of electrical engineering – engineering played a role in all five Toronto centres – wrote in 1989 that 'far from being a drain on the department's resources, participation in the Ontario Centres of Excellence program has greatly improved our research environment and is enabling this department to compete effectively with the best universities in the world for new faculty members.'

The University of Toronto was a participant in 9 of the original 14 federal Centres of Excellence Networks and a principal partner in another on micro-electronics headed by André Salama of electrical engineering. Within a few years, it was participating in all the centres. Like the other Ontario and federal programs, the one on micro-electronics was designed to link universities and industry. In its first phase, Salama's program brought together 16 universities, 8 public sector organizations, and 11 private companies. Another, later, Toronto-based federal centre was on aging, under Victor Marshall, a sociologist in the faculty of medicine. One of the federal centres that was not renewed was on molecular and interfacial dynamics. It had not produced the short-term results that would be of interest to industrial partners. John Polanyi, who had been involved with the program, warned the government – as he had done in the past and would continue to do – that 'quite often, quick returns equate with small returns.'

Nevertheless, what is called 'technology transfer,' that is, the transfer of technology from universities to industry, became an important component of research at the University, and an office of technology transfer was established in Simcoe Hall in 1988 to encourage its development. One successful patent, developed by the biochemist and molecular geneticist David MacLennan and marketed by the University's Innovations Foundation, has brought in almost $5 million in royalties. MacLennan had found a way of eliminating a genetic disease mutation in pigs that was causing huge economic losses in the pork industry. So-called spin-off companies that bring potential revenue to the University are now being formed at the rate of about five a year.

Research in Toronto's teaching hospitals also increased significantly during the 1980s. Most teaching hospitals established research institutes, and they raised funds for research outside the University's then relatively modest fund-raising activities. Charles Hollenberg, the vice-provost of health sciences for part of this period, later would note that it was the hospital research institutes, coupled with the insecurity in Quebec, that allowed Toronto to overtake the previously dominant McGill faculty of medicine in research funding and productivity. Research had always been an activity of the teaching hospitals – the development of the blood-thinner heparin at the Toronto General and of the children's cereal Pablum at the Sick Children's are early examples – though the research was usually closely connected with clinical work.

In 1953, the Hospital for Sick Children had formally established a research institute. Under its director, Aser Rothstein, a Canadian biophysicist who had been hired in the early 1970s from the University of Rochester, the institute developed an excellent reputation for research. 'Research is an elitist activity,' Rothstein once said, 'mediocre research might as well not be done.' By 1980, the institute had a staff complement of more than 500 persons, including clinicians associated with it in various ways, and a budget of over $10 million. It was particularly strong in genetics under its geneticist-in-chief, Louis Siminovitch. Siminovitch was able to attract future stars, such as Lap-Chee Tsui, who would discover the defective gene and molecular defect that were responsible for cystic fibrosis. Today, many believe that Sick Children's is the strongest of the hospitals in research terms, with the largest share of federal Medical Research Council / Canadian Institute for Health Research funding, and with programs cutting across all the granting agency's funding categories.

In 1985, at the usual retiring age of 65, Siminovitch took on a new job, by becoming head of the recently established Mount Sinai Research Institute, later named after its major benefactor, Samuel Lunenfeld. A large addition was built behind the hospital. Researchers were hired from other universities in Canada – a number came from Queen's – and some from the United States. The geneticist Alan Bernstein, who would later succeed Siminovitch as institute director and today is head of the federal Canadian Institute for Health Research, was brought from the Ontario Cancer Institute to head the division of molecular and developmental biology, one of the four divisions of the institute. Bernstein, in turn, was able to recruit noted researchers, such as Tony Pawson from UBC, Janet Rossant, and Alexandra Joyner. The four later would receive a $1 million

Award-winning team from the Mount Sinai Hospital's Lunenfeld Research Institute, in 1991:
from left to right, Tony Pawson, Alan Bernstein, Janet Rossant, and Alex Joyner.

grant from the Howard Hughes Institute for their collaborative work on the genetic basis of disease. In 1995, the institute received a $5 million grant from the federal and Ontario governments and at the same time received a $10 million grant from the Brystol-Myers Squibb Pharmaceutical Research Institute. Moreover, each year, the hospital's fund-raising foundation contributes over $5 million for research. A fund-raising campaign for the hospital in the early 1990s, organized by Jon Dellandrea, later the head of fund-raising at the University, received pledges of $75 million in three years.

With the genetic research being done at the Medical Sciences Building, at Sick Children's, and at the Princess Margaret, and with researchers such as Tak Mak and younger scientists such as James Woodgett and Joseph Penninger, Toronto has become one of the key centres in the world for genetic research. These three researchers from the University's department of biophysics are part of the Amgen Institute of Princess Margaret and the Ontario Cancer Institute. The American biotech company Amgen gave $10 million to found the institute bearing its name. Being connected to the University and the other hospitals, Penninger has stated, is 'like being in an intellectual candy store. All you have to do is call people up and ask for help and you get it.'

Other teaching hospitals could tell similar if less dramatic stories, particularly in the area of clinical medicine. The Toronto General, for example, brought in the biochemist Donald Layne from Connaught Laboratories in the early 1980s and constructed a research building behind the original College Street structure, thereby increasing the hospital's research capacity in such fields as endocrinology and respiratory and heart diseases. Other hospitals also increased their clinical research capacity: the Western in neurological diseases, St Michael's in gastroenterology and cardiovascular disease, Women's College in women's health, the Wellesley in basic immunology, and Sunnybrook in new imaging techniques, cancer treatment, and trauma research.

Sunnybrook is also home for the Institute for Clinical Evaluative Sciences (ICES), which evaluates the effectiveness and efficiency of clinical medical procedures in Ontario. ICES was established in 1992, with the epidemiologist David Naylor (now dean of medicine) as founding chief executive officer and the ubiquitous former president John Evans as inaugural chair of the board of directors. The institute is now headquarters for the largest grouping of health care researchers in Canada. They have published hundreds of peer-reviewed articles on aspects of health-care delivery, along with an influential series of 'practice atlases' focusing on major clinical areas such as cancer, arthritis, and cardiovascular disease.

Senior staff in the hospital institutes are normally cross-appointed to university departments and supervise graduate students. Because the hospital institutes could offer an association with the University as well as good facilities for research, they were able to attract talent from across the country. This caused a measure of uneasiness in the basic science departments in the University, which did not have the hospital institutes' access to research funds or flexibility in recruiting. There were also other problems. The regulation of research and ethical procedures and their enforcement in the hospitals did not keep up with the growth of research, as became evident in the controversy in the 1990s involving the Hospital for Sick Children and the development of a drug to treat the iron overload associated with the disease thalassaemia. The controversy, brought to public attention by the haematologist Nancy Olivieri, had the long-term consequence of convincing everyone that harmonization of the differing hospital rules on research procedures was necessary, particularly in the area of drug trials.

Another problem was that each of the hospitals had its own agenda and coordination of their research activities was difficult to achieve, though each tried not to compete directly in research areas that had been built up by other hospitals. Greater coordination is now developing, however, because the basic science departments in the University regained momentum in the 1990s and forged an academic partnership with the hospital research institutes based on positions of mutual strength. Furthermore, the Ontario government–enforced hospital restructuring that took place beginning in 1996, and later rationalized the clinical roles of the various teaching hospitals, helped reduce the degree of inter-institutional rivalry. In addition, a coordination of activity was strongly encouraged by the fact that the funding agencies were placing a growing premium on inter-institutional and interdisciplinary collaboration.

❧

The University had delayed the start of its own fund-raising campaign. In a feasibility survey conducted by an American consulting firm in 1986, a number of potential major donors had expressed concern about the ability of the University to govern itself. This concern could affect the success of the campaign. It was also clear that donors did not want to contribute to the University's endowment – perhaps its greatest need. Furthermore, the personnel and apparatus for a successful campaign were not in place, and the consulting firm noted that ten professional staff would have to be added. There were, however, positive indications. Dean Prichard's successful campaign to raise $10 million for the Bora Laskin Law Library helped persuade the University that donors were indeed willing to contribute to well-conceived projects. Only about 15 per cent of the University's alumni had been giving annually to the Varsity Fund, and Malim Harding, who chaired the fund, believed that a several-fold increase was possible.

The University's 'Breakthrough' campaign to raise $100 million was begun in late 1987 under the chairmanship of Mary Alice Stuart, a 1949 University College graduate, an active community worker, and the head of the local CJRT radio station. A couple of bank presidents apparently had declined an invitation to chair the campaign. Connell has said that he devoted about one-third of his time to fund-raising over a six-year period. The editorial and administrative

Pierre Elliott Trudeau opening the Bora Laskin Law Library in March 1991. Robert McGavin, chair of the governing council, is on the left, and President Robert Prichard and Dean Robert Sharpe are on the right.

offices of the University of Toronto Press were moved out of the 'Press building' on King's College Circle to make way for the development team. The campaign was a success, and raised about $135 million. The Polanyi name helped. Even before the official launch, $1 million was pledged by the Jackman Foundation to support research by Polanyi and future scientists, and a chair in Polanyi's name became one of the featured goals of the campaign. The humanities, however, did relatively poorly.

Some donations came unexpectedly. A gift in 1987, for example, from the land developer Mark Tanz and his brother and sister – all U of T graduates – created the U of T's Tanz Centre for Research in Neurodegenerative Diseases in the faculty of medicine, located in the former Botany Building at the corner of College Street and University Avenue. Their mother had died the previous year from Alzheimer's disease, and Tanz had contacted the University to see what work was being done on Alzheimer's. As it turned out, a project in that area was being considered for the campaign. A few years earlier, the physiologists Donald McLachlan and Harold Atwood and others had proposed a centre for degenerative diseases such as Alzheimer's, Parkinson's, and ALS (Lou Gehrig's disease).

The Tanz family agreed to donate $4 million and the Alzheimer's Association of Ontario $5 million, and Tanz undertook to lead a campaign to raise an additional $8.5 million. McLachlan became the centre's first director and built a staff of more than 50 researchers. One of the senior researchers, the neurologist Peter St George-Hyslop, who would take over as director, was the principal investigator of a team that found the gene that causes early-onset Alzheimer's disease.

The Tanz Centre moved into the renovated Botany Building after the department of botany had moved to its new home in the recently opened Earth Sciences Centre on the south-west campus. The Earth Sciences Centre had been in the works for more than ten years. A commitment by the Davis government to Jim Ham had been revoked when Peterson took over, but was later restored as part of the University's capital appropriation. It had not taken inflation into account, however, and consequently there were serious cost overruns. 'This project,' Connell later said, 'cost me more hours of sleep than any other ... As building costs rocketed upwards this turned into a financial disaster of the first magnitude.' As a result, the Breakthrough campaign included $12 million to complete the project. 'Unless we get that building paid for,' Connell wrote to Gordon Cressy, the vice-president of development, ' it will be a terrible millstone around our necks, negating much of the beneficial effect of the campaign.' A scaled-down version opened in 1989, containing botany, forestry, geology, and the Institute for Environmental Studies. Physical geography, which was to have been included in the complex, took over the old forestry building on St George Street. The Earth Sciences Centre was eventually paid off during Prichard's tenure as president.

Many people within the University shared the concerns identified by the fund-raising consultants about the way in which the University governed itself. In December 1986, the governing council asked Edward Stansbury, a former vice-president of planning at McGill – with three degrees in physics from the University of Toronto – to survey opinion on the campus about the overall effectiveness of Toronto's unicameral governing structure. His report set forth a depressing list of complaints. The faculty association agreed with Stansbury that something should be done. Its president, Michael Finlayson, wrote to the chairman of the governing council, St Clair Balfour: 'It will not come as a surprise to you, I suppose, that members of my Executive share [Stansbury's] view that substantial changes are required in our system of governance ... There are intolerable weaknesses in the system of governance at the University of

Toronto.' President Connell, though not as negative about the system as Stansbury, also wanted changes. He was attracted to the system at the University of Western Ontario, 'where the Senate functioned well as a lower house, dealing effectively with all substantial issues of university governance, including the budget.' Connell's *Renewal 1987*, released at about the same time as Stansbury's report, urged changes in the system of government.

With the University about to embark on a fund-raising campaign, Connell wanted to get the festering governance issue settled. The deans of arts and science, graduate studies, medicine, and engineering asked Connell to move reform of university governance to the top of the renewal agenda. The arts and science dean Robin Armstrong warned, 'Unless something is done about governance, I believe the rest will be more difficult.' A series of position papers was produced by the governing council and others, and a number of special meetings of the council were held.

The executive committee of the governing council eventually decided to recommend to the governing council that it reform the unicameral system through its by-laws and not seek legislation for more fundamental change. The faculty association was not pleased. Its new president, philosopher Fred Wilson, had wanted a return to a bicameral system with a senate and a board of governors. So had the majority of the academic administrators. In a survey, 52 academic administrators preferred bicameralism, and only 12 a reformed unicameral structure. A nine-point plan to reform governance was to be put to a meeting of the governing council on December 3, 1987 by Joan Randall, the vice-chair of the council, and engineering professor Michael Uzumeri. This was also to be the meeting at which the council would approve the $100 million Breakthrough fund-raising campaign.

A few days before the meeting, the *Globe and Mail* headlined the news that the faculty association had censured President Connell and Provost Foley. A copy of the censure had been hand-delivered to the *Globe*. The direct issue was a relatively minor change in the academic appointments policy – an appeal process following a pre-tenure review. The administration and the faculty association had agreed upon the change at the end of the previous academic year. Foley, however, wanted a change in the proposal, following a negative reaction to the appeal process from the academic administrators. She decided not to bring the provision before the academic affairs committee, though other parts of the agreement were introduced. The association considered that the failure to bring the entire package before the committee was a breach of the agreement that had been reached. It was also considered a breach of the formal memorandum of agreement, a view disputed by the administration.

The association in its censure also criticized Connell's 'lack of leadership' on a number of issues, including his handling of the soon-to-be-launched fund-raising campaign. There was shock and bewilderment in Simcoe Hall, particularly as the censure came on the eve of the announcement of the campaign. 'However strongly the faculty may have felt,' the *Globe* stated in an editorial, 'it did not come knocking on the door of a president known for his quiet courtesy. It preferred the surprise tactic of an explosion of public rage.' At the governing council meeting on December 3, Connell received prolonged applause and a standing ovation. The members of the governing council condemned the censure. Roger Beck, the dean of humanities at Erindale, termed it a 'strange manoeuvre,' and Mike Uzumeri of civil engineering, who had been actively involved with the association in the past, called the censure 'inexplicable, unexpected, unreasonable and shrill.'

It is not easy to determine what lay behind this extreme measure. It reflected a number of concerns over Connell's conduct, including his position on the divestment of South African securities and – of considerable importance to the faculty association – the failure of the administration and the association to agree on the precise wording of proposals for pay equity for women. The association also had a concern that if the governing council was restructured to give the faculty a greater voice in policy making, the association would lose some of its present power. In particular, it probably feared that Connell wanted to change article 2 of the memorandum of agreement – the frozen policies provision – which required approval by the faculty association for any change in those policies. In fact, Connell wanted such a change. He had written in *Renewal 1987* that article 2 'constitutes a major limitation on the powers assigned to the Council under the University of Toronto Act.' Moreover, the faculty association was annoyed that it had not been more involved in the restructuring process. It was feeling marginalized. The censure was therefore a dramatic signal that the association was not to be written off.

The governing council unanimously approved the nine-point plan on governance, which provided that the academic affairs committee and the planning and resources committee be combined into a large academic board that would have a majority of academics and academic administrators. Unlike what had happened in previous debates on governance, most student groups were resigned to the proposals. SAC's university affairs commissioner, Brian Burchell, who was also a member of the governing council, supported the changes. A working group was set up to flesh out the plan. The legislative rule about not having a committee without a majority of governing council members was to be circumvented by having decisions of the board approved by the executive committee of the council, which could, if it thought necessary, pass the matter on to the governing council. Furthermore, the rule established in the late 1970s that the council could not tamper with administration proposals – all they could do was accept, reject, or send them back for reconsideration – would be changed to permit amendments by the council and its committees. On May 19, 1988, the governing council unanimously approved a new 114-member academic board, consisting of 28 academic administrators, 49 elected faculty members, and 37 others, of whom 16 would be students. There would also be a business board consisting of 25 members and a university affairs board of 20 members, both of which would have a majority of governing council members.

The University now had a credible governing structure. It has worked well, and the call for a return to bicameralism has died down. Aspects of the old bicameral system in effect had been introduced through the new governing structures. Michael Marrus, who was chair of the academic board from 1990 to 1996, stressed formality of procedure. 'The major challenge I faced,' he later wrote, 'was to legitimize this assembly as the highest instance of academic decision-making in the University.' The members always stood to speak, and had to identify themselves. The meetings rarely finished after the time agreed upon. 'It was a matter of great pride to me,' he said, 'that we almost always finished, somehow, at that precise time, often to the minute.' In his view, 'the standing of the Academic Board was high – and has remained so.' His successor, Roger Beck, takes the same view, stating that 'the reformed Governing Council and the Academic Board, in my frankly partisan view, have worked extraordinarily well.'

⁂

The renewal of the faculty was another important objective for Connell. The new Centres of Excellence and government-sponsored chairs helped bring some new blood to the sciences. The humanities were not as fortunate. They had been assisted to a limited extent, however, by a $750,000 grant from the Mellon Foundation in the early 1980s – the first it had made for such a purpose outside the United States – to finance young faculty members in the humanities for a period of years. 'If we're going to have people capable of teaching graduate students in 1990,' said John Leyerle, the dean of the School of Graduate Studies, 'we've got to bring them on board now.' Appointments could be linked to pending retirements. A financial program to encourage early retirements also assisted in permitting new hirings.

The University of Toronto continued to require retirement at the age of 65. The policy was challenged in the courts by the U of T historian Norman Zacour and the associate chief librarian Ritvars Bregzis, along with others from other Ontario universities. Supported by the faculty association and both the federal and provincial associations of university teachers, the plaintiffs argued that the policy was a violation of the Canadian Charter of Rights and Freedoms, whose equality provision (section 15) came into force in April 1985. Some universities speculated that the universities would lose the case and made relatively generous arrangements with their faculty for continuing employment past age 65. On the advice of Provost Frank Iacobucci, the University of Toronto predicted that it would win the case. It did, and owing to the subsequent retirements of the many faculty members who had been hired in the 1960s, Toronto was able to hire junior faculty in the 1990s when a number of other universities could not. Of course, the policy also meant that many valuable senior faculty members who could continue to make a contribution were forced into retirement. Some divisions, such as the faculties of law and engineering, have been able both to renew the faculty and to find ways of using retired professors effectively in the teaching program as well as supporting their research.

One important change made in the late 1980s was to introduce long-range budgeting, designed to achieve financial equilibrium. Previously, most budgets had been fixed each year. That meant that it was difficult for divisions to do long-range planning because divisional budgets could change drastically from year to year. 'The greatest incentive of all' to divisional planning, wrote Daniel Lang, the assistant vice-president of planning who had been working in Simcoe Hall since the 1970s and in Connell's words 'provided the continuity and much of the genius' for planning at the University, 'is predictability and stability.' 'A process that offers some guarantees for the future,' Lang went on to say, 'even when the future is perilous and unpromising provides the security needed to plan and make commitments to plans. Planning must be a visible, continuous process, not a series of disconnected studies or task force reports which are wedded to particular times, circumstances or personalities.'

The solution adopted was to develop a five-year budget, based on a series of assumptions, with guarantees to divisions of a certain level of support during that period. On June 29, 1990 – the day before Connell left the presidency – he was able to send a memo to his successor, Robert Prichard, containing the most recent long-range budget projections. 'I am satisfied,' he told Prichard, 'that we are on target with our budget strategy, and if anything there has been a modest improvement in our circumstances, to the extent that the accumulative deficit will now reach its peak at approximately $19 million. You will recall that previous projections had a deficit of nearly $30 million.'

By the summer of 1987 – after the publication of *Renewal 1987* – Connell had announced that he would not seek a second term in office. He felt that by the time he left he would successfully have laid the foundations on which a new president could build. He would have been a university president for thirteen years when his term was up at the end of June 1990 – seven years at Western and six at Toronto. A search committee, under the governing council chair, Joan Randall, was established in January 1989. One internal candidate, Robert Prichard, and three external candidates, all long-serving and respected university presidents – James Downey of the University of New Brunswick, Arnold Naimark of Manitoba, and William Saywell of Simon Fraser – were interviewed. Prichard was chosen in October 1989. The faculty association president, Fred Wilson, was positive: 'He's got a good record, he's well liked in his faculty and he's respected as a scholar, administrator and fund raiser.' David Askew, the president of the staff association, agreed, saying: 'All indications suggest he'll be an active president.' The SAC president, Charles Blattberg, noted that the president-elect 'seems genuinely interested in improving the undergraduate experience.' Rosalie Abella, then chair of the Ontario Law Reform Commission, of which Prichard was a member, called Prichard 'a leader who is allergic to failure.'

Connell also was pleased. He had hoped Prichard would succeed him, having worked closely with him during the previous six years and having relied heavily on his advice. Prichard had been a member of the President's Advisory Committee and the Provost's Advisory Committee and had led the administration's team in one set of negotiations with the faculty association. Their styles, however, would be very different. Prichard was dynamic and outgoing, Connell cautious and low-key. A letter from Prichard to Connell in March 1989, commenting on one of Connell's somewhat pessimistic – though realistic – drafts on a particular issue, nicely reveals the difference in their approach. 'We should begin to build a mood that better days are still possible,' Prichard wrote, 'because often the mood we set will become a self-fulfilling prophecy.'

chapter forty-one

1994

❦

RAISING THE SIGHTS

In the spring of 1994, President Prichard would complete the assembly of his own personally selected team of four vice-presidents. Connell had had six. Prichard's would remain with him throughout his tenure and into that of the next president, Robert Birgeneau. It would prove to be an effective team. Prichard, with his characteristic enthusiasm, would describe them as 'the best vice-presidents in Canada.'

Michael Finlayson became vice-president for administration and human resources in 1994, expanding his existing portfolio of human resources, which he had taken on in 1991. He had previously been chair of history, but, more important, earlier he had been president of the faculty association on two separate occasions, each for a two-year period. Finlayson knew the politics of the association and its leaders. During the nine years he conducted salary negotiations for the University, agreements were reached voluntarily, and resort to binding arbitration proved necessary on only one occasion. Relations with the faculty association during the 1990s, though rarely smooth, did not have the debilitating effect they had had during the presidencies of Connell and Ham.

In July 1993, Adel Sedra, the chair of electrical engineering, succeeded Joan Foley as provost. Sedra too had been active in the faculty association. He had been a member of the association's council from 1978 until 1985 and had been one of the key players in the achievement of binding arbitration in the early 1980s. He had also been one of the original members of the academic board and,

Robert Prichard, rear, and his four vice-presidents in the fall of 1999: from left to right,
Michael Finlayson, Jon Dellandrea, Heather Munroe-Blum, and Adel Sedra.

for a number of years, until he was appointed provost, was chair of the board's
budget committee. 'We have to plan, change and move,' he said on his appointment as provost.

The third member of the team chosen by Prichard was Heather Munroe-
Blum, appointed as vice-president for research and international relations in
1993. An epidemiologist with a background in social work, she had been dean of
social work since 1989. 'As a young social worker in psychiatry,' she recalled, 'we
were taught to intervene, but where was the evidence that a particular interven-
tion was going to make a difference?' This question had led her into epidemiol-
ogy: 'I learned that research isn't the answer to everything but that with the right
questions, consideration to values and having a research base, you could be
much more effective in making change happen.'

To complete the group, Jon Dellandrea, the head of fund-raising at Mount
Sinai Hospital, was hired by the University in 1994 as vice-president and chief

development officer. He held a BA in English literature obtained in the early 1970s from Scarborough College and a doctorate in 1987 from OISE on – appropriately – corporate support and university development. A member of the Varsity Blues football team from 1969 to 1973 and named to the All-Canadian team in 1972, he played both offensive and defensive positions. He had been part of the Update campaign launched at the University in the 1970s and then had become vice-president and head of fund-raising at the University of Waterloo. The Waterloo campaign's goal was $21 million, but it raised $86 million. He had been similarly successful at Mount Sinai Hospital.

⊛

The early years of Prichard's presidency were difficult ones, both at the University and in his personal life. His youngest son, Jay, was diagnosed with brain cancer in 1992, and following surgery at the Hospital for Sick Children, was treated with chemotherapy and radiation. Prichard spent many nights at the hospital sleeping at Jay's side. He knew the hospital well because his own father, who had come with his family from England in 1950 when Prichard was a year old, had spent his career there as head of neurology. Eight years after the initial treatment, Jay has been doing very well. 'He finished runner-up in the public speaking contest at his school,' Prichard reported with pride.

Prichard's installation had taken place in October 1990. 'The current plight of our universities,' he told those in Convocation Hall, 'is desperate ... Our universities have been progressively ravaged for almost 20 years. We have reached the point where quality is more than suffering – it is being lost.' One of those on the platform was the recently elected NDP premier, Bob Rae, who was a friend of Prichard's, the two having attended U of T law school at the same time. But the new premier had other problems, and the financial picture for the University did not improve. Like his immediate predecessors, Prichard had to continue to cut budgets. He urged the University community 'to get the word out and keep it out as to how much damage' was being done by the inadequate funding. Between 1991 and 1998, the complement of full-time faculty and staff was reduced from 8,000 to 6,500.

The department of athletics and recreation, for example, faced a cut of over $1 million to its base budget. In 1992, it was announced that Varsity Stadium was to be closed and several intercollegiate teams discontinued, including men's

Warm-up exercises on the back campus before a Varsity football game in the fall of 1974.
Hart House and Soldiers' Tower are on the left, and the Laidlaw Library of University College
is on the right. Note that the then incomplete CN Tower can barely be seen rising above
University College.

football and women's ice hockey. Both alumni and students, however, worked to
save the teams. A lobby group made up of ex-football players, the 'Friends of
Football,' promised half the quarter of a million dollars required annually, and a
group of women lawyers sparked a similar campaign for women's hockey. In
addition, student activity fees were substantially raised. The graduate students'
and part-time students' associations objected to the increase, saying that it was
'unfair to force students, who seem uninterested in football, judging from game
attendance records, to pay more for it.' The teams survived, however, and the
following year the football team won the Vanier Cup as the Canadian intercollegiate champions, defeating the Calgary Dinosaurs 37–34. The women's hockey
team has become one of the strongest in Canada. It contributed five members to
Canada's first women's Olympic hockey team in 1998.

Another pressure facing the department of athletics was to ensure that the facilities for men and women at the athletic centre did not favour men, and that women's intercollegiate teams received equal funding. Bruce Kidd, dean of the faculty of physical education and health, strongly supported equality. 'If we fail to have a budget that gives men and women equality,' Kidd warned, 'we are going to be open to tremendous criticism.' Several years later, parts of the interior of the athletic centre were redesigned to provide better and equal facilities for women. Hart House – to cite another example of budget cuts – was forced to discontinue serving regular lunches and dinners in the Great Hall. It was losing $20,000 a month and would have to triple its daily number of 350 customers to break even. Unfortunately, no benefactors came to the aid of meals in the Great Hall.

The cutbacks had unexpected consequences for the faculty of medicine. A management consultant's report had suggested that eliminating about 80 support staff positions would save some $3 million a year. The positions were cut, but it was later discovered that the university procedures requiring prior consultation with the affected staff members had not been properly followed. The president took the blame for the errors made by Simcoe Hall. The event, however, provoked a crisis in the medical faculty, and Dean John Dirks, who had served four years of a six-year term as dean, resigned to bring to a close what he described as the 'divisive debate.' He had earlier been responsible for introducing problem-based learning to the medical school. (Dirks went on to be head of health sciences at the Aga Khan University in Pakistan and also became president of the Toronto-based Gairdner Foundation, which gives out international awards for significant achievements in the medical field.) Behind the immediate crisis was the widely held view in the medical faculty that greater openness and wider consultation was necessary. Arnold Aberman, the chair of medicine, who had been a vocal critic of Dirks' administration, subsequently became dean and followed a course of openness and consultation by keeping in close touch with the departmental chairs, who now reported directly to him and not through an associate dean. Aberman became well known for his flow of correspondence and faxes. Few administrators in the University produced as many e-mails or replied as rapidly to those received.

Prichard had been stung by the events, but, as with other issues during his administration, he was quick to apologize and to learn from the experience. One result was a determination to ensure that all important decisions, such as the one that had triggered the crisis, be discussed formally by what was known in Evans' time as 'Simcoe Circle' and in the 1990s as PVP (president and vice-presidents and various other senior administrators). Although many in Simcoe Hall, including the president, had known about and supported the dismissals, the proposal had never come before PVP. If it had, perhaps someone might have questioned the process, or even the decision to dismiss the staff. Munroe-Blum noted that from then on Prichard 'used PVP to debate, refine principles, and develop strategy for virtually every major issue confronting his administration,' including academic planning. A follow-up of the medical controversy was to make the dean of medicine a vice-provost, so that Simcoe Hall would be kept better informed of what was happening in the vast medical empire, and so that, at the same time, the dean would be involved in decision making at the highest levels in Simcoe Hall. There had previously been a vice-provost for health sciences, but that person had never been dean of medicine.

Throughout the 1990s, issues involving allegations of racism had to be dealt with. Several days after Prichard's installation, his office was occupied by an anti-racist group, the United Coalition against Racism, which demanded, among other things, that the University establish a racial harassment advocacy centre and that classes be cancelled on Martin Luther King Day for a teach-in on racism. Prichard defused the situation by appointing two special advisers, Mimi Rossi, a black paediatrician who was assistant dean of student affairs in the faculty of medicine, and Jack Wayne, a sociologist who had been director of the Transitional Year Program. Prichard told the governing council, 'There is much we can and must do to improve the racial climate.' 'The community around us has changed faster than we have changed ourselves,' he said in December 1990, after receiving the report requested from Rossi and Wayne. 'It remains clear to me that we have some catching up to do.' The University adopted several of the report's suggestions, including the establishment of a meeting room for the Native Students' Association, the creation of a presidential advisory committee on race relations, and the setting up of an office of race relations and anti-racism.

In a survey in 1994, about half the members of the student body identified themselves as non-white, yet the number of professors belonging to visible minority groups remained relatively low. At the end of the decade, Chandrakant Shah of the department of public health sciences published statistics showing that fewer than 9 per cent of the faculty members identified themselves as belonging to a visible minority group. The recommendation of the Rossi-Wayne report that candidates from minority backgrounds be selected over others who were 'equal academically' had not been brought in as official university policy. The hiring of members of visible minority groups had increased to about 14 per cent of new appointments by the end of the decade, but Shah argued that at that rate of hiring it might be more than fifty years before even 15 per cent of the faculty consisted of members of visible minority groups. University Professor Julia Ching, an expert on China, subsequently noted that 25 per cent of the student body was Chinese, but that only about 3 per cent of the tenured faculty was Chinese.

The University was becoming increasingly aware of the issue. The 1999 provost's planning report, *Raising Our Sights*, referred to the 'rich multi-cultural diversity of our student body and of the surrounding urban and suburban context.' 'On campus,' the report went on, 'these changes are most apparent among our students, but with the wave of faculty appointments that will occur in the next decade, they will come to characterize the faculty as well.' The provost's office in the past few years has emphasized the importance of proactive recruitment by divisions, 'building a broad, deep and diverse pool and ensuring that over time the proportion of visible minority candidates appointed reflects their representation in the pool.'

One contentious case that spanned the decade was that of Kin-Yip Chun, who had been a research associate in the physics department from 1985 to 1994 and had applied for a tenure-stream position on a number of occasions during that period. He was unsuccessful, however, and eventually brought a complaint of discrimination against the University before the Ontario Human Rights Commission. The University took the position that candidates hired into tenure-stream positions had superior qualifications. An earlier investigation within the University conducted by Cecil Yip, the vice-dean of research in the faculty of medicine, had found no discrimination, but did find that Chun had been 'exploited' in his capacity as a researcher in the department.

The Chun issue continued to fester on the campus, and gave rise to protests and disruptions reminiscent of the 1960s. At one governing council session in 1998, for example, some 70 protesters in support of Chun disrupted the meeting, which had to move to another location. The following year, the president's office was occupied for three days by Chun supporters. Although an investigator for the Ontario Human Rights Commission found evidence to support discrimination and recommended that a board of inquiry be estab-

lished, the full Human Rights Commission decided in the summer of 2000 –
after Prichard had left office – not to hold a hearing, citing insufficient evidence
to support the claim of racism. The University and Chun subsequently reached
an agreement that Chun would be brought back to the University as a research
associate without tenure, but with research funds, some compensation for
perceived injustice in the past, and the right to 'apply for any position for which
he is eligible and qualified to apply for.' The case spurred the development of a
policy on research associates. 'The absence of such a policy,' stated Vice-provost
Paul Gooch, 'contributed to the ambiguities of Chun's appointment.'

⊂⊃

Prichard and his vice-presidents were skilled in working with the existing university structures. There was no serious talk of returning to a bicameral system. The
governing council, Prichard noted, 'has been important in giving us the capacity
to legitimize change because all the estates are at the table.' The administration
was also able to work reasonably effectively with the faculty association. Librarian Bonnie Horne, the first woman to head the association, stated in the spring
of 1990 that Prichard's presidency 'will allow us to have a fresh start. With a new
president on both sides there is an opportunity to establish as good a relationship
as possible.'

A number of university policies were changed with the approval of the
association. Consent was necessary because of the so-called frozen policies that
had been specified in the memorandum of agreement entered into in 1977.
Prichard did not view the frozen policies as negatively as Connell had. Their
existence, he believed, meant that it was far less likely that the faculty would seek
to unionize. (By the end of the decade, a number of major Canadian research
universities, such as Queen's, Western, and UBC, had unionized faculties.) A
more detailed conflict of interest policy, requiring, for example, greater disclo-
sure of outside commitments, was eventually agreed to by the association.
Changes in the tenure rules were also brought in, but the faculty association
would not consent to a requirement that candidates for tenure have excellence in
both teaching and research and not just in one of the categories.

Although in late 1992 the business board questioned whether tenure was
necessary, Prichard argued that 'our focus should be on performance, not on the
institution of tenure itself.' Tenure is important in a university. Not only does

the system help to ensure that those given continuing appointments are of high quality, but, as law professor Stephen Waddams argued in the *Bulletin* in response to the business board's speculation, its principal justification is 'to encourage original thought and research by professional scholars ... The only way in which the university can effectively encourage new ideas is to make it clear that they will not bring adverse consequences to their originators, however uncomfortable the ideas may be.' Moreover, argued Sedra, 'our top departments compete with the large public universities in the US. If we changed the tenure system, nobody would look at us.'

Prichard later stated that the University 'is unequivocally committed to tenure, as the centrepiece of both academic freedom and our mission as one of the world's great public research universities.' Tenure decisions – both positive and negative – were carefully reviewed by the president, and on occasion he would call the members of the tenure committee to meet with him to explain their decision. The faculty association, however, took the position that the president was exceeding his authority and brought the issue before a grievance panel, which after a lengthy hearing held that the president indeed was responsible for reviewing tenure decisions. He could not call the members of the tenure committee to justify their actions, however, but instead had to work through the chair of the committee.

The faculty association consented to the clarification of the Haist rules relating to the appointment of academic administrators. These rules are now known as the Perron rules, named after Paul Perron of the French department, the chair of the committee that recommended the changes. Prichard was able to work within the rules to appoint the administrators he thought would forward the objectives of the faculty and the University. Not only did the central administration appoint the members of the search committees that chose deans and principals, but the committees were normally chaired by the provost, who would know Prichard's views on individual candidates. It was usual for Prichard to appear at one of the meetings to give his personal views on the needs of the faculty or college, but he was careful not to discuss specific names.

❦

In 1995, the University was faced with a major budgetary crisis. Mike Harris' Conservative government was elected in Ontario in June 1995, and its 'Common Sense Revolution' hit the Ontario university system in his first budget in November. Ontario was already last among the ten provinces in operating support per student. The University of Toronto would now be faced with a reduction of $56 million dollars in operating support. The University, Prichard said, will 'stay the course' – to use one of his favourite expressions – 'set out in our academic planning process.' 'We will not give up on our objective,' he went on – using words he would repeat on countless occasions – 'of being one of the world's great public research universities.' The University, in fact, was able to 'stay the course' thanks to its long-range budgeting, as well as the planning process that had been started in 1993. The budgeting process had been introduced by Connell and had been refined by Prichard and Sedra. Its multi-year budgets gave the divisions a period of time in which to adjust to the unexpected.

One immediate consequence of the cut was that whereas faculty salaries were frozen, administrative staff salaries were rolled back. This, in turn, helped fuel the unionization of the administrative staff. There were at the time 16 other unions in the University, but the 3,000 members of the administrative staff were not part of one. A certification drive by CUPE in 1990 had narrowly failed to receive support from the required 50 per cent of the eligible voters. In 1998, however, a drive by the Steelworkers of America was supported by 55 per cent of the votes. More than 80 per cent of the 2,400 members of the bargaining unit turned out for the vote.

As chair of the budget committee before becoming provost, Sedra had been interested in academic planning. He had seen the great difficulty in trying to close the faculty of architecture in the 1980s and in dropping forestry's undergraduate program in the early 1990s. Sedra thought there had to be a better process for rationalizing academic resources. Assisted by the political scientist and vice-provost Carolyn Tuohy, he began a new planning process in September 1993. They consulted widely, and on Valentine's Day, 1994 produced a white paper on university objectives, which they entitled *Planning for 2000*. 'The cost of doing nothing,' Tuohy observed, 'is to decline into mediocrity.'

The report, which was endorsed by governing council in March 1994, set out general objectives for the divisions to work with in developing their own divisional plans. 'What we foresee,' the white paper stated, 'is neither a grand design nor a mere aggregation of locally determined divisional plans, but rather a partnership between the centre and the divisions in shaping the University of the twenty-first century.' A number of objectives were set out as well as the strategies

Provost Adel Sedra and Deputy-provost Carolyn Tuohy, the authors of *Planning for 2000*, in 1994.

for achieving them. Among the objectives were linking teaching and research, recruiting and supporting outstanding students, and restructuring areas of study. A program, for example, should not be in the University of Toronto, the document stated, 'unless it is in demand by excellent students' and 'is regarded by peers to be in the top third among similar programs offered in Canada, or is the sole program of its type in Ontario.'

The document formed the basis for working with the divisions in the planning process. The divisions had to take the exercise seriously because success in obtaining the discretionary funds in the budget process depended on a sound divisional plan. As part of the budget process, each division had to surrender a portion of its budget – usually about 1.5 per cent per year – which then became part of what was called the academic priorities fund. This gave the central administration significant power to reshape the University. The planning process helped make change more palatable to the divisions involved. Sedra pointed out that, whereas the parties had experienced difficulties in working together in the past, the new planning process would mean that the academic divisions and the central administration would work together. He cited the example of the faculty of architecture and landscape architecture's working with the central administration to close its undergraduate division and concentrate on graduate work.

A second planning document, *Raising Our Sights*, was produced by Sedra and Tuohy in 1999 to prepare for the planning cycle from 2000 to 2004. The new document made it clear, however, that the earlier white paper remained 'the guiding framework for planning at the University of Toronto.' Three key priorities were identified in the new plan: building the faculty for the twenty-first century, enhancing the educational experience of students, and strengthening academic programs. One important change between the two planning documents was that in the period between the first and the second – without public discussion and without formal authorization from the governing council – the mission of the University was subtly elevated from being that of 'an internationally significant research university' to being a mission 'to rank with the best public research universities of the world.' The second planning report was approved by the governing council. The university's sights indeed had been raised.

❧

The planning process fed into a fund-raising campaign. 'It was not until the planning exercise was completed,' observed Vice-president Jon Dellandrea, 'that the objectives of the proposed campaign were set.' As in Connell's administration, the marketing experts had advised delay until the University had its house in better order. The University was told by the experts that 'the students and to a great extent the faculty talked of alienation, size and lack of community at U of T ... Until some significant strides are made to address these issues, it would be counter-productive to proceed with a lavish marketing campaign that would be undercut by word of mouth at every turn.' The 1994 white paper helped give a sense of direction to the University and encouraged changes to the student experience, such as the previously discussed arts and science option of a first year small-group seminar and an upper year research experience. Moreover, it was increasingly clear that, given the Harris cuts, the University could not achieve its potential without private support.

A campaign to raise $300 million was planned in 1994, following the publication of the white paper. The president of the Bank of Montreal, Tony

Comper, who holds a degree in English literature from the University, became chair of the campaign. Prichard's drive and optimism were crucial to its success. 'He's the biggest cheerleader the U of T has,' Dellandrea told the press. By the time the campaign was publicly launched in the fall of 1997, most of the $300 million had been raised. The goal was reset at $400 million, and later raised to $575 million. When Prichard left office at the end of June 2000, the official tally was $705 million. The campaign had come at a particularly good time because the second half of the 1990s was a time of strong economic activity, which was particularly reflected in the stock market. The campaign continues, and under Robert Birgeneau a new campaign target of $1 billion has been set to be reached by the year 2004.

Unlike previous campaigns, this one concentrated initially on human capital rather than physical facilities. When Prichard assumed office, there were only 14 endowed chairs in the entire University – that is, chairs supported by permanently endowed funds, the income from which paid the salaries of the occupants of the chairs. When he left, there were more than 160 such chairs. A professorial chair was valued at a minimum of $2 million. If a donor contributed $1 million, the University would match it with another million. The university money came mainly from the fund that had been built up with the pension savings the University had put aside following the agreement it had made in the 1980s with the faculty association. Over a four-year period, during which the University did not have to contribute to the pension plan, the University had accumulated about $150 million in a fund, called the endowed adjustment fund. There was pressure to use this fund for current needs, but Prichard wanted to protect it. The matching scheme would do so by locking in the funds in support of senior faculty positions. The first endowed chairs matched by the University were given in 1994 by the business associates John Bahen and Joseph Tanenbaum for two chairs in civil engineering, and the hundredth endowed chair was in Canadian studies at University College given by Warren Goldring, the founder of AGF mutual funds. The 150th chair, established in the year 2000, was in law and public policy (the law faculty's seventeenth endowed chair), given by friends and associates in the name of Robert Prichard and his spouse, lawyer Ann Wilson.

One concern that arose over the creation of these chairs was that few were going to the humanities. The professions, such as medicine, engineering, law, and business, were getting a disproportionate share of the resources raised. Chancellor Hal Jackman stepped forward and gave $5 million to attract 'internationally renowned' scholars in the humanities. The gift was of sufficient importance to the University that it was double-matched by the University to create a $15 million endowment fund for five chairs of $3 million each. A number of other contributions to the humanities followed. The former chancellor Rose Wolfe gave money for a chair in Holocaust studies, the Yewpick Lee Charitable Foundation of Hong Kong endowed a chair in the culture and philosophy of Chinese civilization, and the newspaper baron Conrad Black gave money for one of two chairs in Christianity and culture at St Michael's College – to select only three of many examples. Still, up until the end of the decade, the humanities as well as the social sciences did not do as well as the professions and the sciences.

Some major contributions, such as the Davenport gift, were from those with a long association with the University. Edna Street had graduated from household science in 1929, the same year that her future husband, John Davenport, graduated from chemical engineering. The couple were married three years later in the Hart House chapel. John had been secretary of the Hart House library committee. They later moved to the United States, but kept in touch with Toronto and the University. Claude Bissell's diary has an entry for June 5, 1969: 'met with Davenports – Engineering /29 who had given $20,000 for a student loan fund.' Seventy years after their graduation, a lawyer in Florida telephoned the University about a possible gift from an unnamed client. John Davenport had died earlier, and his wife wanted to do something to honour his name. (Some of the University's largest gifts, such as the David Dunlap Observatory and the Wallberg Memorial Building, have come about in this way.) The lawyer was put through to the chair of chemistry, Martin Moscovits, who suggested an endowed chair of $1 million. The lawyer took the idea back to his client and reported that she was thinking of something bigger. Moscovits then boldly suggested a cluster of chairs. Again the lawyer phoned back saying that his client was thinking of something more substantial. 'It's too bad your client isn't thinking in the order of $10 million,' Moscovits replied, 'because that would be the cost of a major new chemistry research facility.' Mrs Davenport was then identified, and she agreed to provide that sum plus an additional $3 million on her death to help support the three-storey addition to the Lash Miller Chemical Laboratories.

A substantial gift of $7.5 million was given by a relatively recent graduate, Jeffrey Skoll, who had graduated from electrical and computer engineering in

John Davenport graduated from chemical engineering in 1929, and his future wife, Edna Street, graduated from household science the same year. They were married in Hart House three years later. She donated funds after her husband's death for a major addition to the chemistry building.

1987. It was, in fact, only when Dellandrea and his group read in the *Globe and Mail* about Skoll's having made a fortune from his 'dot.com' company eBay that the fund-raisers became aware of him. Dellandrea visited Skoll at his offices in San Jose, California. According to Dellandrea, 'the first meeting lasted a little over 19 minutes and started with Jeff Skoll saying, "I know you're busy and I'm busy so let's get down to talking about what it is you wish to discuss."' In the course of the brief meeting, Skoll remarked that he had had a good engineering education at Toronto, but felt he had not acquired enough business expertise.

Jeff Skoll, a graduate of electrical and computer engineering in 1987 and a founder
of the 'eBay' company.

Skoll had gone on to take an MBA at Stanford University. About a month later,
another meeting was held in California – this time lasting about 45 minutes –
with Dellandrea and Skoll's fourth year supervisor at Toronto, Safwat Zaky. At
that meeting, Skoll agreed to consider a proposal to provide the lead gift to fund
a joint engineering/business degree. He subsequently made a commitment to
endow three chairs in what would be known as the Jeffrey Skoll BASc/MBA
program, as well as to provide support for the new Centre for Information
Technology.

At the end of Prichard's term as president, two other very large gifts were
announced, a $25 million gift from the cable and communications executive Ted

Rogers and his spouse Loretta Rogers, and a $50 million donation from the Samuel McLaughlin Foundation. Ted Rogers made the gift, to the department of electrical and computer engineering, to honour the memory of his father, Edward, the inventor of the batteryless radio receiver. Henceforth, the department would be named after Edward S. Rogers, Sr. The bulk of the money would be used for undergraduate and graduate scholarships. With various matching amounts from the University and the Ontario government, a minimum of 85 graduate awards would be created, each valued at approximately $20,000 per year.

In addition, $3 million from the Rogers gift would be used to build and equip the Rogers AT&T Wireless Communications Laboratories for wireless technology research. The laboratory would be located in the new Bahen Centre for Information Technology, then under construction on St George Street north of the Koffler Centre. The engineering graduate John Bahen had donated $6 million towards the construction of the centre, which would bring closer together the department of computer engineering and the arts and science department of computer science. The Bahen Centre, stated Michael Charles, the dean of engineering, 'will provide the opportunity for an even greater level of codisciplinary interaction between computer scientists and computer and electrical engineers. Many of the most important developments occur where disciplines converge.'

The McLaughlin Foundation gift will have as profound an effect on cellular and biomolecular research in the University and its affiliated hospitals as the Rogers donation will have on computer science and engineering. The foundation was set up about fifty years ago by Sam McLaughlin, a pioneer in the Canadian auto industry. 'Who will remember Sam McLaughlin in 2001?' he had asked. 'Let's wrap it up then.' The foundation gave $50 million of the remaining funds to establish the R. Samuel McLaughlin Centre at the University of Toronto and at its teaching hospitals. The gift was matched by the Ontario government and by the hospitals, making a total of $150 million. The centre would be located at various places in the University and at the hospitals, and would include a new site for cellular and biomolecular research to be built on Taddle Creek Road between the Mining and FitzGerald buildings and to be physically connected to the Medical Sciences and other surrounding buildings. 'Researchers often used to move to the States saying Canada can't compete,' said James Woodgett of the department of medical biophysics and the Princess Margaret Hospital. 'That excuse has gone out the window with this initiative.'

Chancellor Rose Wolfe at her last convocation, June 1997. Wendy Cecil-Cockwell, the chair of the governing council, is on the left.

The number of large gifts made by individuals who were students in the 1950s is striking, and perhaps reflects the opening sentence of an earlier chapter, which noted that 'it was good to be a student in the 1950s.' Many previously mentioned graduates from the 1950s – Bahen (1954) and his wife, Margaret (1952), Jackman (1953), Rogers (1956), and Tanenbaum (1955) – did well in business and remembered the University. Other major donors from the 1950s include Leslie Dan, Peter Munk, and Joseph Rotman. Dan contributed $8 million towards a new $44 million pharmacy building, to be named for him, that will double the number of students enrolled in pharmacy. It will be constructed on the site of the present greenhouse at the corner of Queen's Park and College Street. Peter Munk and his associated companies donated $6.4 million for the renovated former Devonshire House, which now houses the Munk Centre for International Studies – a partnership between the University and Trinity College. Ted Rogers contributed funds for a new library for Trinity College in the centre, named after his father-in-law, John Graham. Under the centre's director, political scientist Janice Stein, it is the home of 11 graduate and undergraduate centres and programs specializing in international studies. Joseph Rotman and his wife, Sandra, donated $18 million towards the building and the program of the Rotman School of Management on St George Street. The number of Jewish contributors within this group is also striking. The fact that Rose Wolfe, highly respected in the Jewish community, had been chancellor of the University from 1991 to 1997 may have been a factor in drawing the community more closely into the University, as was Jon Dellandrea's knowledge of the Jewish community from his years as head of development at Mount Sinai Hospital.

Several of these gifts and research contracts provoked controversy. Some people believed strongly that the University was becoming too close to big business. 'We are not the Loblaws of science and technology or knowledge,' stated engineering professor Ursula Franklin. 'Industry can jolly well do their own research and employ our graduates.' Philosopher Bill Graham, the president of the faculty association, in a series of articles in 1998 entitled 'Corporatism and the University,' expressed concern about the lack of debate on the direction of the University. 'Since the 1980s the view that the purpose of the university is to contribute to the economic growth of the province and the nation has been gaining strength and acceptance,' he wrote. 'As more and more academics become dependent on private funding to carry on their work, it becomes increasingly difficult to think critically and dispassionately about other visions of the purpose of the University.' The *Varsity* was an especially outspoken critic of the administration on these issues. Even the business-minded *Globe and Mail* editorialized about arrangements 'whose intimacies expose both universities and their donors to historically rooted doubts about the wisdom of it all.'

Concern focused particularly on four gifts: Joseph Rotman's donations to management studies, Peter Munk's for the Munk Centre for International Studies, Nortel's to set up the Nortel Institute for Telecommunications, and the Toronto Stock Exchange's for a capital markets institute to be run jointly by the faculties of management and of law. In all these cases, the donors did not just give the money and leave it to the University to spend it, but they wanted some further involvement in the overall operations. A similar controversy, it will be recalled, had erupted shortly after the First World War concerning major gifts to the medical faculty by Timothy Eaton and the Rockefeller Foundation: the Eatons had a major say in the selection of the holder of the Eaton chair, and in both cases there were obligations placed on the University with respect to future financial support of the relevant medical departments. In the case of the stock exchange gift, the donor's involvement was minor, in that it gave the president of the exchange a place on an advisory committee that was to be selected by the two deans. The Nortel agreement, however, went somewhat further and specified that the search committee process for chairs and tenure-stream positions should be 'conducted in consultation with Nortel.' The Rotman donation required the setting up of an international academic advisory committee of external business people that would be consulted on faculty appointments, and the Munk donation gave the Barrick International Advisory Board (Barrick Gold is controlled by Munk) the right to 'provide such assistance and resources ... as the Board may in its discretion consider appropriate and the Council [of the Munk Centre] will be receptive thereto.' The faculty association president, Graham, complained that in the case of the Munk gift 'the vagueness, ambiguities and lack of specific protection for academic freedom and crucial University policies was scary.' 'What was entailed,' he asked, 'by saying the Council "will be receptive" to the Board's advice?' Both the Rotman and the Munk gifts were to be given over a period of years – ten in the case of the Munk gift and eleven for Rotman's – and the donors could withdraw future funding if dissatisfied with the progress made. The terms thus gave the donors potential influence over the conduct of the recipient.

The outcry caused the Rotman, Munk, and Nortel agreements to be re-drafted to minimize the possibility of outside influence. 'Mr. Munk wishes it to be unequivocally clear,' Prichard told the academic board, 'that it was not his intention to place any constraint on the university's autonomy or the freedom of its members.' The provost's office subsequently brought in guidelines to reaffirm the University's dedication to the principle of academic freedom. The first of these states that 'at the heart of the university lies the commitment to academic freedom, which may not be abridged.' The second states that 'the university values and will protect its integrity, autonomy and academic freedom, and does not accept gifts when a condition of such acceptance would compromise these fundamental principles.' Another provides that it is the University which creates advisory bodies with the agreement of the relevant academic unit or units. 'The guidelines,' said Graham, 'are a substantial improvement over what we had before – which was nothing.' Graham noted that 'the medieval scholar had to worry about the church ... We have to concern ourselves with the directing power of money. It's a seductive and driving influence.'

The controversy surrounding the Munk donation spilled over into the ceremony in the fall of 1997 at which the former US president George Bush – a member of Barrick's International Advisory Board – was awarded an honorary degree by the University. Twenty-eight faculty members, led by Ursula Franklin, quietly walked out of the hall as political scientist Jean Smith started to read the citation, in part because they disapproved of Bush's record and in part because it was thought that the degree had been arranged to suit Munk's interests. This was the most controversial honorary doctorate since the one awarded to Adlai Stevenson, the American ambassador to the United Nations, in the 1960s during the Vietnam war. As it turned out, one of the least controversial and most celebrated degrees ever awarded by the University was also associated with the Munk Centre. It was given in February 2000 to Archbishop Desmond Tutu, who took part in the inaugural conference at the centre, entitled 'Justice, Memory and Reconciliation.'

The ability to match donor funds was an important part of the fund-raising campaign. It was particularly important in acquiring funds for student scholarships and bursaries. The University knew that it had to acquire funds for needy students if it was to raise fees, as it hoped to do. It announced that it would match contributions to endow student aid. Independently, the provincial government had been developing its own incentive program to encourage support for student aid and launched a matching scheme several months after U of T's program was under way. U of T adapted quickly to what became a double match.

The government's matching program for Ontario universities cost the province $300 million, and Toronto received a little over $100 million of that sum. This double match meant that a contribution of $1,000 for student aid would result in an increase of $2,000 in the endowment. The University of Toronto was able to raise over $100 million in student aid, and the total student-aid endowment now amounts to half a billion dollars. The total university endowment at present is about $1.2 billion. It had been a little over $200 million in 1990. The next-highest endowments in Canada are at McGill and UBC, which have endowments of about $600 million, and Alberta is not far behind. The Toronto endowment, which amounts to about $24,000 per full-time equivalent student, is, however, far below those of a number of US public universities, such as Michigan, with $52,000 per full-time student, and Virginia, with $65,000. It does not come anywhere close to Princeton's $900,000, Harvard's $750,000, or MIT's $300,000 per student.

Although student fees for basic undergraduate programs continue to be regulated by the Ontario government, and universities thereby are prevented from raising fees on their own, a number of professional programs, such as management studies, law, medicine, and dentistry, as well as of graduate programs, were completely deregulated. This allowed the universities to set their own tuition policies in these fields, and the University of Toronto made the decision to raise significantly the tuition fees for professional programs, but only modestly those for doctoral programs. Moreover, the Ontario government has been allowing fees to rise by a set amount in regulated programs. Between 1995 and 2000, tuition fees for first-entry arts and science students at Toronto have increased by more than 50 per cent, and professional fees, such as in medicine, have more than doubled. Some Ontario universities now get 50 per cent of their operating budget from tuition fees; Toronto gets about 30 per cent from that source. The annual income from tuition fees at U of T amounted to $50 million at the beginning of the decade and more than $200 million at the end.

A seventeen–person provostial task force, co-chaired by Deputy Provost Tuohy and Vice-provost Derek McCammond, recommended in early 1998 that no student be prevented from entering or completing a program of study because of financial need, and that all U of T students should know on entry what the maximum tuition fee will be over their course of study. Prichard was delighted. The University should be able to say to students, he stated, 'If you're admitted to U of T, we will work with you to ensure you have the resources necessary to get here.' The guarantee, approved by the governing council in April 1998, was unique for Canadian universities. The new policy stated that 'no student offered admission to a program at the University of Toronto should be unable to enter or complete the program due to lack of "financial means."'

At the beginning of the decade, the University spent about $12 million a year on financial support for its students. At the end of the decade, the figure was in excess of $50 million. Research by the task force showed, according to Tuohy, that over the course of the decade 'there doesn't seem to be any evidence we are losing lower-income students.' The *Varsity* was not convinced, however, and said editorially, 'It is idiotic that the report refuses to recognize the magnitude of the problem it is facing.' It criticized the research, based on student postal codes, calling it 'one of the loopiest bits of useless research we have ever seen.' Subsequent direct surveys of students by Vice-provost Ian Orchard reinforced the findings by the task force that the proportion of students from low-income families had not declined in an era of increased tuition. The debate will continue. One thing is clear, however: the *Varsity* was at least as critical of the administration in the 1990s as it was in the 1890s.

chapter forty-two

1997

❦

MOVING UP PARNASSUS

In 1997, a particularly significant change in government funding took place that greatly assisted the University of Toronto. Both the Ontario and the federal government began to invest large sums of money for research and development in the universities. The University of Toronto, with the strongest research base in Canada, received a substantial share of these new funds. Provincial formula funding, which had tended to homogenize the Ontario universities, would no longer determine the fate of the University of Toronto.

In earlier periods, the Ontario government had provided about 85 per cent of Toronto's basic operating funds through formula funding, with about 15 per cent coming from tuition. By the end of the 1990s, however, Ontario's contribution was down to 60 per cent. When research funding and other sources of income, such as tuition, private gifts, and interest on the endowment, were taken into account, formula funding was responsible for only about one-third of the total University of Toronto operating budget of over a billion dollars. Indeed, formula funding to the University had gone down over the decade – from roughly $400 million to roughly $350 million. Ontario's contribution to the operating funds of its universities continued to be significantly below that of every other province.

The Ontario government had assisted research at Ontario universities – and particularly the University of Toronto – through the Centres of Excellence program started in the 1980s, but it was only after a report from an Ontario government-appointed committee in late 1996 entitled 'Future Directions for Postsecondary Education,' chaired by the economist and former principal of Queen's University David Smith, that non-formula special purpose funding by the Ontario government was significantly increased. Prichard called it 'the best report on higher education released in Canada in the last 25 years.' The Smith report emphasized the importance of post-secondary education, noting that 'university research contributes greatly to our economic competitiveness' – a message that was attractive to the Harris government. Within days of the release of the report, Ontario announced that there would be no further funding cuts for universities and community colleges. The report urged Ontario to develop a research policy and to increase the funds available to the universities for research overhead and research infrastructure. 'We urge the Province,' the report stated, 'to consider a policy of focusing more of its limited resources on promoting excellence in research, through directing funds to ... [support] research over-heads ... to be distributed on the basis of measures of quality.'

So many new Ontario and federal programs have been established over the past few years that one can easily get lost in the complexity of the various programs and the many acronyms by which they are known. A particularly important Ontario program has been the competitive 'Challenge Fund,' created in 1998 to support research operations, including support for researchers and, to a certain extent, research infrastructure. The program, currently valued at $500 million over ten years, requires a match of one-third of the amount of any award from industry. Toronto has received almost half of these awards. They have been given, for example, to the Energenius Centre for Advanced Technology ($15 million), to the Bell University Labs ($12 million), to the Nortel Institute ($9 million), to the faculty of dentistry's Advanced Biomaterials and Regenerative Surgery Research Unit ($5 million), and to John Polanyi and his colleagues (about half a million dollars) to investigate how to imprint patterns of molecular size on a silicon chip through chemical reactions.

Another program, created in 1998, that has given Toronto about half the total sum available is the Premier's Research Excellence Awards, which provide graduate student support to faculty members who win awards. Furthermore, in 1999 the 'SuperBuild' fund was announced, to support the infrastructure necessary for an expansion of student enrolment and for research. Two examples of expanding enrolment areas that have received SuperBuild funds are the Bahen Centre for Information Technology ($24 million) on the St George campus and

Artist's sketch of the Bahen Centre for Information Technology, on St George Street near College Street. Note the incorporation into the design of the house that formerly contained the offices of the *Varsity*.

a program in communication, culture, and information technology, in partnership with Sheridan College ($27 million), at Erindale College (renamed the University of Toronto at Mississauga in 1998). Most recently, the province has adopted a number of the recommendations made in a provincial report on university research by Vice-president Heather Munroe-Blum, in particular the recommendation that the province increase the overhead allocation for provincially funded research to 40 per cent of the direct costs of the projects.

The Ontario Innovation Trust has been matching awards given by the federal government's Canada Foundation for Innovation (CFI). The federal CFI program of close to $2 billion provides funds on a competitive basis – with matching funds from the universities and their industrial partners – for major infrastructure developments. Toronto, with about 8 per cent of Canada's university faculty, has attracted about 15 per cent of these federal awards, but it has also received 40 per cent of the amount that Ontario provided in matching funds. Success in one program, therefore, often has a multiplier effect.

The CFI program, whose president is David Strangway and whose chairman is John Evans, was launched in 1997. It has contributed funds to such undertakings as the projected Centre for Cellular and Biomolecular Research ($25 million), led by James Friesen of the Banting and Best Department of Medical

Research, and a functional imaging research network (about $10 million), headed by the neuropsychologist Donald Stuss. Other significant amounts have been awarded, for example, for a physical sciences computer network, to the Lash Miller Chemical Laboratories, to Scarborough's Centre for Integrative Research on Stress and the Brain, and to Mississauga's Centre for Applied Biosciences and Biotechnology. Almost all the CFI money has gone to medicine, engineering, and science. Toronto, with its affiliated teaching hospitals, received about $70 million from the CFI in 1999 and another $35 million the following year – and these sums were matched by the Ontario government. Moreover, the federal government has announced that the CFI will be extended to 2005, and another billion dollars added to the pot. The sums are remarkable when compared, for example, to the $10,000 that Vincent Bladen was able to find for John Polanyi's path-breaking work in the 1950s.

The multiplier effect of success in achieving funds from one source can clearly be seen in the program announced by the federal government in late 1999 to create 2,000 endowed chairs at Canadian universities in celebration of the new millennium. The government had been warned in a confidential report by the Prime Minister's Advisory Council on Science and Technology that the brain drain was not a myth, and was causing serious problems for universities, particularly in those areas that were driving Canada's economic growth. Prichard and others from the University had publicly expressed grave concern over the loss of leading scholars. 'Not a week goes by these days without a "retention battle,"' Sedra told the press. The federal finance minister, U of T graduate Paul Martin, announced the new program, saying, 'These will be new research positions at Canadian universities designed to attract the best researchers from around the world, and to retain the best from across Canada.' Prichard called it 'the single most important step forward in the past decade for Canada's research capacity.'

The allocation of these chairs among Canadian universities has been made according to each university's success in receiving competitively awarded funds from the three federal granting agencies: the Medical Research Council (MRC), now called the Canadian Institutes for Health Research (CIHR); the Natural Sciences and Engineering Research Council (NSERC); and the Social Sciences and Humanities Research Council (SSHRC). The funding for all these bodies has increased over the past few years, particularly for the council for health research. Because the University of Toronto has done well in the competition for the funds of these councils, at least 250 new endowed research chairs will be

Philosopher Bill Graham, a former president of the University of Toronto Faculty Association. Photograph taken in 1992.

allocated to it. The university with the next-highest number of chairs is McGill, with 162, and it is followed by the University of British Columbia, with 160. The importance of these new chairs to the University of Toronto and its teaching hospitals is enormous. The value of the chairs to the University of Toronto will amount to some $40 million a year in perpetuity, which is the equivalent of close to a billion dollars in endowment funds. The process of selecting the chairs at Toronto, which are to be 'clustered in key areas of academic priority and research strength,' began in June 2000.

The extent of the federal government's contribution to the health of universities through these programs – as well as the generous millennium student scholarships inaugurated in the year 2000, which will fund more than 100,000 Canadian students each year for ten years – has not been seen since the late 1950s, when the federal government followed the advice of the Massey Commission and provided funds to help finance the growth of the university system. The faculty association, however, has expressed concern about the implication of the new chairs program. Its president, Bill Graham, returned to the concerns he had expressed earlier over donor control of the University's agenda in private funding. Because the number of chairs depends on the total funds that were available from each granting council and each university's share of those funds, relatively few new chairs at the University of Toronto will go to the humanities and social sciences. About 85 per cent of the 250 chairs at the University will go to medicine, the natural sciences, and engineering. 'This massive restructuring of our University,' Graham wrote in the faculty association's newsletter, 'is taking place without any real debate in the Academic Board and the Governing Council ... The issue is the corporate take-over of our University.'

The administration argues, however, that additional resources free up funds that can then be reallocated internally. So, for example, it points out that the University has been generously supporting the library system, which is primarily used by the humanities and social sciences. Over $40 million a year is devoted to the central library system, and when the divisional libraries are added, the figure is over $60 million. Toronto is ranked third among university libraries in North America and has recently become the top-ranked library of any public university on the continent. How the University will maintain a proper balance among disciplines will be one of the major subjects of debate within the University in the coming decade.

The development of these various sources of government funding has been a priority of Simcoe Hall. 'Most of these sources of funds,' Prichard pointed out, 'are interdependent.' 'If you check out of any one category of funding, you are almost certain to disadvantage yourself in a variety of sources of funding.' The advantage to the University of a diversification of revenue sources, he added, allows for diversification of risks. Toronto is no longer as dependent on the provincial operating grant as it once was. Putting together a proposal today, he observed, requires considerable creativity. A number of sources of funding have to be tapped. The new Centre for Cellular and Biomolecular Research, for example, has combined funds from the Canada Foundation for Innovation, the provincial fund (the Ontario Innovation Trust) that matches this source, the SuperBuild fund, and private donations.

The new government programs have obviously helped the University of Toronto. 'The combined force of all these programs,' Prichard noted, 'almost all of which are based on competition and where the results are dynamically inter-related, is to generate far greater differentiation of outcome for Canada's universities.' 'All these federal and provincial initiatives,' he wrote, 'are putting wind in our sails. At present, we have a quite remarkable alignment of federal and provincial forces all blowing basically in the same direction. As a result, for institutions like the University of Toronto which has, in effect, a very large spinnaker, we are going to pick up a lot of speed and leave a lot of distance between us and other institutions ... This phenomenon may not last. But for now, it is blowing away many cobwebs of the homogeneity forced upon the university system.'

❧

The 1990s also saw an enhancement of the physical beauty of the University. The key event was the revitalization of St George Street, which divides the downtown campus – the 'great divide,' as it has been known. The street had been widened to four lanes in the 1940s – a time when no one talked seriously about extending the campus west of St George Street. After development took place on the west campus, Bissell had tried to move the street underground from Hoskin Avenue to College Street. 'Only in this way,' he argued, 'can we unify the campus, liberate the pedestrians and assure the free flow of motor traffic.' But the plan proved to be too expensive. In 1994, a competition was organized by the University to develop ideas about the street. Twenty submissions were received, but 'no single perfect vision surfaced.'

That summer, Trinity graduate Judy Matthews went to see Prichard and offered $1 million towards the redesign of the street. She had an interest in planning and architecture: she had taken a master's degree in urban planning at York University, and her great-grandfather was E.J. Lennox, who had designed Toronto's old city hall. The University gladly accepted the donation. Working with Elizabeth Sisam's planning team at the University, the city of Toronto provided the additional funds required and hired outside planners. The street was narrowed by 8 feet, the sidewalks were widened, and flowers and trees were planted. The prize-winning remodelled street was opened officially in October 1996, on a cold and rainy afternoon. 'Wait for spring,' Matthews told those attending the ceremony, 'when there will be another 220 trees, pedestrian lighting and gates – it will be quite a different street.' Which indeed it is.

Matthews did not stop there. She helped promote the development of a plan for the many open spaces of the University – spaces that comprise almost 60 per

A rejuvenated St George Street, officially opened in October 1996.

cent of the University's 140 acres of downtown land. 'Open space,' she said, 'plays an important part in city life ... Toronto has no large central park like New York. King's College Circle and Queen's Park are Toronto's version.' The University subsequently hired a number of outside consultants to develop an open space plan. The primary objectives identified in the master plan were approved in principle by the governing council in May 1999. Six demonstration projects were proposed. Estimated to cost over $30 million, the plan, once implemented, would transform the University – more green space, more trees, fewer cars, less concrete, and greater recognition of the importance of pedestrians. Matthews is the fund-raising officer leading this initiative under Jon Dellandrea.

King's College Circle and the roads and paths leading to it would be given new life. Trees would be planted west of Hart House and Wycliffe College, and parking eliminated on Tower Road, leading to Soldiers' Tower. More trees would be planted on Hoskin Avenue and Harbord Street. Taddle Creek would again surface on the campus. With the use of rain water, parts of the creek would be re-created along Philosopher's Walk, and McCaul's Pond, which was buried as a sewer in the 1880s, would reappear close to its original site south-east of Hart House. The grounds surrounding the old Knox College on Spadina Crescent would be revitalized, and Willcocks Street on the west campus would have more open space and less traffic – a familiar but unfulfilled hope over the years. Professor Michael Marrus, the head of the governing council's design advisory committee, wholly supported the plan and was optimistic about its implementation. 'Who would have predicted that the St. George Street project would have been feasible?' he asked. 'Now we have a kind of momentum out of that project that is carrying us forward.'

The first stage of the implementation would focus on King's College Circle. 'The Circle has deteriorated enormously,' Matthews stated. 'Cars have intruded into the fabric of the university.' Over $2 million has been set aside by the University for the project, with other funds to come from the fund-raising campaign. A grander tree-lined entrance would lead from College Street to King's College Circle. The concrete and asphalt in front of Convocation Hall, where graduates mingle with their family and friends after graduation, would become a plaza. For the most part, parking would be eliminated around the circle, and more trees would be planted. A bold part of the plan – though one not included in the first phase – is to give greater prominence to the Wellesley Street entrance to the University. It would be done by eliminating the flyover on Queen's Park Crescent constructed in the late 1940s, and reintroducing a ground-level entrance to the University, complete with traffic lights to slow down the traffic and allow safer pedestrian access. A planning firm from Pennsylvania that had worked on the University of Pennsylvania campus and at other universities was selected to develop the first stage.

Greater awareness of the importance of art in the University became evident during the decade. Planners were encouraged to include outdoor art as part of their buildings, and in 1996 a new art gallery opened – the University of Toronto Art Centre. About 7,000 square feet of space was provided in the Laidlaw Wing of University College to house three existing collections: University College's own collection, works of art acquired by the University over the years, and the magnificent Malcove collection. A list of what the University owned and where the objects were located had not been made until the late 1970s. A painting by the nineteenth-century French painter Fantin-Latour, for example, was found abandoned in the basement of the Galbraith Building.

The Malcove collection is particularly impressive. The New York psychoanalyst Lillian Malcove had acquired more than 500 fine pieces, with a particular

Proposed design for a plaza in front of Convocation Hall.

emphasis on medieval Christian art, and wanted the collection left to a university with an outstanding medieval program. She investigated a number of universities, and on her death in 1982 left her collection to the University of Toronto. A new gallery on the St George campus was clearly necessary. The Malcove's superb sixteenth-century painting by the German Renaissance master Lucas Cranach, showing Eve offering Adam an apple, with a snake overhead, was soon on display in the Art Centre.

The new Art Centre complemented Hart House's splendid Canadian art collection and the temporary shows in Hart House's Justina M. Barnicke Gallery. Art galleries were also established at the Scarborough and Mississauga campuses. Although the Royal Ontario Museum is now no longer officially part of the University – it separated in the mid-1960s so as to be able to attract its own funding from the government and the private sector – it continues to enrich the cultural life of the University.

The new University of Toronto Art Centre was a success. Its space, however, was limited and was not properly climate-controlled. Thanks to an anonymous donor in 1997, the gallery was able to double its size in University College. It reopened in the spring of 2000. The real purpose of the gallery, according to its then director David Silcox, best known for his books on the Canadian artist David Milne, is to support teaching and scholarship. An exhibit planned for 2001, 'The Ambidextrous Polymath,' will be devoted to the art and life of Sir Daniel Wilson, the University's second president. Wilson, who could draw with both hands, in his early years worked with the great English artist J.M.W. Turner.

University plans called for the construction of numerous new buildings on the campus. In the past, the University had had to deal with ratepayers' groups who objected to plans for specific buildings, such as the Robarts Library and the athletic centre. This discussion inevitably slowed down the process of getting approval from the city of Toronto, and also created public relations problems for the University. A new process was developed that culminated in an agreement with the city in 1997 – with the support of local ratepayers' groups – to permit the development of more than twenty specific sites on the downtown campus. These sites included all those the University needed for its current plans, plus additional sites that may be required in the foreseeable future. In exchange, the city was assured that the University would extend and maintain its heritage sites, and that future buildings would conform to certain guidelines.

The sites include that of the Banting and Best Institutes on College Street at the south-east end of the campus, and the area behind the faculty of education building on the north-west corner of Bloor and Spadina. The agreement with the city allows for the redevelopment of the Varsity Stadium lands and of the old Knox College, for an addition to the north side of Sidney Smith Hall, for development on the site of the parking lot behind Simcoe Hall, for expansion behind the Sigmund Samuel Library building, and for redevelopment of St Michael's lands on Wellesley Street, east of Queen's Park Crescent – to cite some further examples. Moreover, it has permitted the development of a number of sites for which detailed planning had already begun, such as the Bahen Centre for Information Technology north of the Koffler Centre, the Davenport Building on St George Street, the cellular and molecular biology building on Taddle Creek Road, and the new graduate student residence at the corner of Spadina Avenue and Harbord Street.

In 1997, the governing council set up a physical planning and design advisory committee to review design policy, select future architects, and consider the design of future university buildings. 'Now is the time,' argued planning professor Alan Waterhouse in the *Bulletin*, 'to uncover and remake the whole process of architectural decision making and commissioning if we are to rescue what is valuable and restore some vestige of visual excellence to the campus.' Alex Waugh of Woodsworth College, who chaired the body that had recommended the physical planning committee, stated, 'We need to open up our planning, make it more accountable to the larger community – not just architects, but people who want the campus to look good.'

The plans for Varsity Stadium changed over the decade, as the University's finances improved and new priorities emerged. At one point, the land was to be used for commercial development, a luxury hotel, and condominiums, plus athletic facilities. Objections by various student groups slowed things down. The University then realized that it needed more land for student residences, and in 1999 it was announced that the site would be developed for athletic facilities and student housing. The new plans include a much smaller grandstand – perhaps seating 5,000 persons – an eight-lane track that is slightly narrower than international standards, and an indoor skating rink. The president of the Students' Administrative Council, Chris Ramsaroop, had appealed to the governing council to stop the earlier commercial project, and expressed delight at the outcome: 'It was a David and Goliath battle – students should take credit for this. It shows the power of the little people.'

At all three campuses, the university policy is to offer housing to all entering students who seek places. At the end of the decade, only 17 per cent of the student body could be housed in residences. John Browne of Innis College, who has chaired the committee on residence development, noted in 1999 that the number of applicants for residence on the various campuses had almost tripled in the previous six years. An additional 2,500 places would have to be constructed. A graduate students' residence for 450 students was built at the corner of Spadina Avenue and Harbord Street. Unlike the athletic centre, which turned its back on Spadina – the ill-fated Spadina Expressway was still a possibility when the athletic centre was planned – the new residence faces the street and is a

Graduate House, at the north-east corner of Harbord Street and Spadina Avenue,
officially opened in 2000.

western gateway to the campus, with its massive and controversial sign 'University of Toronto' overhanging half the width of Harbord Street. The architecture dean, Larry Richards, calls the building 'fantastic' – some local residents call it an 'eyesore' – and he has described the sign as 'a rhetorical piece that, I think, just baffles people. I like that part of it a lot.' There will be a residence complex for Woodsworth College at the south-east corner of St George and Bloor, and other residences are being planned.

The Students' Administrative Council, which was in need of additional space, had also objected, without success, to the tearing down of the temporary building east of University College. A sixteen-person committee, chaired by Vice-provost Ian Orchard, was established to study student needs. It identified a number of pressing concerns, including a place for students to worship. 'If you're Christian,' said Margaret Hancock, a committee member and warden of Hart House, 'there are numerous chapels on campus so there isn't a problem, but if you're Islamic, for example, and have to pray five times a day, there aren't many places close to your classroom.'

Opposition to the tearing down of some old houses on St George Street for the Bahen Centre for Information Technology resulted in changes to its design. The nineteenth-century building that housed the *Varsity* and other student activities at the corner of St George and Russell streets, as well as two buildings to the south, were to be taken down to make way for the centre. The Toronto Heritage Board recommended that the *Varsity* building be saved, but not the other two. A compromise was reached. The façade and other parts of the historical house were incorporated into the centre. The *Varsity* and forty other student organizations were given space in the Sussex Court apartments at the corner of Sussex Avenue and Huron Street.

⮿

Plans were prepared to expand enrolment on all three campuses to meet the future growth of demand for university places. The growth will be the result principally of what the U of T economist David Foot referred to in his book *Boom Bust & Echo* as the growing up of the 'echo kids,' that is, the children of the post-war baby boomers. (The book has been enormously successful. 'No non-fiction book published in this country,' the *Globe and Mail* observed, 'has sold so many copies in so short a time. Ever.') The increase in enrolment will also be due in part to the increase in the number of persons returning to university to upgrade their skills. It was predicted that demand for post-secondary places in Ontario at the end of the first decade of the new millennium might result in permanent growth of 40 per cent. To add to the problem, there will be a temporary crisis in enrolment early in the new millennium on account of the so-called double cohort caused by the planned elimination of grade 13 in the province. This change will create a demand for places by graduates from both grade 12 and grade 13 in the year 2003.

The University of Toronto explored how it would meet the need and concluded that, with appropriate new government funding, the principal growth will be at Scarborough and Mississauga, where enrolment will increase by about 50 per cent on each campus. All the growth at Scarborough will be in the co-op programs (planned mixes of work and study), the aim being eventually to enrol over half the students in such programs. A large component of the Mississauga increase (about 1,000 students) would be in a proposed joint program with Sheridan College – a community college in the western end of the greater Toronto area – in communication, culture, and information technology.

The St George campus, it was concluded, will grow by fewer than 5,000 students. None of this growth will be in first-entry programs, that is, entry directly from high school. One of the significant changes in the 1990s was to cut down on the University's first-entry programs. Most programs now require a degree or a number of years of university before entry: architecture, forestry, nursing, occupational therapy, pharmacy, and physical therapy all became second-entry. As of the year 2000, only four programs in the University – arts and science, engineering, physical education and health, and music – allow entry from high school. Arts and science and engineering are, of course, very large programs. The increase in numbers that will occur in second-entry and doctoral-stream programs will further raise the average age of students on campus, which had been rising over the years with the integration of generally older part-time degree students into the regular programs.

Graduate students have been given greater support. The University promised to give all doctoral students a minimum of $12,000 a year plus tuition for their first four years. The decision – accelerated by a strike by the University's teaching assistants in 1999 – will help ensure that Toronto's graduate programs attract some of the best national and international students. 'It's not just getting them here but also seeing them through,' observed Provost Adel Sedra. 'It has been shown that lack of sufficient funding causes graduate students to take longer to complete their degree which is not good for anybody.' There has also been a change in the administration of graduate programs, following a report in 1996 of a task force chaired by Sedra and the graduate school dean, Jon Cohen. Much of the day-to-day work is now done at the department level and not by the graduate school. Many of those in positions of power, such as Prichard, Sedra, and Marrus, had been frustrated, when administering their own disciplines' graduate programs, by what they considered the 'bureaucratic tendencies' of the graduate school. One reason why the graduate school had been given greater control in the 1960s was to ensure the quality of those teaching and supervising graduate students. With the tightening of hiring and tenure procedures, however, and with the graduate dean having a representative on tenure committees, the former distinction between those who should and those who should not be members of the graduate faculty no longer made sense. The graduate school therefore became much smaller, and took on a supervisory and entrepreneurial role for the promotion of graduate education, with a mandate to ensure consistency and high standards across the divisions.

&

In the fall of 1998, Prichard was nearing the end of his second five-year term as president. He decided to step down, even though it was reasonably certain he would have been invited to serve another term. He wanted to return to teaching, he stated. 'Great universities require both continuity and renewal,' he wrote to Wendy Cecil-Cockwell, the chair of the governing council. 'I was very pleased to have served for a decade,' he went on, 'but believe the moment is now right for a new President to set our agenda and lead us forward. The University is in fundamentally good shape.' In his last report in the *U of T Magazine*, Prichard was characteristically enthusiastic: 'After a very difficult period in the first half of the 1990s, numerous developments nationally and provincially suggest we are on the cusp of one of the most exciting and productive periods in the university's history. Indeed, our prospects may have never been better.' Under his leadership, the University was prospering, financially and academically.

Its library was second only to Harvard's in acquisitions. The University's endowment was double that of any other Canadian university. Toronto was far and away the leading university in Canada in grants and awards per faculty member. In the year 1999–2000, for example, it won three of the four prestigious Killam prizes in medicine and science, awarded by the Canada Council – they went to Paul Brumer of chemistry, Fergus Craik of psychology, and Tony Pawson of medical genetics and microbiology. Similarly, University of Toronto professors have won the National Research Council's Steacie prize, given to a young scientist or engineer, for four of the past six years, the prize in the year 2000 going to chemist Ian Manners. There has been comparable success with prizes and awards of the Royal Society of Canada and other bodies.

For seven years – from 1994 until 2000 – Toronto has ranked first in the medical/doctoral university category in the annual survey of Canadian universities conducted by *Maclean's* magazine. How it will do in subsequent surveys remains to be seen. In 1991, the first year of the survey, Toronto had ranked fourth among the participating universities. The next year, the universities were divided into broad categories, and Toronto ranked second after McGill in the

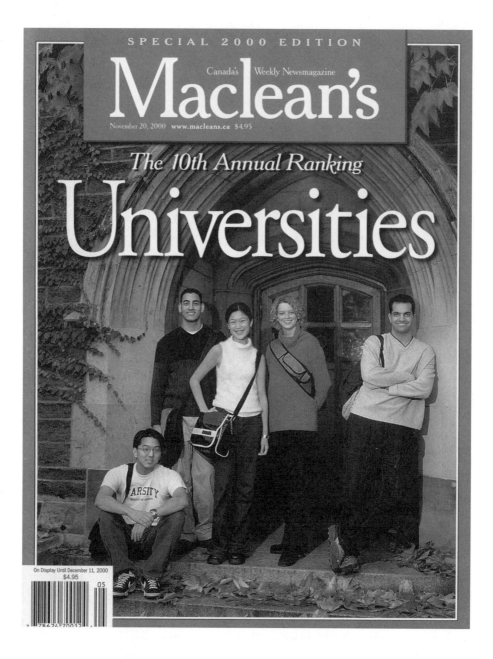

Cover of the November 2000 issue of *Maclean's* magazine, featuring its tenth annual ranking
of universities in Canada. The students, standing in front of one of the west doorways of
Hart House, are, from left to right: Jin David Kim, English; Jameel Lalji, computer science
and sociology; Amy Cheng, biological science; Morwenna White, French;
and Arvin Hariri, biological chemistry.

research university group. The following year, it ranked third after McGill and Queen's. In 1994, however – for the first time – Toronto topped the list. Moreover, its reputation continued to grow. In 1999, *Maclean's* surveyed more than 5,000 high school guidance counsellors, academic administrators, and others. Toronto's reputation, according to the survey, came first for research universities in three out of four categories – highest quality, leaders of tomorrow, and best overall. It came second after McMaster as the university with a reputation for being the most innovative.

A fifteen–member search committee, chaired by Wendy Cecil-Cockwell, began its search for a new president in March 1999. Robert Birgeneau, the 57-year-old dean of science at the Massachusetts Institute of Technology, was selected. The governing council approved the appointment for a seven-year term at the end of November 1999. 'An inspired appointment,' said Prichard. 'There could be no better choice to lead U of T into the next century.'

Birgeneau was – as he had to be under the University of Toronto Act – a Canadian citizen. He was also a U of T graduate, having entered St Michael's College on a full scholarship to study classics and then switched to mathematics and physics, and graduated in 1963. He had been a member of the Putnam mathematical team that competed successfully against other North American teams. His wife, Mary Catherine, was a St Michael's graduate in English. Like Prichard, who met his wife on the first day of law school, Birgeneau met his wife on the first day of university. He completed a doctorate in physics at Yale in 1966, and joined the MIT faculty in 1975. In the interval, he did scientific work at the Bell Laboratories in New Jersey. The winner of a number of prestigious awards for his work on solid-state physics, using both neutron and x-ray scattering techniques, he has published an impressive total of more than 350 articles. In 1988, he became chair of physics at MIT, and three years later he was appointed dean of science.

Birgeneau had been in the news while at MIT for his support of women members of his faculty who had complained to him about unfair treatment by their male colleagues. He took steps to change the situation. 'We were finally recognized,' said a woman biologist at MIT. 'He was instrumental in correcting inequalities.' For many years, Birgeneau had had a strong concern with inequality. While at Yale, he and his wife, who was a social worker, had spent considerable time with New Haven's black community, and later he spent a summer at a predominantly black college in South Carolina. He also became involved in the

Robert Birgeneau, shortly after taking office on July 1, 2000.

Jewish 'refusenik' movement in Russia and was a spokesman on its behalf. 'I was a child of the 60s,' Birgeneau said. 'I knew society wasn't going to change if people didn't act.' 'One of my primary goals,' he has said, 'will be to increase the diversity of the faculty so that it properly reflects the wonderfully heterogeneous community that it serves.'

The new president took over on July 1, 2000. He inherited the largest university in North America (among those that belong to the American Association of Universities) in number of students. Its three campuses have more than 50,000 full-time and part-time students, about 3,000 full-time equivalent faculty, and a substantially greater number of staff positions. 'The University of Toronto is an outstanding institution on the brink of truly international stature,' was Birgeneau's prediction on his appointment.

2000

⸺◈⸺

A WALK THROUGH THE CAMPUS

From the time I started this project, my plan was to take the story up to around the year 2000. The concluding chapter, I thought, perhaps might record a personal stroll through the St George campus on the last day of 1999, in which I reflected on the past and maybe speculated on the future. I was not sure where to start the walk, or, indeed, whether I would actually go on it. As it turned out, on December 30, 1999, the optometrist phoned to say that my new lenses had arrived. I could pick them up at the Eaton Centre the next morning.

While waiting to have them fitted, I map out a rough itinerary. I would start from the Eaton Centre, walk over to University Avenue, and then up to the campus. It is a mild, overcast day, with only slight traces of snow on the ground. Not a bad day for a stroll through the University, though I had been hoping to see it blanketed in a layer of newly fallen snow and under a clear sky. The University is officially closed, so I will not be able to observe the great diversity of the student body. Nor will I be around at midnight to hear the anticipated crash of computers, which, in any event, seems unlikely. Before I left home, it was already the year 2000 in Japan, and the lights had not gone out there.

As I walk along Queen Street over to University Avenue, I think about how intimately connected the city has been with the University. The Eaton family, for example, endowed the chair of medicine. Joseph Flavelle, a key member of the board of governors in the early part of the century, was the controlling shareholder of Simpsons, across the street (now The Bay), and O.D. Vaughan, the vice-president of Eaton's, was the second-last chairman of the board of governors of the University. The old city hall, which I pass, is a reminder that the city endowed two chairs at the University in the nineteenth century, following a dispute involving Queen's Park land.

The old city hall was the scene of the celebrations for the last turn of the century – in 1901, not 1900. Twenty strokes of the bells from the newly erected bell tower were rung after the twelve strokes of midnight. Will the university bells ring tonight? The new city hall has direct links with the University. In the mid-1950s, Peter Richardson and other architecture students blocked the solid but unexciting design that had been commissioned by the city fathers without a competition. The subsequent competition was run by the professor of architecture, Eric Arthur. So the University can claim some credit for Viljo Revell's imposing structure and its influence on the architecture of the city.

As I pass Osgoode Hall, I recall Robert Baldwin, the treasurer of the Law Society of Upper Canada, who as premier was primarily responsible for the demise of King's College in 1849 and the start of the so-called godless University of Toronto. A significant turning point in the history of the University. I can also picture Bruce Dunlop and Horace Krever and about forty other University of Toronto law students picketing Osgoode Hall a hundred years later, seeking recognition for the University's law school, which eventually was accorded in 1957.

At Queen Street and University Avenue, I envision the procession that started on foot from that exact corner on a cloudless day in the spring of 1842 to lay the cornerstone of the first university building, on the site of the present legislative building. The ceremonial party included Bishop John Strachan, the president of King's College, who had obtained the college's charter from George IV in 1827, and the governor general, Sir Charles Bagot, along with other dignitaries, and was accompanied by the First Incorporated Dragoons with their waving plumes. Fifteen hundred people sat on a wooden platform in Queen's Park to witness the ceremony. There is now no sign of the original King's College building, which was later used as a 'lunatic asylum' until it was torn down to make way for the present legislative building.

Passing the US consulate, I think of Strachan and others wanting a university in Upper Canada in order to prevent students from having to go to the United States and being exposed there to corrupting republican views. 'Some may become fascinated with that liberty which has degenerated into licentiousness,'

Strachan wrote, 'and imbibe, perhaps unconsciously, sentiments unfriendly to things of which Englishmen are proud.' Throughout the history of the University, reaction to American influence has played an important role in determining its direction. The Massey Commission later noted that universities have been a force in the determination of Canadian culture. In the 1920s, for example, the University of Toronto was the centre of cultural life in Toronto. Federal funding of universities, which started in the late 1950s, might help – it was thought – prevent American cultural domination of Canada.

Instead of the soldiers of the 43rd Regiment lining the route to the King's College site, there are now insurance companies and hospitals. Each hospital has its own history. Mount Sinai Hospital was founded because Jews were not permitted on staff at the Toronto General Hospital across the street. Times have changed: three of the last four Sir John and Lady Eaton professors of medicine at the Toronto General have been Jewish, the last two coming directly from Mount Sinai. The present Mount Sinai building was constructed because the foundations of the former, smaller hospital to the south could not support a major addition: Taddle Creek ran under it. The creek, which flowed from Wychwood Park, off Bathurst Street, through the University and then down to the lake, was a source of delight for the University, and in much earlier times for First Nations people. In the 1860s and 1870s, there was a pond with fish in it beside University College. The creek, however, later became a matter of concern on account of the stench from the sewage that was being dumped into it by the residents of the village of Yorkville, upstream. It was buried below ground in 1884. The University now has tentative plans to re-create the pond and parts of the creek.

I pass the Hospital for Sick Children, famous throughout the world, and the Princess Margaret Hospital, Canada's premier centre for cancer research and treatment. And then the massive Toronto General Hospital. The hospital moved from near the Don River to its present site on College Street just before the First World War. I look up at the old private patients' pavilion where I was born – it is scheduled for demolition – and pass the small building donated by the two Shields sisters, Agnes and Jane, as an emergency hospital. One can barely see their names chiselled into the stone. Across College Street are the Banting and Best Institutes. Am I right, I wondered, in saying that the discovery of insulin in 1922 may actually have held back the University's future medical research by resulting in the concentration of most of the research money on Banting, who was not, it appears, a particularly good scientist? But the discovery did bring fame to the University.

I look up at Queen's Park and think of all the magnificent houses that stood around the park. Many were bought by the University and used for various academic divisions, such as Mayor William Howland's house, for a women's residence and later the School of Nursing. The houses south of the legislature have all been torn down, but many north and east of the legislative buildings are still standing – the biscuit manufacturer William Christie's house on the corner of Wellesley and Queen's Park, which now belongs to St Joseph's College, a women's college that is part of St Michael's, and another house used by the Centre for Medieval Studies, one of the jewels in Toronto's crown.

On the north side of College Street, I pass the greenhouses of the old Botany Building. I recall that the greenhouses, which are to be taken down to accommodate the new Leslie Dan pharmacy building, contain a plant that is said to bloom every hundred years. The former Botany Building is now the Tanz Neuroscience Building, having been renovated as the result of a generous donation by Mark Tanz, just one of the many wealthy businessmen – like Leslie Dan – who graduated in the easy times of the 1950s and subsequently have made significant contributions to the University. The glass hydro building at the south-west corner of College and Queen's Park was the site of the Royal Conservatory of Music, where I managed to pass some piano exams – like many others growing up in Toronto. I think of Boyd Neel asking why 90 per cent of its students played only the piano. The conservatory, however, started Glenn Gould on his way. There was also an opera school, which produced such stars as Lois Marshall, Teresa Stratas, and Jon Vickers. I pass the FitzGerald Building, named after John FitzGerald, the founder of the Connaught Laboratories and the School of Hygiene. And then the Mining Building, with its no-nonsense look, which the alumni association – formed in 1900 – successfully lobbied the government to finance.

I'm now in engineering territory. The faculty dominates the south end of the campus, with buildings crowded together and some tucked in behind other buildings. The Haultain Building, for example, is completely hidden from view. The Sandford Fleming Building is attached to the Galbraith Building, which stretches to St George Street. The engineering faculty is an immense operation, with over 1,000 graduate students. The faculty is now spilling over to the other side of St George Street. Eric Arthur complained that the area felt like Lower

Manhattan, with 90 per cent coverage and very little green space. An earlier professor of architecture had told the 1906 royal commission that the faculty was too big to remain on the campus. 'Ultimately,' he said, 'the whole University will be forced to move, on account of the city.' Fortunately, his advice was not accepted, nor was that of C.D. Howe, the reconstruction minister after the Second World War, who thought the University should move to the temporary home for engineering students at Ajax. 'It seems to me,' Howe wrote to Eric Phillips, the chairman of the board, 'that you will be driven out of the city eventually, and I doubt if there is any more suitable location' than Ajax.

And now there is King's College Road and the magnificent view of University College, completed in 1859. Governor General Edmund Walker Head had wanted it to face west, but it is hard to picture it facing in any other direction than south. The Anglican-dominated King's College had been closed in 1849 and the non-denominational University of Toronto established. John McCaul, who had been president of King's, became president of the University of Toronto. Bishop Strachan went on to create another university – Trinity College on Queen Street West. The round building attached to the west side of University College was originally the chemistry laboratory, named after the first professor of chemistry, Henry Croft. For safety reasons, it was not directly connected with University College. I think back to Toronto's unwise decision not to hire the biologist Thomas Huxley and the physicist John Tyndall, who applied for positions in the 1850s. The noted physiologist A.B. Macallum wrote fifty years later that had Huxley and Tyndall been appointed, 'Toronto, as a seat of learning ... would more than rival the leading universities of this Continent.'

In researching and writing this history, I never felt that I really knew President McCaul. He left no journals or similar documents. His successor, Daniel Wilson, on the other hand, left a diary and many letters, and through them I developed a fondness for him. A University College residence now bears his name. There is an historical plaque commemorating Wilson between the college and the residence. McCaul had a short street running south from College Street and one of the houses in the 'Sir Dan' residence named after him. Wilson's less-than-effective successor, James Loudon, had only a house in the residence.

As one walks up King's College Road, one has Convocation Hall on the left, a gift from the alumni. I think of all of the memorable events I have attended there – law dean Caesar Wright's funeral, Claude Bissell's address to the University in 1969 during the height of the student activism of the 1960s, the memorial service for Northrop Frye in 1981, and the graduations of my wife, our three children, and myself. There is almost certainly no one living today who remembers being in Convocation Hall for Robert Falconer's installation address in 1907, when he carefully laid out the future direction of the University under the new system of governance established by another turning point – the University Act of 1906. The day after his address, he complained that it was wrong to allocate seats in the front rows for dignitaries. The more I got to know Falconer, the more I liked him. Canon Cody was less successful as a president, but his period in office covered difficult times – the depression and the Second World War.

On the right-hand side of King's College Road was the engineering 'Skulehouse,' built in 1878, and the old medical school, constructed in 1903, both of which were torn down to make way for the new Medical Sciences Building. A plaque on the wall outside the McLeod Auditorium in the medical building – he received the Nobel prize along with Banting in 1922 – records the fact that insulin was discovered on that exact site. I think of A.B. Macallum and Ramsay Wright, who did so much for medical research at the University before the First World War. The zoology building on the west campus is named after Wright, but all Macallum got was an annual lecture, though there was an unsuccessful move in the 1980s to name the medical school after him.

Then – as I continue around King's College Circle – the old library, with its elaborate doorway modelled after that of a twelfth-century Scottish abbey, and which contained large wooden tables with green-shaded lamps, where I often studied as a student. The library was constructed after the fire of 1890 and was to have had a teardrop-shaped dome similar to that of Sacré-Coeur church in Paris. It was the main university library until the Sigmund Samuel building was added to it in the mid-1950s. They are both now part of the Gerstein Science Information Centre. The humanities and social science collection is now primarily in the Robarts Library.

I walk past the observatory. It was originally built in the early 1850s, just south of what is now Convocation Hall, and then rebuilt on its present site in 1908 – with a different configuration. It now serves as the main office of the Students' Administrative Council. I glance at the two cannons – recovered from a French ship sunk by General Wolfe in Louisbourg harbour and donated to the University by the first graduating class of the twentieth century – menacingly facing the legislative building, in effect saying 'hands off.'

Then I try the door of Hart House's Arbor Room. Time for a coffee. Closed. I remember the early 1950s, when the Arbor Room was first created, and women were allowed in – but only after 3 o'clock in the afternoon. The House itself, in fact, is open, but the hall porter tells me that it will close at 6 o'clock and that, as far as she knows, there will be no carillon concert to welcome the year 2000. I pause outside at the memorial tablets beside Soldiers' Tower and look for some of the names of those who lost their lives in the Great War – the sons of President Loudon, Chancellor William Meredith, the medical dean Alexander Primrose, the historian George Wrong, and others. I think of J.K. Macalister, a law graduate and Rhodes scholar in the 1930s, and his fellow graduate Frank Pickersgill, who were dropped behind enemy lines during the Second World War to assist the French resistance, and were captured, tortured, and executed in Buchenwald.

The quadrangle of University College – my college – is empty. I walk along the old cloisters. The Junior Common Room, not surprisingly, is locked. I think of the cow that the students in the 1870s led to the top of the bell tower above the JCR, and left there, after tying its tail to the bell. One can picture other scenes: Eliza Balmer and other women students demurely but resolutely insisting upon admission to the college in the early 1880s; the fire of 1890, which gutted much of the college; President Loudon breaking up student skirmishes with a fire hose in the early 1890s; Mackenzie King leading the student strike of 1895. The ghost of Reznikoff, who is said to have been killed and buried in the foundations of the college, did not appear as I walked through the college grounds. If he were ever to make his presence felt, it would surely have been on this day.

I walk up to Hoskin Avenue – named after John Hoskin, the first chairman of the board of governors under the University Act of 1906. The back campus is deserted, one of the many sites considered and fortunately rejected for what became the Robarts Library. I think of the fierce competition that used to take place each fall on the back campus for the Mulock Cup. Sir William Mulock deserves to be remembered also for his role in the 1880s in bringing about the federation of the denominational colleges and the re-establishment of the medical faculty. He later became chancellor of the University and died in office in 1944 at the age of 100.

Interfaculty football is a thing of the past. The cup is now given for supremacy in men's rugger. I have been told that women's rugger is the fastest-growing intercollegiate women's sport at the University. In the spring, the back campus – and the front campus – will be dominated by mixed softball teams. I pass beneath the large elm trees beside Whitney Hall, some of which may have been standing when King's College received its royal charter in 1827. E.C. Whitney, the brother of the premier, donated money for Whitney Hall and for one of the four sides of the Devonshire Place residence. The University could not get a donor for the fourth side, but the residence was built anyway. It has now been reconstructed as the Munk Centre for International Studies and the John Graham Library of Trinity College.

Massey College, on the other side of Devonshire Place, the first and still the only graduate college in the University, was opened in 1963, the fifth of the Massey family's great gifts to the University – the household science building, Victoria's Annesley Hall and Burwash Hall, and Hart House being the others. A fellow of Massey College, I go to the hall porter's lodge to wish the porter a happy new year, but the gate is locked. Then past Trinity, which moved from its Queen Street site in the 1920s – there are two foundation stones in the front gateway of the college – and up Philosopher's Walk, wondering whether the plan to bring Taddle Creek back to the surface will actually be realized.

Then I climb the outside stairway between the faculty of music and the faculty of law. The law school, occupying Joseph Flavelle's grand house, is celebrating its fiftieth anniversary. Only one light is on in the offices on the west side. I see the office Bora Laskin once occupied, and Frank Iacobucci's old office – my earlier office was beside Frank's – and the office Rob Prichard will have when he returns from his sabbatical at Harvard. (As we know now, Prichard did not return to teach at the law school, but joined the *Toronto Star* organization.) Then the Edward Johnson Building, and the thought that the music school is named after the opera man and the opera theatre after Sir Ernest MacMillan, the music man. I think of some of the memorable concerts I have attended in the building – including those in celebration of John Beckwith's retirement and John Weinzweig's eightieth birthday.

I cross Queen's Park when there is a lull in the traffic. Like the students, I figure, Why take the underground passageway, when one can risk one's life crossing the road? Into the quiet Victoria University enclave in front of Old Vic, the first building put up by Victoria when it moved from Cobourg in the early 1890s. The Act of 1887, which brought about federation of Victoria, St Michael's, and, later, Trinity, was another important turning point in the University's fortunes. I admire the clean lines of Northrop Frye Hall and the E.J. Pratt

Library, named after two distinguished professors of English at Victoria. I glance at the Isabel Bader Theatre, being constructed behind the main building. It will serve also as a large lecture hall and will help bring more students to Victoria College, part of a continuing determination – like the new college programs – to make the colleges more than simply residences in the life of the student body.

I cut through to St Michael's College, the home of the world-famous Pontifical Institute of Mediaeval Studies and of Marshall McLuhan, perhaps Toronto's best known academic – after all, he appeared in a Woody Allen movie. I look over at Carr Hall, designed by Ernest Cormier, who designed the Supreme Court building in Ottawa as well as Pierre Trudeau's house in Montreal. Then I enter St Basil's Church. The church and the surrounding administration buildings are the oldest in the University still standing in their original location. One of the Basilian priests informs me that there will be no bells at midnight.

At the corner of Yonge and St Mary streets is the University of Toronto Press, now a relatively independent operation and reasonably content to be situated off the campus. There is no point in walking over there. The Press is just a floor of an office building – the printing and distribution centre is on north Dufferin Street – but there resides the premier academic press in Canada and one respected throughout the world for its scholarly series, such as the *Dictionary of Canadian Biography* and the 89-volume *Collected Works of Erasmus*.

Up to Bloor Street and into the Colonnade to purchase some Godiva chocolates for my wife for New Year's Eve, thinking how lucky Victoria was to acquire and keep the Bloor Street frontage as an endowment. I do not go into the household science building, constructed in 1906 at the corner of Bloor and Queen's Park, though Club Monaco, which rents space from Victoria, is open. Most customers would not realize that a swimming pool for women is still there, hidden under the floor. Nor would they know that the first two women given full-time academic positions in the University – the chemist Clara Benson and the school's principal, Annie Laird – worked there. The fine Pre-Raphaelite stained-glass windows in the building show women tending to household tasks and men hunting and harvesting.

Then along Bloor Street, passing the Royal Ontario Museum, no longer an official part of the University. I can see the plaque commemorating W.A. Parks, the palaeontologist who brought the first dinosaur skeletons to the museum, and another commemorating Charles Currelly, the first director of the archaeology section of the museum. There is no plaque, however, for Sir Edmund

Walker, for many years the cultured chairman of the University's board of governors, without whose determination the museum might not have been built. The museum is open, but I resist the temptation to go in. One can see from Bloor Street the Ming tomb with the stone camels that children (including the author) used to climb up on when the tomb was outside the building. I pass the gates at the northern entrance to Philosopher's Walk, where in the nineteenth century Taddle Creek surfaced above ground. The gates were originally located at the top of Queen's Park at Bloor Street, but were moved when Queen's Park was widened after the Second World War. I notice for the first time an old plaque commemorating a visit of royalty in 1901. One is constantly discovering new things about the campus.

I look up at McMaster Hall, beside Philosopher's Walk, once the home of McMaster University and later of Toronto's department of political economy. I think of my favourite undergraduate classes there – the memorable lectures on economic history by Karl Helleiner, one of the relatively few refugee academics taken into the University before the Second World War, and the international relations seminar by Jim Eayrs. The building is now the home of the Royal Conservatory of Music and looks a bit old and tired across the street from the classy Hotel Inter-Continental, and may look even worse when Varsity Stadium and Varsity Arena are replaced with new residences and athletic facilities. Varsity Stadium is quiet, as it usually is these days. I picture the events in the 1920s and the 1950s, the golden years for spectator team sports at the University. I think of the freezing cold December day in 1926 when the University of Toronto lost the Grey Cup to the Ottawa Senators, and of the Varsity Grads hockey team that won Olympic gold in 1928 at St Moritz, undefeated and unscored-against.

Across the road is the faculty of social work, which has come a long way from the social service course begun around the time of the First World War. Harry Cassidy, the dynamic director after the Second World War, would be pleased with its growth. The twelve-storey OISE building is next door. OISE was established as an institute separate from the faculty of education, located farther west on Bloor Street, and now has been merged with the faculty – to the benefit of both institutions. My wife did her PhD at the institute as a mature student, and I have a soft spot for its ability to cater to the needs of such students.

I glance at the York Club, at the corner of St George and Bloor, where the old board of governors made many of the key decisions for the University. There has been no comparable venue following the elimination of the board of governors under the 1971 unicameral governing structure inherited by John Evans when he became president in 1972. The important decisions then were initiated in morning sessions in Evans' presidential office, attended by the senior officials who constituted what was called 'Simcoe Circle.' The unicameral governing structure is unique among major universities in North America – its introduction marked another major turning point in the University's history.

I walk south on Devonshire Place, hoping to be able to go through the lovely passageways of Woodsworth College, the degree-granting part-time college, which now has more than 1,000 full-time and many times that number of part-time students, and clearly fills an important need in the community. I go by the Margaret Fletcher Day Care Centre, the subject of fierce debates in the 1970s, but now taken for granted. Woodsworth College is closed, and I cut through a side passage to St George Street. I continue to marvel at the transformation of the street that has taken place through Judy Matthews' determination and her gift for its redevelopment.

The view south is dominated, of course, by the Robarts Library, crucial to the development of graduate studies in the humanities and social sciences in the University. The top three storeys were added at a late stage to accommodate the needs of other Ontario universities using the library. It is said to be the largest academic library building in the world. Thirty years after its construction, we have reluctantly learned to like it. It is flanked on the south by the Fisher Rare Book Library – from the inside one of the most dramatic sights in the University – and on the north by the building housing the faculty of information studies and the institute for policy analysis and named for Claude Bissell. Bissell was primarily responsible for the library and the growth of the University in the 1960s.

Walking south on St George Street, I pass the Rotman School of Management, with its growing reputation, and ponder the fact that business schools across North America, unlike most other professional schools, are named after individual donors. Across the road is Innis College, named after the University's pre-eminent social scientist, Harold Innis. From the corner of St George and Hoskin one can see the athletic centre – the women's and the men's buildings now united. I can also see the controversial giant sign on the new graduate residence that forms the words 'University of Toronto' stretching out over Harbord Street.

I can see, too, the Skydome in the distance, and remain grateful that it did not end up on Bloor Street, as some hoped it would. Beside it is the CN Tower, visible from many places in the University.

I continue south on St George Street. The west campus has never reached the aesthetic potential that was promised in the early plans, which would have barred vehicles and had large open spaces. Instead, buildings were constructed using the existing street pattern: the McLennan Physical Laboratories, named after the distinguished head of physics, who with luck might have had a Nobel prize for his work; Sidney Smith Hall, housing various departments in the faculty of arts and sciences, and named after the University's sixth president; New College, the first university-owned college built since University College; and so on. There was to have been a bust of Sidney Smith in the building named in his memory, but the board chairman Eric Phillips and others did not like what the sculptor produced. Phillips probably wanted something that showed what he described as Smith's 'complicated simplicity,' not an easy characteristic to represent.

One can see the signs of more construction farther south on St George Street – an addition to the chemistry building, the home of the Nobel laureate John Polanyi, and a centre for information technology, both the result of the University's recent successful fund-raising campaign and its ability to acquire government funds through competitions. The money for the chemistry addition was donated by Edna Davenport in honour of her late husband, John, two obviously satisfied graduates of the 1920s, and the lead gift for the information technology centre was given by the alumni John and Margaret Bahen. Polanyi has a special place in this history. His Nobel prize and George Connell's document on 'renewal' I see as turning points in the fortunes of the University, after the fifteen difficult years of underfunding experienced by Presidents John Evans, Jim Ham, and David Strangway.

I take Willcocks Street and walk through the elaborate Earth Sciences Centre, which effectively integrates some old buildings in a modern structure, to Spadina Avenue, wondering what will become of the old Knox College on Spadina Circle. I return to Huron Street, passing the administration building, which has the department of philosophy on its top floors. Perhaps philosophers can thrive in inelegant surroundings better than lawyers. Next door is the faculty of architecture, located in the old dental building – one can still see the word 'infirmary' over the side door – a functional building that never won an architectural prize. The architecture building, it should be noted, is the only building in the University with most of its lights on. I assume that many architecture students still have major projects to complete before the new term commences.

I pass the Clarke Institute of Psychiatry, named after a former head of psychiatry and dean of medicine, and arrive back at College Street. The Koffler Centre – the former city of Toronto reference library – is open, or at least the U of T Bookstore is. I glance at the new Fields Institute of Mathematics and think of J.C. Fields, one of the many faculty members who received their doctorates from Johns Hopkins University in the nineteenth century – a university that had an important influence on the University of Toronto. I also think of Fields' doctoral student Sam Beatty and of other members of the department of mathematics, whose undergraduate students consistently won the North American Putnam prize for student mathematicians in the 1940s. I remember that Robert Birgeneau, the recently appointed president of the University from MIT, who will take office on July 1, 2000, was a member of a successful Putnam team when he was a maths and physics student at the University in the 1960s.

What will Birgeneau's contribution be to the development of the University of Toronto as a major teaching and research institution? How will he build on the foundations laid by his predecessors? One challenge facing the University is to find ways of supporting the humanities and social sciences, which generally have not benefited from the shower of private and government funding experienced in recent years by the sciences, engineering, and medicine. Further, how can the University find the right balance between applied and fundamental research, so that, in the words of engineering professor Ursula Franklin, we do not become 'the Loblaws of science and technology or knowledge?' Still another challenge, brought forward most prominently by the faculty association, is to guard against what the former association president Bill Graham has called 'the corporate take-over of our University.' Finally, the increase of fees throughout the University means that maintaining accessibility will remain a challenge.

Recent planning documents have stated that Toronto's mission is 'to rank with the best public research universities of the world.' The dynamic and always optimistic Rob Prichard has observed that the University of Toronto is 'on the cusp of one of the most exciting and productive periods in the university's history.' Similarly, Birgeneau at the time of his appointment predicted that the University is 'on the brink of truly international stature.' Whether Toronto achieves its mission is a question that must be left to the next historian of the University.

It is now 4 o'clock, and, in the company of my thoughts and the chocolates, I take a taxi home to await the year 2000.

SOURCES AND CREDITS

PRINCIPAL SOURCES

The notes below list only the principal documents on which I relied in writing the history. The alphabetical bibliography that follows this section is limited to the items cited here. Detailed note references are contained in a separate document available at the University of Toronto Archives and on the University of Toronto Press' website (www.utppublishing.com). In addition, a hard copy of the notes may be purchased separately through the University of Toronto Press (*Notes to the University of Toronto: A History*, ISBN 0-08020-8526-1, Marketing Manager, University of Toronto Press, 10 St. Mary Street, Suite 700, Toronto, Ontario M4Y 2W8). The notes on the website and in the hard copy are keyed to individual pages, paragraphs, and specific words of the text. They are numbered to make future reference to them easier. The Archives also contain my notes, correspondence, copies of drafts of the chapters of the book, and photocopies of much of the material my research assistants and I collected. There is also a separate loose-leaf binder for each chapter of the book, containing photocopies of the relevant excerpts of the material cited in the footnotes.

An exceptionally valuable book for most of this history was Brian McKillop's magisterial study of higher education in Ontario from 1791 to 1951, *Matters of Mind* (1994). Other books in the Ontario Historical Studies Series have also been used extensively. The *Dictionary of Canadian Biography* proved indispensable for many of the earlier chapters. The latest volume (volume 14) of the *Dictionary* includes persons who died before 1920. The obituaries contained in the Royal Society of Canada's publications have also been useful, as have two earlier books on the history of the University of Toronto, *The University of Toronto and Its Colleges* (1906) and W.S. Wallace, *A History of the University of Toronto* (1927). J. George Hodgins' published collection of documents on higher education in the nineteenth century, *Documentary History of Education in Upper Canada*, was extremely valuable. I have also used, of course, the archival material contained in the University of Toronto Archives, including material collected in the 1970s and early 1980s by Professors Robin Harris and Gerald Craig for a planned but uncompleted history of the University, as well as material in the Ontario Archives, the National Archives, and in various other archives at the University of Toronto and elsewhere.

Chapter 1: A Charter for King's College (1826)

Chapter 2: Laying the Cornerstone (1842)

Chapter 3: The Creation of the University of Toronto and Trinity College (1849)

I was fortunate to have been able to use two as yet unpublished manuscripts relating to King's College, Elizabeth Pearce's PhD thesis for OISE, completed in 1998 ('King's College') and John Slater's work on the history of philosophy at the University of Toronto ('Philosophy at Toronto'). In these and later chapters I relied heavily on Brian McKillop's book (*Matters of Mind*) and W.S. Wallace's history of the U of T (*A History of the University of Toronto*), as well as on J.G. Hodgins' collection of documents (*Documentary History of Education in Upper Canada*). In addition, I had available to me Gerald Craig's material in the U of T Archives collected in the 1970s and meant to be used for his history of the U of T in the nineteenth century, a work that because of his ill health was not completed. Fortunately, Craig prepared a number of important entries for the *Dictionary of Canadian Biography*. I relied also on the writings of numerous historians, among them Maurice Careless (*The Union of the Canadas* and *The Pre-Confederation Premiers*), Roger Hall on the legislative buildings (*A Century to Celebrate*), John Moir on religion (*Church and State in Canada West*), William Westfall ('The Divinity 150 Project'), T.A. Reed (*History of the University of Trinity College*), and J.L.H. Henderson ('Founding of Trinity College'). I also used various books relating to other universities, such as the University of London (Negley Harte, *The University of London*), McGill (Stanley Frost, *McGill University*), Queen's (Hilda Neatby, *Queen's University*), and Victoria (C.B. Sissons, *A History of Victoria University*). Douglas Richardson's book on University College (*A Not Unsightly Building*) and Eric Arthur's book on Toronto (*Toronto: No Mean City*) are important for this as well as for later chapters.

Chapter 4: Starting Over (1850)

For discussions of the early medical schools, I used R.D. Gidney and W.P.J. Millar (*Professional Gentlemen*), Charles Godfrey (*John Rolph*), and Sandra McRae's thesis ('The Scientific Spirit'); for the Victoria Medical School, C.B. Sissons (*A History of Victoria*); for Rev. Beaven, John Slater's manuscript ('Philosophy at Toronto'); for early legal education, Blaine Baker ('Legal Education in Upper Canada'), Ian Kyer and Jerome Bickenbach (*The Fiercest Debate*), Christopher Moore (*The Law Society of Upper Canada*), and Gidney and Millar, as above; and for St Michael's, Father Lawrence Shook (*Catholic Post-Secondary Education*) as well as W.S. Wallace (*A History*) and Brian McKillop (*Matters of Mind*).

Chapter 5: New Professors (1853)

Again, I used W.S. Wallace (*A History*) and Brian McKillop (*Matters of Mind*); for Daniel Wilson, his letters and journals and Elizabeth Hulse (*Thinking with Both Hands*); for the UC Lit, Charles Levi's thesis ('Where the Famous People Were?'); and for discussions of Huxley and Tyndall, A.B. Macallum's article ('Huxley and Tyndall at the University of Toronto').

Chapter 6: Building University College (1856)

The material used included Douglas Richardson (*A Not Unsightly Building*), Geoffrey Simmins (*Fred Cumberland*), Elizabeth Hulse (*Thinking with Both Hands*), the John Langton letters (in *CHR*), Wilson's journal, and, again, W.S. Wallace (*A History*) and Brian McKillop (*Matters of Mind*).

Chapter 7: Saving the University (1860)

The material used included Elizabeth Hulse (*Thinking with Both Hands*), C.B. Sissons (*History of Victoria* and *Egerton Ryerson*), W.J. Loudon (*Sir William Mulock* and *Sketches*), as well as Wilson's journal, W.S. Wallace (*A History*), and Brian McKillop (*Matters of Mind*).

Chapter 8: Science and Technology (1871)

Again, I used W.S. Wallace (*A History*) and Brian McKillop (*Matters of Mind*), and also C.R. Young (*Early Engineering Education*), Trevor Levere (*Research and Influence*), W.A.E. McBryde ('History of the Chemistry Department'), D.F. Forward (*History of Botany*), E.H. Craigie (*History of Zoology*), Yves Gingras (*Physics and the Rise of Scientific Influence*), John Slater ('Philosophy at Toronto'), Elizabeth Hulse (*Thinking with Both Hands*), Richard White (*The Skule Story*), Wilson's journal, and James Loudon's memoirs.

Chapter 9: The Admission of Women (1880)

For the admission of women, I relied on Anne Ford (*A Path Not Strewn with Roses*), Wilson's journals, Paula LaPierre's thesis ('The First Generation'), Nancy Thompson's thesis ('The Controversy over the Admission of Women'), R.D. Gidney and W.P.J. Millar (*Professional Gentlemen*), Elizabeth Hulse (*Thinking with Both Hands*), Jean O'Grady (*Margaret Addison*), John Squair's article ('Admission of Women'), articles by M.E. Spence ('Once There Were no Women') and E. Gardiner ('A Reminiscence'), W.S. Wallace (*A History*), and Brian McKillop (*Matters of Mind*).

Chapter 10: Federation (1883)

For material on federation, I used C.B. Sissons (*History of Victoria*), Harold Averill and Gerald Keith ('A Railway to the Moon'), *The University of Toronto and Its Colleges*, Marguerite Van Die (*An Evangelical Mind*), Lawrence Shook (*Catholic Post-Secondary Education*), Charles Johnston (*McMaster University*); speeches by G.S. French ('Prelude to Federation'), J.M.S. Careless ('Beginning a New Life'), and Neil Semple ('Federation'); Wilson's journals; and, as usual, W.S. Wallace (*A History*) and Brian McKillop (*Matters of Mind*).

Chapter 11: More New Professors (1887)

For Ashley and Mavor, I used Sara Burke (*Seeking the Highest Good*), Alan Bowker ('Truly Useful Men'), and Ian Drummond (*Political Economy*); for Alexander, Heather Murray (*Working in English*); and for Baldwin and Hume, Tory Hoff ('The Controversial Appointment') and John Slater ('Philosophy at Toronto').

Chapter 12: Medicine (1887)

For material on medicine, I used R.D. Gidney and W.P.J. Millar (*Professional Gentlemen* and 'Reorientation of Medical Education'), Sandra McRae ('Scientific Spirit'), A.A. Primrose ('The

Faculty of Medicine' in *The University of Toronto*), Wilson's journals, Charles Godfrey (*Aikins*), James Loudon memoirs, W.J. Loudon (*Sir William Mulock*), W.E. Gallie ('Medical Alumni Oration'), W.S. Wallace (*A History*), Michael Bliss (*William Osler*), *Return to an order ... giving the report ... of the Senate*, Brian McKillop (*Matters of Mind*), and Harold Averill and Gerald Keith ('Railway to the Moon'); for Trinity, T.A. Reed (*Trinity College*) and G.W. Spragge ('The Trinity Medical College'); and for women and medicine, Gidney and Millar (*Professional Gentlemen*), Anne Ford (*A Path Not Strewn*), Lykke De la Cour and Rose Sheinin ('The Ontario Medical College for Women'), and Sandra McRae ('Scientific Spirit').

Chapter 13: Law, Dentistry, and Other Professions (1889)

For material on law, I used Ian Kyer and Jerome Bickenbach (*The Fiercest Debate*), Blaine Baker ('Legal Education'), R.D. Gidney and W.P.J. Millar (*Professional Gentlemen*), Christopher Moore (*The Law Society*), J.M. Young ('Faculty of Law'), Law Society of Upper Canada minutes, and Curtis Cole ('Legal Education in Ontario'); for material on dentistry, D.W. Gullett (*History of Dentistry*), Anne Dale ('J.B. Wilmott'), and *Ontario Dental Association: A Profile*; for material on pharmacy, E.W. Steib ('Pharmaceutical Education'), and Steib et al. ('Women in Ontario Pharmacy'); and for material on the Ontario Agricultural College, A.M. Ross (*The College on the Hill*) and C.C. James ('The Ontario Agricultural College').

Chapter 14: The Fire and New Construction (1890)

For material on the University College fire, I used Douglas Richardson (*A Not Unsightly Building*), Robert Blackburn (*Evolution of the Heart*), Wilson's journals, Loudon's memoirs, and W.S. Wallace (*A History*); for the new library, Robert Blackburn (*Evolution*); for the gymnasium and athletics, T.A. Reed (*Blue and White*), A.E.M. Parkes ('Women's Athletics'), and Helen Gurney (*Women's Sports*); and for the chemistry building, W.A.E. McBryde ('History of the Chemistry Department').

Chapter 15: The Strike (1895)

Material on the strike and the events leading to it is very extensive. I used the following principal sources, apart from archival records and newspapers: Sara Burke ('Co-education'), Robert Blackburn ('Toronto Student Strike'), Hector Charlesworth (*Candid Chronicles*), H.S. Ferns and B. Ostry (*Age of Mackenzie King*), the W.L. Mackenzie King diaries, the *Varsity*, theses by Alan Bowker ('Truly Useful Men') and W.D. Meikle ('And Gladly Teach'), W.S. Wallace (*A History*), Robert Bothwell (*Laying the Foundation*), the 1895 'Report on Discipline in the University,' Loudon's memoirs, and A.M. Chisholm ('When I Went to College').

Chapter 16: Graduate Studies (1897)

I was helped particularly by Peter Ross' thesis ('The Origins and Development of the Ph.D.') and article ('The Establishment of the Ph.D. at Toronto'). I also used the 1906 U of T history (*The University of Toronto*), A.B. Macallum ('Foundation of the Board'), John Slater ('Philosophy at Toronto'), Robin Harris ('Graduate Studies in Toronto' and *History of Higher Education*), and James Greenlee (*Falconer*); on graduate studies in the history department, Robert Bothwell (*Laying the Foundation*); on the PhD in England, Renate Simpson (*How the Ph.D. Came to*

Britain); and on Clara Benson and household science, Ruby Heap ('From the Science of Housekeeping') and Kerrie Kennedy ('Womanly Work').

Chapter 17: The Turn of the Century and the Rise of the Alumni Association (1901)

For material on the Alumni Association, I used the U of T *Monthly*, John Squair ('Alumni Associations'), R.A. Reeve ('McLennan and the Alumni Association'), H.H. Langton (*Sir John Cunningham McLennan*), the *Varsity*, Loudon's memoirs, *The University of Toronto and Its Colleges*, W.S. Wallace (*A History*), and *Educational Monthly of Canada*; for engineering, Richard White (*Skule Story*), C.R. Young (*Early Engineering*), Robin Harris and Ian Montagnes (*Cold Iron*), B.G. Levine (*A Century of Skill*), and H.V. Nelles (*Politics of Development*); and for Whitney, Charles Humphries ('*Honest Enough to Be Bold*' and 'James Whitney and the University of Toronto').

Chapter 18: Whitney and the Royal Commission (1905)

For this section, I used the *Report of the Royal Commission* of 1906 and its various appendices, Charles Humphries ('*Honest Enough to Be Bold*' and 'James Whitney and the University of Toronto'), Michael Bliss (*A Canadian Millionaire*), James Greenlee (*Falconer*), Brian McKillop (*Matters of Mind*), W.S. Wallace (*A History*), *The University of Toronto and Its Colleges*, D.B. Macdonald's and James Loudon's memoirs, G.P. de T. Glazebrook (*Sir Edmund Walker*), and the Goldwin Smith papers at Cornell University.

Chapter 19: Robert Falconer Chosen (1907)

Material on the selection of Falconer is drawn primarily from James Greenlee (*Falconer*) and Michael Bliss (*A Canadian Millionaire* and *Sir William Osler*) and their research notes; other sources include the *Monthly*, W.S. Wallace (*A History*), Charles Humphries ('*Honest Enough to be Bold*'), C.B. Sissons (*History of Victoria*), D.B. Macdonald's memoirs, and the archival papers of Joseph Flavelle at Queen's University, of Edmund Walker at U of T, and of Goldwin Smith at Cornell University. Material on the establishment of the University Settlement House can be found in Sara Burke (*Seeking the Highest Good*); on the extension department, in J.A. Blyth *A Foundling at Varsity*; on forestry, in J.W.B. Sisam (*Forestry Education at Toronto*), the *Monthly*, and Robin Harris' research material; on St Michael's College, in Lawrence Shook (*Catholic Post-Secondary Education*), E.J. McCorkell (*Father Henry Carr* and *Henry Carr – Revolutionary*), Irene Poelzer ('Father Henry Carr'), and Henry Carr ('J.R. Teefy').

Chapter 20: Falconer's Early Years (1908)

For astronomy material, I used C.A. Chant (*Astronomy in the University of Toronto*), R.A. Jarrell (*Cold Light of Dawn*), I.R. Dalton and G.D. Garland ('The Old Observatory'), the *Monthly*, and James Loudon's memoirs; for the Eakins and Jackson controversies, James Greenlee (*Falconer*), Michiel Horn (*Academic Freedom*), C.B. Sissons (*Victoria University*), and minutes of the hearing and the *Report of the Special Committee* of 1909; for the separate college for women controversy, minutes of the University Women's Club and the United Alumnae, Paula LaPierre ('The First Generation'), Alyson King ('Second Generation of Women Students'), M.J. Brown ('*A Disposition to Bear*'), and the *Monthly*; for the Margaret Eaton School, Heather Murray ('Making the

Modern' and *Working in English*) and Dorothy Jackson (*History of Three Schools*); for enrolment and finances, James Greenlee (*Falconer*); for appointments, Greenlee (*Falconer*), Michael Bliss (*A Canadian Millionaire*), Horn (*Academic Freedom*), and the Namier file in the Falconer papers.

Chapter 21: Education, Medicine, and the Museum (1909)

Material on the thermodynamics building is contained in the *Monthly* and in R.W. Angus ('New Laboratories'), as well as in Richard White (*Skule Story*) and C.R. Young (*Early Engineering Education*). The sources for education were the *Monthly*, the *Report of the Royal Commission* of 1906, W.S. Wallace (*A History*), D.C. Masters (*Henry John Cody*), Robin Harris ('Professional Education'), H.T.J. Coleman ('The University Schools'), Jack Batten (*UTS*), and John Seath's 1917 report to the minister of education. For the TGH, I relied heavily on Michael Bliss' biography of Flavelle (*A Canadian Millionaire*) and Bliss' comprehensive notes and documents on the TGH, which he lent to me and which include an extensive collection of relevant Flavelle papers from Queen's University as well as the minutes of the hospital's board of trustees and other hospital documents; other TGH sources include the 1906 *Report of the Royal Commission*, W.G. Cosbie (*Toronto General Hospital*), the correspondence between Ernest Jones and Sigmund Freud in R.A. Paskauskas (*Complete Correspondence*), and J.T.H. Connor on the history of TGH (*Doing Good*); for the reorganization of the TGH, I used James Greenlee (*Falconer*), and Connor. For Women's College Hospital, I used Geraldine Maloney ('Women's College Hospital'), and for the hospitals in general, Edward Shorter (*A Century of Radiology*). The principal sources for the ROM were C.T. Currelly (*I Brought the Ages Home*), Lovat Dickson (*The Museum Makers*), various *Monthly* volumes and ROM publications, the 1906 *Report of the Royal Commission*, and G.P. de T. Glazebrook (*Sir Edmund Walker*); for zoology, E.H. Craigie (*History of the Department of Zoology*) and J.R. Dymond ('The Royal Ontario Museum of Zoology'); for mineralogy, T.L. Walker ('Royal Ontario Museum: Mineralogy'); for geology, E.S. Moore ('Royal Ontario Museum of Geology'), W.A. Parks, ('Geology'), and '150 Years of Geology'; for palaeontology, Madeleine Fritz ('Royal Ontario Museum of Palaeontology' and 'William Arthur Parks'); and, generally, various Royal Society of Canada obituaries.

Chapter 22: The Great War (1914)

Sources on the First World War include James Greenlee (*Falconer*), Brian McKillop (*Matters of Mind*), the U of T *Roll of Service*, Barbara Wilson (*Ontario and the First World War*), Donald Smith ('Lost Youth'), Desmond Morton and Glenn Wright (*Winning the Second Battle*), various issues of the *Monthly*, and the *President's Reports*; on the German professors, James Greenlee (*Falconer*), McKillop (*Matters of Mind*), and Michiel Horn (*Academic Freedom*); on the National Research Council, Mel Thistle (*The Inner Ring*), Yves Gingras (*Physics and the Rise of Scientific Research*), McKillop (*Matters of Mind*), and Trevor Levere (*Research and Influence*); on engineering, Richard White (*Skule Story*), W.H. Ellis ('The University and Industrial Research'), and the *Monthly*; on aeronautics, Gordon Patterson (*Pathway to Excellence*) and the *Monthly*; on physics, H.H. Langton (*John McLennan*); on occupational therapy, W.J. Dunlop ('History of Occupational Therapy'), A.A. Primrose ('Ontario Society of Occupational Therapy'), and the Helen LeVesconte oral interview; on physical therapy, Ruby Heap ('Physiotherapy Education'); on the Connaught Laboratories, Paul Bator and Andrew Rhodes (*Within Reach of Everyone*), Robert Defries (*The First Fifty Years*), C.B. Farrar ('FitzGerald'), and McKillop (*Matters of Mind*).

Chapter 23: Post War (1919)

For Soldiers' Tower, I used the *Monthly* and Ian Montagnes (*Uncommon Fellowship*); for return-
ing soldiers, James Greenlee (*Falconer*) and Brian McKillop (*Matters of Mind*); for Hart House,
Montagnes (*Uncommon Fellowship*), David Kilgour (*A Strange Elation*), Vincent Massey (*What's
Past Is Prologue*), Karen Finlay (*The Force of Culture*), Hart House committee minutes, the
Monthly, and the *Graduate*; for Trinity College, T.A. Reed (*History of Trinity College*) and the
Trinity University Review; for the Cody royal commission on university finances, Greenlee
(*Falconer*), McKillop (*Matters of Mind*), Edward Stewart's thesis ('The Role of the Provincial
Government'), the *Report of the Royal Commission* of 1921, submissions to the royal commis-
sion, and the *Monthly*; for the 1922–3 select committee and the medical controversy, Greenlee
(*Falconer*), R.B. Kerr and D. Waugh (*Duncan Graham*), and the Robin Harris material on post-
war development; for university extension work, the *Monthly*, Allen Tough ('Adult Education'),
J.A. Blyth (*A Foundling at Varsity*), and the Robin Harris material on extension.

Chapter 24: Research and Graduate Studies (1922)

Material on Banting is drawn mainly from the work of Michael Bliss – his two books (*Banting*
and *The Discovery of Insulin*) and his articles ('Build It and They Will Come' and 'Rewriting
Medical History'); these were supplemented by Brian McKillop (*Matters of Mind*), Susan
Belanger ('Continuing the Banting Legacy'), Sandra McRae ('The Scientific Spirit'), and various
Royal Society of Canada and Royal Society of London obits. For graduate studies, I relied on
Peter Ross ('The Establishment of the Ph.D.'), James Greenlee (*Falconer*), Mel Thistle (*The
Inner Ring*), McKillop (*Matters of Mind*), Robin Harris' material on graduate studies, RSC and
RS obits, the *Monthly*, and the *President's Reports*; for physics, on Yves Gingras (*Physics and the
Rise of Scientific Research*), Elizabeth Allin (*Physics at the U of T*), and Gordon Shrum (*Gordon
Shrum*); for chemistry, on W.A.E. McBryde ('History of the Chemistry Department' and
'William Lash Miller'); for philosophy, on John Slater ('Philosophy at Toronto'); for the Pontifi-
cal Institute, on Martin Dimnik (*Jubilee 1989*), Alexander Reford ('St. Michael's College'), and
Lawrence Shook (*Catholic Post-Secondary Education*); for history, on Robert Bothwell (*Laying the
Foundation*); for political economy, on Ian Drummond (*Political Economy*); for sociology, on
Harry Hiller (*Society and Change*) and R. Helmes-Hayes, (*A Quarter Century of Sociology*); and
for engineering, on Richard White (*Skule Story*).

Chapter 25: Good Years (1926)

Brian McKillop (*Matters of Mind*) was particularly helpful; also useful were James Greenlee
(*Falconer*) and D.C. Masters (*Cody*), as well as the Royal Society of Canada obits, the Falconer
papers, the *Monthly*, the *Varsity*, and several of the oral interviews. For the various disciplines
discussed in the chapter, I used McKillop (*Matters of Mind*), Claude Bissell (*Halfway up Parnassus*), Kathleen Coburn (*In Pursuit of Coleridge*), W.W. Briggs (*North American Classicists*),
Robert Bothwell (*Laying the Foundation*), C.D. Rouillard (*French Studies*), R.C.B. Risk ('W.P.M.
Kennedy'), Ian Kyer and Jerome Bickenbach (*The Fiercest Debate*), John Beckwith (*Music at
Toronto*), Ezra Schabas (*Sir Ernest MacMillan*), F.V. Winnett and W.S. McCullough ('Department of Near Eastern Studies'), Alan Latta ('German at the U of T'), and Maddalena Kuitunen
and Julius Molinaro ((*Italian Studies*); for athletics, T.A. Reed (*Blue and White*), the *Varsity*,

the Sports Hall of Fame website, *Torontonensis*, the daily papers, Helen Gurney (*Women's Sports*), A.E.M. Parkes ('Women's Athletics'), Patrick Okens ('Rowing at the University of Toronto'), R. Kollins and P. Carson ('Varsity Blues Football'), Brian McFarlane (*Canadian Women's Hockey*), and Stephen Thiele (*History of the Grey Cup*).

Chapter 26: Depressing Times (1931)

For the discussion of academic freedom, I used the wealth of material in Michiel Horn (*Academic Freedom*), Brian McKillop (*Matters of Mind*), James Greenlee (*Falconer*), R.D. Francis (*Frank H. Underhill*), and D.C. Masters (*Henry John Cody*); for Cody's appointment, Masters (*Cody*) and the Robin Harris memo and files; for the depression, McKillop (*Matters of Mind*), Masters (*Cody*), the Robin Harris memo, John Saywell (*Mitchell Hepburn*), Paul Axelrod (*Making a Middle Class*), and Edward Stewart ('Role of the Provincial Government'); for fine arts, Dorothy Farr ('Fine Art Department'); for nursing, 'School of Nursing'; for the ROM, Lovat Dickson (*Museum Makers*), L.C. Walmsley (*Bishop in Honan*), C.T. Currelly (*I Brought the Ages Home*), ROM documents in the ROM, and the Thomas McIlwraith papers in the U of T Archives; for geography, Marie Sanderson (*Griffith Taylor*), Nancy Christie ('Griffith Taylor and the Ecology of Geography'), and Patrick Naughton ('The Development of the Department of Geography'); and for the David Dunlap Observatory, C.A. Chant (*Astronomy*), the *Monthly*, and David Dunlap Observatory pamphlets.

Chapter 27: The Second World War (1939)

For the war and the University of Toronto, I used Brian McKillop (*Matters of Mind*), D.C. Masters (*Henry John Cody*), the *University of Toronto Memorial Book*, Donald Avery (*The Science of War*), Richard White (*Skule Story*), and the U of T *Monthly*. For refugees, I used Masters (*Cody*), James Greenlee (*Falconer*), Irving Abella and Harold Troper (*None Is Too Many* and 'Canada and the Refugee Intellectual'), L.D. Stokes ('Gerhard Herzberg'), Michael Bliss (*Banting*), Paul Bator (*Within Reach of Everyone*), and Michiel Horn (*Academic Freedom*); for internees, Paula Draper ('Muses behind Barbed Wire'), Masters (*Cody*), Donald Avery (*Reluctant Host*), and John Slater ('Philosophy at Toronto'); for student life, Paul Axelrod (*Making a Middle Class*); for mathematics, G. de B. Robinson (*Mathematics Department*) and the *Varsity Graduate*; for women and the war, Nancy Kiefer and Ruth Pierson ('The War Effort and Women's Students'); for medical admissions, R.D. Gidney and W.P.J. Millar ('Medical Students' and 'Admissions in Medicine'), and W.P.J. Millar ('Jewish Medical Students'); for Underhill, Horn (*Academic Freedom*), R.D. Francis (*Frank H. Underhill*), Masters (*Cody*), and McKillop (*Matters of Mind*); for scientific research, Avery (*The Science of War*), McKillop (*Matters of Mind*), C.P. Stacey (*Arms, Men and Governments*), Wilfrid Eggleston (*Scientists at War* and *National Research in Canada*), D.J. Goodspeed (*Defence Research Board*), Michael Bliss (*Banting*), Peter Allen ('The Franks Flying Suit'), Paul Bator (*Within Reach of Everyone*), G.R. Lindsey (*No Day Long Enough*), T.M. Gibson and M.H. Harrison (*Into Thin Air*), and John Bryden (*Deadly Allies*).

Chapter 28: Changing the Guard (1944)

Material on students in the post-war period was drawn from Brian McKillop (*Matters of Mind*), Peter Neary ('Canadian Veterans'), E.A. Corbett (*Sidney Earle Smith*), the *Varsity*, and the

Monthly. On the changing of the guard, I used D.C. Masters (*Henry John Cody*), Corbett (*Sidney Earle Smith*), McKillop (*Matters of Mind*), Claude Bissell (*Vincent Massey* and *Halfway up Parnassus*), the board of governors *Minutes*, the *Monthly*, the *Varsity Graduate*, Royal Society of Canada obits, and the Cody, Sidney Smith, Massey, and Drew papers; on women, Alison Prentice (*Canadian Women*) and McKillop (*Matters of Mind*); on engineering, Richard White (*Skule Story*), Robin Harris and Ian Montagnes (*Cold Iron*), the *Monthly*, and the *Varsity Graduate*; on defence, Donald Avery (*Science of War*), D.J. Goodspeed (*Defence Research Board*), and Stuart Leslie (*Cold War and American Science*); on aerospace, Gordon Patterson (*Pathway to Excellence*), Ben Etkin ('Beginnings'), the *Varsity Graduate*, and the *Bulletin*; on computer science, Michael Williams ('UTEC and Ferut'), J.N.P. Hume ('Systems Software'), various speeches, interviews, and publications ('Early Canadian Developments' and 'Presentation at Los Alamos') by C.C. Gotlieb, the *Varsity Graduate*, and the *Bulletin*.

Chapter 29: 'Easy Street' (1950)

Throughout this chapter, I used material from the *Varsity*, *Torontonensis*, the *Bulletin*, and various alumni publications, such as the *Monthly* and the *Varsity Graduate*. On student life, I used Paul Axelrod (*Scholars and Dollars*), Claude Bissell (*Halfway Up Parnassus*), Seymour Kanowitch ('Students' Administrative Council'), and Charles Levi ('S.A.C. Historical Project'); on sports, R. Kollins and P. Carson ('Varsity Blues Football'), Patrick Okens ('Rowing at the University of Toronto'), T.A. Reed (*Blue and White*), Andrew Podnieks (*Canada's Olympic Teams*), John Court ('Out of the Woodwork'), and Helen Gurney (*Women's Sports*), as well as the Sports Hall of Fame website; on Hart House, Ian Montagnes (*An Uncommon Fellowship*), David Kilgour (*A Strange Elation*), Claude Bissell (*Vincent Massey*), Boyd Neel (*My Orchestras*), and Hart House committee minutes; on international students, N. Kelly and M. Trebilcock (*The Making of the Mosaic*), Kay Riddell (*International Student Centre*), and FROS reports; on the cold war, Michiel Horn (*Academic Freedom*), Steve Hewitt (*Spying 101*), E.W. Schrecker (*No Ivory Tower*), and Chandler Davis ('The Purge'); and on Infeld, Horn (*Academic Freedom*), Leopold Infeld (*Why I Left Canada*), John Stachel ('Einstein and Infeld'), and Jack Dimond ('Memo to President Prichard').

Chapter 30: Planning for Growth (1955)

On predictions of future university growth, I used E.F. Sheffield ('University and College Enrolment'), Paul Axelrod (*Scholars and Dollars*), Claude Bissell (*Halfway up Parnassus*), and Brian McKillop (*Matters of Mind*); on planning at the University of Toronto, 'Report of the Plateau Committee,' Eric Arthur (1949 report), W.A. Osbourne (1957 report), and Geoffrey Simmins (*Ontario Association of Architects*); on Smith, E.A. Corbett (*Sidney Earle Smith*), Bissell (*Parnassus* and diaries), McKillop (*Matters of Mind*), Thomas Goudge (address), and Caesar Wright (senate speech); on the general course, Edgar McInnis ('Report on Pass and General Courses'); on salaries, Bill Nelson (*Search for Faculty Power*), the James Conacher oral interview, Robin Harris ('Development of the Faculty Association'), and Corbett (*Sidney Earle Smith*); on graduate studies and Harold Innis, the 1947 'Report on Graduate Studies,' Donald Creighton (*Harold Adams Innis*), Bissell (*Parnassus*), Harris ('Graduate Studies'), various issues of *Explorations*, and Moffat Woodside ('Special Committee on the Humanities').

Chapter 31: Financing Expansion (1958)

Throughout this chapter, I made use of Bissell's *Halfway up Parnassus* as well as his diaries and journals, and also of various University of Toronto publications, including the *Varsity News*, the *Monthly*, the *Alumni Bulletin*, the *Varsity Graduate*, the *Bulletin*, and the *Magazine*. For financing the expansion, I used Paul Axelrod (*Scholars and Dollars*), David Stager ('Federal Government Grants'), Glen Jones ('Governments, Governance, and Canadian Universities'), Brian McKillop (*Matters of Mind*), D.C. Masters (*Henry John Cody*), Ernest Sirluck (*First Generation*), the 1951 report of the Massey Commission, Claude Bissell (*Vincent Massey*), and Paul Litt (*The Muses, the Masses, and the Massey Commission*); for music, John Beckwith (*Music at Toronto*), Ezra Schabas (*Sir Ernest MacMillan*), Ezra Schabas and Carl Morey (*Opera Viva*), and Boyd Neel (*My Orchestras*); for the business school, Vincent Bladen (*Bladen on Bladen*), the Bladen and Warren Main oral interviews, and John Sawyer ('The Rotman School' and 'From Commerce to Management'); for social work, J.R. Graham ('History of the University of Toronto School of Social Work' and 'Charles Eric Hendry'), J.R. Graham and A. Al-Krenawi ('Contested Terrain'), *Teach Us to Care*, Allan Irving ('Social Science Research' and his thesis on Cassidy), and Sara Burke (*Seeking the Highest Good*); and for law, Ian Kyer and Jerome Bickenbach (*The Fiercest Debate*), Christopher Moore (*The Law Society of Upper Canada*), and John Arnup ('The 1957 Breakthrough').

Chapter 32: New Colleges (1960)

Claude Bissell's diaries and book (*Halfway up Parnassus*) were valuable for this chapter, as were various planning documents and University of Toronto publications, including the *Varsity Graduate*, the *Varsity News*, the *Bulletin*, and the *Magazine*. For York University, I used Paul Axelrod (*Scholars and Dollars*) and Murray Ross (*The Way Must Be Tried*); for New College and Innis College, Bissell's *Parnassus* and diaries, D.G. Ivey ('New College'), Peter Russell '('Memo on Innis College'), and Linda Poulos ('The Multi-Faculty Concept and Innis College'); for Scarborough College, D.C. Williams ('The Development of Scarborough and Erindale Colleges'), John Ball (*The First Twenty-Five Years*), the 1963 report of the Off-Campus College Committee,' Wynne Plumptre ('Scarborough's Noble Experiment'), and the 1971 'Report on the Status and Future of Scarborough College'; and for Erindale, John Percy (*Erindale College*), the 1965 'Report on Erindale College,' Paul Fox's letter, and the Peter Robinson and Tuzo Wilson oral interviews.

Chapter 33: Graduate Studies: From Massey College to the Robarts Library (1962)

In this chapter, I used Ernest Sirluck (*First Generation*), Claude Bissell (*Parnassus* and *The Imperial Canadian*, and the diaries), Robert Blackburn (*Evolution of the Heart*), Paul Axelrod (*Scholars and Dollars*), J.B. Macdonald (*Chances and Choices*), the *Varsity Graduate*, the *Bulletin*, and a number of reports on graduate studies, including the 1947 'Report on Graduate Studies,' *Graduate Studies in the University of Toronto* (1965, the Laskin report), and *Report to Study the Development of Graduate Programmes* (1966, the Spinks report).

Chapter 34: Multidisciplinary Endeavours (1963)

Material on the University of Toronto Press was drawn from Marsh Jeanneret (*God and Mammon*), Eleanor Harman ('Founding a University Press'), and Francess Halpenny ('Scholarly

Publishing'). For centres and institutes, I relied on graduate school documents, Ernest Sirluck (*First Generation*), Claude Bissell (*Halfway up Parnassus* and the diaries), various articles in the *Bulletin*, the *Monthly*, and the *Varsity Graduate*, and the *President's Reports*, *Canadian Who's Who* entries, graduate handbooks, and graduate school calendars. For the Erasmus series, I used Robert Fulford ('Erasmus of Toronto') and J.K. McConica and R.M. Schoeffel ('Collected Works of Erasmus'); for criminology, John Edwards ('Centre of Criminology'); for the REED project, A.F. Johnston ('Records of Early English Drama'); for Russian and East European studies, Gordon Skilling (*The Education of a Canadian*); and for Marshall McLuhan, Philip Marchand (*Marshall McLuhan*) and W.T. Gordon (*Marshall McLuhan*).

Chapter 35: Engineering and Medicine (1966)

For this section, I used Bissell's *Parnassus* and diaries; also helpful were Bissell's presidential files, various oral interviews, University of Toronto publications such as the *Varsity Graduate* and the *Bulletin*, and the *Canadian Who's Who* and press releases on University Professors. For engineering, I used Richard White (*Skule Story*), presidential files on the Ford Foundation grant, R.R. McLaughlin ('History of the Ford Foundation Grant'), Paul Axelrod (*Scholars and Dollars*), Gordon Patterson (*Pathway to Excellence*), Ben Etkin ('Beginnings'), and Henry O'Beirne ('Institute of Biomedical Engineering'); for medicine, the 1964 'Report of the Special Committee,' the Henry Borden memoirs, various memos from John Evans and George Connell, the 1968 'Report from Consultants on Medical Education' (the Commonwealth Fund report), and Paul Axelrod (*Scholars and Dollars*); for the hospitals, J.T.H. Connor (*Toronto's General Hospital*), Irene McDonald (*History of St. Michael's Hospital*), and Leslie Barsky (*History of Toronto's Mount Sinai Hospital*); and for the Ontario Cancer Institute and medical biophysics, H.E. Johns ('Department of Medical Biophysics'), draft chapters by Ernest McCulloch ('The Ontario Cancer Institute'), Edward Shorter (*A Century of Radiology*), and Louis Siminovitch ('Louis Siminovitch').

Chapter 36: Student Activism (1967)

I used a number of memoirs for this section, including Claude Bissell (*Halfway up Parnassus*), Robin Ross (*Short Road Down*), Ernest Sirluck (*First Generation*), Robert Blackburn (*Evolution of the Heart*), Kenneth McNaught (*Conscience and History*), Jill Conway (*True North*), and Bob Rae (*From Protest to Power*). I also used Bill Nelson (*Search for Faculty Power*), Michiel Horn (*Academic Freedom* and 'Students and Academic Freedom'), Patricia Jasen ('Student Critique of the Arts Curriculum'), Doug Owram (*Born at the Right Time*), Cyril Levitt (*Children of Privilege*), Tom Warner (*Never Going Back*), John Hagan (*Northern Passage*), Bissell's diaries, Donald Forster's papers, various University of Toronto publications such as the *Bulletin*, the *Varsity Graduate*, and the *Varsity*, and a number of official reports such as *University Government in Canada* (the Duff-Berdahl report), *Undergraduate Instruction in Arts and Science* (the Macpherson report), and *Towards Community in University Government*, (the CUG report).

Chapter 37: A New Act (1971)

The books I used for this chapter include Claude Bissell (*Halfway up Parnassus*), Robin Ross (*Short Road Down*), Bill Nelson (*Search for Faculty Power*), Ernest Sirluck (*First Generation*), and Jill Conway (*True North*). I also used Bissell's diaries and the oral interviews with Henry Borden,

John Evans, Donald Forster, William Harris, Sydney Hermant, and Frances Ireland. In addition, I used the *Bulletin, Debates and Proceedings of the Legislature*, the *President's Reports*, and the 1966 'Report on Academic Tenure' (the Haist rules), as well as *Towards Community in University Government* (the CUG report), A.C.H. Hallett. ('Summary of Proceedings of the University-wide Committee'), and John Macdonald ('The Governing Council System').

Chapter 38: Sliding down Parnassus (1975)

In this chapter and all the subsequent chapters, I made extensive use of the *Bulletin* as well as of various e-mails, letters, and conversations (mentioned in the notes) with many of the persons who took part in the events described. I made extensive use also of a number of taped oral interviews conducted by the University in the mid-1980s, including interviews with John Evans, Donald Forster, Arthur Kruger, William Harris, and Frances Ireland. For the financing of universities, I used Paul Axelrod (*Scholars and Dollars*), Jill Conway (*True North*), John Macdonald (*Chances and Choices*), Michiel Horn (*Academic Freedom*), and various speeches by Evans; for the faculty association, Bill Nelson (*Search for Faculty Power*) and the memorandum of agreement; for the colleges, *Undergraduate Instruction in Arts and Science* (the Macpherson report), various memoranda of understanding and agreements, Robin Harris ('Victoria in Federation'), Alexander Reford ('St. Michael's College'), and arts and science calendars; for Woodsworth College, the 1970 'Report of the Advisory Committee on Extension' (the Colman report), Norma Grindal ('Before Woodsworth College'), Arthur Kruger and Peter Silcox ('Woodsworth at Ten'), and the 1998 'Review of Woodsworth College'; for food sciences, Bissell (*Halfway up Parnassus*) and various reports; and for the School of Hygiene, various reports, Harding le Riche ('School of Hygiene'), and Paul Bator (*Within Reach of Everyone*).

Chapter 39: Financial and Other Concerns (1980)

Understandably, there was less secondary material available for this and later chapters than for any previous chapter. The books I used included Paul Axelrod (*Scholars and Dollars*), Jill Conway (*True North*), Anne Ford (*A Path Not Strewn with Roses*), Bill Nelson (*Search for Faculty Power*), and George Connell (*Renewal 1987*). I made extensive use of various University of Toronto publications, including the *Bulletin*, the *Varsity Graduate*, and the *Magazine*, and of oral interviews, particularly the one with James Ham. In addition, I had helpful face-to-face, telephone, and e-mail conversations with a number of people, including George Connell, David Cook, Kendall Cork, Harvey Dyck, Dan Lang, Michael Finlayson, Joan Foley, Frank Iacobucci, Marnie Paikin, Robert Prichard, Terrence Wardrop, John Whitten, Fred Wilson, and various members of the search committees for Ham, Forster, and Connell. Finally, I was helped by a collection of papers by Connell and by memos he prepared specifically for me.

Chapter 40: Moving Forward (1986)

I made extensive use of the *Bulletin* and the *Magazine*, as well as of George Connell's *Renewal 1987*; I also used Connell's presidential papers, his memos to me, and two volumes of his speeches and other documents. For government finances, I used Dan Lang (*University Finances in Ontario*); for engineering, Richard White (*Skule Story*); for medicine, Leslie Barsky (*Toronto's Mount Sinai Hospital*) and the Connell memos, the hospital websites, and conversations with a number of people, in particular Arnold Aberman, John Dirks, Charles Hollenberg, David MacLennan, David Naylor, Aser Rothstein, and Cecil Yip; for fundraising, the Marts and Lundy study; and for governance issues, Bill Nelson (*Search for Faculty Power*) and E.J. Stansbury ('Report on the Unicameral Governing Structure').

Chapter 41: Raising the Sights (1994)

Chapter 42: Moving up Parnassus (1997)

There were relatively few records in the archives for this period, and consequently I relied to a great extent on the U of T *Bulletin*, the U of T *Magazine*, the U of T *National Report*, the *UTFA Newsletter*, the *Varsity, The Independent, The Newspaper*, 'Campaign Quarterly' and other campaign documents, the *Globe and Mail*, the *Toronto Star, Maclean's*, and *Toronto Life*. Dan Lang's *University Finances in Ontario* was also helpful. In addition, I used interviews with and memos and e-mails from some of the principal players, including Arnold Aberman, Susan Bloch-Nevitte, Robert Birgeneau, Michael Charles, David Cook, Ron Daniels, Jon Dellandrea, John Dirks, Martin England, Michael Finlayson, Joan Foley, Paul Gooch, Bruce Kidd, Dan Lang, Michael Marrus, Robert McNutt, Judy Matthews, Carole Moore, Heather Munroe-Blum, Janice Oliver, Paul Perron, Robert Prichard, Adel Sedra, David Silcox, Elizabeth Sisam, Carolyn Tuohy, Bob White, Paul Williams, and Cecil Yip. The major documents used include *Planning for 2000* and *Raising Our Sights*, site planning documents, and the open-space plan.

Epilogue: A Walk through the Campus (2000)

Just about all the sources used for this section can be found in the listings for earlier chapters.

BIBLIOGRAPHY

———— ∞ ————

Only the material cited in the section on sources is cited in this bibliography. The entries are in alphabetical order (with those under 'Report' in chronological order) and are not divided into books, articles, theses, archival sources, etc. To cite all the material consulted during the course of this project would require hundreds of pages of text. Even citing all the note references in a bibliography would produce too long a document to be included in this book. Presidential papers and most other archival sources found in the University of Toronto Archives are not listed in the bibliography.

Abella, Irving, and Harold Troper. 'Canada and the Refugee Intellectual.' In Jarrell C. Jackman and Carla M. Borden, eds, *The Muses Flee Hitler: Cultural Transfer and Adaptation*. Washington: Smithsonian Institution Press, 1983
– *None Is Too Many: Canada and the Jews of Europe, 1933–1948*. Toronto: Lester, 1991
Allen, Peter. 'The Remotest of Mistresses: The Story of Canada's Unsung Tactical Weapon: The Franks Flying Suit.' *Canadian Aviation Historical Society Journal* 21 (Winter 1983)
Allin, Elizabeth J. *Physics at the University of Toronto*. Toronto: University of Toronto Press, 1981
Alumni Bulletin
Angus, Robert W. 'The New Laboratories of the University of Toronto, for Steam, Gas, and Hydraulic Work.' *Applied Science*, February 1910
The Arbour
Arnup, John. 'The 1957 Breakthrough.' *Law Society Gazette* 18 (1982)
Arthur, Eric. 'Report of the Committee Approved by the Board of Governors on April 22nd, 1948 on the Siting of Buildings and the Physical Growth of the University,' June 1, 1949. UTA/A75-0019/012(01)

– *Toronto: No Mean City*. 3rd ed. Toronto: University of Toronto Press, 1986

Ash, Marinell. 'The Early Years.' In Elizabeth Hulse, ed., *Thinking with Both Hands: Sir Daniel Wilson in the Old World and the New*. Toronto: University of Toronto Press, 1999

Averill, Harold, and Gerald, Keith. 'A Railway to the Moon: Daniel Wilson and the University of Toronto.' In Elizabeth Hulse, ed., *Thinking with Both Hands: Sir Daniel Wilson in the Old World and the New*. Toronto: University of Toronto Press, 1999

Avery, Donald H. *Reluctant Host: Canada's Response to Immigrant Workers, 1896–1995*. Toronto: McClelland and Stewart, 1995

– *The Science of War: Canadian Scientists and Allied Military Technology during the Second World War*. Toronto: University of Toronto Press, 1998

Axelrod, Paul. *Making a Middle Class: Student Life in English Canada during the Thirties*. Montreal: McGill-Queen's University Press, 1990

– *Scholars and Dollars: Politics, Economics, and Universities of Ontario, 1945–1980*. Toronto: University of Toronto Press, 1980

Baker, G. Blaine. 'Legal Education in Upper Canada, 1785–1889: The Law Society as Educator.' In David H. Flaherty, ed., *Essays in the History of Canadian Law*, vol. 2. Toronto: Osgoode Society, 1983

Ball, John L. *The First Twenty-Five Years*. Toronto: Scarborough College, 1989

Barsky, Leslie Marrus. *From Generation to Generation: A History of Toronto's Mount Sinai Hospital*. Toronto: McClelland and Stewart, 1998

Bator, Paul A. *Within Reach of Everyone: A History of the University of Toronto School of Hygiene and the Connaught Laboratories Limited*, vol. 2, *1955 to 1975, with an Update to the 1990s*. Toronto: Canadian Public Health Association, 1995

Bator, Paul A., and Andrew James Rhodes. *Within Reach of Everyone: A History of the University of Toronto School of Hygiene and the Connaught Laboratories*, vol. 1, *1927–1955*. Ottawa: Canadian Public Health Association, 1990

Batten, Jack. *UTS: 75 Years of Excellence*. Toronto: University of Toronto Schools, 1985

Beckwith, John. *Music at Toronto: A Personal Account*. Toronto: University of Toronto Press, 1995

Belanger, Susan E. 'Continuing the Banting Legacy: The Banting Research Foundation, 1925–1995, 70 Years of Medical Research in Canada.' Toronto: Banting Research Foundation, 1995

Bissell, Claude. Diaries. UTA/B88-0091

– *Halfway up Parnassus: A Personal Account of the University of Toronto, 1932–1971*. Toronto: University of Toronto Press, 1974

– *The Imperial Canadian: Vincent Massey in Office*. Toronto: University of Toronto Press, 1986

– *The Young Vincent Massey*. Toronto: University of Toronto Press, 1981

Blackburn, Robert H. *Evolution of the Heart: A History of the University of Toronto Library Up to 1981*. Toronto: University of Toronto Press, 1989

– 'Mackenzie King, William Mulock, James Mavor, and the University of Toronto Student Strike of 1895.' *Canadian Historical Review* 69 (December 1988)

Bladen, Vincent. *Bladen on Bladen*. Toronto: Scarborough College, 1978

Bliss, Michael. *Banting: A Biography*. 2nd paperback ed. Toronto: University of Toronto Press, 1992

– 'Build It and They Will Come: Why Insulin Was Discovered in Toronto.' Address given at the 'Medicine in Toronto, 200 Years' symposium, October 16, 1993

– *A Canadian Millionaire: The Life and Business Times of Sir Joseph Flavelle, Bart., 1858–1939.* Toronto: Macmillan, 1978

– *The Discovery of Insulin.* Toronto: University of Toronto Press, 1982

– Research notes on Frederick Banting, the discovery of insulin, and Joseph Flavelle

– 'Rewriting Medical History: Charles Best and the Banting and Best Myth.' *Journal of the History of Medicine* 48 (July 1993)

– *William Osler: A Life in Medicine.* Toronto: University of Toronto Press, 1999

Blyth, J.A. *A Foundling at Varsity: A History of the Division of University Extension, University of Toronto.* Privately published, 1976

Board of Governors. Minutes. UTA/A70-0024

Borden, Henry. 'Memoirs.' National Archives of Canada, MG30, A86, v. 4

Bothwell, Robert. *Laying the Foundation: A Century of History at University of Toronto.* Toronto: Department of History, University of Toronto, 1991

Bowker, Alan F. 'Truly Useful Men: Maurice Hutton, George Wrong, James Mavor, and the University of Toronto, 1880–1927.' PhD thesis, University of Toronto, 1975

Briggs, Ward W., ed. *Biographical Dictionary of North American Classicists.* Westport, Connecticut: Greenwood, 1994

Brown, M. Jennifer. *'A Disposition to Bear the Ills ...': Rejection of a Separate College by University of Toronto Women.* Toronto: The Women in Canadian History Project, 1977

Bryden, John. *Deadly Allies: Canada's Secret War, 1937–1947.* Toronto: McClelland and Stewart, 1989

Burke, Sara Z. 'New Women and Old Romans: Co-education at the University of Toronto, 1884–1895.' *Canadian Historical Review,* June 1999

– *Seeking the Highest Good: Social Service and Gender at the University of Toronto, 1888–1937.* Toronto: University of Toronto Press, 1996

Campaign News

Campaign Quarterly

Canadian Who's Who (various volumes)

Careless, J.M.S. 'Beginning a New Life in Toronto.' Undated and unpublished speech

– ed. *The Pre-Confederation Premiers: Ontario Government Leaders, 1841–1867.* Toronto: University of Toronto Press, 1980

– *The Union of the Canadas: The Growth of Canadian Institutions.* Toronto: McClelland and Stewart, 1967

Carr, Henry. 'The Very Reverend J.R. Teefy, C.S.B., LL.D.' *Canadian Catholic Historical Association Report* 7 (1939–40)

Chant, C.A. *Astronomy in the University of Toronto: The David Dunlap Observatory.* Toronto: University of Toronto Press, 1954

Charlesworth, Hector. *More Candid Chronicles.* Toronto: Macmillan, 1928

Chisholm, Arthur M. 'When I Went to College.' *University of Toronto Monthly* 26 (November 1926)

Christie, Nancy J. 'Pioneering for a Civilized World: Griffith Taylor and the Ecology of Geography.' *Scientica Canadensis* 17:1–2

Coburn, Kathleen. *In Pursuit of Coleridge.* Toronto: Clarke, Irwin, 1993

Cole, Curtis. 'A Hand to Shake the Tree of Knowledge: Legal Education in Ontario, 1871–1889.' *Interchange*, Autumn 1986

Coleman, H.T.J. 'The University Schools.' *University of Toronto Monthly* 10 (1910)

Connell, George E. *Renewal 1987: A Discussion Paper on the Nature and Role of the University of Toronto*. March, 1987

Connor, J.T.H. *Doing Good: The Life of Toronto's General Hospital in the Nineteenth and Twentieth Centuries*. Toronto: University of Toronto Press, 2000

Conway, Jill Ker. *True North: A Memoir*. Toronto: Knopf, 1994

Corbett, E.A. *Sidney Earle Smith*. Toronto: University of Toronto Press, 1961

Cosbie, W.G. *The Toronto General Hospital, 1819–1965: A Chronicle*. Toronto: Macmillan, 1975

Court, John P.M. 'Out of the Woodwork: The Wood Family's Benefactions to Victoria College.' In Neil Semple, ed., *Canadian Methodist Historical Society Papers*, vol. 11. 1997

Craig, G.M. *Upper Canada: The Formative Years*. Toronto: McClelland and Stewart, 1963

Craigie, E. Horne. *A History of the Department of Zoology of the University of Toronto Up to 1962*. Toronto: University of Toronto Press, 1966

Creighton, Donald. *Harold Adams Innis: Portrait of a Scholar*. Toronto: University of Toronto Press, 1957

Currelly, Charles Trick. *I Brought the Ages Home*. Toronto: Ryerson, 1956

Dale, Anne. 'J.B. Wilmott.' *Dictionary of Canadian Biography* 14

Dalton, I.R., and G.D. Garland. 'The Old Observatory's Noble History.' *The Cannon*, October 31, 1980

The David Dunlap Observatory: The First Fifty Years, 1935–1985. Toronto: University of Toronto, 1985

Davis, Chandler. 'The Purge.' Repr. from *A Century of Mathematics in America*. Providence: American Mathematical Society, 1988

Dawson, R. MacGregor. *William Lyon Mackenzie King: A Political Biography, 1874–1923*. Toronto: University of Toronto Press, 1959

Debates and Proceedings of the Legislature of the Province of Ontario

Defries, Robert D. *The First Fifty Years*. Toronto: University of Toronto Press, 1968

De la Cour, Lykke, and Rose Sheinin. 'The Ontario Medical College for Women 1883 to 1906: Lessons from Gender-separatism in Medical Education.' In Marianne Ainley, ed., *Despite the Odds: Essays in Canadian Women and Science*. Montreal: Vehicule, 1990

Dickson, Lovat. *The Museum Makers: The Story of the Royal Ontario Museum*. Toronto: Royal Ontario Museum, 1986

Dictionary of Canadian Biography 1–20

Dimnik, Martin, ed. *Jubilee 1989: Pontifical Institute of Mediaeval Studies Foundation 1929 – Papal Charter 1939*. Toronto: Pontifical Institute of Mediaeval Studies, 1989

Dimond, Jack. 'Memo to President Prichard re Prof. Leopold Infeld,' June 15, 1994

Draper, Paula Jean. 'Muses behind Barbed Wire: Canada and the Interned Refugees.' In Jarrell C. Jackman and Carla M. Borden, eds, *The Muses Flee Hitler: Cultural Transfer and Adaptation*. Washington: Smithsonian Institution Press, 1983

Drew, George Alexander. Papers. National Archives of Canada, MG32, C3

Drummond, Ian M. *Political Economy at the University of Toronto: A History of the Department, 1888–1982*. Toronto: Governing Council of the University of Toronto, 1983

Duff, James, and Robert Berdahl. *University Government in Canada: Report of a Commission*

Sponsored by the Canadian Association of University Teachers and the Association of Universities and Colleges in Canada. Toronto: University of Toronto Press, 1966

Dunlop, W.J. 'A Brief History of Occupational Therapy.' *Canadian Journal of Occupational Therapy* 1:1 (1933)

Dymond, J.R. 'The Royal Ontario Museum of Zoology.' UTA/A83-0036/019

Educational Monthly of Canada

Edwards, John LL. J. 'Directing the Development of a University Centre of Criminology.' In A.N. Doob and E.L. Greenspan, eds, *Perspectives in Criminal Law: Essays in Honour of John LL.J. Edwards.* Aurora: Canada Law Book, 1985

Eggleston, Wilfrid. *National Research in Canada: The NRC, 1916–1966.* Toronto: Clarke, Irwin, 1978

– *Scientists at War.* Toronto: Oxford University Press, 1950

Ellis, W.H. 'The University and Industrial Research.' *Applied Science* 10:5 (June 1916)

Etkin, Ben. 'Beginnings.' *Canadian Aeronautics and Space Journal* 45:2 (June 1999)

Evans, A. Margaret. *Sir Oliver Mowat.* Toronto: University of Toronto Press, 1992

Excellence, Accessibility, Responsibility: Report of the Advisory Panel on Future Directions for Postsecondary Education. www.edu.gov.on.ca/eng/document/reports/futuree.html

'Extract from Report to the Minister of Education from the Superintendent.' UTA/A83-0036/007

Falconer, Robert. 'Development in the University of Toronto.' *University of Toronto Monthly* 13 (1913)

– 'The Needs of the University of Toronto.' *University of Toronto Monthly* 9 (1908)

Farr, Dorothy. 'The Fine Art Department of the University of Toronto – A History.' UTA/A83-0036/005

Farrar, C.B. 'I Remember J.G. FitzGerald.' *American Journal of Psychiatry* 120:1 (1963)

Ferns, H.S., and B. Ostry. *The Age of Mackenzie King: The Rise of the Leader.* London: Heinemann, 1955

Finlay, Karen. *The Force of Culture: Vincent Massey and Canadian Sovereignty.* Forthcoming, University of Toronto Press

Flavelle, Joseph. Papers. Queen's University Archives

Ford, Anne Rochon. *A Path Not Strewn with Roses: One Hundred Years of Women at the University of Toronto, 1884–1984.* Toronto: University of Toronto Press, 1985

Forster, Donald. Papers. UTA/B83-0040

Forward, Dorothy F. *The History of Botany at the University of Toronto.* Toronto: Botany Department, University of Toronto, 1977

Fox, Paul. 'Letter to M.L. Friedland.' March 23, 1998

Francis, R.D. *Frank H. Underhill, Intellectual Provocateur.* Toronto: University of Toronto Press, 1986

Fraser, Brian J. *Church, College, and Clergy: A History of Theological Education at Knox College, Toronto, 1844–1944.* Montreal: McGill-Queen's University Press, 1995

French, G.S. 'Prelude to Federation.' Undated and unpublished speech

Fritz, Madeleine A. 'The Royal Ontario Museum of Palaeontology.' UTA/P78-0626

– 'William Arthur Parks.' Toronto: Royal Ontario Museum, 1971

Frost, Stanley Brice. *McGill University: For the Advancement of Learning.* Montreal: McGill-Queen's University Press, 1980

Bibliography

Fulford, Robert. 'Erasmus of Toronto.' *Journal of Scholarly Publishing*, April 1999

Gallie, William E. 'First Annual Medical Alumni Oration.' *Medical Graduate* 3 (1956–7)

Gardiner, E. 'A Reminiscence.' *Sesame* 1:1 (1897)

Gibbs, Elizabeth, ed. *Debates of the Legislative Assembly of United Canada*. Montreal: Centre de recherche en histoire économique du Canada français, 1977

Gibson, Frederick W. *'To Serve and Yet Be Free': Queen's University*, vol. 2, *1917–1961*. Kingston: McGill-Queen's University Press, 1983

Gibson, T.M., and M.H. Harrison. *Into Thin Air: A History of Aviation Medicine in the RAF*. London: Robert Hale, 1984

Gidney, R.D., and W.P.J. Millar. 'Medical Students at the University of Toronto, 1910–1940: A Profile.' *Canadian Bulletin of Medical History* 13 (1996)

– *Professional Gentlemen: The Professions in Nineteenth-Century Ontario*. Toronto: University of Toronto Press, 1994

– 'Quality and Quantity: The Problem of Admissions in Medicine at the University of Toronto, 1910–51.' *Historical Studies in Education* 9:2 (Fall 1997)

– 'The Reorientation of Medical Education in Late Nineteenth-Century Ontario: The Proprietary Medical Schools and the Founding of the Faculty of Medicine at the University of Toronto.' *Journal of the History of Medicine* 49 (1994)

Gingras, Yves. *Physics and the Rise of Scientific Research in Canada*. Trans. Peter Keating. Montreal: McGill-Queen's University Press, 1991

Glazebrook, G.P. de T. *Sir Edmund Walker*. Oxford: Oxford University Press, 1933

Globe and Mail

Godfrey, Charles. *Aikins of the U of T Medical Faculty*. Madoc, Ontario: Codam, 1998

– *John Rolph: Rebel with Causes*. Madoc, Ontario: Codam, 1993

Goodspeed, D.J. *A History of the Defence Research Board of Canada*. Ottawa: Queen's Printer, 1958

Gordon, W. Terrence. *Marshall McLuhan: Escape into Understanding*. Toronto: Stoddart, 1997

Gotlieb, Calvin C. 'Early Canadian Developments in Computers and Electronics.' In C.E. Law et al., eds, *Perspectives in Science and Technology: The Legacy of Omond Solandt*. Kingston: Queen's Quarterly, 1994

– 'Transcript of Presentation Given at Los Alamos.' Los Alamos: University of California Los Alamos Scientific Laboratory, 1976

Goudge, T.A. 'Address Given at the Staff Meeting in Honour of Sidney Smith, January 11, 1958.' UTA/A83-0036/039

The Graduate

Graduate Studies in the University of Toronto. Report of the President's Committee on the School of Graduate Studies, 1964–1965 (Laskin report)

Graham, John R. 'Charles Eric Hendry (1903–1979): The Pre-war Formative Origin of a Leader of Post World-War II Canadian Social Work Education.' *Canadian Social Work Review* 11 (1994)

– 'A History of the University of Toronto School of Social Work.' PhD thesis, University of Toronto, 1996

Graham, J.R., and A. Al-Krenawi. 'Contested Terrain: Two Competing Views of Social Work at the University of Toronto, 1914–1945.' Forthcoming in *Canadian Social Work Review*

Greenlee, James G. President Search Committee notecards

– *Sir Robert Falconer: A Biography.* Toronto: University of Toronto Press, 1988

Grindal, Norma. 'The Six Years before Woodsworth College.' *The Arbor* 4 (Winter 1984)

Gullett, D.W. *A History of Dentistry in Canada.* Toronto: University of Toronto Press, 1971

Gurney, Helen. *A Century to Remember: Women's Sports at the University of Toronto.* Toronto: U of T Women's T-Holders' Association, 1993

Hagan, John. *Northern Passage: American War Resisters in Canada.* Cambridge, Massachusetts: Harvard University Press, 2001

Hall, Roger. *A Century to Celebrate / Un Centenaire à fêter, 1893–1993.* Toronto: Dundurn, 1993

Hallett, A.C.H. 'Summary of Proceedings of the University-wide Committee, June 1–3, 1970.' UTA/A77-0019/061

Halpenny, Francess. 'The Ambience of Scholarly Publishing in Canada, 1955–1975.' Unpublished draft ms., 1998

Hamilton, John. 'Problems of the School and University,' December 10, 1973. UTA/A85-0044

Harman, Eleanor. 'Founding a University Press.' UTA/A83-0036/020

Harris, Robin. 'The Development of the University of Toronto Faculty Association.' UTA/A83-0036/001

– 'Developments, 1919–1932.' UTA/A91-0020/001

– 'Extension.' UTA/A83-0036/001

– 'Graduate Studies in Toronto: The Role of the Dean.' Speech delivered on March 12, 1986 at University College

– *A History of Higher Education in Canada, 1663–1960.* Toronto: University of Toronto Press, 1976

– 'Professional Education.' UTA/A83-0036/001

– 'Victoria in Federation with the University of Toronto.' In *From Cobourg to Toronto: Victoria College in Retrospect.* Toronto: Chartres, 1986

Harris, Robin S., and Ian Montagnes, eds. *Cold Iron and Lady Godiva: Engineering Education at Toronto, 1920–1972.* Toronto: University of Toronto Press, 1972

Harte, Negley. *The University of London, 1836–1986.* London: Athlone, 1986

Heap, Ruby. 'From the Science of Housekeeping to the Science of Nutrition: Pioneers in Canadian Nutrition and Dietetics at the University of Toronto's Faculty of Household Science, 1900–1950.' In Elizabeth Smyth et al., *Challenging Professions: Historical and Contemporary Perspectives on Women's Professional Work.* Toronto: University of Toronto Press, 1999

– 'Training Women for a New "Women's Profession": Physiotherapy Education at the University of Toronto, 1917–1940.' *History of Education Quarterly* 35 (Summer 1995)

Helmes-Hayes, R., ed. *A Quarter Century of Sociology at the University of Toronto, 1963–1988.* Toronto: Canadian Scholars Press 1988

Henderson, J.L.H. 'The Founding of Trinity College, Toronto.' *Ontario History* 44 (1952)

Hendriks, Martha. 'An Institutional History of the Department of Computer Science at the University of Toronto, 1948–1971,' January 6, 1992. Unpublished paper

Hewitt, Steve. *Spying 101: The RCMP's Secret Activities at Canadian Universities.* Forthcoming, University of Toronto Press

Hiller, Harry. *Society and Change: S.D. Clark and the Development of Canadian Sociology.* Toronto: University of Toronto Press, 1982

Hodgins, J. George. *Documentary History of Education in Upper Canada.* 28 vols. Toronto: Warwick Bros and Rutter, 1894–1910

Hoff, Tory. 'The Controversial Appointment of James Mark Baldwin to the University of Toronto in 1889.' MA thesis, Carleton University, 1980

Horn, Michiel. *Academic Freedom in Canada: A History*. Toronto: University of Toronto Press, 1999

– 'Students and Academic Freedom in Canada.' *Historical Studies in Education* 11:1

Hoy, Claire. *Bill Davis*. Toronto: Methuen, 1985

Hulse, Elizabeth, ed. *Thinking with Both Hands: Sir Daniel Wilson in the Old World and the New*. Toronto: University of Toronto Press, 1999

Hume, J.N. Patterson. 'Development of Systems Software for the Ferut Computer at the University of Toronto, 1952 to 1955.' *IEEE Annals of the History of Computing* 16:2 (1994)

Humphries, Charles W. *'Honest Enough to Be Bold': The Life and Times of Sir James Pliny Whitney*. Toronto: University of Toronto Press, 1985

– 'James P. Whitney and the University of Toronto.' In Edith G. Firth, ed. *Profiles of a Province: Studies in the History of Ontario*. Toronto: Ontario Historical Society, 1967

Hunter, R.S. *Rowing in Canada since 1848*. Hamilton: Davis-Lisson, 1933

'Implementation Committee on the Faculty of Food Sciences, University of Toronto, Final Report,' February 2, 1973. UTA/A79-0057/019

The Independent

Infeld, Leopold. *Why I Left Canada: Reflections on Science and Politics*. Ed. Lewis Pyenson. Trans. Helen Infeld. Montreal: McGill-Queen's University Press, 1978

Irving, Allan. 'Social Science Research in the University: An Examination of the Views of Harry Cassidy and Harold Innis.' *Canadian Journal of Higher Education* 10 (1980)

Ivey, D.G. 'New College, 1962–1974.' Unpublished document

Jackson, Dorothy N.R. *A Brief History of Three Schools*. Toronto: T. Eaton Co. Ltd, 1953

James, C.C. 'The Ontario Agricultural College.' *University of Toronto Monthly* 3 (1903)

Jarrell, Richard A. *The Cold Light of Dawn: A History of Canadian Astronomy*. Toronto: University of Toronto Press, 1988

Jasen, Patricia. 'In Pursuit of Human Values (or "Laugh When You Say That"): The Student Critique of the Arts Curriculum in the 1960s.' In Paul Axelrod and John G. Reid, eds, *Youth, University, and Canadian Society: Essays in the Social History of Higher Education*. Montreal: McGill-Queen's University Press, 1989

Jeanneret, Marsh. *God and Mammon: Universities as Publishers*. Toronto: Macmillan, 1989

Johns, Dr and Mrs H.E. 'History of the Department of Medical Biophysics, University of Toronto,' November 1973. UTA/A83-0036/011

Johnson, Robert E. 'Centre for Russian and East European Studies: Director's Five-Year Report, 1989–93,' November 1993

Johnston, Alexandra F. 'Records of Early English Drama in Retrospect.' In Gillian Fenwick, ed., 'The Endangered Editor: Papers of the 34th Annual Conference on Editorial Problems.' Draft ms.

Johnston, Charles M. *McMaster University*, vol. 1, *The Toronto Years*. Toronto: University of Toronto Press, 1976

Jones, Glen. 'Governments, Governance, and Canadian Universities.' In J. Smart, ed. *Higher Education: Handbook of Theory and Research*, vol. 11. San Francisco: Jossey-Bass, 1996

The Jubilee Volume of Wycliffe College. Toronto: Wycliffe College, 1927

Kanowitch, Seymour. 'From Social Committee to Student Union: A History of the Students' Administrative Council, 1955–56 to 1966–67.' UTA/A83-0036/031

Kelly, Ninette, and Michael Trebilcock. *The Making of the Mosaic: A History of Canadian Immigration Policy*. Toronto: University of Toronto Press, 1998

Kennedy, Kerrie J. 'Womanly Work: The Introduction of Household Science at the University of Toronto.' MA thesis, University of Toronto, 1995

Kerr, David. 'A Short History of the Department of Geography, University of Toronto.' Address delivered at the 50th anniversary of the department, October, 1985

Kerr, Robert B., and Douglas Waugh, eds. *Duncan Graham: Medical Reformer and Educator*. Toronto: Dundurn, 1989

Kiefer, Nancy, and Ruth Roach Pierson. 'The War Effort and Women Students at the University of Toronto, 1939–1945.' In Paul Axelrod and John Reid, eds, *Youth, University, and Canadian Society: Essays in the Social History of Higher Education*. Montreal: McGill-Queen's University Press, 1989

Kilgour, David, ed. *A Strange Elation: Hart House, The First Eighty Years*. Toronto: Hart House, 1999

King, Alyson. 'Centres of "Home-like Influence": Residences for Women at the University of Toronto.' *Material History Review* 49 (Spring 1999)

– 'The Experience of the Second Generation of Women Students at Ontario Universities.' PhD thesis, University of Toronto, 1999

King, John. *McCaul, Croft, Forneri*. Toronto: Macmillan, 1914

King, William Lyon Mackenzie. *The Mackenzie King Diaries, 1893–1931*. Toronto: University of Toronto Press, 1973

Kollins, Rick, and Paul Carson. 'The History of Varsity Blues Football.' Department of Athletics and Recreation, University of Toronto, 1993

Kruger, Arthur, and Peter Silcox. 'Woodsworth at Ten.' *University of Toronto Graduate*, January/February 1984

Kuitunen, Maddalena, and Julius Molinaro. *A History of Italian Studies at the University of Toronto, 1840–1990*. Toronto: Department of Italian Studies, University of Toronto, 1991

Kyer, C. Ian, and Jerome E. Bickenbach. *The Fiercest Debate: Cecil A. Wright, the Benchers, and Legal Education in Ontario, 1923–1957*. Toronto: Osgoode Society and University of Toronto Press, 1987

Lang, Dan, with Dawn House, Stacey Young, and Glen Jones. *Government Finances in Ontario*. Forthcoming, Winnipeg: Canadian Society for the Study of Higher Education

Langton, H.H. *Sir John Cunningham McLennan: A Memoir*. Toronto: University of Toronto Press, 1939

Langton, John. 'The University of Toronto in 1856.' *Canadian Historical Review* 5 (1924)

Langton, W.A., ed. *Early Days in Upper Canada: From the Backwoods of Upper Canada and the Audit Office of the Province of Canada*. Toronto: Macmillan, 1926

LaPierre, Paula J.S. 'The First Generation: The Experience of Women University Students in Central Canada.' PhD thesis, University of Toronto, 1993

Latta, Alan. 'The Story of German at the University of Toronto.' Notes for a speech given November 7, 1991

le Riche, W. Harding. 'University of Toronto Medical School and School of Hygiene Historical Comments, 1959–1980.' Unpublished paper

Leslie, Stuart. *The Cold War and American Science: The Military-Industrial-Academic Complex and MIT and Stanford*. New York: Columbia University Press, 1993

Levere, Trevor H. *Research and Influence: A Century of Science in the Royal Society of Canada*. Ottawa: Royal Society of Canada, 1998

Levi, Charles. 'Decided Action Has Been Taken: Student Government, Student Activism, and University Administration at the University of Toronto and McGill University, 1930–1950.' MA thesis, York University, revised version, 1994

– 'Doctoral Theses by Discipline, 1915–1939, as Taken from *Doctoral Theses, 1897–1967.*' Memorandum, June 30, 1999

– 'Memorandum on the Supervision of PhD Theses at the University of Toronto, 1915–1939.' Memorandum, July 8, 1999

– 'The S.A.C. Historical Project, 1930–1950.' Privately published, 1992

– 'Where the Famous People Were? The Origins, Activities, and Future Careers of Student Leaders at University College, Toronto, 1854–1973.' PhD thesis, York University, 1998

Levine, Barry G. *A Century of Skill and Vigour*. Toronto: T.H. Best, 1985

Levitt, Cyril. *Children of Privilege: Student Revolt in the Sixties*. Toronto: University of Toronto Press, 1984

Lindsey, George R., ed. *No Day Long Enough: Canadian Science in World War II*. Toronto: Canadian Institute of Strategic Studies, 1997

Litt, Paul. *The Muses, the Masses, and the Massey Commission*. Toronto: University of Toronto Press, 1992

Loudon, James. 'Memoirs of James Loudon.' UTA/B72-0031/016(11)

Loudon, William James. *Sir William Mulock: A Short Biography*. Toronto: Macmillan, 1932

– *Sketches of Student Life*. 7 vols. Toronto: Macmillan, 1923–37

Luckyj, George. 'Department of Slavic Language and Literature,' 1973. UTA/B88-0007/002(042)

Macallum, A.B. 'The Foundation of the Board of Graduate Studies.' *University of Toronto Monthly* 16 (February 1916)

– 'Huxley and Tyndall at the University of Toronto.' *University of Toronto Monthly* 2 (1901)

Macdonald, D.B. 'Partial Memoirs of the Rev. D.B. Macdonald,' 1953. UTA/B83-1295

Macdonald, John B. *Chances and Choices: A Memoir*. Vancouver: UBC and UBC Alumni Assoc., 2000

– 'The Governing Council System of the University of Toronto, 1972–1977: A Review of the Unicameral Experiment,' December 1977

Macklem, T.C.S. 'Federation Days.' *Trinity University Review*, January 1927

Maclean's

Maloney, Geraldine. 'The Women's College Hospital as a Teaching Institution.' UTA/A83-0036/012

Marchand, Philip. *Marshall McLuhan: The Medium and the Messenger*. Toronto: Vintage, 1998

Marts and Lundy. 'Feasibility Study Report Prepared for the University of Toronto, Toronto, Ontario, Canada,' July 1986. Document forwarded by Marts and Lundy, New Jersey, August 2000

Massey, Vincent. Papers. UTA/B87-0082

– *What's Past Is Prologue*. Toronto: Macmillan, 1963

Masters, D.C. *Henry John Cody: An Outstanding Life*. Toronto: Dundurn, 1995

McBryde, W.A.E. 'History of the Chemistry Department.' Unpublished ms., 1999

– 'William Lash Miller.' Proof for American Chemical Society, 1989

– 'William Lash Miller: Canada's Unique Chemist.' *Journal of Canadian Studies* 26:3 (Fall 1991)

McConica, J.K., and R.M. Schoeffel. 'The Collected Works of Erasmus.' *Scholarly Publishing*, July 1979

McCorkell, Edmund J. *Father Henry Carr*. Toronto: Basilian Teacher, 1964

– *Henry Carr – Revolutionary*. Toronto: Griffin House, 1971

McCulloch, Ernest. 'The Ontario Cancer Institute (OCI): A Brief Account.' Undated ms.

McDonald, Irene. *For the Least of My Brethren: A Centenary History of St. Michael's Hospital*. Toronto: Dundurn, 1992

McFarlane, Brian. *Proud Past, Bright Future: One Hundred Years of Canadian Women's Hockey*. Toronto: Stoddart, 1994

McInnis, Edgar. 'Report of the Committee to Investigate the Pass and General Courses.' UTA/A83-0036/004

McKillop, A.B. *Contours of Canadian Thought*. Toronto: University of Toronto Press, 1987

– *Matters of Mind: The University in Ontario, 1791–1951*. Toronto: University of Toronto Press, 1994

McLaughlin, R.R. 'History of the Ford Foundation Grant to the Faculty of Applied Science and Engineering in the University of Toronto,' April 25, 1963. UTA/A73-0019/001

McLuhan, Marshall. 'Harold Innis.' *Explorations* 25 (June 1969)

McNaught, Kenneth. *Conscience and History: A Memoir*. Toronto: University of Toronto Press, 1999

McRae, Sandra Frances. 'The "Scientific Spirit" in Medicine at the University of Toronto, 1880–1910.' PhD thesis, University of Toronto, 1987

Meikle, William D. 'And Gladly Teach: G.M. Wrong and the Department of History at the University of Toronto.' PhD thesis, Michigan State University, 1977

Millar, W.P.J. '"We Wanted Our Children Should Have It Better": Jewish Medical Students at the University of Toronto.' Unpublished CHA paper, May 20, 2000

Mills, Judy, and Irene Dombra, eds. *University of Toronto Doctoral Theses, 1897–1967*. Toronto: University of Toronto Press, 1968

Moir, John S. *Church and State in Canada West: Three Studies in the Relation of Denominationalism and Nationalism, 1841–1867*. Toronto: University of Toronto Press, 1959

Montagnes, Ian. *An Uncommon Fellowship: The Story of Hart House*. Toronto: University of Toronto Press, 1969

Moore, Christopher. *The Law Society of Upper Canada and Ontario's Lawyers, 1797–1997*. Toronto: University of Toronto Press, 1997

Moore, E.S. 'The Royal Ontario Museum of Geology.' UTA/A83-0036/019

Morgan, Henry James, ed. *The Canadian Men and Women of Our Time*. Toronto: William Briggs, 1912

Moriarty, Catherine. *John Galbraith, 1846–1914: Engineer and Educator*. Toronto: Faculty of Applied Science and Engineering, University of Toronto, 1989

Morton, Desmond, and Glenn Wright. *Winning the Second Battle: Canadian Veterans and the Return to Civilian Life, 1915–1930*. Toronto: University of Toronto Press, 1987

Murray, Heather. 'Making the Modern: Twenty Five Years of the Margaret Eaton School of Literature and Expression.' *Essays in Theatre* 10 (November 1991)

– *Working in English: History, Institution, Resources*. Toronto: University of Toronto Press, 1996

Naughton, Patrick W. 'The Development of the Department of Geography at the University of Toronto.' Student paper, 1977

Neary, Peter. 'Canadian Universities and Canadian Veterans of World War II.' In Neary and Jack Granatstein, *The Veteran's Charter and Post–World War II Canada*. Montreal: McGill-Queen's University Press, 1998

Neatby, Hilda. *'And Not to Yield': Queen's University, 1841–1917*. Kingston: McGill-Queen's University Press, 1978

Neel, Boyd. *My Orchestras and Other Adventures*. Toronto: University of Toronto Press, 1985

Nelles, H.V. *The Politics of Development: Forests, Mines, and Hydro-Electric Power in Ontario, 1849–1941*. Toronto: Macmillan, 1974

Nelson, William H. *The Search for Faculty Power: The University of Toronto Faculty Association, 1942–1992*. Toronto: Canadian Scholars Press, 1993

The Newspaper

Nowry, Laurence. *Man of Mana: Marius Barbeau*. Toronto: New Canada, 1995

O'Beirne, Henry. 'History of the Institute of Biomedical Engineering, 1962 to 1987.' Unpublished ms.

Office of the President of the University of Toronto. Papers. UTA/various accessions

O'Grady, Jean. *Margaret Addison: A Biography*. Montreal: McGill-Queen's University Press, 2001

Okens, Patrick. 'Blues before Sunrise: Rowing at the University of Toronto.' MA thesis, University of Toronto, 1999

Oliver, Peter. *G. Howard Ferguson: Ontario Tory*. Toronto: University of Toronto Press, 1977

'150 Years of Geology at the University of Toronto.' Toronto: Department of Geology, University of Toronto, 1998

The Ontario Dental Association: A Profile: The First One Hundred Years. Ontario Dental Association, 1967

Ontario Public Records and Archives Department. 'Newspaper Hansard'

Oral Interview with Vincent Bladen. UTA/B74-0038

Oral Interview with Henry Borden Transcript. UTA/B87-0044

Oral Interview with James Conacher. UTA/B86-0041

Oral Interview with John Evans. UTA/B86-0044

Oral Interview with Donald Forster. UTA/B86-0043

Oral Interview with James Ham. UTA/B90-0001

Oral Interview with William Harris. UTA/B86-0049

Oral Interview with Sydney Hermant. UTA/B78-0022

Oral Interview with Frances Ireland. UTA/B86-0052

Oral Interview with Arthur Kruger. UTA/B86-0062

Oral Interview with Helen LeVesconte Transcript. UTA/B76-0008

Oral Interview with Warren Main. UTA/B86-0060

Oral Interview with Peter Robinson. UTA/B86-0081

Oral Interview with Tuzo Wilson. UTA/B86-0064

Osbourne, W.A. 'Report of the Advisory Planning Committee to the Board of Governors, University of Toronto, September 12, 1957.' UTA/A83-0036/026

Owram, Doug. *Born at the Right Time: A History of the Baby Boom Generation*. Toronto: University of Toronto Press, 1996

Parkes, A.E.M. 'The Development of Women's Athletics at the University of Toronto,' 1961

Parks, W.A. 'The Royal Ontario Museum: Geology.' *University of Toronto Monthly* 14 (1914)

Paskauskas, R. Andrew, ed. *The Complete Correspondence of Sigmund Freud and Ernest Jones, 1908–1939*. Cambridge, Massachusetts: Belknap, 1993

Patterson, Gordon N. *Pathway to Excellence: UTLAS – The First Twenty-Five Years*. Toronto: Institute for Aerospace Studies, 1977

Pearce, Elizabeth Helen. 'King's College: Purpose and Accountability in Higher Education: The Dilemma of King's College, 1827–1853.' PhD thesis, Ontario Institute for Studies in Education, 1998

Percy, John R., ed. *Erindale College: The First Twenty-Five Years*. December, 1992

Planning for 2000: A Provostial White Paper on University Objectives, University of Toronto, February 14, 1994. University of Toronto Bulletin, February 21, 1994

Plumptre, Wynne. 'Scarborough's Noble Experiment.' *University of Toronto Graduate*, May 1972

Podnieks, Andrew. *Canada's Olympic Teams: The Complete History, 1920–1998*. Toronto: Doubleday, 1997

Poelzer, Irene. 'Father Henry Carr and the Federated Model for Catholic Higher Education in Canada.' In *The Basilian Way of Life and Higher Education*. Saskatoon: St Thomas More College, 1995

Poulos, Linda Nye. 'An Examination of the Multi-Faculty Concept at the University of Toronto and Innis College, 1956–1980.' Unpublished report, May 1980

Prentice, Alison, et al. *Canadian Women: A History*. Toronto: Harcourt Brace Jovanovich, 1988

President's Reports

Primrose, A.A. 'The Faculty of Medicine.' In *The University of Toronto and Its Colleges, 1827–1906*. Toronto: University Library, 1906

– 'Ontario Society of Occupational Therapy.' *University of Toronto Monthly* 29 (1928)

Proceedings and Transactions of the Royal Society of Canada

'A Provisional Plan for Two Off-Campus Colleges in the University of Toronto,' Off-Campus College Committee, 1963. UTA/A72-0026/001

Rae, Bob. *From Protest to Power: Personal Reflections on a Life in Politics*. Toronto: Penguin, 1997

Raising Our Sights: The Next Cycle of White Paper Planning, Key Priorities for 2000–2004, January 6, 1999. University of Toronto Bulletin, January 18, 1999

Rea, K.J. *The Prosperous Years: The Economic History of Ontario, 1939–1975*. Toronto: University of Toronto Press, 1985

Reaney, James. *The Dismissal: Or Twisted Beards and Tangled Whiskers*. Erin, Ontario: Porcépic, 1978

Reed, T.A. *The Blue and White: A Record of Fifty Years of Athletic Endeavour at the University of Toronto*. Toronto: University of Toronto Press, 1944

– ed. *A History of the University of Trinity College, Toronto, 1852–1952*. Toronto: University of Toronto Press, 1952

Reeve, R.A. 'Professor McLennan and the Alumni Association,' *University of Toronto Monthly* 15 (1915)

Reford, Alexander. 'St. Michael's College at the University of Toronto, 1958–1978: The Frustrations of Federation.' *CCHA Historical Studies* 61 (1995)

'Report of the Commissioners on the Discipline in the University of Toronto,' 1895. UTA/B75-0013 (002)

Report of the Royal Commission on the University of Toronto. Toronto: L.K. Cameron, 1906

'Report of the Committee re Faculty of Education, University of Toronto, October 16, 1906.' UTA/A83-0036/007

Report of the Special Committee to the Board of Governors, University of Toronto, Adopted 20th December, 1909. Toronto: University of Toronto Press, 1909

'Report of a Special Committee on the Organisation of the Faculty of Education,' May 6, 1910. UTA/A83-0036/007

Report of the Royal Commission on University Finances. Toronto: Clarkson W. James, 1921

Report of the Special Committee Appointed by the Legislature to Inquire into the Organization and Administration of the University of Toronto. Toronto: Clarkson W. James, 1923

'Report of the President's Committee on Graduate Studies,' 1947, Harold Innis, chair. UTA/A83-0036/016

Report of the Royal Commission on National Development in the Arts, Letters, and Sciences, 1949–1951. Ottawa: Edmond Cloutier, 1951 (Massey Commission report)

'Report of the Plateau Committee to the Senate, June 5, 1956.' UTA/A75-0019/12

Report of the Off-Campus College Committee. 'A Provisional Plan for Two Off-Campus Colleges in the University of Toronto,' 1963. UTA/A72-0026/001

'Report of the Board of Governors' Special Committee on the Future Development of the Faculty of Medicine, May 1964.' UTA/A86-0019/001

'Report of the Presidential Advisory Committee on Erindale College,' June 1965. UTA/A75-0021/004

'Report on Academic Tenure Submitted by the Presidential Advisory Committee on Academic Appointments and Tenure,' 1966 (Haist rules). UTA/A75-0021/079

Report to the Committee on University Affairs and the Committee of Presidents of Provincially-Assisted Universities of the Commission to Study the Development of Graduate Programmes in Ontario Universities. Toronto, 1966 (Spinks report)

'Report from Consultants on Medical Education to Chairman of the Board of Governors, University of Toronto,' May 1968 (Commonwealth Fund report). UTA/A75-0025/30(02)

'Report of the Presidential Advisory Committee on Extension,' July 1970 (Colman report)

'Report of the Presidential Committee on the Status and Future of Scarborough College,' 1970–71 (Hare report)

'Report to the Provost of the University of Toronto from the Programme Committee on Household Science,' November 1, 1974. UTA/A79-0057/022

'Report of the Committee to Review the Undergraduate Programme to the Dean of the Faculty of Arts & Science.' *University of Toronto Bulletin*, May 5, 1979

Return to an Order passed by the Legislative Assembly on the 24th day of April, 1893 giving the report of the Committee of the Senate of the University of Toronto appointed to inquire into the erection of the Biological Building .... Ontario Department of Education, 1894

'Review of Woodsworth College,' February 1998. Document forwarded by Noah Meltz

Richardson, Douglas, ed. *The New Woodsworth College.* Undated

– *A Not Unsightly Building: University College and Its History.* Toronto: Mosaic, 1990

Riddell, Kay. *The International Student Centre – How It All Began.* Toronto, 1985

Risk, R.C.B. 'The Many Minds of W.P.M. Kennedy.' *University of Toronto Law Journal* 48 (1998)

Robinson, G. de B. *The Mathematics Department in the University of Toronto*. Toronto: Department of Mathematics, University of Toronto, 1979

Ross, Alexander M. *The College on the Hill: A History of the Ontario Agricultural College, 1874–1974*. Toronto: Copp Clark, 1974

Ross, Alexander M., and Terry Crowley. *The College on the Hill: A New History of the Ontario Agricultural College, 1874–1999*. Toronto: Dundurn, 1999

Ross, Murray. *The Way Must Be Tried: Memoirs of a University Man*. Toronto: Stoddart, 1992

Ross, Peter N. 'The Establishment of the PhD at Toronto: A Case of American Influence.' *History of Education Quarterly*, Fall 1973

– 'The Origins and Development of the PhD Degree at the University of Toronto, 1871–1932.' EdD thesis, University of Toronto, 1972

Ross, Robin. *The Short Road Down: A University Changes*. Toronto: University of Toronto Press, 1984

Rouillard, C.D., ed. *French Studies at the University of Toronto, 1853–1993*. Toronto: Department of French, University of Toronto, 1994

Russell, Peter. 'Memo on Innis College,' July, 1998

Sanderson, Marie. *Griffith Taylor: Antarctic Scientist and Pioneer Geographer*. Ottawa: Carleton University Press, 1988

Sawyer, John. 'From Commerce to Management: The Evolution of Business Education at the University of Toronto.' In Barbara Austin, ed., *Capitalizing Knowledge: Essays on the History of Business Education in Canada*. Toronto: University of Toronto Press, 2000

– 'The Rotman School: A Historical Perspective, 1901–1998.' Draft article, June 30, 1998

Saywell, John. *'Just Call Me Mitch': The Life of Mitchell F. Hepburn*. Toronto: University of Toronto Press, 1991

Schabas, Ezra. *Sir Ernest MacMillan: The Importance of Being Canadian*. Toronto: University of Toronto Press, 1994

Schabas, Ezra, and Carl Morey. *Opera Viva: The Canadian Opera Company: The First Fifty Years*. Toronto: Dundurn, 2000

'The School of Nursing.' Excerpt from the School of Nursing calendar of 1956–57. UTA/A83-0036/013

Schrecker, Ellen W. *No Ivory Tower: McCarthyism and the Universities*. New York: Oxford University Press, 1986

Seath, John. 'Extract from Report to the Minister of Education from the Superintendent, 1917.' UTA/A83-0036/007

Semple, Neil. 'Federation and the New "Old Vic."' Undated and unpublished notes of a speech

Sheffield, E.F. 'Canadian University and College Enrolment Projected to 1965.' In J.F. Leddy, ed., *Proceedings of the National Conference of Canadian Universities 1955*

Shook, Lawrence K. *Catholic Post-Secondary Education in English-speaking Canada: A History*. Toronto: University of Toronto Press, 1971

Shore, Marlene. *The Science of Social Redemption: McGill, the Chicago School, and the Origins of Social Research in Canada*. Toronto: University of Toronto Press, 1987

Shorter, Edward. *A Century of Radiology in Toronto*. Toronto: Wall and Emerson, 1995

Shrum, Gordon. *Gordon Shrum: An Autobiography*. Vancouver: University of British Columbia Press, 1986

Siminovitch, Louis. 'Louis Siminovitch.' In G.A. Kenney-Wallace, et al., eds, *In Celebration of Canadian Scientists: A Decade of Killam Laureates*. Ottawa, 1990

Simmins, Geoffrey. *Fred Cumberland: Building the Victorian Dream*. Toronto: University of Toronto Press, 1997

– *Ontario Association of Architects: A Centennial History, 1889–1989*. Toronto: Ontario Association of Architects, 1989

Simpson, Renate. *How the PhD Came to Britain: A Century of Struggle for Postgraduate Education*. Sturminster Newton, England: Direct Design, 1983

Sirluck, Ernest. *First Generation: An Autobiography*. Toronto: University of Toronto Press, 1996

Sisam, J.W.B. *Forestry Education at Toronto*. Toronto: University of Toronto Press, 1961

Sissons, C.B. *Egerton Ryerson: His Life and Letters*, vol. 2. Toronto: Clark Irwin, 1947

– *A History of Victoria University*. Toronto: University of Toronto Press, 1952

Skilling, Gordon. *The Education of a Canadian: My Life as a Scholar and Activist*. McGill-Queen's University Press, 2000

Slater, John G. 'Philosophy at Toronto.' Unpublished ms., 2000

Smith, Donald B. 'Lost Youth.' *University of Toronto Graduate*, Autumn 1989

Smith, Goldwin. Papers. Cornell University

Spence, M.E. 'Once There Were No Women at Varsity.' *University of Toronto Monthly* 33 (1933)

Spragge, George W. 'The Trinity Medical College.' *Ontario History* 58 (1966)

Squair, John. 'Admission of Women to the University of Toronto and University College.' Pamphlet, 1924, in the University of Toronto Pamphlet collections, and also found in B84-0003/002

– 'Alumni Associations in the University of Toronto.' Toronto: University of Toronto Press, 1922

Stacey, C.P. *Arms, Men, and Governments: The War Policies of Canada, 1939–1945*. Ottawa: Queen's Printer, 1970

Stachel, John. 'Einstein and Infeld, Seen through Their Correspondence.' Unpublished paper, undated

Stager, David A.A. 'Federal Government Grants to Canadian Universities.' *Canadian Historical Review* 54:3 (September 1973)

Stansbury, Edward J. 'Report on the Unicameral Governing Structure of the University of Toronto,' March 10, 1987. UTA/A94-0013/027

Steib, Ernst W. 'A Century of Formal Pharmaceutical Education in Ontario.' *Canadian Pharmaceutical Journal* 116 (1983)

Steib, Ernst W., et al. 'Women in Ontario Pharmacy, 1867–1927.' *Pharmacy in History* 28 (1986)

Stewart, Edward E. 'The Role of the Provincial Government in the Development of the Universities of Ontario, 1791–1964.' EdD thesis, University of Toronto, 1970

Stokes, Lawrence D. 'Canada and an Academic Refugee from Nazi Germany: The Case of Gerhard Herzberg.' *Canadian Historical Review* 57 (1976)

Teach Us to Care and Not to Care: Fiftieth Anniversary, 1914–1964, School of Social Work, University of Toronto. 1964

Thiele, Stephen. *Heroes of the Game: A History of the Grey Cup*. Norval, Ontario: Moulin, 1997

Thistle, Mel. *The Inner Ring: The Early History of the National Research Council of Canada*. Toronto: University of Toronto Press, 1966

Thompson, Nancy Ramsay. 'The Controversy over the Admission of Women to University College, University of Toronto.' MA thesis, University of Toronto, 1974

Torontonensis

Toronto Star

Tough, Allen M. 'The Development of Adult Edcation at the University of Toronto before 1920.' MA thesis, University of Toronto, 1962

Towards Community in University Government: Report of the Commission on the Government of the University of Toronto. Toronto: University of Toronto Press, 1970 (CUG report)

Trigger, Bruce G. '*Prehistoric Man* and Daniel Wilson's Later Canadian Ethnology.' In Elizabeth Hulse, ed., *Thinking with Both Hands: Sir Daniel Wilson in the Old World and the New.* Toronto: University of Toronto Press, 1999

Trinity University Review

Undergraduate Instruction in Arts and Science: Report of the Presidential Advisory Committee on Undergraduate Instruction in the Faculty of Arts and Science, University of Toronto. Toronto: University of Toronto Press, 1967 (Macpherson report)

University Government in Canada: Report of a Commission Sponsored by the Canadian Association of University Teachers and the Association of Universities and Colleges in Canada. Toronto: University of Toronto Press, 1966 (Duff-Berdahl report)

University of Toronto Alumni Magazine

The University of Toronto and Its Colleges, 1827–1906. Toronto: University Library, 1906

University of Toronto Bulletin

University of Toronto Campus Master Plan Discussion Draft, 1991. Document forwarded by Elizabeth Sisam

University of Toronto Graduate

University of Toronto Magazine

University of Toronto Memorial Book, Second World War, 1939–1945. Toronto: Soldiers' Tower Committee, 1994

University of Toronto Monthly

University of Toronto National Report

University of Toronto Open Space Master Plan Working Report, October 1998

University of Toronto Register of Graduates, 1920. Toronto: University of Toronto Press, 1921

University of Toronto Roll of Service, 1914–1918. Toronto: University of Toronto Press, 1921

UTFA Newsletter

Van Die, Marguerite. *An Evangelical Mind: Nathanael Burwash and the Methodist Tradition in Canada, 1839–1918.* Montreal: McGill-Queen's University Press, 1989

Varsity

Varsity News

Walker, Sir Edmund. Papers. Thomas Fisher Rare Book Library

Walker, T.L. 'The Royal Ontario Museum: Mineralogy.' *University of Toronto Monthly* 14 (1914)

Wallace, W. Stewart. *A History of the University of Toronto, 1827–1927.* Toronto: University of Toronto Press, 1927

Walmsley, Lewis C. *Bishop in Honan: Mission and Museum in the Life of William C. White.* Toronto: University of Toronto Press, 1974

Warner, Tom. *Never Going Back: Lesbian and Gay Activism and Organising in Canada at the End of the 20th Century.* Forthcoming, University of Toronto Press

Westfall, William. 'The Divinity 150 Project.' Unpublished draft, 1998

White, Richard. *The Skule Story: The University of Toronto Faculty of Applied Science and Engineering, 1873–2000*. Toronto: University of Toronto Press, 2000

Williams, David C. 'The Development of Scarborough and Erindale Colleges and Their Relationship to the Queen's Park Campus,' December 6, 1963. UTA/A72-0026/001

Williams, Michael R. 'UTEC and Ferut: The University of Toronto's Computation Centre.' *IEEE Annals of the History of Computing* 16:2 (1994)

Wilson, Barbara M., ed. *Ontario and the First World War, 1914–1918: A Collection of Documents*. Toronto: University of Toronto Press, 1977

Wilson, Daniel. 'Sir Daniel Wilson's Journal.' In UTA/Langton Family Papers/B65-0014/004

Winnett, Fred V., and W. Stewart McCullough. 'A Brief History of the Department of Near Eastern Studies (formerly Oriental Languages) in the University of Toronto to 1976–1977.' Unpublished ms., 1978. UTA/B2000-0009

Woodside, Moffat. 'Report of the Special Committee on the Humanities,' February 1, 1954. UTA/A83-0036/019

Wright, Caesar. 'Senate Speech on Sidney Smith,' November 8, 1957. UTA/A83-0036/039

Wrong, George M. 'Report of the Committee Appointed to Enquire in Regard to a Possible College for Women,' March 10, 1909. UTA/A67-0007/026

Young, C.R. *Early Engineering Education at Toronto*. Toronto: University of Toronto Press, 1958

Young, J. McGregor. 'The Faculty of Law.' In *The University of Toronto and Its Colleges, 1827–1906*. Toronto: University Library, 1906

Zeller, Suzanne. 'Merchants of Light: The Culture of Science in Daniel Wilson's Ontario, 1853–1892.' In Elizabeth Hulse, ed., *Thinking with Both Hands: Sir Daniel Wilson in the Old World and the New*. Toronto: University of Toronto Press, 1999

PICTURE CREDITS

⁓

Chapter 1 (1826)

Town of York: Metro Toronto Reference Library, J. Ross Robertson Collection, T10339; Strachan: Trinity College Archives, P1278/0005; 1827 charter: U of T Development Office; King's College property: U of T Archives, A65-0004/0.192; Fowler's design: Ontario Archives, Horwood Collection, AO 3623 C 11-438-01(411)-2.

Chapter 2 (1842)

Approach to King's College: U of T Archives, A65-0004/0.196; Bagot: Fisher Library, Sproatt Collection, Ms. Collection 147; Victoria College: United Church Archives, Victoria University, 91.161P/350 N; McCaul: U of T Archives, A73-0033 (neg. 2001-31.1); Croft: U of T Archives, B2000-0024/001(08); Legislative buildings: Metro Toronto Reference Library, J. Ross Robertson Collection, T10249.

Chapter 3 (1849)

King's College residence: U of T Archives, B79-1006; Tender: U of T Archives, A73-0022/005(02) (neg. 2001-31.2); Robert Baldwin: Metro Toronto Reference Library, J. Ross Robertson Collection, T15007; Trinity College: U of T Development Office.

Chapter 4 (1850)

Beaven and the monkey: from *University of Toronto Monthly*, volume 30 at 221 (neg. 2001-31.3); University gates at College and Yonge streets: U of T Archives, A65-0004/0.64; McCaul: U of T Archives, A65-0004/135.131; Soulerin: St Michael's College Archives, photo 1865, no. 2; St Michael's College: St Michael's College Archives, photo 1870, no. 6.

Chapter 5 (1853)

Toronto in 1854: City of Toronto, EDCT-Culture Division, The Market Gallery; Wilson: Fisher Library, Sproatt Collection, Ms. Coll. 147; Cherriman: U of T Archives, A73-0003/ 001(21); Hincks: U of T Archives, A65-0004/240.23; Chapman: U of T Archives, B2000-002/003(02); Forneri: U of T Archives, A73-0003/001(41).

Chapter 6 (1856)

Carvings in University College rotunda: U of T Archives, A65-0004/1.4; Carvings in University College rotunda: U of T Archives, A65-0004/1.7; Workers in front of Croft Chapter House: U of T Archives, A65-0004/1.12; East Wing of University College: U of T Archives, A65-0004/1.9; Bell tower: U of T Development Office; Workers in front of University College: U of T Archives, B98-0033/025P.

Chapter 7 (1860)

University College before the fire of 1890: U of T Archives, A65-0004/1.16; McCaul's Pond: U of T Archives, B65-0025/001P; Ryerson: United Church Archives, Victoria University, 76.001P/5741 N; University College 'foot ball team': U of T Archives, A73-0046/001; Fenian monument: U of T Archives, A65-0004/0.188.

Chapter 8 (1871)

University College Natural Science Club: U of T Archives, A73-0003/002(60); Wright: U of T Archives, A65-0004/16.19; Loudon: U of T Archives, B2000-0024/001(10); Engineering building: U of T Archives, A65-0004/009; Galbraith: U of T Archives, B2000-0020/011P(11).

Chapter 9 (1880)

Houston: U of T Archives, A77-0049:0027 (neg. 2001-31.4a); Gullen: United Church Archives, 91.161P/1006 N; Balmer: U of T Archives, A73-0026/018(17)0001; Salter: U of T Archives, A73-0026/396(17)0001; Three women graduates: U of T Archives, taken from the 1885 graduation picture, P78-0030/(01)01; Annesley Hall: United Church Archives, 91.161P/ 417 N; Women's hockey: U of T Archives, B90-0044/001(11).

Chapter 10 (1883)

Mulock: U of T Archives, B2000-0024/001(05); Nelles: United Church Archives, 76.001P/ 4835; Burwash: United Church Archives, 76.002P/4 N; Knox College: Notman Collection, McCord Museum, McGill University; McMaster University: U of T Development Office; Teefy: St Michael's College Archives, Michael Joseph Ferguson, photo album 3; Victoria University: U of T Archives, A65-0004/50.5.

Chapter 11 (1887)

'Varsity Base Ball Club, 1887': U of T Archives, A65-0004/0.215; Ashley: from Ian Drummond, *Political Economy at the University of Toronto: A History of the Department, 1888–*

1982 (1983); Mavor: U of T Archives, B85-0018/001P (neg. 95-19.2); Alexander: U of T Archives, B84-1137/(01) (neg. 2001-31.6a); Hume: U of T Archives, A73-0026/018(17); Wilson: U of T Archives, A73-0026/517(99)0003 (neg. 97-05.1).

Chapter 12 (1887)

Woman's Medical College: U of T Archives, P78-0120(03); Aikins: History of Medicine Collection, U of T; Geikie: Metro Toronto Reference Library, 920.0713 B24; Biology Building: Metro Toronto Reference Library, T12958; Macallum: U of T Archives, B66-0005/001(12); Medical school: U of T Development Office (Eric Trussler); Macklem and others: Trinity College Archives, P1527/0001.

Chapter 13 (1889)

Duff: Law Society of Upper Canada Archives, P58; Martin: Law Society of Upper Canada Archives, P291; Dentistry building: U of T Development Office; Pharmacy building: U of T Archives, A65-0004/120.37; Ontario Agricultural College: University of Guelph, McLaughlin Library, Archival and Special Collections.

Chapter 14 (1890)

Program for *conversazione*: U of T Archives, A76-0002/001/.0016; University College, after the fire: U of T Archives, A65-0004/1.85; Blake: U of T Archives, B2000-0024/001(04); University library: U of T Archives, A65-0004/3.22.

Chapter 15 (1895)

1895 graduation picture: U of T Archives, B91-0010 (neg. 2001-31.17); 1895 graduation picture (banner): U of T Archives, B91-0010 (neg. 2001-31.16); Wrong: U of T Archives, B91-0010 (neg. 2001-31.21); Dale: U of T Archives, B91-0010 (neg. 2001-31.20); Tucker: U of T Archives, B91-0010 (neg. 2001-31.19); Montgomery: U of T Archives, B 91-0010 (neg. 2001-31.18); The *Varsity*: U of T Archives, Feb. 20, 1895; University College cloisters: U of T Archives, A65-0004/1.177.

Chapter 16 (1897)

King's MA thesis: U of T Archives, T79-00075.(83); Scott: U of T Archives, 1897 graduating class in arts, A77-0046:0009 (neg. 2001-31.8a); McLennan: U of T Archives, B89-0017/003P (neg. 99-48.02); Miller: U of T Archives, A73-0003/001(64); Benson: U of T Archives, A73-026/027(30); Laird: U of T Archives, A78-0041/012(37); Household science building: U of T Archives, A78-0050/006/(12).

Chapter 17 (1901)

Loudon: from *The University of Toronto: 1827-1906* (1906); Mining Building: U of T Archives, A65-0004/7.3; Sod-turning ceremony: U of T Archives, B71-0006/001(19); Convocation Hall: 2000-0030/0011(07) (Max Fleet).

Chapter 18 (1905)

King's College Circle: U of T Archives, A65-0004/0.214; Devonshire Place: U of T Development Office; Royal commission of 1906: U of T Archives, A73-0003/002(39); Hutton: from 1903 *Torontonensis*.

Chapter 19 (1907)

Falconer: U of T Archives, A65-0004/135.28; Carr: St Michael's College Archives, photo 1905, no. 2; Installation procession: U of T Archives, A73-0003/002(45); Convocation Hall: U of T Archives, A73-0051/001:0003; University Settlement House: University Settlement Recreation Centre Collection in the City of Toronto Archives, SC24#6.

Chapter 20 (1908)

Old observatory: U of T Development Office; Eakin: U of T Archives, A78-0041/006(23); Cartwright: Trinity College Archives; Biology lab: U of T Archives, A65-0004/5.28.

Chapter 21 (1909)

Faculty of education: U of T Archives, A65-0004/14.1; Flavelle House: City of Toronto Archives, SC 568, item 340; Toronto General Hospital: U of T Archives, A65-0004/120.43; Jones: from Ernest Jones, *Free Associations: Memoirs of a Psycho-Analyst* (1959); Royal Ontario Museum: U of T Archives, B79-1000; Fritz: Royal Ontario Museum.

Chapter 22 (1914)

Sopwith Camel: U of T Archives, A65-0004/0.221 (G.R. Anderson); MacDowell: U of T Archives, A73-0026/536; McCrae: U of T Archives, B66-1000:0001; Underhill: from R.D. Francis, *Frank Underhill: Intellectual Provocateur* (1986); Innis: U of T Archives, B72-0003/034(07) (neg. 94-39.3); Bethune: U of T Archives, A73-0014.(02) (Robert Lansdale – neg. 731055-10); Salonika: U of T Archives, A80-0021/004(10); McLennan's pass: U of T Archives, B89-0017/003P (neg. 2001-31.10); Connaught Laboratories: property of James FitzGerald; Red Cross Room: U of T Archives, A65-0004/140.85.

Chapter 23 (1919)

Soldiers' Tower: U of T Archives, A65-0004/2.A22; Hart House: U of T Archives, A78-0050/003(04); Great Hall: U of T Archives, A65-0004/2.79; Trinity College: U of T Development Office; Simcoe Hall: U of T Development Office; Falconer: U of T Archives, A65-0004/135.88.

Chapter 24 (1922)

Banting and Best: U of T Archives, A78-0041/001(53); Laboratory: U of T Archives, A65-0004/4.23; McLeod: History of Medicine Collection, U of T; Collip: History of Medicine Collection, U of T; McMurrich: U of T Archives, A73-0003/001(56); Brett: U of T Archives, A65-0004/21.10; Gilson: St Michael's College Archives, photo 1929, no. 32; Pontifical Institute: U of T Development Office (Eric Trussler).

Chapter 25 (1926)

Convocation: U of T Archives, A65-0004/0.79; Kennedy: U of T Archives, A78-0041/011(48); Finkelman: U of T Archives, A78-0041/007(08); 'Varsity Grads' Olympic hockey: U of T Archives, A79-0060/020(30); Women's hockey: from 1926 *Torontonensis*; Olympic crew: U of T Archives, B73-0017P/001; MacMillan: MacMillan family photo; Women undergraduates: City of Toronto Archives, James Collection, 2534.

Chapter 26 (1931)

Underhill: U of T Archives, A78-0041/022(38); Cody and Henry: Ontario Archives, AO 1929 F980; White: Royal Ontario Museum Collection; Royal Ontario Museum: A65-0004/17.107; Taylor: U of T Archives, A65-0004/135.1404; Astronomy department: U of T Archives, A78-0041/028(03) (Jack Marshall).

Chapter 27 (1939)

King and Queen: U of T Archives, A73-0050/002P; Macalister and LePan: from Douglas LePan, *Macalister, or Dying in the Dark* (1995); Helleiner: Helleiner family photo; Keyfitz and Putnam Competition: U of T Development Office (Jack Marshall); Fackenheim: U of T Development Office (David Lloyd); Levy: U of T Development Office (Eric Trussler); Tank: U of T Archives, A68-0003/002; Hart House Library: U of T Archives, A73-0050/002; Banting: U of T Archives, A78-0041/001(46); Franks: U of T Development Office (Robert Lansdale).

Chapter 28 (1944)

Smith and Cody: U of T Archives, A78-0041/020(14) (J.G. Merrill); Mulock: U of T Archives, A78-0041/016(34); Phillips and Massey: U of T Archives, A78-0041/017(30); Wallberg Memorial Building: U of T Archives, A78-0050/007(18); Patterson: U of T Development Office (Chris Lund); UTEC computer: U of T Archives, B2001-0014.

Chapter 29 (1950)

Cheerleaders: U of T Archives, A78-0051/004(33); The *Varsity*: from 1956 *Torontonensis*; Engineering students: U of T Archives, A78-0041/027(16) (Herb Nott); Onyschuk: U of T Archives, A78-0041/028(22); Stulac: U of T Archives, A78-0041/028(18) (Nat Turofsky); Women's basketball: from 1953 *Torontonensis*; McCulley: U of T Archives, A78-0041/013(42) (Jack Marshall); Sutherland: Hart House Archives; Riddell: U of T Archives, A78-0041/018(20) (Jack Marshall); Einstein and Infeld: from Leopold Infeld, *Why I Left Canada* (1978).

Chapter 30 (1955)

Aerial view of campus: U of T Development Office; McKinnon: U of T Development Office (Dennis Hall); Arthur: U of T Development Office (Robert Lansdale – neg. 701170-21); Smith: U of T Development Office (Verner Reed); Creighton: U of T Archives, A78-0041/005(02); Innis: U of T Archives, A78-0041/011(06).

Chapter 31 (1958)

Bissell's installation: U of T Development Office (Ken Bell); Physics building: U of T Development Office; Sidney Smith Hall: U of T Development Office (Jack Marshall); Massey Commission: U of T Archives, A78-0041/015(22); Music building: U of T Archives, A78-0041/016(43) (Jack Marshall); Main: U of T Archives, A78-0041/015(06) (Jack Marshall); Cassidy: U of T Archives, A78-0041/003(69); Law professors: Faculty of Law Archives.

Chapter 32 (1960)

York University: U of T Development Office; New College: U of T Development Office (Jack Marshall); Innis College: U of T Archives, A78-0050/005(06) (Robert Lansdale); Map of Scarborough and Erindale: U of T Development Office; Williams: U of T Archives, A78-0041/023(41) (Herb Nott); Scarborough College: U of T Development Office (Ken Bell); Plumptre: U of T Archives, A78-0041/017(41) (Robert Lansdale); Erindale College: U of T Development Office (Robert Lansdale – neg. 711068-17); Moon rock: U of T Development Office (Robert Lansdale – neg. 691258-19).

Chapter 33 (1962)

Massey College: U of T Development Office (Ken Bell); Davies: U of T Development Office; Laskin Committee: U of T Development Office; OISE: U of T Development Office; Laskin: U of T Archives, A78-0041/012(52) (Robert Lansdale); Robarts Library: U of T Development Office (Robert Lansdale).

Chapter 34 (1963)

University of Toronto Press: U of T Development Office (Robert Lansdale – neg. 761011-106); Frye: U of T Archives, A78-0041/007(42) (Jack Marshall); Valdés and Hutcheon: U of T Development Office (Rob Allen); McLuhan: U of T Development Office; Pratt and Skilling: U of T Development Office (Jack Marshall); Robson: U of T Archives, B98-0033/026P (Robert Lansdale); Johnston: U of T Development Office (Jewel Randolph).

Chapter 35 (1966)

Demolition of SPS: U of T Archives, A78-0041/027(14) (Jack Marshall); James Ham: U of T Archives, A78-0041/029(05) (Jack Marshall); Medical Sciences Building: U of T Development Office (Robert Lansdale – neg. 691217-25/24); Sunnybrook Hospital: U of T Development Office; Peters: U of T Archives, B96-0019/001(07); Johns: U of T Development Office (Jack Marshall); Arthur Ham: U of T Archives, A78-0041/009(21) (Jack Marshall); Siminovitch: U of T Development Office; Masui: U of T Development Office (Greg Holman).

Chapter 36 (1967)

Protest: U of T Archives, A78-0041/021(26) (Jack Marshall); Commission on University Government: U of T Archives, A78-0041/029(31) (Robert Lansdale); Macpherson committee: U of T Archives, A78-0041/027(20) (Jack Marshall); Caput meeting: U of T Development

Office (Robert Lansdale – neg. 691255); Bissell at sit-in: U of T Development Office; Pollution Probe: U of T Development Office (Robert Lansdale – neg. 701283-22).

Chapter 37 (1971)

Hallett: U of T Archives, A78-0041/009(20) (Robert Lansdale); Evans and Sword: U of T Development Office (Robert Lansdale – neg. 711235-60); Evans and Harding: U of T Archives, B78-0041/009(32); Alumni members: U of T Archives, A78-0041/027(08) (Robert Lansdale); President's Council: U of T Development Office (Robert Lansdale – neg. 721030-2).

Chapter 38 (1975)

Koffler Centre: U of T Development Office (Ian Crysler); Nelson: U of T Development Office (Robert Lansdale – neg. 711009-52); Smith: U of T Development Office; Iacobucci: U of T Development Office; Memorandum of agreement: U of T Development Office (Steve Behal); Ivey and Hume: U of T Development Office (Henry Fox); Woodsworth College: Woodsworth College Collection; FitzGerald Building: U of T Development Office (Jack Marshall).

Chapter 39 (1980)

James Ham's installation: U of T Development Office; Earth Sciences Centre: U of T Development Office (Jewel Randolph); Forster: U of T Development Office (Steve Behal); Connell: U of T Archives, A78-0041/004(34); Women's studies: U of T Archives, A78-0050/005(17) (Robert Lansdale); Babb affair: U of T Development Office (Steve Behal).

Chapter 40 (1986)

Polanyi: from John Polanyi (Richard Palmer); Connell: U of T Development Office (Greg Holman); National Scholars program: U of T Development Office (Steve Behal); Teaching awards: U of T Development Office (Steve Behal); Pawson et al.: Mount Sinai Hospital Archives; Trudeau: U of T Development Office (Jewel Randolph).

Chapter 41 (1994)

Prichard and vice-presidents: U of T Development Office (Laura Arsiè); Football on back campus: U of T Archives, A78-0041/028(22) (Robert Lansdale); Sedra and Tuohy: U of T Development Office (Andre Souroujon); Davenports: U of T Development Office; Skoll: U of T Development Office (Brian Smale/Clixpix); Wolfe: U of T Development Office (Susan King).

Chapter 42 (1997)

Bahen Centre: Office of Operations and Services, Simcoe Hall; Graham: U of T Development Office (Jewel Randolph); St George Street: from *Canadian Architect*, April 1998; Convocation Hall plaza: from 'King's College Circle Precinct: Schematic Design'; Graduate House: from Office of Operations and Services, Simcoe Hall; *Maclean's* ranking: *Maclean's* (Rino Noto); Birgeneau: *Maclean's* (Peter Bregg).

READERS OF
THE COMPLETE MANUSCRIPT

I was fortunate in having a large number of knowledgeable readers of the complete manuscript. The review process was valuable for finding errors and omissions and helped me shape the final manuscript. I am grateful for the time and effort they put into the task.

John Beattie
Michael Bliss
David Bronskill
Adrian Brook
Craig Brown
Sara Burke
Alan Cairns
George Connell
David Cook
Anne Innis Dagg
Ron Daniels
Jack Dimond
Jacalyn Duffin
Ben Etkin
John Evans
Michael Finlayson
Joan Foley
Paul Fox
Judy Friedland
Robert Gidney
Paul Gooch

James Greenlee
Donald Guthrie
Francess Halpenny
Bill Harnum
Michiel Horn
Frank Iacobucci
Alexandra Johnston
Richard Landon
Dan Lang
Michael Marrus
James McConica
Michael McCulloch
Brian McKillop
Wynn Millar
Ian Montagnes
Heather Murray
Bill Nelson
Patrick Okens
Paul Perron
Melissa Pitts
John Polanyi

Graham Rawlinson
Peter Richardson
Richard Risk
Peter Russell
Edward Safarian
Ann Schabas
Ezra Schabas
Ron Schoeffel
Robert Sharpe
Ernest Sirluck
Elizabeth Sisam
John Slater
Boris Stoicheff
David Strangway
Jack Sword
Stephen Travis
Stephen Waddams
Richard White
Katrina Wyman

INDEX

Page numbers in italics refer to illustrations.

Corrigan, Beatrice, 294, 497
Corry, Alex, 441
Cotter, Graham, *555*
Couchiching Conference, 335
Coughtry, Graham, 391
Coventry, Alan, 312
Cox, George, 240
Coxeter, H.S.M., 345, 346
Craigie, E. Horne, 323
Craigie, James, 359
Craik, Fergus, 457, 661
Cranach, Lucas, 655
Crawford, H.J., 238
Creighton, Donald, 305, 318, *413*, 417–18, 479, 496; *Sir John A. Macdonald*, 493
Cressy, Gordon, 617
Crighton, 'Hec,' 313
Crispo, John, 434
Croft, Henry, *21*, 28, 34, 47, 71, 84, 671; and construction of University College, 56; at School of Practical Science, 83; as teacher, 79; and University Rifle Corps, 73; women at lectures of, 88
Crofts, George, 326–7
Crombie, David, 580
Crombie, Ernestus, 47
Crooks, Adam, 36, 71–2, 73, 74, 80, 82, 86–7
Crossley, Kathleen, 353
Cumberland, Frederic, 30, 54, 56–8, 153, 396
Cumberland House (St George Street), 57, *395*, 396, 432, 438, 493
Cunningham, Frank, 449
Currelly, Charles, 246–8, 327–8, 330, 675
curriculum: choice of subjects, 533, 571; first-entry programs, 660; for general arts, 413–14; Macpherson committee on undergraduate instruction, 531–3, 567; proposal to eliminate three-year degree, 607; Ryerson's criticism of, 66; subjects taught by colleges, 102, 106, 108–9, 110, 136, 206, 568–9; undergraduate arts and science, 571, 607
Curtis, Wilfred, 443, 444–5

Dadson, D.F., 471, 474
Dale, William, 158, 160, *161*, 162, 169, 171, 172, 188
Dalhousie University, 120, 139, 233
Dalziel, Ann, *444*
Dan, Leslie, 641, 670
dances and dancing: prohibition of, 167; during wartime, 255, 339
Daniells, Roy, 294
Daniels, Ron, 442
Darling and Pearson (architects), 194, 196, 216, 241, 247, 278
Darwin, Charles, 49, xi; impact of his ideas, 50–2, 77, 105, 124; *On the Origin of Species*, 50
Davenport, Edna (née Street), 637–8, *638*, 678
Davenport, John, 637–8, *638*, 678
Davenport Building (St George Street), 656–7, 678
David Dunlap Observatory (Richmond Hill), 226, 332–4, *333*, 637
Davies, Robertson, 465, *466*, 487–8; *Deptford Trilogy*, 466; *Fortune My Foe*, 394
Davis, Chandler, 396
Davis, Donald, 393
Davis, Herbert, 304
Davis, Murray, 393
Davis, Natalie Zemon, 396, 481, 537, 591
Davis, William (Bill), 451, 470, 471, 548, 553, 561, 587
Dawson, McGregor: *Government of Canada*, 493
Dawson, William, 89
Dean, William: *Economic Atlas of Canada*, 493; *Historical Atlas of Canada*, 493
dean of women, 231, 419, 425
de Blaquière, Peter, 32, 38
de Charbonnel, Armand, 38
Defence Research Board, 356, 375, 376, 379
Delahcy, Charlie, *310*
deLeeuw, J.H., 504
Dellandrea, Jon, 613, *625*, 625–6, 636, 638, 642, 653
Delsarte, François, 230